Contents

> If you're revising for the **AS exams**, you'll need the topics marked with an AS stamp. (AS)
> If you're revising for the **A-Level exams**, you'll need the **whole book**.
> Further information about what's required for AS is given on some pages.

Core Pure Mathematics (CP)

Further Pure Mathematics 1 (FP1)

Further Statistics 1 (FS1)

AS & A-Level

Further Maths

Exam Board: Edexcel

Taking AS or A-Level Further Maths? Kudos. From now on, people you've never met will stop you in the street to shake your hand and comment on how great your shoes are.

Your shoes are great, by the way. But they probably won't help you get to grips with complex loci, Poisson distributions or feasible regions. That's what this CGP book is for.

It's packed with the clearest study notes and worked examples you'll find anywhere, plus plenty of exam-style questions (with step-by-step answers included at the back). And with the free Online Edition, you can read it all on your computer or tablet!

Did you say free Online Edition?

Sure did. Just go to **cgpbooks.co.uk/extras** and enter this code:

2376 7973 9066 4894

This code only works for one person. If somebody else has used
this book before you, they might have already claimed the Online Edition.

A-Level revision? It has to be CGP!

Published by CGP

Editors:
Liam Dyer, Sammy El-Bahrawy, Will Garrison, Shaun Harrogate, Ceara Hayden, Paul Jordin,
Charles Kitts, Tom Miles, Andy Park, Aidan Smith, Ben Train, Ruth Wilbourne, Dawn Wright

ISBN: 978 1 78294 869 8

With thanks to Elizabeth Best, Alastair Duncombe, Allan Graham, Glenn Rogers and David Ryan for the proofreading.

With thanks to Emily Smith for the copyright research.

Clipart from Corel®
Printed by Elanders Ltd, Newcastle upon Tyne.

Based on the classic CGP style created by Richard Parsons.

Further Mechanics 1 (FM1)

Decision Mathematics 1 (D1)

Proof

This might just be the most important section in the whole book — proof is a vital part of maths and so had better be a vital part of your revision. If you don't believe me, let me prove it...

Proofs appear Everywhere in Further Maths

Proof questions can go with almost any topic and they can appear all over your exam paper. You might be asked to prove that things are **equal**, that things are **not equal**, that a statement is **true** or that it is **false**.

You should already know a few ways of proving things, but here's a quick reminder:

Proof by exhaustion
This is where you split the problem into a number of cases and prove the statement for each in turn.

Proof by deduction
You work up from things that you know are true until you reach the desired result. This is sometimes called a 'direct proof'.

Proof by contradiction
For this one, you prove that the opposite of the statement is impossible, so the statement must be true.

Disproof by counter-example
This is an easy one — you just find a single case to show the statement can't be true. If I said all even numbers are multiples of 4, you could disprove it by using 6 as a counter-example.

For Proof by Induction, Assume True for k and then Prove for k + 1

Proof by **mathematical induction** is a powerful method of proof that can be used to show a statement is true for every positive integer. It's a **four-step** process:

Proof by Induction
1) **Show** that the statement is true for an **initial value** (usually $n = 1$). This is the **base case**.
2) **Assume** that the statement is true for some **arbitrary value** $n = k$.
3) Using your assumption in step 2, **prove** that the statement is true for $n = k + 1$. This is the **inductive step**.
4) Write a **concluding statement** to explain how the previous steps have proven the result. It should say something like this: "If the statement is true for $n = k$ then we have shown it is true for $n = k + 1$. As we've shown it is true for $n = 1$, the statement must be true for all $n \geq 1$."

1) You're showing that **if** a statement is true for some value k, then it's true for $(k + 1)$. This then means it's also true for $(k + 2)$, $(k + 3)$, etc. But you **know** from Step 1 that it **is** true for an initial value — therefore it's true for **all** integer values higher than the initial value.

2) Don't forget about **step 1** — without it, the rest of the proof **doesn't work**. Think of induction as a **ladder**: the inductive step proves that if you're on one rung you can climb onto the **next rung**. But that's pretty useless if you can't get onto the **bottom rung** — that's what the base case is for.

3) You'll need to **read the question** carefully to figure out which **initial value** to use. If the question says "for all positive integers" then use $n = 1$, but if another range is given then use the **lowest value** — e.g. if the question said "for $n \geq 0$" then you'd use $n = 0$ as the initial value.

4) Remember that $\mathbb{N}$ and $\mathbb{Z}^+$ both mean the **positive** integers and $\mathbb{Z}_0^+$ means the **non-negative** integers.

Proof by induction can seem a bit weird to start with. Take some time to get your head round it and make sure you're happy before carrying on.

Use Induction for Divisibility Proofs

One situation where induction is really useful is for proving that expressions are **divisible** by a certain integer.

The inductive step of the process can be **fiddly** for these types of proof, but they usually follow the same **pattern**.

To guarantee the top marks, use proof by seduction.

For an expression f(n), the trick is to **manipulate f(k + 1)** so that it's expressed using the **terms that made up f(k)**. Then rearrange these to make terms with the required divisibility — one of these should be a **multiple of f(k)**.

Proof

Example: Prove that, for positive integers n, $8^n - 3^n$ is always divisible by 5.

Let $f(n) = 8^n - 3^n$.

1) Show that it's true for $n = 1$: $f(1) = 8^1 - 3^1 = 8 - 3 = 5$, which is divisible by 5.
   So the statement is true for $n = 1$.

2) Assume it's true for $n = k$, i.e. $f(k) = 8^k - 3^k$ is divisible by 5.

   $f(k)$ contains 8^k and 3^k so write $f(k + 1)$ in terms of those.

3) Now consider $n = k + 1$: $f(k + 1) = 8^{k+1} - 3^{k+1} = 8 \times 8^k - 3 \times 3^k$
   $= (5 + 3) \times 8^k - 3 \times 3^k$
   $= 5 \times 8^k + 3(8^k - 3^k)$
   $= 5 \times 8^k + 3f(k)$

   Split up the terms so $f(k + 1)$ can be written as a multiple of $f(k)$ plus something that's a multiple of 5.

   5×8^k is divisible by 5, and $3f(k)$ is divisible by 5 (by the assumption in step 2), so their sum $f(k + 1)$ is divisible by 5.

4) In conclusion: **We have shown that if the statement is true for $n = k$, then it is true for $n = k + 1$. Since we have shown it to be true for $n = 1$, it must be true for all $n \geq 1$.**

Example: Prove that $27(23^n) + 17(10^{2n}) + 22n$ is divisible by 11 for all $n \in \mathbb{N}$.

Let $f(n) = 27(23^n) + 17(10^{2n}) + 22n$.

1) If $n = 1$ then $f(1) = 27(23^1) + 17(10^{2 \times 1}) + 22 = 621 + 1700 + 22 = 2343 = 11 \times 213$
   So the statement is true for $n = 1$.

2) Assume it's true for $n = k$, i.e. $f(k) = 27(23^k) + 17(10^{2k}) + 22k$ is divisible by 11.

3) Now consider $n = k + 1$: $f(k + 1) = 27(23^{k+1}) + 17(10^{2(k+1)}) + 22(k + 1)$
   $= 23 \times 27(23^k) + 10^2 \times 17(10^{2k}) + 22(k + 1)$
   $= (22 + 1) \times 27(23^k) + (99 + 1) \times 17(10^{2k}) + 22k + 22$
   $= 22 \times 27(23^k) + 99 \times 17(10^{2k}) + 22 + f(k)$

   Each of the four terms is divisible by 11, so $f(k + 1)$ is divisible by 11.

4) In conclusion: **We have shown that if the statement is true for $n = k$, then it is true for $n = k + 1$. Since we have shown it to be true for $n = 1$, it must be true for all $n \in \mathbb{N}$.**

Practice Questions

Q1 Use induction to prove that $15^n - 3^n$ is divisible by 12 for all positive integer values of n.

Q2 Show by induction that $4^n + 7^n + 10^n$ is divisible by 3 for all $n \in \mathbb{Z}_0^+$.

Q3 Prove that $2^{6n} + 3^{2n-2}$ is divisible by 5 for all $n \in \mathbb{N}$.

Q4 Show that $2^{n+2} + 3^{2n+1}$ is divisible by 7 for all non-negative integers n.

Q5 Prove that $3^{2n+2} + 8n - 9$ is divisible by 8 for all $n \in \mathbb{Z}^+$.

Exam Questions

Q1 Prove by induction that $(2^{3n-3})(3^{n-1}) - 1$ is divisible by 23 for all integers $n \geq 2$. **[5 marks]**

Q2 Prove by induction that $f(n) = 2^{2n+1} + 4(7^n)$ is divisible by 6 for all integers $n \geq 1$. **[5 marks]**

Labour by induction — assume you're pregnant with n = k babies...

Proof by induction is quite a simple idea, but can be used in loads of different ways. As well as for divisibility proofs, it's really useful for proving things to do with powers of matrices and summation of series. We'll get round to covering those on p.24 and p.40-41. And if it can be used in Question K, consider if it can be used in Question K + 1...

Complex Numbers

The square root of a negative number has never made sense — until now. Thanks to complex numbers, so many equations that were once unsolvable, now have solutions. So, without any further ado...

Imaginary Numbers are the Square Roots of Negative Numbers

1) **Real numbers** are the ones you've been using all your life — they make up the entire number line and consist of both rational and irrational numbers.

2) Real numbers aren't the only type of numbers though — there are also things called **imaginary numbers.**

3) Every imaginary number is a multiple of the **imaginary unit**, **i**, defined as:

$$i = \sqrt{-1} \qquad i^2 = -1$$ From this, you get: $\ i^3 = i^2 \times i = -1 \times i = -i, \quad i^4 = i^2 \times i^2 = -1 \times -1 = 1$

4) You can perform operations on imaginary numbers like you would on other numbers:

Examples: $\ i + i = 2i \qquad 7i^2 = 7 \times -1 = -7 \qquad \sqrt{-2} = \sqrt{2}\sqrt{-1} = \sqrt{2}\,i \qquad (4i)^3 = 4^3 i^3 = 64 \times -i = -64i$

Some books might use the letter j for imaginary numbers.

Complex Numbers have Real and Imaginary Parts

1) A **complex number** has the **general form** $a + bi$, where a and b are real numbers.

2) a is the **real part** and b is the **imaginary part** — they're written as $\text{Re}(a + bi) = a$ and $\text{Im}(a + bi) = b$ respectively.

3) To **add** or **subtract** complex numbers, just add or subtract the real and imaginary parts separately.

Examples: If $z_1 = 3 + 4i$ and $z_2 = 6 - 2i$, work out each of the following:

a) $z_1 + z_2 \quad = (3 + 4i) + (6 - 2i) = 3 + 4i + 6 - 2i = (3 + 6) + (4i - 2i) = \mathbf{9 + 2i}$

b) $z_2 - z_1 \quad = (6 - 2i) - (3 + 4i) = 6 - 2i - 3 - 4i = (6 - 3) + (-2i - 4i) = \mathbf{3 - 6i}$

A general complex number is often given the letter z, and the set of all complex numbers is denoted by $\mathbb{C}$.

4) You can **multiply** complex numbers by putting them into **brackets** and expanding.

5) The **answer** will usually be another complex number — but you might get just a real or an imaginary number.

6) Look for any ways of **simplifying** your answer — for instance, writing any i^2 terms as real numbers.

Example: For the complex numbers $s = 3 - 7i$ and $t = 5 + 4i$, find st.

$st = (3 - 7i)(5 + 4i) = 15 + 12i - 35i - 28i^2 = 15 - 23i - 28i^2$
$\qquad = 15 - 23i - (28 \times -1) = \mathbf{43 - 23i}$

Every Complex Number has a Complex Conjugate

1) The **conjugate** of the complex number $z = a + bi$ is written as $z^* = a - bi$ (sometimes written $\bar{z}$).

2) The **real** part stays the **same** but the **sign changes** on the **imaginary** part.
So for example, if $z = 5 + 13i$ then $\mathbf{z^* = 5 - 13i}$. And if $z = -2i - 7$ then $\mathbf{z^* = 2i - 7}$.

3) Dividing complex numbers is a bit trickier than the other operations — you have to use the **complex conjugate**:

Example: Write $\dfrac{2 + 2i}{3 - i}$ as a complex number in the form $a + bi$.

This is similar to rationalising the denominator when working with surds.

① Multiply top and bottom by the complex conjugate of the denominator.

The conjugate of $3 - i$ is $3 + i$:
$$\frac{(2 + 2i)(3 + i)}{(3 - i)(3 + i)} = \frac{6 + 2i + 6i + 2i^2}{9 + 3i - 3i - i^2}$$

② Simplify the numerator and denominator.

$$\frac{6 + 2i + 6i + 2i^2}{9 + 3i - 3i - i^2} = \frac{6 + 8i - 2}{9 - (-1)} = \frac{4 + 8i}{10}$$

③ Separate into real and imaginary parts, and simplify any fractions.

$$\frac{4 + 8i}{10} = \frac{4}{10} + \frac{8i}{10} = \frac{2}{5} + \frac{4}{5}i$$

The denominator zz will always be a real number.*

Complex Numbers

Solve Equations by Equating the Real and Imaginary parts

1) When you're given an equation involving complex numbers, you can **equate** the real parts and the imaginary parts **separately**. You can then form a pair of **simultaneous equations**.

2) You'll have to **substitute** $x + y$i into an equation to represent a complex number — like in the examples below.

Example: Solve the equation $z^* + 5iz = 2 + 34i$.

Let $z = x + y$i, then $z^* = x - y$i.

$z^* + 5iz = x - y\text{i} + 5\text{i}(x + y\text{i}) = x - y\text{i} + 5x\text{i} + 5y\text{i}^2 = x - y\text{i} + 5x\text{i} - 5y = (x - 5y) + (5x - y)\text{i}$

$$\Rightarrow (x - 5y) + (5x - y)\text{i} = 2 + 34\text{i}$$

Equate the real parts and imaginary parts separately: ①$x - 5y = 2$ ②$5x - y = 34$

Solve these equations simultaneously: $5 \times$①: $5x - 25y = 10$

$5 \times$①$-$②: $-24y = -24 \Rightarrow y = 1$

Plug this value for y into one of the equations: $x - 5(1) = 2 \Rightarrow x = 7$

Combine x and y back into a complex number: $z = x + y$i, so $z = 7 + \mathbf{i}$

Two complex numbers are equal if and only if their real and imaginary parts are equal.

Example: Find the square roots of $8 + 6i$.

Let $\sqrt{8 + 6\text{i}} = x + y$i, then $8 + 6\text{i} = (x + y\text{i})^2 = x^2 + 2xy\text{i} + y^2\text{i}^2 = x^2 + 2xy\text{i} - y^2 = (x^2 - y^2) + 2xy\text{i}$

Equate the real and imaginary parts separately: ①$x^2 - y^2 = 8$ ②$2xy = 6 \Rightarrow y = \dfrac{3}{x}$

Solve simultaneously by substituting ② into ①: $x^2 - \dfrac{9}{x^2} = 8 \Rightarrow x^4 - 9 = 8x^2 \Rightarrow x^4 - 8x^2 - 9 = 0$

$$(x^2 + 1)(x^2 - 9) = 0$$

x and y must both be real numbers. $\longrightarrow$ $x^2 = -1$ has no real solutions.

$x^2 = 9 \Rightarrow x = 3$ and $x = -3$.

Plug these values for x back into the other equation: When $x = 3$, $y = 1$, and when $x = -3$, $y = -1$

So the roots are $\mathbf{3 + i}$ and $\mathbf{-3 - i}$.

Practice Questions

Q1 Write the real part, imaginary part and complex conjugate of each of these numbers:
a) $3 + 2$i   b) $-11 - 8$i   c) 5 d) 17i

Q2 Write the following numbers as complex numbers in the form $a + b$i:
a) $(9 + 3\text{i}) - (5 - 2\text{i})$ b) $(4 - 6\text{i})(3\text{i} - 2)$ c) $\dfrac{3\text{i} + 5}{2 - 9\text{i}}$

Q3 For the following complex numbers, write down the complex conjugate and compute zz^*:
a) $6 - 3$i   b) $-8 + 2$i   c) 14i   d) 12

Exam Questions

Q1 Complex numbers z_1 and z_2 are given by $z_1 = 3 + 4\text{i}$ and $z_2 = 1 - 2\text{i}$.
Giving your answers in the form $x + y$i, where x and y are real numbers, find:
a) $2z_1 - z_2$ [2 marks]
b) $(z_1 z_1^*)(z_2 z_2^*)$ [3 marks]
c) $\dfrac{z_1}{z_2}$ [3 marks]

Q2 Solve the following equations, giving your answers in the form $a + b$i:
a) $3iz^* + 4z = -1 - 6\text{i}$ [3 marks]
b) $4iz - 2z^* = 28 - 14\text{i}$ [3 marks]
c) $z^2 = \text{i}$ [4 marks]

$\sqrt{-1}$ love complex numbers...

After all these years, it turns out you actually can find the square root of negative numbers... The best thing is, the root of a complex number is also a complex number, so there's no need to invent any other types of numbers.

Complex Roots of Polynomials

If a graph doesn't touch the x-axis, it doesn't have any roots, right? Not so fast...

Quadratic Equations might have Complex Roots

1) Every polynomial of **degree** n has exactly n **roots**. (Repeated roots are counted multiple times — e.g. for $f(x) = (x - 1)^4$, the root $x = 1$ is counted 4 times.) This is part of the **fundamental theorem of algebra**, or **FTA**.

2) Consider the **quadratic equation** $ax^2 + bx + c = 0$ where a, b and c are **real**. If $b^2 - 4ac < 0$, then there are **no real roots**. But by the FTA, there **must be** two complex roots.

3) Complex roots occur in **conjugate pairs**, so if $z = p + iq$ is a root then so is $z^* = p - iq$. This is true for **any polynomial** with **real coefficients**.

Example: Solve $2x^2 + 2x + 13 = 0$.

$a = 2$, $b = 2$ and $c = 13$

$$x = \frac{-2 \pm \sqrt{2^2 - (4 \times 2 \times 13)}}{4} = \frac{-2 \pm \sqrt{4 - 104}}{4}$$

$$= \frac{-2 \pm \sqrt{-100}}{4}$$

$$= \frac{-2 \pm \sqrt{100}\sqrt{-1}}{4}$$

Notice the solutions are a conjugate pair.

$$= \frac{-2 \pm 10i}{4}$$

$$= -0.5 \pm 2.5i$$

So $x = -0.5 + 2.5i$ and $x = -0.5 - 2.5i$

Example: Find the quadratic equation with real coefficients that has a complex root $2 + 3i$.

The other root of the quadratic is **2 − 3i**.

So, $(x - (2 - 3i))(x - (2 + 3i)) = 0$

$\Rightarrow x^2 - (2 + 3i)x - (2 - 3i)x + (2 - 3i)(2 + 3i) = 0$

$\Rightarrow x^2 - 2x - 3ix - 2x + 3ix + 4 + 6i - 6i - 9i^2 = 0$

$\Rightarrow x^2 - 4x + 4 + 9 = 0$

$\Rightarrow x^2 - 4x + 13 = 0$

Cubic Equations can have both Real and Complex Roots

The FTA tells you that cubic equations have **three roots** in total. Complex roots come in pairs, so cubic equations either have **3 real roots**, or **1 real root and 1 pair of complex conjugate roots**.

Example: Show that −1 is a root of the equation $x^3 - 2x^2 + 2x + 5 = 0$, and find the other two roots.

1) Substitute $x = -1$ into the equation:
$(-1)^3 - 2(-1)^2 + 2(-1) + 5 = -1 - 2 - 2 + 5 = 0$, so **−1 is a root.**

2) Divide the cubic equation by $(x + 1)$ to get a quadratic factor:

$$\begin{array}{r} x^2 - 3x + 5 \\ x + 1 \overline{)\, x^3 - 2x^2 + 2x + 5} \\ -(x^3 + x^2) \\ \hline -3x^2 + 2x \\ +(3x^2 + 3x) \\ \hline 5x + 5 \\ -(5x + 5) \\ \hline 0 \end{array}$$

If −1 is a root, then $(x + 1)$ is a factor of the cubic equation.

3) Find the other roots, where $x^2 - 3x + 5 = 0$, using the quadratic formula.

$$x = \frac{3 \pm \sqrt{(-3^2) - (4 \times 1 \times 5)}}{2} = \frac{3 \pm \sqrt{9 - 20}}{2}$$

$$= \frac{3 \pm \sqrt{-11}}{2}$$

$$= \frac{3 \pm \sqrt{11}i}{2}$$

So the other two roots are:

$$x = \frac{3}{2} + \frac{\sqrt{11}}{2}i \text{ and } x = \frac{3}{2} - \frac{\sqrt{11}}{2}i$$

Example: Let $f(x) = 2x^3 - 5x^2 + 7x - 6$. Given that $(2x - 3)$ is a factor of $f(x)$, find all 3 roots of $f(x)$.

1) One root is $2x - 3 = 0 \Rightarrow x = \frac{3}{2}$

2) Divide the cubic equation by $(2x - 3)$ to get a quadratic factor:

$$\begin{array}{r} x^2 - x + 2 \\ 2x - 3 \overline{)\, 2x^3 - 5x^2 + 7x - 6} \\ -(2x^3 - 3x^2) \\ \hline -2x^2 + 7x \\ +(2x^2 - 3x) \\ \hline 4x - 6 \\ -(4x - 6) \\ \hline 0 \end{array}$$

3) Find the other roots, where $x^2 - x + 2 = 0$, using the quadratic formula.

$$x = \frac{1 \pm \sqrt{(-1^2) - (4 \times 1 \times 2)}}{2} = \frac{1 \pm \sqrt{1 - 8}}{2}$$

$$= \frac{1 \pm \sqrt{-7}}{2}$$

$$= \frac{1 \pm \sqrt{7}i}{2}$$

So the three roots are:

$$x = \frac{1}{2} + \frac{\sqrt{7}}{2}i, \ x = \frac{1}{2} - \frac{\sqrt{7}}{2}i \text{ and } x = \frac{3}{2}$$

Complex Roots of Polynomials

Some *Quartic Equations* have no *Real Roots*

A **quartic equation** is a polynomial with an x^4 term (and nothing higher). So by the FTA it must have four roots, which can be: **4 real roots**, **2 real roots and 1 pair of complex conjugate roots** or **2 pairs of complex conjugate roots**.

Example: A quartic equation is given by
$f(x) = x^4 - x^3 - 3x^2 + 17x - 30$.
Given that $f(-3) = f(2) = 0$,
find the other two roots of $f(x)$.

1) $(x + 3)$ and $(x - 2)$ are factors of $f(x)$
$\Rightarrow (x + 3)(x - 2) = x^2 + x - 6$ is also a factor.

$$
\begin{array}{r}
x^2 - 2x + 5 \\
x^2 + x - 6 \overline{\smash{)}\ x^4 - x^3 - 3x^2 + 17x - 30} \\
-(x^4 + x^3 - 6x^2) \\
\hline
-2x^3 + 3x^2 + 17x \\
+(2x^3 + 2x^2 - 12x) \\
\hline
5x^2 + 5x - 30 \\
-(5x^2 + 5x - 30) \\
\hline
0
\end{array}
$$

This is an example of a quartic equation that has one pair of complex roots and 2 real roots

2) Find the other roots, where $x^2 - 2x + 5 = 0$, using the quadratic formula.

$$x = \frac{2 \pm \sqrt{(-2)^2 - (4 \times 1 \times 5)}}{2} = \frac{2 \pm \sqrt{-16}}{2}$$

$$= 1 \pm 2i$$

So the other two roots are: $x = 1 + 2i$ and $x = 1 - 2i$

Example: Two roots of a quartic equation are $1 + 2i$ and $3 - 4i$.
What is the quartic equation?

$1 + 2i$ is a root $\Rightarrow (1 + 2i)^* = 1 - 2i$ is a root
$3 - 4i$ is a root $\Rightarrow (3 - 4i)^* = 3 + 4i$ is a root
So the quartic equation is:
$[x - (1 + 2i)][(x - (1 - 2i)][(x - (3 - 4i)][(x - (3 + 4i)]$
$= (x^2 - 2x + 5)(x^2 - 6x + 25)$
$= x^4 - 8x^3 + 42x^2 - 80x + 125$

This is an example of a quartic equation with 2 pairs of complex roots and no real roots.

Practice Questions

In the following questions, all polynomials have real coefficients.

Q1 Give the missing roots of the following:
  a) A quadratic equation where one of the roots is $1 - 7i$
  b) A quartic equation where two of the roots are $2i$ and $5i - 2$

Q2 Find the quadratic function $f(x)$ that satisfies $f(1 + i) = 0$

Q3 By factorising the following polynomials, determine how many real roots and how many complex roots they each have:
  a) $x^3 - x^2 + x - 1$ b) $x^4 - 16$ c) $x^2 + 1$ d) $x^4 - 2x^3 - x^2 + 2x$

Q4 Explain why a cubic equation can't have 3 complex roots, but a quartic equation can have 4 complex roots.

Steve was adamant that he had hair, and couldn't accept that the roots were imaginary

Exam Questions

Q1 The function $g(x)$ is given by $g(x) = x^4 - 2x^3 + 15x^2 - 134x + 290$.
Given that $3 - i$ is a root of $g(x)$, find the other three roots. [7 marks]

Q2 The function $f(x)$ is given by $f(x) = x^3 - 4x^2 + 17x - 26$.
  a) Given that $f(x) = (x - 2)(x^2 + ax + b)$, find the values of a and b. [2 marks]
  b) Hence, find the three roots of the equation $x^3 - 4x^2 + 17x - 26 = 0$. [3 marks]

Q3 $f(x) = x^3 + px^2 + qx - 20$, where p and q are real numbers.
Given that $f(2) = f(1 - 3i) = 0$, find the values of p and q. [3 marks]

The exam is real and the numbers are imaginary — don't get it mixed up...

If in your pre-complex numbers life it upset you that there were "unsolvable" quadratics, I bet you're chuffed to bits now. And just because the solutions aren't real doesn't mean they're not useful — being able to find complex solutions to polynomials crops up in all sorts of places, such as in aerospace engineering and quantum mechanics.

Argand Diagrams

*Argand diagrams are a bit like a 2D number line for complex numbers. If complex numbers still seem
a bit abstract and weird, then hopefully these couple of pages will make things clearer.*

Complex Numbers can be represented Geometrically

1) **Complex numbers** can be represented by points on an
   Argand diagram. It's similar to a **Cartesian coordinate system**,
   but on an Argand diagram the **x-axis** becomes the **real axis**
   and the **y-axis** becomes the **imaginary axis**.

2) **Real numbers** are represented by points on the **real axis**
   and **imaginary numbers** by points on the **imaginary axis**.

3) The complex number $z = x + yi$ is represented by the
   point $(\text{Re}(z), \text{Im}(z)) = (x, y)$ on the Argand diagram.

4) z and its conjugate, z^*, will appear **symmetrically**
   about the **real axis** on an Argand diagram.

This coordinate system is also called the complex plane.

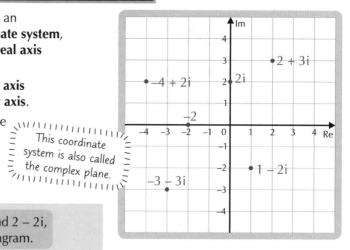

Example: Show the complex numbers $-3 + 3i$ and $2 - 2i$,
and their conjugates, on an Argand diagram.

The conjugate of $-3 + 3i$ is **$-3 - 3i$**.
The conjugate of $2 - 2i$ is **$2 + 2i$**.

*Notice how the complex numbers
and their conjugates appear an equal
distance above and below the real axis.*

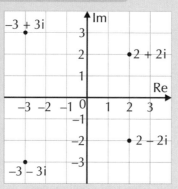

Many philosophers grappled with
the big question — if one axis is
imaginary, is a diagram real or not?

The Argand Diagram can be used for Addition and Subtraction

1) Complex numbers can be represented by **vectors from the origin** on an Argand diagram.

2) Then to add or subtract complex numbers you just **add or subtract** their **vectors**.

Example: Complex numbers z_1 and z_2 are represented by vectors on the Argand
diagram on the right. Draw vectors representing $(z_1 + z_2)$ and $(-z_1 - z_2)$.

$z_1 + z_2$:

$-z_1 - z_2$:

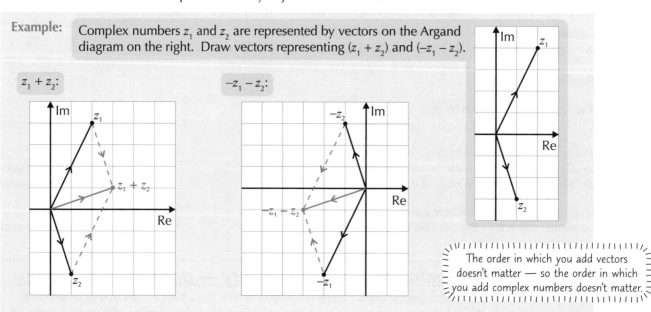

*The order in which you add vectors
doesn't matter — so the order in which
you add complex numbers doesn't matter.*

Argand Diagrams

Every *Number* has a *Modulus* and an *Argument*

1) Recall that the **modulus** of a real number x, written $|x|$, is the **size** (or **length**) of the number — it's always a positive value.

2) This idea of the length of a number can be extended to the complex numbers. For $z = x + yi$, you can work out the modulus using **Pythagoras' theorem**: $|z| = \sqrt{x^2 + y^2}$.

3) Remember to only ever take the **positive square root.**

4) The **argument** of a complex number z, written **arg** z, is the angle between the **positive real axis** and the vector representing the complex number.

5) The argument is usually given in **radians**, where $-\pi < \arg z \leq \pi$. (This is sometimes called the **principal** argument.) So, measuring **anticlockwise** from the real axis gives a **positive** argument.

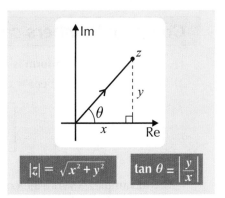

$$|z| = \sqrt{x^2 + y^2} \qquad \tan \theta = \left|\frac{y}{x}\right|$$

6) For $z = x + yi$, you can work out the angle, θ, between the vector and the real axis using $\theta = \tan^{-1}\left|\dfrac{y}{x}\right|$. You might have to do a bit more work to get the argument — see the example below:

All positive real numbers have an argument of 0, and all negative real numbers have an argument of π.

Example: Find the modulus and principal argument of the following complex numbers to 2 decimal places:
 a) $z_1 = 3 - 4i$ b) $z_2 = -4 + 2i$

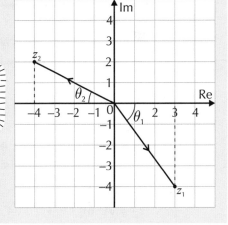

a) $|z_1| = \sqrt{3^2 + (-4)^2} = \sqrt{25} = 5$

$\theta_1 = \tan^{-1}\left(\dfrac{4}{3}\right) = 0.9272...$ radians

So arg $z_1 = $ **−0.93 radians (2 d.p)**

It's helpful to sketch the complex numbers on an Argand diagram.

b) $|z_2| = \sqrt{(-4)^2 + 2^2} = \sqrt{20} = 2\sqrt{5} = $ **4.47 (2 d.p)**

$\theta_2 = \tan^{-1}\left(\dfrac{2}{4}\right) = 0.4636...$ radians

But θ_2 is the angle made with the <u>negative</u> real axis:

So arg $z_2 = \pi - 0.4636...$ radians = **2.68 radians (2 d.p)**

Practice Questions

Q1 Plot the complex numbers $s = 1 + 4i$ and $t = -4 - 5i$ on an Argand diagram and use these points to plot $t + s$.

Q2 Find the modulus for each of the following:
 a) $5 - 6i$ b) $-4 + 4i$ c) $7i$ d) -9

Q3 Find the argument in radians to 2 d.p. for each of the following:
 a) $2 - 6i$ b) $-9 + 3i$ c) 8 d) $-5i$

Exam Questions

Q1 Complex numbers s and t are given by $s = 2 - 5i$ and $t = 5 - 4i$.
 a) Show s, t and $s - t$ on the same Argand diagram. [3 marks]
 b) Find $|st|$. [3 marks]
 c) Show that $\arg(s) + \arg(t) = \arg(st)$, giving any angles in radians. [3 marks]

Q2 The complex number z is given by $z = 8 - bi$, where b is a positive real number.
 a) $|z| = 10$. Find the value of b. [1 mark]
 b) Draw z and z^* on the same Argand diagram. [2 marks]
 c) Use your answers to parts a) and b) to find $\arg(z)$ and $\arg(z^*)$ in radians, to 2 d.p. [2 marks]

Q3 Given that $-3 + i$ and $4 - 2i$ are roots of a quartic $f(x)$, find and plot all roots of $f(x)$ on an Argand diagram. [3 marks]

A grand diagram, don't you think...?

Argand diagrams are a fantastic way of seeing how the imaginary numbers fit with the real numbers. They're not just floating somewhere completely separate to the reals — they're right next to them, but going in a different direction...

Modulus-Argument Calculations

You can use the stuff you've just learnt about modulus and argument to do all sorts of cool things, including writing complex numbers in a completely different form. I use the word 'cool' very loosely...

Complex Numbers can be written in Modulus-Argument Form

1) **Modulus-argument form** is a way of writing complex numbers using the **modulus** and **argument**.

2) For a complex number $z = x + yi$ the **modulus-argument form** is:

$$z = r(\cos \theta + i \sin \theta)$$ where $r = |z|$ and $\theta = \arg z$.

Example: Write the complex numbers $z_1 = 2 - 5i$, $z_2 = -1 + 4i$ and $z_3 = -6 - 3i$ in modulus-argument form, giving any angles in radians to 2 d.p.

We need to find the modulus and principal argument of each of the complex numbers.
It's helpful to draw a sketch of the three complex numbers.

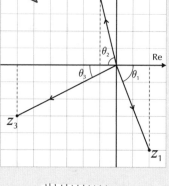

$z_1 = 2 - 5i$:

$|z_1| = \sqrt{2^2 + (-5)^2} = \sqrt{29}$, $\theta_1 = \tan^{-1}\left(\frac{5}{2}\right) = 1.1902...$

θ_1 is below the positive real axis, so the argument must be negative:

$\Rightarrow \arg z_1 = -1.19$ radians (2 d.p)

$\Rightarrow z_1 = \sqrt{29}\,(\cos(-1.19) + i\sin(-1.19))$

$z_2 = -1 + 4i$:

$|z_2| = \sqrt{(-1)^2 + 4^2} = \sqrt{17}$, $\theta_2 = \tan^{-1}\left(\frac{4}{1}\right) = 1.3258...$

θ_2 is the angle made with the <u>negative</u> real axis:

$\arg z_2 = \pi - 1.3258... = 1.82$ radians (2 d.p)

$\Rightarrow z_2 = \sqrt{17}\,(\cos(1.82) + i\sin(1.82))$

$z_3 = -6 - 3i$:

$|z_3| = \sqrt{(-6)^2 + (-3)^2} = \sqrt{45} = 3\sqrt{5}$, $\theta_3 = \tan^{-1}\left(\frac{3}{6}\right) = 0.4636...$

$\Rightarrow \arg z_3 = -(\pi - 0.4636...) = 0.4636... - \pi = -2.68$ radians (2 d.p)

$\Rightarrow z_3 = 3\sqrt{5}\,(\cos(-2.68) + i\sin(-2.68))$

It's easy to check if you've converted correctly — just plug the numbers in on a calculator and you should end up with the original complex number.

Multiply Complex Numbers using the Modulus-Argument Form

1) Consider the complex numbers $z_1 = r_1(\cos \theta_1 + i \sin \theta_1)$ and $z_2 = r_2(\cos \theta_2 + i \sin \theta_2)$:

$z_1 z_2 = r_1(\cos \theta_1 + i \sin \theta_1)\, r_2(\cos \theta_2 + i \sin \theta_2)$
$= r_1 r_2[\cos \theta_1 \cos \theta_2 - \sin \theta_1 \sin \theta_2 + i(\sin \theta_1 \cos \theta_2 + \sin \theta_2 \cos \theta_1)]$.

Then, by using the sin and cos addition formulas, we get:

$$z_1 z_2 = r_1 r_2 [\cos (\theta_1 + \theta_2) + i \sin (\theta_1 + \theta_2)]$$

2) So the product of z_1 and z_2 has **modulus** $r_1 r_2$ and **argument** $\theta_1 + \theta_2$. If $\theta_1 + \theta_2$ is outside the range $-\pi < \theta \le \pi$, then you'll have to add or subtract multiples of 2π until it's within the range.

Example: Find the product of $z_1 = 5(\cos \frac{\pi}{2} + i \sin \frac{\pi}{2})$ and $z_2 = 4(\cos \frac{2\pi}{3} + i \sin \frac{2\pi}{3})$.
Give your answer in modulus-argument form.

$z_1 z_2 = 5(\cos \frac{\pi}{2} + i \sin \frac{\pi}{2}) \times 4(\cos \frac{2\pi}{3} + i \sin \frac{2\pi}{3}) = (5 \times 4)[\cos\left(\frac{\pi}{2} + \frac{2\pi}{3}\right) + i\sin\left(\frac{\pi}{2} + \frac{2\pi}{3}\right)]$

Make sure you give the argument as a value between $-\pi$ and π.

$= 20[\cos\left(\frac{3\pi}{6} + \frac{4\pi}{6}\right) + i\sin\left(\frac{3\pi}{6} + \frac{4\pi}{6}\right)]$

$= 20[\cos\left(\frac{7\pi}{6}\right) + i\sin\left(\frac{7\pi}{6}\right)] = 20[\cos\left(-\frac{5\pi}{6}\right) + i\sin\left(-\frac{5\pi}{6}\right)]$

Modulus-Argument Calculations

Divide Complex Numbers using the Modulus-Argument Form

1) If $z_1 = r_1(\cos\theta_1 + i\sin\theta_1)$ and $z_2 = r_2(\cos\theta_2 + i\sin\theta_2)$ are complex numbers, then:

$\dfrac{z_1}{z_2} = \dfrac{r_1(\cos\theta_1 + i\sin\theta_1)}{r_2(\cos\theta_2 + i\sin\theta_2)}$. Multiplying top and bottom by $(\cos\theta_2 - i\sin\theta_2)$ gives:

$\dfrac{z_1}{z_2} = \dfrac{r_1(\cos\theta_1 + i\sin\theta_1)(\cos\theta_2 - i\sin\theta_2)}{r_2(\cos\theta_2 + i\sin\theta_2)(\cos\theta_2 - i\sin\theta_2)} = \dfrac{r_1[\cos\theta_1\cos\theta_2 + \sin\theta_1\sin\theta_2 + i(\sin\theta_1\cos\theta_2 - \cos\theta_1\sin\theta_2)]}{r_2[\cos^2\theta_2 + \sin^2\theta_2]}$

Then, by using the sin and cos addition formulas along with the identity $\cos^2\theta + \sin^2\theta \equiv 1$, we get:

$$\frac{z_1}{z_2} = \frac{r_1}{r_2}[\cos(\theta_1 - \theta_2) + i\sin(\theta_1 - \theta_2)]$$

2) So **dividing** z_1 by z_2 gives a complex number with **modulus** $\dfrac{r_1}{r_2}$ and **argument** $\theta_1 - \theta_2$.

Example: Given that $p = 28[\cos\left(-\frac{3\pi}{4}\right) + i\sin\left(-\frac{3\pi}{4}\right)]$ and $q = 8(\cos\frac{2\pi}{5} + i\sin\frac{2\pi}{5})$, find $\frac{p}{q}$, giving your answer in the form $a + ib$, where a and b are given to 2 d.p.

$\dfrac{p}{q} = \dfrac{28\left(\cos\left(-\frac{3\pi}{4}\right) + i\sin\left(-\frac{3\pi}{4}\right)\right)}{8\left(\cos\frac{2\pi}{5} + i\sin\frac{2\pi}{5}\right)} = \dfrac{28}{8}[\cos\left(-\frac{3\pi}{4} - \frac{2\pi}{5}\right) + i\sin\left(-\frac{3\pi}{4} - \frac{2\pi}{5}\right)]$

$= \dfrac{7}{2}[\cos\left(-\frac{23\pi}{20}\right) + i\sin\left(-\frac{23\pi}{20}\right)]$

$= -3.1185... + 1.5889...i = \mathbf{-3.12 + 1.59i}$ **(2 d.p.)**

Summary:

If the modulus-argument forms of z_1 and z_2 are $z_1 = r_1(\cos\theta_1 + i\sin\theta_1)$ and $z_2 = r_2(\cos\theta_2 + i\sin\theta_2)$:

$|z_1 z_2| = |z_1||z_2| = r_1 r_2$ $\qquad \left|\dfrac{z_1}{z_2}\right| = \dfrac{|z_1|}{|z_2|} = \dfrac{r_1}{r_2}$ $\qquad \arg(z_1 z_2) = \arg(z_1) + \arg(z_2) = \theta_1 + \theta_2$ $\qquad \arg\left(\dfrac{z_1}{z_2}\right) = \arg(z_1) - \arg(z_2) = \theta_1 - \theta_2$

You should try to learn these results off by heart.

Practice Questions

Q1 Write each of the following numbers in modulus-argument form giving angles in radians to 2 d.p.
   a) $16 - 13i$　　　b) $-3 + 10i$　　　c) $-8 - 9i$

Q2 Find the product of $z_1 = 6(\cos\frac{\pi}{6} + i\sin\frac{\pi}{6})$ and $z_2 = 5(\cos\frac{\pi}{3} + i\sin\frac{\pi}{3})$.
   Give your answer in the form $a + ib$.

Q3 Given that $p = 32[\cos\left(-\frac{3\pi}{8}\right) + i\sin\left(-\frac{3\pi}{8}\right)]$ and $q = 12[\cos\left(-\frac{4\pi}{5}\right) + i\sin\left(-\frac{4\pi}{5}\right)]$,
   find $\frac{p}{q}$, giving your answer in modulus-argument form.

Exam Questions

Q1 The complex number z is given by $z = -5 + 12i$. For the parts a), b) & c) give any angles in radians to 2 d.p.
   a) Write z in modulus-argument form. [3 marks]
   b) Find the value of $\frac{2z^*}{z^2}$. Give your answer in modulus-argument form. [4 marks]
   c) Find the square roots of z. Give your answers in modulus-argument form. [7 marks]

Q2 Let $z_1 = 3 + 2i$ and $z_2 = -3 - 5i$.
   a) Write z_1 and z_2 in modulus-argument form, giving any angles in radians to 2 d.p. [4 marks]
   b) Compute $\frac{z_1}{z_2}$, giving your answer in the form $a + ib$, where a and b are given to 2 d.p. [3 marks]

No, the modulus is 4. Ok, let's not have a modulus-argument...

Finding the modulus of complex numbers is the easy bit — just use Pythagoras' theorem. Finding the argument is trickier — make sure you know which angle the tan formula is giving you, then use it to work out the argument. It all becomes much easier once you practise it — so if you haven't already, you know what to do...

Complex Loci

You will have seen loci before at GCSE — you will have been given a description of a locus in plain English. The loci here are similar, but a bit more mathsy — lots of lovely equations. And complex numbers, of course.

A **Locus** of **Points** can be described by an **Equation**

Before we get going on the **complex loci**, it's worth having a quick recap of normal loci. When you're asked to find a **locus of points** for a certain **rule**, you need to give an **equation** that is **always satisfied** by that rule.

Example: Let P be the set of points (x, y) that are 5 units from the origin. Find the locus of P.

1) The set of points a fixed distance from a single point is a circle.

2) So the locus of points is the equation for a circle with centre $(0, 0)$ and radius $5 \Rightarrow x^2 + y^2 = 25$

Complex Loci are points on an **Argand Diagram**

Real loci are plotted on Cartesian axes, whereas **complex loci** are plotted on an **Argand diagram**.

Example: A complex number, z, is represented by the point P in the Argand diagram. z satisfies $|z - 3 + 4i| = 4$. Sketch the locus of P.

Set $z = x + yi$ and recall that $|z| = \sqrt{x^2 + y^2} \Rightarrow |z|^2 = x^2 + y^2$

So, $|z - 3 + 4i|^2 = 4^2 \Rightarrow |(x + yi) - 3 + 4i|^2 = 16$

$\Rightarrow |(x - 3) + (y + 4)i|^2 = 16 \Rightarrow \left(\sqrt{(x-3)^2 + (y+4)^2}\right)^2 = 16$

$\Rightarrow (x - 3)^2 + (y + 4)^2 = 16$

A locus of points must be the only points in the plane to obey the given rule.

So, this equation describes **circle centred** at **(3, –4)**, with **radius 4.**

More generally, $|z - (x + yi)| = r$ describes a circle centred at (x, y) with radius r.

Complex Loci can also describe **Lines**

1) Equations of the form $|z - a| = |z - b|$, where a and b are complex numbers, describe **straight lines**. By writing $z = x + yi$ and squaring both sides, you can find the **straight line equation** of the locus.

Example: If $|z + 2 - i| = |z + 3i|$, construct the locus of z.

If $z = x + yi$, then: $|x + yi + 2 - i| = |x + yi + 3i|$

$\Rightarrow |(x + 2) + (y - 1)i| = |x + (y + 3)i|$

$\Rightarrow |(x + 2) + (y - 1)i|^2 = |x + (y + 3)i|^2$

$\Rightarrow (x + 2)^2 + (y - 1)^2 = x^2 + (y + 3)^2$

$\Rightarrow x^2 + 4x + 4 + y^2 - 2y + 1 = x^2 + y^2 + 6y + 9$

$\Rightarrow 4x - 2y + 5 = 6y + 9 \Rightarrow 4x - 4 = 8y \Rightarrow y = \frac{1}{2}x - \frac{1}{2}$

This is the locus of z, constructed on the right.

Remember that x and y are the real and imaginary parts, so your line equation will go on an Argand diagram.

2) The equation $\mathbf{arg\,(z - a) = \theta}$ represents complex loci called **half-lines** — they are straight lines that start at a specific point and only continue in **one direction**. First, you'll find the **line equation**, and then you'll have to **think carefully** about which values are **valid** for the locus.

3) When **sketching** a half-line, use an **arrow** to indicate the direction that it's valid. Often an **unshaded** circle is used to show the locus **excludes** an endpoint and a **shaded** circle shows it **includes** the endpoint.

Example: For $\arg(z - 5 - 2i) = \frac{\pi}{4}$, construct the locus of z.

If $z = x + yi$, then: $\arg[(x - 5) + (y - 2)i] = \frac{\pi}{4} \Rightarrow \tan^{-1}\left(\frac{y - 2}{x - 5}\right) = \frac{\pi}{4}$

$\Rightarrow \frac{y - 2}{x - 5} = \tan\frac{\pi}{4} = 1 \Rightarrow y - 2 = x - 5 \Rightarrow y = x - 3$

If $x < 5$ and $y < 2$, the complex number $(x - 5) + (y - 2)i$ would be in the bottom-left quadrant of the Argand diagram — i.e. its argument **can't** be $\frac{\pi}{4}$.

If $x = 5$ and $y = 2$, its argument is $0 \neq \frac{\pi}{4}$. So the locus is restricted to $x > 5, y > 2$.

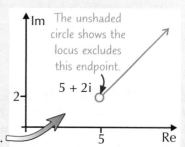

The unshaded circle shows the locus excludes this endpoint.

Complex Loci

Complex Numbers can be used to describe Regions

1) If a complex locus is an **equation**, it describes a **line** or a **curve**.
   But if the complex locus is an **inequality**, then it will describe a **region**.

2) Sometimes a region will be described by the set of points that satisfy **more than one** inequality. If it is,
   it could be written in set notation, so make sure you're familiar with what all the set symbols mean.

Example: a)   Shade in the region represented by $|z - 2 + i| < 3$.

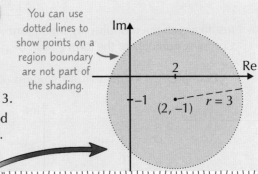

You can use dotted lines to show points on a region boundary are not part of the shading.

Firstly, solve the inequality as if it was an equation like we did on the previous page:
Set $z = x + yi$ and square both sides.
$|(x + yi) - 2 + i|^2 = 3^2 \Rightarrow (x - 2)^2 + (y + 1)^2 = 9$
The equation describes a circle centred at $(2, -1)$, with radius 3.

1) Now pick a point **inside** the circle (the centre is usually a good one), plug in the numbers and see if the inequality is satisfied.
   $(2 - 2)^2 + (-1 + 1)^2 = 0 < 9$

2) Conclude which region you're looking for.
   The point at the centre of the circle satisfies the inequality, so **the correct region is the inside of the circle.**

*If the centre didn't satisfy the inequality, then the correct region would be everything **outside** the circle.*

b)   Hence, sketch the set of points $A = \{z \in \mathbb{C} : |z - 2 + i| < 3\} \cap \{z \in \mathbb{C} : |z + 2 - i| > |z + 3i|\}$.

1) Work out which points satisfy each subset, one at a time.

2) From part a), $|z - 2 + i| < 3$ means that the points will be inside the circle of radius 3 centred at $(2, -1)$.

3) From the previous page, $|z + 2 - i| > |z + 3i|$ means the points must also satisfy $y < \frac{1}{2}(x - 1)$.

4) Pick a point to test, such as $(0, 0)$. It does not satisfy $y < \frac{1}{2}(x - 1)$, which means the origin is not part of the shaded region.

5) So, shade the region that satisfies $y < \frac{1}{2}(x - 1)$ **and** is inside the circle of radius 3 centred at $(2, -1)$.

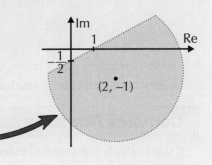

Practice Questions

Q1 Describe and sketch the locus of z when: a) $|z| = 6$ b) $|z + 8| = |z - 4|$ c) $\arg(z + 2 + 2i) = \frac{2\pi}{3}$

Q2 On an Argand diagram, shade in the regions represented by: Parts a) and c) have two inequalities here. Make sure your set of points satisfy both.
   a) $1 \leq |z + 2i| \leq 3$ b) $|z + 6| \geq |z + i|$
   c) $0 \leq \arg(z + 2 + 3i) \leq \frac{\pi}{3}$, and find the Cartesian equations of the straight lines that bound the region.

Exam Questions

Q1 The point P represents a complex number z on an Argand diagram such that $|z - 12i| = 2|z - 9|$
Find the equation of the locus of P, and describe its shape.   [4 marks]

Q2 The point Q represents a complex number z on an Argand diagram such that $\arg(z - 5) = -\frac{3\pi}{4}$
a) Sketch, on an Argand diagram, the locus of Q as z varies.   [2 marks]
b) Find **two** complex numbers for which both $|z + 4 + 3i| = 6$ and $\arg(z - 5) = -\frac{3\pi}{4}$ [5 marks]

Q3 Sketch the set of points $A = \{z \in \mathbb{C} : |z - 2i| > |z|\} \cap \{z \in \mathbb{C} : \frac{3\pi}{4} \leq \arg(z - 2) \leq \pi\}$ on an Argand diagram.   [5 marks]

I'm still not sure how I'd describe the region where I live...

A lot of this stuff here should be fairly familiar — you'll have seen equations of circles and lines before, but you're just sticking them on an Argand diagram this time. That half-line business is a bit trickier though, so watch out for that one — if you're unsure which half of the line you need, just try a couple of different values to help you figure it out.

Exponential Form of Complex Numbers

Grab a cup of tea and get ready for this one — you're about to see a relation that some people have described as 'the most remarkable formula in mathematics'. Personally, I'd give it an 11 out of 10.

Euler related the **Exponential Function** and **Trigonometric Functions**

Euler's relation will crop up throughout this section so it's **important** that you remember it:

$$e^{i\theta} = \cos\theta + i\sin\theta$$

Just like with the modulus-argument form, θ is restricted to the interval $-\pi < \theta \leq \pi$.
Complex numbers of the form $e^{i\theta}$ can be plotted on an Argand diagram. Each point lies on the unit circle.

Example: Plot the following points on an Argand diagram:

a) $e^{i\frac{\pi}{6}}$

$e^{i\frac{\pi}{6}} = \cos\frac{\pi}{6} + i\sin\frac{\pi}{6}$

$= \frac{\sqrt{3}}{2} + \frac{1}{2}i$

b) $e^{i\frac{2\pi}{3}}$

$e^{i\frac{2\pi}{3}} = \cos\frac{2\pi}{3} + i\sin\frac{2\pi}{3}$

$= -\frac{1}{2} + \frac{\sqrt{3}}{2}i$

c) $e^{-i\frac{\pi}{4}}$

$e^{-i\frac{\pi}{4}} = \cos\left(-\frac{\pi}{4}\right) + i\sin\left(-\frac{\pi}{4}\right)$

$= \frac{\sqrt{2}}{2} - \frac{\sqrt{2}}{2}i$

d) $e^{i\pi}$

$e^{i\pi} = \cos\pi + i\sin\pi$

$= -1$

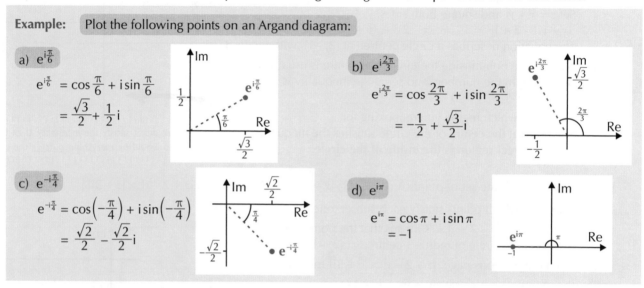

Once you've learnt about **Maclaurin series** (see pages 44-45), you'll be able to **derive** Euler's relation.

Complex Numbers can be written in **Exponential Form**

If you multiply both sides of **Euler's relation** by r, the left-hand side of the relation becomes the **exponential form** of the complex number. The right-hand side becomes the **modulus-argument** form of the complex number z, where $|z| = r$ and $\arg(z) = \theta$.

$$re^{i\theta} = r(\cos\theta + i\sin\theta)$$

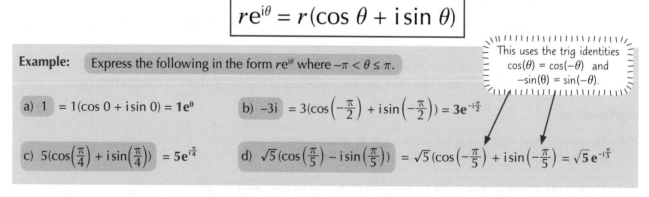

Example: Express the following in the form $re^{i\theta}$ where $-\pi < \theta \leq \pi$.

This uses the trig identities $\cos(\theta) = \cos(-\theta)$ and $-\sin(\theta) = \sin(-\theta)$.

a) $1 = 1(\cos 0 + i\sin 0) = \mathbf{1e^0}$

b) $-3i = 3\left(\cos\left(-\frac{\pi}{2}\right) + i\sin\left(-\frac{\pi}{2}\right)\right) = \mathbf{3e^{-i\frac{\pi}{2}}}$

c) $5\left(\cos\left(\frac{\pi}{4}\right) + i\sin\left(\frac{\pi}{4}\right)\right) = \mathbf{5e^{i\frac{\pi}{4}}}$

d) $\sqrt{5}\left(\cos\left(\frac{\pi}{5}\right) - i\sin\left(\frac{\pi}{5}\right)\right) = \sqrt{5}\left(\cos\left(-\frac{\pi}{5}\right) + i\sin\left(-\frac{\pi}{5}\right)\right) = \mathbf{\sqrt{5}\,e^{-i\frac{\pi}{5}}}$

You can use **Euler's relation** to express the trig functions in exponential form. You'll need to **memorise** these for the exam — they won't be given to you in the formula booklet.

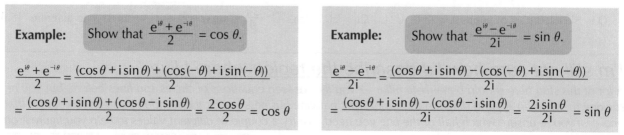

Example: Show that $\dfrac{e^{i\theta} + e^{-i\theta}}{2} = \cos\theta$.

$\dfrac{e^{i\theta} + e^{-i\theta}}{2} = \dfrac{(\cos\theta + i\sin\theta) + (\cos(-\theta) + i\sin(-\theta))}{2}$

$= \dfrac{(\cos\theta + i\sin\theta) + (\cos\theta - i\sin\theta)}{2} = \dfrac{2\cos\theta}{2} = \cos\theta$

Example: Show that $\dfrac{e^{i\theta} - e^{-i\theta}}{2i} = \sin\theta$.

$\dfrac{e^{i\theta} - e^{-i\theta}}{2i} = \dfrac{(\cos\theta + i\sin\theta) - (\cos(-\theta) + i\sin(-\theta))}{2i}$

$= \dfrac{(\cos\theta + i\sin\theta) - (\cos\theta - i\sin\theta)}{2i} = \dfrac{2i\sin\theta}{2i} = \sin\theta$

Exponential Form of Complex Numbers

You can **Multiply** and **Divide** complex numbers using **Euler's Relation**

1) Multiplication and division in exponential form follow the same rules as multiplication and division in modulus-argument form.

2) Suppose the **exponential form** of complex numbers z_1 and z_2 are $z_1 = r_1 e^{i\theta_1}$ and $z_2 = r_2 e^{i\theta_2}$. Then the **product** is given by:

$$z_1 z_2 = r_1 r_2 e^{i(\theta_1 + \theta_2)}$$

3) Similarly, the **ratio** is given by:

$$\frac{z_1}{z_2} = \frac{r_1}{r_2} e^{i(\theta_1 - \theta_2)}$$

Sharon thought she was the most beautiful thing in the world, until she saw the equation $e^{i\pi} + 1 = 0$.

Example: Given that $s = 6(\cos\frac{3\pi}{2} + i\sin\frac{3\pi}{2})$ and $t = 3(\cos\frac{3\pi}{4} + i\sin\frac{3\pi}{4})$, find the following, giving your answers in the form $re^{i\theta}$ where $-\pi < \theta \le \pi$:

a) st

$s = 6e^{i\frac{3\pi}{2}}$, $t = 3e^{i\frac{3\pi}{4}}$

$st = 6e^{i\frac{3\pi}{2}} \times 3e^{i\frac{3\pi}{4}} = 18e^{i(\frac{3\pi}{2} + \frac{3\pi}{4})} = 18e^{i(\frac{6\pi}{4} + \frac{3\pi}{4})} = 18e^{i(\frac{9\pi}{4})} = 18e^{i\frac{\pi}{4}}$

> As $\sin\theta$ and $\cos\theta$ are both 2π-periodic, so is $e^{i\theta}$.
> i.e. $e^{i\theta} = e^{i(2\pi + \theta)} = e^{i(4\pi + \theta)}$, etc.
> Here, you subtract 2π to get θ in the right range.

b) $\frac{t}{s}$

$\frac{t}{s} = \frac{3e^{i\frac{3\pi}{4}}}{6e^{i\frac{3\pi}{2}}} = \frac{1}{2}e^{i(\frac{3\pi}{4} - \frac{3\pi}{2})} = \frac{1}{2}e^{i(\frac{3\pi}{4} - \frac{6\pi}{4})} = \frac{1}{2}e^{-i\frac{3\pi}{4}}$

c) $\frac{s^3}{t}$

$\frac{s^3}{t} = \frac{6^3 e^{i(\frac{3\pi}{2} + \frac{3\pi}{2} + \frac{3\pi}{2})}}{3e^{i\frac{3\pi}{4}}} = 72e^{i(\frac{9\pi}{2} - \frac{3\pi}{4})} = 72e^{i(\frac{15\pi}{4})} = 72e^{-i\frac{\pi}{4}}$

Practice Questions

Q1 Find three values of θ such that $e^{i\theta} = 1$.

Q2 Write each of the following numbers in exponential form giving angles in radians in the range $-\pi < \theta \le \pi$ to 2 d.p.
   a) $16 - 13i$ b) $-3 + 10i$ c) $-8 - 9i$

Q3 For the following complex numbers, find st and $\frac{t}{s}$, giving your answers in the form $re^{i\theta}$ where $-\pi < \theta \le \pi$.
   a) $s = 2(\cos\frac{\pi}{8} + i\sin\frac{\pi}{8})$, $t = 5(\cos\frac{\pi}{7} - i\sin\frac{\pi}{7})$
   b) $s = 3(\cos\frac{3\pi}{4} + i\sin\frac{3\pi}{4})$, $t = 4(\cos\left(-\frac{\pi}{3}\right) + i\sin\left(-\frac{\pi}{3}\right))$

Q4 By writing $\sin\theta$ and $\cos\theta$ in exponential form, prove that:
   a) $\cos^2\theta + \sin^2\theta = 1$ b) $2\cos\theta\sin\theta = \sin 2\theta$

Q5 By writing -1 using Euler's relation, find a real value for $(-1)^i$, giving your answer to 3 significant figures.

Exam Questions

Q1 Express the number $3 - (3\sqrt{3})i$ in the form $re^{i\theta}$, where $-\pi < \theta \le \pi$. [3 marks]

Q2 By converting to exponential form, find $[32(\cos\left(-\frac{3\pi}{8}\right) + i\sin\left(-\frac{3\pi}{8}\right))]^4$.
   Give your answer in modulus-argument form, expressing the modulus as 2^a where a is an integer. [3 marks]

How many mathematicians does it take to change a light bulb? $-e^{i\pi}$...

I'm not going to pretend all maths is exciting and, if you've come this far, you've had to do some boring bits. But your patience has been rewarded with the wonderful Euler's relation — it's pretty incredible, being able to link exponentials and trig functions via complex numbers. It's likely to be on the exam too, so make sure you learn it well.

De Moivre's Theorem

De Moivre's theorem is one you're going to need to use in your exams — so learn it and learn it well.
It was proven before Euler's relation but to be fair to Euler, de Moivre was born 40 years before him...

De Moivre's Theorem also connects Complex Numbers to Trigonometry

Here's another **useful formula**, known as **de Moivre's** theorem. For all integer values of n:

$$(\cos\theta + i\sin\theta)^n = \cos n\theta + i\sin n\theta$$

Example: Use induction to prove de Moivre's theorem for positive integer values of n.

When $n = 1$, the theorem is true: $\quad$ LHS $= (\cos\theta + i\sin\theta)^1 = (\cos\theta + i\sin\theta) =$ RHS

Assume the theorem is true when $n = k$,
for any positive integer value of k: $\quad$ $(\cos\theta + i\sin\theta)^k = (\cos k\theta + i\sin k\theta)$

Now, when $n = k + 1$:

$\qquad\qquad$ LHS $= (\cos\theta + i\sin\theta)^{k+1}$

$\qquad\qquad\qquad = (\cos\theta + i\sin\theta)^k(\cos\theta + i\sin\theta)$

Use the assumption here: $\qquad = (\cos k\theta + i\sin k\theta)(\cos\theta + i\sin\theta)$

Expand the brackets: $\qquad = [(\cos k\theta)(\cos\theta) - (\sin k\theta)(\sin\theta)]$
$\qquad\qquad\qquad\qquad\qquad + i[(\sin k\theta)(\cos\theta) + (\cos k\theta)(\sin\theta)]$

Use the trigonometric addition formulas: $\qquad = \cos(k\theta + \theta) + i\sin(k\theta + \theta)$

$\qquad\qquad\qquad = \cos((k+1)\theta) + i\sin((k+1)\theta) =$ RHS

We have shown that if the statement is true for $n = k$, then it is true for $n = k + 1$.
Since we have shown it to be true for $n = 1$, it must be true for all $n \geq 1$.

1) It's easy to show that de Moivre's theorem holds for $n = 0$:
$(\cos\theta + i\sin\theta)^0 = \cos(0 \times \theta) + i\sin(0 \times \theta) = 1 + 0i = 1$ for every value of θ.

2) You can **show** that de Moivre's theorem holds for **all negative integers** too.

3) You can also **extend** the proof of de Moivre's theorem to get the following formula:

$$[r(\cos\theta + i\sin\theta)]^n = r^n(\cos n\theta + i\sin n\theta)$$

You've got this one in the formula booklet — huzzah!

Use De Moivre's Theorem to Solve Equations involving High Powers

De Moivre's theorem can be used to **work out calculations** that would otherwise be difficult
and take a long time to answer. Here are a couple of **examples** of the theorem in action.

Example: Calculate $z = (\cos\frac{7\pi}{4} - i\sin\frac{7\pi}{4})^8$. Simplify your answer fully.

De Moivre's theorem.

$z = (\cos\frac{7\pi}{4} - i\sin\frac{7\pi}{4})^8 = \left(\cos\left(-\frac{7\pi}{4}\right) + i\sin\left(-\frac{7\pi}{4}\right)\right)^8 = \cos\left(-\frac{7\pi}{4} \times 8\right) + i\sin\left(-\frac{7\pi}{4} \times 8\right)$

$\qquad\qquad\qquad\qquad = \cos(-14\pi) + i\sin(-14\pi) = 1$

$\cos\theta = \cos(-\theta)$ and $-\sin\theta = \sin(-\theta)$.

Example: Calculate $(2\sqrt{3} + 6i)^8$. Give your answer in modulus-argument form, with $-\pi < \theta \leq \pi$.

If $z = (2\sqrt{3} + 6i)$ then $|z| = \sqrt{(2\sqrt{3})^2 + 6^2} = \sqrt{48}$ and $\arg(z) = \tan^{-1}\left(\frac{6}{2\sqrt{3}}\right) = \frac{\pi}{3}$

$(2\sqrt{3} + 6i)^8 = [\sqrt{48}(\cos\frac{\pi}{3} + i\sin\frac{\pi}{3})]^8 = 48^4\left(\cos\frac{8\pi}{3} + i\sin\frac{8\pi}{3}\right) = 48^4\left(\cos\frac{2\pi}{3} + i\sin\frac{2\pi}{3}\right)$

There are **other ways** of answering questions like this — for instance, you could **expand the brackets** one by one,
or you could use the **binomial expansion**. But de Moivre's is miles **quicker** than either of these methods.

De Moivre's Theorem

You can express *Multiple-Angle* trig functions as trig *Powers*...

If you're given a **multiple-angle trig function**, such as **sin $n\theta$**, you can use de Moivre's theorem to **rewrite** this in terms of **powers** of sin θ. So $\sin n\theta = a\sin\theta + b\sin^2\theta + c\sin^3\theta + ...$, where a, b, c, etc., are coefficients to be found.

Example: Express cos 5θ in terms of powers of cos θ.

Use **de Moivre's theorem** and **binomial expansion** to express the multiple angles in terms of powers:

$\cos 5\theta + i\sin 5\theta = (\cos\theta + i\sin\theta)^5$
$= \cos^5\theta + 5i\cos^4\theta\sin\theta + 10i^2\cos^3\theta\sin^2\theta + 10i^3\cos^2\theta\sin^3\theta + 5i^4\cos\theta\sin^4\theta + i^5\sin^5\theta$
$= \cos^5\theta + 5i\cos^4\theta\sin\theta - 10\cos^3\theta\sin^2\theta - 10i\cos^2\theta\sin^3\theta + 5\cos\theta\sin^4\theta + i\sin^5\theta$

Equate the **real parts** of the equation:

$\cos 5\theta = \cos^5\theta - 10\cos^3\theta\sin^2\theta + 5\cos\theta\sin^4\theta$

To find sin 5θ you would equate the imaginary parts of the expansion.

$= \cos^5\theta - 10\cos^3\theta(1 - \cos^2\theta) + 5\cos\theta(1 - \cos^2\theta)^2$

$= \cos^5\theta - 10\cos^3\theta + 10\cos^5\theta + 5\cos\theta - 10\cos^3\theta + 5\cos^5\theta = \mathbf{16\cos^5\theta - 20\cos^3\theta + 5\cos\theta}$

Example: Express tan 4θ in terms of powers of tan θ.

$\tan 4\theta = \dfrac{\sin 4\theta}{\cos 4\theta}$ so find expressions for **sin 4θ** and **cos 4θ**.

$\cos 4\theta + i\sin 4\theta = (\cos\theta + i\sin\theta)^4$
$= \cos^4\theta + 4i\cos^3\theta\sin\theta + 6i^2\cos^2\theta\sin^2\theta + 4i^3\cos\theta\sin^3\theta + i^4\sin^4\theta$
$= \cos^4\theta + 4i\cos^3\theta\sin\theta - 6\cos^2\theta\sin^2\theta - 4i\cos\theta\sin^3\theta + \sin^4\theta$

Equate the **real** and **imaginary parts** of the expression:

$\cos 4\theta = \cos^4\theta - 6\cos^2\theta\sin^2\theta + \sin^4\theta$ $\sin 4\theta = 4\cos^3\theta\sin\theta - 4\cos\theta\sin^3\theta$

So, $\tan 4\theta = \dfrac{4\cos^3\theta\sin\theta - 4\cos\theta\sin^3\theta}{\cos^4\theta - 6\cos^2\theta\sin^2\theta + \sin^4\theta}$

Now divide through by $\cos^4\theta$ to give $\tan 4\theta = \dfrac{4\tan\theta - 4\tan^3\theta}{1 - 6\tan^2\theta + \tan^4\theta}$

...and express trig *Powers* as *Multiple-Angle* functions

There are a couple of **important** formulas to learn before you can change from **powers** to **multiple angles**.
If $z = \cos\theta + i\sin\theta$ then $z^n = \cos n\theta + i\sin n\theta$ and $z^{-n} = \cos(-n\theta) + i\sin(-n\theta) = \cos n\theta - i\sin n\theta$. Rearrange these to get:

$$\boxed{\dfrac{z^n + z^{-n}}{2} = \cos n\theta}$$ and $$\boxed{\dfrac{z^n - z^{-n}}{2i} = \sin n\theta}$$

These can be further rearranged into the forms $z^n + \dfrac{1}{z^n} = 2\cos n\theta$ and $z^n - \dfrac{1}{z^n} = 2i\sin n\theta$.

Example: Express $\cos^3\theta$ in terms of multiple angles of cos θ.   *Find terms in the form $(z^n + z^{-n})$ to use the first formula.*

If $z = \cos\theta + i\sin\theta$ then $2\cos\theta = z + z^{-1}$

$(2\cos\theta)^3 = 2^3\cos^3\theta = (z + z^{-1})^3 = z^3 + 3z + 3z^{-1} + z^{-3} = (z^3 + z^{-3}) + 3(z + z^{-1}) = 2\cos 3\theta + 6\cos\theta$

So, $\cos^3\theta = \dfrac{2\cos 3\theta + 6\cos\theta}{2^3} = \dfrac{\cos 3\theta + 3\cos\theta}{4}$

Using the two formulas above and this method, you can write any power of cos θ and sin θ in terms of multiple angles.

Example: Express $\sin^4\theta$ in terms of multiple angles of cos θ.

If $z = \cos\theta + i\sin\theta$ then $2i\sin\theta = z - z^{-1}$

$(2i)^4\sin^4\theta = (z - z^{-1})^4 = z^4 - 4z^2 + 6 - 4z^{-2} + z^{-4} = (z^4 + z^{-4}) - 4(z^2 + z^{-2}) + 6 = 2\cos 4\theta - 8\cos 2\theta + 6$

So, $\sin^4\theta = \dfrac{2\cos 4\theta - 8\cos 2\theta + 6}{(2i)^4} = \dfrac{\cos 4\theta - 4\cos 2\theta + 3}{8}$

De Moivre's Theorem

Use *De Moivre's Theorem* to find the *Sum* of a *Geometric Series*

1) The sum of a **geometric series** can be written as: $\sum_{k=0}^{n-1} ar^k = a\left(\dfrac{1-r^n}{1-r}\right)$

2) By replacing the r^k term with $(\cos\theta + i\sin\theta)^k$, you can then apply **de Moivre's theorem** to geometric series and get some **interesting** results.

Example: Using de Moivre's theorem, show that $\sum_{k=0}^{n-1}(\cos\dfrac{\pi}{n} + i\sin\dfrac{\pi}{n})^k = i\cot\dfrac{\pi}{2n} + 1$.

1) Identify a and r for a geometric series and plug into the formula:

$$a = (\cos\tfrac{\pi}{n} + i\sin\tfrac{\pi}{n})^0 = 1, \; r = (\cos\tfrac{\pi}{n} + i\sin\tfrac{\pi}{n}) \Rightarrow \sum_{k=0}^{n-1}(\cos\tfrac{\pi}{n} + i\sin\tfrac{\pi}{n})^k = 1 \times \left(\frac{1-(\cos\tfrac{\pi}{n} + i\sin\tfrac{\pi}{n})^n}{1-(\cos\tfrac{\pi}{n} + i\sin\tfrac{\pi}{n})}\right)$$

Apply de Moivre's theorem here: $\longrightarrow$ $= \dfrac{1-(\cos\pi + i\sin\pi)}{1-(\cos\tfrac{\pi}{n} + i\sin\tfrac{\pi}{n})} = \dfrac{2}{1-(\cos\tfrac{\pi}{n} + i\sin\tfrac{\pi}{n})}$

2) Use $(\cos\tfrac{\pi}{n} + i\sin\tfrac{\pi}{n}) = e^{i\frac{\pi}{n}}$ and multiply top and bottom by $e^{-i\frac{\pi}{2n}}$:

$$\Rightarrow \frac{2}{1-(\cos\tfrac{\pi}{n} + i\sin\tfrac{\pi}{n})} = \frac{2}{1-e^{i\frac{\pi}{n}}} = \frac{2e^{-i\frac{\pi}{2n}}}{e^{-i\frac{\pi}{2n}} - e^{i\frac{\pi}{2n}}}$$

3) Consider the identity $\sin\theta = \dfrac{e^{i\theta} - e^{-i\theta}}{2i}$ and rearrange:

$$2i\sin\theta = e^{i\theta} - e^{-i\theta} \Rightarrow -2i\sin\theta = -(e^{i\theta} - e^{-i\theta}) = e^{-i\theta} - e^{i\theta}. \text{ Let } \theta = \tfrac{\pi}{2n}, \text{ then } e^{-i\frac{\pi}{2n}} - e^{i\frac{\pi}{2n}} = -2i\sin\tfrac{\pi}{2n}.$$

So $\dfrac{2e^{-i\frac{\pi}{2n}}}{e^{-i\frac{\pi}{2n}} - e^{i\frac{\pi}{2n}}} = \dfrac{2e^{-i\frac{\pi}{2n}}}{-2i\sin\tfrac{\pi}{2n}} = \dfrac{2\left(\cos\left(-\tfrac{\pi}{2n}\right) + i\sin\left(-\tfrac{\pi}{2n}\right)\right)}{-2i\sin\tfrac{\pi}{2n}}$ $\longleftarrow$ Convert back to modulus-argument form.

$$= \frac{\cos\tfrac{\pi}{2n} - i\sin\tfrac{\pi}{2n}}{-i\sin\tfrac{\pi}{2n}} = \frac{-\cos\tfrac{\pi}{2n}}{i\sin\tfrac{\pi}{2n}} + 1 = -\frac{1}{i}\cot\tfrac{\pi}{2n} + 1 = i\cot\tfrac{\pi}{2n} + 1 \text{ as required.}$$

You can simplify this by multiplying top and bottom by i.

Practice Questions

Q1 Use de Moivre's theorem to calculate $(\cos\tfrac{3\pi}{8} - i\sin\tfrac{3\pi}{8})^4$, giving your answer in the form $a + bi$.

Q2 Use de Moivre's theorem to calculate $(2 + 2\sqrt{3}\,i)^7$. Give your answer in modulus-argument form.

Q3 Use de Moivre's theorem to prove that $\cos^n(k\pi) = \cos(kn\pi)$ for all integers, n and k.

Q4 For $n \geq 0$, prove that if $(\cos\theta + i\sin\theta)^n = \cos n\theta + i\sin n\theta$, then $(\cos\theta + i\sin\theta)^{-n} = \cos(-n\theta) + i\sin(-n\theta)$ and deduce that de Moivre's theorem holds for every negative integer.

Exam Questions

Q1 Using $z^n - z^{-n} = 2i\sin n\theta$, show that $\sin^3\theta = \tfrac{1}{4}(3\sin\theta - \sin 3\theta)$. [5 marks]

Q2 a) Use de Moivre's theorem to show that $\sin 6\theta = \sin 2\theta(16\sin^4\theta - 16\sin^2\theta + 3)$. [5 marks]
    b) Hence solve the equation $\sin 6\theta = \sin 2\theta$. Give your answers in radians in the interval $-\pi < \theta \leq \pi$. [6 marks]

Q3 Find $\sum_{k=0}^{\infty}\left(\tfrac{1}{3}\right)^k(\cos k\theta + i\sin k\theta)$ using de Moivre's theorem, giving your answer in the from $a + bi$ where a and b are functions of $\cos\theta$ and $\sin\theta$ only. [5 marks]

Higher powers of complex numbers — De Moivre-llous...

Let's be honest — this stuff is hard. There's no short cut to success here, but knowing the common trigonometric rules and double angle formulas off by heart can really help you out when you're knee deep in computation. De Moivre's theorem will probably appear somewhere on your exam so getting to grips with it will be worth your time.

Roots of Unity

These pages on roots of unity are a brilliant way of wrapping up this section — they bring together pretty much everything you've seen so far. 'Unity' is a fancy maths word that here just means '1' — so roots of unity are roots of 1.

n^{th} Roots Of Unity satisfy $z^n = 1$

1) When you're trying to find the nth **roots of unity**, you want to find z, where $z^n = 1$:
   - Let $z = re^{i\theta}$. Then $z^n = 1 \Rightarrow (re^{i\theta})^n = 1 \Rightarrow r^n e^{in\theta} = 1e^{i2\pi k}$, for all integers k.
   - You can now **equate parts**. $r^n = 1$, so as r is a positive real number, **$r = 1$**.
     You also get $e^{in\theta} = e^{i2\pi k} \Rightarrow e^{in\theta - i2\pi k} = 1 \Rightarrow e^{i(n\theta - 2\pi k)} = 1 \Rightarrow i(n\theta - 2\pi k) = 0$
     $i \neq 0$, so $n\theta - 2\pi k = 0 \Rightarrow n\theta = 2\pi k \Rightarrow \boldsymbol{\theta = \dfrac{2k\pi}{n}}$ for all integers k.

   If you're unsure about this, you can use Euler's relation to check that $e^{i2\pi k} = 1$

2) So the nth roots of unity are: $\boxed{\omega = e^{i\frac{2k\pi}{n}}}$, where k is any integer.
   ω ('omega') is commonly used to denote a root of unity.

3) As $e^{i\theta}$ is **2π-periodic**: $\omega = e^{i\frac{2k\pi}{n}} = e^{i\left(\frac{2k\pi}{n} \pm 2\pi\right)} = e^{i\left(\frac{2k\pi}{n} \pm 4\pi\right)} = e^{i\left(\frac{2k\pi}{n} \pm 6\pi\right)} = \dots$
   To avoid repeating roots, we can restrict k to the interval $\boldsymbol{0 \leq k \leq n-1}$.

4) When plotted on an Argand diagram, each root of unity appears on the unit circle, at **intervals** of $\dfrac{2\pi}{n}$ radians.

5) $z^n - 1$ is a polynomial with **real coefficients**, so the roots of the equation come in **conjugate pairs** — i.e. $z^n = 1 \Rightarrow (z^*)^n = 1$. So when all the roots are plotted, the graph will be **symmetrical** about the real axis.

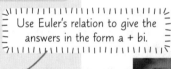

Example: Find every cube root of unity. Give your answers in the form $a + bi$, where a and b are exact real numbers.

The cube roots of unity are $\omega = e^{i\frac{2k\pi}{3}}$, where $k = 0, 1, 2$.

Use Euler's relation to give the answers in the form $a + bi$.

$k = 0$: $\omega = e^{i\frac{2(0)\pi}{3}} = e^0 = 1$

$k = 1$: $\omega = e^{i\frac{2(1)\pi}{3}} = e^{i\frac{2\pi}{3}} = \cos\dfrac{2\pi}{3} + i\sin\dfrac{2\pi}{3} = -\dfrac{1}{2} + \dfrac{\sqrt{3}}{2}i$

$k = 2$: $\omega = e^{i\frac{2(2)\pi}{3}} = e^{i\frac{4\pi}{3}} = \cos\dfrac{4\pi}{3} + i\sin\dfrac{4\pi}{3} = -\dfrac{1}{2} - \dfrac{\sqrt{3}}{2}i$

Colin and Anne's shared love of crackers was the root of their unity.

You can find the nth roots of Any Real Number

Finding the nth root of **any real number** a is fairly similar to finding roots of unity.
$z^n - a$ is a polynomial of degree n, so it has n roots. So $\boldsymbol{z^n = a}$ **has n solutions**.

Example: Find all solutions to $z^5 = -36$, giving your answers in the form $a + bi$ to two decimal places.

Rewrite both sides of the equation in exponential form.

Let $z = re^{i\theta}$. Then $z^5 = (re^{i\theta})^5 = r^5 e^{i5\theta}$, and $-36 = 36 \times -1 = 36e^{i(\pi + 2\pi k)}$, for all integers k.

So $r^5 e^{i5\theta} = 36e^{i(\pi + 2\pi k)}$, for all integers k.

Equate parts: $r^5 = 36 \Rightarrow r = \sqrt[5]{36}$

Remember that $r > 0$.

and $e^{i5\theta} = e^{i(\pi + 2\pi k)} \Rightarrow 5\theta = \pi + 2\pi k \Rightarrow \theta = \dfrac{(2k+1)\pi}{5}$

To avoid repeating the roots, restrict k to the interval $0 \leq k \leq n-1$

So $z = \sqrt[5]{36}\, e^{i\frac{(2k+1)\pi}{5}}$, for $k = 0, 1, 2, 3, 4$.

Evaluate z for each value of k:

$k = 0$: $z = \sqrt[5]{36}\, e^{i\frac{\pi}{5}} = \sqrt[5]{36}(\cos\dfrac{\pi}{5} + i\sin\dfrac{\pi}{5}) = 1.6566\dots + 1.2035\dots i$

$k = 1$: $z = \sqrt[5]{36}\, e^{i\frac{3\pi}{5}} = \sqrt[5]{36}(\cos\dfrac{3\pi}{5} + i\sin\dfrac{3\pi}{5}) = -0.6327\dots + 1.9474\dots i$

$k = 2$: $z = \sqrt[5]{36}\, e^{i\pi} = \sqrt[5]{36}(\cos\pi + i\sin\pi) = -2.0476\dots$

$k = 3$: $z = \sqrt[5]{36}\, e^{i\frac{7\pi}{5}} = \sqrt[5]{36}(\cos\dfrac{7\pi}{5} + i\sin\dfrac{7\pi}{5}) = -0.6327\dots - 1.9474\dots i$

$k = 4$: $z = \sqrt[5]{36}\, e^{i\frac{9\pi}{5}} = \sqrt[5]{36}(\cos\dfrac{9\pi}{5} + i\sin\dfrac{9\pi}{5}) = 1.6566\dots - 1.2035\dots i$

So the solutions to $z^5 = -36$ are: $z = \boldsymbol{-2.05,\ 1.66 \pm 1.20i,\ -0.63 \pm 1.95i}$ to 2.d.p.

Roots of Unity

You can also find n^{th} roots of Complex Numbers

Every number has **n n^{th} roots**, even if it's **imaginary** or **complex**. But for complex α, the polynomial $z^n - \alpha$ **doesn't** have real coefficients, so the nth roots of α no longer come in conjugate pairs.

Example: a) Find all solutions to $z = (8i)^{\frac{1}{3}}$, leaving your answers in exact form.

You're asked to find all solutions to $z = (8i)^{\frac{1}{3}} \Rightarrow z^3 = 8i$

Let $z = re^{i\theta} \Rightarrow z^3 = (re^{i\theta})^3 = r^3e^{i3\theta}$. Write 8i in exponential form: $8i = 8e^{i\frac{\pi}{2}} = 8e^{i\left(\frac{\pi}{2} + 2\pi k\right)}$, for all integers k.

$\Rightarrow r^3e^{i3\theta} = 8e^{i\left(\frac{\pi}{2} + 2\pi k\right)}$

Equating parts gives: $r^3 = 8 \Rightarrow r = 2$ and $e^{i3\theta} = e^{i\left(\frac{\pi}{2} + 2\pi k\right)} \Rightarrow 3\theta = \frac{\pi}{2} + 2\pi k = \frac{\pi}{2}(4k + 1) \Rightarrow \theta = \frac{\pi}{6}(4k + 1)$

So $z = 2e^{i\frac{\pi}{6}(4k+1)}$, where $k = 0, 1, 2$.

$k = 0:\ z = 2e^{i\frac{\pi}{6}} = 2(\cos\frac{\pi}{6} + i\sin\frac{\pi}{6}) = 2\left(\frac{\sqrt{3}}{2} + \frac{1}{2}i\right) = \sqrt{3} + i$

$k = 1:\ z = 2e^{i\frac{5\pi}{6}} = 2(\cos\frac{5\pi}{6} + i\sin\frac{5\pi}{6}) = 2\left(-\frac{\sqrt{3}}{2} + \frac{1}{2}i\right) = -\sqrt{3} + i$

$k = 2:\ z = 2e^{i\frac{9\pi}{6}} = 2e^{i\frac{3\pi}{2}} = 2(\cos\frac{3\pi}{2} + i\sin\frac{3\pi}{2}) = -2i$

This is the same method used for real numbers. You can apply the same idea to complex numbers too.

b) Prove that the solutions to $z = (8i)^{\frac{1}{3}}$, form an equilateral triangle when plotted on an Argand diagram.

First, plot the solutions found in part a) — this is shown on the right.

To show that this is an equilateral triangle, it's enough to show that all three sides have the same length.

X and Y have the same imaginary value, so $|XY| = 2\sqrt{3}$

Use Pythagoras to work out $|XZ|$:

$|XZ| = \sqrt{(\sqrt{3} - 0)^2 + (1 - (-2))^2} = \sqrt{12} = 2\sqrt{3}$

It's easy to see that $|YZ|$ will be the same as $|XZ|$, because the shape has symmetry about the imaginary axis.

So $|XY| = |XZ| = |YZ| = 2\sqrt{3}$, so the cube roots of 8i **form an equilateral triangle**.

So, the cube roots of 8i form an equilateral triangle. This can be **generalised** — the nth roots of **any number** form the vertices of a **regular n-gon**, inscribed on a circle **centred at zero** on an Argand diagram. (Here, **inscribed** means all the vertices lie **on the circumference** of the circle.)

The roots of unity have some Interesting Properties

You can **generate** the nth roots of unity from just **one root** — i.e. if you take a **particular** n^{th} root of unity, ω, you can multiply it by itself to give **all** the other n^{th} roots. So $1, \omega, \omega^2, ..., \omega^{n-1}$ is just a **different** way of writing the roots of unity.

Example: a) Show that the nth roots of unity may be written in the form $1, \omega, \omega^2, \omega^3, ..., \omega^{n-1}$, where ω is a single n^{th} root of unity.

You know that the nth roots of unity are $\omega = e^{i\frac{2k\pi}{n}}$, where $k = 0, 1, 2, ..., n - 1$.

Consider the root where $k = 1$ — i.e. $\omega = e^{i\frac{2\pi}{n}}$.

Then $\omega^2 = \left(e^{i\frac{2\pi}{n}}\right)^2 = e^{i\frac{4\pi}{n}}$, $\omega^3 = \left(e^{i\frac{2\pi}{n}}\right)^3 = e^{i\frac{6\pi}{n}}$, ..., $\omega^{n-1} = \left(e^{i\frac{2\pi}{n}}\right)^{n-1} = e^{i\frac{2(n-1)\pi}{n}}$, $\omega^n = \left(e^{i\frac{2\pi}{n}}\right)^n = e^{i2\pi} = 1 = \omega^0$.

But these are just $e^{i\frac{2k\pi}{n}}$, where $k = 0, 1, 2, ..., n - 1$. So $1, \omega, \omega^2, ..., \omega^{n-1}$, are the nth roots of unity.

b) Prove by counter-example that **not every** ω will generate the other n^{th} roots of unity.

Consider the 4th roots of unity — you can show that they are: $1, i, -1$ and $-i$.

Take the fourth root $\omega = -1$. Then $\omega^2 = 1$, $\omega^3 = -1$, and so on.

So by starting with $\omega = -1$, you can never generate the fourth roots i or $-i$.

So, **not every root of unity can generate all of the other roots**.

If you start with i or −i, you do generate all the roots.

Another property of the nth roots of unity (for $n > 1$) is that when you **add** them all together, you **always** get **zero**. (You'll be asked to prove this in the Exam Questions on the next page.)

Roots of Unity

Use **Complex Roots of Unity** to solve **Geometric Problems**

You could be given a question on a **Cartesian** coordinate grid that may seem **unrelated** to complex numbers. But by **imagining** the coordinate grid as an **Argand diagram**, you can turn a **nasty geometric problem** into something a tad more **straightforward**.

Example: A regular heptagon is inscribed in a circle centred at the origin. Given that the vertex V_0 has the coordinates $(-\sqrt{8}, \sqrt{8})$, find the other 6 vertices. Give your answers to 2 decimal places.

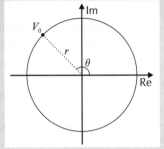

1) Imagine the coordinate grid as an Argand diagram — then the vertex $(-\sqrt{8}, \sqrt{8})$ is at the point $-\sqrt{8} + \sqrt{8}\,i$

2) Write $-\sqrt{8} + \sqrt{8}\,i$ in exponential form: $r = \sqrt{(-\sqrt{8})^2 + (\sqrt{8})^2} = 4$, $\theta = \frac{3\pi}{4}$.
   $$\Rightarrow -\sqrt{8} + \sqrt{8}\,i = 4e^{i\frac{3\pi}{4}}$$

3) The heptagon is inscribed on a circle centred at the origin — i.e. each point will be evenly spaced out in intervals of $\frac{2\pi}{7}$ radians.
   So the vertices are at $V_k = 4e^{i\left(\frac{3\pi}{4} + \frac{2\pi k}{7}\right)}$, for $k = 0, 1, ..., 6$.

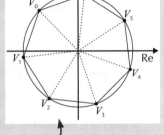

4) You're given V_0 in the question — evaluate V_k for all the other values of k (2 d.p.):
   $k = 1$: $V_1 = 4e^{i\left(\frac{3\pi}{4} + \frac{2\pi}{7}\right)} = 4e^{i\left(\frac{29\pi}{28}\right)} = 4(\cos\left(\frac{29\pi}{28}\right) + i\sin\left(\frac{29\pi}{28}\right)) = -3.97 - 0.45i.$

   $k = 2$: $V_2 = 4e^{i\left(\frac{3\pi}{4} + \frac{4\pi}{7}\right)} = 4e^{i\left(\frac{37\pi}{28}\right)} = 4(\cos\left(\frac{37\pi}{28}\right) + i\sin\left(\frac{37\pi}{28}\right)) = -2.13 - 3.39i.$

   $k = 3$: $V_3 = 4e^{i\left(\frac{3\pi}{4} + \frac{6\pi}{7}\right)} = 4e^{i\left(\frac{45\pi}{28}\right)} = 4(\cos\left(\frac{45\pi}{28}\right) + i\sin\left(\frac{45\pi}{28}\right)) = 1.32 - 3.78i.$

   ...and so on: $V_4 = 3.78 - 1.32i$, $V_5 = 3.39 + 2.13i$, $V_6 = 0.45 + 3.97i$

5) Convert back to Cartesian coordinates — the missing six vertices are:
   (–3.97, –0.45), (–2.13, –3.39), (1.32, –3.78), (3.78, –1.32), (3.39, 2.13) and **(0.45, 3.97).**

Practice Questions

Q1 Find every fifth root of unity, giving your answers in the form $a + bi$ to 2 d.p. Plot them on an Argand diagram.

Q2 Find every root of the equation $f(z) = z^4 - 12$, giving your exact answers in the form $a + bi$.

Q3 Calculate $(\cos\frac{3\pi}{8} + i\sin\frac{3\pi}{8})^{\frac{1}{4}}$, giving all of your answers in the form $a + bi$ to 2 decimal places.

Q4 a) Explain why the regular n-gon formed by the nth roots of a positive real number, α, always has a vertex on the real axis of an Argand diagram.

   b) Given that every regular n-gon has a line of symmetry through each vertex, explain why $(a + ib)^n = \alpha \Rightarrow (a - ib)^n = \alpha$ where α is a positive real number.

Exam Questions

Q1 Plot the square formed by the 4th roots of $2 - 2i\sqrt{3}$ on an Argand diagram. [5 marks]

Q2 By writing the nth roots of unity as $1, \omega, \omega^2, ..., \omega^{n-1}$, where ω is an nth root of unity ($n > 1$), prove that the sum of the nth roots of unity is zero. [3 marks]

Q3 Solve the equation $z^3 = 27i$, giving all 3 of your solutions in the form $e^{i\theta}$, where $-\pi < \theta \le \pi$. [4 marks]

Q4 A regular pentagon is inscribed in a circle centred at the origin. Given that one vertex is at $(-1, -\sqrt{3})$, find the coordinates of the other four vertices to 2 decimal places. [5 marks]

There are no more numbers to discover — what am I meant to do now..?

Well that's pretty much everything you need to know about complex numbers. By now, you should have realised how important de Moivre's theorem and Euler's relation are when you're faced with complex number problems. Knowing these like the back of your hand will be a massive help when you're in the exam. So practise, practise, practise.

Matrices

A matrix is a collection of numbers set out in rows and columns. They're a bit like vectors and come in useful for all kinds of things, such as describing transformations and solving simultaneous equations.

The **Dimension** of a Matrix is its **Size**

1) The contents of matrices are called **elements**. Matrices are usually named using a bold or underlined **capital letter**.

2) The **dimension** of a matrix is given in the form **m × n**, where **m** is the number of **rows** and **n** is the number of **columns**. If m = n, you've got a **square matrix**.

$$M = \begin{pmatrix} 4 & 1 & 2 \\ 2 & 3 & 7 \end{pmatrix} \rbrace \, \textbf{m rows}$$

Here, m = 2 and n = 3, so **M** is a 2 × 3 matrix.

n columns

3) Matrices can be **added** together, **subtracted** from each other and **multiplied** by **scalars** or **other matrices**.

4) You can only perform these operations if the matrices have the **right dimensions**. If two matrices have the right dimensions to let you carry out a particular operation on them, they're said to be **conformable** for that operation.

5) A **zero matrix** is a matrix where all the elements are zero. It's usually denoted by a bold or underlined **0**.

$$\begin{pmatrix} 0 & 0 & 0 \\ 0 & 0 & 0 \end{pmatrix}$$ This is the 2 × 3 zero matrix.

Matrices can be **Added** or **Subtracted** if they have the **Same Dimension**

Two matrices are conformable for **addition** and **subtraction** only if they have the **same dimension**.

Example: C, D, E and F are matrices such that $C = \begin{pmatrix} 2 & 4 \\ 1 & 3 \end{pmatrix}$, $D = (2 \ \ 3)$, $E = \begin{pmatrix} 5 & -2 \\ -3 & 2 \end{pmatrix}$, $F = \begin{pmatrix} 3 \\ 5 \end{pmatrix}$.

Which of these matrices are conformable for addition?

You can only add or subtract matrices with the same dimension.
C and **E** are both 2 × 2 matrices, so **C and E are conformable for addition.**
The dimension of **D** is 1 × 2, and of **F** is 2 × 1 — these are different so they aren't conformable for addition.

Adding and subtracting matrices is really easy — you simply add or subtract the **corresponding elements**.

Example: For the matrices $A = \begin{pmatrix} 6 & 2 \\ 5 & 3 \\ 8 & 4 \end{pmatrix}$ and $B = \begin{pmatrix} 1 & 2 \\ 3 & 4 \\ 5 & 0 \end{pmatrix}$, find: (i) A + B, (ii) A − B.

Check that the matrix dimensions are the same — if not, they can't be added.

Both matrices have a dimension of 3 × 2, so you can add or subtract the corresponding elements:

(i) $\begin{pmatrix} 6 & 2 \\ 5 & 3 \\ 8 & 4 \end{pmatrix} + \begin{pmatrix} 1 & 2 \\ 3 & 4 \\ 5 & 0 \end{pmatrix} = \begin{pmatrix} 6+1 & 2+2 \\ 5+3 & 3+4 \\ 8+5 & 4+0 \end{pmatrix} = \begin{pmatrix} 7 & 4 \\ 8 & 7 \\ 13 & 4 \end{pmatrix}$

(ii) $\begin{pmatrix} 6 & 2 \\ 5 & 3 \\ 8 & 4 \end{pmatrix} - \begin{pmatrix} 1 & 2 \\ 3 & 4 \\ 5 & 0 \end{pmatrix} = \begin{pmatrix} 6-1 & 2-2 \\ 5-3 & 3-4 \\ 8-5 & 4-0 \end{pmatrix} = \begin{pmatrix} 5 & 0 \\ 2 & -1 \\ 3 & 4 \end{pmatrix}$

You can **Multiply** a Matrix by a **Scalar**

A **scalar** is just a number. To **multiply** a matrix by a scalar, simply multiply **each element** by the scalar.

Example: For the 2 × 2 matrix $A = \begin{pmatrix} 4 & 5 \\ -1 & 3 \end{pmatrix}$, find 4A and $\frac{1}{2}$A.

Multiply each element in the matrix **A** by the given scalar:

$$4A = 4\begin{pmatrix} 4 & 5 \\ -1 & 3 \end{pmatrix} = \begin{pmatrix} 4\times4 & 4\times5 \\ 4\times-1 & 4\times3 \end{pmatrix} = \begin{pmatrix} 16 & 20 \\ -4 & 12 \end{pmatrix}$$

$$\frac{1}{2}A = \frac{1}{2}\begin{pmatrix} 4 & 5 \\ -1 & 3 \end{pmatrix} = \begin{pmatrix} \frac{1}{2}\times4 & \frac{1}{2}\times5 \\ \frac{1}{2}\times-1 & \frac{1}{2}\times3 \end{pmatrix} = \begin{pmatrix} 2 & \frac{5}{2} \\ -\frac{1}{2} & \frac{3}{2} \end{pmatrix}$$

Matrices

Multiplying *One Matrix* by *Another Matrix* is a bit trickier

1) For matrices **A** and **B**, you can only find **A** × **B** if the number of **columns** in **A** equals the number of **rows** in **B**.

2) So if **A** has dimension m × n and **B** has dimension n × k, then **A** × **B** has dimension m × k.

3) If **A** and **B** are **square matrices**, you can also find **B** × **A**. However, apart from a few special cases, **B** × **A** ≠ **A** × **B**. To put that in maths-speak, matrix multiplication is **not commutative**.

4) You can multiply more than two matrices together. Matrix multiplication is **associative** — this means that **A** × **B** × **C** = (**A** × **B**) × **C** = **A** × (**B** × **C**).

To find matrix A × B:

If **A** is an m × n matrix and **B** is an n × k matrix, then to find the element in row i and column j of the matrix **A** × **B**:

1) Look at the ith row of **A** and the jth column of **B**. Multiply the first element of the row by the first element of the column, the second element of the row by the second element of the column, and so on.

2) Add together the products from step 1.

That might sound a bit confusing, but it's really not that bad — an example should make things clearer:

Example: Given that $\mathbf{A} = \begin{pmatrix} 1 & 3 \\ 2 & 4 \end{pmatrix}$ and $\mathbf{B} = \begin{pmatrix} 0 & 1 & 4 \\ 1 & 3 & 5 \end{pmatrix}$, find **AB**.

*A × B is often written as **AB**.*

1) First calculate the dimensions of the matrices: $(2 \times 2)(2 \times 3) = (2 \times 3)$

2) Find the elements of **AB** one at a time.

These are the same, so you can multiply these matrices.

Start by multiplying the first row of **A** by the first column of **B**:

$$\mathbf{AB} = \begin{pmatrix} 1 & 3 \\ 2 & 4 \end{pmatrix} \times \begin{pmatrix} 0 & 1 & 4 \\ 1 & 3 & 5 \end{pmatrix} = \begin{pmatrix} 1\times0+3\times1 & \cdot & \cdot \\ \cdot & \cdot & \cdot \end{pmatrix} = \begin{pmatrix} 3 & \cdot & \cdot \\ \cdot & \cdot & \cdot \end{pmatrix}$$

Row 1 of A and column 1 of B combine to give the element in row 1, column 1 of AB.

3) Now repeat this for all the other elements of AB:

$$\mathbf{AB} = \begin{pmatrix} 1 & 3 \\ 2 & 4 \end{pmatrix} \times \begin{pmatrix} 0 & 1 & 4 \\ 1 & 3 & 5 \end{pmatrix} = \begin{pmatrix} 1\times0+3\times1 & 1\times1+3\times3 & 1\times4+3\times5 \\ 2\times0+4\times1 & 2\times1+4\times3 & 2\times4+4\times5 \end{pmatrix} = \begin{pmatrix} 3 & 10 & 19 \\ 4 & 14 & 28 \end{pmatrix}$$

Check the answer has the right dimension — it's a 2 × 3 matrix, as expected.

You can multiply square matrices by themselves:

Example: Given that $\mathbf{A} = \begin{pmatrix} 1 & 2 \\ 3 & 4 \end{pmatrix}$, find $\mathbf{A}^2$.

When you multiply two square matrices, the dimension of the answer is the same as the dimension of the original matrices.

$$\mathbf{A}^2 = \mathbf{A} \times \mathbf{A} = \begin{pmatrix} 1 & 2 \\ 3 & 4 \end{pmatrix} \times \begin{pmatrix} 1 & 2 \\ 3 & 4 \end{pmatrix} = \begin{pmatrix} 1\times1+2\times3 & 1\times2+2\times4 \\ 3\times1+4\times3 & 3\times2+4\times4 \end{pmatrix} = \begin{pmatrix} 7 & 10 \\ 15 & 22 \end{pmatrix}$$

Multiplying by the *Identity Matrix* has no effect

The **identity matrix**, **I**, is a special matrix which multiplies a matrix **A** to give **A**.
This means that **AI** = **IA** = **A** — it's the matrix equivalent of multiplying by 1.

The identity matrix is always a **square** matrix — i.e. it's an $n \times n$ matrix, for **all** positive integers n. In the **diagonal** going from top-left to bottom-right, every element is **1**, and all **other** elements in the matrix are **zero**.

2 × 2 identity matrix

$$\begin{pmatrix} 1 & 2 \\ 3 & 4 \end{pmatrix} \times \begin{pmatrix} 1 & 0 \\ 0 & 1 \end{pmatrix} = \begin{pmatrix} 1\times1+2\times0 & 1\times0+2\times1 \\ 3\times1+4\times0 & 3\times0+4\times1 \end{pmatrix} = \begin{pmatrix} 1 & 2 \\ 3 & 4 \end{pmatrix}$$

$$\mathbf{A} \quad \times \quad \mathbf{I} \qquad\qquad\qquad\qquad = \quad \mathbf{A}$$

3 × 3 identity matrix

$$\begin{pmatrix} 4 & 3 & 2 \\ 1 & 5 & 3 \\ 2 & 7 & 1 \end{pmatrix} \times \begin{pmatrix} 1 & 0 & 0 \\ 0 & 1 & 0 \\ 0 & 0 & 1 \end{pmatrix} = \begin{pmatrix} 4 & 3 & 2 \\ 1 & 5 & 3 \\ 2 & 7 & 1 \end{pmatrix}$$

$$\mathbf{A} \quad \times \quad \mathbf{I} \quad = \quad \mathbf{A}$$

Matrices

Use Proof by Induction with Powers of Matrices

You can use proof by induction (see p.2) to prove a given formula for the nth power of a matrix.

Example: For the matrix $M = \begin{pmatrix} 1 & 0 \\ 2 & 3 \end{pmatrix}$, show that for any positive integer n, $M^n = \begin{pmatrix} 1 & 0 \\ 3^n - 1 & 3^n \end{pmatrix}$.

1) First, show that it's true for n = 1:

When $n = 1$, $M^n = M^1 = M = \begin{pmatrix} 1 & 0 \\ 2 & 3 \end{pmatrix} = \begin{pmatrix} 1 & 0 \\ 3 - 1 & 3 \end{pmatrix} = \begin{pmatrix} 1 & 0 \\ 3^1 - 1 & 3^1 \end{pmatrix}$, so the statement is true for $n = 1$.

2) Assume that it's true for n = k:

Assume that for some positive integer k, $M^k = \begin{pmatrix} 1 & 0 \\ 3^k - 1 & 3^k \end{pmatrix}$.

3) Prove that it's true for n = k + 1:

$M^{k+1} = M^k M = \begin{pmatrix} 1 & 0 \\ 3^k - 1 & 3^k \end{pmatrix} \times \begin{pmatrix} 1 & 0 \\ 2 & 3 \end{pmatrix} = \begin{pmatrix} 1 \times 1 + 0 \times 2 & 1 \times 0 + 0 \times 3 \\ (3^k - 1) \times 1 + 3^k \times 2 & (3^k - 1) \times 0 + 3^k \times 3 \end{pmatrix}$

$= \begin{pmatrix} 1 & 0 \\ 3 \times 3^k - 1 & 3 \times 3^k \end{pmatrix} = \begin{pmatrix} 1 & 0 \\ 3^{k+1} - 1 & 3^{k+1} \end{pmatrix}$

So if the statement is true for $n = k$, then it is also true for $n = k + 1$.

Make sure you show all the steps in your working really clearly when answering proof questions.

4) Make a concluding statement:

If the statement is true for $n = k$, we have shown that it's true for $n = k + 1$.
As we have shown that it is true for $n = 1$, the statement must be true for all positive integers n.

Practice Questions

Q1 For the matrices $A = \begin{pmatrix} 2 & 4 \\ 6 & 8 \end{pmatrix}$ and $B = \begin{pmatrix} 1 & 5 \\ 3 & 7 \end{pmatrix}$, find:

    a) $A + B$,   b) $B - A$,   c) $A - B$.

Q2 For the matrices $C = \begin{pmatrix} 2 & -2 \\ -1 & 1 \end{pmatrix}$ and $D = \begin{pmatrix} 0 & 2 \\ 4 & 1 \end{pmatrix}$, find:

    a) $3C$,   b) $\frac{1}{4}D$,   c) CD,   d) DC.

Q3 Consider the six matrices below:

$M = \begin{pmatrix} 2 & 3 & 3 \\ 3 & 1 & 2 \\ 1 & 0 & 0 \end{pmatrix}$, $N = \begin{pmatrix} 1 & 0 \\ 0 & 1 \end{pmatrix}$, $P = \begin{pmatrix} 2 & 3 & 1 \\ 3 & 1 & 2 \end{pmatrix}$, $Q = \begin{pmatrix} 2 & 3 \\ 3 & 1 \\ 1 & 2 \end{pmatrix}$, $R = \begin{pmatrix} 1 & 0 & 0 \\ 0 & 1 & 0 \end{pmatrix}$, $S = \begin{pmatrix} 2 & 0 \\ 0 & 2 \end{pmatrix}$

    a)   Which pairs of matrices are conformable for addition?

    b)   Are any of the matrices identity matrices? If so, which ones?

    c)   Are any of the matrices zero matrices? If so, which ones?

    d)   Which pairs of matrices are conformable for multiplication? Make clear the order of multiplication.

Exam Questions

Q1 Prove that $\begin{pmatrix} 1 & 1 & 0 \\ 0 & 0 & 3 \\ 0 & 0 & 1 \end{pmatrix}^n = \begin{pmatrix} 1 & 1 & 3(n-1) \\ 0 & 0 & 3 \\ 0 & 0 & 1 \end{pmatrix}$ for all positive integers n.   [6 marks]

Q2 $A = \begin{pmatrix} 3 & 0 \\ x & 1 \end{pmatrix}$, $B = \begin{pmatrix} y & 2 \\ 1 & z \end{pmatrix}$

    a) Given that $AB = \begin{pmatrix} 3 & 6 \\ 1 & 2 \end{pmatrix}$, find x, y and z.   [3 marks]

    b) Calculate BA.   [1 mark]

The Matrix isn't an easy topic — you'll see how deep the rabbit hole goes...

Matrix algebra is a whole new world of maths — and this is just the tip of the iceberg. Adding, subtracting and multiplying matrices can be fiddly so be careful with your arithmetic and double check your answers to avoid slips.

Matrix Transformations

Just like vectors can be used to describe movement, matrices can be used to describe transformations of two- and three-dimensional space. You might want to grab your pencil and graph paper for this one...

Transformations can be Represented by Matrices

1) Think about the 2D (x, y)- or the 3D (x, y, z)-space. If you perform a **linear transformation** on the space — such as a **reflection**, **rotation**, **stretch** or **enlargement** — each of these points might be moved somewhere else.

2) You can represent each of the **points** as a **column vector x** (e.g. (3, 2) would be $\begin{pmatrix} 3 \\ 2 \end{pmatrix}$) and any **transformation** as a **matrix M**.

3) **Left-multiply** the vector **x** by the matrix **M** (this just means multiply with **M** on the left) to get the position vector of its **image** — i.e. the position vector of the **new point** after the transformation:

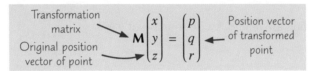

Transformation matrix → Original position vector of point → $\mathbf{M}\begin{pmatrix} x \\ y \\ z \end{pmatrix} = \begin{pmatrix} p \\ q \\ r \end{pmatrix}$ ← Position vector of transformed point

4) The **size** of **M** depends on the **dimension** of the space. **M** will be 2 × 2 if you're in 2D, or 3 × 3 if you're in 3D.

Use (1, 0) and (0, 1) to find the Transformation Matrix

You might be given a transformation and asked to work out **which matrix** represents it. To do this, take some **simple vectors** and **imagine** where the transformation would move them to.

For transformations in 2D, we use the vectors **(1, 0)** and **(0, 1)**. Their **images** under the transformation become the **columns** for the transformation matrix.

Position vectors can be written as rows or columns — but must be columns when you're multiplying by the matrix.

Example: Find the matrix **M** representing a reflection in the *x*-axis.

Look at what happens to $\begin{pmatrix} 1 \\ 0 \end{pmatrix}$ and $\begin{pmatrix} 0 \\ 1 \end{pmatrix}$ under a reflection in the *x*-axis:

$$\begin{pmatrix} 1 \\ 0 \end{pmatrix} \to \begin{pmatrix} 1 \\ 0 \end{pmatrix} \qquad \begin{pmatrix} 0 \\ 1 \end{pmatrix} \to \begin{pmatrix} 0 \\ -1 \end{pmatrix}$$

Then **M** is the matrix formed by using these vectors as columns: $\mathbf{M} = \begin{pmatrix} 1 & 0 \\ 0 & -1 \end{pmatrix}$

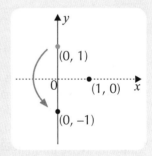

We can check that this is right: $\begin{pmatrix} 1 & 0 \\ 0 & -1 \end{pmatrix}\begin{pmatrix} x \\ y \end{pmatrix} = \begin{pmatrix} x + 0 \\ 0 - y \end{pmatrix} = \begin{pmatrix} x \\ -y \end{pmatrix}$. So, x doesn't change,

and y is sent to −y. This is exactly what happens when you reflect in the x-axis, so our matrix **M** is correct.

Perform Matrix Multiplication to find the Transformations

If you're given a matrix **M**, you can take position vectors (e.g. **(1, 0)** and **(0, 1)**), and **left-multiply** by **M**. By looking at how the position vectors have **changed**, you can work out the **transformation** that **M** represents:

Example: Describe the transformation represented by $\mathbf{M} = \begin{pmatrix} 3 & 0 \\ 0 & 3 \end{pmatrix}$.

Left-multiplying by **M**:

You could just read off the matrix where (1, 0) and (0, 1) are sent under the transformation — their new position vectors are the columns of the matrix.

$$\begin{pmatrix} 3 & 0 \\ 0 & 3 \end{pmatrix}\begin{pmatrix} 1 \\ 0 \end{pmatrix} = \begin{pmatrix} 3 \\ 0 \end{pmatrix}$$

$$\begin{pmatrix} 3 & 0 \\ 0 & 3 \end{pmatrix}\begin{pmatrix} 0 \\ 1 \end{pmatrix} = \begin{pmatrix} 0 \\ 3 \end{pmatrix}$$

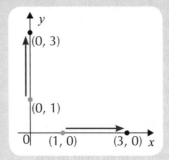

So the transformation is an **enlargement, centred at the origin, with scale factor 3.**

Derek's $\begin{pmatrix} 6 & 0 \\ 0 & 6 \end{pmatrix}$ pills had worked a treat.

Matrix Transformations

Rotations are Harder to Describe

Rotations about the origin $(0, 0)$ have slightly **trickier** matrices than stretches or enlargements. But there's a clever trick that uses **trig values** — recall that coordinates on the unit circle can be written as $(x, y) = (\cos \theta, \sin \theta)$.

Look at what happens to the position vectors $\begin{pmatrix} 1 \\ 0 \end{pmatrix}$ and $\begin{pmatrix} 0 \\ 1 \end{pmatrix}$ when rotated anticlockwise about the origin by an angle of θ:

$$\begin{pmatrix} 1 \\ 0 \end{pmatrix} = \begin{pmatrix} \cos 0 \\ \sin 0 \end{pmatrix} \rightarrow \begin{pmatrix} \cos \theta \\ \sin \theta \end{pmatrix}, \quad \begin{pmatrix} 0 \\ 1 \end{pmatrix} = \begin{pmatrix} \cos \frac{\pi}{2} \\ \sin \frac{\pi}{2} \end{pmatrix} \rightarrow \begin{pmatrix} \cos \left(\frac{\pi}{2} + \theta \right) \\ \sin \left(\frac{\pi}{2} + \theta \right) \end{pmatrix} = \begin{pmatrix} -\sin \theta \\ \cos \theta \end{pmatrix}$$

Then the matrix representing an anticlockwise rotation of θ is $\begin{pmatrix} \cos \theta & -\sin \theta \\ \sin \theta & \cos \theta \end{pmatrix}$.

You can show this using the angle addition formulas.

($-\sin \theta$, $\cos \theta$) *($\cos \theta$, $\sin \theta$)*

Example: Describe the transformation that the matrix $\mathbf{M} = \begin{pmatrix} -\dfrac{\sqrt{2}}{2} & -\dfrac{\sqrt{2}}{2} \\ \dfrac{\sqrt{2}}{2} & -\dfrac{\sqrt{2}}{2} \end{pmatrix}$ represents.

You can find out the position vectors of $(1, 0)$ and $(0, 1)$ under the transformation directly from the matrix.

The position vectors are the columns of $\mathbf{M}$.

$$\begin{pmatrix} 1 \\ 0 \end{pmatrix} \rightarrow \begin{pmatrix} -\dfrac{\sqrt{2}}{2} \\ \dfrac{\sqrt{2}}{2} \end{pmatrix} \quad \begin{pmatrix} 0 \\ 1 \end{pmatrix} \rightarrow \begin{pmatrix} -\dfrac{\sqrt{2}}{2} \\ -\dfrac{\sqrt{2}}{2} \end{pmatrix}$$

This is a rotation. To find the angle, use the trig equations:

Use CAST to work out all the possible angles between 0 and 2π.

$$\cos \theta = -\frac{\sqrt{2}}{2} \Rightarrow \theta = \frac{3\pi}{4}, \frac{5\pi}{4}$$

$$\sin \theta = \frac{\sqrt{2}}{2} \Rightarrow \theta = \frac{\pi}{4}, \frac{3\pi}{4}$$

The angle in common is $\theta = \dfrac{3\pi}{4}$ and we know that $\dfrac{\pi}{2} < \theta < \pi$ since $(1, 0)$ has been sent to the top-left quadrant — so this angle works.

Thus, **M** represents a **rotation about the origin**, anticlockwise through $\dfrac{3\pi}{4}$.

Draw the original points and the new ones under the transformation to get an idea of the type of transformation.

By studying the images of $(1, 0)$ and $(0, 1)$, you can see this looks like a rotation of more than a quarter turn but less than a half turn.

Always compare the size of your angle against where you know $(1, 0)$ and $(0, 1)$ have been sent to. If they don't correspond, something's gone wrong.

There could be Multiple Transformations

1) Transformations that occur one after the other are called **successive transformations**.

2) Each individual transformation will have its own matrix representation, and the overall **total transformation** has a matrix representation formed by **multiplying** these matrices.

3) If **M** represents the first transformation and **N** represents the second transformation, then to transform the vector **x** you do **NMx**.

4) Recall that $\mathbf{NMx} = \mathbf{N(Mx)} = \mathbf{(NM)x}$ — i.e. you can either do the two transformations to **x** one at a time (working right to left), or you can find the total transformation and do this to **x**.

5) You can have **any** number of transformations. Make sure you perform the multiplication in the **order** the transformations happen — i.e. write the matrices **from right to left**.

Example: What is the image of the point $(3, 1)$ under the stretch represented by the matrix **A** followed by the enlargement represented by the matrix **B**, where:

$$\mathbf{A} = \begin{pmatrix} 2 & 0 \\ 0 & 1 \end{pmatrix} \text{ and } \mathbf{B} = \begin{pmatrix} \dfrac{3}{2} & 0 \\ 0 & \dfrac{3}{2} \end{pmatrix}.$$

We perform the stretch first so **A** must be closest to the vector.

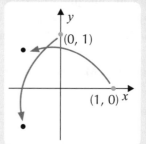

$$\begin{pmatrix} a \\ b \end{pmatrix} = BA \begin{pmatrix} 3 \\ 1 \end{pmatrix}$$

Image under A

$$= \begin{pmatrix} \dfrac{3}{2} & 0 \\ 0 & \dfrac{3}{2} \end{pmatrix} \begin{pmatrix} 2 & 0 \\ 0 & 1 \end{pmatrix} \begin{pmatrix} 3 \\ 1 \end{pmatrix}$$

$$= \begin{pmatrix} \dfrac{3}{2} & 0 \\ 0 & \dfrac{3}{2} \end{pmatrix} \begin{pmatrix} 6 \\ 1 \end{pmatrix}$$

$$= \begin{pmatrix} 3 & 0 \\ 0 & \dfrac{3}{2} \end{pmatrix} \begin{pmatrix} 3 \\ 1 \end{pmatrix} = \begin{pmatrix} 9 \\ \dfrac{3}{2} \end{pmatrix}$$

Matrix of total transformation

Matrix Transformations

It's all *Similar* in *Three Dimensions*

We've focused on 2D so far, but you'll need to know some 3D matrix transformations too.
Luckily, then, it's not all that different — you just have to make a few tweaks.

> Rotations in 3D about one of the axes work the same way as rotations in 2D, but leave the axis of rotation fixed.

Example: Determine the matrix representing an anticlockwise rotation by θ about the x-axis.

Just like with 2D transformations, we look at what happens to a few vectors under this transformation.
In 3D, we use **(1, 0, 0)**, **(0, 1, 0)** and **(0, 0, 1)**.

$$\begin{pmatrix} 1 \\ 0 \\ 0 \end{pmatrix} \to \begin{pmatrix} 1 \\ 0 \\ 0 \end{pmatrix} \qquad \begin{pmatrix} 0 \\ 1 \\ 0 \end{pmatrix} \to \begin{pmatrix} 0 \\ \cos\theta \\ \sin\theta \end{pmatrix} \qquad \begin{pmatrix} 0 \\ 0 \\ 1 \end{pmatrix} \to \begin{pmatrix} 0 \\ -\sin\theta \\ \cos\theta \end{pmatrix}$$

Again, simply use these to write the columns of **M**:

$$\mathbf{M} = \begin{pmatrix} 1 & 0 & 0 \\ 0 & \cos\theta & -\sin\theta \\ 0 & \sin\theta & \cos\theta \end{pmatrix}$$

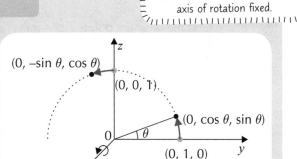

Practice Questions

Q1 Find the matrices that represent the following 2D transformations:
   a) a reflection in the line $y = x$,
   b) an enlargement about $(0, 0)$ of scale factor k,
   c) a stretch parallel to the y-axis of scale factor r,
   d) an anticlockwise rotation of $\frac{\pi}{2}$ about the origin.

Q2 Find the matrices that represent the following 3D transformations:
   a) a reflection in the (y, z)-plane,
   b) an anticlockwise rotation of α about the y-axis, viewed on the diagram above with the y-axis pointing out.

Q3 Describe the transformation represented by the matrix:

> ← Be careful with this question — your perspective of the axes will make a difference. Viewed from the other side, an anticlockwise rotation becomes a clockwise rotation.

   a) $\begin{pmatrix} 0 & -1 \\ -1 & 0 \end{pmatrix}$,
   b) $\begin{pmatrix} \frac{3}{5} & -\frac{4}{5} \\ \frac{4}{5} & \frac{3}{5} \end{pmatrix}$,
   c) $\begin{pmatrix} 1 & 0 \\ 0 & 1 \end{pmatrix}$,
   d) $\begin{pmatrix} 1 & 0 & 0 \\ 0 & 1 & 0 \\ 0 & 0 & -1 \end{pmatrix}$.

Q4 A square has vertices at $(2, 0)$, $(0, 2)$, $(-2, 0)$ and $(0, -2)$.
   a) Write down the single matrix that represents a stretch by a scale factor of 2, parallel to the x-axis, followed by an anticlockwise rotation through an angle θ centred on the origin. Leave your answer in terms of θ.
   b) If $\theta = \frac{\pi}{6}$, what are the coordinates of the vertices of the shape under the transformation?

Exam Questions

Q1 The matrices $\mathbf{P} = \begin{pmatrix} \frac{3}{7} & \frac{2}{7} \\ \frac{1}{7} & \frac{3}{7} \end{pmatrix}$, $\mathbf{Q} = \begin{pmatrix} 11 & -3 \\ -5 & 2 \end{pmatrix}$ and $\mathbf{R} = \begin{pmatrix} 0 & 2 \\ 1 & 1 \end{pmatrix}$ represent the transformations T, U and V respectively.

   a) A single transformation W is obtained by combining these transformations in the order U, followed by V, followed by V again, followed by T. Find the matrix **S** representing W. [3 marks]

   b) Interpret W geometrically. [1 mark]

Q2 A student claims that $\mathbf{M} = \begin{pmatrix} -\frac{1}{2} & \frac{\sqrt{3}}{2} \\ -\frac{\sqrt{3}}{2} & -\frac{1}{2} \end{pmatrix}$ represents an anticlockwise rotation about the origin by an angle $\frac{2\pi}{3}$.

   Either show that the student is right or explain why they are not, giving the true description of the transformation **M**. [3 marks]

Transformations — matrices in disguise...

When you're describing transformations in the exam, don't leave any scrap of detail out — you need to mention the centres of any rotations, enlargements or stretches, the equations of any lines of reflection, the angles or scale factors, and the directions of any changes. Don't give the examiner any reason to mark you down, got it?

Invariant Points and Lines

Transformations can make the plane look a whole lot different — but just like in life, some things never change. These things are called invariants.

An **Invariant Point** is a point that **Doesn't Move**

Not all points in the plane are affected by a transformation. The ones that stay **fixed** are called **invariant points**.

Example: Find the invariant points of the transformation represented by the matrix $N = \begin{pmatrix} 2 & 3 \\ 0 & -1 \end{pmatrix}$.

The image of an invariant point under the transformation is the original point, so $N\begin{pmatrix} x \\ y \end{pmatrix} = \begin{pmatrix} x \\ y \end{pmatrix}$.

$$\begin{pmatrix} 2 & 3 \\ 0 & -1 \end{pmatrix}\begin{pmatrix} x \\ y \end{pmatrix} = \begin{pmatrix} x \\ y \end{pmatrix} \Rightarrow \begin{pmatrix} 2x + 3y \\ -y \end{pmatrix} = \begin{pmatrix} x \\ y \end{pmatrix}$$

If two matrices are equal then all their elements are equal, so equate the elements to obtain simultaneous equations:

① $2x + 3y = x$ ② $-y = y \Rightarrow y = 0 \Rightarrow 2x = x \Rightarrow x = 0$

So the only invariant point under this transformation is **(0, 0)**.

Example: Find all the invariant points of the transformation represented by the matrix $A = \begin{pmatrix} 1 & 0 & 0 \\ 0 & -1 & 0 \\ 0 & 0 & 1 \end{pmatrix}$.

The invariant points satisfy the matrix equation:

$$A\begin{pmatrix} x \\ y \\ z \end{pmatrix} = \begin{pmatrix} x \\ y \\ z \end{pmatrix} \Rightarrow \begin{pmatrix} 1 & 0 & 0 \\ 0 & -1 & 0 \\ 0 & 0 & 1 \end{pmatrix}\begin{pmatrix} x \\ y \\ z \end{pmatrix} = \begin{pmatrix} x \\ y \\ z \end{pmatrix}$$

① $x = x \Rightarrow x$ can take any value
② $-y = y \Rightarrow y = 0$
③ $z = z \Rightarrow z$ can take any value

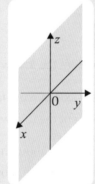

Since invariant points are the solutions to linear simultaneous equations with no constant terms, there will either be infinitely many invariant points (if the points form a line or plane) or just one (the origin).

So the invariant points are $(x, 0, z)$, i.e. the whole (x, z)-**plane**.

Points on **Invariant Lines** are mapped onto the **Invariant Line**

Some **lines** are left **unchanged** by transformations even though the points on them are moved.

An **invariant line** under a transformation is a line with the following property — the image of any point on the line is also **on the line**. This just says that the line stays the same but the points move about on it.

Example: What are the invariant lines of the transformation represented by the matrix $\begin{pmatrix} 0 & 1 \\ 1 & 0 \end{pmatrix}$?

To do this with matrices, we're going to need the position vector of a general point on the invariant line:

Write the line as $y = mx + c$. Then, using the parameter $x = t$, a general point is of the form $\begin{pmatrix} t \\ mt + c \end{pmatrix}$.

Next, find its image under the transformation: $\begin{pmatrix} 0 & 1 \\ 1 & 0 \end{pmatrix}\begin{pmatrix} t \\ mt + c \end{pmatrix} = \begin{pmatrix} mt + c \\ t \end{pmatrix}$

Use this to get the image of the line: $x = mt + c$ and $y = t$, so the line can be written $y = \dfrac{x - c}{m} = \dfrac{1}{m}x - \dfrac{c}{m}$

The line is meant to be invariant. This means the image of the line should just be the original line $y = mx + c$. Let's equate the gradients and y-intercepts of the two equations.

$\dfrac{1}{m} = m \Rightarrow 1 = m^2 \Rightarrow m = \pm 1$ $-\dfrac{c}{m} = c \Rightarrow c = -cm$ *c might be zero so don't cancel them*

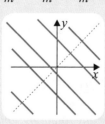

When $m = 1$, $c = -c \Rightarrow c = 0$. When $m = -1$, $c = c \Rightarrow c$ is any value.

So the invariant lines are $y = x$ and $y = -x + c$ for any c.

All the points on this line are invariant so the line must also be invariant.

Invariant Points and Lines

Example: Find the equation of any invariant lines through the origin of the transformation whose matrix is $\mathbf{Q} = \begin{pmatrix} 2 & 3 \\ 0 & -1 \end{pmatrix}$.

Since the lines we want go through the origin, they are of the form $y = mx$ (the y-intercept $c = 0$). First, find its image under the transformation.

The position vector of a general point on the line is $\begin{pmatrix} t \\ mt \end{pmatrix}$.

$$\mathbf{Q}\begin{pmatrix} t \\ mt \end{pmatrix} = \begin{pmatrix} 2 & 3 \\ 0 & -1 \end{pmatrix}\begin{pmatrix} t \\ mt \end{pmatrix} = \begin{pmatrix} 2t + 3mt \\ -mt \end{pmatrix} = \begin{pmatrix} (2 + 3m)t \\ -mt \end{pmatrix}$$

Now you need to work out the equation of the image line from this general position vector.

① $x = (2 + 3m)t$ Rearranging ①: $t = \dfrac{x}{2 + 3m}$

② $y = -mt$

Substituting into ②: $y = -m\dfrac{x}{2 + 3m} = -x\dfrac{m}{2 + 3m}$

So $-\dfrac{m}{2 + 3m}$ is the gradient of the image line for this transformation.

Since you're looking for invariant lines, you want the original and image line to be the same. This means their gradients must be the same:

$$m = -\frac{m}{2 + 3m} \Rightarrow m(2 + 3m) = -m \Rightarrow 3m^2 + 3m = 0$$
$$\Rightarrow 3m(m + 1) = 0$$
$$\Rightarrow m = 0, \ m = -1$$

Therefore the invariant lines are $y = 0$ and $y = -x$.

Overall, the hotel was good but the buffet was a little invariant.

Practice Questions

Q1 Find the invariant points of the transformation with matrix:

a) $\begin{pmatrix} 1 & 0 \\ 0 & -1 \end{pmatrix}$,   b) $\begin{pmatrix} r & 0 \\ 0 & -r \end{pmatrix}$,   c) $\begin{pmatrix} \cos\theta & 0 & -\sin\theta \\ 0 & 1 & 0 \\ \sin\theta & 0 & \cos\theta \end{pmatrix}$.

Q2 Find the equations of the invariant lines for the following transformations in the (x, y)-plane:

a) an enlargement, centred at the origin, of scale factor $a > 0$, $a \neq 1$,

b) a stretch parallel to the x-axis of scale factor $b > 0$, $b \neq 1$,

c) a rotation about the origin through an angle of   i) π,   ii) $\theta \neq n\pi$ for any integer n.

Q3 Find the invariant lines through the origin of the transformation represented by the matrix:

a) $\begin{pmatrix} 3 & 1 \\ 0 & 2 \end{pmatrix}$,   b) $\begin{pmatrix} 0 & -1 \\ -1 & 0 \end{pmatrix}$,   c) $\begin{pmatrix} 1 & -3 \\ 2 & 4 \end{pmatrix}$.

Exam Question

Q1 The matrix $\mathbf{R} = \begin{pmatrix} 2 & -1 \\ 2 & 4 \end{pmatrix}$ represents a transformation T in two-dimensional space.

a) Explain the difference between an invariant line and a line of invariant points.   [2 marks]

b) Find all the invariant points of T.   [3 marks]

c) Show that T has no invariant lines through the origin.   [5 marks]

Finding invariant lines is just one of mytrix...

If you recognise the transformation from the matrix, it's not too tricky to figure out the invariant points and lines just by imagining the transformation being carried out in your head. But it's a good idea to get into the habit of working through the method each time so you know how to go about it when the matrix is a bit more complicated.

Determinants

These pages are only about square matrices, so you can forget about any others for now — lucky you...

Every Square Matrix has a Determinant

1) The **determinant** of a **square** matrix is a **special value** that we can calculate from its **elements**.

2) If the determinant of a matrix is **zero**, we say the matrix is **singular**. Matrices with a **non-zero** determinant are **non-singular**.

The determinant of a matrix A can be written |A| or det A.

3) You work it out differently depending on the **size** of the matrix — you need to know how to do it for **2 × 2** and **3 × 3** matrices.

For a 2 × 2 matrix $\mathbf{M} = \begin{pmatrix} a & b \\ c & d \end{pmatrix}$, det $\mathbf{M} = \begin{vmatrix} a & b \\ c & d \end{vmatrix} = ad - bc$

For a 3 × 3 matrix, the **minor determinant** A of an element a is the determinant of the 2 × 2 matrix formed by **covering up** the **row** and **column** of a. We use these to find the determinant of the 3 × 3 matrix:

For a 3 × 3 matrix $\mathbf{M} = \begin{pmatrix} a & b & c \\ d & e & f \\ g & h & i \end{pmatrix}$, det $\mathbf{M} = \begin{vmatrix} a & b & c \\ d & e & f \\ g & h & i \end{vmatrix} = a\begin{vmatrix} e & f \\ h & i \end{vmatrix} - b\begin{vmatrix} d & f \\ g & i \end{vmatrix} + c\begin{vmatrix} d & e \\ g & h \end{vmatrix}$

These are A, B and C, the minor determinants of a, b and c.

Watch out for this pesky minus.

There are other formulas for the determinant of a 3 × 3 matrix, e.g. det M = aA − dD + gG.

Example: Calculate the determinant of: a) $\mathbf{A} = \begin{pmatrix} 2 & 3 \\ 5 & 1 \end{pmatrix}$, b) $\mathbf{B} = \begin{pmatrix} 2 & 3 & 2 \\ 0 & 4 & 5 \\ 1 & 3 & 7 \end{pmatrix}$.

a) det $\mathbf{A} = |\mathbf{A}| = \begin{vmatrix} 2 & 3 \\ 5 & 1 \end{vmatrix} = (2 \times 1) - (3 \times 5) = 2 - 15 = -13$

b) det $\mathbf{B} = 2\begin{vmatrix} 4 & 5 \\ 3 & 7 \end{vmatrix} - 3\begin{vmatrix} 0 & 5 \\ 1 & 7 \end{vmatrix} + 2\begin{vmatrix} 0 & 4 \\ 1 & 3 \end{vmatrix} = 2(4 \times 7 - 5 \times 3) - 3(0 \times 7 - 5 \times 1) + 2(0 \times 3 - 4 \times 1) = 33$

The Determinant is a Transformation Scale Factor

The determinant is linked to **transformations**. If **M** is the matrix representing the transformation T, then det **M** is the **area scale factor** for a 2D transformation, or a **volume scale factor** for a 3D transformation. If det M is **negative**, then it tells you that T involves a **reflection**.

Example: A hexagon has been transformed by $\begin{pmatrix} 3 & 4 \\ 9 & 1 \end{pmatrix}$. It now has an area of 11. What was its original area?

Work out the determinant: $\begin{vmatrix} 3 & 4 \\ 9 & 1 \end{vmatrix} = (3 \times 1) - (4 \times 9) = -33$

If the original area is A then $33A = 11$ as the determinant is the scale factor. (The minus represents a reflection, but areas are all positive so we don't need to include it in the calculation.) So, $A = \frac{11}{33} = \frac{1}{3}$.

There are some Important Rules of Determinants

These properties are true for all n × n matrices.

1) If **A** has a row or column which is all zeros, $|\mathbf{A}| = 0$.
2) If **A** has two rows or two columns which are identical, $|\mathbf{A}| = 0$.
3) If you can get **B** from **A** by multiplying one row or column of **A** by a scalar k then $|\mathbf{B}| = k|\mathbf{A}|$.
4) For any two matrices, $|\mathbf{AB}| = |\mathbf{BA}|$.
5) If you can get **B** from **A** by swapping two rows or two columns then $|\mathbf{B}| = -|\mathbf{A}|$.
6) If **B** can be obtained from **A** by adding a scalar multiple of one row/column of A to another row/column of **A**, then $|\mathbf{B}| = |\mathbf{A}|$.

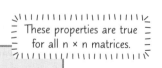
See the next page for some examples of this one.

Determinants

Adding Rows or Columns doesn't change the determinant

You can use the **rules** on the previous page to find determinants of **tricky-looking matrices**. The one you'll need the most often is the **sixth rule**. By adding or subtracting different rows or columns you can get, for example:

C1 just means 'Column 1'.

$$\begin{vmatrix} a & b & c \\ d & e & f \\ g & h & i \end{vmatrix} \xrightarrow{\substack{\text{new } C1 = \\ \text{old } C1 + C2}} = \begin{vmatrix} a+b & b & c \\ d+e & e & f \\ g+h & h & i \end{vmatrix}, \qquad \begin{vmatrix} a & b & c \\ d & e & f \\ g & h & i \end{vmatrix} \xrightarrow{\substack{\text{new } R2 = \\ \text{old } R2 - 2R1}} = \begin{vmatrix} a & b & c \\ d-2a & e-2b & f-2c \\ g & h & i \end{vmatrix}$$

Example: Given that $\begin{vmatrix} 7 & 2x & 4 \\ 3q+3x & xq+x^2 & 2q+2x \\ x-(3+p) & -p & x-(p+2) \end{vmatrix} = 0$, find x in terms of p and q.

To decide which rows or columns to **add** or **subtract**, look for **common factors** in a row or column.

$$\begin{vmatrix} 7 & 2x & 4 \\ 3q+3x & xq+x^2 & 2q+2x \\ x-(3+p) & -p & x-(p+2) \end{vmatrix} \xrightarrow{\substack{\text{Factorise the} \\ \text{second row.}}} = \begin{vmatrix} 7 & 2x & 4 \\ 3(x+q) & x(x+q) & 2(x+q) \\ x-(3+p) & -p & x-(p+2) \end{vmatrix}$$

Use the 3rd rule to take out the scalar.
$$\longrightarrow = (x+q) \begin{vmatrix} 7 & 2x & 4 \\ 3 & x & 2 \\ x-(3+p) & -p & x-(p+2) \end{vmatrix} \xrightarrow{\substack{\text{new } R3 = \\ \text{old } R3 + R2}} = (x+q) \begin{vmatrix} 7 & 2x & 4 \\ 3 & x & 2 \\ x-p & x-p & x-p \end{vmatrix}$$

Again, take out the scalar.
$$\longrightarrow = (x+q)(x-p) \begin{vmatrix} 7 & 2x & 4 \\ 3 & x & 2 \\ 1 & 1 & 1 \end{vmatrix} \xrightarrow{\substack{\text{new } R1 = \\ \text{old } R1 - 2R2}} = (x+q)(x-p) \begin{vmatrix} 1 & 0 & 0 \\ 3 & x & 2 \\ 1 & 1 & 1 \end{vmatrix}$$

It's now simple to find the determinant of the remaining matrix.
$$\longrightarrow = (x+q)(x-p)(x-2) = 0 \quad \Rightarrow \quad x = 2, x = p \text{ or } x = -q$$

Practice Questions

Q1 Find the determinants of the following matrices:

a) $\begin{pmatrix} 3 & 11 \\ 5 & 1 \end{pmatrix}$,
b) $\begin{pmatrix} 2 & \sqrt{2} \\ -4 & -22 \end{pmatrix}$,
c) $\begin{pmatrix} 4 & 0 & 4 \\ -3 & 7 & \frac{1}{3} \\ -1 & 2 & 9 \end{pmatrix}$,
d) $\begin{pmatrix} 5 & -3 & 2 \\ 3 & -9 & 0 \\ 2 & -4 & 3 \end{pmatrix}$.

Q2 A square with sides of length 3 is transformed by $\begin{pmatrix} 3 & 1 \\ 2 & 11 \end{pmatrix}$. What is the area of the new shape?

Q3 The matrix $\begin{pmatrix} 1 & 3 & 0 \\ 2 & 5 & 6 \\ 4 & 9 & 7 \end{pmatrix}$ has determinant 11. State the determinant of:

a) $\begin{pmatrix} 12 & 7 & 1 \\ 0 & 0 & 0 \\ 9 & 3 & 2 \end{pmatrix}$,
b) $\begin{pmatrix} 2 & 1 & 3 \\ 19 & 2 & 7 \\ 2 & 1 & 3 \end{pmatrix}$,
c) $\begin{pmatrix} 3 & 1 & 0 \\ 5 & 2 & 6 \\ 9 & 4 & 7 \end{pmatrix}$,
d) $\begin{pmatrix} 1 & 3 & 1 \\ 2 & 5 & 8 \\ 4 & 9 & 11 \end{pmatrix}$,
e) $\begin{pmatrix} 7 & 21 & 0 \\ 2 & 5 & 6 \\ 4 & 9 & 7 \end{pmatrix}$.

Exam Question

Q1 The matrix $\mathbf{S} = \begin{pmatrix} x-2a & 2b & x^2 \\ 1 & a & a-2x \\ 0 & b & x^2-ax \end{pmatrix}$ is singular. Find the possible values of x in terms of a and b. [7 marks]

If I spent less time working out determinants, maybe I wouldn't be singular...

Sign errors and arithmetical slips — the timeless enemy of any maths student. A 3 × 3 determinant has nine different numbers to take care of and a bunch of ways to add and multiply them together. Take it steady so you don't mess up.

Inverting Matrices

Inverses appear everywhere so it's no surprise matrices might have them too. These go hand in hand with determinants, so don't even think about reading on without getting to grips with those first.

Some Square Matrices have Inverses

When a square matrix is multiplied by its **inverse**, it gives the identity matrix.
So the inverse of a matrix **A**, written A^{-1}, is such that $AA^{-1} = A^{-1}A = I$.

Some matrices are **not invertible**. In order to find out whether a matrix
has an inverse you must first calculate the **determinant** of the matrix.

If the matrix is **singular** (has zero determinant),
then the matrix has **no inverse**.

$$\begin{pmatrix} 1 & 2 \\ 3 & 4 \end{pmatrix}\begin{pmatrix} -2 & 1 \\ \frac{3}{2} & -\frac{1}{2} \end{pmatrix} = \begin{pmatrix} -2 & 1 \\ \frac{3}{2} & -\frac{1}{2} \end{pmatrix}\begin{pmatrix} 1 & 2 \\ 3 & 4 \end{pmatrix} = \begin{pmatrix} 1 & 0 \\ 0 & 1 \end{pmatrix}$$

$$A \times A^{-1} = A^{-1} \times A = I$$

Use the Determinant to find the Inverse

For a 2 × 2 matrix $A = \begin{pmatrix} a & b \\ c & d \end{pmatrix}$, the inverse is $\dfrac{1}{\det A}\begin{pmatrix} d & -b \\ -c & a \end{pmatrix}$

Example: For the matrix $A = \begin{pmatrix} 5 & 3 \\ 7 & 6 \end{pmatrix}$: a) Determine if **A** has an inverse. If so, find A^{-1}.

b) Hence or otherwise find **B**, given that $BA = \begin{pmatrix} 17 & 12 \\ 22 & 15 \end{pmatrix}$.

a) Find the determinant of **A**: $5 \times 6 - 3 \times 7 = 30 - 21 = 9$ Since $|A| \neq 0$, the inverse **exists**.

Using the formula for inverting a 2 × 2 matrix, $A^{-1} = \dfrac{1}{9}\begin{pmatrix} 6 & -3 \\ -7 & 5 \end{pmatrix}$.

b) $BA = \begin{pmatrix} 17 & 12 \\ 22 & 15 \end{pmatrix} \Rightarrow BAA^{-1} = \begin{pmatrix} 17 & 12 \\ 22 & 15 \end{pmatrix}A^{-1} \Rightarrow B = \begin{pmatrix} 17 & 12 \\ 22 & 15 \end{pmatrix}A^{-1}$ (because $BAA^{-1} = BI = B$)

$\Rightarrow B = \begin{pmatrix} 17 & 12 \\ 22 & 15 \end{pmatrix}\dfrac{1}{9}\begin{pmatrix} 6 & -3 \\ -7 & 5 \end{pmatrix} = \dfrac{1}{9}\begin{pmatrix} 18 & 9 \\ 27 & 9 \end{pmatrix} = \begin{pmatrix} 2 & 1 \\ 3 & 1 \end{pmatrix}$

Scalars can be taken out of matrices and multiplied in whatever order you like.

Higher Dimensions mean Harder Inverses

A matrix of dimension 2 × 2 is pretty easy to invert — it's **tougher** to invert 3 × 3 matrices. Usually you'll be able to use your **calculator** to invert matrices, so make sure you know how — but you still need to know how to do it **by hand**. You could be asked to **show your working** or invert a matrix with **unknown values**, which your calculator can't do.

Inverting a 3 × 3 matrix

Here's the method for inverting the general 3 × 3 matrix $M = \begin{bmatrix} a & b & c \\ d & e & f \\ g & h & i \end{bmatrix}$.

1) Start off by finding the **determinant**, det **M**. If it's zero, then you **can't** invert the matrix.

2) Find the **minor determinant** (see p.30) of the nine elements and call them A, B, C, etc.

3) Form the **matrix of cofactors**. Its elements are the minor determinants in the **positions** corresponding to the elements which they belong to, with **minus** signs in the **even** positions. $\begin{pmatrix} A & -B & C \\ -D & E & -F \\ G & -H & I \end{pmatrix}$

4) Form the **adjoint matrix**, adj **M** — that's the **transpose** of the matrix of cofactors. To transpose a matrix, turn the columns into rows and the rows into columns. This is essentially **reflecting** the matrix in the **diagonal** from top-left to bottom-right. $\begin{pmatrix} A & -D & G \\ -B & E & -H \\ C & -F & I \end{pmatrix}$

5) The **inverse** is the adjoint over the determinant: $M^{-1} = \dfrac{\text{adj } M}{\det M} = \dfrac{1}{\det M}\begin{bmatrix} A & -D & G \\ -B & E & -H \\ C & -F & I \end{bmatrix}$.

Inverting Matrices

Example: Find the inverse of $M = \begin{pmatrix} 3 & 1 & 2 \\ 2 & 1 & 5 \\ 4 & 2 & 1 \end{pmatrix}$.

1) The first task is to find $|M|$: $\begin{vmatrix} 3 & 1 & 2 \\ 2 & 1 & 5 \\ 4 & 2 & 1 \end{vmatrix} = 3\begin{vmatrix} 1 & 5 \\ 2 & 1 \end{vmatrix} - 1\begin{vmatrix} 2 & 5 \\ 4 & 1 \end{vmatrix} + 2\begin{vmatrix} 2 & 1 \\ 4 & 2 \end{vmatrix} = 3 \times (-9) - (-18) + 2 \times 0 = -9$

Since det $M \neq 0$, we can invert M.

2) Now we need to find all the minor determinants. We already know the first three — they're the 2×2 determinants used to calculate det M.
We'll call these $A = -9$, $B = -18$ and $C = 0$. The others are:

$$D = \begin{vmatrix} 1 & 2 \\ 2 & 1 \end{vmatrix} = -3, \qquad E = \begin{vmatrix} 3 & 2 \\ 4 & 1 \end{vmatrix} = -5, \qquad F = \begin{vmatrix} 3 & 1 \\ 4 & 2 \end{vmatrix} = 2,$$

$$G = \begin{vmatrix} 1 & 2 \\ 1 & 5 \end{vmatrix} = 3, \qquad H = \begin{vmatrix} 3 & 2 \\ 2 & 5 \end{vmatrix} = 11, \qquad I = \begin{vmatrix} 3 & 1 \\ 2 & 1 \end{vmatrix} = 1$$

Don't forget to put a minus in the even positions.

3) Use these to get the matrix of cofactors: $\begin{pmatrix} A & -B & C \\ -D & E & -F \\ G & -H & I \end{pmatrix} = \begin{pmatrix} -9 & -(-18) & 0 \\ -(-3) & -5 & -2 \\ 3 & -11 & 1 \end{pmatrix} = \begin{pmatrix} -9 & 18 & 0 \\ 3 & -5 & -2 \\ 3 & -11 & 1 \end{pmatrix}$

4) The adjoint matrix is the transpose of this: $\text{adj } M = \begin{pmatrix} -9 & 3 & 3 \\ 18 & -5 & -11 \\ 0 & -2 & 1 \end{pmatrix}$

5) Finally, the inverse is the adjoint over the determinant: $\dfrac{1}{-9}\begin{pmatrix} -9 & 3 & 3 \\ 18 & -5 & -11 \\ 0 & -2 & 1 \end{pmatrix} = \begin{pmatrix} 1 & -\frac{1}{3} & -\frac{1}{3} \\ -2 & \frac{5}{9} & \frac{11}{9} \\ 0 & \frac{2}{9} & -\frac{1}{9} \end{pmatrix}$

Practice Questions

Q1 Where possible, find the inverse of the following matrices. You should <u>not</u> use your calculator.

a) $A = \begin{pmatrix} 2 & 3 \\ 1 & 0 \end{pmatrix}$, b) $B = \begin{pmatrix} 3 & 6 \\ 4 & 8 \end{pmatrix}$, c) $C = \begin{pmatrix} 1 & -1 \\ 1 & 1 \end{pmatrix}$, d) $D = \begin{pmatrix} 1 & 2 & 1 \\ 3 & 0 & 2 \\ 1 & 4 & 3 \end{pmatrix}$, e) $E = \begin{pmatrix} 3 & 2 & 1 \\ 1 & 2 & 1 \\ 1 & 4 & 2 \end{pmatrix}$.

Q2 Using the matrices from Q1, find X in each case: a) $AX = C$, b) $XA = C$, c) $DX = E$, d) $XD = E$.

Q3 The point (x, y) is sent to $(3, 7)$ under the transformation represented by $\begin{pmatrix} 2 & 3 \\ 1 & -2 \end{pmatrix}$. Find (x, y).

Q4 Multiply $B^{-1}A^{-1}$ by AB to show that $(AB)^{-1} = B^{-1}A^{-1}$ for all non-zero, non-singular square matrices.

Exam Questions

Q1 $M = \begin{pmatrix} a & x & 2 \\ 1 & 0 & 1 \\ x & 1 & 2 \end{pmatrix}$

a) Suppose that M is singular and x and a are unknown real values.
   i) Find the possible values of x in terms of a, simplifying as far as possible. [3 marks]
   ii) For what values of a does M exist? [1 mark]
b) Now suppose that M is non-singular and $a = 2$. Find M^{-1}, in terms of x. [5 marks]

Q2 A matrix M is *involutory* if it is invertible, and $M = M^{-1}$.
Show that for involutory matrices A, B and C, if $ABCB^2A^3 = I$, then $B = C$. [4 marks]

Struggling to find your identity? Just multiply by your inverse...

Inverting a matrix by hand can be fiddly, so don't make things harder for yourself — if you have a scalar outside the matrix, only multiply it inside if it simplifies the answer. And make use of your calculator to check your answers after.

Matrices and Simultaneous Equations

You know how to solve by elimination, you know how to solve by substitution. Now get ready to solve by matrices...

Use the **Inverse Matrix** to solve **Simultaneous Equations**

You can write a system of equations in **matrix form** by creating a matrix out
of the **coefficients** and vectors out of the **variables** and **constants**:

① $a_1x + b_1y + c_1z = p$
② $a_2x + b_2y + c_2z = q$
③ $a_3x + b_3y + c_3z = r$

$$\begin{pmatrix} a_1 & b_1 & c_1 \\ a_2 & b_2 & c_2 \\ a_3 & b_3 & c_3 \end{pmatrix}\begin{pmatrix} x \\ y \\ z \end{pmatrix} = \begin{pmatrix} p \\ q \\ r \end{pmatrix}$$
$$\mathbf{M} \times \mathbf{x} = \mathbf{N}$$

To solve, use the **inverse** of the
coefficient matrix and left-multiply:

$$\mathbf{x} = \mathbf{I}\,\mathbf{x} = \mathbf{M}^{-1}\mathbf{M}\,\mathbf{x} = \mathbf{M}^{-1}\mathbf{N}$$

Example: Use matrices to solve the following set of linear equations:
$$2x + 3y + z = 1, \quad x + 2y + z = 2, \quad 3x + y + z = 0$$

1) Write the equations in matrix form:
$$\begin{pmatrix} 2 & 3 & 1 \\ 1 & 2 & 1 \\ 3 & 1 & 1 \end{pmatrix}\begin{pmatrix} x \\ y \\ z \end{pmatrix} = \begin{pmatrix} 1 \\ 2 \\ 0 \end{pmatrix}$$

2) Find the inverse of the coefficient matrix:
$$\frac{1}{3}\begin{pmatrix} 1 & -2 & 1 \\ 2 & -1 & -1 \\ -5 & 7 & 1 \end{pmatrix}$$

3) Left-multiply to solve:
$$\mathbf{x} = \begin{pmatrix} x \\ y \\ z \end{pmatrix} = \frac{1}{3}\begin{pmatrix} 1 & -2 & 1 \\ 2 & -1 & -1 \\ -5 & 7 & 1 \end{pmatrix}\begin{pmatrix} 1 \\ 2 \\ 0 \end{pmatrix} = \frac{1}{3}\begin{pmatrix} -3 \\ 0 \\ 9 \end{pmatrix}$$
$$\Rightarrow x = -1, y = 0, z = 3$$

Sub your solution back into the equations to check it's right.

Geometrically, a unique
solution (x, y, z) corresponds
to an intersection of three
planes at the point (x, y, z).

There may be a **Unique Solution**, **No Solution** or **Infinitely Many Solutions**

There are **three** possible outcomes when you attempt to solve three linear equations in three variables:

1) There could be a **unique** solution (like in the example above).

2) There are **infinitely** many solutions.

3) There exists **no solution**.

If there exists a unique solution or infinitely many, we
say that the equations are consistent.
If there is no solution, the equations are inconsistent.

If there are **no** or **infinitely** many solutions, the **determinant** of the coefficient matrix will be **zero** and so there is
no inverse. In this instance, you'd have to solve the equations using some of your other techniques.

Example: Use matrices to solve the following sets of linear equations:

a) $\quad x - 2y + z = 1$
$\quad\quad 2x + 3y + 2z = 0$
$\quad\quad x + 5y + z = -1$

b) $\quad x + 2y - z = 2$
$\quad\quad -3x - 6y + 3z = 7$
$\quad\quad 4x - y + z = 2$

a) $$\begin{pmatrix} 1 & -2 & 1 \\ 2 & 3 & 2 \\ 1 & 5 & 1 \end{pmatrix}\begin{pmatrix} x \\ y \\ z \end{pmatrix} = \begin{pmatrix} 1 \\ 0 \\ -1 \end{pmatrix}$$

Both of these have determinant zero.
They aren't invertible so there isn't a
unique solution.

b) $$\begin{pmatrix} 1 & 2 & -1 \\ -3 & -6 & 3 \\ 4 & -1 & 1 \end{pmatrix}\begin{pmatrix} x \\ y \\ z \end{pmatrix} = \begin{pmatrix} 2 \\ 7 \\ 2 \end{pmatrix}$$

If you add together the first and third equations, notice
that you get the second one. So this isn't really a brand
new equation — it's just a **combination** of the others.

Rearrange the third equation and sub into the second:
$$z = -1 - x - 5y \Rightarrow 2x + 3y + 2(-1 - x - 5y) = 0$$
$$\Rightarrow -7y - 2 = 0 \Rightarrow y = -\frac{2}{7}$$

Rearrange the unused first equation:
$$x = 1 + 2y - z = 1 + \left(2 \times -\frac{2}{7}\right) - z = \frac{3}{7} - z$$

$$\Rightarrow (x, y, z) = \left(\frac{3}{7} - t, \ -\frac{2}{7}, \ t\right)$$

*Use a parameter to represent the 'free' variable — that's
the one that can take any value and defines the others.*

The planes intersect
along a line
(this is sometimes
called a 'sheaf').

If you multiply the first equation by -3,
you would get $-3x - 6y + 3z = -6$. This is
almost the same as the second equation,
except the constants are **different**.

If we were to subtract them from
one another, we would get $0 = 13$, a
contradiction.

So these equations are **inconsistent** and
there is **no solution**.

The three planes have
no common intersections
(although here there are
intersections between
some of the planes).

Matrices and Simultaneous Equations

Matrix equation problems might be **Really Wordy**

The system of equations might be **hidden** in the **context** of a question.
You'll need to read it **closely** and **decide** what's been asked for.

Example: Charlotte is entering a talent competition. She has a 15-minute slot and intends to perform acrobatics, play the banjo and do some card tricks.

She will spend triple the amount of time performing acrobatics compared to the time spent doing card tricks. She will spend 1 minute longer playing the banjo than she will doing card tricks.

Form and solve a matrix equation to determine how much time Charlotte will spend on each part of her routine in minutes and seconds. You may assume that no time is lost between parts of the routine.

The first step in these questions is working out what the variables should be. You want to determine the time spent on three activities:

a = time spent on acrobatics, b = time spent on banjo, c = time spent on cards

Now work out what the equations should be. Every part of the question will give you a bit of necessary information.

Total time is 15 minutes $\Rightarrow a + b + c = 15$

Acrobatics should be three times longer than cards $\Rightarrow a = 3c \Rightarrow a - 3c = 0$

Banjo should be 1 minute longer than cards $\Rightarrow b = c + 1 \Rightarrow b - c = 1$

Now write the system in matrix form and solve it. Make sure you give your answers in the context of the question.

$$\begin{pmatrix} 1 & 1 & 1 \\ 1 & 0 & -3 \\ 0 & 1 & -1 \end{pmatrix}\begin{pmatrix} a \\ b \\ c \end{pmatrix} = \begin{pmatrix} 15 \\ 0 \\ 1 \end{pmatrix} \Rightarrow \begin{pmatrix} a \\ b \\ c \end{pmatrix} = \frac{1}{5}\begin{pmatrix} 3 & 2 & -3 \\ 1 & -1 & 4 \\ 1 & -1 & -1 \end{pmatrix}\begin{pmatrix} 15 \\ 0 \\ 1 \end{pmatrix} = \frac{1}{5}\begin{pmatrix} 42 \\ 19 \\ 14 \end{pmatrix} = \begin{pmatrix} 8.4 \\ 3.8 \\ 2.8 \end{pmatrix}$$

Charlotte should spend:

8.4 minutes performing acrobatics, 3.8 minutes playing the banjo and 2.8 minutes doing card tricks

0.4 mins = 0.4 × 60 secs = 24 secs, and 0.8 mins = 0.8 × 60 secs = 48 secs

$\Rightarrow$ **8 mins, 24 secs** performing acrobatics, **3 mins, 48 secs** playing the banjo, **2 mins, 48 secs** doing card tricks

Practice Questions

HINT: Move all constants to the RHS and variables to the LHS.

Q1 Using matrices where possible, solve the following sets of simultaneous equations:

a) $5x - 2 = -1$
    $3x + 2y - z = y$
    $x + y - 2z = 1$

b) $x + y - 1 = 0$
    $2x + 2y = 2$
    $x - 3y = z$

c) $x + y - z = 0$
    $x + y - z = 2$
    $2x + 2y - 2z = 2$

d) $x - y + z = 3$
    $2y - 2z + 6 = 2x$
    $3x - 3y + 3z = 9$

e) $2z = -(x + y)$
    $x - y + z = 2$
    $3(x - y + z) = 9$

Q2 For each of the sets of simultaneous equations in Q1, interpret your answers geometrically.

Exam Question

Q1 Roger is landscaping his garden. The costs of materials at his local garden centre are:

- gravel: £160 per cubic metre
- clay: £150 per cubic metre
- soil: £135 per cubic metre

Roger buys a total of 2 cubic metres of gravel, clay and soil. He buys twice as much gravel as he does clay.

One week later, Roger finds that due to rainfall, his clay has expanded in volume by 5%, and his soil has expanded in volume by 0.2%. After this expansion, he now has a total of 1.1 cubic metres of clay and soil.

By forming and solving a matrix equation, calculate the amount of money that Roger spent on each of gravel, clay and soil, to the nearest penny.

[7 marks]

The only thing Charlotte can't do is solve matrix equations for you...

Your calculator will come in useful for matrix equations questions. Use it to find the inverse (or to find it doesn't exist) and then to check your answers if there's a unique solution — but, as always, you still need to show all your working.

Roots of Polynomials

There are handy rules, known as Vieta's formulas, that relate the roots of a polynomial equation to its coefficients. You can use these to evaluate expressions involving the roots without needing to find the values of the roots themselves.

The **Roots** of a **Quadratic Equation** are α and β

Given a **quadratic** equation, you can work out the **sum** and the **product** of the roots using the following:

> *If the quadratic only has one distinct root, α, then replace β with α in the equations.*

If the quadratic equation $ax^2 + bx + c = 0$ has roots α and β then $\alpha + \beta = -\dfrac{b}{a}$ and $\alpha\beta = \dfrac{c}{a}$.

Example: If $x^2 - 5x + 7 = 0$ has roots α and β, write down the following values without solving the equation:

(i) $\alpha + \beta$ $a = 1$ and $b = -5$ so $\alpha + \beta = -\dfrac{-5}{1} = 5$

(ii) $\alpha\beta$ $a = 1$ and $c = 7$ so $\alpha\beta = \dfrac{7}{1} = 7$

(iii) $\alpha^2 + \alpha\beta + \beta^2$ $(\alpha + \beta)^2 = \alpha^2 + 2\alpha\beta + \beta^2$

So, $\alpha^2 + \alpha\beta + \beta^2 = (\alpha + \beta)^2 - \alpha\beta$
$= 5^2 - 7 = 25 - 7 = 18$

> *Find an equivalent expression which only involves the sum and product of the roots.*

In part (iii), you had to **rewrite** the expression you were given in terms of $\alpha + \beta$ and $\alpha\beta$ only. This comes up quite often — you have to **rearrange** an expression to get it in terms of the **things you know**.

Example: α and β are the roots of a quadratic equation. Their sum is 4 and their product is 9. Without solving the equation find the value of:

a) $\dfrac{1}{\alpha} + \dfrac{1}{\beta}$

$\dfrac{1}{\alpha} + \dfrac{1}{\beta} = \dfrac{\beta}{\alpha\beta} + \dfrac{\alpha}{\alpha\beta}$

$= \dfrac{\alpha + \beta}{\alpha\beta}$

$= \dfrac{4}{9}$

> *It's a good idea to learn the results for $\dfrac{1}{\alpha} + \dfrac{1}{\beta}$ and $\alpha^3 + \beta^3$.*

b) $\alpha^3 + \beta^3$

$(\alpha + \beta)^3 = (\alpha + \beta)(\alpha + \beta)(\alpha + \beta)$
$= (\alpha + \beta)(\alpha^2 + 2\alpha\beta + \beta^2)$
$= \alpha^3 + 2\alpha^2\beta + \alpha\beta^2 + \alpha^2\beta + 2\alpha\beta^2 + \beta^3$
$= \alpha^3 + 3\alpha^2\beta + 3\alpha\beta^2 + \beta^3$
$= \alpha^3 + \beta^3 + 3\alpha\beta(\alpha + \beta)$

So $\alpha^3 + \beta^3 = (\alpha + \beta)^3 - 3\alpha\beta(\alpha + \beta)$
$= 4^3 - (3 \times 9 \times 4) = -44$

The **Roots** of a **Cubic Equation** are α, β and γ

You can link the **coefficients** of a **cubic** equation to its **roots** with the following formulas:

> *If the cubic has just two distinct roots, replace γ with α in the equations. If the cubic has only one distinct root, replace both β and γ with α.*

If the cubic equation $ax^3 + bx^2 + cx + d = 0$ has roots α, β and γ then:
$$\alpha + \beta + \gamma = -\frac{b}{a}, \quad \alpha\beta + \alpha\gamma + \beta\gamma = \frac{c}{a} \text{ and } \alpha\beta\gamma = -\frac{d}{a}$$

Example: The equation $x^3 + 12x^2 - 6x + 5 = 0$ has three distinct roots α, β and γ. Without solving the equation, find the values of:

a) $\alpha + \beta + \gamma$, $\alpha\beta + \alpha\gamma + \beta\gamma$ and $\alpha\beta\gamma$.

$\alpha + \beta + \gamma = -\dfrac{12}{1} = -12$, $\alpha\beta + \alpha\gamma + \beta\gamma = \dfrac{-6}{1} = -6$ and $\alpha\beta\gamma = -\dfrac{5}{1} = -5$

b) $\alpha^2 + \beta^2 + \gamma^2$.

Write the expression you want in terms of the expressions you worked out in (i).

$(\alpha + \beta + \gamma)^2 = \alpha^2 + \beta^2 + \gamma^2 + 2\alpha\beta + 2\alpha\gamma + 2\beta\gamma$

So, $\alpha^2 + \beta^2 + \gamma^2 = (\alpha + \beta + \gamma)^2 - 2(\alpha\beta + \alpha\gamma + \beta\gamma)$

$\alpha^2 + \beta^2 + \gamma^2 = (-12)^2 - 2(-6) = 144 + 12 = 156$

Roots of Polynomials

The **Roots** of a **Quartic Equation** are α, β, γ and δ

A **quartic** equation is a polynomial with an x^4 term in it (and no higher powers).
The **roots** of a quartic equation can also be linked to its **coefficients**:

If the quartic equation $ax^4 + bx^3 + cx^2 + dx + e = 0$ has roots α, β, γ and δ then:

$$\alpha + \beta + \gamma + \delta = -\frac{b}{a}, \quad \alpha\beta + \alpha\gamma + \alpha\delta + \beta\gamma + \beta\delta + \gamma\delta = \frac{c}{a},$$

$$\alpha\beta\gamma + \alpha\beta\delta + \alpha\gamma\delta + \beta\gamma\delta = -\frac{d}{a} \text{ and } \alpha\beta\gamma\delta = \frac{e}{a}$$

If there are any repeated roots, replace the repeated roots with α as before.

You might see these written as $\sum\alpha$ (for $\alpha + \beta + \gamma + \delta$), $\sum\alpha\beta$ (for $\alpha\beta + \alpha\gamma + \alpha\delta + \beta\gamma + \beta\delta + \gamma\delta$) and
$\sum\alpha\beta\gamma$ (for $\alpha\beta\gamma + \alpha\beta\delta + \alpha\gamma\delta + \beta\gamma\delta$). Remember that $\sum$ means '**sum of**'.

> **Example:** A quartic equation has roots α, β, γ and δ, where $\sum\alpha = 4$, $\sum\alpha\beta = 5.5$, $\sum\alpha\beta\gamma = -8$
> and $\alpha\beta\gamma\delta = 6$. Given that the coefficient of x^4 is 2, find the quartic equation.
>
> $-\frac{b}{a} = 4$ and $a = 2$, so $b = -8$ $\qquad$ $\frac{c}{a} = 5.5$ so $c = 11$ $\qquad$ $-\frac{d}{a} = -8$ so $d = 16$ $\qquad$ $\frac{e}{a} = 6$ so $e = 12$
>
> So the equation is $2x^4 - 8x^3 + 11x^2 + 16x + 12 = 0$.

The **Roots** might be **Complex Numbers**

The relationships between the roots and the coefficients work for both real and complex roots
(in fact, **all** the examples so far have had complex roots). Remember that if a complex number
is a root, then its **complex conjugate** is also a root (see p.6-7).

> **Example:** The equation $x^3 - 5x^2 + mx + n = 0$ has roots α, β and γ.
> If $\alpha = 1 + 2i$, what are the values of m and n?
>
> Since $1 + 2i$ is a root, $1 - 2i$ is also a root, so $\beta = 1 - 2i$.
>
> In the equation, $a = 1$ and $b = -5$. So $\alpha + \beta + \gamma = 5 \Rightarrow \gamma = 3$.
>
> $m = \alpha\beta + \alpha\gamma + \beta\gamma = (1 + 2i)(1 - 2i) + 3(1 + 2i) + 3(1 - 2i) = 11$
> and $n = -\alpha\beta\gamma = -3(1 + 2i)(1 - 2i) = -15$

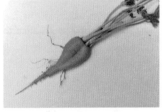

β was a bit complex, but α still liked him better than all the other roots.

Practice Questions

Q1 The equation $2x^3 + 8x^2 - 6x + 21 = 0$ has roots α, β and γ. Write down the values of:
a) $\alpha\beta\gamma$ $\qquad\qquad$ b) $\alpha\beta + \alpha\gamma + \beta\gamma$ $\qquad\qquad$ c) $\alpha + \beta + \gamma$

Q2 A cubic equation has roots α, β and γ, where $\alpha + \beta + \gamma = -\frac{5}{3}$, $\alpha\beta + \alpha\gamma + \beta\gamma = 7$ and $\alpha\beta\gamma = 10$.
Given that the coefficient of x^3 is 3, find the cubic equation.

Q3 The equation $(x + 3)(x + 5) = -7$ has roots α and β.
a) Write down the values of $\alpha + \beta$ and $\alpha\beta$. $\qquad\qquad$ b) Find the value of $\frac{\alpha^2 + \beta^2}{\alpha\beta}$.

Q4 The equation $x^4 - 6x^3 + 3x^2 + 7x - 9 = 0$ has roots α, β, γ and δ.
Find the value of $\frac{1}{\alpha} + \frac{1}{\beta} + \frac{1}{\gamma} + \frac{1}{\delta}$.

Exam Questions

Q1 The equation $2x^3 + 4x^2 + 14x - 11 = 0$ has roots α, β and γ. Find the value of $(4 + \alpha)(4 + \beta)(4 + \gamma)$. $\qquad$ [3 marks]

Q2 The equation $x^3 - gx^2 + h = 0$ has roots α, β and γ. Find the value of $\alpha^3 + \beta^3 + \gamma^3$ in terms of g and h. $\qquad$ [4 marks]

Q3 The equation $x^4 - 12x^3 + 49x^2 + rx + 60 = 0$ has roots α, β, γ and δ.
If $\alpha = 2$ and $\beta = 6$, what is the value of r? $\qquad$ [6 marks]

A polynomial's favourite road trip — Root 66...

To understand where all these formulas involving roots come from, have a go at deriving them for yourself.
E.g. if α, β are the roots, then $a(x - \alpha)(x - \beta) = ax^2 + bx + c$ — so you can use this to derive the equations for the roots.

Related Roots

The roots of one equation might be linked to those of another by a linear relationship, e.g. one equation with roots α, β and γ and another with roots $2\alpha + 3$, $2\beta + 3$ and $2\gamma + 3$. Here you'll see how to find equations with such related roots.

Method 1 — Write the New Roots in terms of What You Know

If you know one **equation**, and you're told the **rule** linking its **roots** with a second **unknown** equation, you can use the **formulas** you saw on the previous couple of pages to find that equation. So, for a **cubic equation**:

> *You can adapt this method for a quadratic or quartic equation.*

1) Find the **sum** $\alpha + \beta + \gamma$, the **sum of pairs** $\alpha\beta + \alpha\gamma + \beta\gamma$ and the **product** $\alpha\beta\gamma$, where α, β and γ are the roots of the **given** cubic equation.

2) By using the linear relationship of the **related roots**, write the sum, sum of pairs and product of the **new roots** in terms of the equivalent expressions for the original roots.

3) **Substitute** the values you found in **step 1)** into the expressions you wrote in **step 2)**.

4) Use the results to write the **new equation**.

Example: The quadratic equation $2x^2 + 12x - 9 = 0$ has roots α and β. Find the equation whose roots are $\alpha - 2$ and $\beta - 2$.

Find $\alpha + \beta$ and $\alpha\beta$ using the coefficients of the given equation.

$$\alpha + \beta = -\frac{12}{2} = -6$$
$$\alpha\beta = -\frac{9}{2}$$

Find the sum and product of the new roots in terms of $\alpha + \beta$ and $\alpha\beta$, and substitute in the values.

$$(\alpha - 2) + (\beta - 2) = (\alpha + \beta) - 4 = -6 - 4 = -10$$
$$(\alpha - 2)(\beta - 2) = \alpha\beta - 2\alpha - 2\beta + 4$$
$$= \alpha\beta - 2(\alpha + \beta) + 4 = -\frac{9}{2} - 2(-6) + 4 = \frac{23}{2}$$

Pick values for the coefficients in the new equation that satisfy the values found for the sum and product of the roots.

So, in the new equation: $-\dfrac{b}{a} = (\alpha - 2) + (\beta - 2) = -10$,

so let $a = 1$ and $b = 10$.

$$\frac{c}{a} = (\alpha - 2)(\beta - 2) = \frac{23}{2}, \text{ so } c = \frac{23}{2}$$

So the equation is $x^2 + 10x + \dfrac{23}{2} = 0 \Rightarrow \mathbf{2x^2 + 20x + 23 = 0}$

Choosing different values of a, b and c would give you an equation that could be simplified to this one. Always give the equation with integer coefficients, and cancel any common factors of the coefficients.

Example: The cubic equation $x^3 - 5x^2 + 3x - 2 = 0$ has roots α, β and γ. Find a cubic equation with roots $4\alpha + 1$, $4\beta + 1$ and $4\gamma + 1$.

Find $\alpha + \beta + \gamma$, $\alpha\beta + \alpha\gamma + \beta\gamma$ and $\alpha\beta\gamma$.

$$\alpha + \beta + \gamma = 5, \ \alpha\beta + \alpha\gamma + \beta\gamma = 3, \ \alpha\beta\gamma = 2$$

Find the sum, sum of pairs and product of the new roots.

$$(4\alpha + 1) + (4\beta + 1) + (4\gamma + 1) = 4(\alpha + \beta + \gamma) + 3 = 4 \times 5 + 3 = \mathbf{23}$$

$$(4\alpha + 1)(4\beta + 1) + (4\alpha + 1)(4\gamma + 1) + (4\beta + 1)(4\gamma + 1)$$
$$= (16\alpha\beta + 4\alpha + 4\beta + 1) + (16\alpha\gamma + 4\alpha + 4\gamma + 1) + (16\beta\gamma + 4\beta + 4\gamma + 1)$$
$$= 8(\alpha + \beta + \gamma) + 16(\alpha\beta + \alpha\gamma + \beta\gamma) + 3$$
$$= 8 \times 5 + 16 \times 3 + 3 = \mathbf{91}$$

$$(4\alpha + 1)(4\beta + 1)(4\gamma + 1)$$
$$= 64\alpha\beta\gamma + 16\alpha\beta + 16\alpha\gamma + 4\alpha + 16\beta\gamma + 4\beta + 4\gamma + 1$$
$$= 64\alpha\beta\gamma + 16(\alpha\beta + \alpha\gamma + \beta\gamma) + 4(\alpha + \beta + \gamma) + 1$$
$$= 64 \times 2 + 16 \times 3 + 4 \times 5 + 1 = \mathbf{197}$$

Find values for the coefficients of the new equation, and write down the equation.

So, in the new equation: $-\dfrac{b}{a} = 23$, so let $a = 1$ and $b = -23$

$$\frac{c}{a} = 91, \text{ so } c = 91$$
$$-\frac{d}{a} = 197, \text{ so } d = -197$$

So the equation is $\mathbf{x^3 - 23x^2 + 91x - 197 = 0}$.

Related Roots

Method 2 — Use a *Substitution* to find the *New Equation*

You might find this alternative method easier to use for some polynomials:

> 1) Take the expression relating the **root** α of the original equation to the corresponding **new root** and **set it equal** to another letter, say y. Then rearrange to **express α in terms of y**.
>
> 2) **Substitute** the expression for α into the **original equation**.
>
> 3) **Rearrange** or **simplify** the new equation.

Example: The cubic equation $x^3 + 2x^2 - 5x + 1 = 0$ has roots α, β and γ.
Find a cubic equation with roots $\alpha + 1$, $\beta + 1$ and $\gamma + 1$.

1) Let $y = \alpha + 1$, then $\alpha = y - 1$.

2) Substitute $\alpha = y - 1$ into $x^3 + 2x^2 - 5x + 1$: $(y - 1)^3 + 2(y - 1)^2 - 5(y - 1) + 1 = 0$.

   α is a root, so substituting the expression for α into the polynomial gives O.

3) Expand the brackets and simplify: $y^3 - 3y^2 + 3y - 1 + 2(y^2 - 2y + 1) - 5y + 5 + 1 = 0$

   It doesn't matter what variable you use for the equation, so it's fine to leave it in terms of y. $y^3 - y^2 - 6y + 7 = 0$

Example: The quartic equation $2x^4 + 5x^3 + 4x^2 - 7x + 11 = 0$ has roots α, β, γ and δ.
Find a quartic equation with roots 3α, 3β, 3γ and 3δ.

1) Let $y = 3\alpha$, then $\alpha = \dfrac{y}{3}$.

2) Substitute $\alpha = \dfrac{y}{3}$ into $2x^4 + 5x^3 + 4x^2 - 7x + 11$: $2\left(\dfrac{y}{3}\right)^4 + 5\left(\dfrac{y}{3}\right)^3 + 4\left(\dfrac{y}{3}\right)^2 - 7\left(\dfrac{y}{3}\right) + 11 = 0$

3) Simplify the equation: $\dfrac{2y^4}{81} + \dfrac{5y^3}{27} + \dfrac{4y^2}{9} - \dfrac{7y}{3} + 11 = 0$

   Always give your answer with integer coefficients. $2y^4 + 15y^3 + 36y^2 - 189y + 891 = 0$

Practice Questions

All equations in your answers should be given with <u>integer coefficients</u>.

Q1 The quadratic equation $3x^2 + 4x + 9 = 0$ has roots α and β.
Use Method 1 to find the quadratic equation with roots 4α and 4β.

Q2 The cubic equation $x^3 + 6x^2 - 2x + 7 = 0$ has roots α, β and γ.
Use Method 1 to find the cubic equation with roots $\alpha + 2$, $\beta + 2$ and $\gamma + 2$.

Q3 The cubic equation $x^3 - 3x^2 + 7x - 4 = 0$ has roots α, β and γ.
Use Method 2 to find the cubic equation with roots $2\alpha - 1$, $2\beta - 1$ and $2\gamma - 1$.

Q4 The quartic equation $x^4 + 9x^2 + 13 = 0$ has roots α, β, γ and δ.
Use Method 2 to find the quartic equation with roots $\alpha + 3$, $\beta + 3$, $\gamma + 3$ and $\delta + 3$.

Exam Questions

Q1 The cubic equation $3x^3 - 2x^2 - 4x - 6 = 0$ has roots α, β and γ.
Find the cubic equation with roots $3\alpha + 2$, $3\beta + 2$ and $3\gamma + 2$.
Your answer should have integer coefficients. [5 marks]

Q2 The quartic equation $5x^4 + 11x + 8 = 0$ has roots α, β, γ, and δ.

a) Use the substitution $x = 1 - 2u$ to obtain a quartic equation in terms of u. [2 marks]

b) Hence find the values of $\dfrac{1-\alpha}{2} + \dfrac{1-\beta}{2} + \dfrac{1-\gamma}{2} + \dfrac{1-\delta}{2}$ and $\left(\dfrac{1-\alpha}{2}\right)\left(\dfrac{1-\beta}{2}\right)\left(\dfrac{1-\gamma}{2}\right)\left(\dfrac{1-\delta}{2}\right)$. [3 marks]

He clearly dyes his equations — just look at those roots...

It's a good idea to learn both methods, but unless the question tells you what to do, it's up to you which method you use. As a bit of extra practice, try doing the examples on p.38 using Method 2, and those on p.39 using Method 1.

Summation of Series

These pages are all about nifty ways to add lots of numbers together. If you're finding the sum of a series of numbers, such as the squares of integers, then there are formulas that will save you from having to add them together yourself.

Make sure you're happy with the Basics

You'll have already seen some facts about series in A Level Maths. Here's a quick recap of a couple of important formulas — remember that $\sum\limits_{r=1}^{n}$ means "the sum from $r = 1$ up to $r = n$."

$\sum\limits_{r=1}^{n} 1$ means add n lots of 1 together.

The formula is $\sum\limits_{r=1}^{n} 1 = n$

$\sum\limits_{r=1}^{n} r$ means $1 + 2 + 3 + \ldots + (n - 1) + n$

The formula is $\sum\limits_{r=1}^{n} r = \frac{1}{2} n(n + 1)$

> You need to LEARN these two formulas — they won't be given in the formula booklet.

There are also Formulas for r^2 and r^3

$\sum\limits_{r=1}^{n} r^2$ means $1^2 + 2^2 + 3^2 + \ldots + (n - 1)^2 + n^2$

The formula is $\sum\limits_{r=1}^{n} r^2 = \frac{1}{6} n(n + 1)(2n + 1)$

$\sum\limits_{r=1}^{n} r^3$ means $1^3 + 2^3 + 3^3 + \ldots + (n - 1)^3 + n^3$

The formula is $\sum\limits_{r=1}^{n} r^3 = \frac{1}{4} n^2(n + 1)^2$

> These two formulas are given in the formula booklet.

You can Prove these Formulas by Induction

For a reminder on how to use proof by induction, see page 2.

Example: Prove that when n is a positive integer, $\sum\limits_{r=1}^{n} r^2 = \frac{1}{6} n(n + 1)(2n + 1)$.

First, show it's true when $n = 1$.

When $n = 1$, LHS $= \sum\limits_{r=1}^{1} r^2 = 1^2 = 1$

and RHS $= \frac{1}{6}(1)(1 + 1)(2 \times 1 + 1) = \frac{1}{6}(1)(2)(3) = 1$

So the statement is **true for $n = 1$.**

Then show that if it's true for $n = k$, it's also true for $n = k + 1$.

Assume the statement is true for $n = k$, so $\sum\limits_{r=1}^{k} r^2 = \frac{1}{6} k(k + 1)(2k + 1)$.

Then $\sum\limits_{r=1}^{k+1} r^2 = \sum\limits_{r=1}^{k} r^2 + (k + 1)^2 = \frac{1}{6} k(k + 1)(2k + 1) + (k + 1)^2$

> Look out for common factors — it'll help you avoid dealing with big polynomials.

$= \frac{1}{6}(k + 1)[k(2k + 1) + 6(k + 1)]$

$= \frac{1}{6}(k + 1)[2k^2 + 7k + 6]$

$= \frac{1}{6}(k + 1)(k + 2)(2k + 3)$

$= \frac{1}{6}(k + 1)((k + 1) + 1)(2(k + 1) + 1)$

Remember to write a concluding statement.

We have shown that if the statement is true for $n = k$, then it is true for $n = k + 1$. Since we have shown it to be true for $n = 1$, it must be true for all $n \geq 1$.

Summation of Series

The formula for the sum of r^3 can be proved in a similar way.

Example: Prove that when n is a positive integer, $\sum_{r=1}^{n} r^3 = \frac{1}{4} n^2 (n+1)^2$.

When $n = 1$, LHS $= \sum_{r=1}^{1} r^3 = 1^3 = 1$

and RHS $= \frac{1}{4}(1^2)(1+1)^2 = \frac{1}{4}(1)(2)^2 = 1$

So the statement is **true for $n = 1$**.

Assume the statement is true for $n = k$, so $\sum_{r=1}^{k} r^3 = \frac{1}{4} k^2 (k+1)^2$

Then $\sum_{r=1}^{k+1} r^3 = \sum_{r=1}^{k} r^3 + (k+1)^3 = \frac{1}{4} k^2 (k+1)^2 + (k+1)^3$

$\qquad = \frac{1}{4}(k+1)^2 [k^2 + 4(k+1)]$

$\qquad = \frac{1}{4}(k+1)^2 [k^2 + 4k + 4]$

$\qquad = \frac{1}{4}(k+1)^2 (k+2)^2$

$\qquad = \frac{1}{4}(k+1)^2 ((k+1) + 1)^2$

This follows exactly the same method as the previous example — show the statement's true for $n = 1$, then show that if it's true for $n = k$, it's also true for $n = k + 1$.

We have shown that if the statement is true for $n = k$, then it is true for $n = k + 1$. Since we have shown it to be true for $n = 1$, it must be true for all $n \geq 1$.

During his summation, Hamish began to wonder if the audience were entirely engaged.

Proof by induction isn't only useful for the standard summation results — you can use it to prove the summation formulas for many different series. Give these Practice and Exam Questions a go to see how it works for yourself.

Practice Questions

Q1 Use proof by induction to show that $\sum_{r=1}^{n} r = \frac{1}{2} n(n+1)$, when n is any positive integer.

Q2 Use proof by induction to show that $\sum_{r=1}^{n} (r-1)(r+2) = \frac{1}{3} n(n+4)(n-1)$, when n is any positive integer.

Q3 Use proof by induction to show that $\sum_{r=1}^{n} \frac{1}{(r+1)(r+2)} = \frac{n}{2(n+2)}$, when n is any positive integer.

Q4 Use proof by induction to show that $\sum_{r=1}^{n} 3^r = \frac{3}{2}(3^n - 1)$, when n is any positive integer.

Exam Questions

Q1 Use proof by induction to show that $\sum_{r=1}^{n} r^2(r+1) = \frac{1}{12} n(n+1)(n+2)(3n+1)$, when n is any positive integer. [6 marks]

Q2 a) Use proof by induction to show that $\sum_{r=1}^{n} r(r-3) = \frac{1}{3} n(n+1)(n-4)$, when n is any positive integer. [6 marks]

b) For what value of n is $\sum_{r=1}^{n} r(r-3) = 10 \sum_{r=1}^{n} r$ true? [3 marks]

Q3 a) Use proof by induction to show that $\sum_{r=1}^{n} r(r!) = (n+1)! - 1$, when n is any positive integer. [6 marks]

b) For what value of n does $\sum_{r=1}^{n} r(r!)$ equal 23? [3 marks]

There are two more exciting episodes to come in this series...

The next page explains another method for showing a formula for the summation of a polynomial expression is correct — but if the question tells you to use proof by induction, make sure you use that method. When you're working out the sum for $n = k + 1$, remember what you're aiming for — that'll help you rearrange things to get the result you need.

Using Summations

Here's a couple of pages of handy tricks you can use to figure out summations. If you're doing AS Level, once you reach the end of this page, head straight to the practice questions — you don't need to learn the method of differences.

Split Summations into Bits you Know

If an expression can be written as a polynomial of degree 3 or less, you can find a formula for its summation by splitting up the sum and using the standard results for $\sum_{r=1}^{n} 1$, $\sum_{r=1}^{n} r$, $\sum_{r=1}^{n} r^2$ and $\sum_{r=1}^{n} r^3$.

$$\sum_{r=1}^{n}(ar^3 + br^2 + cr + d) = a\sum_{r=1}^{n}r^3 + b\sum_{r=1}^{n}r^2 + c\sum_{r=1}^{n}r + d\sum_{r=1}^{n}1$$

Use this method to find the formula for the summation of an expression that can be written as a polynomial:

1) **Expand any brackets** and **rearrange** to get the expression into the form of a **polynomial**.

2) Split up the summation into sums of the **separate terms** (see above).

3) Substitute in the **formulas** from p.40 for $\sum_{r=1}^{n} r^3$, $\sum_{r=1}^{n} r^2$, $\sum_{r=1}^{n} r$ and $\sum_{r=1}^{n} 1$.

4) **Simplify** your expression where possible.
The **question** might tell you the form the expression should take.

Example: Show that $\sum_{r=1}^{n}(r+3)(r-1) = \frac{1}{6}n(n-1)(an+b)$, where a and b are integers to be found.

1) Expand the brackets. $\quad \sum_{r=1}^{n}(r+3)(r-1) = \sum_{r=1}^{n}(r^2 + 2r - 3)$

2) Split into sums of the separate terms. $\quad = \sum_{r=1}^{n}r^2 + 2\sum_{r=1}^{n}r - 3\sum_{r=1}^{n}1 \longleftarrow$ *Don't forget to sum the constant term.*

3) Use the standard formulas. $\quad = \frac{1}{6}n(n+1)(2n+1) + 2 \times \frac{1}{2}n(n+1) - 3n$

4) Simplify and factorise to get the expression into the required form.
$\quad = \frac{1}{6}n[(n+1)(2n+1) + 6(n+1) - 18]$

$\quad = \frac{1}{6}n[2n^2 + 3n + 1 + 6n + 6 - 18]$

$\quad = \frac{1}{6}n(2n^2 + 9n - 11)$

$\quad = \frac{1}{6}n(n-1)(2n + 11)$

Look Carefully at the Limits

The sum won't necessarily be from $r = 1$ up to $r = n$, so always check what the limits are (the little numbers at the top and bottom of the summation symbol).

Example: Find $\sum_{r=9}^{25} r^3$.

To find the sum from $r = 9$ to $r = 25$, use the standard r^3 summation formula and subtract off the bit that you don't need, i.e. the sum from $r = 1$ to $r = 8$.

$\sum_{r=1}^{n} r^3 = \frac{1}{4}n^2(n+1)^2$

$\sum_{r=9}^{25} r^3 = \sum_{r=1}^{25} r^3 - \sum_{r=1}^{8} r^3$

$\quad = \frac{1}{4}25^2(26)^2 - \frac{1}{4}8^2(9)^2$

$\quad = 105\ 625 - 1296 = \mathbf{104\ 329}$

Example: Show that $\sum_{r=k+1}^{2k} r^2 = \frac{1}{6}k(2k+1)(7k+1)$.

$\sum_{r=1}^{n} r^2 = \frac{1}{6}n(n+1)(2n+1)$

$\sum_{r=k+1}^{2k} r^2 = \sum_{r=1}^{2k} r^2 - \sum_{r=1}^{k} r^2 \longleftarrow$ *Split the sum into parts involving the standard results.*

$\quad = \frac{1}{6}2k(2k+1)(4k+1) - \frac{1}{6}k(k+1)(2k+1)$

$\quad = \frac{1}{6}k(2k+1)[2(4k+1) - (k+1)]$

$\quad = \frac{1}{6}k(2k+1)(7k+1)$

Section 4 — CP: Further Algebra and Functions

Using Summations

Use the *Method of Differences* for *Fractions*

1) If an expression can be written as the **difference of similar terms**, then you can work out summations using the **method of differences**.

2) The method lets you **cancel** many of the **terms**, so that only the values **close to the upper and lower limits** of the sum actually **contribute** to the sum.

3) It's really handy for expressions that can be written as **partial fractions** — have a look at the example below to see how it works. It can also be used to prove some standard summation results — see Practice Question 3.

Example: Show that $\sum_{r=1}^{n}\frac{2}{(r+2)(r+4)} = \frac{n(7n+25)}{12(n+3)(n+4)}$

First, rewrite the expression using partial fractions.

$$\frac{2}{(r+2)(r+4)} = \frac{A}{r+2} + \frac{B}{r+4} = \frac{A(r+4)+B(r+2)}{(r+2)(r+4)} = \frac{(A+B)r+(4A+2B)}{(r+2)(r+4)}$$

Equating coefficients: $A + B = 0$ and $4A + 2B = 2 \Rightarrow -2B = 2 \Rightarrow B = -1$ and $A = 1$.

$$\Rightarrow \frac{2}{(r+2)(r+4)} = \frac{1}{r+2} - \frac{1}{r+4}$$

You could also use the substitution method to find the partial fractions.

Write out the first few and last few terms in the sum.

$$\sum_{r=1}^{n}\frac{2}{(r+2)(r+4)} = \sum_{r=1}^{n}\left[\frac{1}{r+2} - \frac{1}{r+4}\right]$$

$$= \left(\frac{1}{3}-\frac{1}{5}\right)+\left(\frac{1}{4}-\frac{1}{6}\right)+\left(\frac{1}{5}-\frac{1}{7}\right)+\left(\frac{1}{6}-\frac{1}{8}\right) + \dots$$

$$\dots + \left(\frac{1}{(n-3)+2}-\frac{1}{(n-3)+4}\right)+\left(\frac{1}{(n-2)+2}-\frac{1}{(n-2)+4}\right)$$

$$+\left(\frac{1}{(n-1)+2}-\frac{1}{(n-1)+4}\right)+\left(\frac{1}{n+2}-\frac{1}{n+4}\right)$$

Look for terms that cancel — the only $\frac{1}{r+2}$ terms that won't be cancelled are $\frac{1}{3}$ and $\frac{1}{4}$.

The only $\frac{1}{r+4}$ terms that won't be cancelled are $\frac{1}{n+3}$ and $\frac{1}{n+4}$.

$$= \frac{1}{3}-\frac{1}{5}+\frac{1}{4}-\frac{1}{6}+\frac{1}{5}-\frac{1}{7}+\frac{1}{6}-\frac{1}{8} + \dots$$

$$\dots + \frac{1}{n-1}-\frac{1}{n+1}+\frac{1}{n}-\frac{1}{n+2}+\frac{1}{n+1}-\frac{1}{n+3}+\frac{1}{n+2}-\frac{1}{n+4}$$

$$= \frac{1}{3}+\frac{1}{4}-\frac{1}{n+3}-\frac{1}{n+4}$$

Put over a common denominator and simplify to get the required result.

$$= \frac{4(n+3)(n+4)+3(n+3)(n+4)-12(n+4)-12(n+3)}{12(n+3)(n+4)}$$

$$= \frac{7(n^2+7n+12)-24n-84}{12(n+3)(n+4)}$$

$$= \frac{7n^2+25n}{12(n+3)(n+4)} = \frac{n(7n+25)}{12(n+3)(n+4)}$$

Practice Questions

If you're doing AS Level, you only need to do Practice Question 1 and Exam Question 1.

Q1 Show that $\sum_{r=1}^{n}r^2(r-4) = \frac{n(n+1)}{12}(an^2+bn+c)$, where a, b and c are integers to be found.

Q2 a) Use the method of differences to show that $\sum_{r=1}^{n}\frac{1}{r(r+1)} = \frac{n}{n+1}$. b) Find $\sum_{r=12}^{50}\frac{1}{r(r+1)}$.

Q3 Use the method of differences to prove that $\sum_{r=1}^{n}r = \frac{1}{2}n(n+1)$. Hint: use $r = \frac{1}{2}(r(r+1)-r(r-1))$.

Exam Questions

Q1 Show that $4 + \sum_{r=1}^{n}(r+1)(r+4) = \frac{1}{3}(n+1)(n+2)(n+6)$. [6 marks]

Q2 a) Show that $\frac{2}{(r+2)(r+3)(r+4)}$ can be written in the form $\frac{A}{(r+2)(r+3)} + \frac{B}{(r+3)(r+4)}$, where A and B are constants to be found. [2 marks]

b) Use the method of differences to show that $\sum_{r=1}^{n}\frac{1}{(r+2)(r+3)(r+4)} = \frac{n(n+7)}{24(n+3)(n+4)}$. [5 marks]

Summations and series — know your limits...

There were a few different ideas on these two pages, so make sure you're happy with all of them. A question might tell you which method to use when you're proving something involving series, so always read it carefully.

Maclaurin Series

You'll need your differentiating skills for this topic — so refresh your memory now if you're feeling at all rusty.

A Maclaurin series is a way of Representing a Function

If a function and all its derivatives have finite, real values at $x = 0$, then the function can be expressed as a **Maclaurin series**. The Maclaurin series of a function f(x) is a **polynomial**, where the **coefficients** of the powers of x are determined by f(x) and its **derivatives**, evaluated at $x = 0$. The series are usually **infinite**, but an **approximation** of a function can be found by considering a limited number of terms.

This is the expression for the rth term in the series. $r = 0$ gives the first term, $r = 1$ gives the second and so on...

$$f(x) = f(0) + xf'(0) + \frac{x^2}{2!}f''(0) + \frac{x^3}{3!}f'''(0) + \dots + \frac{x^r}{r!}f^{(r)}(0) + \dots$$

To find the Maclaurin series of a function:

1) Work out the first few **derivatives** of f(x), and an expression for the rth derivative where possible.

$f^{(r)}(x)$ is the rth derivative of f(x).

2) **Evaluate** f(x) and each of these derivatives at **$x = 0$**.

3) Plug these into the Maclaurin series **formula** to get a polynomial — **simplify** the coefficients where possible.

Example: Find the Maclaurin series for f(x) = e^x

1) f'(x) = e^x So all the derivatives of f(x) equal e^x.
2) f(0) = f'(0) = f''(0) = ... = e^0 = 1.
3) So the Maclaurin series is:

$$f(x) = f(0) + xf'(0) + \frac{x^2}{2!}f''(0) + \frac{x^3}{3!}f'''(0) + \dots + \frac{x^r}{r!}f^{(r)}(0) + \dots$$

$$e^x = 1 + x + \frac{x^2}{2!} + \frac{x^3}{3!} + \dots + \frac{x^r}{r!} + \dots$$ ← *This series is valid for all values of x.*

The Maclaurin racing team hadn't managed to secure as much funding as their better-known rivals.

Example: Find the Maclaurin series for f(x) = $\sin x$

1) f'(x) = $\cos x$, f''(x) = $-\sin x$, f'''(x) = $-\cos x$, $f^{(4)}(x)$ = $\sin x$, $f^{(5)}(x)$ = $\cos x$, etc. ← *There is a repeating pattern in the derivatives.*
2) $\sin(0)$ = 0, so f(0) = 0 and $f^{(n)}(0)$ = 0 for all even powers of n.
   $\cos(0)$ = 1, so f'(0) = 1, f'''(0) = -1, $f^{(5)}(0)$ = 1, etc.
3) So the Maclaurin series is:

$$f(x) = f(0) + xf'(0) + \frac{x^2}{2!}f''(0) + \frac{x^3}{3!}f'''(0) + \dots$$

$$\sin x = x - \frac{x^3}{3!} + \frac{x^5}{5!} - \dots + (-1)^r \frac{x^{2r+1}}{(2r+1)!} + \dots$$ ← *This series is valid for all values of x.*

You need to be able to Recognise Standard Maclaurin Series

The results for **e^x** and **$\sin x$** in the examples above are **well-known** Maclaurin series that you need to be able to **recognise**. There are three other Maclaurin series that you need to be familiar with. Two of these are only **valid** for certain values of x — you don't need to be able to work out these ranges, but you need to be able to **use** them.

1) For **$\cos x$**, the series only includes even powers of x:
$$\cos x = 1 - \frac{x^2}{2!} + \frac{x^4}{4!} - \dots + (-1)^r \frac{x^{2r}}{(2r)!} + \dots \quad \text{valid for all } x$$

2) $\ln x$ and its derivatives are undefined at $x = 0$, so the Maclaurin series for **$\ln(1 + x)$** is usually considered instead:
$$\ln(1 + x) = x - \frac{x^2}{2} + \frac{x^3}{3} - \dots + (-1)^{r+1} \frac{x^r}{r} + \dots \quad \text{valid for } -1 < x \leq 1$$

3) Another standard result is the one for **$(1 + x)^n$**:
$$(1 + x)^n = 1 + nx + \frac{n(n-1)}{1 \times 2}x^2 + \dots + \frac{n(n-1)\dots(n-r+1)}{1 \times 2 \times \dots \times r}x^r + \dots$$
When n is a positive integer, this is valid for all x. Otherwise, it's valid for $-1 < x < 1$.

Maclaurin Series

Use the standard results to find Maclaurin series of Compound Functions

You can use the standard Maclaurin series to find the Maclaurin series of **more complicated** functions involving e^x, $\sin x$, etc., **without** having to start from scratch. This avoids lots of tricky differentiation. If you're asked for e.g. "the first four non-zero terms", you're looking for powers of x with non-zero coefficients, starting from x^0.

Example: Find the first four non-zero terms in the Maclaurin series for $f(x) = \ln(1 - 4x)$.

Write down the series you know.
$$\ln(1 + x) = x - \frac{x^2}{2} + \frac{x^3}{3} - \frac{x^4}{4} + \dots$$

Then replace x with $-4x$ and simplify.
$$\ln(1 - 4x) = -4x - \frac{(-4x)^2}{2} + \frac{(-4x)^3}{3} - \frac{(-4x)^4}{4} - \dots$$

You need to find the powers of the constant (−4) as well as x — watch those signs...

$$= -4x - \frac{16x^2}{2} - \frac{64x^3}{3} - \frac{256x^4}{4} - \dots$$

$$= -4x - 8x^2 - \frac{64x^3}{3} - 64x^4 - \dots$$

For what range of values of x is the series valid?

$\ln(1 + x)$ is valid for $-1 < x \le 1$, so $\ln(1 - 4x)$ is valid where $-1 < -4x \le 1$.

So the series is valid for $-\frac{1}{4} \le x < \frac{1}{4}$. ← *Remember that dividing by a negative reverses the inequality.*

Multiply standard results to find the series for a Product of Functions

Example: Find the first four non-zero terms in the Maclaurin series for $f(x) = e^{2x} \cos x$.

Substitute $2x$ into the series for e^x, and write down the one for $\cos x$.

$$e^x = 1 + x + \frac{x^2}{2!} + \frac{x^3}{3!} + \dots$$

$$e^{2x} = 1 + 2x + \frac{(2x)^2}{2!} + \frac{(2x)^3}{3!} + \dots = 1 + 2x + 2x^2 + \frac{4x^3}{3} + \dots$$

$$\cos x = 1 - \frac{x^2}{2!} + \frac{x^4}{4!} - \dots = 1 - \frac{x^2}{2} + \frac{x^4}{24} - \dots$$

Multiply the two series together — you only need to consider terms that make a power of x that is 3 or less.

$$e^{2x} \cos x = \left(1 + 2x + 2x^2 + \frac{4x^3}{3} + \dots\right)\left(1 - \frac{x^2}{2} + \frac{x^4}{24} + \dots\right)$$

$$= 1 + 2x + 2x^2 - \frac{x^2}{2} + \frac{4x^3}{3} - x^3 + \dots$$

$$= 1 + 2x + \frac{3x^2}{2} + \frac{x^3}{3} + \dots$$

Practice Questions

Q1 Show that the Maclaurin series for $\cos x$ is: $\quad 1 - \frac{x^2}{2!} + \frac{x^4}{4!} - \dots + (-1)^r \frac{x^{2r}}{(2r)!} + \dots$

Q2 Show that the Maclaurin series for $\ln(1 + x)$ is: $\quad x - \frac{x^2}{2} + \frac{x^3}{3} - \dots + (-1)^r \frac{x^r}{r} + \dots$

Q3 Show that the Maclaurin series for $(1 + x)^n$ is: $\quad 1 + nx + \frac{n(n-1)}{1 \times 2} x^2 + \dots + \frac{n(n-1)(n-2)}{1 \times 2 \times \dots \times r} x^r + \dots$

Q4 Find the first three non-zero terms in the Maclaurin series for $f(x) = \sin x \cos x$.

Exam Questions

Q1 Use the Maclaurin series for e^x and $\sin x$ to find the first four non-zero terms in the Maclaurin series for $f(x) = e^{\sin x}$. [5 marks]

Q2 Use Maclaurin series to prove Euler's relation, $e^{ix} = \cos x + i \sin x$. [4 marks]

Q3 a) Find the first four non-zero terms in the Maclaurin series for $\ln((1 + 2x)^3(1 - x))$. [5 marks]
   b) For what values of x is the series valid? [4 marks]

That's the end of this series of topics...

The Maclaurin series for e^x, $\sin x$, $\cos x$ and $\ln(1 + x)$ are given in the formula booklet, but you still need to be familiar with what they look like — so get try to get them fixed in your head, and just use the booklet as a back-up.

Volumes of Revolution

*The next two pages are about using integration to find volumes. If you're studying for **AS Level**, once you've learnt this first page, go straight onto the questions — you **don't** need to be able to use parametric equations to find volumes.*

You have to find the Volume of an area Rotated About the x-Axis...

If you're given a **definite** or **improper** integral, the solution you come up with is the **area under the graph** between the two **limits**. If you now **rotate** that area 2π radians **about the x-axis**, you'll come up with a **solid** — and this is what you want to find the **volume** of. The **formula** for finding the **volume of revolution** is:

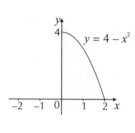

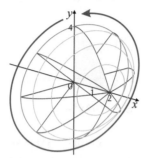

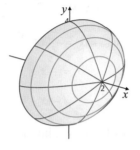

$$V = \pi \int_{x=x_1}^{x=x_2} y^2 \, dx$$

where y is a function of x (i.e. $y = f(x)$) and x_1 and x_2 are the limits of x.

Example: R is the area enclosed by the curve $y = \sqrt{6x^2 - 3x + 2}$, the x-axis and the lines $x = 1$ and $x = 2$. Find the volume V of the solid formed when R is rotated 2π radians about the x-axis.

Don't forget to square y — you might think it's obvious, but it's easily done.

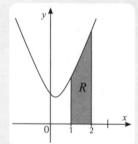

If $y = \sqrt{6x^2 - 3x + 2}$, then $y^2 = 6x^2 - 3x + 2$.

Putting this into the formula gives:

$$V = \pi \int_1^2 6x^2 - 3x + 2 \, dx = \pi \left[2x^3 - \frac{3}{2}x^2 + 2x \right]_1^2$$

$$= \pi \left(\left[2(2)^3 - \frac{3}{2}(2)^2 + 2(2) \right] - \left[2(1)^3 - \frac{3}{2}(1)^2 + 2(1) \right] \right)$$

$$= \pi \left([16 - 6 + 4] - \left[2 - \frac{3}{2} + 2 \right] \right) = \pi \left(14 - 2\frac{1}{2} \right) = 11\frac{1}{2}\pi$$

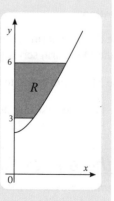

The volume of last night's revolution had really disrupted Donna's sleeping pattern.

...or the Volume of an area Rotated About the y-Axis

Instead of rotation about the x-axis, you might be asked to find the volume when an area is rotated about the **y-axis** instead. You do this using this **formula**:

$$V = \pi \int_{y=y_1}^{y=y_2} x^2 \, dy$$

This time, you need to **rearrange** the equations to get x^2 **on its own** (you'll often be given a function that **already** has x^2 in it). The limits are **horizontal lines**, e.g. $y = 1$ and $y = 2$.

Example: R is the area enclosed by the curve $y = \sqrt{x^2 + 5}$, the y-axis and the lines $y = 3$ and $y = 6$. Find the volume V of the solid obtained from R by rotating it 2π radians about the y-axis.

First, rearrange the equation to get x^2 on its own:

$$y = \sqrt{x^2 + 5} \Rightarrow y^2 = x^2 + 5 \quad \text{so } x^2 = y^2 - 5.$$

Now integrate:

$$V = \pi \int_3^6 y^2 - 5 \, dy = \pi \left[\frac{1}{3}y^3 - 5y \right]_3^6$$

$$= \pi \left(\left[\frac{1}{3}(6)^3 - 5(6) \right] - \left[\frac{1}{3}(3)^3 - 5(3) \right] \right)$$

$$= \pi(42 - (-6)) = 48\pi$$

Volumes of Revolution

You can use *Parametric Equations* to find a *Volume*

Remember that curves can have **parametric equations** — where x and y are **functions of t**.
You can integrate these and you also need to be able to calculate their volumes of revolution.
Here are the **formulas** you need, for a curve with parametric equations $x = f(t)$ and $y = g(t)$ and limits t_1 and t_2.

For a rotation about the x-axis:

$$V = \pi \int_{t=t_1}^{t=t_2} y^2 \frac{dx}{dt}\, dt$$

Or for a rotation about the y-axis:

$$V = \pi \int_{t=t_1}^{t=t_2} x^2 \frac{dy}{dt}\, dt$$

> Don't be put off if the equations use some other parameter instead of t (e.g. **trig** equations often use θ) — just change $\frac{dx}{dt}$ to $\frac{dx}{d\theta}$ and dt to $d\theta$ (or whatever the **parameter** is).

Example: A curve is given by the parametric equations $x = 2t$, $y = \sin 3t$. Find the volume formed when the area bounded by the curve, the x-axis and the lines $x = 0$ and $x = 2\pi$ is rotated 2π radians about the x-axis.

1) First of all, $\frac{dx}{dt} = 2$.

2) Change the limits:
   $x = 0$, so $2t = 0 \Rightarrow t = 0$
   $x = 2\pi$, so $2t = 2\pi \Rightarrow t = \pi$

3) Squaring y gives $y^2 = \sin^2 3t$.

> Don't forget to change the limits from x to t.

4) Put the expressions for y^2, $\frac{dx}{dt}$ and the new limits into the formula:

$$V = \pi \int_0^\pi 2\sin^2 3t\, dt = \pi \int_0^\pi 1 - \cos 6t\, dt$$

$$= \pi \left[t - \frac{1}{6}\sin 6t \right]_0^\pi$$

$$= \pi \left[\pi - \frac{1}{6}\sin 6\pi \right] - \pi \left[0 - \frac{1}{6}\sin 0 \right]$$

$$= \pi \left[\pi - \frac{1}{6}(0) \right] - 0 = \pi^2$$

> This uses the identity $\cos 2t \equiv 1 - 2\sin^2 t$ — don't forget to double the coefficient of t.

Practice Questions

If you're doing <u>AS Level</u>*, you only need to do Practice Question 1 and Exam Question 2.*

Q1 What is the volume of the solid formed when the area enclosed by the curve $y = \sqrt{5 - 2x^2}$, the y-axis and the lines $y = 2$ and $y = 1$ is rotated 2π radians about the y-axis? Give an exact answer.

Q2 What sort of shape would you obtain by rotating the curve defined by the parametric equations $x = a\cos t$, $y = a\sin t$ by π radians around either of the axes? What would be its volume?

Q3 Find the volume of the solid obtained when the area enclosed by the y-axis, the lines $y = 1$ and $y = \pi + 1$ and the curve defined by the parametric equations $x = \cos 2\theta$, $y = 2\theta + 1$ is rotated 2π radians about the y-axis.

Exam Questions

Q1 A curve is defined by the parametric equations $x = 2t + 1$, $y = a\sec t$. Find the exact volume of the solid obtained when the area enclosed by this curve, the x-axis and the lines $x = 1 + \frac{\pi}{3}$ and $x = 1 + \frac{\pi}{2}$ is rotated 2π radians about the x-axis, leaving your answer in terms of a and simplifying as far as possible. [4 marks]

Q2 The graph below shows part of a curve with equation $y = \dfrac{\sqrt{2}}{(2x-1)^{\frac{1}{2}}}$.
The region R is the area enclosed by this curve, the x-axis and the lines $x = 1$ and $x = 4$.

A geography student is to make a scale model of a volcano using the solid obtained by rotating the region R a full revolution about the x-axis. The height of the real volcano, measured in the x-direction, is known to be 3 km.

a) Using the model, find the volume within the volcano.
   Give an exact answer. [3 marks]

b) Calculate the diameter, to 3 significant figures, of the volcano at:
   i) its widest point,   ii) its peak. [3 marks]

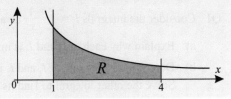

Come the revolution, I will have to kill you all...

Not to be confused with the French Revolution, the Industrial Revolution or the bloody CGP Revolution, volumes of revolution is just part of Further Maths A-Level. So don't go overthrowing your teachers and not letting them eat cake.

Improper Integrals

Oh boy, this page is a treat — you'll be integrating things that people thought were impossible...

Improper Integrals might have a Limit of Infinity...

An integral with a **limit of infinity** is exactly what it sounds like — it's an integral where the upper limit is ∞ or the lower limit is $-\infty$ (or maybe even both). You can't just stick $x = \infty$ or $x = -\infty$ into an expression — you have to **replace infinity** with a value, a, and think about what happens as a **approaches** infinity (written '$a \to \infty$').

Example: Find the value of the improper integral $\int_2^\infty x^{-\frac{3}{2}}\,dx$.

Replace ∞ with a and integrate as you normally would, making sure to include the limit notation:

$$\int_2^\infty x^{-\frac{3}{2}}\,dx = \lim_{a\to\infty}\int_2^a x^{-\frac{3}{2}}\,dx = \lim_{a\to\infty}[-2x^{-\frac{1}{2}}]_2^a = \lim_{a\to\infty}\left[-2a^{-\frac{1}{2}} - (-2\,(2)^{-\frac{1}{2}})\right] = \lim_{a\to\infty}\left[\frac{-2}{\sqrt{a}} + \frac{2}{\sqrt{2}}\right] = \lim_{a\to\infty}\left[\sqrt{2} - \frac{2}{\sqrt{a}}\right]$$

As $a \to \infty$, $\dfrac{2}{\sqrt{a}} \to 0$ so $\int_2^\infty x^{-\frac{3}{2}}\,dx = \lim_{a\to\infty}\left[\sqrt{2} - \dfrac{2}{\sqrt{a}}\right] = \sqrt{2} - 0 = \sqrt{2}$

Sometimes, the limit as $a \to \infty$ is **not a finite number** like in the above example. Instead, the integral goes to infinity as a tends to infinity. In these cases, we say the integral **does not exist** or is **undefined**, i.e. it doesn't have a finite value.

...or they could have an Undefined Value

An integral with an **undefined value** is an **improper** integral where one of the limits or a value between the limits has an undefined value when put into the expression for the integral. To solve, use the same method as above.

Example: Explain why the integral $\int_0^{16} x^{-\frac{1}{2}}\,dx$ is improper, and solve it.

At the lower limit $x = 0$, $x^{-\frac{1}{2}} = \dfrac{1}{\sqrt{x}}$ is undefined and so the integral is improper.

Replace 0 with a, and integrate:

$$\int_0^{16} x^{-\frac{1}{2}}\,dx = \lim_{a\to0+}\int_a^{16} x^{-\frac{1}{2}}\,dx = \lim_{a\to0+}[2x^{\frac{1}{2}}]_a^{16} = \lim_{a\to0+}\left[2\sqrt{16} - 2\sqrt{a}\right]$$
$$= \lim_{a\to0+}\left[8 - 2\sqrt{a}\right]$$

As $a \to 0+$, $2\sqrt{a} \to 0$ and so $\int_0^{16} x^{-\frac{1}{2}}\,dx = 8 - 0 = \mathbf{8}$

> When the value you replace with a is finite, you might approach it from below or above. Since you're integrating over the values $a \le x \le 16$, you want to know what happens as $a \to 0$ from above. This is written $a \to 0+$. You would write $a \to 0-$ if you were approaching from below.

In this example, the undefined point was one of the limits — it was at the end of the **interval of integration**. But the undefined point could be somewhere in the **middle** of the interval. If this was the case, you'd have to **split** the integral into two, one either side of the undefined point. Then you have two integrals with an undefined limit — work them out like in the example and **add** them together at the end.

Practice Questions

Q1 Why are the following integrals improper?　　a) $\displaystyle\int_0^{41} \frac{1}{x^3}\,dx$　　b) $\displaystyle\int_{-2}^2 \frac{\sin x}{x^2}\,dx$

Q2 Explain why $\displaystyle\int_3^\infty (x+1)^{-\frac{5}{2}}\,dx$ is an improper integral and find its value.

Exam Question

Q1 Consider the integrals $I_1 = \displaystyle\int_{-\infty}^{-1} \frac{1}{x^2}\,dx$ and $I_2 = \displaystyle\int_{-1}^0 \frac{1}{x^2}\,dx$.

 a) Explain why each of I_1 and I_2 is improper. 　　　　　　　　　　　　　　　　[1 mark]

 b) Determine which **one** of I_1 and I_2 is undefined, giving a reason for your answer.
 　Solve the other integral to find its finite value. 　　　　　　　　　　　　　　[4 marks]

Oi, there ain't nothing improper about the way I speak...

So there are two types of improper integral, and sometimes they can't be defined. As long as you can show whether or not it's improper, and whether or not it can be defined, then you're sorted.

Mean Value of a Function

The mean value of discrete data is a value somewhere in the middle that represents the data as a whole. You can find a similar value for continuous data by modelling it as a function and finding the mean value of that function.

You can find the **Mean Value** of a **Function**

The **area** under the curve $y = f(x)$ between the values $x = a$ and $x = b$ is $\int_a^b f(x)\, dx$ (shown as Area M below).

You can draw a **horizontal line** somewhere on the graph so that when it forms a **rectangle** between $x = a$ and $x = b$ the area is the **same** as under the curve (shown as Area N below).

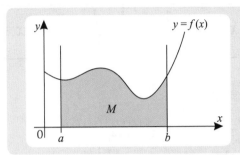 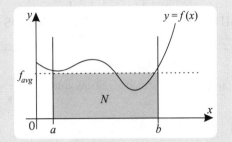

The **height** of this horizontal line is known as the **mean value of the function**, and is often written as 'f_{avg}'.

Using the equation for the area of a rectangle, you know that $N = f_{avg} \times (b - a)$.

Also, $M = N$ so $\int_a^b f(x)\, dx = f_{avg} \times (b - a)$. So the **formula** for the mean value is:

$$f_{avg} = \frac{1}{b-a} \int_a^b f(x)\, dx$$

Example: Find the mean value of the function $f(x) = 3x^3 - 6x^2 + 1$ between the y-axis and $x = 2$.

The y-axis is the line $x = 0$, so in the formula above, $a = 0$ and $b = 2$. Write out the formula using the values given, and solve:

$$f_{avg} = \frac{1}{2-0} \int_0^2 3x^3 - 6x^2 + 1\, dx = \frac{1}{2}\left[\frac{3}{4}x^4 - 2x^3 + x\right]_0^2 = \frac{1}{2}\left[\left(\frac{3}{4}(2)^4 - 2(2)^3 + 2\right) - \left(\frac{3}{4}(0)^4 - 2(0)^3 + 0\right)\right]$$

$$= \frac{1}{2}\left[(12 - 16 + 2) - 0\right] = \frac{1}{2}(-2) = -1.$$

Practice Questions

Q1 Find the mean value of the function $f(x) = \frac{x^4}{5} + 9x^2 - 3$ on the interval $-1 \le x \le 4$.

Q2 The function $f(x) = x^2 - a$, where a is a constant, has a mean value of $f_{avg} = 15$ between the values $x = 3$ and $x = 6$. Find a.

Q3 Find the exact mean value of the function $f(x) = \sin 2x + 18\,000$ between the values $x = 0$ and $x = \frac{\pi}{2}$.

Exam Questions

Q1 a) Fully factorise the expression $x^3 + 3x^2 - 4x - 12$. [2 marks]

    b) The function $f(x) = 3x^2 + 6x - 4$ has a mean value of 56 on the interval $2 \le x \le b$. Find b. [4 marks]

Q2 A stationery company is attempting to forecast their net income. They model their forecast using the function

$$f(t) = \sin t + 2\cos 3t + \frac{t}{t^2 + 3},$$

where t represents time in months and $t = 0$ is the present day. The company wishes to know if they will have made a profit or a loss after six months.

    a) Calculate the mean value of the model function for the next six months, to 3 significant figures. [3 marks]

    b) Hence, conclude whether the company will make a profit in the next six months according to the model. Give a reason for your answer. [2 marks]

Mean value? Nahhhh, it's really more of a lovely value...

The maths on this page is nothing new, really — it's just your bog-standard integration, with a little division thrown in. But you should understand the theory behind it — it's pretty nifty.

Calculus with Inverse Trig Functions

This page covers some not-too-nasty differentiation of some kinda weird functions. You should have seen inverse trig functions before, but here's a quick reminder: $\sin^{-1} x = \arcsin x$, $\cos^{-1} x = \arccos x$ and $\tan^{-1} x = \arctan x$.

Use the **Chain Rule** to **Differentiate Inverse Trig**

Examiners love asking you to find the **derivative** of **inverse trig functions**, so make sure you understand and remember each step of the example below. The other two functions are done in a similar way. Don't worry too much about **memorising** the results — you'll be given these in your **formula booklet**.

$$\frac{d}{dx}\arcsin x = \frac{1}{\sqrt{1-x^2}}$$

$$\frac{d}{dx}\arccos x = \frac{-1}{\sqrt{1-x^2}}$$

$$\frac{d}{dx}\arctan x = \frac{1}{1+x^2}$$

Example: $y = \arcsin x$. Show that $\dfrac{dy}{dx} = \dfrac{1}{\sqrt{1-x^2}}$.

1) If $y = \sin^{-1} x$, then $\sin y = x$.

2) Differentiate with **respect to** x using the **chain rule**:

$$\cos y \frac{dy}{dx} = 1 \Rightarrow \frac{dy}{dx} = \frac{1}{\cos y}$$

> Watch out —
> $\sin^{-1} x \neq 1/\sin x$

3) You can rearrange the **identity** $\sin^2 \theta + \cos^2 \theta = 1$ to get sin back in the denominator:

$$\sin^2 y + \cos^2 y = 1 \Rightarrow \cos^2 y = 1 - \sin^2 y \Rightarrow \cos y = \sqrt{1 - \sin^2 y}$$

$$\Rightarrow \frac{dy}{dx} = \frac{1}{\sqrt{1 - \sin^2 y}}$$

Oscar was having trouble with his own identity.

4) But $\sin y = x$, so $\sin^2 y = (\sin y)^2 = x^2$. So $\dfrac{dy}{dx} = \dfrac{1}{\sqrt{1-x^2}}$.

Combine these results with others to Differentiate More Functions

You can use these results just like any other derivative — for example in chain, product or quotient rules.

Example:
a) Differentiate $y = \arccos (x^2 - 1)$ with respect to x.
   Simplify your answer as far as possible.

b) Hence find the gradient of the curve $y = \arccos (x^2 - 1)$ when $x = 1.4$.

a) Use the **chain rule**. Let $u = (x^2 - 1)$. Then $y = \arccos u$.

Differentiate u with respect to x, and y with respect to u: $\quad \dfrac{du}{dx} = 2x, \quad \dfrac{dy}{du} = \dfrac{-1}{\sqrt{1-u^2}}$

So you get $\dfrac{dy}{dx} = \dfrac{dy}{du} \times \dfrac{du}{dx} = \dfrac{-2x}{\sqrt{1-u^2}} = \dfrac{-2x}{\sqrt{1-(x^2-1)^2}}$ Substitute $u = (x^2 - 1)$ back into the equation

Now simplify: $\dfrac{dy}{dx} = \dfrac{-2x}{\sqrt{1-(x^2-1)^2}} = \dfrac{-2x}{\sqrt{1-(x^4-2x^2+1)}} = \dfrac{-2x}{\sqrt{2x^2-x^4}}$

$$\Rightarrow \frac{dy}{dx} = \frac{-2x}{\sqrt{x^2(2-x^2)}} = \frac{-2x}{x\sqrt{2-x^2}} = \frac{-2}{\sqrt{2-x^2}}$$

Expand the brackets and cancel terms down

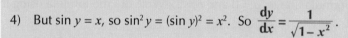

Take a factor of x^2 and then take it outside the root

b) From part a), you know that $\dfrac{dy}{dx} = \dfrac{-2}{\sqrt{2-x^2}}$. Putting $x = 1.4$ into this gives:

$$\frac{dy}{dx} = \frac{-2}{\sqrt{2-1.4^2}} = \frac{-2}{\sqrt{2-1.96}} = \frac{-2}{\sqrt{0.04}} = \frac{-2}{0.2} = -10.$$

Calculus with Inverse Trig Functions

Some *Integrals* require *Trig Substitutions*

Now that you've found the derivatives of inverse trig functions, you can **work backwards** and **integrate**.
This might require a **substitution** using a **trig** function. Keep an eye out for these crafty integrals.

$$\int \frac{1}{\sqrt{a^2-x^2}}\, dx = \arcsin \frac{x}{a} + C \quad (|x| < a) \qquad\qquad \int \frac{1}{a^2+x^2}\, dx = \frac{1}{a}\arctan \frac{x}{a} + C$$

These are in the formula booklet.

Example: a) Show that $\int \frac{1}{\sqrt{a^2-x^2}}\, dx = \arcsin \frac{x}{a} + C$.   b) Hence solve $\int_{-1.5}^{1.5} \frac{1}{\sqrt{9-x^2}}\, dx$.

a) **Rewrite** so that it's in a form useful for substitution: $\displaystyle \int \frac{1}{\sqrt{a^2\left(1-\frac{x^2}{a^2}\right)}}\, dx = \int \frac{1}{a\sqrt{1-\left(\frac{x}{a}\right)^2}}\, dx$

Let $\frac{x}{a} = \sin u$. Then $x = a \sin u$. **Differentiating** this gives: $\frac{dx}{du} = a \cos u$, so $dx = a \cos u \, du$.

Putting all these **substitutions** into the integral gives:

$$\int \frac{1}{a\sqrt{1-\sin^2 u}}\, a \cos u \, du = \int \frac{1}{a \cos u}\, a \cos u \, du = \int 1\, du = u + C = \mathbf{\arcsin \frac{x}{a} + C}$$

Rearrange $\sin^2 \theta + \cos^2 \theta = 1$ Rearranging $\frac{x}{a} = \sin u$ gives $u = \arcsin \frac{x}{a}$.

b) $\displaystyle \int_{-1.5}^{1.5} \frac{1}{\sqrt{9-x^2}}\, dx = \left[\arcsin \frac{x}{3}\right]_{-1.5}^{1.5} = \arcsin 0.5 - \arcsin(-0.5)$

$$= \frac{\pi}{6} - \left(-\frac{\pi}{6}\right) = \frac{\pi}{3}$$

Practice Questions

Q1 Show that:

   a) if $y = \arccos x$, then $\dfrac{dy}{dx} = \dfrac{-1}{\sqrt{1-x^2}}$,   b) if $y = \arctan x$, then $\dfrac{dy}{dx} = \dfrac{1}{1+x^2}$.

Q2 Differentiate $y = \arctan\left(\dfrac{1}{x}\right)$ with respect to x. What is the gradient of the curve $y = \arctan\left(\dfrac{1}{x}\right)$ when $x = 4$?

Exam Questions

Q1 a) Show that $\int \dfrac{1}{a^2+x^2}\, dx = \dfrac{1}{a}\arctan \dfrac{x}{a} + C$.   [4 marks]

   b) Hence find the value of $\int_{-8}^{8} \dfrac{1}{x^2+16}\, dx$, giving your answer in the form $p \arctan q$, where p and q are rational

      numbers. You may use the fact that $-\tan x = \tan(-x)$.   [3 marks]

Q2 A theme park has received design plans for a new roller coaster. One of the peaks of the roller coaster is shown in
the sketch. It is known that this part of the roller coaster can be modelled by a curve with equation
$y = \dfrac{1}{2}\arctan 2x + x\sqrt{1-x^2}$, where one unit in both the x- and y-directions is equivalent to 100 m.

   a) The peak occurs at 77 m from the origin in the x-direction, to the nearest metre.
      Using this value, find the height of the peak above the origin to the nearest metre.
      [2 marks]

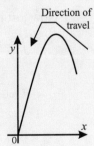

Direction of travel

   b) The park's safety policy states that no part of the roller coaster design can be
      approved if it contains a drop steeper than a fixed threshold. The policy states
      that for every metre travelled in the x-direction, the height should not drop more
      than 4 m. For the purpose of this model, assume the drop is steepest at the origin.
      Determine whether or not the drop is allowed under this policy.   [5 marks]

Arcsin — they say they come in two-by-twos...

See, this page isn't too bad, is it? Most of the tricky stuff is in your formula booklet and you can work the rest out so long as you know your identities and how to use the chain, product and quotient rules. No trouble at all...

Integration with Partial Fractions

You've seen before how to break down a scary-looking algebraic fraction into partial fractions. This comes in handy when you're integrating — you could try integration by parts on the original fraction, but it would get pretty messy.

The **Denominator** can include **Factors** of the form **$ax^2 + c$**

So far, you've dealt with partial fractions that had combinations of **linear factors** like $ax + b$ or $(ax + b)^2$ in the **denominator**. Now, you might also come across **quadratic factors** of the form $ax^2 + c$. Luckily, they're not much harder.

Watch out for difference of two squares factors. You can handle them as quadratic factors but it's usually easier to split them like this.

You **split** the fractions up like this. Notice the **difference** when there's a quadratic factor. You need to include a **linear numerator**.

$$\frac{4x^2 + 3x + 5}{(x + 1)(x^2 + 1)} \text{ can be written as } \frac{A}{(x + 1)} + \frac{Bx + C}{(x^2 + 1)}$$

$$\frac{2x^2 - 1}{x(x^2 - 1)} \text{ can be written as } \frac{A}{x} + \frac{B}{(x + 1)} + \frac{C}{(x - 1)}$$

$$\frac{7x - 1}{(x + 2)^2} \text{ can be written as } \frac{A}{(x + 2)} + \frac{B}{(x + 2)^2}$$

$$\frac{5x + 10}{(4x^2 - 3)(2x^2 + 1)} \text{ can be written as } \frac{Ax + B}{(4x^2 - 3)} + \frac{Cx + D}{(2x^2 + 1)}$$

This is just the square of a linear factor (a repeated factor) — it's not the same as a quadratic factor.

Once you've split your original fraction into the right partial fractions, you can work out what the **letters** need to be by using **substitution** or by **equating coefficients**, just like you normally would.

If you need to integrate a fraction of the form $\frac{Ax + B}{f(x)}$, it's usually a good idea to split it into two fractions — one for each term in the numerator. The fraction becomes $\frac{Ax}{f(x)} + \frac{B}{f(x)}$ and you can integrate each of these separately.

Example: Find   a) $\int \frac{4x^2 + 3x + 5}{(x + 1)(x^2 + 1)} \, dx$,   b) the exact value of $\int_0^{\sqrt{3}} \frac{4x^2 + 3x + 5}{(x + 1)(x^2 + 1)} \, dx$.

a) To start off, convert the fraction in the integral into partial fractions:

$$\frac{4x^2 + 3x + 5}{(x + 1)(x^2 + 1)} = \frac{A}{(x + 1)} + \frac{Bx + C}{(x^2 + 1)} \Rightarrow 4x^2 + 3x + 5 = A(x^2 + 1) + (Bx + C)(x + 1)$$

$$\Rightarrow 4x^2 + 3x + 5 = Ax^2 + A + Bx^2 + Bx + Cx + C$$

Comparing x^2 terms: $4 = A + B$ (equation 1)

Comparing x terms: $3 = B + C$ (equation 2)

Comparing constants: $5 = A + C$ (equation 3)

Solving these simultaneous equations gives: $A = 3, B = 1, C = 2$

So $\frac{4x^2 + 3x + 5}{(x + 1)(x^2 + 1)} = \frac{3}{(x + 1)} + \frac{x + 2}{(x^2 + 1)} = \frac{3}{(x + 1)} + \frac{x}{(x^2 + 1)} + \frac{2}{(x^2 + 1)}$

Splitting up the second fraction like this will make integrating easier.

Now just integrate term by term:

$$\int \frac{3}{(x + 1)} + \frac{x}{(x^2 + 1)} + \frac{2}{(x^2 + 1)} \, dx = 3 \ln |x + 1| + \frac{1}{2} \ln |x^2 + 1| + 2 \arctan x + C$$

$$= \ln \left| (x + 1)^3 (x^2 + 1)^{\frac{1}{2}} \right| + 2 \arctan x + C$$

If you're integrating a fraction where the degree of the numerator is one less than the degree of the denominator, you might be able to use the rule $\int \frac{f'(x)}{f(x)} dx = \ln(f(x))$.

b) $\int_0^{\sqrt{3}} \frac{4x^2 + 3x + 5}{(x + 1)(x^2 + 1)} \, dx = \left[\ln |x + 1|^3 (x^2 + 1)^{\frac{1}{2}} | + 2 \arctan x \right]_0^{\sqrt{3}} = \ln((\sqrt{3} + 1)^3 \times 4^{\frac{1}{2}}) + 2 \times \frac{\pi}{3} - (0 + 0)$

$$= \ln(2(\sqrt{3} + 1)^3) + \frac{2\pi}{3}$$

Integration with Partial Fractions

There are Two Special Cases

$$\int \frac{1}{x^2 - a^2}\,dx = \frac{1}{2a}\ln\left|\frac{x-a}{x+a}\right| + C$$

This is equal to $\frac{1}{a}\operatorname{artanh}\frac{x}{a} + C$ — see p.75

$$\int \frac{1}{a^2 - x^2}\,dx = \frac{1}{2a}\ln\left|\frac{a+x}{a-x}\right| + C \quad (|x| < a)$$

These two integrals are no more difficult than the previous example — you can use partial fractions to solve them. You'll find them in the **formula booklet**, and the second one will come up again on page 75.

Example:

a) Show that $\int \frac{1}{x^2 - a^2}\,dx = \frac{1}{2a}\ln\left|\frac{x-a}{x+a}\right| + C$.

b) Hence solve $\int_{10}^{15} \frac{1}{4x^2 - 100}\,dx$.

Give your answer in the form $c \ln d$, where c and d are rational numbers.

a) From partial fractions, $\dfrac{1}{x^2 - a^2} = \dfrac{1}{(x-a)(x+a)} = \dfrac{1}{2a}\left(\dfrac{1}{x-a} - \dfrac{1}{x+a}\right).$

So $\int \dfrac{1}{x^2 - a^2}\,dx = \dfrac{1}{2a}\int \dfrac{1}{x-a} - \dfrac{1}{x+a}\,dx = \dfrac{1}{2a}(\ln|x-a| - \ln|x+a|) + C = \dfrac{1}{2a}\ln\left|\dfrac{x-a}{x+a}\right| + C$

b) $\int_{10}^{15} \dfrac{1}{4x^2 - 100}\,dx = \dfrac{1}{4}\int_{10}^{15} \dfrac{1}{x^2 - 25}\,dx = \dfrac{1}{4}\left[\dfrac{1}{2\times5}\ln\left|\dfrac{x-5}{x+5}\right|\right]_{10}^{15} = \dfrac{1}{40}\left[\ln\dfrac{10}{20} - \ln\dfrac{5}{15}\right] = \dfrac{1}{40}\ln\dfrac{3}{2}$

Practice Questions

Q1 Write $\dfrac{3x - 4}{(x+1)^2(x^2+1)}$ in partial fractions.

Q2 Find $\displaystyle\int_1^2 \dfrac{2x^2 + 5x + 1}{x(x^2+1)}\,dx$ to 3 significant figures. Remember that $\dfrac{d}{dx}\arctan x = \dfrac{1}{x^2+1}$.

Q3 Find $\displaystyle\int_0^1 \dfrac{2}{\pi^2 - x^2}\,dx$. Give an exact answer.

Exam Questions

Q1 Show that $\displaystyle\int_2^3 \dfrac{3x^2 + 3x + 2}{(3x^2+1)(1-x)}\,dx = \dfrac{1}{2}\ln p$, where p is a positive fraction written in its simplest form. [6 marks]

Q2 $f(x) = \dfrac{x+3}{(x^2-4)(x^2+2)}$

   a) Write $f(x)$ in the form $\dfrac{x+a}{b(x^2-4)} - \dfrac{x+c}{d(x^2+2)}$, where a, b, c and d are positive integers. [3 marks]

   b) Show that $\displaystyle\int_0^{\sqrt{2}} f(x)\,dx = \dfrac{1}{8}\ln(3 - 2\sqrt{2}) - \dfrac{1}{6}\ln 2 - \dfrac{\sqrt{2}}{16}\pi$. [6 marks]

Q3 a) Find the exact value of $\displaystyle\int_0^1 \dfrac{1}{9 - 4x^2}\,dx$. [3 marks]

   b) A power station is set to have a new cooling tower installed. The interior of the tower is modelled by the solid of revolution of the curve $y = \dfrac{1}{\sqrt{9 - 4x^2}}$ about the x-axis for $0 \le x \le 1$, shown as the region T in the sketch to the right.

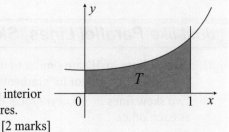

   Using your answer to part a) or otherwise, calculate the volume of the interior of the model of the tower, giving your answer to three significant figures. [2 marks]

It's not the winning that counts, but the taking parts...

There are more logs on this page than a woodchuck would chuck if a woodchuck could chuck logs. So you'll need to be pretty handy with your laws of logs. Memorise them so that you can use them whenever the need arises...

Equations of Lines in 3D

There's nothing like a bit of vector geometry — I can't get enough of the stuff personally. If you're like me then you're in luck here — you might recognise some of this, but there are plenty of new bits to learn too. Right, best crack on...

3D Vectors have *i*, *j* and *k* Components

Here's a quick recap of the **basics** of 3D vectors:

1) 3D vectors can be written either in **column form** as $\begin{pmatrix} x \\ y \\ z \end{pmatrix}$ or in **component form** as $x\mathbf{i} + y\mathbf{j} + z\mathbf{k}$.

2) The **magnitude** (distance between the start and end point) of a vector **a** is written |**a**|.

3) You use **Pythagoras** to work out the magnitude of a vector:

$$|x\mathbf{i} + y\mathbf{j} + z\mathbf{k}| = \sqrt{x^2 + y^2 + z^2}$$

There are Two Forms of Equations for Straight Lines

The equation of a straight line can be written in **vector form** or in **Cartesian form**.

Vector Form

The **vector form** of the equation of a straight line (in two or three dimensions) is:

$$\mathbf{r} = \mathbf{a} + \lambda\mathbf{b}$$ ← direction vector (parallel to the line)

position vector of a general point on the line

position vector of a fixed point on the line

scalar that varies with the point

Cartesian Form

In three dimensions, the **Cartesian form** of the equation of the line $\mathbf{r} = \mathbf{a} + \lambda\mathbf{b}$ is:

$$\frac{x - a_1}{b_1} = \frac{y - a_2}{b_2} = \frac{z - a_3}{b_3}$$

Where (x, y, z) is a general point on the line, $\mathbf{a} = a_1\mathbf{i} + a_2\mathbf{j} + a_3\mathbf{k}$ and $\mathbf{b} = b_1\mathbf{i} + b_2\mathbf{j} + b_3\mathbf{k}$.

You can **derive** the Cartesian form from the vector form of the equation:

For a line $\mathbf{r} = \mathbf{a} + \lambda\mathbf{b}$, if $\mathbf{a} = \begin{pmatrix} a_1 \\ a_2 \\ a_3 \end{pmatrix}$ and $\mathbf{b} = \begin{pmatrix} b_1 \\ b_2 \\ b_3 \end{pmatrix}$ then for any point (x, y, z) on the line $\begin{pmatrix} x \\ y \\ z \end{pmatrix} = \begin{pmatrix} a_1 \\ a_2 \\ a_3 \end{pmatrix} + \lambda\begin{pmatrix} b_1 \\ b_2 \\ b_3 \end{pmatrix}$

So $x = a_1 + \lambda b_1 \Rightarrow \lambda = \frac{x - a_1}{b_1}$, and similarly $\lambda = \frac{y - a_2}{b_2}$ and $\lambda = \frac{z - a_3}{b_3}$

So the equation of the line can be written:

$\frac{x - a_1}{b_1} = \frac{y - a_2}{b_2} = \frac{z - a_3}{b_3} = \lambda$, where λ is variable.

You don't need to learn this, but it helps to see how the forms of the equation are related.

Example: Find a vector equation for the line with Cartesian equation $\frac{x - 4}{3} = \frac{y + 2}{5} = \frac{2 - z}{7}$.

$\frac{x - 4}{3} = \frac{y + 2}{5} = \frac{2 - z}{7} \Rightarrow \frac{x - 4}{3} = \frac{y - (-2)}{5} = \frac{z - 2}{-7} \Rightarrow \mathbf{r} = (4\mathbf{i} - 2\mathbf{j} + 2\mathbf{k}) + \lambda(3\mathbf{i} + 5\mathbf{j} - 7\mathbf{k})$

Just like Parallel Lines, Skew Lines Never Meet

1) **Parallel lines** in 3D are similar to those in 2D. They **never meet** and have the same **direction vector** (or gradient).

2) Two **skew lines** in 3D never meet but **don't** have the same direction vector as each other.

3) Skew lines in 2D don't exist, because in 2D if two lines don't have the same direction vector, they have to meet at some point.

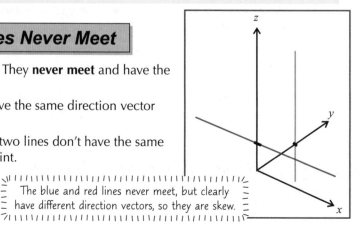

The blue and red lines never meet, but clearly have different direction vectors, so they are skew.

Equations of Lines in 3D

Find the **Point of Intersection** of two Lines with **Simultaneous Equations**

If Line 1, $\mathbf{r}_1 = \begin{pmatrix} 5 \\ 2 \\ -1 \end{pmatrix} + \mu \begin{pmatrix} 1 \\ -2 \\ -3 \end{pmatrix}$, and Line 2, $\mathbf{r}_2 = \begin{pmatrix} 2 \\ 0 \\ 4 \end{pmatrix} + \lambda \begin{pmatrix} 1 \\ 2 \\ -1 \end{pmatrix}$, **intersect**, there'll be a value for μ and a value for λ that result in **the same point for both lines**. This is the **point of intersection**.

> If you're dealing with more than one line, you've got to use different Greek letters for the variable scalar to avoid confusion — that's why Line 1 uses μ instead of λ. You might also see λ_1, λ_2, etc.

Example: Determine whether Line 1 and Line 2 (above) intersect. If they do, find the point of intersection.

1) At the point of intersection, $\begin{pmatrix} 5 \\ 2 \\ -1 \end{pmatrix} + \mu \begin{pmatrix} 1 \\ -2 \\ -3 \end{pmatrix} = \begin{pmatrix} 2 \\ 0 \\ 4 \end{pmatrix} + \lambda \begin{pmatrix} 1 \\ 2 \\ -1 \end{pmatrix}$. This gives three equations:
   ① $5 + \mu = 2 + \lambda$
   ② $2 - 2\mu = 0 + 2\lambda$
   ③ $-1 - 3\mu = 4 - \lambda$

2) Solve the first two **simultaneously**.
   $2 \times$①: $\quad 10 + 2\mu = 4 + 2\lambda$ ④
   ④ − ②: $\quad 8 + 4\mu = 4 \Rightarrow \mu = -1$
   sub. in ②: $\quad 2 - 2(-1) = 0 + 2\lambda \Rightarrow \lambda = 2$

3) Substitute the values for μ and λ into equation ③. If they make the equation **true**, the lines **do** intersect:
   $-1 - (3 \times (-1)) = 4 - 2 \Rightarrow 2 = 2$ — True, so **they do intersect.**

4) Now find the **intersection point**: $\mathbf{r} = \begin{pmatrix} 5 \\ 2 \\ -1 \end{pmatrix} + \mu \begin{pmatrix} 1 \\ -2 \\ -3 \end{pmatrix} = \begin{pmatrix} 5 \\ 2 \\ -1 \end{pmatrix} - 1\begin{pmatrix} 1 \\ -2 \\ -3 \end{pmatrix} \Rightarrow \mathbf{r} = \begin{pmatrix} 4 \\ 4 \\ 2 \end{pmatrix}$

This is the position vector of the point of intersection. Its coordinates are (4, 4, 2).

Practice Questions

Q1 Write the vector $\begin{pmatrix} 1 \\ 4 \\ -7 \end{pmatrix}$ in terms of the standard unit vectors $\mathbf{i}$, $\mathbf{j}$ and $\mathbf{k}$.

Q2 $\mathbf{r}_1 = \begin{pmatrix} 2 \\ -1 \\ 2 \end{pmatrix} + t\begin{pmatrix} -4 \\ 6 \\ -2 \end{pmatrix}$ and $\mathbf{r}_2 = \begin{pmatrix} 3 \\ 2 \\ 4 \end{pmatrix} + u\begin{pmatrix} -1 \\ 3 \\ 0 \end{pmatrix}$
   Find the point of intersection of these two lines in $\mathbf{i}$, $\mathbf{j}$, $\mathbf{k}$ form.

Q3 Find vector equations for the following lines. Give your answer in column vector form and in $\mathbf{i}$, $\mathbf{j}$, $\mathbf{k}$ form.
   a) a straight line through (4, 1, 2), parallel to the vector $3\mathbf{i} + \mathbf{j} - \mathbf{k}$.
   b) a straight line through (2, –1, 1) and (0, 2, 3).

Exam Questions

Q1 Lines l_1 and l_2 have Cartesian equations $\frac{x-3}{5} = \frac{y+1}{3} = \frac{z-3}{7}$ and $\frac{1-x}{2} = \frac{y-7}{4} = \frac{z-9}{3}$ respectively.

   Write down vector equations for l_1 and l_2 in $\mathbf{i}$, $\mathbf{j}$, $\mathbf{k}$ form. [2 marks]

Q2 The quadrilateral ABCD has vertices A(1, 5, 9), B(3, 2, 1), C(–2, 4, 3) and D(–9, 9, 13).

   a) Find the vector $\overrightarrow{AB}$. [2 marks]
   b) C and D lie on line l_1. Using the parameter μ, find a vector equation of l_1 in $\mathbf{i}$, $\mathbf{j}$, $\mathbf{k}$ form. [2 marks]
   c) Find the coordinates of the intersection point of l_1 and the line that passes through AB in $\mathbf{i}$, $\mathbf{j}$, $\mathbf{k}$ form. [5 marks]

I'd normally write a joke here — but I don't want to cross the line...

Nothing too scary here — the vector equation of a line might be familiar already. Even so, the trickier stuff you need to learn relies on these basics, so make sure you know them like the back of your hand. Cover up the key formulas on the previous page and try writing them down from memory. If you haven't quite got it, have another read through.

Scalar Products

The scalar product of two vectors is kind of what it says on the tin — two vectors multiplied together to give a scalar result. But this is Further Maths, so it's going to be trickier than simple multiplying. It even involves a bit of cos-ing.

The **Scalar Product** is a way of **Multiplying Vectors**

The scalar product is often called the dot product.

1) The **scalar product** of two vectors **a** and **b** is written **a.b** (you read this as 'a dot b').

The **definition** of the scalar product is:

$$\mathbf{a.b} = |\mathbf{a}||\mathbf{b}|\cos\theta$$

Where θ is the **angle between the two vectors** when they're both **directed away** from the same point.

Watch out — the correct angle might not always be obvious.

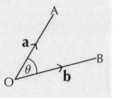

θ is the angle in the definition.

Here you have to continue **b** on so that it's also directed away from the intersection point.

2) The scalar product of two vectors is always a **scalar quantity** — it's **never** a vector.

3) The **scalar product** can be used to calculate the **angle** between two lines:
    a.b = $|\mathbf{a}||\mathbf{b}|\cos\theta$ rearranges to $\cos\theta = \frac{\mathbf{a.b}}{|\mathbf{a}||\mathbf{b}|}$.

To **work out** the scalar product you use this formula:

$$\mathbf{a.b} = a_1b_1 + a_2b_2 + a_3b_3$$

where $\mathbf{a} = \begin{pmatrix} a_1 \\ a_2 \\ a_3 \end{pmatrix}$ and $\mathbf{b} = \begin{pmatrix} b_1 \\ b_2 \\ b_3 \end{pmatrix}$.

This formula is derived from the definition of the scalar product.

4) It's really, really important to put the dot in, as it shows you mean the **scalar product**.
    (If you're doing the Further Pure 1 option, you'll meet another vector product, the cross product — see p.110.)

5) Like normal multiplication, scalar products follow the **commutative law** (i.e. $\mathbf{a.b} = \mathbf{b.a}$) and the **distributive law** (i.e. $\mathbf{a.(b + c)} = \mathbf{a.b} + \mathbf{a.c}$).

Perpendicular Vectors have a **Scalar Product** of **Zero**

1) **Perpendicular** vectors are at **90°** to each other, and **cos 90° = 0**.
    This means that for perpendicular vectors **a** and **b**, the scalar product $\mathbf{a.b} = |\mathbf{a}||\mathbf{b}|\cos 90° = 0$.

2) So for two **non-zero** vectors **a** and **b**: $\boxed{\mathbf{a.b} = 0 \iff \mathbf{a} \text{ and } \mathbf{b} \text{ are perpendicular}}$

3) The unit vectors **i**, **j** and **k** are all **perpendicular** to each other: $\mathbf{i.j} = 1 \times 1 \times 0 = 0$ and $3\mathbf{j.4k} = 3 \times 4 \times 0 = 0$

4) This all assumes that the vectors are **non-zero**, because if either vector was **0**, you'd always get a scalar product of 0, regardless of the angle between them.

Example: Show that the lines $\mathbf{r}_1 = (\mathbf{i} + 6\mathbf{j} + 2\mathbf{k}) + \lambda(\mathbf{i} + 2\mathbf{j} + 2\mathbf{k})$
and $\mathbf{r}_2 = (3\mathbf{i} - \mathbf{j} + \mathbf{k}) + \mu(4\mathbf{i} - 3\mathbf{j} + \mathbf{k})$ are perpendicular.

1) Make sure you've got the right bit of each vector equation — it's the **direction** you're interested in, so it's **b** in $\mathbf{r} = \mathbf{a} + t\mathbf{b}$. $\mathbf{i} + 2\mathbf{j} + 2\mathbf{k}$ and $4\mathbf{i} - 3\mathbf{j} + \mathbf{k}$

2) Find the **scalar product** of the vectors. $(\mathbf{i} + 2\mathbf{j} + 2\mathbf{k}).(4\mathbf{i} - 3\mathbf{j} + \mathbf{k}) = 4 - 6 + 2 = 0$

3) Draw the correct **conclusion**.   The scalar product is 0 so **the lines are perpendicular**.

The Scalar Product of **Parallel Vectors** is the **Product of the Magnitudes**

1) If two (non-zero) vectors are **parallel**, the angle between them is **0°**. And **cos 0° = 1**, so...

Scalar Product of Two Parallel Vectors

$$\mathbf{a.b} = |\mathbf{a}||\mathbf{b}|\cos 0° = |\mathbf{a}||\mathbf{b}|$$

2) Two **i** unit vectors are **parallel** to each other (as are two **j**s or two **k**s).
    So, $\mathbf{j.j} = 1 \times 1 \times 1 = 1$ and $3\mathbf{k.4k} = 3 \times 4 \times 1 = 12$

This works if a and b point in the same direction. If they point in opposite directions, then $\mathbf{a.b} = |\mathbf{a}||\mathbf{b}|\cos 180° = -|\mathbf{a}||\mathbf{b}|$

Scalar Products

Use the **Scalar Product** to find the **Angle** between two **Vectors**

Rearranging the scalar product formula gives you a formula for working out the **angle** θ **between two vectors**:

$$\cos\theta = \frac{\mathbf{a}.\mathbf{b}}{|\mathbf{a}||\mathbf{b}|}$$

Example: Find the angle between the vectors $4\mathbf{i} - 6\mathbf{j} + 3\mathbf{k}$ and $-\mathbf{i} - 5\mathbf{j} - 7\mathbf{k}$, giving your answer in degrees to 1 decimal place.

1) Call the vectors **a** and **b**. Find the **scalar product** of the vectors:
$$\mathbf{a}.\mathbf{b} = a_1 b_1 + a_2 b_2 + a_3 b_3 = -4 + 30 - 21 = 5$$

2) Find the **magnitude** of each vector:
$$|\mathbf{a}| = \sqrt{16 + 36 + 9} = \sqrt{61} \qquad |\mathbf{b}| = \sqrt{1 + 25 + 49} = \sqrt{75}$$
Use Pythagoras to find the magnitude of each vector.

3) Now plug these values into the equation and find the **angle**:
$$\cos\theta = \frac{\mathbf{a}.\mathbf{b}}{|\mathbf{a}||\mathbf{b}|} = \frac{5}{\sqrt{61}\sqrt{75}} = 0.0739... \Rightarrow \theta = \cos^{-1}(0.0739...) = 85.8° \text{ (1 d.p.)}$$

Use the **Same Formula** to find the **Angle** between two **Lines**

1) The angle between two lines $\mathbf{r}_1 = \mathbf{a}_1 + \lambda\mathbf{b}_1$ and $\mathbf{r}_2 = \mathbf{a}_2 + \mu\mathbf{b}_2$ is the angle between the **direction vectors** of the lines — $\mathbf{b}_1$ and $\mathbf{b}_2$. So it's calculated using $\cos\theta = \frac{\mathbf{b}_1.\mathbf{b}_2}{|\mathbf{b}_1||\mathbf{b}_2|}$.

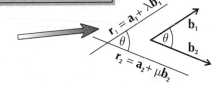

2) The formula might give you an angle **greater than 90°**. If this happens you'll have to **subtract** the angle from 180° to get the **acute angle** between the two lines.

\\\\\\\\\\\\\\\\\\\\\\\\\\
This only applies to lines, not vectors — sometimes the angle between two vectors actually is greater than 90°.
/////////////////////////

Example: Find the acute angle in degrees between the lines
$\mathbf{r}_1 = (-\mathbf{i} + 2\mathbf{j} + 4\mathbf{k}) + \lambda(3\mathbf{i} - 2\mathbf{j} + 8\mathbf{k})$ and $\mathbf{r}_2 = (-6\mathbf{i} + 3\mathbf{k}) + \mu(5\mathbf{i} + 2\mathbf{j} + \mathbf{k})$.

1) Identify $\mathbf{b}_1$ and $\mathbf{b}_2$: $\quad \mathbf{b}_1 = (3\mathbf{i} - 2\mathbf{j} + 8\mathbf{k}), \mathbf{b}_2 = (5\mathbf{i} + 2\mathbf{j} + \mathbf{k})$

2) Find the **scalar product** of the vectors: $\quad \mathbf{b}_1.\mathbf{b}_2 = 15 - 4 + 8 = 19$

3) Find the **magnitude** of each vector: $\quad |\mathbf{b}_1| = \sqrt{9 + 4 + 64} = \sqrt{77}$
$$|\mathbf{b}_2| = \sqrt{25 + 4 + 1} = \sqrt{30}$$

4) Find the **angle**: $\cos\theta = \frac{\mathbf{b}_1.\mathbf{b}_2}{|\mathbf{b}_1||\mathbf{b}_2|} = \frac{19}{\sqrt{77}\sqrt{30}} = 0.395... \Rightarrow \theta = 66.7° \text{ (1 d.p.)}$

Practice Questions

Q1 Find $\mathbf{a}.\mathbf{b}$ if: a) $\mathbf{a} = 3\mathbf{i} + 4\mathbf{j}$ and $\mathbf{b} = \mathbf{i} - 2\mathbf{j} + 3\mathbf{k}$ b) $\mathbf{a} = \begin{pmatrix} 4 \\ 2 \\ 1 \end{pmatrix}$ and $\mathbf{b} = \begin{pmatrix} 3 \\ -4 \\ -3 \end{pmatrix}$

Q2 Find the acute angle, in degrees to 1 decimal place, between the lines
$\mathbf{r}_1 = 2\mathbf{i} - \mathbf{j} + 2\mathbf{k} + t(-4\mathbf{i} + 6\mathbf{j} - 2\mathbf{k})$ and $\mathbf{r}_2 = 3\mathbf{i} + 2\mathbf{j} + 4\mathbf{k} + u(-\mathbf{i} + 3\mathbf{j})$.

Q3 Find a vector that is perpendicular to $3\mathbf{i} + 4\mathbf{j} - 2\mathbf{k}$.

Exam Questions

Q1 The line l_1 between two points A and B has a vector equation $\mathbf{r}_1 = \mathbf{i} + 5\mathbf{j} + 9\mathbf{k} + \lambda(2\mathbf{i} - 3\mathbf{j} - 8\mathbf{k})$.
The line l_2 between two other points C and D has a vector equation $\mathbf{r}_2 = -2\mathbf{i} + 4\mathbf{j} + 3\mathbf{k} + \mu(-7\mathbf{i} + 5\mathbf{j} + 10\mathbf{k})$.
Find the acute angle between l_1 and l_2. Give your answer in degrees to 1 decimal place. [4 marks]

Q2 Point A has the position vector $3\mathbf{i} + 2\mathbf{j} + \mathbf{k}$ and point B has position vector $3\mathbf{i} - 4\mathbf{j} - \mathbf{k}$.
a) Show that AOB is a right-angled triangle. [3 marks]
b) Find the angle ABO in the triangle, in degrees to 1 decimal place, using the scalar product definition. [4 marks]
c) Point C has the position vector $3\mathbf{i} - \mathbf{j}$. Show that triangle OAC is isosceles. [3 marks]

Scalar products? No thanks — snakeskin's not really my thing...

There's a lot to learn here, but it's not too bad once you've got your head around what all of the letters mean. The key thing is to remember the standard forms that the equation of a line comes in. Then when you're faced with the equation of a line you'll be able to recognise the different bits of it, and pick out the vectors you need. Simple, eh?

Plane Geometry

Unsurprisingly, this topic is all about planes. Just what you were hoping for...

An **Equation** for a **Plane** can come in **Vector Form...**

1) The **vector form** of the equation of a plane is similar to the vector equation of a straight line.

2) It's made up of the position vector of a **point on the plane**, and scalar multiples of **two non-parallel vectors that lie in the plane**.

3) This works in the same way as the vector equation of a line — you can get to **any point** in the plane by following a combination of these vectors.

4) You can find a **vector equation** for a plane given **three points** in the plane.

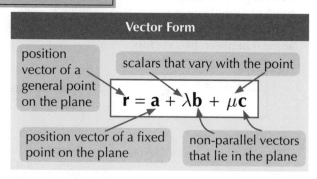

Vector Form

position vector of a general point on the plane

$$\mathbf{r} = \mathbf{a} + \lambda\mathbf{b} + \mu\mathbf{c}$$

scalars that vary with the point

position vector of a fixed point on the plane

non-parallel vectors that lie in the plane

Example: Find an equation in the form $\mathbf{r} = \mathbf{a} + \lambda\mathbf{b} + \mu\mathbf{c}$ for the plane that passes through the points X = (6, –1, 4), Y = (–2, –2, 5) and Z = (11, –3, –8).

1) You need to find the vectors **a**, **b** and **c**.

2) **a** is just any point in the plane, so you can pick $\overrightarrow{OX}$, $\overrightarrow{OY}$ or $\overrightarrow{OZ}$.

$$\overrightarrow{XY} = \overrightarrow{OY} - \overrightarrow{OX} = \begin{pmatrix} -2 \\ -2 \\ 5 \end{pmatrix} - \begin{pmatrix} 6 \\ -1 \\ 4 \end{pmatrix} = \begin{pmatrix} -8 \\ -1 \\ 1 \end{pmatrix}$$

3) **b** and **c** are vectors that lie in the plane, and since the points X, Y and Z lie in the plane, $\overrightarrow{XY}$ and $\overrightarrow{XZ}$ are vectors that lie in the plane.

$$\overrightarrow{XZ} = \overrightarrow{OZ} - \overrightarrow{OX} = \begin{pmatrix} 11 \\ -3 \\ -8 \end{pmatrix} - \begin{pmatrix} 6 \\ -1 \\ 4 \end{pmatrix} = \begin{pmatrix} 5 \\ -2 \\ -12 \end{pmatrix}$$

4) As $\overrightarrow{XY}$ and $\overrightarrow{XZ}$ **aren't parallel**, they are good choices for **b** and **c**.

$$\mathbf{r} = \overrightarrow{OX} + \lambda\overrightarrow{XY} + \mu\overrightarrow{XZ} \Rightarrow \mathbf{r} = \begin{pmatrix} 6 \\ -1 \\ 4 \end{pmatrix} + \lambda\begin{pmatrix} -8 \\ -1 \\ 1 \end{pmatrix} + \mu\begin{pmatrix} 5 \\ -2 \\ -12 \end{pmatrix}$$

... and in **Scalar** or **Cartesian Form**

As well as vector form the equation of a plane can be written in **scalar form** or **Cartesian form**.

Scalar Form

The **scalar form** of the equation of a plane is:

position vector of a general point on the plane

$$\mathbf{r.n} = \mathbf{a.n} = p$$

scalar constant

a normal to the plane

position vector of a fixed point on the plane

So, for example, the scalar form will usually look like
$$\mathbf{r}.(-4\mathbf{i} + 3\mathbf{j} - 6\mathbf{k}) = 4$$
or $\mathbf{r}.\begin{pmatrix} -4 \\ 3 \\ -6 \end{pmatrix} = 4$

The scalar form of the equation uses a **normal** to the plane — this is a vector that's **perpendicular** to the plane, i.e. it's perpendicular to **all vectors** that **lie in the plane**.

Cartesian Form

The **Cartesian form** of the equation $\mathbf{r.n} = p$ is:

$$ax + by + cz + d = 0$$

Where $\mathbf{n} = a\mathbf{i} + b\mathbf{j} + c\mathbf{k}$ and $p = -d$.

You can **derive** the Cartesian form from the scalar form:

For a plane $\mathbf{r.n} = p$, if $\mathbf{n} = \begin{pmatrix} a \\ b \\ c \end{pmatrix}$ and $p = -d$, then for any point (x, y, z) on the plane:
$$\begin{pmatrix} x \\ y \\ z \end{pmatrix} \cdot \begin{pmatrix} a \\ b \\ c \end{pmatrix} = -d \Rightarrow ax + by + cz = -d$$
$$\Rightarrow ax + by + cz + d = 0$$

Example: Write an equation in the form $\mathbf{r.n} = p$ for the plane with Cartesian equation $7x + 3y - 8z - 9 = 0$.

$7x + 3y - 8z - 9 = 0 \Rightarrow 7x + 3y - 8z = 9$

$\Rightarrow (x\mathbf{i} + y\mathbf{j} + z\mathbf{k}).(7\mathbf{i} + 3\mathbf{j} - 8\mathbf{k}) = 9 \Rightarrow \mathbf{r}.(7\mathbf{i} + 3\mathbf{j} - 8\mathbf{k}) = 9$

If you know how the scalar and Cartesian forms are related you can write this answer straight down.

Plane Geometry

*Use **Trigonometry** to find the **Angle** between a **Line** and a **Plane***

1) You find the angle ϕ between a plane $\mathbf{r.n} = p$ and
a line $\mathbf{r} = \mathbf{a} + \lambda\mathbf{b}$ using the angle between the **normal**
to the plane ($\mathbf{n}$) and the **direction vector** of the line ($\mathbf{b}$):

$$\sin\phi = \left|\frac{\mathbf{n.b}}{\|\mathbf{n}\|\mathbf{b}\|}\right|$$

2) You can derive this from the fact that the angle **between the vectors n and b** is θ, where $\cos\theta = \dfrac{\mathbf{n.b}}{|\mathbf{n}\|\mathbf{b}|}$ (see below).

Example: Find the angle between the plane $\mathbf{r}.(3\mathbf{i} + 7\mathbf{j} - \mathbf{k}) = 14$ and the line
$\mathbf{r} = (-\mathbf{i} + 2\mathbf{j} + 4\mathbf{k}) + \lambda(3\mathbf{i} - 2\mathbf{j} + 8\mathbf{k})$. Give your answer in degrees to 1 decimal place.

1) Find the **scalar product** of the vectors $\mathbf{n}$ and $\mathbf{b}$:

$$\mathbf{n} = 3\mathbf{i} + 7\mathbf{j} - \mathbf{k}, \ \mathbf{b} = 3\mathbf{i} - 2\mathbf{j} + 8\mathbf{k}$$
$$\Rightarrow \mathbf{n.b} = (3 \times 3) + (7 \times -2) + (-1 \times 8)$$
$$= 9 - 14 - 8 = -13$$

2) Find the **magnitude** of $\mathbf{n}$ and $\mathbf{b}$:

$$|\mathbf{n}| = \sqrt{9 + 49 + 1} = \sqrt{59}$$
$$|\mathbf{b}| = \sqrt{9 + 4 + 64} = \sqrt{77}$$

3) Plug $\mathbf{n.b}$, $|\mathbf{n}|$ and $|\mathbf{b}|$ into the equation and find the angle ϕ:

$$\sin\phi = \left|\frac{\mathbf{n.b}}{\|\mathbf{n}\|\mathbf{b}\|}\right| = \left|\frac{-13}{\sqrt{59}\sqrt{77}}\right| = 0.192...$$

$$\Rightarrow \phi = \sin^{-1}(0.192...) = \mathbf{11.1°} \ \textbf{(1 d.p.)}$$

---

3) To derive the formula, consider that the normal forms a **right-angled triangle** with the plane and the line.
Depending on the directions of the vectors there are two cases:

Case 1: The angle θ between the two vectors is **less than 90°**.

$\phi = 180° - 90° - \theta = 90° - \theta$

> The angle between the two vectors is the angle in the triangle.

$\sin\phi = \sin(90° - \theta) = \cos\theta$

> $\sin(90° - \theta) \equiv \cos\theta$ is a trig identity.

$= |\cos\theta|$

> θ is less than 90°, so $\cos\theta$ is positive $\Rightarrow \cos\theta = |\cos\theta|$

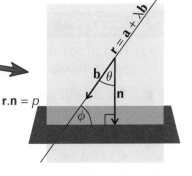

Case 2: The angle θ between the two vectors is **greater than 90°**.

$\phi = 180° - 90° - (180° - \theta) = \theta - 90°$

> The angle between the two vectors lies on a straight line with the angle in the triangle.

$\sin\phi = \sin(\theta - 90°) = -\cos\theta$

> This comes from trig identities.

$= |\cos\theta|$

> θ is greater than 90°, so $\cos\theta$ is negative $\Rightarrow -\cos\theta = |\cos\theta|$

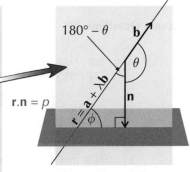

4) So in **both cases** $\sin\phi = |\cos\theta| = \left|\dfrac{\mathbf{n.b}}{\|\mathbf{n}\|\mathbf{b}\|}\right|$.

> You don't need to be able to derive this formula, but if you remember these diagrams you can find the angle without the formula if you need to — it might be easier to remember the formula though.

Here's a yellow plane — now this topic really is all about planes

Section 6 — CP: Further Vectors

Plane Geometry

You can also find the Angle between two Planes

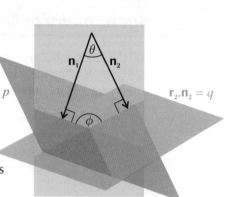

1) You find the angle between two planes $r_1.n_1 = p$ and $r_2.n_2 = q$ using the angle between the **normals** to the planes: n_1 and n_2.

2) Work out the angle between the normals using $\cos\theta = \dfrac{n_1.n_2}{|n_1||n_2|}$.

3) The two normals (which are at 90° to the planes) form a **quadrilateral** with the two planes, so the **angle ϕ between the two planes** is $360° - 90° - 90° - \theta = \mathbf{180° - \theta}$.

4) You might end up with an angle that's **greater than 90°** — if this happens then **subtract** from 180° to get the **acute angle** between the planes.

Example: Find the angle between the planes $r_1.(3i + 7j - k) = 14$ and $r_2.(2i - 2j - 5k) = 9$. Give your answer in degrees to 1 decimal place.

1) Find the **scalar product** of the two normal vectors: $n_1 = 3i + 7j - k$, $n_2 = 2i - 2j - 5k$
$$\Rightarrow n_1 \cdot n_2 = (3 \times 2) + (7 \times -2) + (-1 \times -5) = 6 - 14 + 5 = -3$$

2) Find the **magnitude** of each normal vector:
$$|n_1| = \sqrt{9 + 49 + 1} = \sqrt{59}$$
$$|n_2| = \sqrt{4 + 4 + 25} = \sqrt{33}$$

3) Plug $n_1.n_2$, $|n_1|$ and $|n_2|$ into the equation and find the angle between the two normals:
$$\cos\theta = \frac{n_1 \cdot n_2}{|n_1||n_2|} = \frac{-3}{\sqrt{59}\sqrt{33}} = -0.0679... \Rightarrow \theta = 93.898...°$$

4) Subtract this from 180° to get the angle between the two planes:
$$\phi = 180° - 93.898...° = \mathbf{86.1°\ (1\ d.p.)}$$

Practice Questions

Q1 Find an equation in the form $r = a + \lambda b + \mu c$ for the plane that passes through the points $X = (3, -7, -1)$, $Y = (-2, 0, 4)$ and $Z = (9, -3, 5)$.

Q2 The plane Π passes through the point $(-5, 2, 4)$ and is perpendicular to the vector $(-2, 0, 3)$. Find a Cartesian equation of Π.

Q3 For the following question, give your answers in degrees to 1 decimal place.
   a) Find the acute angle between the planes $r_1.(-4i + 4j - k) = 7$ and $r_2.(3i - 7j - 5k) = 9$.
   b) Find the acute angle between the plane $s_1.(2i + 5j - k) = 14$ and the line $s_2 = (-i + 2j + 4k) + \lambda(3i - 3j + 6k)$.

Exam Questions

Q1 The plane Π_1 has vector equation $r.(-3i - 2j + 3k) = 5$ and the plane Π_2, which passes through the point $(-4i + 3j + 5k)$, is perpendicular to the vector n.

Given that $n = \begin{pmatrix} 1 \\ -3 \\ 5 \end{pmatrix}$:

   a) Find a Cartesian equation for Π_2. [2 marks]
   b) Show that the acute angle between the planes Π_1 and Π_2 is 49.6° to 1 decimal place. [3 marks]

Q2 The plane P is described by the Cartesian equation $-19x - 29y + 26z - 12 = 0$.
   The line l_1 meets the plane P at the point $(2, -8, -7)$ and passes through the point $(1, -4, 2)$.
   Determine to the nearest degree the acute angle between P and l_1. [5 marks]

Remember these equations, or you'll be getting questions plane wrong...

Scalar products — they're everywhere. That means it's crucial you learn all about them and how to use them. There's also a lot of trigonometry sneaking in (classic sneaky trigonometry), so you need to know all the trig identities for the exam. The quicker you can recall them, the easier questions become, and as I'm sure you'll agree, easy = good.

Intersections and Distances

This is the last topic in the vectors section — try not to be too upset. This bit looks tough and the questions on it can be fairly tricky, but if you can remember some rules then you'll be fine. But it's gonna take some learning...

A **Plane** and a **Line Intersect** when both of their **Equations Hold**

To find the **point of intersection** of a line and a plane you **substitute** the equation of the line into the equation of the plane — at the point where they intersect, the equation of the line and the equation of the plane **both hold**.

Example: Find the point of intersection of the line $\mathbf{r} = \begin{pmatrix} 3 \\ -1 \\ 6 \end{pmatrix} + \lambda \begin{pmatrix} 1 \\ 5 \\ -2 \end{pmatrix}$ with the plane $\mathbf{r} \cdot \begin{pmatrix} 8 \\ 2 \\ 5 \end{pmatrix} = 4$.

Finding the Intersection of a Line and Plane

1. Write the equation of the line as a **single vector**.

2. **Substitute** this vector into the equation of the plane.

3. **Solve** to find λ.

4. **Substitute** the value of λ into the equation of the line — this gives the point of intersection.

① $\mathbf{r} = \begin{pmatrix} 3 \\ -1 \\ 6 \end{pmatrix} + \lambda \begin{pmatrix} 1 \\ 5 \\ -2 \end{pmatrix} = \begin{pmatrix} 3+\lambda \\ 5\lambda-1 \\ 6-2\lambda \end{pmatrix}$

You can substitute into either of these forms later on — use the one you find easiest.

② $\begin{pmatrix} 3+\lambda \\ 5\lambda-1 \\ 6-2\lambda \end{pmatrix} \cdot \begin{pmatrix} 8 \\ 2 \\ 5 \end{pmatrix} = 4$

③ $\Rightarrow 8(3 + \lambda) + 2(5\lambda - 1) + 5(6 - 2\lambda) = 4$

$\Rightarrow 24 + 8\lambda + 10\lambda - 2 + 30 - 10\lambda = 4 \Rightarrow 8\lambda = -48 \Rightarrow \lambda = -6$

④ $\mathbf{r} = \begin{pmatrix} 3+\lambda \\ 5\lambda-1 \\ 6-2\lambda \end{pmatrix} = \begin{pmatrix} 3+(-6) \\ (5 \times -6)-1 \\ 6-(2 \times -6) \end{pmatrix} = \begin{pmatrix} -3 \\ -31 \\ 18 \end{pmatrix}$

This is the position vector of the point.

Point of intersection: **(–3, –31, 18)**

Give your answer in Cartesian form unless you're told otherwise.

Two **Planes Intersect** along a **Line**

Any **two non-parallel planes** meet along a line — the **line of intersection**. (Two planes Π_1 and Π_2 are parallel if their normals are parallel.)

The planes meet along the line where the equations of both planes hold.

Example: Find the equation of the line of intersection of the planes $\mathbf{r} \cdot \begin{pmatrix} 7 \\ 3 \\ -2 \end{pmatrix} = 7$ and $\mathbf{r} \cdot \begin{pmatrix} 4 \\ 3 \\ 1 \end{pmatrix} = -11$.

Finding the Intersection of Two Planes

1. Write the equation of each plane in **Cartesian form**.

2. Use **simultaneous equations** to eliminate one variable so that you can express one variable in terms of another.

3. **Substitute** this back into the equation of one of the planes to get an equation in terms of the **eliminated variable**.

4. **Change the subject** of the equation you found in step 2 — this gives you **two different equations** for one variable.

5. Write these as a **single equation** set to equal λ to give you a **Cartesian equation** for the line of intersection.

① $7x + 3y - 2z = 7$ ①
$4x + 3y + z = -11$ ②

② $3x - 3z = 18$ ①–②
$\Rightarrow z = x - 6$

Choose the easiest variable to eliminate.

③ $4x + 3y + x - 6 = -11 \Rightarrow x = -\dfrac{3y+5}{5}$

④ $z = x - 6 \Rightarrow x = z + 6$

⑤ $\Rightarrow x = z + 6 = -\dfrac{3y+5}{5} = \lambda$

You can then convert this into a vector equation if you need to.

Intersections and Distances

Finding the **Perpendicular Distance** between a **Point** and a **Line**...

1) The **shortest** path between a point and a line is always **perpendicular** to the line. For example, if you want to get to a road as fast as possible, you'd take the path that was perpendicular to the road.

2) One method for finding the **perpendicular distance** between a point and a line uses the **scalar product**. Here's how it's done...

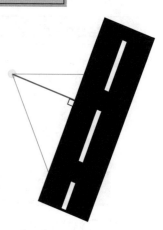

> **Example:** The line l_1 contains the points (1, 5, –9) and (2, 14, 5). Find the perpendicular distance between l_1 and the point, A, whose position vector is (–1, –3, 1).
>
> 1) Find an equation for l_1: ← You could use the position vector of either point for **a**.
>
> $$r = a + \lambda b = i + 5j - 9k + \lambda((2 - 1)i + (14 - 5)j + (5 - (-9))k)$$
> $$r = i + 5j - 9k + \lambda(i + 9j + 14k)$$
> The direction vector **b** is the vector between the two points.
>
> 2) Consider the general point B on l_1. Then:
>
> $$\overrightarrow{AB} = (1 + \lambda - (-1))i + (5 + 9\lambda - (-3))j + (-9 + 14\lambda - 1)k$$
> $$= (2 + \lambda)i + (8 + 9\lambda)j + (-10 + 14\lambda)k$$
>
> 3) If $\overrightarrow{AB}$ is perpendicular to l_1, the scalar product of the direction vectors is zero.
>
> So, $(i + 9j + 14k).[(2 + \lambda)i + (8 + 9\lambda)j + (-10 + 14\lambda)k] = 0$
>
> $\Rightarrow (2 + \lambda) + 9(8 + 9\lambda) + 14(-10 + 14\lambda) = 0 \Rightarrow -66 + 278\lambda = 0 \Rightarrow \lambda = \dfrac{33}{139}$
>
> 4) The perpendicular distance is $|\overrightarrow{AB}|$.
>
> $$|\overrightarrow{AB}| = \sqrt{(2 + \lambda)^2 + (8 + 9\lambda)^2 + (-10 + 14\lambda)^2} = \sqrt{\dfrac{21174}{139}}$$

The shortest path from the yellow dot to the road is along the red line — all other paths are longer.

3) The key thing here is to remember that with a point and a line distance, there is just **one variable** — the variable that tells you where you are on the line.

... and between **a Point** and a **Plane**

1) This bit sounds tricky, but most of the work is just following a **formula**. And better still, you don't even have to remember it.

2) Take a point $\alpha i + \beta j + \lambda k$ and a plane $n_1 x + n_2 y + n_3 z + d = 0$. The **perpendicular distance** between them is:

$$\frac{|n_1 \alpha + n_2 \beta + n_3 \lambda + d|}{\sqrt{n_1^2 + n_2^2 + n_3^2}}$$

This is in the formula book. Hooray!

Steve tried to convince Jane not to look along the path perpendicular to the ground.

> **Example:** Find the perpendicular distance between the point, A, with position vector $-3i + 2j - 10k$ and the plane, Π_1, given by the equation $r.\begin{pmatrix} 4 \\ 3 \\ 1 \end{pmatrix} = -13$.

1) Convert the equation for the plane from scalar form to Cartesian form: $4x + 3y + z + 13 = 0$

2) Identify which number corresponds to each variable: $n_1 = 4, n_2 = 3, n_3 = 1, d = 13, \alpha = -3, \beta = 2, \lambda = -10$

3) Plug in the numbers:

Perpendicular distance = $\dfrac{|(4 \times -3) + (3 \times 2) + (1 \times -10) + 13|}{\sqrt{4^2 + 3^2 + 1^2}} = \dfrac{3}{\sqrt{26}} = $ **0.59 (2 d.p.)**

4) The formula book doesn't mention **points** and **planes** so make sure you know what you're looking for when you see a question on this topic.

Intersections and Distances

Parallel Lines have a constant Perpendicular Distance between them

1) When you work out the perpendicular distance between a point
   and a line, you only have one **variable** to worry about.

2) If you want to find the perpendicular distance between two parallel lines,
   there are **two variables**, one variable telling you where you are on **each** line.

3) But because the lines are **parallel**, they can be **grouped** together as one single variable.

> **Example:** Find the shortest distance between parallel lines l_1 and l_2, where the equation of l_1 is
> $\mathbf{r}_1 = 4\mathbf{i} + 4\mathbf{j} - 5\mathbf{k} + \lambda(2\mathbf{i} + 4\mathbf{j} - 2\mathbf{k})$ and the equation of l_2 is $\mathbf{r}_2 = \mathbf{i} + 4\mathbf{j} - 2\mathbf{k} + \mu(2\mathbf{i} + 4\mathbf{j} - 2\mathbf{k})$.
>
> 1) Let A be any point on l_1 and B be any point on l_2, then
> $$\vec{BA} = \mathbf{r}_1 - \mathbf{r}_2 = (3 + 2(\lambda - \mu))\mathbf{i} + (4(\lambda - \mu))\mathbf{j} + (-3 - 2(\lambda - \mu))\mathbf{k}$$
>
> 2) Set $t = \lambda - \mu$, to give you one less variable to worry about:
> $$\vec{BA} = (3 + 2t)\mathbf{i} + (4t)\mathbf{j} + (-3 - 2t)\mathbf{k}$$
>
> 3) The shortest distance between l_1 and l_2 is just the perpendicular distance between them.
>
>   When $\vec{BA}$ is perpendicular to l_1 and l_2: $[(3 + 2t)\mathbf{i} + (4t)\mathbf{j} + (-3 - 2t)\mathbf{k}].(2\mathbf{i} + 4\mathbf{j} - 2\mathbf{k}) = 0$
> $$\Rightarrow 2(3 + 2t) + 4(4t) - 2(-3 - 2t) = 0 \Rightarrow 12 + 24t = 0 \Rightarrow t = -\frac{1}{2}$$
>
> 4) The perpendicular distance is $|\vec{BA}| = \sqrt{(3 + 2t)^2 + (4t)^2 + (-3 - 2t)^2} = \sqrt{(2)^2 + (-2)^2 + (-2)^2} = \sqrt{12}$

4) To find the shortest distance between **skew lines** (p.54), you need to find the path that is **perpendicular** to
   both lines. You can use a **similar method** to that in the example above — but because the two lines have
   different direction vectors, you need to work out the dot product of $\vec{BA}$ with the direction vectors of **both** l_1
   and l_2 and set each to **zero**. This gives **two simultaneous equations** in λ and μ which must then be solved.

Practice Questions

Q1 Find the perpendicular distance to 3 significant figures between the point, A, whose vector is $4\mathbf{i} + \mathbf{j} - 6\mathbf{k}$

and the plane, Π_1, given by the equation $\mathbf{r}.\begin{pmatrix} -4 \\ 1 \\ -2 \end{pmatrix} = 12$

Q2 Find the Cartesian equation of the line of intersection of the planes $\mathbf{r}.\begin{pmatrix} 6 \\ -4 \\ 1 \end{pmatrix} = 4$ and $\mathbf{r}.\begin{pmatrix} 2 \\ 6 \\ -3 \end{pmatrix} = -9$

Q3 The line l_1 has equation $\mathbf{r}_1 = 3\mathbf{i} - \mathbf{j} + 3\mathbf{k} + \lambda(5\mathbf{i} + 3\mathbf{j} + 7\mathbf{k})$ and line l_2 has equation $\mathbf{r}_2 = \mathbf{i} + 7\mathbf{j} + 9\mathbf{k} + \mu(5\mathbf{i} + 3\mathbf{j} + 7\mathbf{k})$.
   Find the perpendicular distance between them to 3 significant figures.

Exam Questions

Q1 The parallelogram ABCD has vertices A(6, 4, 3), B(7, 7, 1), C(−1, −2, −2) and D(−2, −5, 0).
   Find the perpendicular distance between the lines that pass through $\vec{AB}$ and $\vec{DC}$ to 2 decimal places.   [4 marks]

Q2 a) The plane Π has scalar equation $\mathbf{r}.\begin{pmatrix} -2 \\ 1 \\ 3 \end{pmatrix} = 9$. The point P has coordinates (2, 11, −4).

   The line l passes through P and is perpendicular to Π, intersecting Π at the point N.
   Show that the coordinates of N are (0, 12, −1).   [4 marks]

   b) The point Q has coordinates (−1, −3, 4).
   Find the perpendicular distance from N to the line PQ. Give your answer to 3 significant figures.   [4 marks]

Points on a plane — my new idea for a film...

*This topic can be confusing because there are different methods for working out distances and intersections depending on
what they're between. That's why you have to learn which method is which, but once you've done that, this stuff really
isn't that bad. The best way to get your head around it (and every bit of maths) is to try some questions on it. After you...*

Polar Coordinates and Curves

Up until now, you've been using Cartesian coordinates (x, y) to describe the position of a point in 2D space.
Now you've reached level 7, you've unlocked a new bonus item — polar coordinates. Great news...

Polar Coordinates describe a Point in Space

Polar coordinates give a point in terms of its **distance** from a **fixed point**, and its **angle** from an **initial line**.

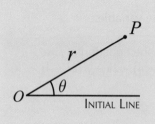

Here, the point P is a **distance r** from point O (the origin, or **pole**), and an **angle θ** from the **initial line**.

So P's polar coordinates are (r, θ).

θ is usually given in **radians**, measured **anticlockwise** from the initial line.

r is usually taken to be **greater than or equal to zero**
(though $r < 0$ might be considered in some situations — see page 67).

You can Convert between Polar and Cartesian Coordinates

1) The fixed point in polar coordinates is usually taken to be the Cartesian **origin**, with the positive x-axis as the initial line.

2) You can turn the diagram above into a **right-angled triangle**, then use **trig** and **Pythagoras** to come up with some **handy identities**. These let you convert between coordinate systems:

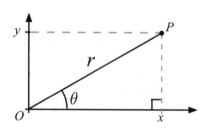

$$x^2 + y^2 = r^2 \qquad x = r \cos\theta$$

$$\tan\theta = \frac{y}{x} \qquad y = r \sin\theta$$

Remember these — they're really important!

3) The angle θ is usually **restricted** to either $0 \le \theta < 2\pi$ or $-\pi < \theta \le \pi$.
This means that each point in space can be uniquely described by a single set of polar coordinates.

4) Finding $\tan^{-1}\left(\frac{y}{x}\right)$ on your calculator won't always give you the correct answer. Think about which **quadrant** the point lies in, and use the **periodicity** of $\tan\theta$ to get the actual value. Drawing a **sketch** is always useful.

Examples: a)   The point Q has polar coordinates $\left(5, \frac{3\pi}{4}\right)$. What are the Cartesian coordinates of Q?

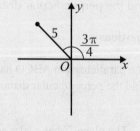

$r = 5$ and $\theta = \frac{3\pi}{4}$, so using the identities:

$$x = r\cos\theta = 5\cos\frac{3\pi}{4} = -\frac{5}{\sqrt{2}}, \qquad y = r\sin\theta = 5\sin\frac{3\pi}{4} = \frac{5}{\sqrt{2}}$$

$\Rightarrow Q$ has Cartesian coordinates $\left(-\frac{5}{\sqrt{2}}, \frac{5}{\sqrt{2}}\right)$ ← Give exact answers where possible.

We can check if our answer is sensible. As Q is in the second quadrant, it will have a negative x-value and a positive y-value, which agrees with our answer.

b)   What are the polar coordinates of the point that has Cartesian coordinates $(-12, -8)$? Give each coordinate to 3 s.f., with $-\pi < \theta \le \pi$.

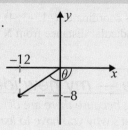

1) $x^2 + y^2 = r^2 \Rightarrow (-12)^2 + (-8)^2 = r^2 \Rightarrow r = \sqrt{208} = 14.422...$

2) $\tan^{-1}\left(\frac{-8}{-12}\right) = 0.5880...$ rad
     But $(-12, -8)$ is in the third quadrant, so for $-\pi < \theta \le \pi$,
     $\theta = \tan^{-1}\left(\frac{-8}{-12}\right) - \pi = 0.5880... - \pi = -2.553...$ rad.

3)   So the polar coordinates are **(14.4, –2.55 rads)** (3 s.f.).

Polar Coordinates and Curves

Polar Coordinates can be used to describe Curves

A **polar equation** gives a curve in terms of r and θ (rather than in terms of x and y, like a Cartesian equation). You might be asked to **sketch** a curve, given its **polar equation**.

There are a few **basic curves** where it's easy to see what's going on.

$r = a$, for $0 \le \theta < 2\pi$, where a is a positive constant.

This **distance** from the pole is **constant**. There's no θ in the equation, so the **angle** from the initial line could be **anything**. This is the description of a **circle**, centred at the **pole**, with **radius** a.

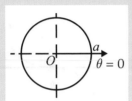

$\theta = \alpha$, where α is a constant, $-\pi < \alpha \le \pi$.

The **angle** from the initial line is **constant**. There's no r in the equation, so the **distance** could be **any** positive value. This is just a **straight line** starting at the **pole**.

You might see $\theta = \alpha$ referred to as a 'half-line'.

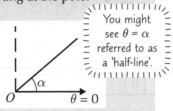

$r = a\theta$ for $0 \le \theta < 2\pi$, where a is a positive constant.

r increases as θ does, so the curve **spirals outwards** from the pole as θ moves from 0 to 2π. The curve will meet the initial line when $\theta = 0$ and $\theta = 2\pi$, i.e. when $r = 0$ and $r = 2a\pi$.

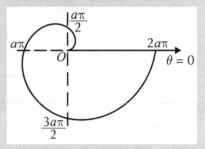

You might need to convert to Cartesian Form

The curve with equation $r = 2a\cos\theta$ is a **circle** of **radius** a, **centred** at $(a, 0)$ and the curve with equation $r = 2b\sin\theta$ is a **circle** of radius b, centred at $(0, b)$. This can be shown by converting to **Cartesian form**, using the **identities** on the previous page:

Example: Sketch the curve given by the equation $r = 6\cos\theta$, for $-\frac{\pi}{2} \le \theta \le \frac{\pi}{2}$.

Multiply both sides of the equation by r and convert to Cartesian coordinates using the identities.

Then complete the square.

$r = 6\cos\theta \Rightarrow r^2 = 6r\cos\theta$
$r^2 = x^2 + y^2$ and $r\cos\theta = x$,
so $r^2 = 6r\cos\theta \Rightarrow x^2 + y^2 = 6x$
$\Rightarrow x^2 - 6x + y^2 = 0$
$(x - 3)^2 - 9 + y^2 = 0$
$(x - 3)^2 + y^2 = 9$

It's a good idea to mark key points on your sketches.

In the x-y plane, this is the **equation of a circle centred** at $(3, 0)$ with **radius 3**. So in the r-θ plane, it will look like this.

The method can also be used to show that $r = p\sec(\alpha - \theta)$ and $r = q\cosec(\beta - \theta)$ are **straight lines**:

Example: Sketch the curve given by the equation $r = 2\sec\left(\frac{\pi}{4} - \theta\right)$.

Using the trig difference formulas.

Use trig identities to get an expression involving $r\cos\theta$ and $r\sin\theta$.

$r = 2\sec\left(\frac{\pi}{4} - \theta\right) \Rightarrow r\cos\left(\frac{\pi}{4} - \theta\right) = 2$
$r\cos\left(\frac{\pi}{4} - \theta\right) = r(\cos\frac{\pi}{4}\cos\theta + \sin\frac{\pi}{4}\sin\theta)$
$= r\left(\frac{\sqrt{2}}{2}\cos\theta + \frac{\sqrt{2}}{2}\sin\theta\right) = \frac{\sqrt{2}}{2}(r\cos\theta + r\sin\theta)$

Then use $x = r\cos\theta$ and $y = r\sin\theta$ and rearrange to find y in terms of x.

So $\frac{\sqrt{2}}{2}(x + y) = 2 \Rightarrow y = 2\sqrt{2} - x$

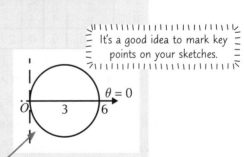

In the x-y plane, this is the equation of a **straight line** with **gradient** -1, **intercepting** the y-axis at the point $(0, 2\sqrt{2})$. So in the r-θ plane, it will look like this.

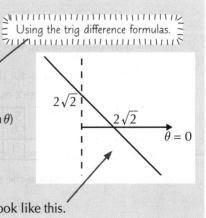

Polar Coordinates and Curves

There are a few other standard types of polar curves you might come across:

1) Curves with equations of the form $r = a \sin k\theta$ and $r = b \cos k\theta$ have **k 'petals'** — see example 1.
2) Curves with equations of the form $r^2 = a^2 \sin 2\theta$ and $r^2 = b^2 \cos 2\theta$ look like a **figure of eight**. The r^2 bit makes their petals slightly wider than $r = a \sin 2\theta$ and $r = b \cos 2\theta$. See example 2.
3) Curves with equations of the form $r = a + b \sin \theta$ and $r = a + b \cos \theta$ ($a > 0$) are called limaçons. When $b = -a$ they are heart-shaped and are called **cardioids** — see example 3.
4) You can sketch these curves using a table of values — remember you only need to consider values of θ where $r \geq 0$, unless a question tells you otherwise.

Example 1: Sketch the curve $r = 2 \sin 2\theta$ in the region $0 \leq \theta < 2\pi$.

1) $\sin 2\theta$ is non-negative for $0 \leq \theta \leq \frac{\pi}{2}$ and $\pi \leq \theta \leq \frac{3\pi}{2}$, so work out the value of r for different values of θ in these ranges:

θ	0	$\frac{\pi}{12}$	$\frac{\pi}{6}$	$\frac{\pi}{4}$	$\frac{\pi}{3}$	$\frac{5\pi}{12}$	$\frac{\pi}{2}$	π	$\frac{13\pi}{12}$	$\frac{7\pi}{6}$	$\frac{5\pi}{4}$	$\frac{4\pi}{3}$	$\frac{17\pi}{12}$	$\frac{3\pi}{2}$
r	0	1	1.7...	2	1.7...	1	0	0	1	1.7...	2	1.7...	1	0

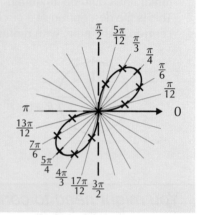

2) Now plot the points from your table and join them up to form the **graph**.
3) You can see that the curve is **symmetrical** about the lines through $\theta = \frac{\pi}{4}$ and $\theta = \frac{3\pi}{4}$, just like the Cartesian curve.

Example 2: Sketch the curve $r^2 = 16 \cos 2\theta$ in the regions $0 \leq \theta \leq \frac{\pi}{4}$, $\frac{3\pi}{4} \leq \theta \leq \frac{5\pi}{4}$ and $\frac{7\pi}{4} \leq \theta < 2\pi$.

1) Fill in a table of the values for $0 \leq \theta \leq \frac{\pi}{4}$ and $\frac{3\pi}{4} \leq \theta \leq \pi$:

The curve is undefined outside these regions as r wouldn't be real.

θ	0	$\frac{\pi}{12}$	$\frac{\pi}{8}$	$\frac{\pi}{6}$	$\frac{\pi}{4}$	$\frac{3\pi}{4}$	$\frac{5\pi}{6}$	$\frac{7\pi}{8}$	$\frac{11\pi}{12}$	π
r	4	3.72...	3.36...	2.82...	0	0	2.82...	3.36...	3.72...	4

2) You could extend the table of values to the other regions of θ, but you can also work out how the rest of the graph will look using **symmetry**:

Since $\cos(2(\theta + \pi)) = \cos(2\theta + 2\pi) = \cos 2\theta$, the values of r in the region $0 \leq \theta \leq \frac{\pi}{4}$, will be the same as the values of r for $\pi \leq \theta \leq \frac{5\pi}{4}$.

Likewise, the values of r in the region $\frac{3\pi}{4} \leq \theta \leq \pi$ will be the same as the values of r for $\frac{7\pi}{4} \leq \theta < 2\pi$.

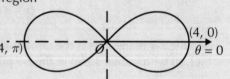

Example 3: Sketch the curve $r = 2(1 - \sin \theta)$ in the region $0 \leq \theta < 2\pi$.

1) $r \geq 0$ for every value of θ.

2) Fill in a table of values for the region $\frac{\pi}{2} \leq \theta \leq \frac{3\pi}{2}$ — you'll be able to work out the rest using symmetry:

θ	$\frac{\pi}{2}$	$\frac{2\pi}{3}$	$\frac{3\pi}{4}$	$\frac{5\pi}{6}$	π	$\frac{7\pi}{6}$	$\frac{5\pi}{4}$	$\frac{4\pi}{3}$	$\frac{3\pi}{2}$
r	0	0.26...	0.58...	1	2	3	3.41...	3.73...	4

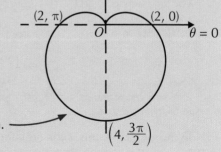

3) Plot the points and use the **symmetry** of $\sin \theta$ to complete the graph.

Polar Coordinates and Curves

Symmetry is often helpful when Sketching Polar Curves

1) Any curve which is a function of **sin $a\theta$ only** will be **symmetrical** about **lines** through $\theta = \frac{\pi}{2a} + \frac{\pi k}{a}$, where $0 \le k < 2a$ and k is an integer. To obtain the corresponding **cos $a\theta$** graph, rotate the **sin $a\theta$** graph $\frac{\pi}{2a}$ radians **clockwise** about the origin.

2) Any curve which is a function of **cos $a\theta$ only** will be **symmetrical** about **lines** through $\theta = \frac{\pi k}{a}$, where $0 \le k < 2a$ and k is an integer. To obtain the corresponding **sin $a\theta$** graph, rotate the **cos $a\theta$** graph $\frac{\pi}{2a}$ radians **anticlockwise** about the origin.

r might Not always be restricted to r ≥ 0

In the exam, always assume that $r \ge 0$ unless the question says **otherwise**. If you need to consider $r < 0$:

$r < 0$ means that the point, or the curve, is positioned in the **opposite direction**, on the **other side** of the pole. So, for example, $\left(-2, \frac{\pi}{2}\right)$ is the same as $\left(2, \frac{3\pi}{2}\right)$ (or $\left(2, -\frac{\pi}{2}\right)$ in the region $-\pi < \theta \le \pi$).

So, for the curve $r = 2\sin 2\theta$ on page 66, the graph would look like this if r was allowed to be negative.

You could've **plotted** a table of values for $\frac{\pi}{2} < \theta < \pi$ and $\frac{3\pi}{2} < \theta < 2\pi$, or instead used the **symmetry** of the curve to fill in the missing bits.

This point is $\left(-2, \frac{3\pi}{4}\right)$.

The parts of the curve that come from negative r-values are drawn with a **dotted line** in this sketch.

Practice Questions

Q1 Give the Cartesian coordinates of the following polar points, to 2 d.p. where appropriate:

a) $\left(6, \frac{7\pi}{8}\right)$ b) $\left(0.4, \frac{\pi}{16}\right)$ c) $\left(3, \frac{41\pi}{22}\right)$ d) $\left(-3, \frac{\pi}{3}\right)$

Q2 Find the exact polar coordinates of the following Cartesian points, for $-\pi < \theta \le \pi$.

a) $(5, -5)$ b) $(-\sqrt{3}, 1)$ c) $(-2, -2\sqrt{3})$

Q3 Sketch the following polar curves for $0 \le \theta < 2\pi$.

a) $r = 5$ b) $\theta = \frac{9\pi}{5}$

Q4 A curve in the r-θ plane is given by the equation $r = \frac{3\theta}{2}$. Sketch the curve for $0 \le \theta < 2\pi$, labelling the points at which it meets the initial line.

Q5 By first converting to Cartesian form, sketch the curve $r = 2\sin\theta$ for $-\pi < \theta \le \pi$.

Alan and Carl's disagreement about which coordinate system is better was really affecting their friendship.

Exam Questions

Q1 Sketch the curve $r = 3\sin 3\theta$ for $0 \le \theta < 2\pi$ and label the points that are furthest from the origin. [3 marks]

Q2 a) Rewrite the polar equation $r = 3\operatorname{cosec}\left(\frac{\pi}{6} - \theta\right)$ as a Cartesian equation. [2 marks]

b) Sketch the curve $r = 3\operatorname{cosec}\left(\frac{\pi}{6} - \theta\right)$, marking the point where it crosses the initial line. [2 marks]

Q3 Sketch the curve $r^2 = 9\sin 2\theta$ for $0 \le \theta < 2\pi$ and label the points that are furthest from the origin. [3 marks]

Q4 Sketch the curve $r = 5 + 4\cos\theta$ for $-\pi < \theta \le \pi$, marking the points where it crosses the initial line. [2 marks]

Polar coordinates — sounds cool...

Working with polar coordinates is tough at first, but with a bit of practice, you'll get used to them fairly quickly. Remember that when drawing polar curves symmetry can be important — almost every trigonometric curve will have at least one line of symmetry, and being able to find it will really save you time in the exam.

Calculus Using Polar Coordinates

Before you get to do some exciting calculus, make sure you know your double angle formulae and the rules for differentiating and integrating trig functions. It'll all become handy once you start this section.

Integrate to find the Area enclosed by a Polar Curve

The **area enclosed by a curve** $r(\theta)$ and the lines $\theta = \alpha$ and $\theta = \beta$ is given by:

$$\text{Area} = \frac{1}{2}\int_{\alpha}^{\beta}[r(\theta)]^2\,d\theta$$

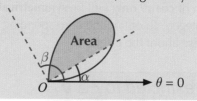

It's just like integrating a Cartesian curve to find the area underneath.

Example: Find the area enclosed by one loop of the curve $r = 2\cos 3\theta$.

Always start integration questions with a quick sketch of the curve to help you see what area you're looking for.

The loops of the curve occur in regions of θ where $r \geq 0$ — you only need one of them.

The curve has a loop for $-\frac{\pi}{6} \leq \theta \leq \frac{\pi}{6}$.

$$\text{Area} = \frac{1}{2}\int_{\alpha}^{\beta}[r(\theta)]^2\,d\theta = \frac{1}{2}\int_{-\frac{\pi}{6}}^{\frac{\pi}{6}}(2\cos(3\theta))^2\,d\theta$$

Use $\cos^2\phi = \dfrac{1 + \cos 2\phi}{2}$ to convert to something integrable.

$$= \int_{-\frac{\pi}{6}}^{\frac{\pi}{6}} 2\cos^2 3\theta\,d\theta = \int_{-\frac{\pi}{6}}^{\frac{\pi}{6}} 1 + \cos 6\theta\,d\theta = \left[\theta + \frac{\sin 6\theta}{6}\right]_{-\frac{\pi}{6}}^{\frac{\pi}{6}}$$

$$= \left[\left(\frac{\pi}{6} + \frac{\sin\pi}{6}\right) - \left(-\frac{\pi}{6} + \frac{\sin(-\pi)}{6}\right)\right] = \frac{\pi}{3}$$

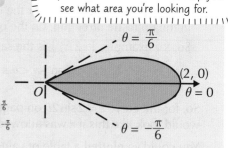

You can also find the Area Between Two Curves

1) To find the area between two curves, **sketch** your curves and identify the **area** you're looking for.

2) **Split the graph** into **sections**, so that each section is **bounded** by **one curve** and **two lines** of the form $\theta = \alpha$. This will involve finding the points where the two curves **meet**.

3) Sometimes the **sum** of all the sections will give you the **total area** required. In other cases, you might need to find the **difference** between sections.

4) Work out the area of **each section** using the method above.

5) Finally, **add or subtract the areas** of each section to obtain your final answer.

Example: Find the exact area between the curves $r_1 = 2$ and $r_2 = 4\cos\theta$.

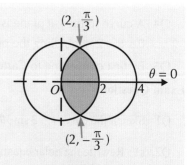

1) Sketch the curves — it's the orange area that you need to find.

2) $r_2 \geq 0$ for $-\frac{\pi}{2} \leq \theta \leq \frac{\pi}{2}$ so you only need to consider θ in that region.

3) Find points where the curves **intersect**:
$$r_1 = r_2 \Rightarrow 2 = 4\cos\theta \Rightarrow \theta = \cos^{-1}\left(\frac{1}{2}\right) = \pm\frac{\pi}{3}$$

4) So use the lines $\theta = \frac{\pi}{3}$ and $\theta = -\frac{\pi}{3}$ to **split the graph** into three **sections**, the **sum** of which is the **total area** you need to find.

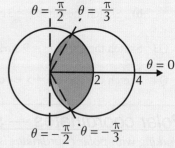

5) **Area of red section** $= \dfrac{1}{2}\displaystyle\int_{-\frac{\pi}{3}}^{\frac{\pi}{3}}[r_1(\theta)]^2\,d\theta = \dfrac{1}{2}\displaystyle\int_{-\frac{\pi}{3}}^{\frac{\pi}{3}} 2^2\,d\theta = 2[\theta]_{-\frac{\pi}{3}}^{\frac{\pi}{3}} = \dfrac{4\pi}{3}$

Area of blue section = **Area of green section**

$$= \frac{1}{2}\int_{\frac{\pi}{3}}^{\frac{\pi}{2}}[r_2(\theta)]^2\,d\theta = \frac{1}{2}\int_{\frac{\pi}{3}}^{\frac{\pi}{2}}(4\cos\theta)^2\,d\theta = \frac{4^2}{2}\int_{\frac{\pi}{3}}^{\frac{\pi}{2}}\frac{1 + \cos 2\theta}{2}\,d\theta$$

$$= 4\left[\theta + \frac{\sin 2\theta}{2}\right]_{\frac{\pi}{3}}^{\frac{\pi}{2}} = 4\left[\left(\frac{\pi}{2} + \frac{1}{2}\sin\pi\right) - \left(\frac{\pi}{3} + \frac{1}{2}\sin\frac{2\pi}{3}\right)\right] = \frac{2\pi}{3} - \sqrt{3}$$

6) So the **total area** is $\dfrac{4\pi}{3} + 2\left(\dfrac{2\pi}{3} - \sqrt{3}\right) = \dfrac{8\pi}{3} - 2\sqrt{3}$

Calculus Using Polar Coordinates

Differentiate to find the Tangent to a Polar Curve

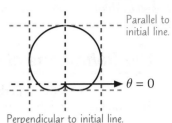

Parallel to initial line.

$\theta = 0$

Perpendicular to initial line.

1) You might be asked to find the **tangent** to a polar curve at the points where the curve is **perpendicular** or **parallel** to the **initial line**.

2) There are tangents **perpendicular** to the initial line at the points where $\dfrac{dx}{d\theta} = 0$.

3) There are tangents **parallel** to the initial line at the points where $\dfrac{dy}{d\theta} = 0$.

Example:

a) A curve has the equation $r = 1 + \sin\theta$, where $-\pi < \theta \le \pi$. Find the coordinates of the points where the tangents are perpendicular to the initial line.

> $r = 1 + \sin\theta$ is the curve shown above. You're looking for the points that have the red dotted lines as tangents.

To find the points where $\dfrac{dx}{d\theta} = 0$, first express x in terms of θ, then differentiate.

$$r = 1 + \sin\theta$$
$$x = r\cos\theta = (1 + \sin\theta)\cos\theta$$
$$\frac{dx}{d\theta} = \cos\theta\cos\theta + (1 + \sin\theta)(-\sin\theta)$$
$$= \cos^2\theta - \sin\theta - \sin^2\theta$$

> Using the product rule.

Now set this equal to zero to find the θ coordinates:

$$\cos^2\theta - \sin\theta - \sin^2\theta = 0 \Rightarrow 1 - \sin^2\theta - \sin\theta - \sin^2\theta = 0$$
$$\Rightarrow 2\sin^2\theta + \sin\theta - 1 = 0 \Rightarrow (2\sin\theta - 1)(\sin\theta + 1) = 0$$
$$\Rightarrow \sin\theta = \frac{1}{2} \text{ or } \sin\theta = -1 \Rightarrow \theta = \frac{\pi}{6}, \frac{5\pi}{6} \text{ or } \theta = -\frac{\pi}{2}$$

> This is the pole — you might see it written as just O.

Then find the corresponding r coordinates.

$$\theta = \frac{\pi}{6} \Rightarrow r = 1 + \sin\frac{\pi}{6} = \frac{3}{2}$$
$$\theta = \frac{5\pi}{6} \Rightarrow r = 1 + \sin\frac{5\pi}{6} = \frac{3}{2}$$
$$\theta = -\frac{\pi}{2} \Rightarrow r = 1 + \sin\left(-\frac{\pi}{2}\right) = 0$$

So the coordinates are $\left(\frac{3}{2}, \frac{\pi}{6}\right)$, $\left(\frac{3}{2}, \frac{5\pi}{6}\right)$ and $\left(0, -\frac{\pi}{2}\right)$.

b) Find the polar equations of the tangents to this curve at these points.

> These are the equations of the red dotted lines.

The tangents perpendicular to the initial line are the lines of constant x. So find the value of x at each point you found in a).

The tangent at the pole is just $\theta = -\frac{\pi}{2}$.

At $\left(\frac{3}{2}, \frac{\pi}{6}\right)$, $x = \frac{3}{2} \times \cos\frac{\pi}{6} = \frac{3\sqrt{3}}{4}$

At $\left(\frac{3}{2}, \frac{5\pi}{6}\right)$, $x = \frac{3}{2} \times \cos\frac{5\pi}{6} = -\frac{3\sqrt{3}}{4}$

Then replace the x with $r\cos\theta$ to find the polar equation of the tangents.

$x = \frac{3\sqrt{3}}{4} \Rightarrow r\cos\theta = \frac{3\sqrt{3}}{4}$ So $r = \frac{3\sqrt{3}}{4}\sec\theta$ is the tangent at $\frac{\pi}{6}$.

$x = -\frac{3\sqrt{3}}{4} \Rightarrow r\cos\theta = -\frac{3\sqrt{3}}{4}$ So $r = -\frac{3\sqrt{3}}{4}\sec\theta$ is the tangent at $\frac{5\pi}{6}$.

Practice Questions

Q1 Find the exact area enclosed by the curve $r = \sin\theta$.

Q2 A curve has the equation $r = 3\sqrt{2} + 3\cos\theta$ where $0 \le \theta \le \pi$.
Find the exact coordinates of the points where the tangents to the curve are perpendicular to the initial line.

Exam Questions

Q1 A curve has the equation $r = \sin\theta + \sqrt{3}\cos\theta$ where $-\pi < \theta \le \pi$.
Find the equations of the tangents to this curve that are parallel to the initial line.   [9 marks]

Q2 A region R is bounded below by the initial line and bounded above by the curves $r_1 = 2\sqrt{3}$ and $r_2 = 4\cos 3\theta$,
where $0 \le \theta \le \frac{\pi}{2}$. Sketch the region R and find its area, giving your answer to 3 significant figures.   [8 marks]

Q3 Circle 1 has equation $r_1 = 1$ and Circle 2 has equation $r_2 = 2\sin\theta$, for $0 \le \theta < 2\pi$. A is the area inside Circle 1
but outside Circle 2. Sketch A and find its area, giving your answer to 3 significant figures.   [9 marks]

I (1 – sin θ) calculus in polar coordinates...

OK, this topic isn't the easiest. But the best way to get good at this stuff is to keep familiarising yourself with polar coordinates, which means slugging your way through some long and tricky questions until you get the hang of it.

Hyperbolic Functions

I used to think nothing could be as exciting as trigonometric functions — until I met their cooler cousins, the hyperbolic functions. Get to grips with these and you'll really be in the clique.

The **Definitions** of **sinh**, **cosh** and **tanh** involve **eˣ**

The definitions of the **hyperbolic functions** are made up of exponential terms e^x and e^{-x}. You won't be given these in the formula booklet, so make sure you **learn** them.

$$\sinh x = \tfrac{1}{2}(e^x - e^{-x})$$

$$\cosh x = \tfrac{1}{2}(e^x + e^{-x})$$

$$\tanh x = \frac{\sinh x}{\cosh x}$$
$$= \frac{e^x - e^{-x}}{e^x + e^{-x}} = \frac{e^{2x} - 1}{e^{2x} + 1}$$

Each hyperbolic function has a **reciprocal**. Their names are like the reciprocal **trig** functions, but with an 'h' stuck on the end:

$$\operatorname{cosech} x = \frac{1}{\sinh x} \qquad \operatorname{sech} x = \frac{1}{\cosh x} \qquad \coth x = \frac{1}{\tanh x}$$

Pronunciations vary, but often: sinh is pronounced 'shine', or 'sinsh'. tanh is pronounced 'tanch', or 'than'. cosh is pronounced, well, 'cosh'. You can probably guess the rest...

Example: Find the value of: a) $\cosh 8 + \sinh 8$, b) $\sinh (\ln 6)$.

a) $\cosh 8 + \sinh 8 = \tfrac{1}{2}(e^8 + e^{-8}) + \tfrac{1}{2}(e^8 - e^{-8}) = e^8 = \textbf{2980.96}$ (2 d.p.)

b) $\sinh (\ln 6) = \tfrac{1}{2}(e^{\ln 6} - e^{-\ln 6})$. But $e^{\ln a} = a$ and $-\ln a = \ln\left(\tfrac{1}{a}\right)$

$\Rightarrow \sinh (\ln 6) = \tfrac{1}{2}\left(6 - \tfrac{1}{6}\right) = \tfrac{1}{2}\left(\tfrac{35}{6}\right) = \dfrac{\textbf{35}}{\textbf{12}}$

Example: Solve $11 \cosh x + 5 \sinh x = 10$. Give your answer in the form $\ln a$, where a is a fraction.

$\tfrac{11}{2}(e^x + e^{-x}) + \tfrac{5}{2}(e^x - e^{-x}) = \tfrac{11}{2}e^x + \tfrac{11}{2}e^{-x} + \tfrac{5}{2}e^x - \tfrac{5}{2}e^{-x} = 8e^x + 3e^{-x}$

$8e^x + 3e^{-x} = 10 \Rightarrow 8e^x + 3e^{-x} - 10 = 0 \Rightarrow 8e^{2x} + 3 - 10e^x = 0 \Rightarrow (2e^x - 1)(4e^x - 3) = 0$

Multiply everything by eˣ to get a 'disguised quadratic'.

$\Rightarrow e^x = \tfrac{1}{2}$ or $e^x = \tfrac{3}{4} \Rightarrow x = \ln\left(\tfrac{1}{2}\right)$ or $x = \ln\left(\tfrac{3}{4}\right)$

Hyperbolic functions have their own **Identities**

Hyperbolic identities look quite similar to **trigonometric identities**. But be warned, there are some subtle **differences**. This identity is really **important**:

Remember, $\cosh^2 x$ means $(\cosh x)^2$ and $\sinh^2 x$ means $(\sinh x)^2$.

$$\cosh^2 x - \sinh^2 x \equiv 1$$

Example: Show that $\cosh^2 x - \sinh^2 x \equiv 1$ for all values of x.

$\cosh^2 x - \sinh^2 x = \left[\tfrac{1}{2}(e^x + e^{-x})\right]^2 - \left[\tfrac{1}{2}(e^x - e^{-x})\right]^2$

$= \tfrac{1}{4}(e^x + e^{-x})^2 - \tfrac{1}{4}(e^x - e^{-x})^2$

$= \tfrac{1}{4}(e^{2x} + 2e^x e^{-x} + e^{-2x}) - \tfrac{1}{4}(e^{2x} - 2e^x e^{-x} + e^{-2x})$

$= \tfrac{1}{4}(4e^x e^{-x}) = \tfrac{1}{4} \times 4 = 1$

More Identities

Divide the identity above by $\cosh^2 x$ or $\sinh^2 x$ to get:
$1 - \tanh^2 x \equiv \operatorname{sech}^2 x$
$\coth^2 x - 1 \equiv \operatorname{cosech}^2 x$

These are the hyperbolic addition formulas:
$\sinh (x + y) \equiv \sinh x \cosh y + \cosh x \sinh y$
$\cosh (x + y) \equiv \cosh x \cosh y + \sinh x \sinh y$

Set $x = y$ in the addition formulas — you'll be given these in the formula booklet:
$\sinh 2x \equiv 2\sinh x \cosh x$
$\cosh 2x \equiv \cosh^2 x + \sinh^2 x$

Hyperbolic Functions

You can **Sketch** the **Graphs** of hyperbolic functions

Sketching hyperbolic functions is no different from sketching any other function.
The **domain** of all of the hyperbolic functions is $x \in \mathbb{R}$. Give it a whirl...

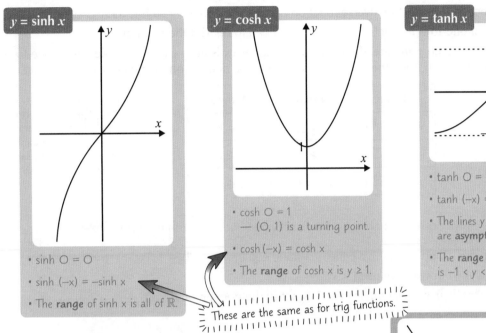

$y = \sinh x$

$y = \cosh x$

$y = \tanh x$

* $\sinh 0 = 0$
* $\sinh(-x) = -\sinh x$
* The **range** of $\sinh x$ is all of $\mathbb{R}$.

* $\cosh 0 = 1$
    — $(0, 1)$ is a turning point.
* $\cosh(-x) = \cosh x$
* The **range** of $\cosh x$ is $y \geq 1$.

* $\tanh 0 = 0$
* $\tanh(-x) = -\tanh x$
* The lines $y = 1$ and $y = -1$ are **asymptotes** to the curve.
* The **range** of $\tanh x$ is $-1 < y < 1$.

These are the same as for trig functions.

Example: Sketch the curve of $y = 2 \cosh \frac{1}{3}x$.

The graph of $\cosh x$ is stretched by a scale factor of 2 vertically...

...and is stretched by a factor of 3 horizontally.

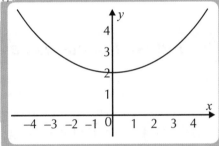

Practice Questions

Q1 Use the definitions to work out $\sinh 0$ and $\cosh 0$.

Q2 Sketch the graphs of $\tanh x$, $\tanh 2x$ and $\coth x$ on the same set of axes, for $-3 < x < 3$.

Q3 Find: a) the value of $\cosh 7$ to 2 decimal places   b) the exact value of $\tanh(\ln 4)$

Q4 Use the definitions of $\sinh x$ and $\cosh x$ to prove the identity $\sinh 2x \equiv 2 \sinh x \cosh x$.

Exam Questions

Q1 Use the fact that $\tanh x = \dfrac{\sinh x}{\cosh x}$ to show that $1 - \tanh^2 x \equiv \text{sech}^2 x$. [2 marks]

Q2 Show that $\sinh x + \sinh y = 2 \sinh\left(\frac{1}{2}(x+y)\right) \cosh\left(\frac{1}{2}(x-y)\right)$ [3 marks]

Q3 a) The curve C_1 is given as $y = 4 \cosh 2x$ and the curve C_2 is given as $y = 7 - e^{2x}$.
Sketch C_1 and C_2 on the same set of axes. Write down the coordinates of the points
of intersection between the axes and each of the curves, and the equations of any asymptotes. [4 marks]

   b) Solve the equation $7 - e^{2x} = 4 \cosh 2x$, giving your answers in an exact form. [5 marks]

Q4 Use the definitions of $\cosh k$ and $\sinh k$ in terms of e^k to show that
$\sinh(A + B) = \sinh A \cosh B + \cosh A \sinh B$. [4 marks]

Q5 Show that $\cosh(ix) = \cos x$ for all x. [4 marks]

Sketching hyperbolic function graphs can be a pain in the asymptote...

Hyperbolic functions. They're not as scary as they sound — even with all the extra h's. In fact, the hardest thing is just being able to pronounce them. Once you've mastered that, it's just a case of tackling the functions themselves...

Inverse Hyperbolic Functions

You'll have seen inverse functions countless times before now, so it'll come as no surprise that hyperbolic functions also have inverses. And they're filled with those lovely natural logarithms too — ooh, what a treat.

There are **Inverse Functions** for sinh, cosh and tanh

1) Recall that for a function $\mathbf{f}(a) = b$, the **inverse** function is $\mathbf{f^{-1}}(b) = a$. So if $x = \sinh y$, then $y = \sinh^{-1} x$.

2) Inverses only exist for **one-to-one** functions, so you may need to **restrict the domain**.

3) The functions $\sinh x$ and $\tanh x$ are already one-to-one, but $\cosh x$ is **not** — we can make $\cosh x$ one-to-one by restricting its domain to $x \geq 0$. Then the inverse, $\cosh^{-1} x$, can be defined on the range of $\cosh y$ — i.e. on $x \geq 1$.

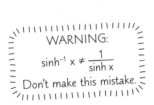
WARNING:
$\sinh^{-1} x \neq \dfrac{1}{\sinh x}$
Don't make this mistake.

Inverse	Domain	Range
$y = \sinh^{-1} x$	$x \in \mathbb{R}$	$y \in \mathbb{R}$
$y = \cosh^{-1} x$	$x \geq 1$	$y \geq 0$
$y = \tanh^{-1} x$	$-1 < x < 1$	$y \in \mathbb{R}$

You might see the inverse of $\sinh x$ written as $\sinh^{-1} x$, arsinh x or arcsinh x — they all mean the same thing. The same goes for cosh and tanh.

Example: Solve $\cosh^2 x - 2 \cosh x - 3 = 0$, leaving your answer in terms of arcosh.

Let $y = \cosh x$. Then we just have the quadratic equation $y^2 - 2y - 3 = 0 \Rightarrow y = 3, -1$.
We've found y but what we need is x:

$-1 = \cosh x$ gives **no solutions** as -1 is not in the domain of arcosh.

$3 = \cosh x \Rightarrow x = \textbf{arcosh } 3$.

The **Inverse Functions** have **Logarithmic Forms**

Hyperbolic functions are defined in terms of **exponentials**, so it shouldn't be too surprising to learn that the inverse hyperbolic functions can be written as the inverse to the exponential — the **natural log**.

$$\text{arsinh } x = \ln(x + \sqrt{x^2 + 1})$$

$$\text{arcosh } x = \ln(x + \sqrt{x^2 - 1})$$

These are all given in your formula booklet.

$$\text{artanh } x = \frac{1}{2} \ln\left(\frac{1 + x}{1 - x}\right)$$

Example: Show that arcosh $x = \ln(x + \sqrt{x^2 - 1})$.

Let $y = \text{arcosh } x$. Then $x = \cosh y = \frac{1}{2}(e^y + e^{-y})$.

Rearrange and multiply by e^y to get a **quadratic**. Then **solve** for e^y:

$$2x = e^y + e^{-y} \Rightarrow e^{2y} - 2xe^y + 1 = 0 \Rightarrow e^y = x \pm \sqrt{x^2 - 1}$$

Take logs: $y = \ln(x \pm \sqrt{x^2 - 1})$. We can ignore $\ln(x - \sqrt{x^2 - 1})$ and just take the positive value:

$$y = \text{arcosh } x = \ln(x + \sqrt{x^2 - 1})$$

If $x < 1$, this is undefined.
If $x = 1$, it's the same as the positive solution.
If $x > 1$, it's less than O but arcosh $x \geq $ O.

Log forms were Wayne's speciality.

Example: Solve $2 \cosh^3 x - 4 \cosh x = 0$. Give the solutions in exact logarithmic form.

First, simplify the equation by dividing by 2: $\cosh^3 x - 2 \cosh x = 0$. Then factorise and solve:

$$\cosh x(\cosh^2 x - 2) = 0 \Rightarrow \cosh x = 0 \text{ or } \cosh^2 x = 2$$

This factor produces no solutions as O is not in the domain of arcosh.

$$\cosh x = \pm\sqrt{2}$$

We only take $+\sqrt{2}$, because $-\sqrt{2}$ is not in the domain of arcosh.

$$x = \text{arcosh } \sqrt{2}$$
$$= \ln(\sqrt{2} + \sqrt{\sqrt{2}^2 - 1}) = \ln(\sqrt{2} + 1)$$

Inverse Hyperbolic Functions

Reflect *in y = x* to *Sketch Inverses*

You can show each of these lovely inverses with a graph too. Just like any other inverse, they're **reflections** of their corresponding hyperbolic function in the line **y = x**.

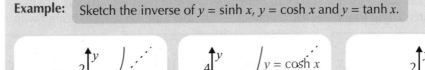

Example: Sketch the inverse of $y = \sinh x$, $y = \cosh x$ and $y = \tanh x$.

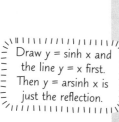

Draw y = sinh x and the line y = x first. Then y = arsinh x is just the reflection.

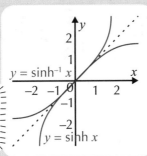
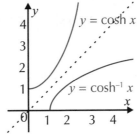
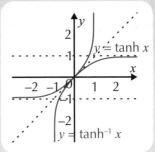

Practice Questions

Q1 Determine whether $\sinh^{-1} x$, $\cosh^{-1} x$ and $\tanh^{-1} x$ exist for each of: a) $x = 0.5$ b) $x = \sqrt{2}$ c) $x = \frac{\pi}{4}$
Where they do exist, work out their exact values.

Q2 Give the domain and range of: a) $\text{arcosh } 2x$ b) $3 \text{ arsinh } x$ c) $\text{artanh } (x + 3)$

Q3 Derive the logarithmic forms for: a) $\text{arsinh } x$ b) $\text{artanh } x$

Q4 Sketch the graphs of these functions on the same axes as their inverse: a) $f(x) = 1 + \sinh x$ b) $g(x) = \coth x$

Exam Questions

Q1 Solve the following equations and explain whether or not $\text{arcosh } x$ is defined for each of your solutions. You should give any logarithmic solutions in the form $\ln (a + \sqrt{b})$, where a and b are integers.

a) $\text{artanh } x = \ln\sqrt{5}$ [4 marks]

b) $\sinh x - 3 \text{ cosech } x = 2$ [4 marks]

Q2 The sketch below shows part of the graph of $y = h(x)$, where $h(x) = \tanh^{-1} (\sin^2 x)$.

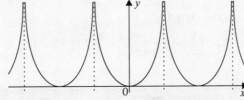

a) By considering the logarithmic definition of $\tanh^{-1} x$, prove that the lines $x = \frac{\pi}{2} + k\pi$ for all integers k correspond exactly to the asymptotes of $y = h(x)$. [4 marks]

b) Find all the values of x such that $h(x) = 0$. [2 marks]

Q3 $f(\theta) = \dfrac{2 \cosh \theta + \sinh 2\theta}{(1 + \sinh \theta)^2 + (\sqrt{2} \sinh \theta + \cosh \theta)(\sqrt{2} \sinh \theta - \cosh \theta)}$

a) Prove that $f(\theta) \equiv \coth \theta$. Explicitly state any hyperbolic identities that you use within your proof. [4 marks]

b) Determine whether $\dfrac{1}{f(\theta)}$ is invertible at $\theta = \pi$, giving a reason for your answer. [1 mark]

c) Solve $\dfrac{1}{f(\theta)} = 1 - 2 \tanh^2 \theta$, leaving any solutions in the form $\theta = \ln \sqrt{a}$, where a is an integer. [3 marks]

Magpies love inverse hyperbolics because they arsinh-y...

The three inverse hyperbolic functions all have different domains and ranges, and you'll need to know which has which to be able to choose the right answers when solving equations. If you're in the exam and not entirely sure, use your calculator to plug in some numbers — e.g. cosh⁻¹ 0 will give you an error so you know 0 isn't in arcosh's domain.

Calculus with Hyperbolics

Just when you thought hyperbolics couldn't get any more fun, here's a bit of calculus. Before you begin, remind yourself of the chain, product and quotient rules — they're going to be your best buddies on these couple of pages.

Hyperbolic Calculus is similar to Trig Calculus

It'll make things a whole lot easier if you try to **remember** these **derivatives**. They're not that different from differentiating **trigonometric** functions — but there are no signs to bother with.

$$\frac{d}{dx}\sinh x = \cosh x \qquad \frac{d}{dx}\cosh x = \sinh x \qquad \frac{d}{dx}\tanh x = \operatorname{sech}^2 x$$

Example: Show that the derivative of $\sinh x$ is $\cosh x$.

Keep in mind the definitions of the hyperbolics in terms of exponentials.

$$\frac{d}{dx}\sinh x = \frac{d}{dx}\left(\tfrac{1}{2}(e^x - e^{-x})\right) = \tfrac{1}{2}(e^x + e^{-x}) = \cosh x.$$

Example: Differentiate $\dfrac{\sinh x}{1 + \cosh x}$.

Use the quotient rule — let $f(x) = \sinh x$ and $g(x) = 1 + \cosh x$

$\Rightarrow f'(x) = \cosh x$ and $g'(x) = \sinh x$

$$\Rightarrow \frac{d}{dx}\left(\frac{\sinh x}{1 + \cosh x}\right) = \frac{d}{dx}\left(\frac{f(x)}{g(x)}\right) = \frac{f'(x)g(x) - f(x)g'(x)}{g^2(x)}$$

$$= \frac{\cosh x(\cosh x + 1) - \sinh^2 x}{(\cosh x + 1)^2}$$

$\cosh^2 x - \sinh^2 x = 1$

$$= \frac{\cosh^2 x - \sinh^2 x + \cosh x}{(\cosh x + 1)^2} = \frac{1 + \cosh x}{(1 + \cosh x)^2} = \frac{1}{1 + \cosh x}$$

Do maths on windows to make the most of the sunsinh.

Once you know the derivatives, **integrating** hyperbolic functions is now fairly straightforward. Sometimes it might help to write the hyperbolic function in its **exponential** form.

Example: Integrate the following: a) $\sinh 3x$, b) $e^{-x}\cosh x$.

Remember: $\displaystyle\int e^{kx} dx = \frac{1}{k}e^{kx} + C$

a) $\displaystyle\int \sinh 3x\, dx = \frac{1}{3}\cosh 3x + C$

b) $\displaystyle\int e^{-x}\cosh x\, dx = \int e^{-x}\left(\tfrac{1}{2}(e^x + e^{-x})\right)dx = \frac{1}{2}\int (1 + e^{-2x})\, dx = \frac{x}{2} - \frac{1}{4}e^{-2x} + C$

Differentiating Inverses involves Squares and Square Roots

Differentiating hyperbolic **inverses** is a bit trickier than it is for the standard hyperbolic functions. Luckily, they're in your **formula booklet** — and you can use the chain, product and quotient rules with them as normal.

$$\frac{d}{dx}\operatorname{arsinh} x = \frac{1}{\sqrt{1 + x^2}}$$

$$\frac{d}{dx}\operatorname{arcosh} x = \frac{1}{\sqrt{x^2 - 1}}$$

$$\frac{d}{dx}\operatorname{artanh} x = \frac{1}{1 - x^2}$$

Example: Show that $\dfrac{d}{dx}\operatorname{arcosh} x = \dfrac{1}{\sqrt{x^2 - 1}}$.

1) Let $y = \operatorname{arcosh} x$ so that $\cosh y = x$.

2) **Differentiate** with **respect** to y: $\dfrac{dx}{dy} = \sinh y$.

3) Write $\sinh y$ **in terms of cosh** y: $\dfrac{dx}{dy} = \sqrt{\cosh^2 y - 1}$.

4) **Substitute** x back in: $\dfrac{dx}{dy} = \sqrt{x^2 - 1}$.

5) **Flip it** upside down: $\dfrac{dy}{dx} = \dfrac{1}{\sqrt{x^2 - 1}}$.

This uses a rearrangement of the identity $\cosh^2 x - \sinh^2 x = 1$.

Section 8 — CP: Hyperbolic Functions

Calculus with Hyperbolics

You can use *Inverse Hyperbolics* to *Integrate Nasty* looking equations

There are yet more **integrations** below that you need to be familiar with — but luckily you'll find them in your **formula booklet**. They do look quite **similar** to some integrations involving **inverse trig**, so make sure you use the right one from the booklet. For trickier integration questions, it could help to use a **substitution**.

$$\int \frac{1}{\sqrt{a^2 + x^2}}\, dx = \text{arsinh}\, \frac{x}{a} + C$$

$$\int \frac{1}{\sqrt{x^2 - a^2}}\, dx = \text{arcosh}\, \frac{x}{a} + C \qquad (x > a)$$

$$\int \frac{1}{a^2 - x^2}\, dx = \frac{1}{a}\, \text{artanh}\, \frac{x}{a} + C$$

$$\qquad\qquad = \frac{1}{2a} \ln \left| \frac{a+x}{a-x} \right| + C \quad (|x| < a)$$

You've seen this integral already on p.53.

Example: Evaluate the following integrals:

a) $\displaystyle\int \frac{1}{\sqrt{x^2 - 36}}\, dx,$ b) $\displaystyle\int \frac{1}{\sqrt{9x^2 + 25}}\, dx$

a) $\displaystyle\int \frac{1}{\sqrt{x^2 - 36}}\, dx = \int \frac{1}{\sqrt{x^2 - 6^2}}\, dx = \text{arcosh}\, \frac{x}{6} + C$

b) Use a substitution here — let $u = 3x$.

Then $\dfrac{du}{dx} = 3 \;\Rightarrow\; dx = \dfrac{du}{3}$

So $\displaystyle\int \frac{1}{\sqrt{9x^2 + 25}}\, dx = \frac{1}{3} \int \frac{1}{\sqrt{u^2 + 25}}\, du$

$\qquad\qquad = \dfrac{1}{3}\, \text{arsinh}\, \dfrac{u}{5} + C = \dfrac{1}{3}\, \text{arsinh}\, \dfrac{3x}{5} + C$

Practice Questions

Q1 Prove that $\dfrac{d}{dx} \tanh x = \text{sech}^2 x$.

Q2 Find the derivative of $\dfrac{x}{\cosh x} - \tanh(3x^2)$ at the point $x = 2$, to 3 significant figures.

Q3 Use the quotient rule to differentiate a) $\text{sech}\, x$,   b) $\text{cosech}\, x$,   c) $\coth x$.

Q4 Calculate $\dfrac{d}{d\phi}(\text{arsinh}(\cosh \phi))$.

Q5 Use integration by parts to calculate the integral $\int x \cosh x\, dx$.

Q6 Evaluate $\displaystyle\int_0^1 \frac{1}{16 - x^2}\, dx$, giving your answer to 3 decimal places.

Exam Questions

Q1 A set of parametric equations is given as $x = 3 \sinh 2t$, $y = 2 \cosh t$.

Use these equations to express $\left(\dfrac{dx}{dt}\right)^2 + \left(\dfrac{dy}{dt}\right)^2$ in terms of $\sinh t$. [4 marks]

Q2 Calculate $\displaystyle\int_0^1 \frac{1}{\sqrt{81x^2 + 4}}\, dx$.

Give your answer in the form $a \ln \left(\dfrac{b + \sqrt{c}}{d} \right)$, where a is a fraction and b, c and d are integers. [4 marks]

Q3 $f(x) = \sinh x + 4 \cosh x$

   a) Show that $f'(x) = \frac{1}{2}(5e^x - 3e^{-x})$. [2 marks]

   b) Hence, solve $f'(x) = \sqrt{10}$. [3 marks]

Q4 The sketch to the right shows the graph of $y = \dfrac{1}{\sqrt{x^2 - 1}}$, for $x \geq 0$.

   a) Use the substitution $x = \cosh u$, $0 < u < \dfrac{\pi}{2}$, to show:

$$\int \frac{1}{\sqrt{x^2 - 1}}\, dx = \ln(x + \sqrt{x^2 - 1}) + C.$$
[4 marks]

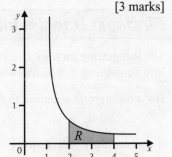

   b) The shaded region R is bounded by the curve, the x-axis and the lines $x = 2$ and $x = 4$. Calculate the exact area of the shaded region R, giving your answer as a single logarithm. [2 marks]

The greatest integral in the universe!!! — no, that's calculus with hyperbole...

If you look really quickly, you might not spot the small differences between calculus with standard trigonometric functions and calculus with hyperbolic functions. Make sure you pay attention to the negative signs — there are fewer for hyperbolics. Hoorah! And remember, a lot of these integrals will appear in the formula booklet — double hoorah!

First Order Differential Equations

You met differential equations in A-Level Maths — but that was just the tip of the iceberg... In this section, you'll meet loads of new types of differential equations (DEs for short), and see how they can be solved and what they're used for.

A *General Solution* makes a *Family of Solution Curves*

A **first order differential equation** is a DE with a **first derivative** in it — i.e. $\frac{dy}{dx}$, $\frac{dx}{dt}$, $\frac{dA}{dt}$, etc.

When solving a first order DE, you first find a **general solution** — one that has an unknown constant, say C. If you change C to **all** its possible values, you get the **family of solution curves**. You can sketch a few **members** of this family of curves by picking some different values of C.

If you're given **specific values** with your differential equation, you can use them to find the **particular solution**.

Example: a) Find the general solution to the differential equation $\frac{dy}{dx} = \frac{y}{x}$, and sketch a few members of the family of solution curves.

b) When $y = 5$, $x = 3$. Find the particular solution.

Recall from A-Level Maths that you can solve simple first order DEs by separating variables.

Separate the variables and integrate both sides:

a) $\frac{dy}{dx} = \frac{y}{x} \Rightarrow \frac{1}{y}\,dy = \frac{1}{x}\,dx \Rightarrow \int \frac{1}{y}\,dy = \int \frac{1}{x}\,dx$

$\Rightarrow \ln|y| = \ln|x| + C$

$\Rightarrow y = e^C x \Rightarrow y = kx$ (where $k = e^C$)

This can now be sketched by plugging in a few different values for k:

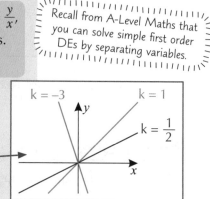

$y = 5$, $x = 3$:   b) $5 = k \times 3 \Rightarrow k = \frac{5}{3} \Rightarrow y = \frac{5}{3}x$

Recognise things that *Look* like the *Product Rule*

For a lot of differential equations, you won't just be able to separate the variables — you'll have to find **another way** to solve them. The **product rule** says that if $f(x) = u(x)v(x)$, then $\frac{df}{dx} = u\frac{dv}{dx} + v\frac{du}{dx}$, where u and v are functions of x.

If you have a differential equation where one side of the equation **looks like** the product rule, then you can solve by **integrating both sides** of the equation.

Example: Find the general solution to the differential equation $x^2\frac{dy}{dx} + 2xy = e^x$.

Notice that the left-hand side is the result of using the product rule:

$\frac{d}{dx}(x^2 y) = x^2\frac{dy}{dx} + 2xy$

Integrate both sides of the equation in the question with respect to x:

$\int \left(x^2\frac{dy}{dx} + 2xy \right) dx = \int e^x\,dx$

$\Rightarrow \int \frac{d}{dx}(x^2 y)\,dx = \int e^x\,dx \Rightarrow x^2 y = e^x + C$

The solution is general because you don't know what C is.

Find and *Use* the *Integrating Factor*

The **integrating factor** can turn a **tricky** differential equation into something that looks like the product rule.

For a differential equation in the form $\frac{dy}{dx} + P(x)y = Q(x)$, the integrating factor $I(x)$ is:

$$I(x) = e^{\int P(x)\,dx}$$

If you **multiply** each term of the DE by the integrating factor, you get: $I(x)\frac{dy}{dx} + I(x)P(x)y = I(x)Q(x)$.

You can use the **chain rule** to show that $\frac{dI}{dx} = I(x)P(x)$, which leaves the DE in the form $I(x)\frac{dy}{dx} + \frac{dI}{dx}y = I(x)Q(x)$.

The **left-hand side** now looks like the product rule, so if you **integrate both sides** you get the **equation**:

$$I(x)y = \int I(x)Q(x)\,dx$$

First Order Differential Equations

Some **Examples** of using the **Integrating Factor**

The integrating factor is a pretty **important** method for solving DEs — knowing it allows you to solve **way more** DEs than you could before. Make sure you understand these **examples**, and then **have a go** yourself.

Example: Find the particular solution to $\frac{dy}{dx} + y \tan x = \sec x$, given that $y = 2$ when $x = 0$.

Find the integrating factor: $P(x) = \tan x$ so $I(x) = e^{\int \tan x\, dx} = e^{\ln \sec x} = \sec x$

The DE is in the form $dy/dx + P(x)y = Q(x)$

Multiply the DE by the IF: $\frac{dy}{dx} \sec x + y \tan x \sec x = \sec^2 x \Rightarrow \frac{d}{dx}(y \sec x) = \sec^2 x$

Integrate both sides: $\int \frac{d}{dx}(y \sec x)\, dx = \int \sec^2 x\, dx \Rightarrow y \sec x = \tan x + C$

$\Rightarrow y = \frac{\tan x + C}{\sec x} \Rightarrow y = \sin x + C \cos x$

$y = 2$ when $x = 0$: $2 = \sin 0 + C \cos 0 \Rightarrow C = 2$, so $y = \sin x + 2 \cos x$

You might need to first **write** a DE before solving it — a classic setup for this is a **mixing problem**:

Example: A tank contains 800 litres of water, mixed with a powdered dye. Pure water is pumped in at a rate of 3 litres/second. The mix is well-stirred, and pumped out at a rate of 4 litres/second.

Find the equation that gives the amount of dye, y, in the tank after t seconds, given that there is a dye concentration of 15 grams/litre at $t = 0$.

If y is the amount of dye in the tank, then $\frac{dy}{dt}$ is the **rate of change** of dye in the tank.

Let V be the volume of the water-dye mix in the tank. Then $\frac{y}{V}$ is the **dye concentration**.
So the amount of dye being pumped out is $4\frac{y}{V}$ grams/second.

The mix is well-stirred, so you can assume that the concentration is equal throughout the whole tank.

V isn't constant — it can be written as a function of time: $V = 800 + 3t - 4t = 800 - t$.

Putting all this together gives a differential equation: $\frac{dy}{dt} = -4\frac{y}{V} \Rightarrow \frac{dy}{dt} + \frac{4y}{800-t} = 0$

So the integrating factor is $I(t) = e^{\int P(t)\, dt} = e^{\int \frac{4}{800-t}\, dt} = e^{-4\ln(800-t)} = (800-t)^{-4}$.

You could use separation of variables here too.

Multiply the DE by the IF: $(800-t)^{-4}\frac{dy}{dt} + 4(800-t)^{-5}y = 0 \Rightarrow \frac{d}{dt}((800-t)^{-4}y) = 0$

$\Rightarrow \int \frac{d}{dt}(y(800-t)^{-4})\, dt = \int 0\, dt \Rightarrow y(800-t)^{-4} = C \Rightarrow y = C(800-t)^4$

At t = 0, there is 800 × 15 g of dye in the tank $\to y(0) = 800 \times 15 = C(800-0)^4 \Rightarrow C = \frac{12\,000}{800^4}$

$\Rightarrow y = 12\,000\left(\frac{800-t}{800}\right)^4$

Practice Questions

Q1 Find the general solution to each of the following, and sketch two members of the family of solution curves:

a) $\frac{dy}{dx} = -\frac{y}{x}$

b) $\frac{dy}{dx} = -\frac{x}{y}$

Q2 Find the integrating factors of the following first order differential equations:

a) $\frac{dy}{dx} + \frac{4y}{x} = e^x \sin x$

b) $\frac{dy}{dx} + \frac{y}{\cos x} = e^{x^2}$

c) $2\frac{dy}{dx} + \frac{y}{\cot x} = 3 \tan x$

Q3 For the differential equation $\frac{dy}{dx} + P(x)y = Q(x)$, show that if $I(x) = e^{\int P(x)\, dx}$, then $\frac{dI}{dx} = I(x)P(x)$.

Exam Question

Q1 The number of caterpillars, C, in a region after t months can be modelled by the equation $\frac{dC}{dt} + \left(\frac{1}{\ln 5}\right)C + 10t = 0$

Find an equation for $C(t)$, given that there are 200 caterpillars at $t = 0$. [5 marks]

General Solution — a clear sign of superhero franchises scraping the barrel...

There's a lot going on in the mixing problem example — make sure you understand why you do each step.
I find that drawing a picture helps — add labels to show what is being pumped in and out of the tank every second.

Second Order Differential Equations

A second order differential equation is a DE with a second derivative in it. Simple. There are lots of different cases that you need to remember here — so make sure you've got your memorising cap on.

Use the **Auxiliary Equation** to tell you the **Form** of the general solution

If you have a **second order differential equation** in the form $a\dfrac{d^2y}{dx^2} + b\dfrac{dy}{dx} + cy = 0$, where a, b and c are all real constants, then there's a **clever method** you can use to find the **general solution**...

Solving the differential equation $a\dfrac{d^2y}{dx^2} + b\dfrac{dy}{dx} + cy = 0$, where a, b and c are real constants

- Write a quadratic using the coefficients: $a\lambda^2 + b\lambda + c = 0$ — this is the **auxiliary equation**.
- Calculate the **discriminant** $b^2 - 4ac$.
- Solve the auxiliary equation and use the table below to determine the **general solution** — A and B are unknown constants.

Discriminant	Roots of the auxiliary equation	General solution of the DE
$b^2 - 4ac > 0$	two distinct real roots: α and β	$y = Ae^{\alpha x} + Be^{\beta x}$
$b^2 - 4ac = 0$	repeated real root: α	$y = (A + Bx)e^{\alpha x}$
$b^2 - 4ac < 0$	two distinct complex roots: $p \pm iq$	$y = e^{px}(A \cos qx + B \sin qx)$

These are a complex conjugate pair.

Example: Find the general solution to the second order differential equation $\dfrac{d^2y}{dx^2} + \dfrac{dy}{dx} - 6y = 0$.

The auxiliary equation is $\lambda^2 + \lambda - 6 = 0$ (a = 1, b = 1 and c = −6)

Find the discriminant: $b^2 - 4ac = 1^2 - 4 \times 1 \times (-6) = 25 > 0$.

Using the table above, the solution will have the form $y = Ae^{\alpha x} + Be^{\beta x}$.

Solve the A.E.: $\lambda^2 + \lambda - 6 = 0 \Rightarrow (\lambda + 3)(\lambda - 2) = 0 \Rightarrow \lambda = -3$ or $\lambda = 2$

So the general solution is $y = Ae^{-3x} + Be^{2x}$

For a **Particular Solution**, you'll need **Two Conditions**

There are **two constants** in the general solution, so if you're asked for a **particular solution**, you need **two** extra pieces of information. Often you'll be given values for y and $\dfrac{dy}{dx}$ when $x = 0$, or values for x and $\dfrac{dx}{dt}$ when $t = 0$.

Example: Find the particular solution to the differential equation $4\ddot{x} + 12\dot{x} + 9x = 0$, given that at $t = 0$, $x = 1$ and $\dot{x} = 3$.

$\dot{x}$ is just another way of writing $\dfrac{dx}{dt}$. Similarly, $\ddot{x} = \dfrac{d^2x}{dt^2}$, $\dddot{x} = \dfrac{d^3x}{dt^3}$, etc.

The auxiliary equation is $4\lambda^2 + 12\lambda + 9 = 0$

Find the discriminant: $b^2 - 4ac = 12^2 - 4 \times 4 \times 9 = 144 - 144 = 0$.

Using the table above, the solution will have the form $x = (A + Bt)e^{\alpha t}$.

Solve the A.E.: $4\lambda^2 + 12\lambda + 9 = 0 \Rightarrow \left(\lambda + \dfrac{3}{2}\right)^2 = 0 \Rightarrow \lambda = -\dfrac{3}{2}$

So the general solution is $x = (A + Bt)e^{-\frac{3}{2}t}$

At t = 0, x = 1: $1 = (A + B(0))e^{-\frac{3}{2}(0)} \Rightarrow A = 1$

Find $\dot{x}$ by differentiating using the product rule: $x = (A + Bt)e^{-\frac{3}{2}t} \Rightarrow \dot{x} = -\dfrac{3}{2}(A + Bt)e^{-\frac{3}{2}t} + Be^{-\frac{3}{2}t}$

At t = 0, $\dot{x}$ = 3: $3 = -\dfrac{3}{2}(A + B(0))e^{-\frac{3}{2}(0)} + Be^{-\frac{3}{2}(0)} \Rightarrow 3 = -\dfrac{3}{2}A + B$

A = 1: $\Rightarrow 3 = -\dfrac{3}{2} + B \Rightarrow B = 3 + \dfrac{3}{2} = \dfrac{9}{2}$

So the particular solution to the differential equation is $x = \left(1 + \dfrac{9}{2}t\right)e^{-\frac{3}{2}t}$

Second Order Differential Equations

Example: Find the general solution to the second order differential equation $\frac{d^2y}{dx^2} - 4\frac{dy}{dx} + 9y = 0$, given that at $x = 0$, $y = -1$ and $\frac{dy}{dx} = -2$.

The auxiliary equation is $\lambda^2 - 4\lambda + 9 = 0$ ($a = 1$, $b = -4$ and $c = 9$)

Find the discriminant: $b^2 - 4ac = (-4)^2 - 4 \times 1 \times 9 = 16 - 36 = -20 < 0$.

From the table, the solution will have the form $y = e^{px}(A \cos qx + B \sin qx)$.

Solve the A.E.: $\lambda^2 - 4\lambda + 9 = 0 \Rightarrow \lambda = \frac{4 \pm \sqrt{(-4)^2 - 4 \times 1 \times 9}}{2} = \frac{4 \pm \sqrt{-20}}{2} = \frac{4 \pm 2\sqrt{-5}}{2} = 2 \pm \sqrt{5}i$

So the general solution is $y = e^{2x}(A \cos \sqrt{5}\,x + B \sin \sqrt{5}\,x)$.

At $x = 0$, $y = -1$: $-1 = A \Rightarrow A = -1$

Use the product rule: $\frac{dy}{dx} = e^{2x}(-\sqrt{5}\,A \sin \sqrt{5}\,x + \sqrt{5}\,B \cos \sqrt{5}\,x) + 2e^{2x}(A \cos \sqrt{5}\,x + B \sin \sqrt{5}\,x)$

At $x = 0$, $\frac{dy}{dx} = -2$: $-2 = \sqrt{5}\,B + 2A \Rightarrow B = 0$

So the particular solution is $y = -e^{2x} \cos \sqrt{5}\,x$

As $B = 0$, $\sin x$ doesn't appear in the particular solution.

Second Order DEs have Applications in Mechanics and Physics

Lots of real-life problems can be **modelled** using second order differential equations — springs (p.83-85), pendulums and electrical circuits are just a few examples.

Example: The current, $I(t)$, in a series circuit satisfies the differential equation $L\frac{d^2I}{dt^2} + R\frac{dI}{dt} + \frac{1}{C}I = 0$. Find a general solution for $I(t)$, given that $L = 2$, $R = 2$ and $C = 0.2$.

L, R and C have **meaning** (they're to do with inductance, resistance and capacitance respectively), but there isn't any new maths here — it's a second order DE that you can **solve**.

Put in the **constants** you've been given: $2\frac{d^2I}{dt^2} + 2\frac{dI}{dt} + 5I = 0$.

The **auxiliary equation** is: $2\lambda^2 + 2\lambda + 5 = 0$

$$\lambda = \frac{-2 \pm \sqrt{2^2 - 4 \times 2 \times 5}}{4} = \frac{-2 \pm \sqrt{-36}}{4} = \frac{-2 \pm 6i}{4} = -\frac{1}{2} \pm \frac{3}{2}i$$

So the **general solution** is: $I(t) = e^{-\frac{1}{2}t}(A \cos \frac{3}{2}t + B \sin \frac{3}{2}t)$

Think about the solution in the context. For large t, $e^{-\frac{1}{2}t}$ is really small, so you'd expect the current to be small after a long period of time.

Practice Questions

Q1 Find the general solutions to the following second order differential equations:

a) $\frac{d^2y}{dx^2} + 16y = 0$

b) $\ddot{x} + 15\dot{x} + 56x = 0$

c) $3\frac{d^2y}{dx^2} - 2\frac{dy}{dx} - 8y = 0$

Q2 Find the particular solution to $\frac{d^2y}{dx^2} - 6\frac{dy}{dx} + 9y = 0$, given that at $x = 0$, $y = -1$ and $\frac{dy}{dx} = 1$.

Exam Question

Q1 A differential equation is given by $\frac{d^2y}{dx^2} = \delta\frac{dy}{dx} - \varepsilon y$, where δ and ε are constants and $\delta^2 = 4\varepsilon$.

At $x = 0$, $y = 0$ and $\frac{dy}{dx} = 1$. At $x = 1$, $\ln y = 4$.

Find the values of δ and ε and give the particular solution to the differential equation. [7 marks]

You enjoyed DEs so much, you've come back for seconds...

Second order differential equations might seem quite scary at first, but there actually isn't much to them. Once you've learnt the different cases and solutions then you're sorted — easy marks for you to pick up in your exam.

Section 9 — CP: Differential Equations

Tougher Second Order Differential Equations

The previous two pages were really just the beginning — these next few pages are going to cover even tougher second order DEs. And if you think you're done with that memorising cap, you can think again...

The **Complementary Function** and the **Particular Integral**

You could be given a DE with a **function** on the right-hand side — i.e. $a\dfrac{d^2y}{dx^2} + b\dfrac{dy}{dx} + cy = f(x)$.

Let $g(x)$ be a solution to $a\dfrac{d^2y}{dx^2} + b\dfrac{dy}{dx} + cy = 0$. And let $h(x)$ be a solution to $a\dfrac{d^2y}{dx^2} + b\dfrac{dy}{dx} + cy = f(x)$.

Then $g(x) + h(x)$ is **also** a solution to $a\dfrac{d^2y}{dx^2} + b\dfrac{dy}{dx} + cy = f(x)$.

(You can show this by putting $y = g + h$ into the differential equation, and rearranging.)

$g(x)$ is known as the **complementary function** (or **CF**), and $h(x)$ is known as the **particular integral** (or **PI**). You need **both bits** for the solution to the DE — so the general solution is: $\boxed{y = CF + PI}$

The previous two pages showed you how to find the CF. Finding the particular integral is a **bit trickier** — you'll need to use a **substitution**. Which substitution you should use depends on whether $f(x)$ is **polynomial**, **trigonometric** or **exponential**. The table below gives a summary:

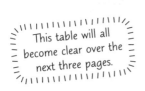
This table will all become clear over the next three pages.

$f(x)$	Substitution
c	γ
$bx + c$	$\beta x + \gamma$
$ax^2 + bx + c$	$\alpha x^2 + \beta x + \gamma$
Pe^{px}	Qe^{px} (or Qxe^{px}, or Qx^2e^{px})
$r\cos\omega x + s\sin\omega x$	$\rho\cos\omega x + \sigma\sin\omega x$

My new function was particularly well received.

You can find the **unknown coefficients** by putting the substitution into the DE, and **equating coefficients**.

To find a **particular solution**, you'll need to use the **boundary conditions** (given values of y, y' or y''). Only put them into the **complete** general solution — don't put them in **too early** when you only have the CF or the PI.

If f(x) is a **Polynomial**, use a **Polynomial Substitution** of the **Same Degree**

To find the **particular integral** when $f(x)$ is a **polynomial**, the substitution you need to use is a polynomial with the **same degree** as $f(x)$. So if there's an x^2 term in $f(x)$, make sure there's an x^2 term in your substitution.

Example: Solve $\dfrac{d^2y}{dx^2} + 2\dfrac{dy}{dx} + y = 9 - x$, given that at $x = 0$, $y = \dfrac{dy}{dx} = 15$.

Just use the method shown on p.78-79 to do this.

You can show that the **complementary function** is $y = (A + Bx)e^{-x}$

$f(x) = 9 - x$, so use the substitution $y = \beta x + \gamma$ to find the **particular integral**:

Differentiate the substitution: $\dfrac{dy}{dx} = \beta$, and $\dfrac{d^2y}{dx^2} = 0$. Substituting these into the DE gives:

$$0 + 2\beta + \beta x + \gamma = 9 - x$$

Equate the coefficients: $\beta x = -x \Rightarrow \beta = -1$, and $2\beta + \gamma = 9 \Rightarrow -2 + \gamma = 9 \Rightarrow \gamma = 11$

So the PI is $y = -x + 11$

$y = CF + PI$: The general solution is $y = (A + Bx)e^{-x} - x + 11$

Now that you have the **complete** general solution, you can use the boundary conditions:

At $x = 0$, $y = 15$: $15 = (A + B(0))e^{-0} - 0 + 11 \Rightarrow A = 4$

Find $\dfrac{dy}{dx}$: $\dfrac{dy}{dx} = -(A + Bx)e^{-x} + Be^{-x} - 1$

At $x = 0$, $\dfrac{dy}{dx} = 15$: $15 = -(A + B(0))e^{-0} + Be^{-0} - 1 \Rightarrow B - A = 16 \Rightarrow B = 20$

So $y = (4 + 20x)e^{-x} - x + 11$

Tougher Second Order Differential Equations

If f(x) is *Exponential*, your *Substitution* will *Depend* on the *CF*

If $f(x) = Pe^{px}$, where p and P are real constants, then you should first **try** the substitution $y = Qe^{px}$.

Example: Find the general solution to $\dfrac{d^2y}{dx^2} + 3\dfrac{dy}{dx} - 10y = 4e^{3x}$.

Find the **complementary function** by finding the general solution to $\dfrac{d^2y}{dx^2} + 3\dfrac{dy}{dx} - 10y = 0$:

Write and solve the auxiliary equation:
$$\lambda^2 + 3\lambda - 10 = 0 \implies (\lambda - 2)(\lambda + 5) = 0 \implies \lambda = 2 \text{ or } \lambda = -5$$
There are two distinct real roots, so the CF is $y = Ae^{2x} + Be^{-5x}$

Use the **substitution** $y = Qe^{3x}$ to find the **PI**:

Find $\dfrac{dy}{dx}$ and $\dfrac{d^2y}{dx^2}$: $\quad \dfrac{dy}{dx} = 3Qe^{3x}$ and $\dfrac{d^2y}{dx^2} = 9Qe^{3x}$

Substitute into the DE: $\quad 9Qe^{3x} + 3(3Qe^{3x}) - 10Qe^{3x} = 4e^{3x}$
$$\implies 8Qe^{3x} = 4e^{3x} \implies 8Q = 4 \implies Q = \frac{1}{2}.$$
So the particular integral is $y = \frac{1}{2}e^{3x}$.

$y = CF + PI$: $\implies$ The general solution is $y = Ae^{2x} + Be^{-5x} + \frac{1}{2}e^{3x}$

If there's **already** a ke^{px} term (where k is a constant) in the **CF**, then the usual substitution of $y = Qe^{px}$ won't work. You'll need to **try** the substitution $y = Qxe^{px}$. And if there's already a kxe^{px} term in the CF, then try $y = Qx^2e^{px}$.

> More generally, if there's a multiple of **f(x)** in the **complementary function**, your usual choice of substitution **won't work**. If this happens, try **multiplying** the substitution by **x** until you find something that does work.

Example: Solve $\dfrac{d^2y}{dx^2} - 4\dfrac{dy}{dx} + 4y = 8e^{2x}$, given that at $x = 0$, $\dfrac{dy}{dx} = 7$ and $\dfrac{d^2y}{dx^2} = 8$.

Find the **complementary function** by finding the general solution to $\dfrac{d^2y}{dx^2} - 4\dfrac{dy}{dx} + 4y = 0$:

Write and solve the auxiliary equation:
$$\lambda^2 - 4\lambda + 4 = 0 \implies (\lambda - 2)^2 = 0 \implies \lambda = 2$$
There is one repeated real root. So the CF is $y = (A + Bx)e^{2x}$.

The complementary function is $y = Ae^{2x} + Bxe^{2x}$. This already contains **both** a ke^{2x} term **and** a kxe^{2x} term, so neither $y = Qe^{2x}$ nor $y = Qxe^{2x}$ will work. So you need to use the **substitution** $y = Qx^2e^{2x}$:

Find $\dfrac{dy}{dx}$ and $\dfrac{d^2y}{dx^2}$: $\quad \dfrac{dy}{dx} = 2Qxe^{2x} + 2Qx^2e^{2x}$

$\implies \dfrac{d^2y}{dx^2} = 2Qe^{2x} + 4Qxe^{2x} + 4Qxe^{2x} + 4Qx^2e^{2x} = 2Qe^{2x} + 8Qxe^{2x} + 4Qx^2e^{2x}$

Sub into the DE: $2Qe^{2x} + 8Qxe^{2x} + 4Qx^2e^{2x} - 4(2Qxe^{2x} + 2Qx^2e^{2x}) + 4Qx^2e^{2x} = 8e^{2x}$
$$\implies 2Q + 8Qx + 4Qx^2 - 4(2Qx + 2Qx^2) + 4Qx^2 = 8$$
$$\implies 2Q = 8 \implies Q = 4$$
So the particular integral is $y = 4x^2e^{2x}$.

$y = CF + PI$: $\implies$ The general solution is $y = (A + Bx)e^{2x} + 4x^2e^{2x} \implies y = (A + Bx + 4x^2)e^{2x}$

Now that you have the **complete** general solution, you can use the boundary conditions:

Find $\dfrac{dy}{dx}$: $\quad \dfrac{dy}{dx} = (B + 8x)e^{2x} + 2(A + Bx + 4x^2)e^{2x}$

At $x = 0$, $\dfrac{dy}{dx} = 7$: $\quad 7 = (B + 8(0))e^{2(0)} + 2(A + B(0) + 4(0)^2)e^{2(0)} = B + 2A$

Find $\dfrac{d^2y}{dx^2}$: $\quad \dfrac{d^2y}{dx^2} = 8e^{2x} + 2(B + 8x)e^{2x} + 2(B + 8x)e^{2x} + 4(A + Bx + 4x^2)e^{2x}$

At $x = 0$, $\dfrac{d^2y}{dx^2} = 8$: $\quad 8 = 8e^{2(0)} + 2(B + 8(0))e^{2(0)} + 2(B + 8(0))e^{2(0)} + 4(A + B(0) + 4(0)^2)e^{2(0)} = 8 + 4A + 4B$

Solve simultaneously: $A + B = 0 \implies B = -A \implies 7 = -A + 2A \implies A = 7 \implies B = -7$.
$$\text{So } y = (4x^2 - 7x + 7)e^{2x}$$

Tougher Second Order Differential Equations

If f(x) is *Trigonometric*, your *Substitution* needs *Both Sin And Cos*

If $f(x) = r \cos \omega x + s \sin \omega x$, then you need to use the substitution $y = \rho \cos \omega x + \sigma \sin \omega x$.
You need to use the full substitution **even if** there's **only** a cos or sin term in $f(x)$ (i.e. if $r = 0$ or $s = 0$)
— if you don't have both a sin and a cos term in the substitution, it **won't work**.

Example: Find the general solution to $\dfrac{d^2y}{dx^2} - 4\dfrac{dy}{dx} + 3y = 6 \cos 3x$.

Find the **complementary function** by finding the general solution to $\dfrac{d^2y}{dx^2} - 4\dfrac{dy}{dx} + 3y = 0$:

$$\lambda^2 - 4\lambda + 3 = 0 \implies (\lambda - 3)(\lambda - 1) = 0 \implies \lambda = 1 \text{ or } \lambda = 3$$

There are two distinct real roots, so the CF is $y = Ae^x + Be^{3x}$

$f(x) = 6 \cos 3x$, so use the substitution $y = \rho \cos 3x + \sigma \sin 3x$
to find the **particular integral**:

Remember to include both sin and cos in the substitution.

Find $\dfrac{dy}{dx}$ and $\dfrac{d^2y}{dx^2}$: $\quad \dfrac{dy}{dx} = -3\rho \sin 3x + 3\sigma \cos 3x$, and $\dfrac{d^2y}{dx^2} = -9\rho \cos 3x - 9\sigma \sin 3x$.

Substituting these into the DE gives:

$-9\rho \cos 3x - 9\sigma \sin 3x - 4(-3\rho \sin 3x + 3\sigma \cos 3x) + 3(\rho \cos 3x + \sigma \sin 3x) = 6 \cos 3x$

$\implies -9\rho \cos 3x - 9\sigma \sin 3x + 12\rho \sin 3x - 12\sigma \cos 3x + 3\rho \cos 3x + 3\sigma \sin 3x = 6 \cos 3x$

$\implies (-6\rho - 12\sigma)\cos 3x + (12\rho - 6\sigma)\sin 3x = 6 \cos 3x$

Equate the coefficients of sin 3x: $\quad 12\rho - 6\sigma = 0 \implies 2\rho = \sigma$

Equate the coefficients of cos 3x: $\quad -6\rho - 12\sigma = 6 \implies -6\rho - 24\rho = -30\rho = 6 \implies \rho = -\dfrac{1}{5}, \sigma = -\dfrac{2}{5}$

So the PI is $y = -\dfrac{1}{5} \cos 3x - \dfrac{2}{5} \sin 3x$

$y = \text{CF} + \text{PI}$: $\quad$ The general solution is $y = Ae^x + Be^{3x} - \dfrac{1}{5} \cos 3x - \dfrac{2}{5} \sin 3x$

Practice Questions

Q1 Show that if $g(x)$ is a solution to $a\dfrac{d^2y}{dx^2} + b\dfrac{dy}{dx} + cy = 0$ and $h(x)$ is a solution to $a\dfrac{d^2y}{dx^2} + b\dfrac{dy}{dx} + cy = f(x)$,
then $g(x) + h(x)$ is also a solution to $a\dfrac{d^2y}{dx^2} + b\dfrac{dy}{dx} + cy = f(x)$

Q2 Find the general solutions to the following:

a) $\dfrac{d^2y}{dx^2} - 2\dfrac{dy}{dx} = 4 \cos 2x + 7 \sin 2x$ $\qquad$ b) $\dfrac{d^2y}{dx^2} - 4y = 24e^{\frac{2}{3}x}$

Q3 Find the particular solution to $\dfrac{d^2y}{dx^2} + 2\dfrac{dy}{dx} + y = x^2 + 2x + 1$ given that at $x = 0$, $y = 7$ and $\dfrac{dy}{dx} = 3$

Exam Question

Q1 $y(x)$ satisfies the differential equation $\dfrac{d^2y}{dx^2} + 2\dfrac{dy}{dx} + 5y = \sin 3x$, for $x \geq 0$

a) Find the general solution to this differential equation. [7 marks]

At $x = 0$, $y = 5$ and $\dfrac{dy}{dx} = 0$.

b) Find the particular solution to this differential equation. [3 marks]

You're on track to be a DE genius — just fulfilling my complimentary function...

These tougher second order DEs aren't really all that tough — they usually just have a lot of steps and take a while.
The good news is that they're probably going to be worth a fair few marks, so get these right and you'll be laughing...

Harmonic Motion

Now for a sneaky bit of mechanics... an object moving with harmonic motion can be described by a second order DE.
These pages will focus on horizontal springs, but you can apply the same principles to other situations too.

Simple Harmonic Motion can be written as a Second Order DE

1) Recall that Newton's Second Law says the overall resultant force = mass × acceleration ($F_{net} = ma$).
   For displacement x, velocity $v = \dfrac{dx}{dt} = \dot{x}$ and acceleration $a = \dfrac{dv}{dt} = \dfrac{d^2x}{dt^2} = \ddot{x}$. Since acceleration is a
   second derivative, you can use the above facts to **write** second order DEs to solve problems in **kinematics**.

2) If an object is moving with **simple harmonic motion (SHM)**, the only force acting on it is **proportional**
   to the **displacement**, but in the **opposite direction** — i.e. $F = -kx$, where k is a positive constant.
   The force **increases** as you get further from the **starting position**.

3) So $F = ma \Rightarrow -kx = ma = m\ddot{x}$, which means $\ddot{x} = -\dfrac{k}{m}x$. This is often written as: $\boxed{\ddot{x} = -\omega^2 x}$

   k/m is written as ω^2 to show the constant is always positive.

4) SHM is clearly a **second order DE** — one that you can easily **solve**:

   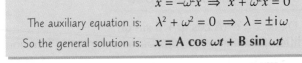

   $$\ddot{x} = -\omega^2 x \Rightarrow \ddot{x} + \omega^2 x = 0$$
   The auxiliary equation is: $\quad \lambda^2 + \omega^2 = 0 \Rightarrow \lambda = \pm i\omega$
   So the general solution is: $\quad x = A\cos\omega t + B\sin\omega t$

   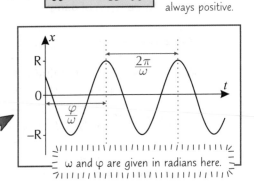

5) You can rewrite the **general solution** using R addition formulas
   (from A-Level Maths) as $x = R\cos(\omega t - \varphi)$ and **sketch** the curve.

6) The displacement **oscillates** either side of the resting position ($x = 0$).
   If **no other forces** act on the object, it'll carry on like this **forever**.

ω and φ are given in radians here.

A **mass on a spring** is one example of a system that has SHM. In this system, k is the **spring constant**
(or stiffness constant), and the spring exerts a 'restoring force' on the mass towards its resting position:

- The 'Resting' diagram on the right shows a **block** with mass m
  resting on a **frictionless surface**, attached to a wall by a **spring**.
  It's at rest, meaning the spring **isn't** being stretched or squished.

- On the 'Extended' diagram, the block is being **held**
  at a **displacement** of x from its resting position.

- When the block is **released**, the block will move back **towards**
  and **past** the resting position, **compressing** the spring, then
  move away again. There is **no friction**, so the mass will continue to **oscillate** forever.

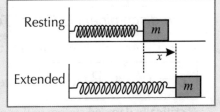

Example: A particle is attached to a spring on a smooth surface, as shown on the right.
The particle (mass 5 kg) is pulled 0.5 m away from its resting position,
A, and released. The spring exerts a force on the particle of $0.8x$ N
towards A, and the particle moves with an initial speed of 0.4 ms⁻¹ towards A.
Find an equation for the displacement, x, of the particle at time t.
Give your answer in the form $x = R\cos(\omega t + \varphi)$, where R, ω and φ are constants to be found.

Take 'right' as positive and use F = ma. $F = ma \Rightarrow -0.8x = 5\ddot{x} \Rightarrow \ddot{x} = -0.16x$
     Rearrange to get $\ddot{x} + 0.16x = 0$ and solve as usual.

Write and solve the auxiliary equation: $\lambda^2 + 0.16 = 0 \Rightarrow \lambda = \sqrt{-0.16} = \pm 0.4i$
     So the **general solution** is $x = A\cos 0.4t + B\sin 0.4t$

Rewrite the general solution using the   This can be written as $x = R\cos(0.4t - \varphi)$
R addition formulas, and find $\dot{x}$.   Then $\dot{x} = -0.4R\sin(0.4t - \varphi)$

At t = 0, x = 0.5: $R\cos(-\varphi) = R\cos\varphi = 0.5$ ①
At t = 0, $\dot{x}$ = −0.4: $-0.4R\sin(-\varphi) = 0.4R\sin\varphi = -0.4 \Rightarrow R\sin\varphi = -1$ ②

Solve the simultaneous equations: $①^2 + ②^2 \Rightarrow R^2 = 1.25 \Rightarrow R = \dfrac{\sqrt{5}}{2}$

     $② \div ① \Rightarrow \tan\varphi = -2 \Rightarrow \varphi = -1.107... = -1.11$ radians (3 s.f)

     So $x = \dfrac{\sqrt{5}}{2}\cos(0.4t + 1.11)$

Harmonic Motion

Damping makes things a bit more Complicated

Simple harmonic motion is '**simple**' because it assumes there's no **resistive force** (e.g. **friction**).
You can **factor in** resistance to make what's called **damped harmonic motion** — 'damping' is essentially the act of **stopping the oscillations**. The model is then more **realistic**, but it does makes the maths a little bit tougher.

Resistance can be **modelled** as being **proportional to the velocity**, acting in the direction **opposite** to motion
— i.e $-r\frac{dx}{dt}$, where r is a non-negative constant. Adding this resistance term to the equation for SHM gives:

$$m\frac{d^2x}{dt^2} = -kx - r\frac{dx}{dt} \Rightarrow \boxed{m\frac{d^2x}{dt^2} + r\frac{dx}{dt} + kx = 0}$$

The auxiliary equation for this DE is $m\lambda^2 + r\lambda + k = 0$, which has discriminant $r^2 - 4mk$.
There are **three** types of **damping**, depending on the value of this **discriminant**.

If the discriminant is Less Than Zero, the system is Underdamped

When $r^2 - 4mk < 0$, the **solution** to the second order DE is $x = e^{pt}(A\cos qt + B\sin qt)$.
Just like on the previous page, you can use the **R addition formulas** to rewrite this as a single trig function:

$$\boxed{x = Re^{pt}\cos(ut - \varphi)}$$ (where $u = \frac{\sqrt{4mk - r^2}}{2m}$, $p = -\frac{r}{2m}$ and R and φ are unknown constants)

By looking at the **graph** for this on the right, you can see
that the oscillations gradually **get smaller** and smaller,
with the maximum displacement tending towards zero.
The system is not damped enough to stop the
oscillations completely — hence it is **underdamped**.

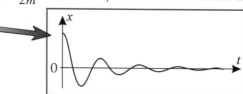

If the discriminant is Equal To Zero, the system is Critically Damped

When $r^2 - 4mk = 0$, the **solution** to the second order DE is:

$$\boxed{x = (A + Bt)e^{-\omega t}}$$ (where $\omega = \frac{r}{2m} = \sqrt{\frac{k}{m}}$ and A and B are unknown constants)

A **critically damped** system will come to rest in the **quickest possible time**.

If the discriminant is Greater Than Zero, the system is Overdamped

When $r^2 - 4mk > 0$, the **solution** to the second order DE is:

$$\boxed{x = Ae^{\alpha t} + Be^{\beta t}}$$ (where $\alpha, \beta = \frac{-r \pm \sqrt{r^2 - 4mk}}{2m}$, α and β are always negative.

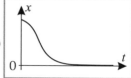

and A and B are unknown constants).

This is **overdamped** because it comes to rest without oscillating,
but takes a **longer time** than a critically damped system.

> **Example:** A particle of mass 17.5 kg is moving on a rough surface. It experiences
> a resistive force equal to its velocity multiplied by a constant, r.
> The particle is attached to a wall by a spring with spring constant k = 0.7 Nm⁻¹.
> Find the value (or range of values) for r that would make the system:
> i) underdamped   ii) overdamped   iii) critically damped

The **auxiliary equation** for this system is $17.5\lambda^2 + r\lambda + 0.7 = 0$.

Find the discriminant: $r^2 - 4 \times 17.5 \times 0.7 = r^2 - 49$

For underdamped: i) $r^2 - 49 < 0 \Rightarrow r^2 < 49 \Rightarrow -7 < r < 7$.
                       r can't be negative, so for an underdamped system, $\mathbf{0 \leq r < 7}$.

Similarly: ii) for overdamped, $r^2 - 49 > 0 \Rightarrow \mathbf{r > 7}$.
              iii) for critically damped, $r^2 - 49 = 0 \Rightarrow \mathbf{r = 7}$.

Harmonic Motion

Forced Vibrations have an External Force

All the examples on the previous two pages are known as **free vibrations** — i.e. they're set in motion and then just **left** to it. If you add an **external** force, you get **forced vibrations**, with a DE that looks like this:

$$m\frac{d^2x}{dt^2} + r\frac{dx}{dt} + kx = F(t)$$

, for some function F(t), often given in terms of sin or cos.

You know how to solve this (p.80-82) — but it's **important** that you understand what it means in the **context**.

Example: A particle of mass 1 kg moves on a horizontal surface. It is attached to a wall by a spring, which exerts a force on the particle of $-2x$ N. The particle also experiences a resistive force to its motion of $2\dot{x}$ and an external force $F(t) = 5 \cos 2t$ N acting in the direction of motion. Find an equation for the displacement of the particle, $x(t)$, given that $x(0) = 1$ and $\dot{x}(0) = -2$.

$F = ma$ gives $F(t) - 2\dot{x} - 2x = 1\ddot{x}$. You can rearrange to get a second order DE: $\ddot{x} + 2\dot{x} + 2x = 5 \cos 2t$.

Find the **complementary function** by working out the general solution to $\ddot{x} + 2\dot{x} + 2x = 0$:

Write and solve the auxiliary equation:

$$\lambda^2 + 2\lambda + 2 = 0 \Rightarrow \lambda = \frac{-2 \pm \sqrt{2^2 - 4 \times 1 \times 2}}{2} = -1 \pm i$$

There are two distinct imaginary roots, so the CF is $x = e^{-t}(A \cos t + B \sin t)$

$F(t) = 5 \cos 2t$, so use the substitution $x = \rho \cos 2t + \sigma \sin 2t$ to find the **particular integral**:

$$\dot{x} = -2\rho \sin 2t + 2\sigma \cos 2t, \quad \ddot{x} = -4\rho \cos 2t - 4\sigma \sin 2t$$
$$\Rightarrow -4\rho \cos 2t - 4\sigma \sin 2t + 2(-2\rho \sin 2t + 2\sigma \cos 2t) + 2(\rho \cos 2t + \sigma \sin 2t) = 5 \cos 2t$$

Equate coefficients:

$-2\rho + 4\sigma = 5$ and $-4\rho - 2\sigma = 0 \Rightarrow \rho = -\frac{1}{2}$ and $\sigma = 1$

So the PI is $-\frac{1}{2} \cos 2t + \sin 2t$

You could also use the R addition formulas in this example.

The complete general solution is $x = e^{-t}(A \cos t + B \sin t) - \frac{1}{2} \cos 2t + \sin 2t$

At $t = 0$, $x = 1$: $\quad x(0) = A - \frac{1}{2} = 1 \Rightarrow A = \frac{3}{2}$

Find $\dot{x}$: $\quad \dot{x} = e^{-t}(-A \sin t + B \cos t) - e^{-t}(A \cos t + B \sin t) + 2 \cos 2t + \sin 2t$

At $t = 0$, $\dot{x} = -2$: $\quad \dot{x}(0) = B - A + 2 = -2 \Rightarrow B = -\frac{5}{2}$

So the **particular solution** to the differential equation is $x = e^{-t}(\frac{3}{2} \cos t - \frac{5}{2} \sin t) - \frac{1}{2} \cos 2t + \sin 2t$

Practice Questions

Hint: the angle follows SHM where $\omega^2 = g/l$. (g is the gravitational constant and l is the length of the pendulum in m)

Q1 A pendulum swings on a string of length 40 cm. Find the angle of displacement from rest, x, after time t has passed, given that $x(0) = 5$ and $\dot{x}(0) = \sqrt{5}$ (take g as 10 ms⁻²)

Q2 a) Find the general solution to $9\ddot{x} + 6\dot{x} + x = 0$. b) State the type of damping in this system.

Q3 a) Find the general solution to $\ddot{x} + 4\dot{x} + x = 0$. b) State the type of damping in this system.

Q4 Find the general solution to $2\ddot{\theta} + 2\dot{\theta} + 3\theta = 0$. Give your answer in the form $\theta(t) = Re^{-pt}\cos(ut - \varphi)$

Exam Question

Q1 A particle with mass m travels in a straight horizontal line through the point O. At a displacement of x metres from O, the particle travels with velocity v ms⁻¹. The only forces acting on the particle are a resistive force of $|2mv|$ and a restoring force of $|10mx|$ that acts towards O. At $t = 0$, $x = 6$ and $v = 0$.

a) Show that the motion of the particle can be modelled by the equation $m\frac{d^2x}{dt^2} = -2m\frac{dx}{dt} - 10mx$. [5 marks]

b) Hence find an equation for the displacement, x, at time t. [6 marks]

Simple Harmonica Motion — oscillate side to side, blowing all the notes...

Whew, that was tough — applied maths right there at its appliediest. It's definitely worth your time going over this stuff to make sure you understand what's going on — it'll really help you relate the equation to the situation.

Coupled First Order Differential Equations

In A-Level Maths you'll have seen that differential equations can be used for modelling populations.
The models were pretty basic though — using coupled first order DEs makes a better model.

Coupled First Order DEs have the Same Variables

Coupled first order DEs are similar to normal **simultaneous** equations — except instead of having two
equations with two unknown variables, you have **two differential equations** with **two unknown functions**
(x and y below) of the same independent variable (usually time, t). They'll be in the form:

$$\frac{dx}{dt} = mx + ny + f(t) \qquad \frac{dy}{dt} = px + qy + g(t)$$

where f and g are functions of t, and m, n, p, and q are constants

It may sound slightly counterintuitive, but the **best** way to solve is to turn them into a single **second order DE**:

- Rearrange one of the equations so that you have x in terms of y (or y in terms of x):

$$\frac{dy}{dt} = px + qy + g(t) \Rightarrow px = \frac{dy}{dt} - qy - g(t) \Rightarrow x = \frac{1}{p}\left[\frac{dy}{dt} - qy - g(t)\right]$$

- Then differentiate with respect to t: $\dfrac{dx}{dt} = \dfrac{1}{p}\left[\dfrac{d^2y}{dt^2} - q\dfrac{dy}{dt} - \dfrac{d}{dt}g(t)\right]$

- Now substitute x and $\dfrac{dx}{dt}$ into the other given equation:

$$\frac{dx}{dt} = mx + ny + f(t) \Rightarrow \frac{1}{p}\left[\frac{d^2y}{dt^2} - q\frac{dy}{dt} - \frac{d}{dt}g(t)\right] = m \times \frac{1}{p}\left[\frac{dy}{dt} - qy - g(t)\right] + ny + f(t)$$

- With a bit of rearranging you get: $\dfrac{d^2y}{dt^2} - (m + q)\dfrac{dy}{dt} + (mq - np)y = \dfrac{d}{dt}g(t) - m{\cdot}g(t) + p{\cdot}f(t)$

The left-hand side might look a bit **nasty**, but you should be able to see that this is just
a second order DE, **exactly** like those you've seen on pages 78-82.
So you can now **solve** this for y, and then **plug in** some values (and functions) to find x.

Example: Functions $x(t)$ and $y(t)$ are given by the equations $\dot{x} = 5x + 7y$ and $\dot{y} = x - y$.
Find the general solutions for the functions $x(t)$ and $y(t)$.
Use the fact that at $t = 0$, $x = 5$ and $y = 3$ to find the particular solutions.

Rearrange the second equation: $\dot{y} = x - y \Rightarrow x = \dot{y} + y$

Differentiate to give $\dot{x}$: $\dot{x} = \ddot{y} + \dot{y}$

Substitute into the first
equation and rearrange: $\dot{x} = 5x + 7y \Rightarrow \ddot{y} + \dot{y} = 5(\dot{y} + y) + 7y$

$\Rightarrow \ddot{y} + \dot{y} = 5\dot{y} + 5y + 7y \Rightarrow \ddot{y} - 4\dot{y} - 12y = 0$

Solve as you would any
second order DE: Auxiliary equation is $\lambda^2 - 4\lambda - 12 = 0$
$\Rightarrow (\lambda + 2)(\lambda - 6) = 0 \Rightarrow \lambda = -2$ or $\lambda = 6$
Two distinct real roots, so the general solution for y is
$y = Ae^{-2t} + Be^{6t}$

Differentiate to find $\dot{y}$: $\dot{y} = -2Ae^{-2t} + 6Be^{6t}$

Find x using y and $\dot{y}$: $x = \dot{y} + y = -2Ae^{-2t} + 6Be^{6t} + Ae^{-2t} + Be^{6t}$

So $x = -Ae^{-2t} + 7Be^{6t}$

When t = 0, x = 5: $5 = -A + 7B$

When t = 0, y = 3: $3 = A + B$

Solve simultaneously: $8 = 8B \Rightarrow B = 1 \Rightarrow A = 2$

So $x = -2e^{-2t} + 7e^{6t}$ and $y = 2e^{-2t} + e^{6t}$

x(t) = no. of left socks,
y(t) = no. of right socks...

...nope, still can't solve it,
even after a second order.

*Don't try and find A and B until
this point — wait till you have
general solutions for both x and y.*

Coupled First Order Differential Equations

Coupled Equations are good for Population Models

In A-Level Maths you'll have come across some DEs that can be used as basic **models** for the **change in population** of one species. But with **two equations** you can now look at the change in population of **two species**, typically a predator and its prey — this is more **realistic**, and more **interesting** too (well *I* think so...).

Example: The population of hares ($100h$) and lynxes ($100x$) on a Canadian island is surveyed, starting in 1990. Their populations can be modelled by the differential equations:
$$\frac{dh}{dt} = -h - x + 4 \quad \text{and} \quad \frac{dx}{dt} = 5h - 3x + 5, \text{ where } t \text{ is time in hundreds of years.}$$
Given that at $t = 0$, $h = 9$ and $x = 3$, find the populations of hares and lynxes on the island at time t after the survey started as predicted by the model.

Rearrange the first equation: $\dot{h} = -h - x + 4 \Rightarrow x = -\dot{h} - h + 4 \Rightarrow \dot{x} = -\ddot{h} - \dot{h}$

Substitute into the second equation: $\dot{x} = 5h - 3x + 5 \Rightarrow -\ddot{h} - \dot{h} = 5h - 3(-\dot{h} - h + 4) + 5 \Rightarrow \ddot{h} + 4\dot{h} + 8h = 7$

Write and solve the auxiliary equation: Auxiliary equation is $\lambda^2 + 4\lambda + 8 = 0 \Rightarrow \lambda = \dfrac{-4 \pm \sqrt{4^2 - 4 \times 1 \times 8}}{2} = -2 \pm 2i$

There are two complex roots, so the CF is $h = e^{-2t}(A \cos 2t + B \sin 2t)$

For the **particular integral**, use the substitution $h = k$. Then $\dot{h} = \ddot{h} = 0$.

So $0 + 4(0) + 8k = 7 \Rightarrow k = \dfrac{7}{8}$

So the **general solution** for h is $h = e^{-2t}(A \cos 2t + B \sin 2t) + \dfrac{7}{8}$

$x = -\dot{h} - h + 4$, so work out $\dot{h}$: $\dot{h} = -2Ae^{-2t}\sin 2t - 2Ae^{-2t}\cos 2t + 2Be^{-2t}\cos 2t - 2Be^{-2t}\sin 2t$

$= e^{-2t}[(2B - 2A)\cos 2t - (2A + 2B)\sin 2t]$

$x = -e^{-2t}[(2B - 2A)\cos 2t - (2A + 2B)\sin 2t] - e^{-2t}(A \cos 2t + B \sin 2t) - \dfrac{7}{8} + 4$

Collect like terms to make the working a bit easier: $= -e^{-2t}[(2B - A)\cos 2t - (2A + B) \sin 2t] + \dfrac{25}{8}$

Use the boundary conditions to find A and B: $h(0) = 9 \Rightarrow A + \dfrac{7}{8} = 9 \Rightarrow A = \dfrac{65}{8}$

$x(0) = 3 \Rightarrow -2B + A + \dfrac{25}{8} = 3 \Rightarrow B = \dfrac{33}{8}$

h(t) and x(t) both have e^{-2t} terms. If t is large, e^{-2t} is very small, so h(t) tends to 7/8 and x(t) tends to 25/8.

Substitute A and B into the general solutions: $h(t) = \dfrac{1}{8}e^{-2t}(65 \cos 2t + 33 \sin 2t) + \dfrac{7}{8}$, $x(t) = -\dfrac{1}{8}e^{-2t}(\cos 2t - 163 \sin 2t) + \dfrac{25}{8}$

Practice Questions

Q1 Given that $\dot{x} = 5x - 2y$ and $\dot{y} = 4x - y$, find the general solutions for the functions $x(t)$ and $y(t)$.

Q2 A model gives the population of two competing species of fish after t years as $1000x$ and $1000y$ respectively.
   a) If $\dot{x} = -x + 2y$, $\dot{y} = 2x - y$, and $x(0) = 10$, $y(0) = 5$, find the population of the species of fish after time t.
   b) Give one reason why this model may be inaccurate.

Exam Question

Q1 Vats A and B have capacities of 10 litres each. At time $t = 0$, both vats are full of pure water.
   - Water with a salt concentration of 1 gram/litre enters into vat A at a rate of 1 litre/minute.
   - Water flows from vat A to vat B at a rate of 3 litres/minute.
   - Water flows from vat B to vat A at a rate of 2 litres/minute.
   - Pure water evaporates from vat B at a rate of 1 litre/minute.

   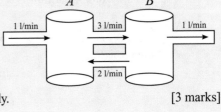

   a) Show that this system can be written as a pair of coupled equations:
   $$\dot{x} = 1 + \frac{2}{10}y - \frac{3}{10}x \qquad \dot{y} = \frac{3}{10}x - \frac{2}{10}y$$
   where $x(t)$ and $y(t)$ are the amounts of salt in vats A and B, respectively. [3 marks]

   b) Hence find the amount of salt in each vat after time t. [14 marks]

I prey these coupled equations don't come up in the exam...

Although coupled DEs make better population models, they're still far from perfect — you're only looking at how those two species interact. In real life there will be many other species and factors that come into play.

The t-formulas

If you thought you knew all there was to know about trigonometry, think again. You're about to see a whole new way of writing the trig functions — and then be dazzled by all its many applications. Believe me, it's beau-TEE-ful...

Use a **Right-Angled Triangle** to **Derive** the **t-formulas**

The **t-formulas** are expressions for **trig** functions involving a special variable, $t = \tan\left(\frac{\theta}{2}\right)$.

$$\sin\theta = \frac{2t}{1+t^2} \qquad \cos\theta = \frac{1-t^2}{1+t^2} \qquad \tan\theta = \frac{2t}{1-t^2}$$

Deriving the t-formulas

1) Draw a **right-angled triangle**.

   Give it an **angle** $\frac{\theta}{2}$, with **side length** t opposite the angle and **side length 1** adjacent to the angle, as shown in the diagram. Then $\tan\left(\frac{\theta}{2}\right) = \frac{\text{opp}}{\text{adj}} = \frac{t}{1} = t$.

2) Work out the **hypotenuse** using **Pythagoras' theorem** — it must be $\sqrt{1+t^2}$.

3) Use **trig** to find the **sine** and **cosine** of the angle:

   $$\sin\left(\frac{\theta}{2}\right) = \frac{\text{opp}}{\text{hyp}} = \frac{t}{\sqrt{1+t^2}} \qquad \cos\left(\frac{\theta}{2}\right) = \frac{\text{adj}}{\text{hyp}} = \frac{1}{\sqrt{1+t^2}}$$

4) Find $\sin\theta$ and $\cos\theta$ using the **double angle formulas**:

   $$\sin\theta = \sin\left(2\times\frac{\theta}{2}\right) = 2\sin\left(\frac{\theta}{2}\right)\cos\left(\frac{\theta}{2}\right) = 2\times\frac{t}{\sqrt{1+t^2}}\times\frac{1}{\sqrt{1+t^2}} = \frac{2t}{1+t^2}$$

   $$\cos\theta = \cos\left(2\times\frac{\theta}{2}\right) = 2\cos^2\left(\frac{\theta}{2}\right) - 1 = 2\times\left(\frac{1}{\sqrt{1+t^2}}\right)^2 - \frac{1+t^2}{1+t^2} = \frac{1-t^2}{1+t^2}$$

5) Divide $\sin\theta$ by $\cos\theta$ to get $\tan\theta$:

   $$\tan\theta = \frac{\sin\theta}{\cos\theta} = \frac{\left(\frac{2t}{1+t^2}\right)}{\left(\frac{1-t^2}{1+t^2}\right)} = \frac{2t}{1-t^2}$$

These derivations assume that the angle $\frac{\theta}{2}$ is **acute**, but the results are true for **any** angle. They can be proved **algebraically** by manipulating the double angle formulas and using the identity $\sin^2\theta + \cos^2\theta \equiv 1$. You can give it a go in **Exam Question 1** at the end of this section.

Example: Suppose $\tan\left(\frac{\theta}{2}\right) = 3$, where $0 \le \theta < 2\pi$.

Find the exact values of $\sin\theta$, $\cos\theta$ and $\tan\theta$.

In which quadrant is θ?

Write down the value of t and substitute it into the t-formulas.

$$t = \tan\left(\frac{\theta}{2}\right) = 3$$

$$\sin\theta = \frac{2\times3}{1+3^2} = \frac{6}{10} = \frac{3}{5}$$

$$\cos\theta = \frac{1-3^2}{1+3^2} = \frac{1-9}{1+9} = -\frac{4}{5}$$

$$\tan\theta = \frac{2\times3}{1-3^2} = -\frac{6}{8} = -\frac{3}{4}$$

To figure out the quadrant, look at which of sin, cos and tan are positive and use CAST.

θ is in the **2nd** (top-left) **quadrant**, since only $\sin\theta$ is positive.

At the village fete, no one could quite agree on the best tea formula.

The t-formulas

Use the t-formulas to **Prove Identities**

The t-formulas can help you **manipulate** trigonometric expressions to prove **identities** — it's often **easier** to work with the variable t than with trig functions. There is often **more than one way** to prove an identity — but if the exam question **tells you** to use t, make sure that you do.

Example: Prove that $\tan\left(\frac{\theta}{2}\right) \equiv \frac{\tan\theta}{\sec\theta + 1}$.

Converting to t: $\text{RHS} \equiv \dfrac{\left(\frac{2t}{1-t^2}\right)}{\left(\frac{1}{\left(\frac{1-t^2}{1+t^2}\right)}\right)+1} \equiv \dfrac{\left(\frac{2t}{1-t^2}\right)}{\left(\frac{1+t^2}{1-t^2}\right)+1} \equiv \dfrac{2t}{1+t^2+1-t^2} = \dfrac{2t}{2} \equiv t \equiv \tan\left(\frac{\theta}{2}\right) = \text{LHS}$

Example: Use the substitution $t = \tan\left(\frac{x}{2}\right)$ to prove that $\dfrac{\sin x - \cos x + 1}{\sin x + \cos x - 1} \equiv \dfrac{\sin x + 1}{\cos x}$.

The LHS looks like the most complicated so let's start there:

$$\text{LHS} = \dfrac{\left(\frac{2t}{1+t^2}\right)-\left(\frac{1-t^2}{1+t^2}\right)+\left(\frac{1+t^2}{1+t^2}\right)}{\left(\frac{2t}{1+t^2}\right)+\left(\frac{1-t^2}{1+t^2}\right)-\left(\frac{1+t^2}{1+t^2}\right)} = \dfrac{2t-1+t^2+1+t^2}{2t+1-t^2-1-t^2} = \dfrac{2t+2t^2}{2t-2t^2} = \dfrac{1+t}{1-t}$$

Now work with the RHS:

$$\text{RHS} = \dfrac{\left(\frac{2t}{1+t^2}\right)+\left(\frac{1+t^2}{1+t^2}\right)}{\left(\frac{1-t^2}{1+t^2}\right)} = \dfrac{2t+1+t^2}{1-t^2} = \dfrac{(1+t)^2}{(1+t)(1-t)} = \dfrac{1+t}{1-t}$$

So the LHS equals the RHS, which proves the identity.

Solve Equations by switching to t

Equations of the form $a\sin x + b\cos x = c$ can be solved using the t-formulas. By writing sin and cos in terms of t and then multiplying out any fractions, you obtain a **polynomial equation** in t that should be easier to solve.

But be careful — the function $t = \tan\left(\frac{x}{2}\right)$ has **asymptotes** at the values $x = (2n+1)\pi$. You won't find solutions at those values of x by solving for t — so always do a separate **check** to see if any of those values are solutions.

Example: Solve $2\cos x + \sin x = 1$ for $0 \le x \le 2\pi$.

> Equations like this might remind you of R addition formula problems that you saw in your standard Maths A-Level. Make sure to use the t-formula if the question says to though.

Write and solve the equation in terms of t:

$$\dfrac{2(1-t^2)}{1+t^2} + \dfrac{2t}{1+t^2} = 1 \implies \dfrac{2-2t^2+2t}{1+t^2} = 1 \implies 2-2t^2+2t = 1+t^2 \implies 3t^2-2t-1 = 0$$
$$\implies t = 1 \text{ or } t = -\frac{1}{3}$$

Switch back to x and solve: $\tan\left(\frac{x}{2}\right) = 1$ or $\tan\left(\frac{x}{2}\right) = -\frac{1}{3}$

Since $0 \le x \le 2\pi$, we need $0 \le \frac{x}{2} \le \pi$.

$\tan\left(\frac{x}{2}\right) = 1 \implies \frac{x}{2} = \frac{\pi}{4}$ — This is the only relevant value between 0 and π.
$\implies x = \frac{\pi}{2}$

For $\tan\left(\frac{x}{2}\right) = -\frac{1}{3}$, $\tan^{-1}\left(-\frac{1}{3}\right) = -0.3217...$

In the correct range, $\frac{x}{2} = -0.3217... + \pi = 2.8198...$

So $x = \textbf{5.64}$ (3 s.f.)

Check for solutions where $\tan\left(\frac{x}{2}\right)$ has asymptotes:

The only asymptote in the range $0 \le x \le 2\pi$ is $x = \pi$.

$2\cos\pi + \sin\pi = -2 + 0 = -2 \ne 1$, so π <u>isn't</u> a solution.

So the solutions to the equation are $x = \frac{\pi}{2}$ and $x = 5.64$.

The t-formulas

Watch out for **Hidden Half Angles**

You could get a question that uses $\tan\left(\frac{x}{2}\right)$ in **disguise** — e.g. you can think of the substitution $t = \tan\left(\frac{x}{4}\right)$ as $t = \tan\left(\frac{\left(\frac{x}{2}\right)}{2}\right)$. In this case, you could use the t-formulas with $\theta = \frac{x}{2}$, so $\sin\left(\frac{x}{2}\right) = \frac{2t}{1+t^2}$ etc.

Example: Show that $\frac{d}{dx}\left(2 + \cos x + 15\sin\left(\frac{x}{2}\right)\right) = \frac{(1-t^2)(15t^2 - 8t + 15)}{2(1+t^2)^2}$, where $t = \tan\left(\frac{x}{4}\right)$.

Since $t = \tan\left(\frac{x}{4}\right)$, you can use the t-formulas with $\theta = \frac{x}{2}$: $\sin\left(\frac{x}{2}\right) = \frac{2t}{1+t^2}$, $\cos\left(\frac{x}{2}\right) = \frac{1-t^2}{1+t^2}$

Do the differentiation first.
$$\frac{d}{dx}\left(2 + \cos x + 15\sin\left(\frac{x}{2}\right)\right) = -\sin x + \frac{15}{2}\cos\left(\frac{x}{2}\right)$$

Use the double angle formulas to write everything in terms of $\theta = \frac{x}{2}$.
$$= -2\sin\left(\frac{x}{2}\right)\cos\left(\frac{x}{2}\right) + \frac{15}{2}\cos\left(\frac{x}{2}\right)$$

Then use the t-formulas.
$$= -2\left(\frac{2t}{1+t^2}\right)\left(\frac{1-t^2}{1+t^2}\right) + \frac{15}{2}\left(\frac{1-t^2}{1+t^2}\right)$$

Simplify to get the final result.
$$= \frac{-4t(1-t^2)}{(1+t^2)^2} + \frac{15(1-t^2)}{2(1+t^2)}$$

Don't multiply out if you don't need to — keep an eye out for common factors.
$$= \frac{-8t(1-t^2) + 15(1-t^2)(1+t^2)}{2(1+t^2)^2}$$
$$= \frac{(1-t^2)(15t^2 - 8t + 15)}{2(1+t^2)^2}$$

Using t as an **Integral Substitution** is called the **Weierstrass Substitution**

If you calculate an integral using the **substitution** $t = \tan\left(\frac{x}{2}\right)$, you're using the **Weierstrass** substitution. Don't worry about the name — it's the method you need to get right.

You're integrating by substitution so you'll need to change **dx to dt**:

$$t = \tan\left(\frac{x}{2}\right) \Rightarrow x = 2\arctan t$$
$$\text{So, } \frac{dx}{dt} = \frac{2}{1+t^2} \Rightarrow dx = \frac{2}{1+t^2}\,dt$$

The Weierstrass substitution is useful for integrals involving **sums** and **differences** of **sines** and **cosines** in **fractions**. By making the **substitution** and using the **t-formulas** for the sine and cosine terms, you can **change** a fraction involving trig functions into a fraction involving the single variable t.

Example: By using an appropriate substitution, find $\int \frac{1}{1 - \sin x + \cos x}\,dx$.

Use the Weierstass substitution $t = \tan\left(\frac{x}{2}\right)$:

Replace each trig function with its t-formula, and don't forget to replace dx with $\frac{2}{1+t^2}\,dt$.
$$\int \frac{1}{1 - \sin x + \cos x}\,dx = \int\left(\frac{1}{1 - \left(\frac{2t}{1+t^2}\right) + \left(\frac{1-t^2}{1+t^2}\right)}\right)\left(\frac{2}{1+t^2}\right)dt$$

Simplify with a common denominator, and cancel down.
$$= \int\left(\frac{1}{\left(\frac{1+t^2 - 2t + 1 - t^2}{1+t^2}\right)}\right)\left(\frac{2}{1+t^2}\right)dt$$
$$= \int\frac{2}{1 + t^2 - 2t + 1 - t^2}\,dt$$
$$= \int\frac{2}{2 - 2t}\,dt$$
$$= \int\frac{1}{1-t}\,dt$$

Integrate once the integrand is in its simplest form. Then rewrite the answer in terms of x.
$$= -\ln|1 - t| + C = -\ln\left|1 - \tan\left(\frac{x}{2}\right)\right| + C$$

The t-formulas

Example: Evaluate the following integrals:

a) $\int_0^{\frac{\pi}{2}} \frac{1}{1+\sin\phi}\,d\phi,$ b) $\int_{\frac{\pi}{3}}^{\frac{\pi}{3}} \sec\theta\,d\theta.$

> It's really easy to forget to include $\frac{2}{1+t^2}$ when you change variables to t. Don't get caught out.

Using the Weierstrass substitution:

a) The new limits after substitution will be $\tan\left(\frac{\left(\frac{\pi}{2}\right)}{2}\right) = \tan\left(\frac{\pi}{4}\right) = 1$ and $\tan 0 = 0$.

$$\int_0^{\frac{\pi}{2}} \frac{1}{1+\sin\phi}\,d\phi = \int_0^1 \left(\frac{1}{1+\left(\frac{2t}{1+t^2}\right)}\right)\left(\frac{2}{1+t^2}\right)dt$$

$$= \int_0^1 \frac{2}{1+t^2+2t}\,dt = \int_0^1 \frac{2}{(t+1)^2}\,dt = \left[-\frac{2}{t+1}\right]_0^1 = -1-(-2) = \mathbf{1}$$

b) The new limits after substitution will be $\tan\left(\frac{\left(\frac{\pi}{3}\right)}{2}\right) = \tan\left(\frac{\pi}{6}\right) = \frac{\sqrt{3}}{3}$ and $\tan\left(\frac{\left(-\frac{\pi}{3}\right)}{2}\right) = -\frac{\sqrt{3}}{3}$.

$$\int_{\frac{\pi}{3}}^{\frac{\pi}{3}} \sec\theta\,d\theta = \int_{-\frac{\sqrt{3}}{3}}^{\frac{\sqrt{3}}{3}} \left(\frac{1+t^2}{1-t^2}\right)\left(\frac{2}{1+t^2}\right)dt$$

$$= \int_{-\frac{\sqrt{3}}{3}}^{\frac{\sqrt{3}}{3}} \frac{2}{1-t^2}\,dt$$

$\ln a - \ln\frac{1}{a} = \ln a + \ln a = 2\ln a$

The integral $\int \frac{1}{1-t^2}\,dt = \frac{1}{2}\ln\left|\frac{1+t}{1-t}\right|$ is in the formula booklet.

$$= \left[\ln\left|\frac{1+t}{1-t}\right|\right]_{-\frac{\sqrt{3}}{3}}^{\frac{\sqrt{3}}{3}} = \ln\left|\frac{1+\frac{\sqrt{3}}{3}}{1-\frac{\sqrt{3}}{3}}\right| - \ln\left|\frac{1-\frac{\sqrt{3}}{3}}{1+\frac{\sqrt{3}}{3}}\right| = 2\ln\left|\frac{1+\frac{\sqrt{3}}{3}}{1-\frac{\sqrt{3}}{3}}\right| = \mathbf{2\ln\left|\frac{3+\sqrt{3}}{3-\sqrt{3}}\right|}$$

Practice Questions

Q1 Express $\frac{1-\cos\theta}{1+\cos\theta}$ in terms of $t = \tan\left(\frac{\theta}{2}\right)$.

Q2 Find the exact values of $\sin\theta$, $\cos\theta$ and $\tan\theta$, and state which quadrant θ lies in, when:

a) $\tan\left(\frac{\theta}{2}\right) = 5,$ b) $\tan\left(\frac{\theta}{2}\right) = \frac{3}{7},$ c) $\tan\left(\frac{\theta}{2}\right) = -\frac{\sqrt{2}}{2}.$

Q3 Use the substitution $t = \tan\left(\frac{\theta}{2}\right)$ to prove that:

a) $\cot\phi + \tan\phi \equiv \sec\phi\,\mathrm{cosec}\,\phi,$ b) $\sec^2\phi \equiv \frac{\mathrm{cosec}\,\phi}{\mathrm{cosec}\,\phi - \sin\phi}.$

Q4 Use the t-formulas to solve the following trigonometric equations for $0 \leq x \leq 2\pi$, giving your answers to 3 significant figures where appropriate:

a) $5\cos x + 3\sin x = 1,$ b) $2\sin\left(\frac{x}{2}\right) = 1 + \cos\left(\frac{x}{2}\right).$

Q5 Use the Weierstrass substitution to find $\int \mathrm{cosec}\,x\,dx.$

Q6 Use the Weierstrass substitution to find the exact value of $\int_{-\frac{\pi}{3}}^{\frac{\pi}{3}} \frac{1}{2+2\cos x}\,dx.$

Exam Questions

Q1 Prove that if $t = \tan\left(\frac{x}{2}\right)$ then $\sin x = \frac{2t}{t^2+1}$ for **any** value of $x \in \mathbb{R}$. [4 marks]

Q2 $f(x) = \dfrac{1}{1+\sin\left(\frac{x}{2}\right)+\cos\left(\frac{x}{2}\right)}$

a) Show that $\int f(x)\,dx = 2\ln\left|1 + \tan\left(\frac{x}{4}\right)\right| + C.$ [5 marks]

b) Find the area enclosed by the curve $y = f(x)$, $y = \sec^2 x$, the y-axis and the line $x = \frac{\pi}{4}$. Give your answer to three significant figures. [5 marks]

Time to relax cos that's the end of trig...

The t-formulas aren't in the formula booklet so you're just gonna have to learn them — make sure you know how to derive them from scratch too. Before cracking on with a t-formula question, write down the formulas you'll need. Then you can quickly refer back when you use them and you might get some marks if things don't go to plan later on.

Taylor Series

I watched a great box set last weekend all about how suits are made. It was called The Tailor Series...
Anyway, flick over to p.44-45 to remind yourself of the Maclaurin Series before viewing the following.

Taylor Series generalise the idea of Maclaurin Series

1) Most functions can be expressed as a **series expansion** —
   you can write them as **infinite series** in powers of x.

2) For the Maclaurin series, these expansions were **focussed on $x = 0$**.

3) The **Taylor series** of a function is a series expansion about any $x = c$ in powers of $(x - c)$.

4) You calculate Taylor series about $x = c$ in a **similar** way to Maclaurin series:

Taylor series will be especially useful for evaluating limits (p.94) and solving differential equations (p.98).

All the derivatives $f^{(n)}(c)$ must be finite for the Taylor series about c to exist.

$$f(x) = f(c) + f'(c)(x - c) + \frac{f''(c)}{2!}(x - c)^2 + \frac{f'''(c)}{3!}(x - c)^3 + ... + \frac{f^{(n)}(c)}{n!}(x - c)^n + ... = \sum_{n=0}^{\infty} \frac{f^{(n)}(c)}{n!}(x - c)^n$$

Evaluate the derivatives at c.

The series should be in powers of $(x - c)$.

Plug in $c = 0$ to get a Taylor series about 0 — in other words, a Maclaurin series.

Example: Find the Taylor series of $\sin x$ about $x = \pi$, up to and including the term in $(x - \pi)^3$.

1) Work out the derivatives:

$f(x) = \sin x$
$f'(x) = \cos x$
$f''(x) = -\sin x$
$f'''(x) = -\cos x$

2) Evaluate the derivatives at $c = \pi$:

$f(\pi) = \sin \pi = 0$
$f'(\pi) = \cos \pi = -1$
$f''(\pi) = -\sin \pi = 0$
$f'''(\pi) = -\cos \pi = 1$

3) Substitute into the formula to get the Taylor series:

$$\sin x = f(\pi) + f'(\pi)(x - \pi) + \frac{f''(\pi)}{2}(x - \pi)^2$$
$$+ \frac{f'''(\pi)}{3 \times 2}(x - \pi)^3 + ...$$
$$= 0 - (x - \pi) + 0 + \frac{1}{6}(x - \pi)^3 + ...$$
$$= -(x - \pi) + \frac{1}{6}(x - \pi)^3 + ...$$

The Taylor series is very close to $\sin x$ for x close to π — even with only two terms.

As x gets further from π, more terms would be needed to give a good approximation.

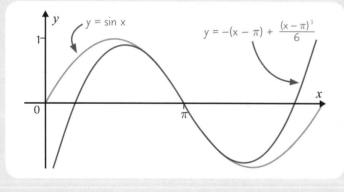

$y = \sin x$

$y = -(x - \pi) + \frac{(x - \pi)^3}{6}$

Example: Show that the Taylor series of $\ln x$ about $x = 2$ is $\ln 2 + \sum_{n=1}^{\infty}\left((-1)^n \frac{(x - 2)^n}{2^n n}\right)$.

$$f(x) = \ln(x), \quad f'(x) = \frac{1}{x}, \quad f''(x) = -\frac{1}{x^2}, \quad f'''(x) = \frac{2}{x^3}, \quad f^{(4)}(x) = -\frac{6}{x^4}, \quad ..., \quad f^{(n)}(x) = (-1)^{n-1}\frac{(n-1)!}{x^n}$$

The sign of the derivatives alternates, which gives the $(-1)^{n-1}$ part. The other part comes from repeatedly differentiating x^{-1}.

There was no Maclaurin series for ln x because its derivatives couldn't be evaluated at $x = 0$. They can, however, be evaluated at $x = 2$ so this Taylor series exists.

$$\Rightarrow \ln x = \ln 2 + \sum_{n=1}^{\infty}\left(f^{(n)}(2)\frac{(x - 2)^n}{n!}\right)$$

$$= \ln 2 + \sum_{n=1}^{\infty}\left((-1)^{n-1}\frac{(n-1)!}{2^n}\frac{(x - 2)^n}{n!}\right)$$

$$= \ln 2 + \sum_{n=1}^{\infty}\left((-1)^{n-1}\frac{(x - 2)^n}{2^n n}\right)$$

Use $\frac{(n-1)!}{n!} = \frac{1}{n}$ to cancel down.

Taylor series only converge to the function for certain values of x (which might be all of $\mathbb{R}$). Outside this range, the series diverges and is no longer valid.

Taylor Series

Approximate f(x) near x = c using Taylor series

You can use a Taylor series about c to **approximate** the **value** of f(x) for x **near** c.

Example:
  a) Find the Taylor series of e^x up to and including the term in $(x-1)^3$.
  b) Use your Taylor series to approximate the value of $e^{1.3}$.
  c) What is the error in your approximation?

a) We're not explicitly told the value of c here — but we are told that the Taylor series will be in powers of $(x-1)$ which means that $c = 1$.
The derivatives of e^x are all e^x so $f^{(n)}(1) = e^1 = e$ for all n.
The Taylor series, up to and including the third power, is then:

When there are dots at the end of the series, it is equal to the function.

$$e^x = e + e(x-1) + \tfrac{e}{2}(x-1)^2 + \tfrac{e}{6}(x-1)^3 + \ldots = e\left(1 + (x-1) + \frac{(x-1)^2}{2} + \frac{(x-1)^3}{6}\right) + \ldots$$

When the series is cut off at a particular power, it is an approximation

b) Approximate by substituting in $x = 1.3$:

$$e^{1.3} \approx e\left(1 + (1.3-1) + \frac{(1.3-1)^2}{2} + \frac{(1.3-1)^3}{6}\right) = e(1 + 0.3 + 0.045 + 0.0045) = \mathbf{1.3495e}$$

c) The true value of $e^{1.3}$ is 3.669296..., so the error is 3.669296... − 1.3495e = **0.000975** (3 s.f.)

If you're not given c, make sure you choose a **sensible** value when creating a Taylor series.
You want one that is **close to the value** of x that you wish to approximate at, but also **easy to work with**.

Example: By constructing an appropriate Taylor series for $f(x) = \sqrt{x}$, find an approximation for $\sqrt{9.5}$.

Choosing $c = 9$ is sensible. It's close to what we want to approximate and $f(9)$ is easy to work with since 9 is a perfect square.

$f(x) = \sqrt{x}$ $f(9) = \sqrt{9} = 3$

$f'(x) = \tfrac{1}{2}x^{-\frac{1}{2}}$ $f'(9) = \tfrac{1}{6}$

$f''(x) = -\tfrac{1}{4}x^{-\frac{3}{2}}$ $f''(9) = -\tfrac{1}{108}$

$f'''(x) = \tfrac{3}{8}x^{-\frac{5}{2}}$ $f'''(9) = \tfrac{1}{648}$

$$\Rightarrow \sqrt{x} = 3 + \tfrac{1}{6}(x-9) + \frac{\left(-\tfrac{1}{108}\right)}{2!}(x-9)^2 + \frac{\left(\tfrac{1}{648}\right)}{3!}(x-9)^3 + \ldots$$

$$= 3 + \frac{x-9}{6} - \frac{(x-9)^2}{216} + \frac{(x-9)^3}{3888} + \ldots$$

$$\Rightarrow \sqrt{9.5} \approx 3 + \frac{0.5}{6} - \frac{0.5^2}{216} + \frac{0.5^3}{3888} = \mathbf{3.08221} \text{ (5 d.p.)}$$

This approximation is correct to 5 decimal places.
It is accurate, because x was sufficiently <u>close</u> to c.

Practice Questions

Q1 Find the Taylor series of $\cos x$ about $x = \frac{\pi}{2}$ up to and including the term in $\left(x - \frac{\pi}{2}\right)^5$.

Q2 Show that the Taylor series of e^x about $x = \ln 3$ is $\sum_{n=0}^{\infty} \frac{3}{n!}(x - \ln 3)^n$.

Q3 a) Find the Taylor series of $\tan x$ about $x = \frac{\pi}{4}$ up to and including the term in $\left(x - \frac{\pi}{4}\right)^2$.

   b) Use your series to approximate $\tan\left(\frac{\pi}{5}\right)$, giving your approximation in terms of π.

   c) Use your calculator to work out the error in your approximation to 3 significant figures.

Exam Question

Q1 a) Find the Taylor series of $x^{\frac{1}{3}}$ about $x = 8$ up to and including the term in $(x-8)^3$.   [4 marks]

   b) Hence, approximate the value of $\sqrt[3]{7.5}$. Give your approximation to 4 decimal places.   [2 marks]

Tinker Taylor Series Pi...

If you're not into your differentiation, I guess you just can't catch a break because this topic is full of it. Loads of marks can be lost to little slips so take it steady and double check your working. It's also a good idea to write down that Taylor series formula from the get-go so you don't forget any of the factorials or powers along the way.

Limits

You've touched on limits before — they're the values that functions get ever and ever closer to.
Sometimes $\lim\limits_{x \to c} f(x) = f(c)$, but what if it's not clear what $f(c)$ is? Read on to find out how to handle it...

Indeterminate Forms have Limits that aren't obvious to Determine

1) An **indeterminate form** is an expression involving **two functions** where the
limit can't be found just by using the limits of the two functions.

2) E.g. if $\lim\limits_{x \to c} f(x) = \lim\limits_{x \to c} g(x) = 0$ then you might guess that $\lim\limits_{x \to c} \dfrac{f(x)}{g(x)} = \dfrac{0}{0}$ ...

3) ...but there isn't such a thing as $\dfrac{0}{0}$ so you've got an indeterminate — you can't **determine** the limit easily.

Luckily, there are a few ways to **deal** with these indeterminate forms.

Use Known Series Expansions to find the limits

1) One way to work out the **limit** of an indeterminate is to work out the limit of its **series expansion** —
that's its **Maclaurin** or **Taylor** series (see p.44-45 and p.92-93 to make sure you're up to speed).

2) Create a series about the **limit** — so a Maclaurin series if $x \to 0$ or a Taylor series about c if $x \to c$.

3) Now that you have a series in **powers** of x or $(x - c)$, it will be **easier** to see what happens as $x \to 0$ or $x \to c$.

4) This method is useful when the series expansion is already **known** —
check your **formula booklet** to see which ones are given to you.

Example: Find $\lim\limits_{x \to 0} \dfrac{1 - \cos x}{x^2 e^{2x}}$.
As $x \to 0$, both $1 - \cos x \to 0$ and $x^2 e^{2x} \to 0$
so this is an indeterminate form.

We know the series for $\cos x$ and e^{2x}: $\cos x = 1 - \dfrac{x^2}{2!} + \dfrac{x^4}{4!} - ...$ and $e^{2x} = 1 + (2x) + \dfrac{(2x)^2}{2!} + \dfrac{(2x)^3}{3!} + ...$

$$\Rightarrow \frac{1 - \cos x}{x^2 e^{2x}} = \frac{1 - \left(1 - \frac{x^2}{2!} + \frac{x^4}{4!} - ...\right)}{x^2\left(1 + 2x + \frac{2^2 x^2}{2!} + \frac{2^3 x^3}{3!} + ...\right)} = \frac{\frac{x^2}{2!} - \frac{x^4}{4!} + ...}{x^2 + 2x^3 + \frac{2^2 x^4}{2!} + \frac{2^3 x^5}{3!} + ...} = \frac{\frac{1}{2!} - \frac{x^2}{4!} + ...}{1 + 2x + \frac{2^2 x^2}{2!} + \frac{2^3 x^3}{3!} + ...}$$

So $\lim\limits_{x \to 0} \dfrac{1 - \cos x}{x^2 e^{2x}} = \lim\limits_{x \to 0} \dfrac{\frac{1}{2!} - \frac{x^2}{4!} + ...}{1 + 2x + \frac{2^2 x^2}{2!} + \frac{2^3 x^3}{3!} + ...} = \dfrac{\frac{1}{2!} - 0 + ...}{1 + 0 + 0 + 0 + ...} = \dfrac{1}{2}$

Divide the numerator and
denominator by the lowest
power of x — that's x^2 here.

L'Hospital's Rule uses Differentiation

You can find the limits of indeterminates of the form $\dfrac{0}{0}$, $\dfrac{\pm\infty}{\pm\infty}$ or $\dfrac{\mp\infty}{\pm\infty}$ by differentiating and using **L'Hospital's Rule**:

If $\lim\limits_{x \to c} f(x)$ and $\lim\limits_{x \to c} g(x)$ are both 0 or both $\pm\infty$ then $\lim\limits_{x \to c} \dfrac{f(x)}{g(x)} = \lim\limits_{x \to c} \dfrac{f'(x)}{g'(x)}$

You might see this
called L'Hôpital's Rule.

c is a real number or $\pm\infty$

The limit might not be clear after the **first round** of differentiation.
You can differentiate **multiple times** so long as you're still working with a $\dfrac{0}{0}$ or $\dfrac{\pm\infty}{\pm\infty}$ form.

Example: Find $\lim\limits_{x \to 0} \dfrac{\tan x}{x}$.

Let $f(x) = \tan x$ and $g(x) = x$. Then $\lim\limits_{x \to 0} f(x) = \lim\limits_{x \to 0} g(x) = 0$.

So use L'Hospital's Rule: $\lim\limits_{x \to 0} \dfrac{\tan x}{x} = \lim\limits_{x \to 0} \dfrac{f(x)}{g(x)} = \lim\limits_{x \to 0} \dfrac{f'(x)}{g'(x)} = \lim\limits_{x \to 0} \dfrac{\sec^2 x}{1} = \dfrac{1}{1} = 1$

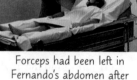

Forceps had been left in
Fernando's abdomen after
the operation — a clear
violation of L'Hospital's Rules.

Some functions are only **defined** for **certain values** of x (e.g. **ln x** is defined for $x > 0$). Think of a graph of ln x —
the curve **only exists** to the **right** of 0, so to find the limit at 0, you could only **approach** it from the right of 0.

This is known as a **one-sided** limit — $\lim\limits_{x \to c^+}$ is the limit as you approach c from the **right** and $\lim\limits_{x \to c^-}$ is the limit as you
approach c from the **left**. **L'Hospital's Rule** still applies to one-sided limits (see Practice Question 4 on the next page).

Limits

There are Other Types of Indeterminates

Indeterminate forms come in lots of other **varieties**. They might look like $0 \times \pm\infty$, $\infty - \infty$, 0^0, 1^∞ or ∞^0.
To use L'Hospital's Rule, you need to **rewrite** them or perform a **substitution** to make them look like $\frac{0}{0}$ or $\frac{\pm\infty}{\pm\infty}$.

> **Example:** Evaluate the following limits using L'Hospital's Rule: a) $\lim\limits_{x \to -\infty} xe^x$, b) $\lim\limits_{x \to \infty} \left(1 + \frac{a}{x}\right)^x$.

a) The indeterminate is of the form $-\infty \times 0$. There are **two ways** to rewrite it — it's not clear which factor should be put in the denominator. Let's try putting the x factor there first:

$$xe^x = \frac{e^x}{\left(\frac{1}{x}\right)} \Rightarrow f(x) = e^x, \ g(x) = \frac{1}{x}$$

Then $\lim\limits_{x \to -\infty} f(x) = \lim\limits_{x \to -\infty} g(x) = 0$ so we have the form $\frac{0}{0}$.

Look at what would happen if you were to **differentiate**:

$$\lim\limits_{x \to -\infty} xe^x = \lim\limits_{x \to -\infty} \frac{e^x}{\left(\frac{1}{x}\right)} = \lim\limits_{x \to -\infty} \frac{e^x}{\left(-\frac{1}{x^2}\right)} = \lim\limits_{x \to -\infty} \frac{e^x}{\left(\frac{2}{x^3}\right)} = \ldots$$

Oh dear — we don't seem to be getting anywhere. In fact, you could keep differentiating forever and the limit wouldn't become clear.

Let's **try again**:

$$xe^x = \frac{x}{e^{-x}} \Rightarrow f(x) = x, \ g(x) = e^{-x}$$

Now, $\lim\limits_{x \to -\infty} f(x) = -\infty$ and $\lim\limits_{x \to -\infty} g(x) = \infty$ so we have $\frac{-\infty}{\infty}$.

Applying L'Hospital's Rule:

$$\lim\limits_{x \to -\infty} xe^x = \lim\limits_{x \to -\infty} \frac{x}{e^{-x}} = \lim\limits_{x \to -\infty} \frac{1}{-e^{-x}} = 0$$

b) The indeterminate is of the form 1^∞. To use L'Hospital's Rule, we're going to make a **substitution** and then introduce some natural **exponentials** and **logs**. To make things clearer, we'll use the notation $\exp u$ instead of e^u.

Let $t = \frac{a}{x}$ so then $x = \frac{a}{t} \Rightarrow \left(1 + \frac{a}{x}\right)^x = (1 + t)^{\frac{a}{t}}$

Use $u = e^{\ln u}$ $\longrightarrow = \exp\left(\ln\left((1 + t)^{\frac{a}{t}}\right)\right)$

Use $\ln(u^v) = v \ln(u)$ $= \exp\left(\frac{a}{t}\ln(1 + t)\right)$

$$= \exp\left(a\frac{\ln(1 + t)}{t}\right)$$

As $x \to \infty$, $t \to 0$.

Since $\lim\limits_{t \to 0} \ln(1 + t) = \lim\limits_{t \to 0} t = 0$,

we have the form $\exp\left(\frac{0}{0}\right)$.

We can apply L'Hospital's Rule by bringing the limit 'inside' the exponential function.

$$\lim\limits_{x \to \infty} \left(1 + \frac{a}{x}\right)^x = \lim\limits_{t \to 0} \exp\left(a\frac{\ln(1 + t)}{t}\right)$$

$$= \exp\left(\lim\limits_{t \to 0} a\frac{\ln(1 + t)}{t}\right)$$

$$= \exp\left(\lim\limits_{t \to 0} a\frac{\left(\frac{1}{1 + t}\right)}{1}\right)$$

$$= \exp a = e^a$$

Practice Questions

Q1 Use the series expansion of $\sin x$ to find $\lim\limits_{x \to 0} \frac{\sin x + x}{x}$.

Q2 Find $\lim\limits_{x \to 0} \frac{4 \arctan x}{\ln(1 + x)}$ using series expansions.

Q3 Find the following limits using L'Hospital's Rule: a) $\lim\limits_{x \to 2} \frac{x^4 - 5x^2 + 4}{x^3 - 7x + 6}$, b) $\lim\limits_{x \to 49} \frac{x - 49}{\sqrt{x} - 7}$.

Try combining the fractions.

Q4 Use L'Hospital's Rule to show that: a) $\lim\limits_{x \to 0^+} x \ln x = 0$, b) $\lim\limits_{x \to \frac{\pi}{2}^+} (\sec x - \tan x) = 0$, c) $\lim\limits_{x \to 1^+} \left(\frac{1}{x - 1} - \frac{1}{\ln x}\right) = -\frac{1}{2}$.

Exam Questions

Q1 Given that $\lim\limits_{x \to 0} \frac{p - q \cos x}{x^2} = 1$, find the values of p and q. [5 marks]

Q2 Find $\lim\limits_{x \to \infty} x^{\frac{1}{x}}$. [5 marks]

Spend plenty of time learning this — but know your limits...

Indeterminate forms can be a tough thing to get your head around — the initial challenge is figuring out that you're dealing with an indeterminate form in the first place. Get a feel for it by letting each x in the expression go off to the limit individually — but remember that this isn't the actual limit. That's where L'Hospital's Rule comes in.

Leibnitz's Theorem

If you liked the product rule for differentiation, you're gonna love this. Think of that as your appetiser, while this is the full course meal — or, well, n courses at least...

Leibnitz's Theorem is an extension of the Product Rule

If you have two functions u and v, then **Leibnitz's theorem** tells you that the **n^{th} derivative** of the **product** uv is:

$$(uv)^{(n)}(x) = \sum_{r=0}^{n} \binom{n}{r} u^{(r)}(x) \, v^{(n-r)}(x)$$

If you see $f^{(0)}(x)$, it just means $f(x)$.

Now would be a good time to remind yourself about the **binomial coefficients**. You can do them on your **calculator**, but you'll need to know the **definition** when you're working out **general** results (see next page).

$$\binom{n}{r} = {}^{n}C_{r} = \frac{n!}{r!\,(n-r)!} = \frac{n \times (n-1) \times \cdots \times 2 \times 1}{[r \times (r-1) \times \cdots \times 2 \times 1] \times [(n-r) \times (n-r-1) \times \cdots 2 \times 1]}$$

The definition of binomial coefficients is in the formula booklet.

It's useful to keep in mind that $\binom{n}{0} = \binom{n}{n} = 1$ and $\binom{n}{1} = \binom{n}{n-1} = n$ for all n.

Example: Calculate the second derivative of $x^3 \ln x$ using Leibnitz's theorem.

Leibnitz's theorem is symmetric in u and v — this means it doesn't matter which factor you choose to be u and which to be v.

Let's set $u(x) = x^3$ and $v(x) = \ln x$.

Since $n = 2$, you're going to need the first and second derivatives of u and v:

$$u^{(0)}(x) = x^3 \qquad\qquad v^{(0)}(x) = \ln x$$
$$u^{(1)}(x) = 3x^2 \qquad\qquad v^{(1)}(x) = \frac{1}{x}$$
$$u^{(2)}(x) = 6x \qquad\qquad v^{(2)}(x) = -\frac{1}{x^2}$$

The arrows show which derivatives to multiply together in the formula.

Then it's just a case of getting the right coefficients and adding them all together. The formula tells you that:

$$(uv)^{(2)}(x) = \binom{2}{0} u^{(0)}(x) \, v^{(2)}(x) + \binom{2}{1} u^{(1)}(x) \, v^{(1)}(x) + \binom{2}{2} u^{(2)}(x) \, v^{(0)}(x)$$

$$= 1 \times (x^3)\left(-\frac{1}{x^2}\right) + 2 \times (3x^2)\left(\frac{1}{x}\right) + 1 \times (6x)(\ln x)$$

$$= -x + 6x + 6x \ln x = x(5 + 6 \ln x)$$

Leibnitz didn't dedicate his life to developing calculus just to be ridiculed with a cheap photo gag.

Example: Find the value of $\dfrac{d^4}{d\phi^4} \cos\phi \, (\sin\phi + \phi^4)$ at the point $\phi = \pi$.

Choose $u(\phi) = \cos\phi$ and $v(\phi) = \sin\phi + \phi^4$. The derivatives are:

$$u^{(0)}(\phi) = \cos\phi \qquad\qquad v^{(0)}(\phi) = \sin\phi + \phi^4$$
$$u^{(1)}(\phi) = -\sin\phi \qquad\qquad v^{(1)}(\phi) = \cos\phi + 4\phi^3$$
$$u^{(2)}(\phi) = -\cos\phi \qquad\qquad v^{(2)}(\phi) = -\sin\phi + 12\phi^2$$
$$u^{(3)}(\phi) = \sin\phi \qquad\qquad v^{(3)}(\phi) = -\cos\phi + 24\phi$$
$$u^{(4)}(\phi) = \cos\phi \qquad\qquad v^{(4)}(\phi) = \sin\phi + 24$$

Using Leibnitz's theorem:

$$\frac{d^4}{d\phi^4}(uv) = (uv)^{(4)}(\phi) = \cos\phi\,(\sin\phi + 24) + 4(-\sin\phi)(-\cos\phi + 24\phi) + 6(-\cos\phi)(-\sin\phi + 12\phi^2)$$
$$\qquad\qquad + 4\sin\phi\,(\cos\phi + 4\phi^3) + \cos\phi\,(\sin\phi + \phi^4)$$

$$= 16\cos\phi\sin\phi + \cos\phi\,(\phi^4 - 72\phi^2 + 24) + \sin\phi\,(16\phi^3 - 96\phi)$$

Evaluating this at $\phi = \pi$:

$$\frac{d^4}{d\phi^4}(uv) = 16 \times -1 \times 0 + (-1)(\pi^4 - 72\pi^2 + 24) + 0 \times (16\pi^3 - 96\pi) = -\pi^4 + 72\pi^2 - 24$$

Leibnitz's Theorem

You might have to find the nth Derivative

It's possible that the examiners will ask you to find the nth derivative but not give you a **specific value** of n. You'll have to carefully use the formula in a more **general** sense.

Example: Show that the nth derivative of $x^2 e^x$ is $e^x(x^2 + 2nx + n(n-1))$.

Start by working out the derivatives.

Write down the first few derivatives to work out how to derive the general n^{th} derivative of u and v.

$u(x) = x^2$, $u^{(1)}(x) = 2x$, $u^{(2)}(x) = 2$, $u^{(3)}(x) = 0$, $u^{(4)}(x) = 0$, ...

So $u^{(r)}(x) = 0$ for all $r \geq 3$.

$v(x) = e^x$, $v^{(1)}(x) = e^x$, $v^{(2)}(x) = e^x$, ...

As you already knew, $v^{(r)}(x) = e^x$ for all $r \geq 0$.

Leibnitz's theorem tells you to match up $u^{(r)}(x)$ with $v^{(n-r)}(x)$. Use the general forms that you've found.

Since $u^{(r)}(x) = 0$ for all $r \geq 3$, $u^{(r)}(x) v^{(n-r)}(x) = 0$ for all $r \geq 3$.
Then we only need to worry about the three terms that involve $r < 3$.

$$u^{(0)}(x) = x^2 \longleftrightarrow e^x = v^{(n)}(x)$$
$$u^{(1)}(x) = 2x \longleftrightarrow e^x = v^{(n-1)}(x)$$
$$u^{(2)}(x) = 2 \longleftrightarrow e^x = v^{(n-2)}(x)$$

Therefore, the nth derivative is:

$$x^2 e^x + n \times 2x\, e^x + \frac{n!}{2!(n-2)!} \times 2e^x = e^x\left(x^2 + 2nx + 2\frac{n!}{2!(n-2)!}\right)$$

These are the binomial coefficients, found using the definition.

$$= e^x\left(x^2 + 2nx + 2\frac{n(n-1)(n-2)(n-3)\cdots \times 2 \times 1}{(2\times 1)\times(n-2)(n-3)\cdots \times 2 \times 1}\right)$$

$$= e^x(x^2 + 2nx + n(n-1))$$

Practice Questions

Q1 Show that the product rule is the same as Leibnitz's theorem when $n = 1$.

Q2 Use Leibnitz's theorem to calculate:

a) $\dfrac{d^5}{dx^5} x^2 \cos x$,   b) $\dfrac{d^4}{dx^4} e^{3x+1} \ln x$.

Q3 Use Leibnitz's theorem to show that:

a) $\dfrac{d^2}{dx^2}(x^4 e^{\sin x}) = x^2 e^{\sin x}(x^2 \cos^2 x - x^2 \sin x + 8x \cos x + 12)$,

b) $\dfrac{d^2}{dx^2}(5\sqrt{x+1}\,\ln x) = -\dfrac{20x + 20 + 5x^2 \ln x}{4x^2 \sqrt{x+1}^3}$.

Exam Questions

Q1 a) If $y = e^{px}\sin(qx)$, use Leibnitz's theorem to find $\dfrac{dy}{dx}$ and $\dfrac{d^2y}{dx^2}$. **[2 marks]**

b) Hence, show that $\dfrac{d^2y}{dx^2} - 2p\dfrac{dy}{dx} + (p^2 + q^2)y = 0$. **[2 marks]**

Q2 a) Show that the nth derivative of $\dfrac{\ln x}{x}$ is $(-1)^n n!\, x^{-(n+1)}\left(\ln x - \sum_{r=1}^{n}\frac{1}{r}\right)$ for $n \geq 1$. **[7 marks]**

b) Evaluate the fourth derivative of $\dfrac{\ln x}{x}$ at $x = 2$, giving your answer in the form $a \ln 2 - b$, where a and b are rational numbers in their simplest form. **[2 marks]**

This stuff will send you to sleep quicker than a general n-aesthetic...

Wow, Leibnitz's theorem is a pretty hefty formula — it could take someone's eye out. Don't try to use it without writing it down first and knowing exactly which bits are multiplied together. The ns and rs make it look spooky, but just remember that as the derivatives of u go up, the derivatives of v go down. And don't forget the coefficients...

Section 11 — FP1: Further Calculus II

Taylor Series and Differential Equations

Ahhh — my two favourite things in one place... aren't actually to do with these pages. Sorry. I was daydreaming about custard creams and cats. Well, I suppose you'd better learn this stuff while you're here. It's all very useful.

Solve Differential Equations using a Series Solution

1) You know how to solve many types of **differential equations** (DEs) already (see p.76–87).
   These equations were **nice** — they had **constant coefficients** and could be solved **explicitly**:

   E.g. $a\dfrac{d^2y}{dx^2} + b\dfrac{dy}{dx} + cy = f(x)$ with constants a, b and c can be solved using the $y = CF + PI$ method (p.80).

2) Differential equations with **non-constant** coefficients (e.g. polynomials or trigonometric functions), often can't
   be solved explicitly. These have to be dealt with in **another way** — one way is by using a **Taylor series** (p.92):

   > **A Taylor series solution, $y(x)$, for a differential equation at $x = x_0$ is:**
   >
   > $$y(x) = y(x_0) + y'(x_0)(x - x_0) + \frac{y''(x_0)}{2!}(x - x_0)^2 + \frac{y'''(x_0)}{3!}(x - x_0)^3 + \dots + \frac{y^{(n)}(x_0)}{n!}(x - x_0)^n + \dots$$
   >
   > If $x_0 = 0$, you get the Maclaurin series.

3) There will also be a number of **initial conditions** — as many as the **order** of the differential equation.
   You'll have to use these to find the unknown **coefficients** in the Taylor series.

4) This means you'll have to keep differentiating the **original equation** to work them all out —
   e.g. if you need a solution up to the term in x^5, then you have to find $y(x_0)$, $y'(x_0)$... up to $y^{(5)}(x_0)$.

5) When you've found a series solution, make it clear that it is a **solution** to the **original**
   differential equation — it sounds **daft**, but you could lose **easy marks** otherwise.

Example: Find a series solution of the differential equation $\dfrac{d^2y}{dx^2} = x\dfrac{dy}{dx} + y$, up to the term in x^4,
given that at $x = 0$, $y = 1$ and $\dfrac{dy}{dx} = 0$.

You're asked to find terms up to x^4, so you need equations involving $\dfrac{d^3y}{dx^3}$ and $\dfrac{d^4y}{dx^4}$.

Rewrite the **original equation** as $y'' = xy' + y$ ①   Writing differential equations in this form is a bit quicker in practice.

Differentiate with respect to x
using the product rule. $\Rightarrow y''' = xy'' + y' + y' \Rightarrow y''' = xy'' + 2y'$ ②

...and again. $\Rightarrow y^{(4)} = xy''' + y'' + 2y'' \Rightarrow y^{(4)} = xy''' + 3y''$ ③

The **initial conditions** are $y(0) = 1$, and $y'(0) = 0$. **Substitute** these values into the equations above.

$$\Rightarrow y''(0) = 0 \times y'(0) + y(0) = 1 \text{ (from ①)}$$

$$\Rightarrow y'''(0) = 0 \times y''(0) + 2y'(0) = 0 \text{ (from ②)}$$

$$\Rightarrow y^{(4)}(0) = 0 \times y'''(0) + 3y''(0) = 3 \text{ (from ③)}$$

You now have all the required **coefficients**: $y(x_0) = 1$, $y'(x_0) = 0$, $y''(x_0) = 1$, $y'''(x_0) = 0$, $y^{(4)}(x_0) = 3$
Put these into the **Taylor series** formula above to get your answer.

So a **series solution** to the DE is $y = 1 + 0x + \dfrac{1}{2!}x^2 + \dfrac{0}{3!}x^3 + \dfrac{3}{4!}x^4 + \dots$ We cut the series off here,
but don't forget there are
(infinitely) more terms.

*y was the original function,
so the answer here is
y = (your series solution)* $y = 1 + \dfrac{1}{2}x^2 + \dfrac{1}{8}x^4 + \dots$

You can **check** your series solution by **substituting** it back into the original DE.

- In the example above, $y = 1 + \dfrac{1}{2}x^2 + \dfrac{1}{8}x^4 + \dots$, so $\dfrac{dy}{dx} = x + \dfrac{1}{2}x^3 + \dots$ and $\dfrac{d^2y}{dx^2} = 1 + \dfrac{3}{2}x^2 + \dots$

- Substitute into the DE, $\dfrac{d^2y}{dx^2} = x\dfrac{dy}{dx} + y$: $1 + \dfrac{3}{2}x^2 + \dots = x(x + \dfrac{1}{2}x^3 + \dots) + 1 + \dfrac{1}{2}x^2 + \dfrac{1}{8}x^4 + \dots$

  $\Rightarrow 1 + \dfrac{3}{2}x^2 + \dots = 1 + \dfrac{3}{2}x^2 + \dots$

- So you know that you've got at least the **first few terms** of the series solution correct.

Taylor Series and Differential Equations

Example: The differential equation E is given by $\dfrac{d^2y}{dx^2} + (x-1)\dfrac{dy}{dx} - xy = 0$, where $y = 1$ and $\dfrac{dy}{dx} = 1$ at $x = 1$.
Find a series solution of E, in ascending powers of $(x-1)$ up to the term in $(x-1)^4$.

Rewrite the **original equation** as $y'' = (1-x)y' + xy$

Differentiate to get y''': $\Rightarrow y''' = (1-x)y'' - y' + xy' + y = (1-x)y'' - (1-x)y' + y$

...and $y^{(4)}$: $\Rightarrow y^{(4)} = (1-x)y''' - y'' - (1-x)y'' + y' + y' = (1-x)y''' - (2-x)y'' + 2y'$

The **initial conditions** are $y(1) = 1$ and $y'(1) = 1$.
Substitute these values in the equations above to get $y''(1) = 1$, $y'''(1) = 1$ and $y^{(4)}(1) = 1$

You can put these **coefficients** into the **Taylor series** formula to get your answer.

This series solution should be familiar — it's the series expansion of e^{x-1} (see p.44).

So a **series solution** of E is $y = 1 + (x-1) + \dfrac{1}{2!}(x-1)^2 + \dfrac{1}{3!}(x-1)^3 + \dfrac{1}{4!}(x-1)^4 + \ldots$

You can find the *Error* if you know the *Exact Solution*

Example: a) Find a series solution of $\dfrac{dy}{dx} = y\cos x$, where $y(\pi) = 1$ up to the term in x^4.
 b) What is the error when using your series solution to approximate $y(\pi + 1)$?

a) Rewrite the **original equation** as $y' = y\cos x$, and **differentiate**:
 $\Rightarrow y'' = -y\sin x + y'\cos x$
 $\Rightarrow y''' = -y\cos x - y'\sin x - y'\sin x + y''\cos x = -y\cos x - 2y'\sin x + y''\cos x$
 $\Rightarrow y^{(4)} = y\sin x - y'\cos x - 2y'\cos x - 2y''\sin x - y''\sin x + y'''\cos x$
 $= y\sin x - 3y'\cos x - 3y''\sin x + y'''\cos x$

The **initial condition** is $y(\pi) = 1$. Use this to find the **other coefficients**.
 $\Rightarrow y'(\pi) = y(\pi)\cos \pi = -1$
 $\Rightarrow y''(\pi) = -y(\pi)\sin(\pi) + y'(\pi)\cos(\pi) = 1$
 $\Rightarrow y'''(\pi) = -y(\pi)\cos(\pi) - 2y'(\pi)\sin(\pi) + y''(\pi)\cos(\pi) = 0$
 $\Rightarrow y^{(4)}(\pi) = y(\pi)\sin(\pi) - 3y'(\pi)\cos(\pi) - 3y''(\pi)\sin(\pi) + y'''(\pi)\cos(\pi) = -3$

So a **series solution** is $y = 1 - (x-\pi) + \dfrac{1}{2}(x-\pi)^2 - \dfrac{1}{8}(x-\pi)^4 + \ldots$

This is the particular solution using the initial conditions.

The latest test series was cancelled due to poor initial conditions.

b) Using the series solution: $y(\pi + 1) \approx 1 - 1 + \dfrac{1}{2} - \dfrac{1}{8} = 0.375$.

You can find the exact solution by **separating variables**: $\int \dfrac{1}{y}\,dy = \int \cos x\,dx \Rightarrow y = e^{\sin x}$

$e^{\sin(\pi + 1)} = 0.431\ldots$, so the **error** is $0.431\ldots - 0.375 = \mathbf{0.0561}$ (3 s.f.).

Practice Questions

Q1 Find a series solution for $\dfrac{dy}{dx} = \dfrac{y}{x} + 1$, up to the term in $(x-1)^2$, given that at $x = 1$, $y = 0$.

Q2 Find a series solution for $\dfrac{d^2y}{dx^2} - \dfrac{dy}{dx} = xy$, up to the term in $(x-1)^4$, given that at $x = 1$, $y = 1$ and $\dfrac{dy}{dx} = 0$.

Exam Questions

Q1 Show that $1 + (x-\pi) + (x-\pi)^2 + \dfrac{1}{6}(x-\pi)^3 + \ldots$ are the first four terms of the
 series solution for $\dfrac{d^2y}{dx^2} = (\sin x)\dfrac{dy}{dx} + 2y$, given that at $x = \pi$, $y = 1$ and $\dfrac{dy}{dx} = 1$. [4 marks]

Q2 Find a series solution of $\dfrac{d^2y}{dx^2} = 5x\dfrac{dy}{dx} - 2y$, up to the term in x^5, given that at $x = 0$, $y = 0$ and $\dfrac{dy}{dx} = 2$. [9 marks]

Where do you find Taylor's eyesies? In between Taylor series...

As you'd expect, if you increase the number of terms in your series, you get a more accurate approximation to the differential equation. And if you can solve the equation exactly, you can check this accuracy by looking at the error.

Reducible Differential Equations

Some differential equations have a bark worse than their bite — they might look so awful that they'd make an onion cry, but a simple trick can quickly turn them into something nice that you've seen before.

Use a **Substitution** to **Transform** a **DE** into something you can **Solve**

The examples coming up all follow the same **three steps**:

① **Use a given substitution** to **transform** the differential equation into a new one with **new variables**.
② **Solve** the **new** differential equation using an **appropriate method**.
③ Give the **general solution** of the **original equation**, by using the substitution again.

This might involve separating variables, auxiliary equations or the integrating factor.

Example: Use the substitution $w = 1 + x - y$ to solve $\dfrac{dy}{dx} = (1 + x - y)^2$.

1) $w = 1 + x - y \Rightarrow \dfrac{dw}{dx} = 1 - \dfrac{dy}{dx} = 1 - w^2$

2) Solve the new equation using **separation of variables**:   *See page 75 for a reminder on hyperbolic functions and integration.*

$$\frac{1}{1 - w^2}\, dw = dx \Rightarrow \int \frac{1}{1 - w^2}\, dw = \int dx \Rightarrow \operatorname{artanh}(w) = x + C \Rightarrow w = \tanh(x + C)$$

3) Give the **general solution** in terms of x and y only:

$$w = 1 + x - y \Rightarrow 1 + x - y = \tanh(x + C) \Rightarrow y = 1 + x - \tanh(x + C)$$

Example: Use the substitution $y = xz$ to solve the differential equation $x^2 \dfrac{d^2 y}{dx^2} - 2x \dfrac{dy}{dx} + (2 - x^2)y = 0$.

1) To use the substitution, you'll need the **derivatives** of y too.

$$y = xz \Rightarrow \frac{dy}{dx} = x\frac{dz}{dx} + z \text{ (by the product rule)}$$

$$\Rightarrow \frac{d^2 y}{dx^2} = x\frac{d^2 z}{dx^2} + \frac{dz}{dx} + \frac{dz}{dx} = x\frac{d^2 z}{dx^2} + 2\frac{dz}{dx}$$

So the **new** DE is $x^2(x\dfrac{d^2 z}{dx^2} + 2\dfrac{dz}{dx}) - 2x(x\dfrac{dz}{dx} + z) + (2 - x^2)xz = 0$

$$\Rightarrow x^3 \frac{d^2 z}{dx^2} + (2x^2 - 2x^2)\frac{dz}{dx} + (-2x + 2x - x^3)z = 0 \Rightarrow x^3(\frac{d^2 z}{dx^2} - z) = 0$$

$$\Rightarrow x^3 = 0 \Rightarrow y = xz = 0 \text{ (which is one solution to the DE) or } \frac{d^2 z}{dx^2} - z = 0.$$

2) You can solve $\dfrac{d^2 z}{dx^2} - z = 0$ using the **auxiliary equation** method (see p.78):

$$\lambda^2 - 1 = 0 \Rightarrow \lambda = \pm 1 \Rightarrow z = Ae^x + Be^{-x}$$

3) $y = xz$, so the other solution to the **original** differential equation is $y = x(Ae^x + Be^{-x})$.

A **Substitution** can **Reduce** the **Order** of the **DE**

Some **second** and **higher order** DEs can 'reduce' to a **lower** order DE, which can be easier to solve. The substitution will involve a **derivative** of one of the variables, so you'll need to **integrate** to find the solution to the higher order DE.

Example: Use the substitution $y' = v$ to solve $xy'' - 5y' = x^3$ *The second order DE has been reduced to a first order DE.*

1) $y' = v \Rightarrow y'' = v'$. Substituting these into $xy'' - 5y' = x^3$ gives $xv' - 5v = x^3 \Rightarrow v' - \dfrac{5}{x}v = x^2$

2) Solve the new equation using the **integrating factor method** (see p.76).

$$I(x) = e^{\int -\frac{5}{x} dx} = e^{-5\ln x} = e^{\ln x^{-5}} = x^{-5}$$

So $x^{-5}v = \int x^{-5}x^2\, dx = \int x^{-3}\, dx = -\dfrac{1}{2}x^{-2} + C \Rightarrow v = -\dfrac{1}{2}x^3 + Cx^5$

3) Integrate v to give the **general solution** in terms of x and y only: *As you don't know C, you can let C ÷ 6 be a new constant (e.g. C₁) for simplicity.*

$$y' = v \Rightarrow y = \int v\, dx = \int -\frac{1}{2}x^3 + Cx^5\, dx = -\frac{1}{8}x^4 + C_1 x^6 + C_2$$

Reducible Differential Equations

Get **Confident** using the **Chain Rule** and **Product Rule**

Substitutions introduce **new variables** — this means some questions will involve using the
chain rule and **product rule** (often more than once). Make sure you're confident using **both**.

Example: Use the substitution $x = e^t$, to solve the differential equation $x^2 \dfrac{d^2y}{dx^2} - 3x\dfrac{dy}{dx} + 3y = 0$.

1) As y is a function of x, and x is a function of t, careful use of the **chain rule** is required.

Find $\dfrac{dx}{dt}$.

$$x = e^t \Rightarrow \dfrac{dx}{dt} = e^t = x$$

Use the chain rule...

$$\dfrac{dy}{dt} = \dfrac{dy}{dx} \times \dfrac{dx}{dt} = x\dfrac{dy}{dx}$$

$\dfrac{dy}{dt}$ is a function of x, so this bit is the chain rule used the first time, but with $\dfrac{dy}{dt}$ in place of y.

...and again.

$$\dfrac{d^2y}{dt^2} = \dfrac{d}{dt}\left(\dfrac{dy}{dt}\right) = \dfrac{d}{dx}\left(\dfrac{dy}{dt}\right) \times \dfrac{dx}{dt} = \dfrac{d}{dx}\left(x\dfrac{dy}{dx}\right) \times x$$

Use the product rule to differentiate $x\dfrac{dy}{dx}$.

$$\Rightarrow \dfrac{d^2y}{dt^2} = \left(x\dfrac{d^2y}{dx^2} + \dfrac{dy}{dx}\right)x = x^2\dfrac{d^2y}{dx^2} + x\dfrac{dy}{dx}$$

So, $x^2\dfrac{d^2y}{dx^2} = \dfrac{d^2y}{dt^2} - \dfrac{dy}{dt}$ (as $x\dfrac{dy}{dx} = \dfrac{dy}{dt}$)

Rewrite the original DE as $\left(\dfrac{d^2y}{dt^2} - \dfrac{dy}{dt}\right) - 3\dfrac{dy}{dt} + 3y = 0 \Rightarrow \dfrac{d^2y}{dt^2} - 4\dfrac{dy}{dt} + 3y = 0$

2) The **auxiliary equation** is $\lambda^2 - 4\lambda + 3 = 0 \Rightarrow (\lambda - 3)(\lambda - 1) = 0 \Rightarrow \lambda = 3$ or $\lambda = 1$
So $y = Ae^{3t} + Be^t$

3) $x = e^t$, so the solution to the **original** differential equation is $y = Ax^3 + Bx$

All of these examples require a '**DE method**' that you've already **seen** (see p.76-87). Make sure you're
comfortable with all the methods, as any of them could crop up in the exam. Now on to the questions...

Practice Questions

Q1 a) Use the substitution $z = \dfrac{y}{x}$ to show that $\dfrac{dy}{dx} = \dfrac{y}{x} + \left(\dfrac{y}{x}\right)^2$ can be written as $x\dfrac{dz}{dx} = z^2$.

   b) Hence show that $y = -\dfrac{x}{\ln x + A}$ is a solution to the differential equation, where A is a constant.

Q2 Use the substitution $y = xz$ to show that $\dfrac{dy}{dx} = \dfrac{x^2 + y^2}{xy - x^2}$ can be written as $x\dfrac{dz}{dx} = \dfrac{z + 1}{z - 1}$.

Q3 Use the substitution $u = \dfrac{d^2y}{dx^2}$ to solve $\dfrac{d^3y}{dx^3} - 25\dfrac{d^2y}{dx^2} = e^x$.

Exam Questions

Q1 a) Use the substitution $x = e^t$, to show that the equation $ax^2\dfrac{d^2y}{dx^2} + bx\dfrac{dy}{dx} + cy = \ln(x)$, where a, b, c $\in \mathbb{R}$,
   can be expressed in the form $a\left(\dfrac{d^2y}{dt^2} - \dfrac{dy}{dt}\right) + b\left(\dfrac{dy}{dt}\right) + cy = t$ **[7 marks]**

   b) Hence find the general solution to the equation $x^2\dfrac{d^2y}{dx^2} - x\dfrac{dy}{dx} - 3y = \ln(x)$ **[10 marks]**

Q2 The differential equation, L, is given by $x^2\dfrac{d^2y}{dx^2} - 2x\dfrac{dy}{dx} = 2y(x^2 - 1)$.

   Use the substitution $y = xz$ to find a general solution to L. **[8 marks]**

Don't let these disguised equations reduce you to tears...

*Reducible differential equations are like guests at a masquerade ball (a reduci-ball?) — they're the same ones you've
seen before but they're wearing fancy masks to hide their faces. When you approach one of these guests, it's best to
just take off their mask before you talk to them. Although, I wouldn't do this at a real ball... it's probably quite rude.*

Parabolas, Ellipses and Hyperbolas

*If you're doing **AS Level**, you only need to know about parabolas and rectangular hyperbolas — that's **p.102** and **105**.*

Conics can be Described in Different Ways

Conic sections or **conics** are the different types of curve you could make if you were to cut through a solid cone — **parabolas**, **ellipses** (including circles) and **hyperbolas** are all conics.
You can describe conics with **Cartesian equations** or **parametric equations**, or as a **locus of points**.

Points on a Parabola are Equidistant to a Focus and Directrix

The standard **Cartesian** equation for a parabola is: $\boxed{y^2 = 4ax}$
The equation $(y - h)^2 = 4a(x - k)$ would translate the
graph of the parabola h units up, and k units to the right.

You'll find the Cartesian and parametric forms for parabolas (and the other conics coming up) in the formula booklet.

The **parametric** equations are: $\boxed{x = at^2 \text{ and } y = 2at}$

Example: A parabola has the parametric equations $x = at^2$ and $y = 2at$.
Show that the Cartesian equation for this parabola is $y^2 = 4ax$.

Rearrange to make t the subject
in the parametric equation for y.
$$y = 2at \Rightarrow t = \frac{y}{2a}$$

Substitute into the
parametric equation for x.
$$x = a\left(\frac{y}{2a}\right)^2 = \frac{ay^2}{4a^2} = \frac{y^2}{4a}$$

Finally, rearrange to give your
answer in the required form.
$$\text{So } y^2 = 4ax$$

Mel and Kim
consider themselves
a good parabolas.

A parabola can also be defined as a **locus**:

A locus is just a set of points that satisfy some rule or equation — there's more about them coming up on p108-109.

> A **parabola** is the **locus** of points $P(x, y)$ for which the
> **distance** from a fixed point (called the **focus**) is the **same**
> as the distance from a straight line (called the **directrix**).

1) In other words, the **ratio** of the **distance** from any point P
   on the parabola to the focus and directrix is **equal to 1**.
2) This ratio is called the **eccentricity** (shown with the letter e).
   So, for a parabola, $e = 1$.
3) For the parabola with equation $y^2 = 4ax$,
   the focus is $(a, 0)$ and the directrix is $x = -a$.

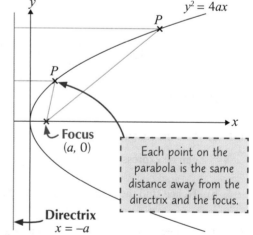

Focus
$(a, 0)$

Each point on the
parabola is the same
distance away from the
directrix and the focus.

Directrix
$x = -a$

Example: Find an equation of the parabola with
focus at $(\frac{1}{2}, 0)$ and directrix at $x + \frac{1}{2} = 0$.

The focus is in the form $(a, 0)$, so use the standard form
for a parabola, $y^2 = 4ax$, with $a = \frac{1}{2}$, to get $y^2 = 2x$.

Example: Find the focus and directrix for the parabola with equation $y^2 = 12(x - 1)$.

The equation is in the standard form for a parabola with $4a = 12$, but with x translated to $(x - 1)$.
For $y^2 = 12x$, $a = 3$, the focus is $(3, 0)$ and the directrix is $x = -3$.
$(x - 1)$ translates the parabola one unit to the right, so the focus for the
parabola $y^2 = 12(x - 1)$ is $(4, 0)$ and the directrix is at $x = -2$.

Parabolas, Ellipses and Hyperbolas

The *Parametric* equations for *Ellipses* use *Cos and Sin*

The **major axis** of an ellipse is its **longest diameter** — it passes through the **centre** and both **foci** of the ellipse (see below).
The **minor axis** is its shortest diameter.

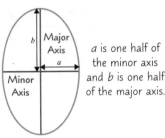

(1) $a > b$

a is one half of the major axis and *b* is one half of the minor axis.

The standard **Cartesian** equation for an ellipse is: $\dfrac{x^2}{a^2} + \dfrac{y^2}{b^2} = 1$

If $a = b$, you can rearrange the equation to get $x^2 + y^2 = r^2$, which is just the equation of a circle.

(2) $b > a$

a is one half of the minor axis and *b* is one half of the major axis.

The **parametric** equations are: $x = a \cos t, \; y = b \sin t$ where $0 \le t < 2\pi$

If you substitute the parametric equation for *x* and *y* into the Cartesian equation you get $\cos^2 t + \sin^2 t = 1$, which is a trig identity you already know.

Example: An ellipse has equation $\dfrac{x^2}{36} + \dfrac{y^2}{16} = 1$

a) Give the parametric equations for this ellipse, in the form $x = f(\theta)$ and $y = g(\theta)$.

b) Point $P(0, y_1)$ lies on the ellipse. Find the value of θ at point P, given that $y_1 > 0$.

a) Use the parametric equations $x = a \cos\theta$ and $y = b \sin\theta$.
$a^2 = 36$ and $b^2 = 16$, so the parametric equations are $x = 6\cos\theta$ and $y = 4\sin\theta$.

b) When $x = 0$, $\dfrac{y^2}{16} = 1$, so $y = \pm 4$.

$y_1 > 0$, so $y_1 = 4 = 4\sin\theta \Rightarrow \theta = \dfrac{\pi}{2}$

> You could also use the parametric equations here.
> If $x = 0$, $6\cos\theta = 0$, which means $\theta = \pi/2$ or $3\pi/2$. As y_1 is > 0, it has to be $\pi/2$.

Ellipses have *two Foci* and *two Directrices*

> Foci is the plural of focus, and directrices is the plural of directrix.

There are **two focus-directrix pairs** — an ellipse can be defined as a **locus** with reference to **one pair**:

> An **ellipse** is the **locus** of points $P(x, y)$ for which the **ratio** of the **distance** from a point to a **focus** and the point to the corresponding **directrix** is a constant e, where $0 < e < 1$.

1) As before, the constant, e, is called the **eccentricity**. For an ellipse, $b^2 = a^2(1 - e^2)$.

2) There are **formulas** to find the foci and directrices:

> These are in the formula booklet.

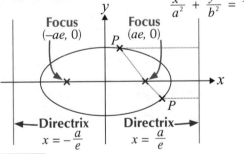

> An ellipse with equation $\dfrac{x^2}{a^2} + \dfrac{y^2}{b^2} = 1$ (where $a > b$) has foci at $(\pm ae, 0)$ and directrices at $x = \pm\dfrac{a}{e}$.

> If $b > a$, the foci will be on the y-axis at $(0, \pm be)$, the directrices will be in the form $y = \pm\dfrac{b}{e}$ and the eccentricity satisfies $a^2 = b^2(1 - e^2)$ instead.

Example: Find the foci and directrices for an ellipse with equation $2x^2 + 8y^2 = 8$.

First, rewrite the equation in the standard form: $\dfrac{x^2}{4} + y^2 = 1$ So $a = 2, b = 1$

Find the eccentricity using the formula: $b^2 = a^2(1 - e^2) \Rightarrow 1 = 4(1 - e^2) \Rightarrow e^2 = \dfrac{3}{4} \Rightarrow e = \dfrac{\sqrt{3}}{2}$

Plug a and e into the formulas for the foci and directrices:

The foci are at $\left(\pm 2 \times \dfrac{\sqrt{3}}{2}, 0\right) = (\sqrt{3}, 0)$ and $(-\sqrt{3}, 0)$.

The directrices are at $x = \pm\dfrac{2}{\frac{\sqrt{3}}{2}} = \pm\dfrac{4}{\sqrt{3}} = \dfrac{4\sqrt{3}}{3}$ and $-\dfrac{4\sqrt{3}}{3}$.

Parabolas, Ellipses and Hyperbolas

Hyperbolas are Related to Hyperbolic Functions

The standard **Cartesian** equation for a hyperbola is:

$$\frac{x^2}{a^2} - \frac{y^2}{b^2} = 1$$

There are **two** ways to write the **parametric** equations:

$$x = a \sec t, \quad y = b \tan t$$ where $0 \le t < 2\pi$

These equations rely on the trig identity $\sec^2 t = 1 + \tan^2 t$.

OR $\quad x = \pm a \cosh t, \quad y = b \sinh t$

These are hyperbolic functions you've seen on p.70.

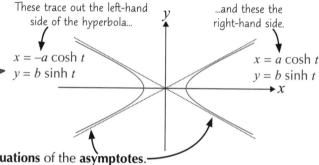

These trace out the left-hand side of the hyperbola...

$x = -a \cosh t$
$y = b \sinh t$

...and these the right-hand side.

$x = a \cosh t$
$y = b \sinh t$

You can find equations for the asymptotes too.

As x and y get **very large**, $\frac{x^2}{a^2} \approx \frac{y^2}{b^2}$, so $y = \pm \frac{b}{a}x$ are the **equations** of the **asymptotes.**

Example: A hyperbola has the parametric equations $x = \pm 2 \cosh t$ and $y = 3 \sinh t$.

a) Show that the Cartesian equation for the curve is $\frac{x^2}{4} - \frac{y^2}{9} = 1$.

b) Find the equations of the asymptotes.

This curve could also be described using
$x = 2 \sec t$ and $y = 3 \tan t$.

a) Rearrange the parametric equations to get **cosh** $t = \frac{x}{2}$ and **sinh** $t = \frac{y}{3}$.

Use the **hyperbolic identity** $\cosh^2 t - \sinh^2 t = 1$:
$$\left(\frac{x}{2}\right)^2 - \left(\frac{y}{3}\right)^2 = \frac{x^2}{4} - \frac{y^2}{9} = 1$$

You'll find the equation for asymptotes in the formula booklet (in a rearranged form).

b) The asymptotes are at $y = \frac{3}{2}x$ and $y = -\frac{3}{2}x$.

Hyperbolas also have Two Focus-Directrix Pairs

A **hyperbola** is the **locus** of points $P(x, y)$ for which the **ratio** of the **distance** from a point to a **focus** and the point to the corresponding **directrix** is a constant e, where $e > 1$.

1) For a hyperbola, $b^2 = a^2(e^2 - 1)$.

2) There are **formulas** to find the foci and directrices:

A hyperbola with equation $\frac{x^2}{a^2} - \frac{y^2}{b^2} = 1$ has foci at $(\pm ae, 0)$ and directrices at $x = \pm \frac{a}{e}$.

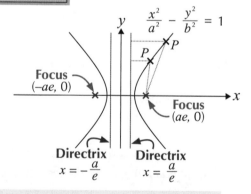

$$\frac{x^2}{a^2} - \frac{y^2}{b^2} = 1$$

Focus $(-ae, 0)$

Focus $(ae, 0)$

Directrix $x = -\frac{a}{e}$

Directrix $x = \frac{a}{e}$

Example: A hyperbola C has equation $\frac{x^2}{100} - \frac{y^2}{25} = 1$.

Find: a) the eccentricity, b) the foci, c) the directrices of the hyperbola

The equation is in the standard form for a hyperbola with $a = 10$ and $b = 5$.

a) Find the eccentricity using the formula:
$$b^2 = a^2(e^2 - 1) \Rightarrow 25 = 100(e^2 - 1) \Rightarrow e^2 = \frac{5}{4} \Rightarrow e = \sqrt{\frac{5}{4}} = \frac{\sqrt{5}}{2}$$

b) Now, plug a and e into the formula $(\pm ae, 0)$ to find the foci:
The foci are at $(5\sqrt{5}, 0)$ and $(-5\sqrt{5}, 0)$.

c) Use $x = \pm \frac{a}{e}$ to find the directrices:
The directrices are at $x = \frac{20}{\sqrt{5}} = 4\sqrt{5}$ and $x = -4\sqrt{5}$.

Parabolas, Ellipses and Hyperbolas

Rectangular Hyperbolas have Perpendicular Asymptotes

If you're doing <u>AS Level</u>, you just need to know what a rectangular hyperbola <u>looks like</u> (see the diagram below on the right) and the <u>Cartesian</u> and <u>parametric equations</u>, which are given in the purple boxes.

In the case where **a = b** in the standard equation of a hyperbola ($\frac{x^2}{a^2} - \frac{y^2}{b^2} = 1$) you get a "**rectangular hyperbola**".

Rectangular hyperbolas have asymptotes that intersect **rectangularly** (are **perpendicular**).

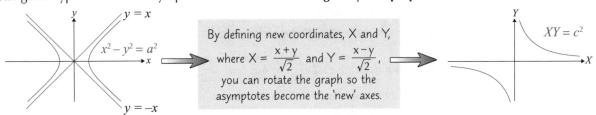

By defining new coordinates, X and Y, where $X = \frac{x+y}{\sqrt{2}}$ and $Y = \frac{x-y}{\sqrt{2}}$, you can rotate the graph so the asymptotes become the 'new' axes.

After this transformation, the equations for a rectangular hyperbola are as follows:

Standard **Cartesian** equation: $\boxed{xy = c^2}$ **Parametric** equations: $\boxed{x = ct,\ y = \frac{c}{t}}$

The **eccentricity** can be found by plugging $a = b$ into the hyperbola eccentricity formula:
$b^2 = a^2(e^2 - 1) \Rightarrow 1 = e^2 - 1 \Rightarrow e^2 = 2 \Rightarrow e = \sqrt{2}$

A rectangular hyperbola with equation $xy = c^2$ has
foci at ($\pm \sqrt{2}\ c, \pm \sqrt{2}\ c$) and **directrices** at $x + y = \pm \sqrt{2}\ c$.

These can be derived from the equations for the foci and directrices of a general hyperbola, using the coordinate transformations defined above.

Practice Questions

If you're doing <u>AS Level</u>, you only need to do Practice Questions 1 a) and 1 c) and Exam Question 1.

Q1 Find a Cartesian equation for each of the following:

a) the parabola A with parametric equations $x = \frac{at^2}{2}$ and $y = at$.

b) the ellipse B with parametric equations $x = 2a \cos t$ and $y = 2b \sin t$.

c) the rectangular hyperbola C with parametric equations $x = c^2 t$ and $y = \frac{c^2}{t}$.

Q2 Give the foci and equations of the directrices for an ellipse with equation $\frac{x^2}{5} + \frac{y^2}{10} = 1$.

Q3 A hyperbola, D, has an eccentricity of 2 and directrices at $x = \pm 1$.

a) Give parametric equations for D in the form $x = \pm a \cosh t$.
and $y = b\sqrt{c}\ \sinh t$, where a, b and c are constants to be found.

b) Give the equations of the asymptotes of D.

Exam Questions

Q1 A parabola P has a focus at $(a, 0)$. a is a positive constant.

A rectangular hyperbola, Q, has parametric equations $x = a\sqrt{2}\ t$ and $y = \frac{a\sqrt{2}}{t}$.

Show that P and Q intersect at the point $R\ (a, 2a)$. **[5 marks]**

Q2 An ellipse E has equation $\frac{x^2}{a^2} + \frac{y^2}{b^2} = 1$.

The point Q, shown on the right, lies on the ellipse.

Given that $b = 3$, and $b > a$, show that the eccentricity of the ellipse is $\frac{2}{3}$. **[4 marks]**

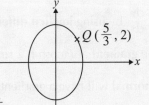

And remember — you can't use conic screwdrivers on wood...

There was a lot of stuff there on conics to take in — thankfully, lots of the formulas are given in the formula booklet, so you don't need to <u>remember</u> them, but you do need to <u>understand</u> what they all mean.

Tangents and Normals to Curves

These two pages pull together the stuff you've just learnt about conics, with the differentiation skills you already have...
*If you're studying **AS Level**, you only need to look at the **first example**, then move on to the questions.*

Use **Implicit Differentiation** or the **Chain Rule** for Conics

You already know how to find **tangents** and **normals** to curves. For **conics**, finding the gradient
you're after can be tricky — you might have to do some **implicit differentiation** or use the **chain rule**.

Example: a) Show that for a parabola with equation $y^2 = 4ax$, $\dfrac{dy}{dx} = \dfrac{2a}{y}$.

Use **implicit differentiation** to find the derivative: $2y\dfrac{dy}{dx} = 4a \implies \dfrac{dy}{dx} = \dfrac{4a}{2y} \implies \boxed{\dfrac{dy}{dx} = \dfrac{2a}{y}}$

If you're doing the AS Level, you don't need to be able to differentiate the equation
— you can just learn the formula for the gradient of a parabola, given in the box.

b) A parabola C has equation $y^2 = 16x$. The line $y = 2$ crosses C at point P.
Find the equation of the normal to C at point P.

A sketch will help you picture the problem.

At point P, $y = 2$ and $y^2 = 16x \implies 4 = 16x \implies x = \dfrac{1}{4}$.

Compare the equation of C with the general equation in a): $4a = 16 \implies a = 4$.

So at $P(\dfrac{1}{4}, 2)$, the gradient of C is $\dfrac{dy}{dx} = \dfrac{2 \times 4}{2} = 4$.

The **normal** will have a gradient of $-1 \div 4 = -\dfrac{1}{4}$.

Find the **equation** of the **normal**: $\quad y - y_1 = m(x - x_1)$

$$y - 2 = -\dfrac{1}{4}(x - \dfrac{1}{4}) \implies y = -\dfrac{1}{4}x + \dfrac{33}{16}$$

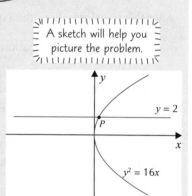

Example: The parametric equations for an ellipse C are $x = \cos t$ and $y = 2\sin t$.
Find the tangent to C at the point $(\dfrac{1}{\sqrt{2}}, \sqrt{2})$.

Find $\dfrac{dy}{dx}$ by using the **chain rule**: $\quad \dfrac{dy}{dx} = \dfrac{dy}{dt} \div \dfrac{dx}{dt} = -\dfrac{2\cos t}{\sin t}$

You could find the Cartesian equation first, and then use implicit differentiation to find the gradient.

At $(\dfrac{1}{\sqrt{2}}, \sqrt{2})$, $\cos t = \dfrac{1}{\sqrt{2}}$ and $2\sin t = \sqrt{2}$, so $\dfrac{dy}{dx} = -\dfrac{2 \times \dfrac{1}{\sqrt{2}}}{\dfrac{\sqrt{2}}{2}} = -2$

Find the **equation** of the **tangent**: $\qquad y - \sqrt{2} = -2(x - \dfrac{1}{\sqrt{2}})$

Rearrange and **simplify**: $\qquad \implies y = -2x + 2\sqrt{2}$

Example: A hyperbola C has equation $x^2 = 1 + \dfrac{y^2}{4}$.
Find the equation for the normal at the point $P(\cosh t, 2\sinh t)$.

The hyperbola can be rearranged to be written in the standard form, with $a = 1$ and $b = 2$.

Find $\dfrac{dy}{dx}$ by using **implicit differentiation**: $\quad 2x = \dfrac{2y}{4}\dfrac{dy}{dx} \implies \dfrac{dy}{dx} = \dfrac{8x}{2y} = \dfrac{4x}{y}$

So the **gradient** at $P(\cosh t, 2\sinh t)$ is: $\quad \dfrac{4\cosh t}{2\sinh t} = \dfrac{2\cosh t}{\sinh t}$

The **normal** will have a gradient of $-1 \div \dfrac{2\cosh t}{\sinh t} = -\dfrac{\sinh t}{2\cosh t}$

Find the **equation** of the **normal** at P: $\quad y - 2\sinh t = -\dfrac{\sinh t}{2\cosh t}(x - \cosh t)$

Multiply both sides by $2\cosh t$: $\quad 2y\cosh t - 4\sinh t\cosh t = -x\sinh t + \sinh t\cosh t$

$$\implies 2y\cosh t + x\sinh t = 5\sinh t\cosh t$$

You can give this answer in the form $y = mx + c$ by dividing by cosh t and rearranging.

Tangents and Normals to Curves

Here's yet *another* example. This time I've sprinkled in a little more algebra.

Example: An ellipse has equation $ax^2 + by^2 = c$, where a, b and c are all positive constants.
Two distinct points on the ellipse, G and H, have tangents which intersect at the point $P(p, q)$.

Show that the gradient of the line that passes through G and H is equal to $-\dfrac{ap}{bq}$.

Find $\dfrac{dy}{dx}$ using **implicit differentiation**: $2ax + 2by \dfrac{dy}{dx} = 0 \Rightarrow \dfrac{dy}{dx} = -\dfrac{ax}{by}$

Let point G have coordinates (x_1, y_1) and H have coordinates (x_2, y_2).

You can call the coordinates anything you want — just make sure the working is easy to follow.

Find the **equation** of the **tangent** at G:

$$y - y_1 = -\frac{ax_1}{by_1}(x - x_1)$$
$$\Rightarrow byy_1 - by_1^2 = -axx_1 + ax_1^2$$
$$\Rightarrow axx_1 + byy_1 = ax_1^2 + by_1^2$$

Use the fact that (x_1, y_1) lies on the **ellipse**: $ax_1^2 + by_1^2 = c$, so $axx_1 + byy_1 = c$

Similarly, you can show the **tangent** at H is: $axx_2 + byy_2 = c$

We're told that both tangents
pass through point $P(p, q)$:

$$apx_1 + bqy_1 = c \text{ and } apx_2 + bqy_2 = c$$
$$\Rightarrow apx_1 + bqy_1 = apx_2 + bqy_2$$
$$\Rightarrow -ap(x_2 - x_1) = bq(y_2 - y_1)$$

Rearrange to get an expression for the
gradient between $G(x_1, y_1)$ and $H(x_2, y_2)$:

$$\frac{y_2 - y_1}{x_2 - x_1} = -\frac{ap}{bq} \text{ as required}$$

Practice Questions

For AS Level, you only need to do Practice Questions 1a), 1d) and 3.

Q1 Give the general equation of the <u>tangent</u> and <u>normal</u>:

   a) for a parabola with equation $y^2 = 4ax$ at the point $(at^2, 2at)$.

   b) for an ellipse with equation $\dfrac{x^2}{a^2} + \dfrac{y^2}{b^2} = 1$ at the point $(a \cos t, \ b \sin t)$.

   c) for a hyperbola with equation $\dfrac{x^2}{a^2} - \dfrac{y^2}{b^2} = 1$ at the point $(a \sec t, \ b \tan t)$.

   d) for a rectangular hyperbola with equation $xy = c^2$ at the point $(ct, \dfrac{c}{t})$.

Q2 The hyperbola H has equation $\dfrac{x^2}{25} - \dfrac{y^2}{36} = 1$.

The tangent at point $P(5 \cosh \alpha, 6 \sinh \alpha)$ passes through the point $(0, 1)$. What is the value of α?

Q3 The normal to the parabola $y^2 = 4ax$ at the point $P(ap^2, 2ap)$ passes through the point Z on the x-axis.
If Z is the focus of the parabola, show that there is only one normal which can satisfy this property.

Exam Question   Only answer this exam question if you're studying for A Level.

Q1 A hyperbola H has equation $\dfrac{x^2}{9} - \dfrac{y^2}{16} = 1$.

   a) Show that the equation for the normal to the hyperbola at $P(3 \sec t, 4 \tan t)$ is
$3x \sin t + 4y = 25 \tan t$. [5 marks]

The normal to the hyperbola at P crosses the x-axis at $R(9e, 0)$, where e is the eccentricity of the hyperbola.
It crosses the positive y-axis at point Q.

   b) Given that $\sin t \neq 0$, find the area of the triangle ORQ, where O is the origin. [8 marks]

It was abnormally hot last week — now I'm a tanned-gent...

Implicit differentiation and the chain rule are key to finding the tangent or normal to a curve — if you're finding one way particularly tricky, it might be worth trying the other method... and you can always use both to check your answer.

Loci Problems

Here you'll get to see how to derive the Cartesian equations of conics from their loci definitions, along with some other loci problems. If you're studying **AS Level**, you only need to look at the **first example**, then go to the questions.

You can Derive **Cartesian** equations for **Conics** from **Loci**

Example: A parabola is the locus of points which are the same distance from a focus and a directrix. Show that the Cartesian equation for a parabola with focus $F = (a, 0)$ and directrix D at $x = -a$ is $y^2 = 4ax$.

Let $P(x, y)$ be a generic point on the parabola.

$PF = \sqrt{(x-a)^2 + y^2}$ and $PD = x + a$

The distance PF is the same as PD, so $\sqrt{(x-a)^2 + y^2} = x + a$

Square both sides:
$$(x - a)^2 + y^2 = (x + a)^2$$
$$\Rightarrow x^2 - 2ax + a^2 + y^2 = x^2 + 2ax + a^2$$
$$\Rightarrow y^2 = 4ax$$

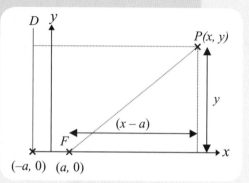

Example: An ellipse is the locus of points for which the ratio of the distance from a point to a focus and the point to a directrix is a constant e, where $0 < e < 1$. Show that an ellipse with focus $F = (ae, 0)$ and directrix D at $x = \dfrac{a}{e}$ has the Cartesian equation $\dfrac{x^2}{a^2} + \dfrac{y^2}{a^2(1 - e^2)} = 1$.

Let $P(x, y)$ be a generic point on the ellipse.

$PF = \sqrt{(x - ae)^2 + y^2}$ and $PD = \dfrac{a}{e} - x$

$PF/PD = e$, so $\sqrt{(x - ae)^2 + y^2} = e\left(\dfrac{a}{e} - x\right)$

Square both sides:
$$(x - ae)^2 + y^2 = e^2\left(\dfrac{a}{e} - x\right)^2$$
$$\Rightarrow x^2 - 2aex + a^2e^2 + y^2 = e^2\left(\dfrac{a^2}{e^2} - \dfrac{2ax}{e} + x^2\right)$$
$$\Rightarrow x^2 - 2aex + a^2e^2 + y^2 = a^2 - 2aex + e^2x^2$$
$$\Rightarrow x^2(1 - e^2) + y^2 = a^2(1 - e^2)$$

Divide by $a^2(1 - e^2)$: $\quad \dfrac{x^2}{a^2} + \dfrac{y^2}{a^2(1 - e^2)} = 1 \quad$ Setting $b^2 = a^2(1 - e^2)$ gives the standard Cartesian equation.

Loci Problems Might Involve a **Chord**

A chord is a straight line segment that connects two points on a curve.

Example: An ellipse has equation $x^2 + \dfrac{y^2}{4} = 1$. The chord PQ of the ellipse has gradient -1. As P and Q vary, the locus of the midpoint M of the chord is a straight line. Find the equation for this locus.

1) The chord is a **straight line** with **gradient -1**, so let the equation of chord PQ be $y = -x + c$.

2) The **endpoints** of the chord satisfy **both** the equation of the **chord** and the equation of the **ellipse**. Substituting $y = -x + c$ into the equation of the ellipse, the x-coordinates of the endpoints are the **roots** of the equation:
$$x^2 + \frac{(-x + c)^2}{4} = 1 \Rightarrow 4x^2 + x^2 - 2cx + c^2 = 4 \Rightarrow 5x^2 - 2cx + c^2 - 4 = 0$$

3) Let x_1 and x_2 be the **roots** of this quadratic, and let the **midpoint** $M = (X, Y)$. Then $X = \dfrac{x_1 + x_2}{2}$. For a quadratic $ax^2 + bx + c = 0$, the **sum of the roots** is equal to $\dfrac{-b}{a}$. So $x_1 + x_2 = \dfrac{2c}{5} \Rightarrow X = \dfrac{c}{5} \Rightarrow c = 5X$

Have a look at p.36 to remind yourself about the rules for roots.

4) The **midpoint** (X, Y) lies on the **chord**, so $Y = -X + c$. Substituting in the expression for c gives:
$$Y = -X + 5X \Rightarrow Y = 4X$$

Loci Problems

Use **Trig Identities** to Eliminate **Parameters**

Example: A hyperbola C has equation $\frac{x^2}{a^2} - y^2 = 1$. The tangent at point Q ($a \sec \theta$, $\tan \theta$) on the hyperbola crosses the x-axis at point A and y-axis at point B.

Find the locus of the midpoint AB.

Use implicit differentiation to find dy/dx.

$$\frac{2x}{a^2} - 2y\frac{dy}{dx} = 0 \quad \Rightarrow \quad \frac{dy}{dx} = \frac{x}{a^2 y}$$

Work out an equation for the tangent at the point Q.

$$y - y_1 = m(x - x_1) \quad \Rightarrow \quad y - \tan \theta = \frac{\sec \theta}{a \tan \theta}(x - a \sec \theta)$$

$$\Rightarrow \quad ay \tan \theta - a \tan^2 \theta = x \sec \theta - a \sec^2 \theta$$

Use the trig identity $\sec^2 \theta - \tan^2 \theta = 1$ to simplify the equation.

$$\Rightarrow \quad a(\sec^2 \theta - \tan^2 \theta) = x \sec \theta - ay \tan \theta$$

$$\Rightarrow \quad x \sec \theta - ay \tan \theta = a$$

Find the coordinates for A and B.

At A, $y = 0 \quad \Rightarrow \quad x \sec \theta = a \quad \Rightarrow \quad x = \frac{a}{\sec \theta}$

At B, $x = 0 \quad \Rightarrow \quad -ay \tan \theta = a \quad \Rightarrow \quad y = -\frac{1}{\tan \theta}$

Use the coordintates of A and B to find the coordinates of the midpoint.

Let (X, Y) be the coordinates of the **midpoint** of the line AB.

$X = \frac{a}{2 \sec \theta}$, $Y = -\frac{1}{2 \tan \theta}$, so $\sec \theta = \frac{a}{2X}$ and $\tan \theta = -\frac{1}{2Y}$

Use $\sec^2 \theta - \tan^2 \theta = 1$ again to eliminate the parameter θ.

So, $(\frac{a}{2X})^2 - (-\frac{1}{2Y})^2 = \frac{a^2}{4X^2} - \frac{1}{4Y^2} = 1$

is the **locus** of the midpoint of the line AB.

Practice Questions

For <u>AS Level</u>, you only need to do Practice Question 2 and Exam Question 1.

Q1 A hyperbola is the locus of points such that the ratio of the distance from a point to a focus and the point to a directrix is a constant e, where $e > 1$.

Show that a hyperbola with focus $F = (ae, 0)$ and directrix D at $x = \frac{a}{e}$ has the Cartesian equation $\frac{x^2}{a^2} - \frac{y^2}{a^2(e^2 - 1)} = 1$.

Q2 A rectangular hyperbola is defined by the equation $xy = 9$.

The tangents at point $P(3p, \frac{3}{p})$ and point $Q(3q, \frac{3}{q})$ on the curve intersect at the point R.

a) Show that the coordinates of R are $(\frac{6pq}{p+q}, \frac{6}{p+q})$.

b) If $pq = -1$, find the equation of the locus of R as p and q vary.

Q3 The tangent to the ellipse $\frac{x^2}{16} + \frac{y^2}{9} = 1$ at the point $P(4 \cos t, 3 \sin t)$ crosses the x-axis at A and y-axis at B. Find an equation for the locus of the midpoint of AB as t varies.

Q4 The normal to the hyperbola $x^2 - 4y^2 = 4$ at point $Q(2 \sec \theta, \tan \theta)$ crosses the x-axis at A and y-axis at B. Find an equation for the locus of the midpoint of AB as θ varies.

Exam Question

Q1 P and Q are two distinct points on a parabola with equation $y^2 = 4x$, with x-coordinates of p^2 and q^2 respectively.

The focus F of the parabola lies on the straight line PQ.

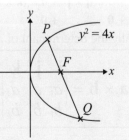

a) Show that $pq = -1$ [5 marks]

b) Hence show that the locus of R, where R is the midpoint of the line PQ, is $y^2 = 2(x - 1)$. [4 marks]

Loki was a whizz at loci — he was a great mythmatician...

Here's a fun fact from Norse mythology — Loki gave birth to an eight-legged horse (called Sleipnir) which later became Odin's trusty steed. I'm not sure how that helps you with this page, but it's important nonetheless... probably.

Vector Cross Product

You've met the scalar product — now it's time to meet the equally useful vector product.

Finding the **Vector Product**

The vector product is often called the cross product.

The **vector product** of two vectors **a** and **b** is written **a** × **b** (you read this as 'a cross b'). The **definition** of the vector product is:

$$\mathbf{a} \times \mathbf{b} = |\mathbf{a}||\mathbf{b}|\sin\theta\,\mathbf{n}$$

A vector product is **calculated** using **two vectors**, but unlike the scalar product, the **result** is **another vector**, not a scalar.

θ is the **angle between the vectors** when they're directed away from the same point.

n is a **unit vector** that's **perpendicular** to both **a** and **b**. So **a** × **b** is always **perpendicular** to both **a** and **b**.

The **Direction** of the **Vector n** matters

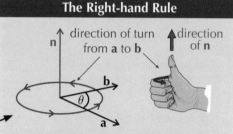

The Right-hand Rule

direction of turn from **a** to **b**   direction of **n**

1) For any two vectors **a** and **b** there are **two** possible unit vectors that are perpendicular to both **a** and **b** — the two unit vectors pointing in **opposite directions** along the line that's perpendicular to **a** and **b**.

2) The **direction of the vector n** in the formula **a** × **b** = |**a**||**b**|sin θ **n** is determined by the **direction of the turn** from **a** to **b** — you can work it out using the **right-hand rule**.

3) The turn from **a** to **b** is in the opposite direction to the turn from **b** to **a**. This means: $\boxed{\mathbf{b} \times \mathbf{a} = -(\mathbf{a} \times \mathbf{b})}$
So the vector product is **not commutative**.

*If your thumb points up for the turn from **a** to **b** then for the reverse turn from **b** to **a** your thumb will point down.*

1) Stick your **right** thumb up.

2) If your **curled fingers** are pointing in the direction of the turn from **a** to **b**...

3) ...then your **thumb** is pointing in the direction of **n**.

4) Using these rules, you can show:

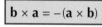

$$\begin{array}{lll} \mathbf{i} \times \mathbf{j} = \mathbf{k} & \mathbf{j} \times \mathbf{k} = \mathbf{i} & \mathbf{k} \times \mathbf{i} = \mathbf{j} \\ \mathbf{j} \times \mathbf{i} = -\mathbf{k} & \mathbf{k} \times \mathbf{j} = -\mathbf{i} & \mathbf{i} \times \mathbf{k} = -\mathbf{j} \end{array}$$

5) The vector product also does **not** obey the **associative law** — i.e. **a** × (**b** × **c**) ≠ (**a** × **b**) × **c**.

Parallel Vectors have a **Vector Product** of **Zero**

This means that **a** × **a** = **O** *for all vectors* **a**.

The angle θ between parallel vectors is **0°** (if they have the same direction) or **180°** (if they have opposite directions), and **sin 0° = sin 180° = 0**.

This means that for parallel vectors **a** and **b**, the vector product **a** × **b** = |**a**||**b**|sin θ **n** = 0.

So for two **non-zero** vectors **a** and **b**: $\boxed{\mathbf{a} \times \mathbf{b} = 0 \Leftrightarrow \mathbf{a} \text{ and } \mathbf{b} \text{ are parallel}}$

The **Vector Product** is the **Determinant** of a 3 by 3 **Matrix**

*p***a** × *q***b** = *pq*(**a** × **b**), *where* **a** *and* **b** *are vectors, and p and q are scalars.*

Let $\mathbf{a} = a_1\mathbf{i} + a_2\mathbf{j} + a_3\mathbf{k}$ and $\mathbf{b} = b_1\mathbf{i} + b_2\mathbf{j} + b_3\mathbf{k}$, then $\mathbf{a} \times \mathbf{b} = (a_1\mathbf{i} + a_2\mathbf{j} + a_3\mathbf{k}) \times (b_1\mathbf{i} + b_2\mathbf{j} + b_3\mathbf{k})$

$= a_1b_1(\mathbf{i} \times \mathbf{i}) + a_2b_2(\mathbf{j} \times \mathbf{j}) + a_3b_3(\mathbf{k} \times \mathbf{k}) + a_1b_2(\mathbf{i} \times \mathbf{j}) + a_2b_1(\mathbf{j} \times \mathbf{i}) + a_1b_3(\mathbf{i} \times \mathbf{k}) + a_3b_1(\mathbf{k} \times \mathbf{i}) + a_2b_3(\mathbf{j} \times \mathbf{k}) + a_3b_2(\mathbf{k} \times \mathbf{j})$

$= 0 \qquad + 0 \qquad + 0 \qquad + a_1b_2\mathbf{k} \quad + a_2b_1(-\mathbf{k}) \quad + a_1b_3(-\mathbf{j}) \quad + a_3b_1\mathbf{j} \qquad + a_2b_3\mathbf{i} \qquad + a_3b_2(-\mathbf{i}).$

This is actually the determinant of a 3 by 3 matrix, which means:

$$\mathbf{a} \times \mathbf{b} = \begin{vmatrix} \mathbf{i} & \mathbf{j} & \mathbf{k} \\ a_1 & a_2 & a_3 \\ b_1 & b_2 & b_3 \end{vmatrix} = (a_2b_3 - b_2a_3)\mathbf{i} - (a_1b_3 - b_1a_3)\mathbf{j} + (a_1b_2 - b_1a_2)\mathbf{k}$$

Example: $\mathbf{a} = (-2\mathbf{i} + 6\mathbf{j} + 3\mathbf{k})$ and $\mathbf{b} = (4\mathbf{i} - 5\mathbf{j} - \mathbf{k})$. Find **a** × **b**.

$$\mathbf{a} \times \mathbf{b} = (-2\mathbf{i} + 6\mathbf{j} + 3\mathbf{k}) \times (4\mathbf{i} - 5\mathbf{j} - \mathbf{k}) = \begin{vmatrix} \mathbf{i} & \mathbf{j} & \mathbf{k} \\ -2 & 6 & 3 \\ 4 & -5 & -1 \end{vmatrix} = (-6 + 15)\mathbf{i} - (2 - 12)\mathbf{j} + (10 - 24)\mathbf{k} = 9\mathbf{i} + 10\mathbf{j} - 14\mathbf{k}$$

Vector Cross Product

The **Vector Product** can be used to find **Areas**

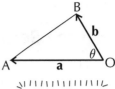

Consider a **triangle** with vertices O, A and B. From GCSE, the formula for the **area** of a triangle is $\frac{1}{2}ab\sin\theta$, where a is the length of the side OA, b is the length of the side OB, and θ is the angle at O. In **vector** form, $\overrightarrow{OA} = \mathbf{a}$ and $\overrightarrow{OB} = \mathbf{b}$.

So the area of the triangle is: $\frac{1}{2}ab\sin\theta = \frac{1}{2}|\mathbf{a}||\mathbf{b}|\sin\theta = \frac{1}{2}|\mathbf{a}||\mathbf{b}||\sin\theta|$ ← $\sin\theta = |\sin\theta|$ for $0 \le \theta \le \pi$

$|\mathbf{n}| = 1$ since $\mathbf{n}$ is a unit vector → $= \frac{1}{2}|\mathbf{a}||\mathbf{b}||\sin\theta||\mathbf{n}| = \frac{1}{2}||\mathbf{a}||\mathbf{b}|\sin\theta\,\mathbf{n}|$

And since θ is the angle between $\mathbf{a}$ and $\mathbf{b}$ (which are both directed **away** from O), $||\mathbf{a}||\mathbf{b}|\sin\theta\,\mathbf{n}| = |\mathbf{a}\times\mathbf{b}|$. So the area of any triangle can be written:

$$A = \frac{1}{2}|\mathbf{a}\times\mathbf{b}|$$

Example: Find the exact area of a triangle with vertices at the points A(−3, −1, 5), B(2, −2, −1) and C(1, 0, −4).

Firstly you need to find vectors $\mathbf{a}$ and $\mathbf{b}$ representing any two sides of the triangle.
Let $\mathbf{a} = (-3-1)\mathbf{i} + (-1-0)\mathbf{j} + (5+4)\mathbf{k} = -4\mathbf{i} - \mathbf{j} + 9\mathbf{k}$ and $\mathbf{b} = (2-1)\mathbf{i} + (-2-0)\mathbf{j} + (-1+4)\mathbf{k} = \mathbf{i} - 2\mathbf{j} + 3\mathbf{k}$

So the area of the triangle ABC $= \frac{1}{2}\left|\begin{matrix} \mathbf{i} & \mathbf{j} & \mathbf{k} \\ -4 & -1 & 9 \\ 1 & -2 & 3 \end{matrix}\right| = \frac{1}{2}|15\mathbf{i} + 21\mathbf{j} + 9\mathbf{k}| = \frac{1}{2}\sqrt{15^2 + 21^2 + 9^2} = \frac{1}{2}\sqrt{747} = \frac{3}{2}\sqrt{83}$

The diagonal of a **parallelogram** splits it into **two congruent triangles**.

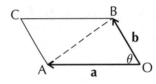

So, the area of the parallelogram on the right is $2 \times \frac{1}{2}|\mathbf{a}\times\mathbf{b}| = |\mathbf{a}\times\mathbf{b}|$.
You can extend this idea to other **quadrilaterals** that can be split into two congruent triangles — the area is $|\mathbf{a}\times\mathbf{b}|$, where $\mathbf{a}$ and $\mathbf{b}$ are **vectors** that represent **adjacent** sides of one of the triangles.

Example: Find the exact area of a parallelogram that has vertices at the points (−4, 2, −3), (0, 3, 3) and (−2, 1, 5).

There is more than one possible parallelogram with only 3 given vertices, but they'll all have the same area.

You need $\mathbf{a}$ and $\mathbf{b}$ to represent adjacent sides of the parallelogram.
Any adjacent vectors work here (see the parallelogram above — the line OC would also split the shape into congruent triangles).
So let $\mathbf{a} = (-4+2)\mathbf{i} + (2-1)\mathbf{j} + (-3-5)\mathbf{k} = -2\mathbf{i} + \mathbf{j} - 8\mathbf{k}$, and $\mathbf{b} = (0+2)\mathbf{i} + (3-1)\mathbf{j} + (3-5)\mathbf{k} = 2\mathbf{i} + 2\mathbf{j} - 2\mathbf{k}$

Then the parallelogram's area $= \left|\begin{matrix} \mathbf{i} & \mathbf{j} & \mathbf{k} \\ -2 & 1 & -8 \\ 2 & 2 & -2 \end{matrix}\right| = |14\mathbf{i} - 20\mathbf{j} - 6\mathbf{k}| = \sqrt{(14)^2 + (-20)^2 + (-6)^2} = \sqrt{632} = 2\sqrt{158}$

Practice Questions

Q1 Find $\mathbf{a}\times\mathbf{b}$ for the following:
 a) $\mathbf{a} = 4\mathbf{i} + 6\mathbf{j}$, $\mathbf{b} = -2\mathbf{j} + 2\mathbf{k}$
 b) $\mathbf{a} = -\mathbf{i} + 3\mathbf{j} + 4\mathbf{k}$, $\mathbf{b} = 3\mathbf{i} + \mathbf{j} - 2\mathbf{k}$
 c) $\mathbf{a} = 3\mathbf{i} + \mathbf{j} - 2\mathbf{k}$, $\mathbf{b} = -\mathbf{i} + 3\mathbf{j} + 4\mathbf{k}$

Q2 Use the vector product to prove that the vectors $4\mathbf{i} + \mathbf{j} - \mathbf{k}$ and $-8\mathbf{i} - 2\mathbf{j} + 2\mathbf{k}$ are parallel.

Q3 Find a vector that's perpendicular to both $5\mathbf{i} - 2\mathbf{j} + 2\mathbf{k}$ and $-9\mathbf{i} + \mathbf{j} + 3\mathbf{k}$.

Exam Questions

Q1 The coordinates of the points A and B are given by $A = (1, a_2, a_3)$ and $B = (1, a_2, -a_3)$ for $a_2, a_3 > 0$. $|\overrightarrow{OA}| = |\overrightarrow{OB}| = 4$ and the area of the triangle OAB is 8, where O is the origin. Find a_2 and a_3, giving your answer in exact form. [6 marks]

Q2 On the right is a kite ABCD. Given that $A = (1, -3, 2)$, $B = (5, -1, 3)$, $C = (17, -3, 6)$ and $D = (5, -5, 3)$, find the exact area of the kite. [5 marks]

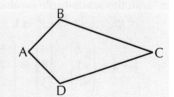

The right-hand rule — giving vector geometry a big thumbs up...

You need to make sure you're really familiar with working out vector products. It's the same as finding the determinant of a 3 by 3 matrix, so if you get the hang of it you've got two skills in one. Also, remember that vector products are a great shortcut to finding areas of shapes and if you forget the shortcut in the exam, you might end up getting lost...

Scalar Triple Product

Is it a scalar product? Is it a vector product? No, it's a scalar triple product... The main thing you can do with the scalar triple product is find volumes of hard-to-pronounce shapes. Seriously, they're a right mouthful...

a.b × c is the **Scalar Triple Product** of **a**, **b** and **c**

From page 110, $\mathbf{b} \times \mathbf{c} = (b_2c_3 - c_2b_3)\mathbf{i} - (b_1c_3 - c_1b_3)\mathbf{j} + (b_1c_2 - c_1b_2)\mathbf{k}$,
where $\mathbf{b} = b_1\mathbf{i} + b_2\mathbf{j} + b_3\mathbf{k}$ and $\mathbf{c} = c_1\mathbf{i} + c_2\mathbf{j} + c_3\mathbf{k}$. So:

$$\mathbf{a}.\mathbf{b} \times \mathbf{c} = a_1(b_2c_3 - c_2b_3) - a_2(b_1c_3 - c_1b_3) + a_3(b_1c_2 - c_1b_2) = \begin{vmatrix} a_1 & a_2 & a_3 \\ b_1 & b_2 & b_3 \\ c_1 & c_2 & c_3 \end{vmatrix}$$

Example: Find $\mathbf{a}.\mathbf{b} \times \mathbf{c}$ where $\mathbf{a} = -2\mathbf{i} + 5\mathbf{j} + \mathbf{k}$, $\mathbf{b} = 3\mathbf{i} - 3\mathbf{j} + \mathbf{k}$ and $\mathbf{c} = \mathbf{i} - 2\mathbf{k}$.

Make sure you always carry out the vector product first, i.e. $\mathbf{a}.(\mathbf{b} \times \mathbf{c})$ not $(\mathbf{a}.\mathbf{b}) \times \mathbf{c}$.

$$\Rightarrow \mathbf{a}.\mathbf{b} \times \mathbf{c} = \begin{vmatrix} -2 & 5 & 1 \\ 3 & -3 & 1 \\ 1 & 0 & -2 \end{vmatrix} = (-2)\begin{vmatrix} -3 & 1 \\ 0 & -2 \end{vmatrix} - 5\begin{vmatrix} 3 & 1 \\ 1 & -2 \end{vmatrix} + 1\begin{vmatrix} 3 & -3 \\ 1 & 0 \end{vmatrix} = -12 + 35 + 3 = 26$$

If any two of **a**, **b** and **c** are **parallel**, then **one row** in the above matrix will be a **multiple** of another. So the **determinant** of the matrix will be 0 (see page 30), which means $\mathbf{a}.\mathbf{b} \times \mathbf{c} = 0$.

a.b × c can be used to find the **Volume** of a **Parallelepiped...**

1) A **parallelepiped** is a 3D shape whose faces are all **parallelograms**. It looks something like this:—

2) The **volume** of a parallelepiped is given by $V = A_p h$, where A_p is the **area** of the base parallelogram and h is the **perpendicular distance** from the bottom face to the top face.

3) As seen on page 111, $A_p = |\mathbf{b} \times \mathbf{c}|$.
Using trigonometry we can see that $h = |\mathbf{a}|\cos\theta$, so $V = |\mathbf{a}||\mathbf{b} \times \mathbf{c}|\cos\theta$.
But h is measured **perpendicular** to **b** and **c**, i.e. **parallel** to $\mathbf{b} \times \mathbf{c}$.
So the angle, θ, between **a** and h is the same as the angle between **a** and $\mathbf{b} \times \mathbf{c}$.
Using the formula for the **scalar product**, we see that the **volume of a parallelepiped** is:

The modulus sign means you don't get a negative value for the volume.

$$V = |\mathbf{a}.\mathbf{b} \times \mathbf{c}|$$

This formula also works for cubes and cuboids.

Example: Find the volume of the parallelepiped that has a vertex at the point (3, 5, 3) connected to vertices at points (–2, –1, 6), (–1, 4, 3) and (–4, –7, 5).

You need vectors **a**, **b** and **c** representing the three edges that meet at (3, 5, 3). It doesn't matter which is which, because changing the order of **a**, **b** and **c** in the scalar triple product formula $\mathbf{a}.\mathbf{b} \times \mathbf{c}$ only changes the sign of the result — i.e. $|\mathbf{a}.\mathbf{b} \times \mathbf{c}|$ stays the same.

See practice question 2.

$$\text{Let } \mathbf{a} = \begin{pmatrix} -2 \\ -1 \\ 6 \end{pmatrix} - \begin{pmatrix} 3 \\ 5 \\ 3 \end{pmatrix} = \begin{pmatrix} -5 \\ -6 \\ 3 \end{pmatrix}, \mathbf{b} = \begin{pmatrix} -1 \\ 4 \\ 3 \end{pmatrix} - \begin{pmatrix} 3 \\ 5 \\ 3 \end{pmatrix} = \begin{pmatrix} -4 \\ -1 \\ 0 \end{pmatrix} \text{ and } \mathbf{c} = \begin{pmatrix} -4 \\ -7 \\ 5 \end{pmatrix} - \begin{pmatrix} 3 \\ 5 \\ 3 \end{pmatrix} = \begin{pmatrix} -7 \\ -12 \\ 2 \end{pmatrix}$$

$$\Rightarrow |\mathbf{a}.\mathbf{b} \times \mathbf{c}| = \left| \begin{vmatrix} -5 & -6 & 3 \\ -4 & -1 & 0 \\ -7 & -12 & 2 \end{vmatrix} \right| = \left| -5\begin{vmatrix} -1 & 0 \\ -12 & 2 \end{vmatrix} - (-6)\begin{vmatrix} -4 & 0 \\ -7 & 2 \end{vmatrix} + 3\begin{vmatrix} -4 & -1 \\ -7 & -12 \end{vmatrix} \right|$$

$$= |-5 \times (-2) + 6 \times (-8) + 3 \times 41| = |85|$$

$\Rightarrow$ **The volume of the parallelepiped = 85**

Even after 9 attempts, Phil still couldn't spell parallelepiped.

Scalar Triple Product

... and the *Volume* of a *Tetrahedron*

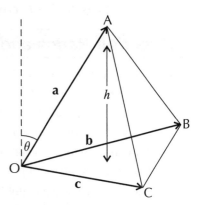

1) A **tetrahedron** (or triangular-based pyramid) is a 3D shape whose 4 faces are all **triangles**, like the one on the right.

2) The formula for working out the **volume**, V, of a tetrahedron is $V = \frac{1}{3} A_t h$, where A_t is the **area** of the base triangle and h is the **perpendicular distance** from the bottom face, OBC, to the top vertex, A.

3) Again, using page 111, $A_t = \frac{1}{2} |\mathbf{b} \times \mathbf{c}|$, and using trigonometry $h = |\mathbf{a}|\cos\theta$. So $V = \frac{1}{6} |\mathbf{b} \times \mathbf{c}||\mathbf{a}|\cos\theta$.

So the volume of a tetrahedron is:

$$V = \frac{1}{6} |\mathbf{a}.\mathbf{b} \times \mathbf{c}|$$

Example: Find the volume of the tetrahedron that has a vertex A such that the three sides connected to A are given by the vectors $8\mathbf{i} - 9\mathbf{k}$, $-7\mathbf{i} + 2\mathbf{j} + 3\mathbf{k}$ and $-2\mathbf{i} + 6\mathbf{j} - 8\mathbf{k}$.

You're given the sides, so you can put them straight into the scalar triple product without needing to know the actual coordinates of the vertices.

So $\mathbf{a} = 8\mathbf{i} - 9\mathbf{k}$, $\mathbf{b} = -7\mathbf{i} + 2\mathbf{j} + 3\mathbf{k}$, $\mathbf{c} = -2\mathbf{i} + 6\mathbf{j} - 8\mathbf{k}$.

$$\Rightarrow |\mathbf{a}.\mathbf{b} \times \mathbf{c}| = \left| \begin{vmatrix} 8 & 0 & -9 \\ -7 & 2 & 3 \\ -2 & 6 & -8 \end{vmatrix} \right| = \left| 8 \begin{vmatrix} 2 & 3 \\ 6 & -8 \end{vmatrix} - 0 \begin{vmatrix} -7 & 3 \\ -2 & -8 \end{vmatrix} + (-9) \begin{vmatrix} -7 & 2 \\ -2 & 6 \end{vmatrix} \right| = |8 \times (-34) - 0 - 9 \times (-38)| = |70|$$

$\Rightarrow$ The volume of the tetrahedron $= \frac{70}{6} = \frac{35}{3}$

The scalar triple product can also be used to find volumes of other shapes whose faces are triangles, squares, rectangles or parallelograms.

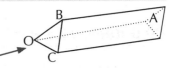

For instance, the volume of this **triangular prism** is given by $V = \frac{1}{2} |\mathbf{a}.\mathbf{b} \times \mathbf{c}|$.

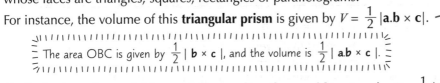

The area OBC is given by $\frac{1}{2}|\mathbf{b} \times \mathbf{c}|$, and the volume is $\frac{1}{2}|\mathbf{a}.\mathbf{b} \times \mathbf{c}|$.

Similarly, the volume of this **parallelogram-based pyramid** is given by $V = \frac{1}{3} |\mathbf{a}.\mathbf{b} \times \mathbf{c}|$.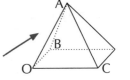

Practice Questions

Q1 Find $\mathbf{a}.\mathbf{b} \times \mathbf{c}$ for $\mathbf{a} = \mathbf{i} - 6\mathbf{k}$, $\mathbf{b} = 8\mathbf{i} + 4\mathbf{j} - 6\mathbf{k}$ and $\mathbf{c} = -4\mathbf{i} + \mathbf{j} - 4\mathbf{k}$.

Q2 Using the fact that the scalar triple product is the determinant of a 3 by 3 matrix, show that
   a) $\mathbf{a}.\mathbf{b} \times \mathbf{c} = -\mathbf{a}.\mathbf{c} \times \mathbf{b}$ and $\mathbf{a}.\mathbf{b} \times \mathbf{c} = -\mathbf{b}.\mathbf{a} \times \mathbf{c}$
   b) $\mathbf{a}.\mathbf{b} \times \mathbf{c} = \mathbf{c}.\mathbf{a} \times \mathbf{b} = \mathbf{b}.\mathbf{c} \times \mathbf{a}$

Exam Questions

Q1 A tetrahedron has vertices at the points
A = (5, −1, 3), B = (0, 4, 6), C = (2, 3, −3) and D = (7, 5, 2).
Find the volume of the tetrahedron ABCD.   **[3 marks]**

Q2 The parallelepiped shown has a volume of 53. Points A, B and C are given by vectors $6\mathbf{i} + 3\mathbf{j} - \mathbf{k}$, $3\mathbf{i} - \mathbf{j} + 4\mathbf{k}$ and $c_1\mathbf{i} + c_3\mathbf{k}$ respectively, and O is the origin. Given that the

equation for the plane CDEF is $\mathbf{r}.\begin{pmatrix} 4 \\ 0 \\ -2 \end{pmatrix} = 2$, find c_1 and c_3 if $c_1, c_3 < 0$.   **[5 marks]**

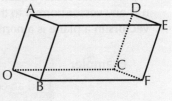

---

a.b × c — easy as 1 2 3, as simple as do re mi...

If you forget that the scalar triple product is the determinant of a 3 by 3 matrix — don't panic. You can always work it out the long way by doing the vector product first then the scalar product. Either way, make sure you do some problems involving the scalar triple product so you know how to use it, because it could be worth a few marks in the exam.

More 3D Geometry

Remember that the vector product of two vectors is always perpendicular to both of them.
So if a problem has the word perpendicular in it, then the vector product will probably help you solve it.

Direction Ratios and Direction Cosines tell you if two Lines are Parallel

1) Let $\mathbf{r}_1 = \mathbf{c} + \lambda\mathbf{a}$ and $\mathbf{r}_2 = \mathbf{d} + \mu\mathbf{b}$ be the vector equations of straight lines,
   where $\mathbf{a} = a_1\mathbf{i} + a_2\mathbf{j} + a_3\mathbf{k}$ and $\mathbf{b} = b_1\mathbf{i} + b_2\mathbf{j} + b_3\mathbf{k}$.

2) $\mathbf{r}_1$ and $\mathbf{r}_2$ are **parallel** if $\mathbf{a} \times \mathbf{b} = (a_2b_3 - b_2a_3)\mathbf{i} - (a_1b_3 - b_1a_3)\mathbf{j} + (a_1b_2 - b_1a_2)\mathbf{k} = \mathbf{0} \Rightarrow \frac{a_2}{a_3} = \frac{b_2}{b_3}, \frac{a_1}{a_3} = \frac{b_1}{b_3}$ and $\frac{a_1}{a_2} = \frac{b_1}{b_2}$
   — in other words if $a_1 : a_2 : a_3 = b_1 : b_2 : b_3$. These are the **direction ratios** of $\mathbf{r}_1$ and $\mathbf{r}_2$ respectively.

3) Another way to see whether $\mathbf{r}_1$ and $\mathbf{r}_2$ are parallel is to find unit vectors in the **directions** of $\mathbf{a}$ and $\mathbf{b}$, and see if
   they're the same (or opposite). So divide each coordinate of $\mathbf{a}$ by $|\mathbf{a}|$ and each coordinate of $\mathbf{b}$ by $|\mathbf{b}|$.
   Then $\mathbf{r}_1$ and $\mathbf{r}_2$ are parallel if: $\frac{\mathbf{a}}{|\mathbf{a}|} = \pm\frac{\mathbf{b}}{|\mathbf{b}|}$, i.e. if $\frac{1}{\sqrt{a_1^2 + a_2^2 + a_3^2}}(a_1\mathbf{i} + a_2\mathbf{j} + a_3\mathbf{k}) = \pm\frac{1}{\sqrt{b_1^2 + b_2^2 + b_3^2}}(b_1\mathbf{i} + b_2\mathbf{j} + b_3\mathbf{k})$.

4) The components in the unit vectors are called the **direction cosines** of $\mathbf{r}_1$ and $\mathbf{r}_2$ respectively.
   This is because $(\frac{a_1}{|\mathbf{a}|}, \frac{a_2}{|\mathbf{a}|}, \frac{a_3}{|\mathbf{a}|}) = (\cos\theta_x, \cos\theta_y, \cos\theta_z)$, where θ_x, θ_y and θ_z are the **angles**
   between $\mathbf{r}_1$ and the **positive** x, y and z-**axes**.

> **Example:** Find the direction ratios of the lines $\mathbf{r}_1 = \mathbf{i} - 3\mathbf{j} - 4\mathbf{k} + \lambda(\frac{1}{\sqrt{3}}\mathbf{i} - 2\mathbf{j})$ and
> $\mathbf{r}_2 = -2\mathbf{i} + 3\mathbf{j} - \mathbf{k} + \mu(-\sqrt{3}\,\mathbf{i} + 6\mathbf{j})$ and state if the lines are parallel or not.
>
> Direction ratio of $\mathbf{r}_1 = \frac{1}{\sqrt{3}} : -2 : 0 = 1 : -2\sqrt{3} : 0$.
> Direction ratio of $\mathbf{r}_2 = -\sqrt{3} : 6 : 0 = 1 : \frac{-6}{\sqrt{3}} : 0 = 1 : -2\sqrt{3} : 0 \Rightarrow \mathbf{r}_1$ and $\mathbf{r}_2$ are parallel.

The equation for a Straight Line can be written using the Vector Product

1) The **vector form** of the equation of a straight line is $\mathbf{r} = \mathbf{a} + \lambda\mathbf{b}$.

2) Since $\mathbf{r} - \mathbf{a}$ is parallel to $\mathbf{b}$, $(\mathbf{r} - \mathbf{a}) \times \mathbf{b} = \mathbf{0}$. This means that every point on $\mathbf{r}$ must satisfy $(\mathbf{r} - \mathbf{a}) \times \mathbf{b} = \mathbf{0}$. So:

> $(\mathbf{r} - \mathbf{a}) \times \mathbf{b} = \mathbf{0}$ is also a vector equation of a straight line with
> direction vector b passing through the point A with position vector a.

> **Example:** The points $(1, -3, 2)$ and $(-4, 4, 1)$ lie on the line l.
> Find the equation for l in the form $(\mathbf{r} - \mathbf{a}) \times \mathbf{b} = \mathbf{0}$.
>
> $\mathbf{a} = \begin{pmatrix} 1 \\ -3 \\ 2 \end{pmatrix}$, $\mathbf{b} = \begin{pmatrix} 1 \\ -3 \\ 2 \end{pmatrix} - \begin{pmatrix} -4 \\ 4 \\ 1 \end{pmatrix} = \begin{pmatrix} 5 \\ -7 \\ 1 \end{pmatrix} \Rightarrow \left(\mathbf{r} - \begin{pmatrix} 1 \\ -3 \\ 2 \end{pmatrix} \right) \times \begin{pmatrix} 5 \\ -7 \\ 1 \end{pmatrix} = \mathbf{0}$

Since $(\mathbf{r} - \mathbf{a}) \times \mathbf{b} = \mathbf{r} \times \mathbf{b} - \mathbf{a} \times \mathbf{b}$, $(\mathbf{r} - \mathbf{a}) \times \mathbf{b} = \mathbf{O}$ can also be written as $\mathbf{r} \times \mathbf{b} = \mathbf{a} \times \mathbf{b}$.

Use Vector Products to convert between Equations of a Plane

A plane with **vector equation** $\mathbf{r} = \mathbf{a} + \lambda\mathbf{b} + \mu\mathbf{c}$ has the **scalar equation** $\mathbf{r}.\mathbf{n} = p$, where
$\mathbf{n}$ is any vector normal to the plane. But the vector product of any **two non-parallel**
vectors in a plane is a **normal** to the plane so $\mathbf{r}.\mathbf{n} = p$ can also be written $\mathbf{r}.\mathbf{b} \times \mathbf{c} = p$.

See page 58 for the standard forms of the equation of a plane.

> **Example:**
> Find an equation in the form $\mathbf{r}.\mathbf{n} = p$ for the plane $\mathbf{r} = \begin{pmatrix} 2 \\ -1 \\ 5 \end{pmatrix} + \lambda\begin{pmatrix} 1 \\ 1 \\ -3 \end{pmatrix} + \mu\begin{pmatrix} -2 \\ 4 \\ 1 \end{pmatrix}$.
>
> $\begin{pmatrix} 1 \\ 1 \\ -3 \end{pmatrix} \times \begin{pmatrix} -2 \\ 4 \\ 1 \end{pmatrix} = \begin{vmatrix} \mathbf{i} & \mathbf{j} & \mathbf{k} \\ 1 & 1 & -3 \\ -2 & 4 & 1 \end{vmatrix} = \begin{pmatrix} 13 \\ 5 \\ 6 \end{pmatrix} \Rightarrow \mathbf{r}.\begin{pmatrix} 13 \\ 5 \\ 6 \end{pmatrix} = \begin{pmatrix} 2 \\ -1 \\ 5 \end{pmatrix}.\begin{pmatrix} 13 \\ 5 \\ 6 \end{pmatrix} = 26 - 5 + 30 = 51 \Rightarrow \mathbf{r}.\begin{pmatrix} 13 \\ 5 \\ 6 \end{pmatrix} = 51$

More 3D Geometry

Finding the **Perpendicular Distance** between **Two Parallel Lines**

1) The **perpendicular distance** between any two **lines** is also the **shortest** distance between them.

2) If vector **m** joins and is perpendicular to the **parallel lines** $\mathbf{r} = \mathbf{a} + \lambda\mathbf{b}$ and $\mathbf{r} = \mathbf{c} + \mu\mathbf{b}$, then:

$\mathbf{m} = (\mathbf{c} + \mu\mathbf{b}) - (\mathbf{a} + \lambda\mathbf{b}) = (\mathbf{c} - \mathbf{a}) + (\mu - \lambda)\mathbf{b}$ for some μ and λ.

Also, $\mathbf{m} \times \mathbf{b} = |\mathbf{m}|\,|\mathbf{b}| \sin 90° = (\mathbf{c} - \mathbf{a}) \times \mathbf{b} + (\mu - \lambda)(\mathbf{b} \times \mathbf{b})$ ← $\mathbf{b} \times \mathbf{b} = \mathbf{0}$

$= (\mathbf{c} - \mathbf{a}) \times \mathbf{b}$

So the perpendicular distance between two parallel lines is: $\dfrac{|(\mathbf{c} - \mathbf{a}) \times \mathbf{b}|}{|\mathbf{b}|}$ ← $= |\mathbf{m}|$

$\mathbf{r} = \mathbf{a} + \lambda\mathbf{b}$

$\mathbf{r} = \mathbf{c} + \mu\mathbf{b}$

Example: The line l_1 contains the points $(1, 5, 5)$ and $(2, -4, 0)$. The line l_2 is parallel to l_1 and contains the point $(-1, -3, 1)$. Find the perpendicular distance between l_1 and l_2.

Use $\mathbf{b} = \begin{pmatrix} 2 \\ -4 \\ 0 \end{pmatrix} - \begin{pmatrix} 1 \\ 5 \\ 5 \end{pmatrix} = \begin{pmatrix} 1 \\ -9 \\ -5 \end{pmatrix} \Rightarrow |\mathbf{b}| = \sqrt{1^2 + 9^2 + 5^2} = \sqrt{107}$, $\mathbf{c} - \mathbf{a} = \begin{pmatrix} -1 \\ -3 \\ 1 \end{pmatrix} - \begin{pmatrix} 1 \\ 5 \\ 5 \end{pmatrix} = \begin{pmatrix} -2 \\ -8 \\ -4 \end{pmatrix}$

$\Rightarrow (\mathbf{c} - \mathbf{a}) \times \mathbf{b} = \begin{vmatrix} \mathbf{i} & \mathbf{j} & \mathbf{k} \\ -2 & -8 & -4 \\ 1 & -9 & -5 \end{vmatrix} = \begin{pmatrix} 4 \\ -14 \\ 26 \end{pmatrix} \Rightarrow |(\mathbf{c} - \mathbf{a}) \times \mathbf{b}| = \sqrt{4^2 + 14^2 + 26^2} = 2\sqrt{222} \Rightarrow \dfrac{|(\mathbf{c} - \mathbf{a}) \times \mathbf{b}|}{|\mathbf{b}|} = \dfrac{2\sqrt{222}}{\sqrt{107}}$

Finding the **Perpendicular Distance** between **Two Skew Lines**

The **perpendicular distance** between two **skew lines** $\mathbf{r} = \mathbf{a} + \lambda\mathbf{b}$ and $\mathbf{r} = \mathbf{c} + \mu\mathbf{d}$ is: $\left| \dfrac{(\mathbf{c} - \mathbf{a}) \cdot (\mathbf{b} \times \mathbf{d})}{|\mathbf{b} \times \mathbf{d}|} \right|$

Example: Find the perpendicular distance between the lines $\mathbf{r} = (-7\mathbf{i} - 4\mathbf{j} + 9\mathbf{k}) + \lambda(-8\mathbf{i} + 6\mathbf{j} + 9\mathbf{k})$ and $\mathbf{r} = (8\mathbf{i} + 2\mathbf{j} + 13\mathbf{k}) + \mu(-2\mathbf{i} + 3\mathbf{j} + 5\mathbf{k})$.

$\mathbf{b} \times \mathbf{d} = \begin{pmatrix} -8 \\ 6 \\ 9 \end{pmatrix} \times \begin{pmatrix} -2 \\ 3 \\ 5 \end{pmatrix} = \begin{vmatrix} \mathbf{i} & \mathbf{j} & \mathbf{k} \\ -8 & 6 & 9 \\ -2 & 3 & 5 \end{vmatrix} = \begin{pmatrix} 3 \\ 22 \\ -12 \end{pmatrix} \Rightarrow |\mathbf{b} \times \mathbf{d}| = \sqrt{3^2 + 22^2 + 12^2} = \sqrt{637} = 7\sqrt{13}$

$\mathbf{c} - \mathbf{a} = \begin{pmatrix} 8 \\ 2 \\ 13 \end{pmatrix} - \begin{pmatrix} -7 \\ -4 \\ 9 \end{pmatrix} = \begin{pmatrix} 15 \\ 6 \\ 4 \end{pmatrix} \Rightarrow (\mathbf{c} - \mathbf{a}) \cdot (\mathbf{b} \times \mathbf{d}) = \begin{pmatrix} 15 \\ 6 \\ 4 \end{pmatrix} \cdot \begin{pmatrix} 3 \\ 22 \\ -12 \end{pmatrix} = 129$. This gives $\left| \dfrac{(\mathbf{c} - \mathbf{a}) \cdot (\mathbf{b} \times \mathbf{d})}{|\mathbf{b} \times \mathbf{d}|} \right| = \dfrac{129}{7\sqrt{13}}$

Practice Questions

Q1 Convert the line with Cartesian equation $\dfrac{x - 4}{3} = \dfrac{y + 2}{5} = \dfrac{2 - z}{7} = \lambda$ into the form $(\mathbf{r} - \mathbf{a}) \times \mathbf{b} = \mathbf{0}$.

Q2 Find an equation in the form $\mathbf{r}.\mathbf{n} = p$ for the plane $\mathbf{r} = (3\mathbf{i} - 3\mathbf{j} + \mathbf{k}) + \lambda(\mathbf{i} - 4\mathbf{j} - 4\mathbf{k}) + \mu(2\mathbf{i} - 5\mathbf{j} + 3\mathbf{k})$.

Exam Questions

Q1 Find the direction cosines of the line $\mathbf{r} = \mathbf{i} - 3\mathbf{j} - 4\mathbf{k} + \lambda(\frac{1}{\sqrt{3}}\mathbf{i} - 2\mathbf{j})$ and hence find the angle, θ, it makes with the positive x, y and z-axes, where $0 < \theta \leq \pi$. Give your answer in radians to 2 decimal places. [3 marks]

Q2 The line l_1 passes through the points $(-5, 4, -7)$ and $(-6, -5, -3)$ and is parallel to the line l_2 that passes through the point $(-2, 0, 2)$. Find the perpendicular distance between the lines l_1 and l_2. [4 marks]

Q3 The line l_1 passes through the points $(3, -1, 4)$ and $(3, 1, 16)$. The line l_2 passes through the points $(-2, 5, 2)$ and $(2, 6, 1)$. Find the perpendicular distance between the lines l_1 and l_2. [5 marks]

Learn this page — it'll skew the odds of acing the exam in your favour...

Questions on the exam that require the vector product won't always tell you to use it, so it's up to you to learn what the vector product can and can't help you to do. Finding areas: Check. Finding perpendicular distances: Check. Converting between equations of a plane: Check. Doing all your revision for you... Unfortunately not.

Numerical Solution of Differential Equations

If you thought you had escaped the clutches of differential equations for good, think again.
These things are like viral videos... they're everywhere and impossible to ignore.

Numerical Methods are needed for DEs you can't solve Exactly

1) Many DEs require a **numerical method** to **approximate** their solution because they can't be solved **analytically**.

2) These methods involve finding the value of a function at **specific values** of x_k, where x_k and x_{k+1} are always a **distance** of h (the **step length**) apart. So, if you know x_k, then $x_{k+1} = x_k + h$ and $x_{k-1} = x_k - h$.

3) A **smaller** step length increases the **accuracy** of the method.

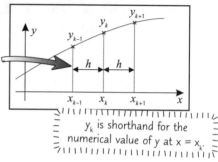

There are **two** numerical methods for **first order DEs** you need to know:

y_k is shorthand for the numerical value of y at $x = x_k$.

Method 1 — find y_{k+1} using y_k

This method, called **Euler's method**, uses a **known** x-value (x_k) and its y-value (y_k), to approximate the value of y_{k+1}:

$$y'(x_k) \approx \frac{y_{k+1} - y_k}{h}$$

which rearranges to

$$y_{k+1} \approx y_k + hy'(x_k)$$

You should spot that this is an **iterative** method.

You might see the notation $\left(\dfrac{dy}{dx}\right)_k$ instead of $y'(x_k)$.

Example: Use a step length, h, of 0.1 to approximate $y(1.2)$ for $y'(x) = \sin(x + y)$, given that at $x = 1$, $y = 1$.

Set the values you know as x_0 and y_0: $x_0 = 1$ and $y_0 = y(1) = 1$

Use the step length to write the other x and y-values:
$x_1 = (x_0 + 0.1) = 1.1$, so $y_1 = y(1.1) = ?$
$x_2 = (x_1 + 0.1) = 1.2$, so $y_2 = y(1.2) = ?$ ← This is what you want to approximate.

Calculate $y'(x_0)$ using the given DE: $y'(x_0) = \sin(x_0 + y_0) = \sin(1 + 1) = \sin 2 = 0.9092...$

Use Euler's method to approximate y_1: $y_1 \approx y_0 + hy'(x_0) = 1 + 0.1 \times \sin 2 = \textbf{1.0909...}$

And again to approximate y_2: $y_2 \approx y_1 + hy'(x_1) = 1.0909... + 0.1 \times \sin(1.1 + 1.0909...) = \textbf{1.1723...}$

So $y_2 = y(1.2) \approx \textbf{1.1723 (4 d.p.)}$

Method 2 — find y_{k+1} using y_k and y_{k-1}

This method gives a **better approximation** than Euler's method. It uses **two** known x-values (x_k and x_{k-1}) and their y-values (y_k and y_{k-1}) to approximate the value of y_{k+1}. If you only know **one** y-value, you will have to use **Euler's method** first to find a **second** y-value.

$$y'(x_k) \approx \frac{y_{k+1} - y_{k-1}}{2h}$$

which rearranges to

$$y_{k+1} \approx y_{k-1} + 2hy'(x_k)$$

Example: Use a step length, h, of 0.01 to approximate $y(1.02)$ for $\dfrac{dy}{dx} = \dfrac{y(x+1)}{x+y}$ given that at $x = 1$, $y = 1$.

Set the values you know as x_0 and y_0: $x_0 = 1$ and $y_0 = y(1) = 1$
The step length is 0.01:
$x_1 = (x_0 + 0.01) = 1.01$, so $y_1 = y(1.01) = ?$
$x_2 = (x_1 + 0.01) = 1.02$, so $y_2 = y(1.02) = ?$

You only know **one** y-value ($y_0 = 1$), so use Euler's method first to find y_1.

Calculate $y'(x_0)$ using the given DE: $y'(x_0) = \dfrac{y_0(x_0 + 1)}{x_0 + y_0} = \dfrac{1(1 + 1)}{1 + 1} = 1$

Use Euler's method to find y_1: $y_1 \approx y_0 + hy'(x_0) = 1 + 0.01 \times 1 = \textbf{1.01}$

You can now approximate y_2 as you know **two** y-values (y_0 and y_1).

Use the formula above ($k = 1$): $y_2 \approx y_0 + 2hy'(x_1) = 1 + 2 \times 0.01 \times \dfrac{1.01(1.01 + 1)}{1.01 + 1.01} = \textbf{1.0201}$

Numerical Solution of Differential Equations

There are **Numerical Methods** for **Second Order DEs** too

With second order DEs, you can use **two** known x-values (x_k and x_{k-1}) and their y-values (y_k and y_{k-1}) to approximate the value of y_{k+1}:

You can derive this by adding the Taylor series expansions of y_{k+1} and y_{k-1}.

$$y''(x_k) \approx \frac{y_{k+1} - 2y_k + y_{k-1}}{h^2}$$

which rearranges to

$$y_{k+1} \approx 2y_k - y_{k-1} + h^2 y''(x_k)$$

Example: Use a step length, h, of 0.2, to approximate $y(1.4)$ for $\frac{d^2y}{dx^2} = x \cos y$, given that at $x = 1$, $y = 0$ and at $x = 1.2$, $y = 0.2$.

You know two x-values and their y-values:

$x_0 = 1$ and $y_0 = y(1) = 0$
$x_1 = (x_0 + 0.2) = 1.2$ and $y_1 = y(1.2) = 0.2$
$x_2 = (x_1 + 0.2) = 1.4$, so $y_2 = y(1.4) = ?$

Calculate $y''(x_1)$ using the DE: $y''(x_1) = x_1 \cos y_1 = 1.2 \cos 0.2 = \mathbf{1.1760...}$

You can now approximate y_2 using the formula above:

$$y_2 \approx 2y_1 - y_0 + h^2 y''(x_1) = 2(0.2) - 0 + 0.2^2 \times 1.1760... = \mathbf{0.4470 \ (4 \ d.p.)}$$

Example: Use a step length of $h = 0.1$ to approximate $y(\ln 2 + 0.2)$ for $y''(x) = \sinh x \cosh x$, given that at $x = \ln 2$, $y = e$ and $y' = 1$.

Set the values you know as x_0 and y_0: $x_0 = \ln 2$ and $y_0 = y(\ln 2) = e$
The step length is 0.1:
$x_1 = (x_0 + 0.1) = \ln 2 + 0.1$, so $y_1 = y(\ln 2 + 0.1) = ?$
$x_2 = (x_1 + 0.1) = \ln 2 + 0.2$, so $y_2 = y(\ln 2 + 0.2) = ?$

You only know **one** y-value ($y_0 = e$), so use Euler's method first to find y_1. *You can only do this as $y'(x_0)$ is known.*

$$y_1 \approx y_0 + hy'(x_0) = e + 0.1 \times 1 = \mathbf{e + 0.1}$$

Calculate $y''(x_1)$ using the DE: $y''(x_1) = \sinh(\ln 2 + 0.1) \cosh(\ln 2 + 0.1) = \mathbf{1.1702...}$

You can now approximate y_2 as you know **two** y-values (y_0 and y_1).

Use the formula above (k = 1): $y_2 = 2y_1 - y_0 + h^2 y''(x_1) = 2(e + 0.1) - e + 0.1^2 \times 1.1702... = \mathbf{2.9300 \ (4 \ d.p.)}$

Practice Questions

Q1 Use the expansions $y(x_0 + h) = y(x_0) + hy'(x_0) + \frac{h^2}{2}y''(x_0) + ...$ and $y(x_0 - h) = y(x_0) - hy'(x_0) + \frac{h^2}{2}y''(x_0) + ...$

to derive: a) $y'(x_0) \approx \frac{y_1 - y_0}{h}$ b) $y'(x_0) \approx \frac{y_1 - y_{-1}}{2h}$ *(Hint: subtract one expansion from the other).*

Q2 Use an appropriate method to approximate $y(10.1)$ for $y'(x) = x^y$, given that at $x = 10$, $y = 1$.

Q3 Use $h = 0.1$ to approximate $y(0.2)$ for $y'(x) = \ln(x + y)$, given that at $x = 0$, $y = e$.

Q4 Use $h = 0.1$ to approximate $y(0.2)$ for $y''(x) = \frac{x^2 y}{1 + y^2}$ given that at $x = 0$, $y = 1$ and at $x = 0.1$, $y = 1.2$.

Exam Question

Q1 $y(x)$ satisfies $\frac{dy}{dx} = 2y(x^2 + xy)$, where at $x = x_0 = 0.1$, $y = y_0 = 1$.

a) Use a step length, h, of 0.1 and $\left(\frac{dy}{dx}\right)_0 \approx \frac{y_1 - y_0}{h}$ to approximate the value of y_1. [3 marks]

b) Use a step length, h, of 0.1 and $\left(\frac{dy}{dx}\right)_1 \approx \frac{y_2 - y_0}{2h}$ to approximate the value of y_2. [3 marks]

c) Hence, give a numerical approximation for y at $x = 0.3$. [1 mark]

Gnomerical method — stand near pond and use fishing rod...

All these numerical methods are explicit — they rely on using known values you've calculated from previous steps. The formulas are sometimes given for the case where k = 0, but knowing the general formula can be really handy.

Simpson's Rule

"Why do we need this rule if we've got the trapezium rule?" I'd be rich if I got a penny for every time I've been asked that. Well, it's usually more accurate — so you'll get a better approximation of the area under a curve.

Use Simpson's Rule to Approximate Area under a Curve

1) The **trapezium rule** approximates the **area** under a curve as the **sum** of the areas of **trapeziums**, where the curve between each **ordinate** is approximately a **straight line**.

2) **Simpson's rule** uses **quadratic polynomials** to approximate each part of the curve instead (as shown here).

3) Generally, Simpson's rule gives a more **accurate approximation** than the trapezium rule.

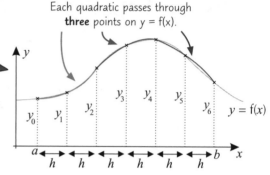

Each quadratic passes through **three** points on y = f(x).

Simpson's Rule

$$\int_a^b y \, dx \approx \frac{h}{3}(y_0 + 4y_1 + 2y_2 + 4y_3 + 2y_4 + 4y_5 + 2y_6 + \ldots + y_n)$$

where n is an **even** number of strips or intervals
and $h = \frac{b-a}{n}$ is the width of each strip

You're not given Simpson's rule in the formula booklet, so use the memory aid below.

If you **group** the terms in Simpson's rule, you get $\frac{h}{3}[(y_0 + 4(y_1 + y_3 + y_5 + \ldots) + 2(y_2 + y_4 + y_6 + \ldots) + y_n]$

An easy way to remember this rearranged form is $\frac{h}{3}$ ['First' + 4 × (Sum of Odds) + 2 × (Sum of Evens) + 'Last']

Example: Use Simpson's rule to find an approximate value for $\int_1^2 \frac{1}{x+2} \, dx$ using 4 strips. Give your answer to 3 d.p.

1) Start by working out the **width** of each strip: $h = \frac{b-a}{n} = \frac{2-1}{4} = 0.25$

2) So, the x-values are $x_0 = 1$, $x_1 = 1.25$, $x_2 = 1.5$, $x_3 = 1.75$, $x_4 = 2$

You might be told the number of ordinates to use instead — don't get caught out. The number of ordinates is n + 1.

3) Set up a **table** and work out the y-values, using the equation in the integral:

x	$y = \dfrac{1}{x+2}$
$x_0 = 1$	$y_0 = \dfrac{1}{3}$
$x_1 = 1.25$	$y_1 = \dfrac{1}{3.25}$
$x_2 = 1.5$	$y_2 = \dfrac{1}{3.5}$
$x_3 = 1.75$	$y_3 = \dfrac{1}{3.75}$
$x_4 = 2$	$y_4 = \dfrac{1}{4}$

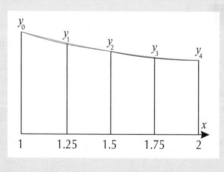

4) Put the y-values into the formula with h and n.

$$\int_1^2 \frac{1}{x+2} \, dx \approx \frac{h}{3}[y_0 + 4(y_1 + y_3) + 2y_2 + y_4]$$

The 'odds' here are y_1 and y_3 and the 'even' is y_2.

$$= \frac{0.25}{3}\left[\frac{1}{3} + 4 \times \left(\frac{1}{3.25} + \frac{1}{3.75}\right) + 2 \times \frac{1}{3.5} + \frac{1}{4}\right]$$

$$= 0.288 \text{ (3 d.p.)}$$

The **exact** answer is $[\ln(x+2)]_1^2 = \ln 4 - \ln 3 = 0.288$ (3 d.p.).
So in this example, Simpson's rule gives a **very good approximation**.

Simpson's Rule

Increase the Number of Strips to Improve an Estimate

Even with a few strips, the Simpson's rule can give a pretty good estimate for the area under a curve.
If you want to **improve** your estimate though, just use **more strips**.

You can also calculate the **error** in your approximation if you know the **exact** solution to the integral.

Example: Use Simpson's rule to find an approximate value for $\int_0^\pi \cosh x \, dx$, and the error to 2 d.p, using: a) 4 strips b) 6 strips.

The **exact solution** is $\int_0^\pi \cosh x \, dx$
$= \sinh(\pi) - \sinh(0) = \mathbf{11.549}$ (3 d.p.)

a) 4 strips $\Rightarrow h = \dfrac{b-a}{n} = \dfrac{\pi}{4}$

x	$y = \cosh x$
$x_0 = 0$	$y_0 = \cosh 0 = 1$
$x_1 = \dfrac{\pi}{4}$	$y_1 = \cosh \dfrac{\pi}{4}$
$x_2 = \dfrac{\pi}{2}$	$y_2 = \cosh \dfrac{\pi}{2}$
$x_3 = \dfrac{3\pi}{4}$	$y_3 = \cosh \dfrac{3\pi}{4}$
$x_4 = \pi$	$y_4 = \cosh \pi$

$\int_0^\pi \cosh x \, dx \approx \dfrac{h}{3}[y_0 + 4(y_1 + y_3) + 2y_2 + y_4]$
$= \dfrac{\pi}{12}[1 + 4(\cosh \dfrac{\pi}{4} + \cosh \dfrac{3\pi}{4}) + 2\cosh \dfrac{\pi}{2} + \cosh \pi]$
$= \mathbf{11.571}$ (3 d.p.)
The **error** is $11.571 - 11.549 = \mathbf{0.02}$ (2 d.p.)

b) 6 strips $\Rightarrow h = \dfrac{b-a}{n} = \dfrac{\pi}{6}$

x	$y = \cosh x$
$x_0 = 0$	$y_0 = \cosh 0 = 1$
$x_1 = \dfrac{\pi}{6}$	$y_1 = \cosh \dfrac{\pi}{6}$
$x_2 = \dfrac{\pi}{3}$	$y_2 = \cosh \dfrac{\pi}{3}$
$x_3 = \dfrac{\pi}{2}$	$y_3 = \cosh \dfrac{\pi}{2}$
$x_4 = \dfrac{2\pi}{3}$	$y_4 = \cosh \dfrac{2\pi}{3}$
$x_5 = \dfrac{5\pi}{6}$	$y_5 = \cosh \dfrac{5\pi}{6}$
$x_6 = \pi$	$y_6 = \cosh \pi$

$\int_0^\pi \cosh x \, dx \approx \dfrac{h}{3}[y_0 + 4(y_1 + y_3 + y_5) + 2(y_2 + y_4) + y_6]$
$= \dfrac{\pi}{18}[1 + 4(\cosh \dfrac{\pi}{6} + \cosh \dfrac{\pi}{2} + \cosh \dfrac{5\pi}{6})$
$\qquad + 2(\cosh \dfrac{\pi}{3} + \cosh \dfrac{2\pi}{3}) + \cosh \pi]$
$= \mathbf{11.553}$ (3 d.p.)
The **error** is $11.553 - 11.549 = \mathbf{0.00}$ (2 d.p.)

Practice Questions

Q1 Use Simpson's rule with 4 strips to calculate the following to 4 d.p.:

a) $\int_2^6 x^{\frac{3}{2}} \, dx$ b) $\int_\pi^{2\pi} \sinh x \, dx$ c) $\int_2^3 x \ln x \, dx$

Q2 a) Use Simpson's rule with 6 strips to approximate $\int_{\ln 2}^{\ln 16} e^{2x} \, dx$ to 4 d.p.

b) What is the error in your approximation to 4 d.p.?

Simpson was always picky with his chicken — he would never order an odd number of strips.

Exam Question

Q1 a) Use Simpson's rule with 5 ordinates to find an approximate value for $\int_4^5 e^{\sqrt{x}} \, dx$. [5 marks]

b) Hence, give an approximate value for $\int_4^5 x + e^{\sqrt{x}} \, dx$. [2 marks]

c) How could you improve the approximation? [1 mark]

The Simpsons rules — anyone who disagrees can eat my shorts...

I don't know about you, but I think Simpson's rule is pretty neat — it gives a good approximation without any tricky integration. You've got to remember the formula though... the 'odds' and 'evens' memory aid should help.

Algebraic Inequalities

*Here's a nice brief section on inequalities. If you're doing **AS Level**, when you get the end of this first page, go straight to the practice questions — you **don't** need to learn about inequalities with modulus signs.*

Add and Subtract to get Zero on one side

1) Multiplying or dividing an inequality by a negative number **changes the direction** of the inequality sign.

2) This causes problems if you multiply or divide by an **algebraic** term or expression — if it can be negative for some values of x, the sign could be **either way round**. You can avoid this by **only adding or subtracting**.

To solve an inequality involving x terms **algebraically**:

- rearrange to get all of the **x terms** on one side (define this as **f(x)**), and 0 on the other.
- find the **critical values** where f(x) = 0.
- find the ranges of x which satisfy the inequality by **sketching a graph** of f(x), or by drawing a **number line** and **testing** a number either side of each **critical value**.

Example: Use algebra to find the set of values of x for which $x^2(x + 3) > 4(x + 3)$.

Don't be tempted to divide by $(x + 3)$ as it could be negative, or even zero.

Rearrange into the form f(x) > O by subtracting 4(x + 3) from both sides:

$$x^2(x + 3) > 4(x + 3)$$
$$\Rightarrow x^2(x + 3) - 4(x + 3) > 0$$

Now fully factorise the left hand side:

$$\Rightarrow (x + 3)(x^2 - 4) > 0 \quad \Rightarrow (x + 3)(x + 2)(x - 2) > 0$$

Find the critical values where f(x) = O:

$(x + 3)(x + 2)(x - 2) = 0$ at critical values $x = -3, -2$ and 2.

Now sketch a graph to find where f(x) > O.

The graph is positive for $-3 < x < -2$ or $x > 2$.

If the question asks for the 'set of values', your answer must be in set notation.

So the **set** of values is $\{x \in \mathbb{R} : -3 < x < -2\} \cup \{x \in \mathbb{R} : x > 2\}$

$y = (x + 3)(x + 2)(x - 2)$

Multiply by the Square of all Denominators

When you square something **real** it can only ever take a **positive value** — so you can multiply or divide by a squared value **without** changing the sign in the inequality.

You still have to avoid dividing by something that could be zero though.

This is particularly handy for inequalities with algebraic fractions — multiply through by the **square of each denominator** and simplify to get a polynomial you can solve.

Example: Find the range of values of x that satisfies the inequality $\dfrac{x}{x-4} \geq \dfrac{2}{x+1}$, where $x \in \mathbb{R}$, $x \neq -1, 4$.

$$\frac{x}{x-4} \geq \frac{2}{x+1}$$

Multiply through by the square of each denominator, i.e. $(x - 4)^2(x + 1)^2$:

$$\Rightarrow \frac{x(x-4)^2(x+1)^2}{x-4} \geq \frac{2(x-4)^2(x+1)^2}{x+1}$$

Cancel down on each side:

$$\Rightarrow x(x-4)(x+1)^2 \geq 2(x-4)^2(x+1)$$

Rearrange into the form f(x) ≥ O... ... then factorise:

$$\Rightarrow x(x-4)(x+1)^2 - 2(x-4)^2(x+1) \geq 0$$
$$\Rightarrow (x-4)(x+1)[x(x+1) - 2(x-4)] \geq 0$$
$$\Rightarrow (x-4)(x+1)(x^2-x+8) \geq 0$$

Find the critical values where f(x) = O:

$(x^2 - x + 8)$ has no real roots, so the critical values are $x = -1$ and $x = 4$.

Draw a number line and test either side of each critical value to find where f(x) ≥ O:

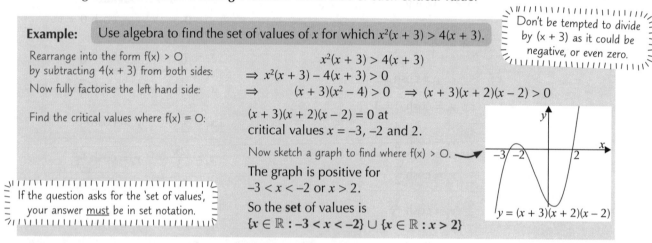

① ② ③

+ve −1 −ve 4 +ve

① Test $x = -2$:
f(−2) = 84 > 0, so f(x) is positive for $x < -1$

② Test $x = 0$:
f(0) = −32 < 0, so f(x) is negative for $-1 < x < 4$.

③ Test $x = 5$:
f(5) = 168 > 0, so f(x) is positive $x > 4$.

Alge-bran: contains a satisfying range of nutritious values.

Or if you prefer...

$$\frac{x}{x-4} - \frac{2}{x+1} \geq O$$
$$\frac{x(x+1) - 2(x-4)}{(x+1)(x-4)} \geq O$$
$$\frac{x^2-x+8}{(x+1)(x-4)} \geq O$$

Then multiply through by the **square** of the denominator.

You're told in the question that $x \neq -1, 4$, so the solution is $x < -1$ and $x > 4$.

Algebraic Inequalities

Squaring can help solve inequalities with Modulus signs...

Squaring both sides of an inequality allows you to get rid of **modulus** signs.
For example: $|x| > 3 \Rightarrow x^2 > 9 \Rightarrow x^2 - 9 > 0 \Rightarrow (x + 3)(x - 3) > 0 \Rightarrow x < -3$ and $x > 3$.

When you have modulus signs around expressions on **both sides of the inequality**,
you can use the following rule:

It also works for $|f(x)| > k$, if k is a positive constant, because $k \equiv |k|$.

$$\text{If } |f(x)| > |g(x)| \text{ then } [f(x)]^2 > [g(x)]^2.$$

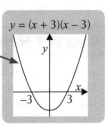

$y = (x + 3)(x - 3)$

Example: Find algebraically the set of values for which $|x + 2| \geq |x^2 - 4|$.

Square both sides to remove the modulus signs:
Factorise $(x^2 - 4)^2$:

$|x + 2| \geq |x^2 - 4| \Rightarrow (x + 2)^2 \geq (x^2 - 4)^2$
$\Rightarrow (x + 2)^2 \geq (x + 2)^2(x - 2)^2$

Now subtract to get in the form $0 \geq f(x)$:
Factorise the right hand side:

$\Rightarrow 0 \geq (x + 2)^2(x - 2)^2 - (x + 2)^2$
$\Rightarrow 0 \geq (x + 2)^2[(x - 2)^2 - 1] \Rightarrow 0 \geq (x + 2)^2(x^2 - 4x + 3)$
$\Rightarrow 0 \geq (x + 2)^2(x - 1)(x - 3)$

Find the critical values where $f(x) = 0$,
and sketch $f(x)$:

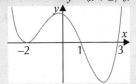

$y = (x + 2)^2(x - 1)(x - 3)$

$(x + 2)^2(x - 1)(x - 3) = 0$ at critical values $x = -2$, 1 and 3.

The graph is **less than or equal to zero**
for $1 \leq x \leq 3$, and it is **also equal to zero**
at $x = -2$.

So the set of values is
$\{x \in \mathbb{R} : 1 \leq x \leq 3\} \cup \{x \in \mathbb{R} : x = -2\}$

Pay close attention to the type of inequality sign at this stage. At repeated roots, such as $(x + 2)$ here, the graph only touches the x-axis, so it would not be considered for $f(x) < 0$.

...but use Graphs to find solutions to |f(x)| > g(x)

If you have **only one** expression with a modulus sign,
squaring may give you **more** solutions than you **need**.
See the example below — the squaring method would give x = 1 as a critical value too, which you don't need.

It's better to **sketch graphs** of the original functions, then work out the critical values from there.

Example: Identify the set of values for which $|x + 2| \geq x^2 - 4$.

1) Sketch $y = |x + 2|$ and $y = x^2 - 4$ on the same axes.

2) You can see that there are two solutions to $|x + 2| = x^2 - 4$,
both for $x + 2 = x^2 - 4 \Rightarrow 0 = x^2 - x - 6 \Rightarrow 0 = (x + 2)(x - 3)$.
So the critical values are at $x = -2$ and 3.

3) From the graphs, $|x + 2| \geq x^2 - 4$ when $-2 \leq x \leq 3$, i.e. when the orange line
is above or touching the green curve. In set notation: $\{x \in \mathbb{R} : -2 \leq x \leq 3\}$

The graphs don't intersect when $-(x + 2) = x^2 - 4$, so you don't have to solve this equation.

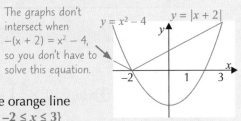

$y = x^2 - 4$ $y = |x + 2|$

Practice Questions

If you're doing AS Level, you only need to do Practice Questions 1 and 2, and Exam Question 1.

Q1 Solve these inequalities algebraically: a) $16x < x(x - 1)^2$,   b) $x^4 - 9x^2 \leq (x + 3)(x - 3)$,   c) $\dfrac{x}{x + 5} \geq 2$, $x \neq -5$

Q2 Use algebra to solve $\dfrac{2}{x - 5} > \dfrac{x}{x - 3}$, giving your answer in set notation.

Q3 Find the range of values for which: a) $2|x| \geq |x + 1|$,   b) $|x^2 - 9| < |x + 3|$,   c) $|x^2 - 9| < x + 3$

Exam Questions

Q1 Solve algebraically $\dfrac{2x}{x + 7} \geq \dfrac{1}{x - 6}$, where $x \in \mathbb{R}$, $x \neq -7, 6$. Give your answer in set notation.   [6 marks]

Q2 a) Show that the inequality $\left|\dfrac{2x}{x - 1}\right| > |x|$ can be written as $f(x) < 0$, where $f(x) = x^2(x - 3)(x + 1)$.   [3 marks]

     b) Hence find the set of values of x that satisfy the inequality for $x \in \mathbb{R}$, $x \neq 1$.   [4 marks]

Inequality Street — a less than appealing box of chocs...

A short and sweet section to round up your revision of Further Pure 1. If you stick to the methods shown here, you shouldn't go far wrong. And give the examiners what they ask for — don't go using graphical methods if they want to see some algebraic manipulation, and if they want a set of values, use set notation. They are very demanding...

Mean and Variance of Discrete Distributions

Remember random variables? They're those variables X whose value is all down to chance — so not at all like your exam grade. This page is all about discrete random variables — they can only take specific individual values.

Discrete Random Variables have an 'Expected Value' or 'Mean'

You can work out the **expected value** (or '**mean**') E(X) for a discrete **random variable** X.
E(X) is a kind of 'theoretical mean' — it's what you'd **expect** the mean of X to be
if you took **loads** of readings. **In practice**, the mean of your results is **unlikely**
to match the theoretical mean exactly, but it should be pretty near.

E(X) is also denoted μ.

If the set of possible values of X (called the **sample space**) is $\{x_1, x_2, x_3, ...\}$, then the expected value of X is:

$$\text{Mean} = \text{Expected Value } E(X) = \sum x_i P(X = x_i) = \sum x_i p_i$$

$p_i = P(X = x_i)$

Example: The probability distribution of X, the number of daughters in a family of 3 children, is shown in the table. Find the expected number of daughters.

x_i	p_i
0	$\frac{1}{8}$
1	$\frac{3}{8}$
2	$\frac{3}{8}$
3	$\frac{1}{8}$

This example assumes that any child being a daughter is independent of any other child being a daughter, and the probability of a child being a daughter is equal to the probability of them not being a daughter — and they both equal $\frac{1}{2}$.

$$\text{Mean} = \sum x_i p_i = \left(0 \times \frac{1}{8}\right) + \left(1 \times \frac{3}{8}\right) + \left(2 \times \frac{3}{8}\right) + \left(3 \times \frac{1}{8}\right)$$
$$= 0 + \frac{3}{8} + \frac{6}{8} + \frac{3}{8} = \mathbf{1.5}$$

The **expected** number of daughters is 1.5 — which sounds a bit weird.
But all it means is that if you check a **large number** of 3-child families, the **mean** will be close to 1.5

The Variance measures how Spread Out the distribution is

You can also find the **variance** of a random variable.
It's the 'expected variance' of a **large number** of readings.

This formula needs $E(X^2) = \sum x_i^2 p_i$ — take each possible value of x, square it, multiply it by its probability and then add up all the results.

$$\text{Variance} = \text{Var}(X) = E(X^2) - [E(X)]^2 = \sum x_i^2 p_i - \left[\sum x_i p_i\right]^2$$

Example: Work out the variance for the '3 daughters' example above.
(cont.)

Var(X) is also written σ^2.

First work out $E(X^2)$:

$$E(X^2) = \sum x_i^2 p_i = \left(0^2 \times \frac{1}{8}\right) + \left(1^2 \times \frac{3}{8}\right) + \left(2^2 \times \frac{3}{8}\right) + \left(3^2 \times \frac{1}{8}\right) = 0 + \frac{3}{8} + \frac{12}{8} + \frac{9}{8} = \frac{24}{8} = 3$$

Now take away the mean squared:

$$\text{Var}(X) = E(X^2) - [E(X)]^2 = 3 - 1.5^2 = 3 - 2.25 = \mathbf{0.75}$$

Example: X has the probability function $P(X = x) = k(x + 1)$ for x = 0, 1, 2, 3, 4.
Find the mean and variance of X.

1) First you need to find k — work out all the probabilities and make sure they add up to 1.
   $P(X = 0) = k \times (0 + 1) = k$. Similarly, $P(X = 1) = 2k$, $P(X = 2) = 3k$, $P(X = 3) = 4k$, $P(X = 4) = 5k$.
   So $k + 2k + 3k + 4k + 5k = 1$, i.e. $15k = 1$ and so $k = \frac{1}{15}$.

   Now you can work out $p_0, p_1, p_2,...$ where $p_1 = P(X = 1)$ etc.

2) Find the mean E(X) first:
   $$E(X) = \sum x_i p_i = \left(0 \times \frac{1}{15}\right) + \left(1 \times \frac{2}{15}\right) + \left(2 \times \frac{3}{15}\right) + \left(3 \times \frac{4}{15}\right) + \left(4 \times \frac{5}{15}\right) = \frac{40}{15} = \frac{8}{3}$$

3) For the variance, you first need $E(X^2)$:
   $$E(X^2) = \sum x_i^2 p_i = \left(0^2 \times \frac{1}{15}\right) + \left(1^2 \times \frac{2}{15}\right) + \left(2^2 \times \frac{3}{15}\right) + \left(3^2 \times \frac{4}{15}\right) + \left(4^2 \times \frac{5}{15}\right) = \frac{130}{15} = \frac{26}{3}$$

4) And then finally:
   $$\text{Var}(X) = E(X^2) - [E(X)]^2 = \frac{26}{3} - \left(\frac{8}{3}\right)^2 = \frac{14}{9}$$

Mean and Variance of Discrete Distributions

These formulas give the *Mean* and *Variance* for a *Linear Function of X*

Watch out for these little jokers in your exam:

$$E(aX + b) = aE(X) + b$$

$$Var(aX + b) = a^2 Var(X)$$

Here, a and b are any numbers.

Example: The discrete random variable X has the probability distribution given in the table.

Find   a) k,   b) $E(X)$,   c) $Var(X)$,   d) $E(3X - 1)$,   e) $Var(3X - 1)$.

a) Remember, the probabilities add up to 1:
$$0.1 + 0.2 + 0.3 + 0.2 + k = 1 \Rightarrow k = 0.2$$

x	2	3	4	5	6
$P(X = x)$	0.1	0.2	0.3	0.2	k

b) Now you can use the formula to find $E(X)$:
$$E(X) = \sum x_i p_i = (2 \times 0.1) + (3 \times 0.2) + (4 \times 0.3) + (5 \times 0.2) + (6 \times 0.2) = \textbf{4.2}$$

c) Next work out $E(X^2)$: $E(X^2) = \sum x_i^2 p_i = (2^2 \times 0.1) + (3^2 \times 0.2) + (4^2 \times 0.3) + (5^2 \times 0.2) + (6^2 \times 0.2) = 19.2$
...and then the variance is easy: $Var(X) = E(X^2) - [E(X)]^2 = 19.2 - 4.2^2 = \textbf{1.56}$

d) You'd expect the question to get harder but it doesn't: $E(3X - 1) = 3E(X) - 1 = 3 \times 4.2 - 1 = \textbf{11.6}$

e) And finally: $Var(3X - 1) = 3^2 Var(X) = 9 \times 1.56 = \textbf{14.04}$

Adjust the formula to work out *E(g(X))*

You could also be asked to work out the expected value of a general **function** of a random variable — that's $E(g(X))$:

$$E(g(X)) = \sum g(x_i) P(X = x_i) = \sum g(x_i) p_i$$

Example: For the discrete random variable X above, find   a) $E(e^X)$,   b) $E(\cosh X)$.
(cont.)

a) $E(e^X) = \sum e^{x_i} p_i = (e^2 \times 0.1) + (e^3 \times 0.2) + (e^4 \times 0.3) + (e^5 \times 0.2) + (e^6 \times 0.2) = \textbf{131.5}$ (1 d.p.)

b) $E(\cosh X) = \sum \cosh(x_i) p_i$
$= (\cosh 2 \times 0.1) + (\cosh 3 \times 0.2) + (\cosh 4 \times 0.3) + (\cosh 5 \times 0.2) + (\cosh 6 \times 0.2) = \textbf{65.8}$ (1 d.p.)

Practice Questions

Q1 The discrete random variable X has a uniform distribution, i.e. $P(X = x) = k$ for $x = 0, 1, 2, 3$ and 4.
Find the value of k and then find the mean and variance of X and of $-2X - 1$.

Q2 A discrete random variable Y has the probability distribution shown in the table, where k is a constant.

y	1	2	3	4
p_i	$\frac{1}{6}$	$\frac{1}{2}$	k	$\frac{5}{24}$

a) Find k.
b) Find $E(Y)$ and $Var(Y)$.
c) Find $E(2Y - 1)$ and $Var(2Y - 1)$.
d) Find $E(3Y^3 + \ln Y)$.

Q3 Use the formula for $E(g(X))$ with $g(X) = aX + b$ to prove that $E(aX + b) = aE(X) + b$.

Exam Question

Q1 The number of red lights encountered on a commuter's drive to work is modelled by the discrete random variable X with the following probability distribution: $p_i = \dfrac{k}{x + 1}$ for $x = 0, 1, 2, 3$.

a) How many red lights should the commuter expect to encounter on each drive to work? [3 marks]
b) Find the expected value and variance of $-X + 1$. [4 marks]
c) Show that the expected value of $\sqrt{X}$ is 0.674, to three decimal places. [2 marks]

Statisticians say: E(Bird in hand) = E(2 Birds in bush)...

The mean and variance here are theoretical values — don't get them confused with the mean and variance of a load of practical observations. You can still take the square root of the variance to get the standard deviation, though. Speaking of variance, get the formula right — the square of the expectation isn't equal to the expectation of the square.

Mean and Variance of Binomial Distribution

You already know what the mean (or expected value) and variance of a random variable are.
And you also know what the binomial distribution is. Put those things together, and you get this page.

For a binomial distribution: **Mean = np**

This formula will be in your **formula booklet**, but it's worth committing to memory anyway.

Mean of a Binomial Distribution
If $X \sim B(n, p)$, then:
Mean (or Expected Value) $= \mu = E(X) = np$

Remember... the expected value is the value you'd **expect** the random variable to take **on average** if you took loads and loads of readings. It's a **"theoretical mean"** — the mean of experimental results is unlikely to match it **exactly**.

Example: If $X \sim B(20, 0.2)$, what is $E(X)$?

$E(X) = np = 20 \times 0.2 = 4$

The probability of getting exactly 5 sixes on your next set of 30 throws $= \binom{30}{5} \times \left(\frac{1}{6}\right)^5 \times \left(\frac{5}{6}\right)^{25} = 0.192$.

So you're much more likely not to get exactly 5 sixes
$(= 1 - 0.192 = 0.808)$.
This is why it only makes sense to talk about the mean as a "long-term average", and not as "what you expect to happen next".

Example: What's the expected number of sixes when you roll a fair dice 30 times? Interpret your answer.

If the random variable X represents the number of sixes in 30 rolls, then $X \sim B(30, \frac{1}{6})$.
So the expected value of X is $E(X) = 30 \times \frac{1}{6} = 5$.

If you were to repeatedly roll the dice 30 times and find the average number of sixes in each set of 30 throws, you would expect it to end up pretty close to 5. And the more sets of 30 rolls you did, the closer to 5 you'd expect the average to be.

For a binomial distribution: **Variance = npq**

Variance of a Binomial Distribution
If $X \sim B(n, p)$, then:
Variance $= Var(X) = \sigma^2 = np(1 - p) = npq$

For a binomial distribution, P(success) is usually called p, and P(failure) is sometimes called q $(= 1 - p)$.

Example: If $X \sim B(20, 0.2)$, find $Var(X)$ and the standard deviation of X.

$Var(X) = np(1 - p) = 20 \times 0.2 \times 0.8 = 3.2$ Standard deviation $= \sqrt{Var(X)} = \sqrt{3.2} = 1.789$ (3 d.p.)

Practice Questions

Q1 Find the mean and variance of the following random variables.
 a) $X \sim B(20, 0.4)$ b) $X \sim B(30, 0.7)$ c) $X \sim B(45, 0.012)$

Q2 Given that $X \sim B(n, p)$, $E(X) = 1$ and $Var(X) = 0.98$, find n and p.

Exam Questions

Q1 A salesman is giving out leaflets. The probability of a passer-by taking a leaflet is 0.3. During a randomly chosen 1 minute interval, 30 people pass him. The number of people who take a leaflet can be modelled by $X \sim B(30, 0.3)$.
 a) What assumptions have been made in modelling X by this binomial distribution?   [1 mark]
 b) How many people would the salesman expect to take a leaflet?   [1 mark]
 c) Find the variance and standard deviation of X.   [2 marks]

Q2 A random variable X is distributed $X \sim B(25, 0.2)$. Find:
 a) $P(X \le \mu)$ [2 marks]   b) $P(X \le \mu - \sigma)$ [2 marks]   c) $P(X < \mu - 2\sigma)$ [2 marks]

I've had far too much to drink — I need to go np...

Nothing too fancy there. A couple of easy-to-remember formulas, and some stuff about how to interpret these figures which you've seen before. So learn the formulas, put your feet up, and do some crocheting while you've got the time.

The Poisson Distribution

Time to meet the Poisson distribution, named after its French inventor Monsieur Siméon-Denis Distribution...

A **Poisson Distribution** has **Only One Parameter**

A Poisson distribution has just **one parameter**: λ.
If the random variable X follows a Poisson distribution, then you write $X \sim \textbf{Po}(\lambda)$.

Poisson Probability Function

If $X \sim \text{Po}(\lambda)$, then X can take values 0, 1, 2, 3... with probability:

$$P(X = x) = \frac{e^{-\lambda} \lambda^x}{x!}$$

Random variables following a Poisson distribution are discrete.

Example: If $X \sim \text{Po}(2.8)$, find:
a) $P(X = 0)$, b) $P(X = 1)$, c) $P(X = 2)$, d) $P(X < 3)$, e) $P(X \geq 3)$.

Using the probability function:

Remember, 0! = 1.

a) $P(X = 0) = \dfrac{e^{-2.8} \times 2.8^0}{0!} = e^{-2.8} = 0.06081... = \textbf{0.061}$ (3 d.p.)

b) $P(X = 1) = \dfrac{e^{-2.8} \times 2.8^1}{1!} = e^{-2.8} \times 2.8 = 0.17026... = \textbf{0.170}$ (3.d.p.)

X is Poisson and so it is discrete — it can only take whole values. So P(X < 3) is the same as P(X ≤ 2).

c) $P(X = 2) = \dfrac{e^{-2.8} \times 2.8^2}{2!} = \dfrac{e^{-2.8} \times 2.8^2}{2 \times 1} = 0.23837... = \textbf{0.238}$ (3 d.p.)

All the normal rules of probability apply.

d) $P(X < 3) = P(X \leq 2) = P(X = 0) + P(X = 1) + P(X = 2)$
$= 0.06081... + 0.17026... + 0.23837...$
$= 0.46945... = \textbf{0.469}$ (3 d.p.)

You could also use the Poisson cumulative distribution function here (see p.127).

e) $P(X \geq 3) = 1 - P(X < 3) = 1 - 0.46945... = \textbf{0.531}$ (3 d.p.)

For a Poisson distribution: **Mean = Variance = λ**

For a Poisson distribution, the **mean** and the **variance** are the **same** — and they both equal λ, the Poisson **parameter**. Remember that and you've probably learnt the most important Poisson fact. Ever.

Mean and Variance of a Poisson Distribution

If $X \sim \text{Po}(\lambda)$, then:

Mean (or Expected Value) $= \mu = E(X) = \lambda$

Variance $= \text{Var}(X) = \sigma^2 = \lambda$

If you were given some sample data, you could assess how suitable the Poisson distribution is as a model by seeing whether the mean and variance of the data were approximately equal.

Example: If $X \sim \text{Po}(7)$, find: a) $E(X)$ and $\text{Var}(X)$,
b) the standard deviation of X.

a) It's Poisson, so $E(X) = \text{Var}(X) = \lambda = 7$

b) Then the standard deviation is $\sqrt{\lambda} = \sqrt{7} = \textbf{2.646}$ (3 d.p.)

Cal was well-prepared for another round of poison distribution.

Example: If $X \sim \text{Po}(1)$, find: a) $P(X \leq \mu)$, b) $P(X \leq \mu - \sigma)$.

$E(X) = \mu = 1$, and $\text{Var}(X) = \sigma^2 = 1 \Rightarrow \sigma = 1$.

a) $P(X \leq \mu) = P(X \leq 1) = P(X = 0) + P(X = 1) = \dfrac{e^{-1} \times 1^0}{0!} + \dfrac{e^{-1} \times 1^1}{1!}$
$= \textbf{0.736}$ (3 d.p.)

b) $P(X \leq \mu - \sigma) = P(X \leq 0) = P(X = 0) = \dfrac{e^{-1} \times 1^0}{0!} = \textbf{0.368}$ (3 d.p.)

The Poisson Distribution

The Poisson *Parameter* is a *Rate*

The **number of events** that occur, or the **number of things** that are present, in a **particular period** often follows a Poisson distribution. It could be a period of: **time** (e.g. minute, hour, etc.), or **space** (e.g. litre, kilometre, etc.).

> If X represents the **number of events** that occur in a **particular space** or **time**, then X will follow a Poisson distribution as long as:
>
> 1) The events occur **randomly**, and are all **independent** of each other.
> 2) The events happen **singly** (i.e. "**one at a time**").
> 3) The events happen (on average) at a **constant rate** (either in space or time).
>
> The Poisson parameter λ is then the **average rate** at which these events occur (i.e. the average number of events in a given interval of space or time).

So a Poisson distribution wouldn't be suitable if, for example, the events occurred less frequently as time went on.

> **Example:** The random variable X represents the number of a certain type of cell in a particular volume of a blood sample. Assuming that the cells are randomly distributed, and that the concentration of these cells in the blood is, on average, constant, show that X follows a Poisson distribution.

Since the cells are randomly distributed, the '**events**' (i.e. the cells you're interested in) should occur **randomly** and **independently**. As two cells cannot occupy the same space, the cells must occur **singly**, and as the average concentration of cells in a given volume is **constant**, the cells should occur (on average) at a **constant rate**. Because X is the total number of 'events' in a given volume, X must follow a **Poisson** distribution.

The Poisson distribution is *Additive*

Suppose X represents the number of events in **1 unit** of time/space (e.g. 1 minute, hour, m^2, m^3, etc.) and $X \sim Po(\lambda)$.

> The number of events in *a* **units** of time/space follows the distribution $Po(a\lambda)$.

This means the expected number of events that occur is proportional to the length of the period.

Suppose $X \sim Po(\lambda)$ and $Y \sim Po(\phi)$ are independent random variables. Then: $\boxed{X + Y \sim Po(\lambda + \phi)}$

Make sure that X and Y are in the same unit of time/space before using additivity.

> **Example:** Sunflowers grow singly and randomly in a field with an average of 10 sunflowers per square metre. What is the exact probability that a randomly chosen area of 0.25 m^2 contains no sunflowers?

X ~ Po(10)

The number of sunflowers in 1 m^2 follows the distribution $Po(10)$. So the number of sunflowers in 0.25 m^2 must follow the distribution $Po(0.25 \times 10) = \mathbf{Po(2.5)}$.

This means P(no sunflowers) $= \dfrac{e^{-2.5} \times 2.5^0}{0!} = e^{-2.5}$

> **Example:** The number of atoms that decay per second in a sample of radioactive material follows the Poisson distribution $Po(5)$. If the probability of no atoms decaying in t seconds is 0.5, find the value of t.

If the random variable X represents the number of radioactive atoms that decay in t seconds, then $X \sim \mathbf{Po(5t)}$.

This means that $P(X = 0) = \dfrac{e^{-5t}(5t)^0}{0!} = e^{-5t} = 0.5$.

Solving this equation for t:

$e^{-5t} = 0.5 \Rightarrow -5t = \ln 0.5 \Rightarrow t = -\dfrac{\ln 0.5}{5} = \mathbf{0.139}$ (3 d.p.)

> **Example:** R and T represent the number of orders a florist receives for roses and tulips respectively in a 30-minute period. Suppose $R \sim Po(3)$ and $T \sim Po(2)$, and that $R + T$ follows a Poisson distribution.
>
> a) What assumptions have been made to model $R + T$ by a Poisson distribution?
> b) What is the probability that the florist receives a total of exactly 15 orders in 1 hour?

a) The orders for roses need to be **independent** of orders for tulips, and a single order cannot be for more than one type of flower. All the other conditions are satisfied since R and T are known to be Poisson.

b) You can model the total number of orders placed in any 30 minute period by $Po(3 + 2) = Po(5)$. But you need the number of orders in 1 hour, which is 2 × 30 mins. This is distributed $Po(2 \times 5) = \mathbf{Po(10)}$. So, using the probability function for the Poisson distribution, P(15 orders) $= \dfrac{e^{-10} \times 10^{15}}{15!} = \mathbf{0.035}$ (3 d.p.)

The Poisson Distribution

Look up probabilities in **Poisson Tables** or use your **Calculator**

You've probably seen **statistical tables** before — they can also be used to find **Poisson** probabilities.

Example: Sunflowers grow singly and randomly in a field with an average of 10 sunflowers per square metre. Find the probability that a randomly chosen square metre contains:
a) no more than 8 sunflowers,   b) no fewer than 9 sunflowers,   c) exactly 10 sunflowers.

If the random variable X represents the number of sunflowers in 1 m², then $X \sim Po(10)$.

That's right... it's the same field of sunflowers.

a) You need to find $P(X \le 8)$. You could do this "manually" using the probability function but it would include 9 terms. It's quicker and easier to use tables of the Poisson cumulative distribution function (c.d.f.). These show $P(X \le x)$ if $X \sim Po(\lambda)$.

Here's a bit of a Poisson table:
- Find your value of λ (here, 10), and the value of x (here, 8).
- You can quickly see that $P(X \le 8) = \mathbf{0.3328}$.

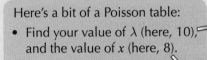
The full Poisson tables can be found on page 288.

Poisson Cumulative Distribution Function
Values show $P(X \le x)$, where $X \sim Po(\lambda)$

$\lambda =$	8.5	9.0	9.5	10.0
$x = 0$	0.0002	0.0001	0.0001	0.0000
1	0.0019	0.0012	0.0008	0.0005
2	0.0093	0.0062	0.0042	0.0028
3	0.0301	0.0212	0.0149	0.0103
4	0.0744	0.0550	0.0403	0.0293
5	0.1496	0.1157	0.0885	0.0671
6	0.2562	0.2068	0.1649	0.1301
7	0.3856	0.3239	0.2687	0.2202
8	0.5231	0.4557	0.3918	0.3328
9	0.6530	0.5874	0.5218	0.4579
10	0.7634	0.7060	0.6453	0.5830
11	0.8487	0.8030	0.7520	0.6968

b) $P(X \ge 9) = 1 - P(X < 9)$
$= 1 - P(X \le 8)$
$= 1 - 0.3328$
$= \mathbf{0.6672}$

c) $P(X = 10) = P(X \le 10) - P(X \le 9)$
$= 0.5830 - 0.4579$
$= \mathbf{0.1251}$

This matches the value you would get using the probability function with x = 10 and λ = 10.

You can also use your **calculator** to find the probabilities — find the **distribution function** and then tap in the x and λ **values**. Make sure to use the right function: the **pdf** is for finding $P(X = x)$ and the **cdf** is for $P(X \le x)$.

Practice Questions

Q1 If $X \sim Po(8.7)$, find (correct to 4 decimal places):
   a) $P(X = 2)$,   b) $P(X = 1)$,   c) $P(X = 0)$,   d) $P(X < 3)$,   e) $P(X \ge 3)$.

Q2 For the following distributions, find: i) $E(X)$ ii) $Var(X)$ iii) the standard deviation of X.
   a) $Po(8)$,   b) $Po(12.11)$,   c) $Po(84.2227)$

Q3 If $X \sim Po(8)$, use Poisson tables to find:
   a) $P(X \le 2)$,   b) $P(X \le 7)$,   c) $P(X < 9)$,   d) $P(X > 1)$,   e) $P(X > 7)$,   f) $P(X = 6)$.

Q4 In a radioactive sample, atoms decay at an average rate of 2000 per hour.
   Describe the Poisson distributions that the following quantities follow.
   a) The number of atoms decaying per minute.   b) The number of atoms decaying per day.

Exam Question

Q1 A birdwatcher wishes to model the number of birds arriving at a particular barn per hour.

   a) State two conditions needed for a Poisson distribution to be a suitable model. **[2 marks]**

   b) The expected number of birds arriving per hour is 7. Assuming the conditions for a Poisson model are met, find the probability that, in a randomly chosen hour during the day, the number of birds arriving at the barn is:
   i) fewer than 4,   **[2 marks]**   ii) at least 7,   **[2 marks]**   iii) exactly 9.   **[2 marks]**

   c) The birdwatcher keeps treats in the barn for an owl. The owl eats, on average, 3 treats every fortnight. The birdwatcher tops up the treats once every 28 days and wishes to ensure that the probability of the treats running out is less than 0.05. Given that the number of treats eaten by the owl in a given period of time satisfies the conditions for a Poisson distribution, find the least number of treats he should have in the barn immediately after adding more to ensure this. **[4 marks]**

Party at mine tonight — Poisson the message...

The Poisson is a simple distribution to get your head around — but there's plenty here to learn. Make sure you know exactly when a Poisson distribution is appropriate, and what the conditions for its validity mean in a real-world context.

Poisson Approximation to B(n, p)

I know that by now you must have fallen in love with both the Poisson and binomial distributions.
So try not to get too jealous when you see them hanging out without you on this page...

For **Big n** and **Small p** — **Po(np)** is an **Approximation** to **B(n, p)**

Sometimes, a Poisson distribution can be used as an **approximation** to a **binomial distribution**:

> ### Poisson Approximation to the Binomial
>
> Suppose the random variable X follows a binomial distribution, i.e. $X \sim B(n, p)$.
> If   (i) n is large,
> and   (ii) p is small,
> then X can be approximated by the Poisson distribution $Y \sim \text{Po}(np)$.

The mean of the binomial distribution is np, so use that as the mean of your Poisson approximation.

Example: In a school of 1825 students, what is the probability that at least 6 of them were born on June 21st? Use a suitable approximation to find your answer. (You may assume that all birthdays are independent, and are distributed evenly throughout the year. Assume all years consist of 365 days.)

If X represents the number of children in the school born on June 21st, then $X \sim B(1825, \frac{1}{365})$.
You need to find $P(X \geq 6)$. ← *So far so good. However, your binomial tables don't go past n = 50. And working this out 'by hand' isn't easy. But look at those values of n and p...*

Since n is large and p is small, $B(1825, \frac{1}{365})$ can be approximated by $\text{Po}(1825 \times \frac{1}{365}) = \text{Po}(5)$.

So $P(X \geq 6) = 1 - P(X < 6) = 1 - P(X \leq 5)$
$= 1 - 0.6160 = \mathbf{0.3840}$

If you work this out using $B(1825, \frac{1}{365})$ on your calculator, you also get 0.3840 — so this is a very good approximation.

The value of n in the binomial distribution represents **1 unit** in the rate given by the Poisson approximation — in the example above, $n = 1825$ so the **average rate** is 5 pupils born on June 21st per 1825 pupils.

The **Smaller** the value of p, the **Better**

1) To use the Poisson approximation to $B(n, p)$, you ideally want n "**as large as possible**" and p "**as small as possible**". The bigger n is and the smaller p is, the **better** the approximation will be.

2) It's important that p is small because then the **mean** and the **variance** of $B(n, p)$ are **approximately equal** — something you need if $\text{Po}(np)$ is going to be a good approximation.

> If $X \sim B(n, p)$, then $E(X) = np$.
> And if p is small, $(1 - p) \approx 1$ — this means $\text{Var}(X) = np(1 - p) \approx np \times 1 = np$.

Example: A factory forgets to add icing to its chocolate cakes with a uniform probability of 0.02. Use a suitable approximation to find the probability that fewer than 6 of the next 100 cakes made will not be iced.

If X represents the number of "un-iced" cakes, then $X \sim B(100, 0.02)$.
Since n is quite large and p is quite small, $X \sim \text{Po}(100 \times 0.02) = \text{Po}(2)$.
So $P(X < 6) = P(X \leq 5) = \mathbf{0.9834}$
If you work it out using $B(100, 0.02)$, you get 0.9845 so this approximation is accurate to 2 decimal places.

These peas are nowhere near small enough.

Poisson Approximation to B(n, p)

If p is Close To One, Swap Successes with Failures

1) Sometimes, the Poisson approximation can be used if p is **very close to 1**.
2) We do this by transforming the binomial distribution of **successes** into a binomial distribution of **failures**.
3) Suppose Y represents the number of successes and $W = n - Y$ represents the number of failures.
   If $Y \sim B(n, p)$ with $p \approx 1$, then $W \sim B(n, q)$, where $q = 1 - p \approx 0$, so q is **small**.

Example: Another factory adds icing to its chocolate cakes with a uniform probability of 0.99. Use a suitable approximation to find the probability that more than 95 of the next 100 cakes made will be iced.

If Y represents the number of iced cakes produced by this factory, then $Y \sim B(100, 0.99)$.
Here, n is quite large, but p is not small.
However, if you let W represent the number of "un-iced" cakes made, then $W \sim B(100, 0.01)$.
Now you can use a Poisson approximation: $W \sim Po(100 \times 0.01) = Po(1)$.

$$P(Y > 95) = P(W < 5) = P(W \leq 4) = \textbf{0.9963}$$

Since $W = 100 - Y$, $Y > 95$ becomes $100 - W > 95 \Leftrightarrow W < 5$.

Using B(100, 0.01), you get $P(W < 5) = 0.99656...$ so this approximation is very accurate.

Practice Questions

Q1 For each of the following random variables, explain whether it can or cannot be approximated by a Poisson distribution. Where it is possible, state the value of the Poisson parameter that you would use.
   a) $X \sim B(4, 0.4)$
   b) $X \sim B(700, 0.01)$
   c) $X \sim B(850, 0.34)$
   d) $X \sim B(8, 0.1)$
   e) $X \sim B(10\,000, 0.00001)$

Q2 Explain how you would use a Poisson distribution to approximate $Y \sim B(80, 0.9)$.

Exam Question

Q1 When a particular engineer is called out to fix a fault, the probability of him being unable to fix the fault is 0.02. This probability is constant, and independent of any other attempted repairs made on other call-outs.

   a) The engineer's work is assessed after every 400 call-outs. The random variable X represents the number of faults the engineer is unable to fix over those 400 call-outs. Explain why the binomial distribution is an appropriate model for X and state the values of any parameters of such a distribution. [2 marks]

   b) i) Why is it appropriate to use a Poisson distribution to approximate X? [2 marks]
      ii) Write down a Poisson distribution that could be used to approximate X. [1 mark]
      iii) Write down the mean and variance of your Poisson distribution. [1 mark]
      iv) Using your Poisson approximation, calculate the probability that the engineer will be unable to fix fewer than 10 faults over a period of 400 call-outs. [1 mark]

   The probability that the engineer is unable to fix fewer than 10 faults in a sample of 400 call-outs, calculated using the binomial distribution, is 0.7179 to 4 decimal places.

   c) Comment on the accuracy of the approximation in part b). [1 mark]

   When the engineer's apprentice accompanies the engineer on a call-out, the probability of him being able to fix the fault in the company's advertised timescale is always 0.99.

   d) By using an appropriate approximation, determine the probability that the engineer will be able to fix more than 390 faults in the advertised timescale in a sample of 400 call-outs when accompanied by his apprentice. [4 marks]

Cod ≈ haddock — a Poisson approximation...

Remember, remember, remember — this approximation only works if p is very small (or, in the right circumstances, when p is close to 1). Fortunately, exam questions will usually tell you when to use one anyway...

The Geometric Distribution

When you think of the geometric distribution, think "fail, fail,..., fail, succeed!"
So it's a bit like England at the Football World Cup, only the geometric distribution ends in a success.

The **Geometric Distribution** models the **Number Of Trials Until A Success**

That old favourite, the fair dice, should give you an idea of what the geometric distribution is all about:

> **Example:**   You roll a fair dice. Find the probability that you first roll a six:
>   a) on the 4th throw,   b) on the nth throw.

a)   If the first six occurs on the 4th throw, then the first 3 throws must all have landed on 'not a six'.

   So P(first six on 4th throw) $= \left(\frac{5}{6}\right)^3 \times \frac{1}{6} = \frac{125}{1296}$ ⬅ This is the probability of needing 4 trials for the first success.

b)   If the first six occurs on the nth throw, then the first $(n-1)$ throws must all have landed on 'not a six'.

   So P(first six on n^{th} throw) $= \left(\frac{5}{6}\right)^{n-1} \times \frac{1}{6}$ ⬅ This is the probability of needing n trials for the first success.

The **geometric distribution** applies to situations similar to the one in this example. If a random variable X follows the distribution you can write $X \sim \text{Geo}(p)$, where X is the **number of trials** up to and including the first success (in the example, a success is a six, and $p = \frac{1}{6}$). In general, the geometric distribution is defined as follows:

Geometric Probability Function

A random variable X follows a geometric distribution as long as these **conditions** are **satisfied**:

1)   There is a **sequence** of **independent** trials with **only two** possible **outcomes** ("**success**" and "**failure**").
2)   There is a **constant probability**, p, of success at each trial.
3) X is the **number** of trials until the **first success** occurs (**including** the "**successful**" trial itself).

If $X \sim \text{Geo}(p)$, then X can take values 1, 2, 3... with probability:

> Random variables following a geometric distribution have an infinite number of possible values.

$$P(X = x) = p(1 - p)^{x-1}$$

one success   x − 1 failures

> The **sample space** (see p.122) is {1, 2, 3, ...}.
> X **cannot** take the value O since you count the trials up to and **including** the first success.

> **Example:**   A biologist examines blood samples until she finds one carrying a certain antibody. She states that $X \sim \text{Geo}(p)$, where X is the number of samples she looks at up to and including the first containing the antibody and p is the probability of finding the antibody in any sample. What assumptions has the biologist made?

The biologist has assumed that p is **constant** for all the samples she looks at, and that the trials are **independent** — i.e. one sample does not affect another.

Fabiano spent a lot of time mulling over his sample space.

The **Mean** and **Variance** are **Functions** of p

The only **parameter** in $\text{Geo}(p)$ is the probability of success p — so the **mean** and **variance** only depend on this.

Mean and Variance of a Geometric Distribution
If $X \sim \textbf{Geo}(p)$, then:
Mean (or **Expected Value**) $= \mu = E(X) = \dfrac{1}{p}$
Variance $= \text{Var}(X) = \sigma^2 = \dfrac{1-p}{p^2}$

> **Example:**   Find $E(X)$ and $\text{Var}(X)$ for the dice example above.
>
> If X is the number of rolls of the dice until the first six, then $X \sim \text{Geo}\left(\frac{1}{6}\right)$. Using the formulas:
>
> $$E(X) = \frac{1}{\left(\frac{1}{6}\right)} = 6 \quad \text{and} \quad \text{Var}(X) = \frac{1 - \frac{1}{6}}{\left(\frac{1}{6}\right)^2} = 30$$
>
> $E(X) = 6$ means that if you **repeated** the process (i.e rolling a dice until you get a six) **many times**, the **average** number of rolls it would take to get your first six would be **6**.

The Geometric Distribution

Be prepared to *Sum A Geometric Series*

The geometric distribution is linked to the **geometric series** — surely you remember those from regular ol' maths.

Example: Suppose $X \sim \text{Geo}(0.2)$. Calculate the probability that
a) X is between 20 and 39 inclusive, b) X is a multiple of 4.

a) You're asked to find $P(20 \le X \le 39)$. For other distributions, you might have done this using tables or the stats function on your calculator — but that's not possible for $\text{Geo}(p)$.

$$P(20 \le X \le 39) = P(X = 20) + P(X = 21) + P(X = 22) + \ldots + P(X = 39)$$

Factorise out the p and as many $(1-p)$s as possible.
$$= p(1-p)^{19} + p(1-p)^{20} + p(1-p)^{21} + \ldots + p(1-p)^{38}$$
$$= p(1-p)^{19}(1 + (1-p) + (1-p)^2 + \ldots + (1-p)^{19})$$

You could work out each of the 20 probabilities but it would take you a long time.

$$= p(1-p)^{19}\frac{(1-(1-p)^{20})}{1-(1-p)}$$

This is a geometric series with first term $a = 1$, common ratio $r = (1-p)$ and $n = 20$ terms.

$$= (1-p)^{19}(1-(1-p)^{20})$$

It has sum $S_n = \frac{a(1-r^n)}{1-r}$.

$$= 0.8^{19} \times (1-0.8^{20}) = \mathbf{0.0142} \text{ (4 d.p.)}$$

b) If X is a multiple of 4 then $X = 4$ or $X = 8$ or $X = 12$ or... In other words:

$$P(X \text{ a multiple of } 4) = P(X = 4) + P(X = 8) + P(X = 12) + \ldots$$
$$= p(1-p)^3 + p(1-p)^7 + p(1-p)^{11} + \ldots$$
$$= p(1-p)^3(1 + (1-p)^4 + (1-p)^8 + \ldots)$$

This is an infinite geometric series with first term $a = 1$ and common ratio $r = (1-p)^4$.

$$= p(1-p)^3\frac{1}{1-(1-p)^4}$$
$$= 0.2 \times 0.8^3 \times \frac{1}{1-0.8^4}$$

Since $|r| < 1$, we can use $S_\infty = \frac{a}{1-r}$.

$$= \mathbf{0.1734} \text{ (4 d.p.)}$$

Practice Questions

Q1 $X \sim \text{Geo}(0.1)$. Find: a) $P(X = 15)$, b) $E(X)$, c) $\text{Var}(X)$, d) the standard deviation of X.

Q2 $Y \sim \text{Geo}(0.75)$. Calculate the probability that Y is no less than 6 but no greater than 30.

Q3 $Z \sim \text{Geo}(0.45)$. Determine the probability that Z is: a) even, b) odd but $Z \ne 1$, c) a multiple of 5.

Exam Questions

Q1 A game involves throwing 2 unfair, but identical, dice and gaining a double six to start.

a) Given that the mean number of throws needed to start the game is 9, determine the probability of throwing a six on any one of the dice. [3 marks]

b) Calculate (to 3 significant figures) the probability that it takes:

i) 4 throws to start, [1 mark]   ii) at least 3 throws to start. [2 marks]

Q2 A politician is canvassing for support by knocking on doors in a particular area of town. On each doorstep, the householder either supports the politician or does not support them. Let X denote the number of householders who support the politician.

a) i) The politician knocks on 20 doors per day. Assuming that each householder's political opinions are independent of other householders and the probability of a householder not supporting the politician is 0.8, show that the probability that exactly 2 householders support the politician is 0.1369 (to 4 d.p.). [2 marks]

ii) Give a criticism of the assumptions made in part i). [1 mark]

b) The politician canvasses every day and always knocks on 20 doors. Assuming that the canvassing on any day is independent of other days, what is the probability (to 4 d.p.) that the politician will not meet exactly 2 householders who supports them until the tenth day? [2 marks]

eXam ~ Geo(1) — *guaranteed success on the first attempt...*

There's nothing too horrendous about the geometric distribution really. Except the possibility that you might have to sum a series to infinity, that is... Go back and relearn the formulas for these sums and you'll be on to a winner.

The Negative Binomial Distribution

The negative binomial distribution is a bit of a mash-up of some of the distributions you've seen before.
It's the geometric distribution dialled up to r, with a probability function reminiscent of the binomial. Take a look...

NB(r, p) models trials up to the rth Success

A random variable X follows a **negative binomial distribution**, written $X \sim NB(r, p)$, if:

1) There is a **sequence** of **independent** trials with **only two** possible **outcomes** ("**success**" and "**failure**").
2) There is a **constant probability**, p, of success at each trial.
3) X is the **number** of trials until the rth **success** occurs (**including** the "**successful**" trials themselves).

These should look familiar — they're **almost identical** to the conditions
for the **geometric** distribution. Make sure you can tell the **difference**.

Negative Binomial Probability Function

If $X \sim NB(r, p)$, then X can take values $r, r + 1, r + 2,...$ with probability:

$$P(X = x) = \binom{x-1}{r-1} p^r (1 - p)^{x-r}$$

There must be at least r trials
for X to include r successes, so
the sample space is $\{x : x \geq r\}$.

The xth trial is fixed as a success. This is
the number of ways of arranging the other
$r - 1$ successes from the other $x - 1$ trials.

r successes   x − r failures

Example: Given that $X \sim NB(4, 0.65)$, find:
a) $P(X = 5)$, b) $P(X > 6)$, c) $P(X = 2)$.

a) $P(X = 5) = \binom{5-1}{4-1} 0.65^4 (1 - 0.65)^{5-4} = \binom{4}{3} 0.65^4 \times 0.35 = 4 \times 0.65^4 \times 0.35 = \mathbf{0.2499}$ (4 d.p.)

b) $P(X > 6) = 1 - P(X \leq 6) = 1 - (P(X = 4) + P(X = 5) + P(X = 6))$ $X \leq 6$ is equivalent to $4 \leq X \leq 6$ since
$= 1 - 0.17851 - 0.24991 - 0.21867$ X cannot take values less than r = 4.
$= \mathbf{0.3529}$ (4 d.p.)

c) $2 < r = 4$ so $P(X = 2) = \mathbf{0}$

Example: A ten-pin bowler wishes to assess how good he is at bowling a strike. During a training
session, he resets the pins after each attempt. Let S be the random variable representing
the number of attempts the bowler must make until he bowls his 12th strike.

a) Give the assumptions that must be made in order to model the number of attempts
until the 12th strike by a negative binomial distribution.

b) Given that the assumptions in a) are satisfied and the probability of the bowler
bowling a strike at any one attempt is $\frac{6}{7}$, determine the probability that:

i) it takes exactly 20 attempts until the 12th strike,
ii) it takes less than 15 attempts until the 12th strike,
iii) it takes at least 15 attempts, but not exactly 20, until the 12th strike.

a) Each attempt must be **independent** of the others and
the probability of a strike must be **constant** for each attempt.

b) We can use $S \sim NB\left(12, \frac{6}{7}\right)$.

i) $P(S = 20) = \binom{19}{11} \times \left(\frac{6}{7}\right)^{12} \times \left(1 - \frac{6}{7}\right)^8 = 75582 \times \frac{6^{12}}{7^{12}} \times \frac{1}{7^8} = 0.00206192... = \mathbf{0.00206}$ (3 s.f.)

ii) $P(S < 15) = P(S \leq 14) = P(S = 12) + P(S = 13) + P(S = 14)$
$= 0.15726... + 0.26960... + 0.25034... = 0.67721... = \mathbf{0.677}$ (3 s.f.)

iii) $P(S \geq 15, S \neq 20) = P(S \geq 15) - P(S = 20)$
$= 1 - P(S < 15) - P(S = 20)$
$= 1 - 0.67721... - 0.00206192... = 0.32072... = \mathbf{0.321}$ (3 s.f.)

The Negative Binomial Distribution

You'll need to use the Mean and Variance

Just like all the other distributions, you'll have to be able to use the formulas for the **mean** and **variance** of NB(r, p):

> ### Mean and Variance of a Negative Binomial Distribution
>
> If $X \sim$ NB(r, p), then:
>
> **Mean** (or **Expected Value**) $= \mu = E(X) = \dfrac{r}{p}$
>
> **Variance** $=$ Var(X) $= \sigma^2 = \dfrac{r(1-p)}{p^2}$

These are almost the same as the Geo(p) versions — they're just multiplied by r.

Example: If $X \sim$ NB(3, 0.3), find the mean and standard deviation of X.

$E(X) = \dfrac{3}{0.3} = \mathbf{10}$

$\text{Var}(X) = \dfrac{3(1-0.3)}{0.3^2} = \dfrac{70}{3} \Rightarrow \sigma = \sqrt{\dfrac{70}{3}} = \mathbf{4.8305}$ (4 d.p.)

Remember, E(X) is the long-term average of X. If you repeatedly carried out trials until the third success many times, you would expect it to take on average 10 attempts until the third success.

Example: The standard deviation of a random variable Y is known to be 2. Given that Y follows a negative binomial distribution measuring the number of trials until the 8th success, find the probability of a single success.

You know that $Y \sim$ NB(8, p) and you're asked to find p.

Using $\sigma = 2$ and the formula for the variance:

$2 = \sqrt{\dfrac{8(1-p)}{p^2}} \Rightarrow 4 = \dfrac{8-8p}{p^2} \Rightarrow 4p^2 + 8p - 8 = 0$

$\Rightarrow p^2 + 2p - 2 = 0$

$\Rightarrow (p+1)^2 - 1 - 2 = 0$

You only need the positive solution as p is a probability.

$\Rightarrow p = -1 + \sqrt{3} = \mathbf{0.7321}$ (4 d.p.)

Practice Questions

Q1 $X \sim$ NB(7, 0.15). Find: a) P($X = 15$),   b) P($X < 10$),   c) E(X),   d) Var(X).

Q2 The random variable Y follows a negative binomial distribution $Y \sim$ NB(r, p). Given that the mean of Y is 4.5 and the variance is 2.25, find r and p.

Exam Question

Q1 Ken is replenishing towels in a hotel. He visits each room in turn. Not all of the rooms require fresh towels, but those which do only require a single fresh towel. Ken only has 6 towels with him. You may assume that each room needs a fresh towel independently of other rooms and that the probability of a room needing a fresh towel is $\frac{1}{3}$ for all rooms. Let T represent the number of rooms that Ken visits before running out of towels, including the room at which he runs out of towels.

a) State a statistical distribution for T. You should make clear all the parameters of the distribution.   [2 marks]

b) What is the probability that Ken runs out of towels at the kth room he visits?   [1 mark]

c) What is the probability, to 3 significant figures, that the 20th room takes Ken's final towel?   [1 mark]

d) What is the probability, to 3 significant figures, that Ken visits at least 9 rooms before visiting the room which takes his final towel?   [2 marks]

Ken works three days a week, visiting all 20 rooms on the hotel's ground floor. The probability that a room needs a fresh towel is independent from one day to the next. He always starts each day with 6 towels.

e) Given that P($T \leq 20$) ≈ 0.70279, find the probability that Ken has at least one towel left at the end of the day on all three days that he works in a particular week.   [2 marks]

Everyone prefers hanging out with B(n, p) — NB(r, p) is just so negative...

You need to know which distribution to use when you're given a problem. The binomial, geometric and negative binomial have some similarities, but come in useful in different scenarios. Get it straight in your head which is which.

Poisson Hypothesis Tests

Poisson hypothesis tests are similar to bog-standard A-level ones, so you'll have seen lots of this stuff before.

Use a Hypothesis Test to Find Out about the Population Parameter λ

If λ is the rate at which an event occurs in a population and X is the number of those events that occur in a random interval, then X can be used as the **test statistic** for testing theories on λ. You can find the **p-value** (or **critical region**) using either the Poisson c.d.f. on your **calculator** or the **Poisson tables** (see page 288).

Example: A bookshop sells the book '*A complete history of the Poisson distribution*' at a rate of 10 copies a week. The shop's manager reduces the price of the book. In one randomly-selected week after the price change, 16 copies are sold. Use a 10% level of significance to test whether there is evidence that sales increased.

1) Identify the **population parameter** that you're going to test (in context):
   Let λ = the rate at which copies of the book are sold per week.

   The word 'rate' tells you that the situation can be modelled by a Poisson distribution.

2) Write null and alternative **hypotheses** for the population parameter λ:
   $H_0: \lambda = 10$ $H_1: \lambda > 10$ ◄——— *This is a one-tailed test since you're testing whether sales increased.*

3) State the **test statistic** X (the number of 'successes'), and its **sampling distribution** under H_0:
   Let X = number of copies sold in a random week. Under H_0, $X \sim Po(10)$.

4) State the **significance level** of the test. Here it's 10%, so $\alpha = 0.1$.

   You could find the critical region here instead.

5) Find the **p-value** — the probability of a value for your test statistic at least as extreme as the observed value. This is a one-tailed test and you're interested in the upper end of the distribution.

   Using the Poisson c.d.f. on your calculator: $P(X \geq 16) = 1 - P(X \leq 15) = 1 - 0.9512... = 0.0487$ (3 s.f.), and since **0.0487 < 0.1**, the result is significant.

6) Don't forget to write your **conclusion** (in context):

   You could also use the Poisson tables to find this.

   There is evidence at the 10% level of significance to reject H_0 and to suggest that sales have increased.

Hypothesis test Questions can be asked in Different Ways

A question might ask for a critical region with a probability '**as close as possible to**', but perhaps **outside**, the significance level. Remember, for **two-tailed** tests you should **halve** the significance level first.

Example: In a particular coral reef, the mean number of plankton is 7 for each 10 ml of seawater. A marine biologist thinks that a recent rainstorm might have changed this rate. She takes a 10 ml sample of seawater from a random location in the coral reef.

a) Using a 1% level of significance, find the critical region for the marine biologist's theory. The probability of rejection in each tail should be as close as possible to 0.005.

b) Find the actual significance level of a test based on the critical region from part a).

The marine biologist finds 6 plankton in her 10 ml sample.

c) State whether the null hypothesis is rejected.

a) Let λ = the mean number of plankton in 10 ml of seawater. Then $H_0: \lambda = 7$ and $H_1: \lambda \neq 7$.
   Let X = the number of plankton in a randomly-selected sample. Under H_0, $X \sim Po(7)$.
   The probability that X lies within each tail should be **as close to 0.005 as** possible.

   Using your calculator: Lower tail: Upper tail:
   $\qquad\qquad\qquad\qquad$ $P(X \leq 0) = 0.0009...$ $\qquad$ $P(X \geq 15) = 1 - P(X \leq 14) = 1 - 0.9942... = 0.0057...$
   $\qquad\qquad\qquad\qquad$ $P(X \leq 1) = 0.0072...$ $\qquad$ $P(X \geq 16) = 1 - P(X \leq 15) = 1 - 0.9975... = 0.0024...$

   $0.0072...$ is closer to 0.005 than $0.0009...$, and $0.0057...$ is closer to 0.005 than $0.0024...$
   So the critical region is $X \leq 1$ or $X \geq 15$.

   $0.0072...$ and $0.0057...$ are both greater than 0.005.

b) The **actual** significance level is the probability of X being in the critical region (i.e. not just 1%):
   $P(X \leq 1) + P(X \geq 15) = 0.0072... + 0.0057... = \mathbf{0.0130}$ **or 1.30% (3 s.f.)**

c) The observed value of 6 is outside the critical region. **So there is insufficient evidence at the 1% level of significance to support the claim that the mean number of plankton in the seawater has changed.**

Poisson Hypothesis Tests

You can use a *Poisson Approximation* to *B(n, p)* to find *Probabilities*

On page 128 you saw that if $X \sim B(n, p)$ for **large n** and **small p**, then X can be approximated by **Po(np)**. You can use this **approximation** when doing a hypothesis test.

Example: May has a crazy, 20-sided dice, which she thinks might be biased towards the number 1. She rolls the dice 100 times and gets 12 ones. Test May's theory at the 1% level of significance.

If the dice is unbiased, $P(1) = 1 \div 20 = 0.05$.

So, **$H_0: p = 0.05$** and **$H_1: p > 0.05$**, where p is the probability of rolling a 1.
Let X = number of ones in 100 rolls. Under H_0, $X \sim B(100, 0.05)$. $\alpha = 0.01$.

n is large and p is quite small, so $X \sim Po(100 \times 0.05) = Po(5)$.

> The p-value using the binomial c.d.f. is 0.0042..., which is also significant.

$P(X \geq 12) = 1 - P(X \leq 11) = 1 - 0.9945... = 0.0054...$ **$0.0054... < 0.01$**, so it's significant at the 1% level.

There is evidence to reject H_0 and to support May's theory that the dice is biased towards the number 1.

> The evidence provided by this test is strong because $\alpha = 0.01$ is low. This means you can be more confident that you've correctly rejected H_0.

> You could've used the Poisson approximation straight away. Then the hypotheses would be $H_0: \lambda = 5$, $H_1: \lambda > 5$. This wouldn't affect the p-value or outcome of the test.

Practice Questions

Q1 A coffee shop serves 8.5 customers every 10 minutes during rush hour each weekday. After a new staff member is employed, 4 customers are served during a randomly-selected 10 minute period on a weekday rush hour. Use a 10% significance level to test whether the rate of customers served has changed.

Q2 144 eggs are delivered to a shop each week.
The probability that any random egg is broken when it is delivered is 0.0625.

a) Show that the number of broken eggs in a delivery, X, can be approximated by a Poisson distribution.

A new type of packaging is introduced to try and lower the probability of eggs breaking.
In the week after the new packaging is introduced, 3 of the 144 eggs delivered are broken.

b) Using your Poisson approximation, test whether there is enough evidence to suggest that the rate of broken eggs has decreased. Use a 5% significance level.

Exam Question

Q1 In 2007, the number of potholes on a particular stretch of road occurred at a rate of 4 potholes per mile. A council worker is investigating whether the rate of potholes is different in 2017. They model the rate of potholes as a Poisson distribution.

a) State one modelling assumption the council worker has used for this distribution to be valid. [1 mark]

b) Using a 5% level of significance, find the critical values for the council worker's investigation. The probability of rejection in each tail should be as close as possible to 0.025. [4 marks]

On a randomly-selected mile of the road, the council worker finds 11 potholes.

c) State whether there is evidence that the rate of potholes has changed. [1 mark]

d) Find the actual significance level of the test. [1 mark]

Questions on hypothesis testing in exam papers ~ Po(3)...

Make sure you know the steps for general hypothesis testing off by heart — you'll be using them lots in this section:
1) State the hypotheses. 2) State the test statistic and its sampling distribution. 3) Find the p-value or critical region.
4) Compare the probabilities to α (or the observed value to the critical region). 5) Write a conclusion in context.

Geometric Hypothesis Tests

It might help to think of the geometric distribution like your driving test — if at first you don't succeed, try, try again. Let's get into gear and hit the accelerator on geometric hypothesis tests. How are these car puns — exhausting?

Use the **Geometric Series Formulas** to calculate the **p-value**

A **geometric distribution** is a suitable model when you have a sequence of X independent trials, where X is the number of trials until the **first success** occurs, and a constant probability, p, of success at each trial.

To test hypotheses about the distribution, you use X as the test statistic. When you calculate the **p-value** (or find the critical region/values) you have to use the **geometric probability function**, which you saw on page 130:

> If $X \sim \text{Geo}(p)$, then X can take values 1, 2, 3... with probability:
> $$P(X = x) = p(1 - p)^{x-1}$$

Sadly there's no calculator function for the geometric distribution.

The *p*-value is a cumulative probability, so you'll have a sum of probabilities. This means you can use the trusty **geometric series formulas** — like you did on page 131. To decide which formula you want, compare the **observed value** to the **expected value**, $E(X)$, for the geometric distribution.

> If observed value < expected value, use: $S_n = \dfrac{a(1 - r^n)}{1 - r}$
>
> If observed value > expected value, use: $S_\infty = \dfrac{a}{1 - r}$
>
> Remember, a is the first term in the series, r is the common ratio and n is the (finite) number of terms in the series.

Gordon was hooked by the latest geometric series — unfortunately it was infinite.

Calculating the **p-value** is **Easier** than finding the **Critical Region**

The process of geometric hypothesis testing is business as usual, except for the calculation of the **p-value** or **critical region**. You should stick to the **p-value method** if you have the choice — to find the critical region/values the working is more complicated (see the next page).

> **Example:** Kasia suspects that a coin is biased, such that the probability of getting a tail is less than 0.5. She keeps tossing the coin until she gets the first tail on the 5th toss. Use a 5% level of significance to test whether there is evidence that the coin is biased.

Let p = probability of getting a tail. Then $H_0: p = 0.5$ and $H_1: p < 0.5$.

Let X = the number of tosses until she gets a tail. Under H_0, $X \sim \text{Geo}(0.5)$. $\alpha = 0.05$.

The *p*-value is the probability of a value being at least as extreme as the observed value.
On a fair coin you'd expect to get the first tail on the 2nd toss (since $E(X) = \dfrac{1}{0.5} = 2$).
The observed value is 5, so values at least as extreme as this are 5, 6, 7, ... etc.
So the *p*-value is:
$$P(X \geq 5) = P(X = 5) + P(X = 6) + P(X = 7) + ...$$
$$= p(1 - p)^4 + p(1 - p)^5 + p(1 - p)^6 + ...$$
$$= p(1 - p)^4[1 + (1 - p) + (1 - p)^2 + ...]$$
$$= p(1 - p)^4 \frac{1}{1 - (1 - p)}$$
$$= p(1 - p)^4 \frac{1}{p}$$
$$= (1 - p)^4$$
$$= (1 - 0.5)^4 = 0.0625$$

This is an infinite geometric series with a = 1 and r = 1 − p.

Since |r| < 1, you can use $S_\infty = \dfrac{a}{1-r}$.

Since $0.0625 > 0.05$, the result is not significant.
There is insufficient evidence at the 5% significance level to reject H_0 and to suggest that the coin is biased.

You could also have found the p-value by doing
$$P(X \geq 5) = 1 - P(X \leq 4) = 1 - S_4,$$
using $S_n = \dfrac{a(1 - r^n)}{1 - r}$ with a = p, r = 1 − p and n = 4 (or just subtracting the four individual probabilities P(X = 1), P(X = 2), P(X = 3) and P(X = 4) from 1).

Geometric Hypothesis Tests

Use **Both** geometric series **Formulas** to find the **Critical Region**

If you're asked to find the critical **region/values**, it helps to be **general** with the calculations, so you can substitute in different values without having to repeat the calculation.

Example: An exam is designed so that the probability that any random person passes the exam is 0.002. The examiner thinks that this probability is actually different. He finds that the first person to pass the exam is the 1526th person who takes it, and carries out a hypothesis test using a 10% level of significance. Find the critical region of the examiner's hypothesis test, and state his conclusion.

Let p = probability of passing the exam. Then $H_0: p = 0.002$ and $H_1: p \neq 0.002$.

Let X = the number of people who take the exam before someone passes it. Under H_0, $X \sim \text{Geo}(0.002)$.

$\alpha = 0.1$, so the probability that X lies within each tail should be less than 0.05.

Rather than working out the cumulative probabilities for lots of values, it's easier to be general by using a variable, say k, and then substituting in different values.

For the lower tail: $P(X \leq k) = P(X = k) + P(X = k - 1) + ... + P(X = 2) + P(X = 1)$

$$= p(1 - p)^{k-1} + p(1 - p)^{k-2} + ... + p(1 - p) + p$$

$$= p[1 + (1 - p) + ... + (1 - p)^{k-2} + (1 - p)^{k-1}]$$

Use $S_n = \dfrac{a(1 - r^n)}{1 - r}$, with $a = 1$, $r = 1 - p$ and $n = k$.

$$= p\frac{1(1 - (1 - p)^k)}{1 - (1 - p)} = p\frac{1 - (1 - p)^k}{p} = 1 - (1 - p)^k = 1 - 0.998^k$$

Now try values of k: $P(X \leq 26) = 0.0507$ (3 s.f.) and $\mathbf{P(X \leq 25) = 0.0488}$ **(3 s.f.) < 0.05**

For the upper tail: $P(X \geq k) = P(X = k) + P(X = k + 1) + P(X = k + 2) + ...$

$$= p(1 - p)^{k-1} + p(1 - p)^k + p(1 - p)^{k+1} + ...$$

$$= p(1 - p)^{k-1}[1 + (1 - p) + (1 - p)^2 + ...]$$

Use $S_\infty = \dfrac{a}{1 - r}$, with $a = 1$ and $r = 1 - p$.

$$= p(1 - p)^{k-1}\frac{1}{1 - (1 - p)} = p(1 - p)^{k-1}\frac{1}{p} = (1 - p)^{k-1} = 0.998^{k-1}$$

Again, try values of k: $P(X \geq 1497) = 0.05003...$ and $\mathbf{P(X \geq 1498) = 0.0499}$ **(3 s.f.) < 0.05**

The critical region is $X \leq 25$ and $X \geq 1498$.

1526 is inside the critical region, so the result is significant. **There is evidence at the 10% level to reject H_0 and to support the examiner's theory that the probability that someone passes the test is different.**

Practice Question

Q1 An arcade game is supposed to award a prize with probability 0.025. The owner claims that the probability is higher than this. On a particular day, the game awards the first prize on the 4th play. Use a 10% level of significance to test whether there is evidence for the owner's claim.

Exam Questions

Q1 In a UK county, 20% of cars are black. A resident claims that this percentage is lower in his area. He watches cars that go past his house and the 10th car to pass is the first black car. Using a 5% level of significance, find the acceptance region of the resident's claim. State whether there is evidence to reject the null hypothesis. [5 marks]

Q2 A theme park ride breaks down with probability 0.1 on any given day. The owners install a new type of carriage to the ride and think that the probability it breaks down will have changed. After the installation, it takes 39 days for the ride to break down for the first time.

a) Test whether the probability that the ride breaks down has changed, at the 1% significance level. [5 marks]

b) State one assumption required for the model used in part a) to be suitable. [1 mark]

Weak bladder? You might need to test your p-value...

Before you quote the general formulas for p-values and critical regions from the examples here, make sure you understand where they've come from — that way you'll have a better chance of using the right one in the exam. My advice with these is to take your time — it's easy to make a mistake when finding probabilities.

Chi Squared Tests — 1

Chi squared (pronouced 'kai') is yet another fabulous distribution. You need to know how to use it for two types of hypothesis test — 'goodness of fit' and 'contingency table' tests. First up — goodness of fit.

You can **Test** the **Goodness of Fit** of a **Model**

A **goodness of fit test** checks whether a particular distribution is a **suitable model** for some observed data. No matter what the model is (e.g. binomial, Poisson, etc.) you can use the following **steps** to do the test:

1) The **null hypothesis** is that the **model** is **suitable** for the **observed distribution** (so the **alternative hypothesis** is that it's **not suitable**).

2) The test compares **observed values** (O_i) and **expected values** (E_i). Usually these aren't exactly equal — for example, if you rolled a fair dice 60 times you might observe 12 sixes when you'd expected 10 sixes. To calculate the **expected values** you have to use the **probability function** for the distribution you're testing.

$$E_i = N \times P(X = x_i)$$

Here, N is the total number of observations.

The same test statistic is used for contingency table tests, but the calculation of the expected values is different — see p.140.

3) The **test statistic** is X^2 (i.e. the upper case Greek letter 'chi', squared).

$$X^2 = \sum_{i=1}^{n} \frac{(O_i - E_i)^2}{E_i}$$

Here, n is the number of pairs of values to compare. This is given in the formula booklet.

To calculate X^2, all **expected frequencies** must be **at least 5**, so you might have to **combine** some of the E_i.

Example: A stationery shop sells pens in boxes of 25. The shop owner thinks that 4% of these pens are broken. She models the number of broken pens in each box, X, by the distribution $X \sim B(25, 0.04)$. The owner randomly samples 50 boxes of pens and records the number of broken pens in each box in the table below.

Goodness of fit tests are always one-tailed.

Carry out a hypothesis test, at the 5% significance level, to see if the owner's model is suitable for the sample data.

1) State the **hypotheses**. H_0: $X \sim B(25, 0.04)$ is a suitable model for the observed data.
   H_1: $X \sim B(25, 0.04)$ is not a suitable model for the observed data.

2) Create a row to calculate the **expected values**. The model is binomial, so you can either use your calculator or the binomial probability function to find $P(X = x_i)$.

Number of broken pens in a box	0	1	2	3 or more
Observed frequency, O_i	23	19	6	2
Expected frequency, $E_i = N \times P(X = x_i)$	$50 \times 0.3603...$ $= 18.0...$	$50 \times 0.3754...$ $= 18.7...$	$50 \times 0.1877...$ $= 9.38...$	$50 \times 0.0764...$ $= 3.82...$

Try to keep your values unrounded by using your calculator's memory function.

$N = 50$

Find $P(X = 0)$ with the binomial p.d.f. on your calculator with $x = 0$, $n = 25$ and $p = 0.04$ or do $\binom{25}{0} \times (0.04)^0 \times (0.96)^{25}$.

Use the binomial c.d.f. or just do $50 - 18.0... - 18.7... - 9.38...$

3) Calculate the **test statistic** X^2. The '3 or more' column is too small ($3.82... < 5$), so combine it with the previous column to make a '2 or more' column, and add another row to calculate $\frac{(O_i - E_i)^2}{E_i}$.

Number of broken pens in a box	0	1	2 or more	Combining gives:
O_i	23	19	8	$6 + 2$
E_i	18.0...	18.7...	13.2...	$9.38... + 3.82...$
$\frac{(O_i - E_i)^2}{E_i}$	1.37...	0.00280...	2.05...	

$n = 3$ because there are 3 pairs of observed and expected values.

$\frac{(23 - 18.0...)^2}{18.0...}$ $\frac{(19 - 18.7...)^2}{18.7...}$ $\frac{(8 - 13.2...)^2}{13.2...}$

Then the test statistic is $X^2 = \sum_{i=1}^{3} \frac{(O_i - E_i)^2}{E_i} = 1.37... + 0.00280... + 2.05... = 3.433... = \mathbf{3.43}$ **(3 s.f.)**

To be continued...

Chi Squared Tests — 1

Find the **Degrees of Freedom** and **Compare** X^2 to χ^2

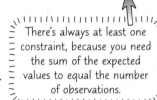
Don't mix up X^2 and χ^2.

Once you've found X^2, there are still a few more steps to go:

4) The **chi squared distribution** (written χ^2, using the lower case chi) has one parameter v, called the **degrees of freedom**. The value of v for a χ^2 distribution depends on the **number of constraints** on the **expected values**.

> **Number of degrees of freedom (v) = number (n) of pairs of values (after combining) – number of constraints**

This usually equals $n - 1$, unless p is estimated from the observed data (for a binomial distribution) or λ is estimated from the observed data (for a Poisson distribution). In these cases $v = n - 2$.

There's always at least one constraint, because you need the sum of the expected values to equal the number of observations.

5) To test for significance, compare X^2 to the χ^2 **statistic** for v degrees of freedom, which is found using the percentage points of the χ^2 distribution **table** (page 289).

> To be **significant** the value of X^2 must be **greater than** the value of $\chi^2_{(v)}$ (the critical value). In this case, you would **reject H_0**.

6) The **conclusion** is that there is evidence to suggest that the model **is suitable** or **is not suitable** for the data.

Example (continued):

4) Find the χ^2 statistic.
Since p isn't estimated from the observed data, $v = 3 - 1 = 2$ degrees of freedom.
Using the table on page 289, with $\alpha = 0.05$, the critical value is $\chi^2_{(2)} = 5.991$.

These are the significance levels.   *These are the degrees of freedom.*

0.100	0.050	0.025	0.010	0.005	v
2.705	3.841	5.024	6.635	7.879	1
4.605	5.991	7.378	9.210	10.597	2
6.251	7.815	9.348	11.345	12.838	3

5) Compare X^2 and χ^2 to test for significance.
Since $3.43 < 5.991$, the result is not significant.

6) Write your conclusion (in context). **There is insufficient evidence, at the 5% level, to reject H_0 and to suggest that the binomial model is not suitable for the observed data.**

Practice Questions

Q1 Look up the values of $\chi^2_{(v)}$ for the following degrees of freedom and significance levels:
a) $v = 10$, $\alpha = 5\%$,   b) $v = 4$, $\alpha = 10\%$,   c) $v = 5$, $\alpha = 1\%$,   d) $v = 2$, $\alpha = 2.5\%$.

Q2 The manufacturers of a 4-sided dice believe that its score can be modelled by a uniform distribution. Test, at the 2.5% level, whether the uniform distribution is a suitable model for the 500 dice rolls below.

Dice score	1	2	3	4
Observed frequency, O_i	113	132	118	137

Exam Question

Q1 Each day a company tests a random sample of the party poppers that it makes.
They believe that the number of party poppers tested until the first one works is modelled by a geometric distribution.
The table below shows the number of party poppers tested until the first one works for 200 randomly-chosen days.

Number of party poppers tested until the first one works	1	2	3	4 or more
Observed frequency, O_i	154	35	7	4

An estimate of the distribution parameter, $p = 0.78$, is calculated from this data.
Use this to carry out a hypothesis test, at the 10% significance level, to see if the company's model is suitable for the sample data.

[10 marks]

Chi squared — the one distribution to rule them all...

You could be asked to do a goodness of fit test on uniform, binomial, Poisson and geometric distributions, so practise finding probabilities for all of them. Questions might give you a table partly filled with some of the expected frequencies to save time in the exam. Remember to combine any columns where $E_i < 5$ — this can be easy to forget.

Chi Squared Tests — 2

Without further ado, let's move on to the other use of the χ^2 distribution you need to know — contingency table tests.

Contingency Tables show Observed Frequencies for Two Variables

Suppose you've got a sample of size N, and you're interested in two different **variables** for each of the N members — where each variable can be **classified** into **different categories**. E.g. eye colour (blue, brown, green, ...), favourite way of cooking potatoes (boiled, roast, baked, ...), etc. You can show this data in a **contingency table**.

You use the **columns** to show the **categories** for one of the variables, and the **rows** to show the other. Then fill in each **cell** in the table with the **number of sample members** that fit that particular **combination** of categories — e.g. 'blue eyes and boiled potatoes'.

This sounds complicated, but it's just a two-way table really.

You can Test whether Two Variables are Independent

With the data in this format, you can do a **contingency table test** of whether the two variables are **independent**. This is similar to a goodness of fit test (p.138-139) — both show significance if $X^2 > \chi^2$. But some bits are different:

1) The **null hypothesis** is always that the **two variables** are **independent** (or **not associated**). So the **alternative hypothesis** is that the **two variables** are **dependent** (or **associated**).

2)
$$\text{Expected values, } E_i = \frac{\text{(row total)} \times \text{(column total)}}{\text{overall total } (N)}$$

3)
$$\text{Number of degrees of freedom } (v) = (r-1) \times (c-1),$$
where r and c are the number of **rows** and **columns** (after combining).

This comes from the constraints on the expected frequencies.

Example: The table on the right shows soil pH and plant growth for a sample of 100 plants. Test at the 5% level whether there is a link between soil pH and growth for these plants.

O_i	Poor growth	Average growth	Good growth	Total
Acidic soil	12	16	4	32
Neutral soil	3	13	14	30
Alkaline soil	3	10	25	38
Total	18	39	43	100

1) State the hypotheses (in context):
   H_0: soil pH and plant growth are independent.
   H_1: soil pH and plant growth are dependent.

2) Draw a second table and calculate the expected values using $E_i = \dfrac{\text{row total} \times \text{column total}}{N}$

E_i	Poor growth	Average growth	Good growth	Total
Acidic soil	5.76	12.48	13.76	32
Neutral soil	5.4	11.7	12.9	30
Alkaline soil	6.84	14.82	16.34	38
Total	18	39	43	100

$\dfrac{32 \times 43}{100} = 13.76$. Here, all $E_i > 5$.

You get the formula for E by saying that under H_0 the ratio of the growth categories should be the same for each type of soil. E.g. $\dfrac{18}{100}$ of each row total should have poor growth.

3) Calculate the test statistic X^2 — you can draw a third table to help.

$\dfrac{(O_i - E_i)^2}{E_i}$	Poor growth	Average growth	Good growth
Acidic soil	6.76	0.992...	6.92...
Neutral soil	1.06...	0.144...	0.0937...
Alkaline soil	2.15...	1.56...	4.58...

$\dfrac{(4 - 13.76)^2}{13.76} = 6.92...$

$$X^2 = \sum \frac{(O_i - E_i)^2}{E_i}$$

$= 6.76 + 1.06... + 2.15... + 0.992... + 0.144...$
$\quad + 1.56... + 6.92... + 0.0937... + 4.58...$
$= 24.3 \text{ (3 s.f.)}$

4) Find the χ^2 statistic. $v = (3-1)(3-1) = \mathbf{4}$ **degrees of freedom**.
   Using the table on page 289, with $\alpha = 0.05$, the critical value is $\chi^2_{(4)} = \mathbf{9.488}$.

5) Compare X^2 and χ^2 to test for significance. Since $\mathbf{24.3 > 9.488}$, the result is significant.

6) Write your conclusion (in context). **There is evidence, at the 5% level, to reject H_0 and to suggest that soil pH and plant growth are dependent.**

Chi Squared Tests — 2

You may need to Merge Rows or Columns in a table

Just like the goodness of fit tests, all of the expected frequencies need to be **greater than 5** for the test to be valid. You can combine **either rows or columns** to make this happen.

> *But remember that you always need at least 2 rows and 2 columns.*

Example: A technology company carries out a hypothesis test to see if product type and point of sale are associated. The table shows the observed frequencies (and expected frequencies in brackets) for a sample of 40 individual sales.

O_i (E_i)	In store	Online	Total
Laptop	19 (16.1)	9 (11.9)	28
Phone	3 (5.175)	6 (3.825)	9
Watch	1 (1.725)	2 (1.275)	3
Total	23	17	40

a) Calculate X^2 by combining the 'Phone' and 'Watch' rows.

b) Test whether product type and point of sale are associated at the 5% level.

a) Combine 'Phone' and 'Watch' into one row (say 'Other'):

Then calculate the value of X^2:

You might want to draw a table with $\frac{(O_i - E_i)^2}{E_i}$.

O_i (E_i)	In store	Online	Total
Laptop	19 (16.1)	9 (11.9)	28
Other	4 (6.9)	8 (5.1)	12
Total	23	17	40

$$X^2 = \sum \frac{(O_i - E_i)^2}{E_i}$$

$$= 0.522... + 0.706... + 1.218... + 1.649... = \mathbf{4.10 \ (3 \ s.f.)}$$

$$\frac{(4 - 6.9)^2}{6.9} = \frac{2.9^2}{6.9} = 1.218...$$

Combining 3 + 1 and 5.175 + 1.725

b) H_0: product type and point of sale are not associated.
H_1: product type and point of sale are associated.
$v = (2 - 1)(2 - 1) = 1$ degree of freedom. With $\alpha = 0.05$, $\chi^2_{(1)} = 3.841$.
Since **4.10 > 3.841**, the result is significant.
There is sufficient evidence at the 5% level to reject H_0 and to suggest that product type and point of sale are associated.

> *Remember to combine columns before using the formula for v. Don't fall into the trap of working out v (without combining) and then subtracting 1.*

Practice Question

Q1 The table on the right shows gender and result for a sample of 80 maths tests. Test whether this sample provides evidence, at the 5% level, that gender and test result are associated.

O_i	Male	Female	Total
Pass	31	28	59
Fail	13	8	21
Total	44	36	80

Exam Question

Q1 The manager of a tourist attraction investigates whether a visitor's review of the attraction is independent of the type of visitor. She takes a sample of 100 reviews and writes the observed frequencies, O_i, and some of the expected frequencies, E_i, in the table below.

O_i (E_i)	Terrible	Poor	Fair	Good	Excellent	Total
Child	13 (5.1)	9 (7.14)	6 (9.18)	5 (6.8)	1 (5.78)	34
Adult	1 (5.25)	2 (7.35)	9 (9.45)	9 (7)	14 (5.95)	35
Concession	1	10 (6.51)	12 (8.37)	6 (6.2)	2 (5.27)	31
Total	15	21	27	20	17	100

a) Find the expected frequency for concessions whose review was 'terrible'. [2 marks]

The manager combines the 'terrible' and 'poor' columns and then calculates $X^2 = 35.7$ (3 s.f.).

b) Explain why the manager has to combine the 'terrible' and 'poor' columns. [1 mark]

c) Test, at the 1% level, whether review and type of visitor are independent. [4 marks]

If your first table falls through it's good to have a contingency table...

You're given the formula for the X^2 test statistic in the formula book, which might help to jog your memory if you've forgotten how to do the test. These questions can be pretty chunky though, so try to learn the many, many steps.

Quality of Tests

By now you must be sick to the back teeth of hypothesis tests. The good news is you've learnt all you need for FS1. The bad news is that you need to know how to measure the quality of a test — this is done by looking at errors.

The **Size** of a test is the **Probability** of being in the **Critical Region**

The result of a hypothesis test can actually be an **error**. There are **two** types of errors that you need to learn:

> - **Type I error** — **rejecting** the null hypothesis, when it is actually **true**.
> - **Type II error** — **not rejecting** the null hypothesis, when it is actually **false**.

To determine the **quality** of a test, you can look at its **size** and **power** — which relate to the **probability** of errors occurring.

You could be asked about any distribution from A-level maths or further maths (e.g. binomial, normal, etc...).

> The **size** of a test is the probability of a **Type I error** — this is the probability of being in the **critical region** given that H_0 is correct.

Example: Tommy and Gina are testing a pile of cards to see if the probability of choosing a spade (with replacement and shuffling), p, is greater than 0.25. Both test at the 1% significance level.

Tommy chooses a card 10 times and records the number of spades.
Gina chooses cards and records the number of cards chosen before she gets 5 spades.

    a) Find the size of Tommy's test.   b) Find the size of Gina's test.

For both tests, H_0: $p = 0.25$ and H_1: $p > 0.25$.

For discrete distributions the size of a test is not the same as the significance level.

a) Let X be the number of spades chosen. Then $X \sim B(10, 0.25)$. $\alpha = 0.01$.

Find the critical region using the binomial c.d.f. on your calculator:
$P(X \geq 6) = 1 - 0.9802... = 0.0197...$ and $P(X \geq 7) = 1 - 0.9964... = 0.0035...$
So the critical region is $X \geq 7$.

Size = P(Type I error) = $P(X \geq 7)$ = **0.00351 (3 s.f.)**

b) Let Y be the number of cards chosen before Gina gets 5 spades. Then $Y \sim NB(5, 0.25)$.
You'd expect to get the 5th spade on the $5 \div 0.25 = 20$th card. If $p > 0.25$ the expected value would be lower than 20, so the critical region is $Y \leq k$, where $P(Y \leq k) < 0.01$.

Gina chooses cards until she gets 5 spades, so $y \geq 5$.

Using the negative binomial probability function (see p.132): $P(Y = y) = \binom{y-1}{r-1} p^r (1-p)^{y-r}$

$P(Y = 5) = 0.0009...$, $P(Y = 6) = 0.0036...$, $P(Y = 7) = 0.0082...$
Add these together to get cumulative probabilities until you get above $\alpha = 0.01$.
$P(Y \leq 5) = 0.0009...$, $P(Y \leq 6) = 0.0009... + 0.0036... = 0.0046...$,
$P(Y \leq 7) = 0.0009... + 0.0036... + 0.0082... = 0.0128...$ So the critical region is $Y \leq 6$.

Size = P(Type I error) = $P(Y \leq 6)$ = **0.00464 (3 s.f.)**

The **Power** of a test is the **Probability** of **Correctly Rejecting** H_0

Another way to measure the quality of a test is to find its **power**.

> The **power** of a test is the probability of correctly rejecting H_0 — so this is equal to $1 - $P(Type II error).

The size and power of a test depend on its significance level — since α affects whether you accept or reject the null hypothesis.

The **power** of a test is a **conditional probability**, since it's **given that** H_0 is actually **false**.

Example: (cont.) The actual probability of choosing a spade is 0.3.
    c) Find the power of Tommy's test.
    d) Find the power of Gina's test.

You could find $1 - $P(Type II error) for parts c) and d), but this is usually more complicated.

c) The critical region for Tommy's test is $X \geq 7$. Since you now know that $p = 0.3$, you would correctly reject H_0 if X is in the critical region, given that $X \sim B(10, 0.3)$.

Using your calculator: Power = $P(X \geq 7 \mid X \sim B(10, 0.3)) = 1 - 0.9894... = $ **0.0106 (3 s.f.)**

d) Similarly, for Gina's test, H_0 is correctly rejected if $Y \leq 6$, given that $Y \sim NB(5, 0.3)$.

Using the negative binomial probability function:
Power = $P(Y \leq 6 \mid Y \sim NB(5, 0.3)) = 0.00243 + 0.008505 = $ **0.0109 (3 s.f.)**

Quality of Tests

The **Power Function** shows **Power** for **Different** values of **p**

Finding the **power function** of a test is **identical** to finding the power, except you use the **general parameter** (e.g. p for binomial distributions, λ for Poisson distributions, etc.) when calculating the probability you need.

A test is of higher **quality** (and therefore more reliable) if its **size is low** and its **power is high**. Changing the **significance level** of the test will affect **both** the size and the power of the test — unfortunately, using a **higher** level of significance will **increase** both (as it will increase the likelihood of rejecting H_0, whether it's true or false), so you **can't** really use it to improve the quality of a test.

> If you substitute the value of the parameter from H_0 into the power function, you should get the size of the test.

Example: e) Show that the power function for Tommy's test is
(cont.) $120p^7(1-p)^3 + 45p^8(1-p)^2 + 10p^9(1-p) + p^{10}$.
    f) Find the power function for Gina's test.
    g) Whose test would you recommend when $p = 0.4$?

> You can draw a graph of a power function for all values of the parameter — this shows how powerful a test is for different values.

e) The null hypothesis is correctly rejected if $X \geq 7$, where $X \sim B(10, p)$:
Power function $= P(X \geq 7 \mid X \sim B(10, p)) = P(X = 7) + P(X = 8) + P(X = 9) + P(X = 10)$

$$= \binom{10}{7}p^7(1-p)^3 + \binom{10}{8}p^8(1-p)^2 + \binom{10}{9}p^9(1-p)^1 + \binom{10}{10}p^{10}(1-p)^0$$

$$= 120p^7(1-p)^3 + 45p^8(1-p)^2 + 10p^9(1-p) + p^{10}$$

> Substituting p = 0.25 into the power functions gives the answers to parts a) and b), and substituting p = 0.3 gives the answers to c) and d).

f) The null hypothesis is correctly rejected if $Y \leq 6$, where $Y \sim NB(5, p)$:
Power function $= P(Y \leq 6 \mid Y \sim NB(5, p)) = P(Y = 6) + P(Y = 5)$
$= 5p^5(1-p) + p^5 = 5p^5 - 5p^6 + p^5 = p^5(6 - 5p)$

g) Substitute $p = 0.4$ into both power functions.
Tommy's power $= 120(0.4)^7(0.6)^3 + 45(0.4)^8(0.6)^2 + 10(0.4)^9(0.6) + (0.4)^{10}$
      $= \mathbf{0.0548}$ **(3 s.f.)**
Gina's power $= 0.4^5(6 - 5(0.4)) = \mathbf{0.04096}$
The power should be as high as possible, so you'd recommend **Tommy's test**.

> Gina's power function looks like this — the test gets more powerful as p increases.

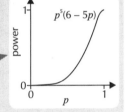

Practice Question

Q1 The heights of fully grown Cumbrian cactus plants are normally distributed with mean 49 cm and standard deviation 5.5 cm. A gardener plans to test whether a new fertiliser will change the value of the mean at the 5% significance level. He gives the fertiliser to a cactus and records its height when it is fully grown.
    a) Find the critical region for the gardener's test.
    b) State the probability of a Type I error for this test.
    c) Find the power of the gardener's test if the new mean height is actually 52 cm.

Exam Question

Q1 Nafisa and Paul are testing a 20-sided dice to see if the probability of rolling a one, p, is less than 0.05. They roll the dice 100 times and record the number of ones scored, X. Nafisa models this using a binomial distribution, while Paul uses a Poisson approximation. Both Nafisa and Paul decide to test at the 5% level of significance.
    a) Explain why Paul's approximation is suitable. State the values of any parameters of Paul's model. [2 marks]
    b) Find the critical region for Paul's test. [2 marks]
    c) State the size of Paul's test. [1 mark]
    d) Find the power function for Paul's test. [3 marks]

Nafisa's test has the power function $100p(1-p)^{99} + (1-p)^{100}$.
    e) Using only your answer to part d), explain whether you'd recommend Nafisa's or Paul's test when $p = 0.03$. [4 marks]

Absolute power corrupts (size) absolutely...

When finding the power function you'll use the probability function for the required distribution — fortunately you're given these in the formula booklet (see p.283-289). Be careful with power and size — they can be easy to mix up.

The Central Limit Theorem

This topic is going to blow your mind — if you hadn't read it in such a trusted book as this one, you probably wouldn't even believe it was true. Turns out, all those distributions you've learnt about have a little something in common...

Even when X **Isn't Normally Distributed**, the **Sample Mean** (approx) **Is**

Suppose that the random variable X follows a normal distribution with mean μ and variance σ^2: $X \sim N(\mu, \sigma^2)$.
If you take a **sample** of size n from this distribution, you should have seen in A-level Maths
that the **sample mean** $\overline{X}$ is also **normally distributed**: $\overline{X} \sim N\left(\mu, \dfrac{\sigma^2}{n}\right)$.

The **Central Limit Theorem** tells you something about the **distribution** of $\overline{X}$ —
even if you **know nothing** at all about the distribution of X:

The Central Limit Theorem (CLT)

Suppose you take a **sample** of n readings from **any distribution** with mean μ and variance σ^2.
- For **large** n, the distribution of the sample mean, $\overline{X}$, is **approximately normal**: $\overline{X} \sim N\left(\mu, \dfrac{\sigma^2}{n}\right)$.
- The **bigger** n is, the **better** the approximation will be. (For $n > 30$, it's pretty good.)

Remember that this is just an approximation. Unless X is normally distributed,
$\overline{X}$ will not be exactly normally distributed.

Example: A random sample of size 50 is taken from a population
that follows a distribution with mean 20 and variance 10.
Estimate the probability that the sample mean is less than 19.

Since n (= 50) is quite large, you can use the Central Limit Theorem.
Here, $\overline{X} \approx\sim N\left(20, \dfrac{10}{50}\right) = N(20, 0.2)$
You need $P(\overline{X} < 19)$. Using the normal cdf function on your calculator:
$\qquad P(\overline{X} < 19) = \mathbf{0.0127}$ (4 d.p.)

Example: Estimate the distribution of the mean of the following random samples:

a) a sample of size 100 from a binomial distribution with 20 trials and success probability 0.5,

b) a sample of size 20 from a Poisson distribution with variance 4,

c) a sample of size 10 000 from a geometric distribution with $P(X = x) = \dfrac{9^{x-1}}{10^x}$.

In each case, briefly comment on the accuracy of the estimate.

---

a) $X \sim B(20, 0.5)$, so $\mu = 20 \times 0.5 = 10$ and $\sigma^2 = 20 \times 0.5 \times (1 - 0.5) = 5$ *Don't get your numbers confused.*
$\qquad \Rightarrow \overline{X} \approx\sim N(10, 5 \div 100) = \mathbf{N(10, 0.05)}$ *We usually denote the number*
of trials (20) and the size of
The size of the sample (= 100) is large and   *the sample (100) by n — but*
so this is a **good approximation**.   *they're very different quantities.*

b) $X \sim Po(4)$, so $\mu = \sigma^2 = 4 \Rightarrow \overline{X} \approx\sim N(4, 4 \div 20) = \mathbf{N(4, 0.2)}$
The size of the sample is only 20, so this approximation may be **poor**.

c) The probability function is of the form $p(1-p)^{x-1} = \dfrac{1}{10} \times \left(\dfrac{9}{10}\right)^{x-1} = \dfrac{9^{x-1}}{10^x} \Rightarrow p = \dfrac{1}{10}$

Therefore, $X \sim Geo\left(\dfrac{1}{10}\right)$, so $\mu = \dfrac{1}{\left(\frac{1}{10}\right)} = 10$ and $\sigma^2 = \dfrac{1 - \frac{1}{10}}{\left(\frac{1}{10}\right)^2} = 90$

$\qquad \Rightarrow \overline{X} \approx\sim N(10, 90 \div 10\,000) = \mathbf{N(10, 0.009)}$
The size of the sample is very large so this approximation would be **very good**.

While this approximation is great, such a large sample would usually be impractical.

The Central Limit Theorem

Example: A housing estate has a wasp infestation. A pest controller conducts a sample of 45 houses to see how many wasps are present. If his sample gives a mean greater than 9, the pest controller will have to report the estate to the health inspector. Given that the actual mean is 10 wasps per house, estimate the probability that the pest controller will send a report.

That's one mean looking sample.

Let the random variable X represent the number of wasps in any one house.

Then $X \sim \text{Po}(10)$.

Since the pest controller's sample size is reasonably large (= 45), the CLT says that you can approximate the distribution of the sample mean with a normal distribution:

$$\overline{X} \approx \sim N(10, 10 \div 45) = N\left(10, \frac{2}{9}\right)$$

Using this approximation and the normal cdf, the probability of the pest controller having to report the estate to the health inspector is:

$$P(\overline{X} > 9) = \textbf{0.9831} \text{ (4 d.p.)}$$

Practice Questions

Q1 Estimate the distribution of the mean of a random sample of size 50 from the following distributions:

a) $X \sim B(20, 0.2)$,   b) $X \sim \text{Geo}(0.9)$,   c) $X \sim \text{Po}(5.5)$.

Q2 A random variable Y follows a negative binomial distribution with $r = 10$ and $p = 0.3$. A random sample of size 36 is taken from the distribution. Estimate the probability that the mean of the sample is:

a) less than 32,   b) greater than 35,   c) between 29 and 37.

Exam Question

Q1 A trainspotter records trains as they go past an observation point and has decided that he will go home once he sees a train painted in a train company's special design. 12% of all trains running past that point have the special design.

a) i) Assuming that the trainspotter has no prior knowledge of which trains will pass the observation point and that trains pass the point independently of one another, suggest a suitable distribution for the number of trains the trainspotter will see before going home, inclusive of the train with the special design. [1 mark]

ii) Find the probability that the trainspotter will see 5 trains before going home. [1 mark]

iii) Find the probability that the trainspotter will see more than 2 trains before going home. [2 marks]

At the same time every day for many years, the trainspotter goes to the observation point and records trains that go past until he sees a train with the special design. The percentage of trains with this design remains constant over these years. On each day, he notes how many trains he sees before going home. He takes a random sample of 55 days to determine how many trains, on average, he sees before going home.

b) i) Suggest a distribution for the mean of this sample, giving the values of any parameters. [2 marks]

ii) If the sample mean is less than 7, the trainspotter has decided he will move to a different line. What is the probability that the trainspotter will move to a different line? [1 mark]

iii) The trainspotter will buy a more expensive camera to photograph the trains if the sample mean is greater than 9. What is the probability that the trainspotter will buy the more expensive camera? [1 mark]

c) What could the trainspotter do to get a more accurate estimate of the mean number of trains he sees before going home? [1 mark]

The distribution doesn't matter, you say? Sounds pretty normal to me...

The hardest part about the Central Limit Theorem is getting to grips with when it's needed. If the exam mentions sample mean, think CLT. Remember, this is only an approximation (unless the population distribution is itself normal), so always make clear that your answers are estimates — and treat them with caution if the sample size is small.

Probability Generating Functions

This section is all about pgfs — which shouldn't be confused with cdfs, pdfs, BFGs or PNEFC.
So if you're a big Preston supporter, what's to follow won't be anywhere near as exciting as you might have hoped...

The pgf is a Sum with Probabilities as Coefficients

If a **discrete** random variable X takes only **integer** values $x \geq 0$ then it has a **probability generating function** (pgf). The pgf is a function that encodes the **probabilities** $P(X = x)$. It's a **power series** in t (i.e. a polynomial of the form $a_0 + a_1 t + a_2 t^2 + a_3 t^3 + ...$), where the **coefficient** of t^x is $P(X = x)$.

Probability Generating Functions

The probability generating function of a **discrete** random variable X taking only **non-negative integer values** is

$$G_X(t) = \sum_x P(X = x)t^x = E(t^X)$$

Remind yourself of the definition of $E(g(X))$ on p.123 to see why this bit is true.

The **formula booklet** will give you that $G_X(t) = E(t^X)$ — but you'll need to **know** that this is the same as $\sum P(X = x)t^x$.

For any pgf, $G_X(0) = P(X = 0)$: $G_X(0) = P(X = 0) + P(X = 1)0^1 + P(X = 2)0^2 + ... = P(X = 0)$

...and $G_X(1) = 1$: $G_X(1) = \sum P(X = x) 1^x = \sum P(X = x) = 1$

Probabilities always sum to 1.

Example: The pgf of Z is $k(2 + 4t + 2t^2)$. Find k.

$$G_Z(1) = k(2 + 4 + 2) = 1 \Rightarrow 8k = 1 \Rightarrow k = \frac{1}{8}$$

Example: You roll a fair six-sided dice. Let the random variable Y represent the result.

What is the probability generating function of Y?

The sample space of Y is $\{1, 2, 3, 4, 5, 6\}$, so the pgf will have terms in t up to t^6.

The probability $P(Y = y) = \frac{1}{6}$ for all possible Y.

So $G_Y(t) = \frac{1}{6}t + \frac{1}{6}t^2 + \frac{1}{6}t^3 + \frac{1}{6}t^4 + \frac{1}{6}t^5 + \frac{1}{6}t^6$

$$= \frac{1}{6}(t + t^2 + t^3 + t^4 + t^5 + t^6)$$

You can check the validity of your pgf by setting t = 1:
$G_Y(1) = \frac{1}{6}(1 + 1^2 + 1^3 + 1^4 + 1^5 + 1^6) = 1$

Example: The random variable X has probability generating function

$$G_X(t) = \frac{1}{5} + \frac{5}{12}t + \frac{1}{4}t^2 + \frac{2}{15}t^3.$$

Find $P(X = x)$ for all $x \geq 0$.

The probability $P(X = x)$ is the coefficient of t^x in $G_X(t)$.

So $P(X = 0) = \frac{1}{5}$, $P(X = 1) = \frac{5}{12}$,

$$P(X = 2) = \frac{1}{4}, \quad P(X = 3) = \frac{2}{15}, \quad P(X \geq 4) = 0$$

Since $t^0 = 1$, the constant term is $P(X = 0)$.

If there is no t^x term in the pgf then $P(X = x) = 0$.

You can find the pgf of a + bX from the pgf of X

If $Y = a + bX$, then its pgf can be found using this formula:

$$G_Y(t) = t^a G_X(t^b)$$

This isn't in the formula booklet — sorry...

Example: X has pgf $\frac{1}{10}(3 + t + t^2 + 2t^3 + 3t^4)$.

Use the pgf of $Y = 3 + 2X$ to find $P(Y = 9)$.

Since $Y = a + bX$, its pgf is:

$$G_Y(t) = t^a G_X(t^b) = t^3 G_X(t^2) = \frac{t^3}{10}(3 + t^2 + (t^2)^2 + 2(t^2)^3 + 3(t^2)^4)$$

Replace each t with t^2 and then multiply by t^3.

Use the constant term as the power on the outside...

$$= \frac{t^3}{10}(3 + t^2 + t^4 + 2t^6 + 3t^8) = \frac{1}{10}(3t^3 + t^5 + t^7 + 2t^9 + 3t^{11})$$

...and the coefficient of X as the power on the inside.

$$\Rightarrow P(Y = 9) = \frac{1}{10} \times 2 = \frac{1}{5}$$

This is the coefficient of t^9 in the pgf.

Probability Generating Functions

The Standard Distributions all have pgfs

The probability generating functions of the **binomial**, **Poisson**, **geometric** and **negative binomial** distributions are all given in the **formula booklet**. They look quite **different** to the pgfs you've seen so far — they're **not** power series. That's because the **sums to infinity** have been **evaluated**, leaving nice expressions in terms of the parameters and t.

Binomial $B(n, p)$	Poisson $Po(\lambda)$	Geometric $Geo(p)$ on 1, 2, ...	Negative binomial $NB(r, p)$ on r, $r + 1$, ...
$(1 - p + pt)^n$	$e^{\lambda(t-1)}$	$\dfrac{pt}{1 - (1-p)t}$	$\left(\dfrac{pt}{1 - (1-p)t}\right)^r$

Example: If $X \sim Geo(p)$, show that the probability generating function $G_X(t) = \dfrac{pt}{1 - (1-p)t}$.

$$G_X(t) = \sum P(X = x)\, t^x = \sum p(1-p)^{x-1}\, t^x = p\sum(1-p)^{x-1}\, t^x = p\left[t + (1-p)t^2 + (1-p)^2 t^3 + ...\right]$$

This is the probability function of Geo(p). See page 130.

The sample space is $\{x : x \geq 1\}$ so the sum starts at $x = 1$, giving first term t.

Some people are closer to infinity than others...

The expression in square brackets is the sum to infinity of a geometric series, so you can replace it with $\dfrac{a}{1-r}$, where $a = t$ is the first term and the common ratio $r = (1-p)t$.

$$\Rightarrow G_X(t) = p\left(\frac{t}{1 - (1-p)t}\right) = \frac{pt}{1 - (1-p)t} \text{ as required.}$$

You can use the pgfs of the distributions to check that the **distributions** are **valid** (i.e. the **probabilities sum to 1**).

Example: Use the probability generating function to check the validity of $X \sim Po(\lambda)$.

The probability generating function of the Poisson distribution is $G_X(t) = e^{\lambda(t-1)}$.
Letting $t = 1$, $\sum P(X = x) = \sum P(X = x)\, 1^x = G_X(1) = e^{\lambda(1-1)} = e^{\lambda \times 0} = 1$,
i.e. the probabilities sum to 1. So the **Poisson is a valid distribution**.

Practice Questions

Q1 The probability distribution of A is shown in the table. What is its probability generating function $G_A(t)$?

a	1	2	3	4
$P(A = a)$	0.2	0.15	0.5	0.15

Q2 A random variable X has probability generating function $k^3(2 + t + 3t^2 + 2t^4)$.
   a) Find k and then write down $P(X = x)$ for all x.
   b) Find the probability generating function of: i) $1 + X$,   ii) $3X$,   iii) $2 + 2X$.

Q3 Use the probability generating functions to check the validity of: a) $B(n, p)$,   b) $Geo(p)$,   c) $NB(r, p)$.

Exam Questions

Q1 a) Use the Maclaurin series expansion of e^x to show that the probability generating function of the Poisson distribution is $e^{\lambda(t-1)}$. [4 marks]

   b) If $X \sim Po(2)$, find the probability generating function of $3X + 5$. [2 marks]

Q2 The function $G_X(t) = \dfrac{1}{26}\left[(kt + 3t^2)^2 + t^5\right]$ is the probability generating function of the discrete random variable X.

   a) Given that $k > 0$, find the value of k. [3 marks]

   b) Write down $P(X = x)$ for all the values of x such that $P(X = x) \neq 0$. [3 marks]

You can generate this joke for yourself...

Don't be put off if a pgf looks a bit weird in the exam. It might have been factorised or rearranged to look a bit more confusing but all the techniques on these pages will still work. And remember that the expression doesn't have to contain all powers of t — so long as the powers are non-negative integers and the coefficients sum to 1, it's a pgf.

Using Probability Generating Functions

Goodness me — you don't seem to have done any calculus since I don't know when.
We need to put that right straight away. Brace yourself...

Differentiate to find the Mean and Variance

If you know the pgf of a random variable, just **differentiate** and **substitute** in $t = 1$ to find its expected value (**mean**).
The expected **variance** isn't much harder. **Differentiate again** and then use the **formula** below.

$$E(X) = G'_X(1)$$

$$\text{Var}(X) = G''_X(1) + G'_X(1) - [G'_X(1)]^2$$

These are in the formula booklet.

Example: If $G_X(t) = 0.04(2 + 3t^3)^2$, find the values of $E(X)$ and $\text{Var}(X)$.

Differentiate to find the **mean**: $G'_X(t) = 0.04 \times 2(2 + 3t^3)(9t^2) = 0.72t^2(2 + 3t^3) = 0.72(2t^2 + 3t^5)$
$$\Rightarrow E(X) = G'_X(1) = 0.72(2 + 3) = \mathbf{3.6}$$

For the **variance**, start by finding the **second derivative**: $G''_X(t) = 0.72(4t + 15t^4)$

Then use the **formula**: $\text{Var}(X) = G''_X(1) + G'_X(1) - [G'_X(1)]^2 = 0.72(4 + 15) + 3.6 - 3.6^2 = \mathbf{4.32}$

Example: You toss a fair coin twice. Let the random variable X represent the number of times the coin lands on heads.
Use the probability generating function to confirm that $E(X) = 1$ and $\text{Var}(X) = \frac{1}{2}$.

To find the probability generating function, you first need the probabilities of all the possible events. The number of heads, X, can either be 0, 1 or 2.

$P(X = 0) = P(\text{no heads}) = P(\text{tail then tail}) = \frac{1}{2} \times \frac{1}{2} = \frac{1}{4}$

$P(X = 1) = P(\text{1 head}) = P(\text{head then tail or tail then head}) = \frac{1}{2} \times \frac{1}{2} + \frac{1}{2} \times \frac{1}{2} = \frac{1}{4} + \frac{1}{4} = \frac{1}{2}$

$P(X = 2) = P(\text{2 heads}) = P(\text{head then head}) = \frac{1}{2} \times \frac{1}{2} = \frac{1}{4}$

So, $G_X(t) = \frac{1}{4} + \frac{1}{2}t + \frac{1}{4}t^2 = \frac{1}{4}(1 + 2t + t^2)$

$$G'_X(t) = \frac{1}{4}(2 + 2t) \Rightarrow E(X) = G'_X(1) = \frac{1}{4}(2 + 2) \Rightarrow \mathbf{E(X) = 1}$$

$$G''_X(t) = \frac{1}{4}(2) = \frac{1}{2} \Rightarrow \text{Var}(X) = G''_X(1) + G'_X(1) - [G'_X(1)]^2 = \frac{1}{2} + 1 - 1 \Rightarrow \mathbf{\text{Var}(X) = \frac{1}{2}}$$

Find E(X) and Var(X) for the Standard Distributions using the pgf

The formulas above for the **mean** and **variance** work with the pgfs of the **standard distributions** too.
You might be asked to **derive** or **prove** the standard expressions for $E(X)$ or $\text{Var}(X)$ using their pgfs.

Example: If $X \sim \text{Po}(\lambda)$, find $E(X)$ and $\text{Var}(X)$ using the pgf $G_X(t)$.

The probability generating function of $\text{Po}(\lambda)$ is $G_X(t) = e^{\lambda(t-1)}$.

Differentiating once:
$$G'_X(t) = \lambda e^{\lambda(t-1)} \Rightarrow E(X) = G'_X(1) = \lambda e^0 = \lambda$$

Differentiating again:
$$G''_X(t) = \lambda^2 e^{\lambda(t-1)} \Rightarrow \text{Var}(X) = G''_X(1) + G'_X(1) - (G'_X(1))^2 = \lambda^2 + \lambda - \lambda^2 = \lambda$$

So for a Poisson distribution, $\mathbf{E(X) = \text{Var}(X) = \lambda}$

You saw that this was the case on page 125.

Which of the standard distributions would the distribution of these standards follow if they are distributed in a standard distribution? *

*If they're randomly distributed independently, singly and constantly, it's Poisson... But who would want to distribute their standards in such a non-standard way?!

Using Probability Generating Functions

The *pgf* of a *Sum of Variables* is the *Product* of their *pgfs*

If X and Y are two **independent** random variables and you know their probability generating functions, you can quickly find out the probability generating function of $X + Y$:

$$G_{X+Y}(t) = G_X(t) \times G_Y(t)$$

X and Y must be independent for this to be true.

This is in the **formula booklet**, but you're going to need to know how to use it.

Example: X and Y are independent random variables. X has probability generating function $G_X(t) = \frac{1}{15}(2 + 10t + t^2 + 2t^3)$ and $Y \sim B(20, 0.1)$. Find the probability generating function of $X + Y$ and use it to find $P(X + Y = 0)$.

You're told that the random variables are independent so you just need to multiply together $G_X(t)$ and $G_Y(t)$ to get $G_{X+Y}(t)$:

The binomial pgf is $(1 - p + pt)^n$.

$$G_{X+Y}(t) = G_X(t) \times G_Y(t) = \frac{1}{15}(2 + 10t + t^2 + 2t^3) \times (1 - 0.1 + 0.1t)^{20} = \frac{1}{15}(2 + 10t + t^2 + 2t^3)(0.9 + 0.1t)^{20}$$

Setting $t = 0$ in $G_{X+Y}(t)$ will give you $P(X + Y = 0)$. So $P(X + Y = 0) = \frac{1}{15} \times 2 \times 0.9^{20} = \mathbf{0.0162}$ (3 s.f.)

This is because you're looking for the constant term in the expansion.

Example: You toss a fair coin twice and roll a fair dice once. Let the random variables X and Y represent the number of heads that resulted from the coin tosses and the result of the dice roll respectively. Find the probability generating function of $X + Y$, and show that $P(X + Y = 2)$ is equal to the coefficient of t^2.

You've seen already that $G_X(t) = \frac{1}{4}(1 + 2t + t^2)$ (on p.148) and $G_Y(t) = \frac{1}{6}(t + t^2 + t^3 + t^4 + t^5 + t^6)$ (on p.146).

Then $G_{X+Y}(t) = \frac{1}{4}(1 + 2t + t^2) \times \frac{1}{6}(t + t^2 + t^3 + t^4 + t^5 + t^6) = \frac{1}{24}(1 + 2t + t^2)(t + t^2 + t^3 + t^4 + t^5 + t^6)$

$$= \frac{1}{24}(t + 3t^2 + 4t^3 + 4t^4 + 4t^5 + 4t^6 + 3t^7 + t^8)$$

The event $X + Y = 2$ is the number of heads and the result of the dice totalling 2. This can happen if there are no heads and the dice lands on a 2 ($X = 0$, $Y = 2$) or there is 1 head and the dice lands on a 1 ($X = 1$, $Y = 1$). Then $P(X + Y = 2) = \frac{1}{4} \times \frac{1}{6} + \frac{1}{2} \times \frac{1}{6} = \frac{1}{24} + \frac{1}{12} = \frac{3}{24}$. This matches the coefficient of t^2 in $G_{X+Y}(t)$.

Since Y cannot take the value 0, the combination X = 2, Y = 0 isn't possible.

Practice Questions

Q1 Find $E(X)$ and $Var(X)$ for the random variables with pgf: a) $\frac{1}{20}(6 + 5t^2 + 3t^4 + 2t^6 + 4t^8)$, b) $\frac{1}{16}(t^2 + 1)^4$.

Q2 Assuming that the random variables in Q1 are independent, what is the probability that their sum equals 0?

Q3 Use the probability generating function to derive the mean and variance of: a) $B(n, p)$, b) $Geo(p)$.

Exam Question

Q1 The random variable X represents the result when a fair tetrahedral dice labelled 1, 2, 3, 4 is rolled. The random variable Y follows a Poisson distribution with parameter $\lambda = 6$. X and Y are known to be independent.

a) Find the probability generating function of $K = X + Y$. [2 marks]

b) Show that the variance of K is $\frac{29}{4}$. [8 marks]

That's enough stats — I can't differentiate one distribution from the other...

Be careful how you handle those derivatives when working out $E(X)$ and $Var(X)$ — you need to differentiate with respect to t, not x, p, r, λ or any of the other letters that seem to keep popping up in Further Maths. As for the pgf of $X + Y$ — well that couldn't be simpler... so long as X and Y are independent. Be sure that one doesn't affect the other.

Momentum and Impulse

If you're after some Further Mechanics, you've come to the right place — there's a delicious bit of momentum to whet your appetite, followed by a lip-smacking impulse entrée. Sink your teeth into this lot...

Momentum has Magnitude and Direction

1) Momentum is a measure of how much "umph" a **moving object** has, due to its **mass** and **velocity**:

The unit of momentum is $kgms^{-1}$ or Ns. → Momentum = Mass × Velocity

2) Momentum is a **vector**, so the **sign** of the velocity is important when calculating momentum.

3) Total momentum **before** a collision equals total momentum **after** a collision — this idea is called "**Conservation of Momentum**".

> **Momentum before = momentum after**
> $$m_1u_1 + m_2u_2 = m_1v_1 + m_2v_2$$

Example: Particles A and B, each of mass 5 kg, move in a straight line with velocities 6 ms⁻¹ and 2 ms⁻¹ respectively. After collision, particle A continues in the same direction with velocity 3.2 ms⁻¹. Find the velocity of B after impact.

Before

A (5kg) 6 ms⁻¹   B (5kg) 2 ms⁻¹

After

A (5kg) 3.2 ms⁻¹   B (5kg) v

Draw 'before' and 'after' diagrams to help you see what's going on.

Taking 'right' as positive:

Using conservation of momentum: $m_Au_A + m_Bu_B = m_Av_A + m_Bv_B$

$(5 \times 6) + (5 \times 2) = (5 \times 3.2) + (5 \times v_B)$

$40 = 16 + 5v_B$

So $v_B = \textbf{4.8 ms}^{-1}$

v_B is positive, so B must be moving to the right.

Example: Particles A and B, of mass 6 kg and 3 kg, are moving directly towards each other at speeds of 2 ms⁻¹ and 1 ms⁻¹ respectively. Given that B rebounds with speed 3 ms⁻¹ in the opposite direction to its initial velocity, find the velocity of A after the collision.

Before

A (6kg) 2 ms⁻¹   1 ms⁻¹ B (3kg)

After

A (6kg) v B (3kg) 3 ms⁻¹

Taking 'right' as positive:

$(6 \times 2) + (3 \times -1) = (6 \times v) + (3 \times 3)$

$9 = 6v + 9$

$v = \textbf{0 ms}^{-1}$

Masses Joined Together have the Same Velocity

Particles that **stick together** after impact are said to "**coalesce**". After that you can treat them as just **one object**.

Example: Two particles of mass 40 g and M kg move directly towards each other with speeds of 6 ms⁻¹ and 3 ms⁻¹ respectively. Given that the particles coalesce after impact and move with a speed of 2 ms⁻¹ in the same direction as that of the 40 g particle's initial velocity, find M.

Before

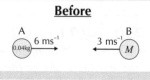

A (0.04kg) 6 ms⁻¹   3 ms⁻¹ B (M)

After

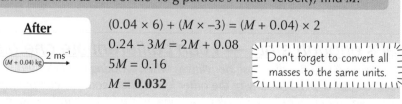

(M + 0.04) kg 2 ms⁻¹

$(0.04 \times 6) + (M \times -3) = (M + 0.04) \times 2$

$0.24 - 3M = 2M + 0.08$

$5M = 0.16$

$M = \textbf{0.032}$

Don't forget to convert all masses to the same units.

Momentum and Impulse

Impulse is *Change in Momentum*

1) If a **constant force F** acts on an object for a **time t**, the **impulse I** of the force is defined as: | Impulse $(I) = Ft$ |

2) Impulse can also be defined as the **change in momentum** of the object: | Impulse $(I) = mv - mu$ |

3) The **units** of impulse are **Ns**. The two formulas can be shown to be **equivalent** by making 'a' the subject of the constant acceleration equation $v = u + at$, and substituting that into $F = ma$.

Example: A body of mass 500 g is travelling in a straight line. Find the magnitude of the impulse needed to increase its velocity from 2 ms⁻¹ to 5 ms⁻¹.

This is called the impulse-momentum principle.

Impulse = Change in momentum
$= mv - mu = (0.5 \times 5) - (0.5 \times 2) = $ **1.5 Ns**

Pea flicking — the art of giving a pulse an impulse.

Impulses always *Balance* in *Collisions*

During **impact** between particles A and B, the impulse that A gives to B is the **same** as the impulse that B gives to A, but in the opposite direction.

Example: A mass of 2 kg moving at 2 ms⁻¹ collides with a mass of 3 kg which is moving in the same direction at 1 ms⁻¹. The 2 kg mass continues to move in the same direction at 1 ms⁻¹ after impact. Find the impulse given by the 2 kg mass to the other mass.

Using "conservation of momentum":
$(2 \times 2) + (3 \times 1) = (2 \times 1) + 3v$
So $v = 1\frac{2}{3}$ ms⁻¹

Impulse (on B) $= mv - mu$ (for B)
$= (3 \times 1\frac{2}{3}) - (3 \times 1)$
$= $ **2 Ns**

Before / **After** diagrams: A (2kg) 2 ms⁻¹, B (3kg) 1 ms⁻¹; After: A (2kg) 1 ms⁻¹, B (3kg) v

The impulse B gives to A is $(2 \times 1) - (2 \times 2) = -2$ Ns. Aside from the different direction, you can see it's the same — so you didn't actually need to find v for this question.

Practice Questions

Q1 Each diagram represents the motion of two particles moving in a straight line. Find the missing mass or velocity (all masses are in kg and all velocities are in ms⁻¹).

a) Before: (5) 3→ (4) 1→ After: (5) 2→ (4) v→

b) Before: (5) 3→ (4) 1→ After: (9) v→

c) Before: (m) 6→ (8) 2→ After: (m) 2→ (8) 4→

Q2 A ball of mass 300 g is moving with a velocity of 5 ms⁻¹. An impulse of 2 Ns acts on the ball in the opposite direction to the ball's initial velocity. Find the ball's new velocity.

Exam Question

Q1 Two particles of mass 0.8 kg and 1.2 kg are travelling in the same direction along a straight line with speeds of 4 ms⁻¹ and 2 ms⁻¹ respectively until they collide. After the collision the 0.8 kg mass has a velocity of 2.5 ms⁻¹ in the same direction. The 1.2 kg mass then continues with its new velocity until it collides with a mass of m kg travelling with a speed of 4 ms⁻¹ in the opposite direction to it.

Given that both particles are brought to rest by this collision, find the mass m. [5 marks]

Doctor, this man is sick — 'im pulse is very weak...

...a little bit like that pun actually. Anyway, naff humour aside, make sure you've got your head round all of this straight line momentum and impulse stuff, 'cos there's a bunch more problems coming up. I bet you can't wait.

Momentum and Impulse Problems

Let's keep up the momentum with some more examples of momentum and impulse in action.

You'll Need to Make Modelling Assumptions

For these 'real-life' examples, some **assumptions** make your life a whole lot easier:

- spherical objects can be modelled as **particles**, so collisions are **direct** and there's **no spinning** going on.
- surfaces can be modelled as **smooth**, so there's no **friction** and the motion is in a **straight line**.

With modelling, you can use the conservation of momentum and the impulse-momentum principle as usual:

Example: A 20 g ball is dropped 1 m onto horizontal ground. Immediately after rebounding the ball has a speed of 2 ms⁻¹. Find the impulse given to the ball by the ground. How high does the ball rebound? Take $g = 9.8$ ms⁻².

Take 'down' as positive.

First you need to work out the ball's speed as it reaches the ground:

List the variables you're given: $u = 0$ ← The ball was dropped, so it started with $u = 0$.
$s = 1$
$a = 9.8$ ← Acceleration due to gravity.
$v = ?$

Choose an equation containing u, s, a and v:
$$v^2 = u^2 + 2as$$
$$v^2 = 0^2 + (2 \times 9.8 \times 1)$$
$$v = 4.4271... \text{ ms}^{-1}$$

The sign is really important. Make sure that down is positive throughout this part of the question.

Now work out the impulse as the ball hits the ground and rebounds:

Impulse $= mv - mu$
$= (0.02 \times -2) - (0.02 \times 4.4271...)$
$= -0.129$ Ns (to 3 s.f.)

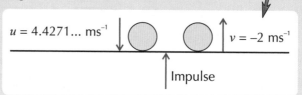

Impulse

Finally you need to use a new equation of motion to find s (the greatest height the ball reaches after the bounce). This time take 'up' as positive:

List the variables: $u = 2$
$v = 0$ ← $v = 0$ at the ball's greatest height.

a is negative because the ball is decelerating. → $a = -9.8$
$s = ?$

$$v^2 = u^2 + 2as$$
$$0^2 = 2^2 + (2 \times -9.8 \times s)$$
$$s = 0.204 \text{ m (to 3 s.f.)}$$

Example: Two snooker balls A and B have a mass of 0.17 kg and 0.16 kg respectively. The balls are initially at rest on a snooker table. Ball A is given an impulse of magnitude 1.19 Ns towards ball B. Modelling the snooker table as a smooth horizontal plane, find the speed of ball A before it collides with B.

Impulse $= mv - mu$
$\Rightarrow 1.19 = (0.17 \times v) - (0.17 \times 0) = 0.17v$
$\Rightarrow v = \dfrac{1.19}{0.17} = 7$ ms⁻¹

The balls collide and move away in the direction A was travelling in before the collision. Find the speed of ball A after the collision, given that the speed of ball B is 4 ms⁻¹.

Using conservation of momentum:
$(0.17 \times 7) + (0.16 \times 0) = 0.17v + (0.16 \times 4)$
So, $v = 3.24$ ms⁻¹ (3 s.f.)

Momentum and Impulse Problems

Treat **Connected** Particles as **Coalesced** Particles

Connected particles joined by a 'light, inextensible string' can be dealt with in the same way as **coalesced** particles. When the string becomes **taut**, there is a **'jerk'** in the string that gives an **impulse** to the particles, after which they act as one particle travelling at a **common speed**.

Example: Two particles A and B of equal mass M are joined by a light, inextensible string. They are moving in opposite directions with speeds of 3 ms^{-1} and 5 ms^{-1}. After the string becomes taut, the particles move in the same direction with a common speed, v.

    a) Find the common speed, v.
    b) Find the impulse given by the string.

First, think about any **modelling assumptions** — 'inextensible' means the string **won't stretch** and 'light' means you can assume the string has **no mass**.

Before

3 ms^{-1} ← (M) ～ (B)(M) → 5 ms^{-1}

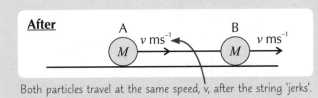

After

    A
    (M) v ms^{-1} ←   B (M) v ms^{-1} →

Both particles travel at the same speed, v, after the string 'jerks'.

a) Take 'right' as positive.

Using conservation of momentum:
$(M \times -3) + (M \times 5) = 2Mv$
$2M = 2Mv$
So, $v = \textbf{1 ms}^{-1}$

Here, we're treating A and B as one 'coalesced' particle.

b) To work out the impulse given by the string, just look at one particle:

Impulse (on A) $= mv - mu$
                    $= (M \times 1) - (M \times -3)$
                    $= \textbf{4}M \textbf{ Ns}$

The impulse on B has the same magnitude as the impulse on A but in the opposite direction ($-4M$ Ns), as you'd expect.

Practice Questions

Q1 A particle of mass 450 g is dropped 2 m onto a floor. It rebounds to two thirds of its original height. Find the impulse given to the particle by the ground.

Q2 A paintball is fired horizontally from a paintball gun. The mass of the paintball is 3 g, and the mass of the gun is 3 kg. Given that the gun experiences a recoil with initial speed 0.08 ms^{-1}, find the initial speed of the paintball.

Exam Question

Q1 Two balls of mass 100 g and 400 g are initially at rest, connected by a slack string. The heavier ball is struck and moves away from the lighter ball with a speed of 4 ms^{-1}.

After the string becomes taut, the balls move with a common speed, v.

    a) Show that the common speed, v, is equal to 3.2 ms^{-1}.   [3 marks]

    b) Find the magnitude of the impulse exerted on the 400 g ball at the moment the string becomes taut.   [2 marks]

    c) Describe any assumptions you have made in your model.   [2 marks]

The perils of internet shopping — the midnight impulse buy...

It often helps to write down all the bits of information you know before you start plugging numbers into formulas, especially when you've got quite a wordy question where some key info mightn't be immediately obvious. If these pages just weren't enough for you, then boy are you in for a treat.

Momentum and Impulse in 2D

The examples you've seen so far have just covered things moving and colliding in a straight line.
*It's time to take it up a notch and move into the next dimension... look out for those **i** and **j** vectors — we're going 2D...*

Momentum is Conserved in 2D Collisions

Conservation of momentum also applies to objects that don't collide in a straight line:

> **Momentum before = momentum after**
> $$m_1\mathbf{u}_1 + m_2\mathbf{u}_2 = m_1\mathbf{v}_1 + m_2\mathbf{v}_2$$

This is the vector form of the equation you saw on p.150.

Since **velocity** is a **vector** and mass is a scalar, **momentum** must be a **vector**.

Example: Two particles, A (of mass 5 kg) and B (of mass 3 kg), collide with initial velocities of $\mathbf{u}_A = (4\mathbf{i} + 3\mathbf{j})$ ms^{-1} and $\mathbf{u}_B = (-2\mathbf{i} + 7\mathbf{j})$ ms^{-1} respectively. Following the collision, particle A has a velocity of $-2\mathbf{i}$ ms^{-1}.
Given that the particles do not coalesce, find B's velocity after the collision.

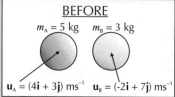

BEFORE
m_A = 5 kg m_B = 3 kg
$\mathbf{u}_A = (4\mathbf{i} + 3\mathbf{j})$ ms^{-1} $\mathbf{u}_B = (-2\mathbf{i} + 7\mathbf{j})$ ms^{-1}

Drawing diagrams will help you understand what's going on.

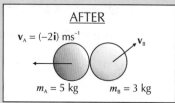

AFTER
$\mathbf{v}_A = (-2\mathbf{i})$ ms^{-1} $\mathbf{v}_B$
m_A = 5 kg m_B = 3 kg

Don't be put off by the vector notation. Plug the numbers into the formula and rearrange to find $\mathbf{v}_B$:

$$m_A\mathbf{u}_A + m_B\mathbf{u}_B = m_A\mathbf{v}_A + m_B\mathbf{v}_B$$

$$5(4\mathbf{i} + 3\mathbf{j}) + 3(-2\mathbf{i} + 7\mathbf{j}) = 5(-2\mathbf{i}) + 3\mathbf{v}_B$$
$$\Rightarrow 20\mathbf{i} + 15\mathbf{j} - 6\mathbf{i} + 21\mathbf{j} = -10\mathbf{i} + 3\mathbf{v}_B$$
$$\Rightarrow 3\mathbf{v}_B = 24\mathbf{i} + 36\mathbf{j}$$
$$\Rightarrow \mathbf{v}_B = 8\mathbf{i} + 12\mathbf{j}$$

So B's new velocity is **(8i + 12j) ms^{-1}**.

You can use the Impulse-Momentum Principle in 2D

Unsurprisingly, you can write the **impulse** equation using vectors too:

> **Impulse = final momentum − initial momentum**
> $$\mathbf{I} = \mathbf{F}t = m\mathbf{v} - m\mathbf{u}$$

$\mathbf{I} = \mathbf{F}t$ is valid when a constant force acts on the object.

As **force** is a **vector** and **time** is a **scalar**, **impulse** must be a **vector**.

Example: A ball (m = 0.1 kg) travels with a velocity of $(5\mathbf{i} + 12\mathbf{j})$ ms^{-1} before receiving an impulse of **I** Ns.
a) If the ball's new velocity is $(15\mathbf{i} + 22\mathbf{j})$ ms^{-1}, find **I**.
b) The impulse **I** was due to a constant force **F**, acting for 0.05 s. Find **F**.

a) Again, it's just a matter of plugging the numbers in:
$\mathbf{I} = m\mathbf{v} - m\mathbf{u}$, where m = 0.1, $\mathbf{v}$ = 15$\mathbf{i}$ + 22$\mathbf{j}$ and $\mathbf{u}$ = 5$\mathbf{i}$ + 12$\mathbf{j}$.

$$\mathbf{I} = 0.1(15\mathbf{i} + 22\mathbf{j}) - 0.1(5\mathbf{i} + 12\mathbf{j})$$
$$= 1.5\mathbf{i} + 2.2\mathbf{j} - 0.5\mathbf{i} - 1.2\mathbf{j}$$
$$= 1\mathbf{i} + 1\mathbf{j} = \mathbf{i} + \mathbf{j}.$$

So the ball received an impulse of **(i + j) Ns**.

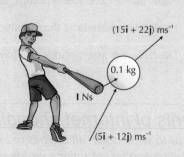

(15i + 22j) ms^{-1}
0.1 kg
I Ns
(5i + 12j) ms^{-1}

b) $\mathbf{I} = \mathbf{F}t$, so $\mathbf{F} = \dfrac{1}{0.05}(\mathbf{i} + \mathbf{j})$ N = **(20i + 20j) N**.

Momentum and Impulse in 2D

Use **Pythagoras** and **Trig** for the **Magnitude** and **Angle** of **Impulse**

With vectors, you can use the **i** and **j** components to form a **right-angled triangle**. Then simply use **basic trig** and **Pythagoras** to find any **angles**, or the **magnitude** (scalar size) of impulses or velocities.

Example: A badminton player smashes a shuttlecock ($m = 0.005$ kg) with an impulse of $(0.035\mathbf{i} - 0.065\mathbf{j})$ Ns, where **i** is horizontal and **j** is vertical. If the shuttle was initially travelling at $(-3\mathbf{i} + \mathbf{j})$ ms^{-1}, find its speed after the smash, and the angle it makes with the horizontal.

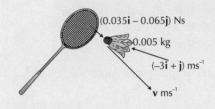

(0.035**i** – 0.065**j**) Ns
0.005 kg
(–3**i** + **j**) ms^{-1}
v ms^{-1}

1) Find the final velocity as a vector first, so: $\mathbf{I} = m\mathbf{v} - m\mathbf{u}$, where $\mathbf{I} = 0.035\mathbf{i} - 0.065\mathbf{j}$, $m = 0.005$ and $\mathbf{u} = -3\mathbf{i} + \mathbf{j}$.

$0.035\mathbf{i} - 0.065\mathbf{j} = 0.005\mathbf{v} - 0.005(-3\mathbf{i} + \mathbf{j})$
$\Rightarrow 0.035\mathbf{i} - 0.065\mathbf{j} = 0.005\mathbf{v} + 0.015\mathbf{i} - 0.005\mathbf{j}$
$\Rightarrow 0.005\mathbf{v} = 0.02\mathbf{i} - 0.06\mathbf{j}$
$\Rightarrow \mathbf{v} = (0.02\mathbf{i} - 0.06\mathbf{j}) \div 0.005 = 4\mathbf{i} - 12\mathbf{j}$ ms^{-1}

2) Draw a right-angled triangle of the velocity vector:

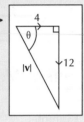

3) Use Pythagoras to find the speed (the **magnitude** of the velocity): $|v| = \sqrt{4^2 + 12^2} = \mathbf{12.6\ ms^{-1}}$ to 3 s.f.

4) Use trig to find the angle of motion with the horizontal: $\theta = \tan^{-1}\left(\frac{12}{4}\right) = \mathbf{71.6°}$ (3 s.f.) below the horizontal.

Finding the magnitude of a vector this way should be familiar to you from A-Level Maths.

Practice Questions

Q1 Find the velocity of a particle of mass 0.1 kg, travelling at $(\mathbf{i} + \mathbf{j})$ ms^{-1}, after receiving an impulse of:
   a) $2\mathbf{i} + 5\mathbf{j}$ Ns   b) $-3\mathbf{i} + \mathbf{j}$ Ns   c) $-\mathbf{i} - 6\mathbf{j}$ Ns   d) $4\mathbf{i}$ Ns.

Q2 A 2 kg particle, travelling at $(4\mathbf{i} - \mathbf{j})$ ms^{-1}, receives an impulse, **Q**, changing its velocity to $(-2\mathbf{i} + \mathbf{j})$ ms^{-1}. Find:
   a) **Q**   b) $|\mathbf{Q}|$, in Ns to 3 s.f.   c) the angle **Q** makes with **i**, in degrees to 3 s.f.

Q3 Two particles A and B collide, where $m_A = 0.5$ kg and $m_B = 0.4$ kg. Their initial velocities are $u_A = (2\mathbf{i} + \mathbf{j})$ ms^{-1} and $u_B = (-\mathbf{i} - 4\mathbf{j})$ ms^{-1}. Find, to 3 s.f.:
   a) the speed of B after impact if A moves away from the collision at a velocity of $(-\mathbf{i} - 2\mathbf{j})$ ms^{-1},
   b) their combined speed after the impact if they coalesce instead.

Exam Question

Q1 A particle of mass 0.4 kg receives an impulse of $(3\mathbf{i} - 8\mathbf{j})$ Ns, where **i** is horizontal and **j** is vertical. Just before the impulse, the velocity of the particle is $(-12a\mathbf{i} + 2a\mathbf{j})$ms^{-1}, where a is a positive constant, and it has a speed of $\sqrt{37}$ ms^{-1}.

   a) Show that $a = \frac{1}{2}$. [2 marks]

   b) Find the speed of the particle immediately after the impulse. Give your answer in ms^{-1} to 3 s.f. [5 marks]

   c) Find the angle between the motion of the particle and the horizontal following the impulse. Give your answer in degrees to 3 s.f. [2 marks]

Mo' mentum mo' problems...

*The theory here is the same as it was in 1 dimension — you've just got to mind your **i**'s and **j**'s. Drawing a picture of the situation helps when you're trying to visualise the particles bouncing in all directions. Or, you could draw inspirational doodles and think about that emo type you fancy who sits at the back of class. Less productive though...*

Work and Energy

Hello, good evening, welcome to Section 24 — where <u>work</u> and <u>energy</u> are tonight's chef's specials...

You Can Find the **Work Done** by a Force Over a Certain **Distance**

When a force is acting on a particle, you can work out the **work done** by the force using the formula:

> **Work done = force (F) × distance moved in the direction of the force (s)**

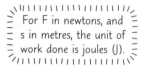
For F in newtons, and s in metres, the unit of work done is joules (J).

E.g. if an object is pushed **4 m** across a horizontal floor by a force of magnitude **12 N** acting horizontally, the **work done** by the force will be $12 \times 4 = \textbf{48 J}$

> **Example:** A rock is dragged across horizontal ground by a rope attached to the rock at an angle of 25° to the horizontal. Given that the work done by the force is 470 J and the tension in the rope is 120 N, find the distance the rock is moved.
>
> 120 N   Work done = horizontal component of force × s
> $470 = 120 \cos 25° \times s$
> $s = \textbf{4.32 m}$ (3 s.f.)
>
> *Because the force and the distance moved have to be in the same direction.*

A Particle Moving **Up a Rough Slope** does Work against **Friction and Gravity**

> **Example:** A block of mass 3 kg is pulled 9 m up a rough plane inclined at an angle of 20° to the horizontal by a force, T. The block moves at a constant speed. The work done by T against friction is 154 J.
>
> Find: a)   the work done by T against gravity
>   b)   the coefficient of friction between the block and the plane.

You can always use mgh to find work done against gravity.

a)   Work done against gravity = mgh
     $= 3g \times 9 \sin 20°$
     $= \textbf{90.5 J}$ (3 s.f.)

You need to use the vertical height, because it's only vertically that T does work against gravity.

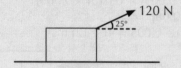

R N
T N
F N
20° $3g$ N

Remember — for a moving particle, F = μR, where μ is the coefficient of friction and R is the normal reaction.

b)   Use $F = ma$ and resolve perpendicular to the slope (so $a = 0$) to find R:
     $R - 3g \cos 20° = m \times 0$
     $\Rightarrow R = 3g \cos 20°$

Particle is moving, so:
     $F = \mu R$
     $= \mu \times 3g \cos 20°$

Work done by T against friction
     $= F \times s = 154$
So, $\mu \times 3g \cos 20° \times 9 = 154$
     $\mu = \textbf{0.619}$ (3 s.f.)

The bit of T that is working against friction must be equal to F as the block is moving with constant speed (i.e. a = 0), so you can just use F here.

A **Moving Particle** Possesses **Kinetic Energy**

Any particle that is **moving** has **kinetic energy** (K.E.). You can find the kinetic energy of a particle using the formula:

> $\text{K.E.} = \frac{1}{2}mv^2$

You need to learn this formula — you won't be given it in the exam.

If mass, m, is measured in kg and velocity, v, in ms^{-1}, then kinetic energy is measured in joules.

> **Example:**   An ice skater of mass 60 kg is moving at a constant velocity of 8 ms^{-1}. Find the ice skater's kinetic energy.
>
> Kinetic energy $= \frac{1}{2}mv^2 = \frac{1}{2} \times 60 \times 8^2 = \textbf{1920 J}$

Work and Energy

Work Done *is the same as the* Change *in a Particle's* Kinetic Energy

Work done by a **resultant force** to **change the velocity** of a particle moving
horizontally is equal to the change in that particle's kinetic energy:

$$\text{Work done by resultant force = change in kinetic energy} \Rightarrow \text{Work done} = \tfrac{1}{2}mv^2 - \tfrac{1}{2}mu^2 = \tfrac{1}{2}m(v^2 - u^2)$$

Example:
A block *P* of mass 6 kg is pulled along a rough horizontal plane by a force of 40 N,
acting parallel to the plane. The block travels 4 m in a straight line between two points
on the plane, *A* and *B*. The coefficient of friction between *P* and the plane is 0.35.

a) Find the work done against friction in moving *P* from *A* to *B*.

At *B*, *P* has a speed of 8 ms⁻¹.

b) Calculate the speed of *P* at *A*.

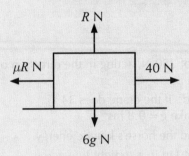

a) $R - 6g = 0$ ← There's no acceleration
perpendicular to the
plane, so use F = ma
with a = O to find R.

$\Rightarrow R = 6g.$

$F = \mu R$
$= 0.35 \times 6 \times g = 20.58$ N

Work against friction = Fs
$= 20.58 \times 4$
$= \textbf{82.3 J}$ (3 s.f.)

Multiply the resultant force
acting on P by the distance
moved to find the work done.

b) Work done by the resultant force = $\tfrac{1}{2}mv^2 - \tfrac{1}{2}mu^2$

$(40 - \mu R) \times 4 = \tfrac{1}{2} \times 6 \times 8^2 - \tfrac{1}{2} \times 6 \times u^2$

$77.68 = 192 - 3u^2$

$u^2 = 38.10...$

So, speed of *P* at *A*, $u = \textbf{6.17 ms}^{-1}$ (3 s.f.)

Gravitational Potential Energy *is all about a Particle's* Height

The gravitational potential energy (G.P.E.) of a particle can be found using the formula:

$$\boxed{\text{G.P.E.} = mgh} \quad \Longleftarrow \quad \text{You need to learn this formula as well.}$$

If mass (*m*) is measured in kg, acceleration due to gravity (*g*) in ms⁻² and the vertical height (*h*) above some
base level in m, then G.P.E. is measured in **joules, J**.

The **greater the height** of a particle above the 'base level', the **greater** that particle's gravitational **potential energy**.

Example:
A lift and its occupants have a combined mass of 750 kg. The lift moves vertically from the ground
to the first floor of a building, 6.1 m above the ground. After pausing, it moves vertically to the
17th floor, 64.9 m above the ground. Find the gravitational potential energy gained by the lift and
its occupants in moving:

a) from the ground floor to the first floor,

b) from the first floor to the 17th floor.

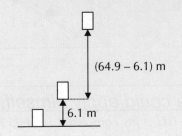

a) G.P.E. gained = $mg \times$ increase in height
$= 750 \times 9.8 \times 6.1$
$= \textbf{44 800 J}$ (3 s.f.)

b) G.P.E. gained = $mg \times$ increase in height
$= 750 \times 9.8 \times (64.9 - 6.1)$
$= \textbf{432 000 J}$ (3 s.f.)

Work and Energy

Gravitational Potential Energy Always uses the Vertical Height

When you're working out the gravitational potential energy of a particle, the value of h you use should **always, always, always** be the **vertical height** above the 'base level'. This means that for a particle moving on a **slope**, it's only the **vertical component** of the distance you're interested in:

Example: A roller skater has a mass of 65 kg. The skater starts from rest at a point X and skates down a slope inclined at 15° to the horizontal. She travels 40 m down the line of greatest slope. Find the gravitational potential energy lost by the skater.

The skater has moved a distance of 40 m down the slope, so this is a vertical distance of: 40 sin 15° m.

G.P.E. $= mgh$
$= 65 \times 9.8 \times 40 \sin 15°$
$= 6590 \text{ J} = \textbf{6.59 kJ}$ (both to 3 s.f.)

Perry desperately wanted to increase his gravitational potential energy...

Practice Questions

Q1 A crate is pushed across a smooth horizontal floor by a force of 250 N, acting in the direction of motion. Find the work done in pushing the crate 3 m.

Q2 A crane lifts a concrete block 12 m vertically at constant speed. If the crane does 34 kJ of work against gravity, find the mass of the concrete block. Take $g = 9.8 \text{ ms}^{-2}$.

Q3 A horse of mass 450 kg is galloping at a speed of 13 ms⁻¹. Find the horse's kinetic energy.

Q4 An ice skater of mass 65 kg sets off from rest. After travelling 40 m in a straight line across horizontal ice, she has done 800 J of work. Find the speed of the ice skater at this point.

Q5 A cyclist has a mass of 67 kg (including her bike). She cycles 120 m up a slope with a 9° incline. Find the increase in the combined gravitational potential energy of the cyclist and her bike.

Exam Questions

Q1 A car of mass 1500 kg is towed 320 m along a straight horizontal road by a rope attached to a pick-up truck. The rope is attached to the car at an angle of 40° to the horizontal and the tension in the rope is 800 N. The car experiences a constant resistance to motion from friction.

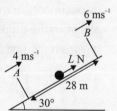

a) Find the work done by the towing force. [3 marks]

b) Over the 320 m, the car increases in speed from 11 ms⁻¹ to 16 ms⁻¹. Assuming that the magnitude of the towing force remains constant at 800 N, find the coefficient of friction between the car and the road. [4 marks]

Q2 A skier is pulled up a sloping plane by a force, L, acting parallel to the plane which is inclined at an angle of 30° to the horizontal. The skier has a mass of 90 kg and he experiences a constant frictional force of 66 N as he moves up the slope. The skier passes through two gates, A and B, which are 28 m apart. His speed at gate A is 4 ms⁻¹. At gate B, his speed has increased to 6 ms⁻¹. Find:

a) the work done against friction in moving from gate A to gate B, [1 mark]

b) the increase in the skier's kinetic energy and gravitational potential energy as he moves from gate A to gate B. [4 marks]

Particle P has so much potential — if only he could apply himself...

There shouldn't be anything earth-shattering on these three pages — I'd bet my completed 1994-95 Premier League sticker album that you've seen both of these types of energy before. Still, it's worth refreshing yourself for what's next.

The Work-Energy Principle

Those pages refreshing your memory on potential and kinetic energy weren't just for fun and giggles. Behold...

Mechanical Energy is the Sum of a Particle's Kinetic and Potential Energies

Over the next few pages, you're going to see a fair bit about '**mechanical energy**'.
This is nothing to freak out about — it's just the sum of the kinetic and potential energies of a particle:

> **Total Mechanical Energy = Kinetic Energy + Gravitational Potential Energy (+ Elastic Potential Energy)**

You'll find out all about **elastic potential energy** in the next section — it's on p.164, if you're interested.
In the calculations coming up, you can ignore elasticity, and just use K.E. and G.P.E.

Learn the Principle of Conservation of Mechanical Energy

The **principle of conservation of mechanical energy** says that:

> **If there are no external forces doing work on an object, the total mechanical energy of the object will remain constant.**

An **external force** is any force other than the weight of the object, e.g. friction, air resistance, tension in a rope, etc. This means that the sum of **potential** and **kinetic** energies remains the **same** throughout an object's motion.
This is a **pretty useful** bit of knowledge:

Robert and Borky were experts at conserving energy.

Example: A BASE jumper with mass 88 kg jumps from a ledge on a building.
When he is 150 m above the ground, he is travelling at 6 ms^{-1} towards the ground.
He releases his parachute at a point 60 m above the ground.

a) Find the kinetic energy of the jumper when he is 150 m above the ground.

b) Use the principle of conservation of mechanical energy to find the jumper's kinetic energy and speed at the point where he releases his parachute.

c) State one assumption you have made in modelling this situation.

a) K.E. at 150m = $\frac{1}{2}mu^2 = \frac{1}{2} \times 88 \times (6)^2$
   $= 1584 = $ **1580 J** (3 s.f.)

You can just use the change in height here, as it's the change in P.E. that you're interested in.

b) Decrease in G.P.E. as he falls:
   $mgh = 88 \times 9.8 \times (150 - 60)$
   $= 77\ 616$ J

Using conservation of mechanical energy: Increase in K.E. = Decrease in G.P.E.

So, K.E. when parachute released − K.E. at 150 m = Decrease in G.P.E.

$\Rightarrow$ K.E. when parachute released = 77 616 + 1584 = **79 200 J**

Use K.E. = $\frac{1}{2}mv^2$ to find the speed when the parachute is released:
$\frac{1}{2}mv^2 = 79\ 200 \Rightarrow \frac{1}{2} \times 88 \times v^2 = 79\ 200$

$\Rightarrow v = \sqrt{\dfrac{79\ 200}{\frac{1}{2} \times 88}} = $ **42.4 ms^{-1}** (3 s.f.)

If you don't assume this, then you can't use the principle of conservation of mechanical energy.

c) That the only force acting on the jumper is his weight.

The Work-Energy Principle

The **Work Done** on an Object is **Equal** to the **Change in Mechanical Energy**

1) As you saw on the previous page, if there are **no external forces** doing work on an object, then the total mechanical energy of the object remains **constant**.

2) So, if there *is* an **external force** doing work on an object, then the **total mechanical energy** of the object must **change**.

3) This leads to the **work-energy principle**:

> The work done on an object by external forces is equal to the change in the **total mechanical energy** of that object.

4) The work-energy principle is pretty similar to the result on p157. It's generally **more useful** though, because you can use it for objects moving in any direction — not just horizontally.

Example: A particle of mass 3 kg is projected up a rough plane inclined at an angle θ to the horizontal, where $\tan\theta = \frac{5}{12}$. The particle moves through a point A at a speed of 11 ms^{-1}.

The particle continues to move up the line of greatest slope and instantaneously comes to rest at a point B before sliding back down the plane.

The coefficient of friction between the particle and the slope is $\frac{1}{3}$.

a) Use the work-energy principle to find the distance AB.

Let x = distance from A to B.

You're told to use the work-energy principle, so first find the change in total mechanical energy:

Change in K.E. of the particle = Final K.E. − Initial K.E.

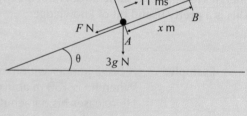

$$= \tfrac{1}{2}mv^2 - \tfrac{1}{2}mu^2 = 0 - \left(\tfrac{1}{2} \times 3 \times 11^2\right) = \textbf{−181.5 J}$$

Change in G.P.E. of the particle = $mg \times$ (change in height)

$$= 3gx\sin\theta = 3gx \times \tfrac{5}{13} = \frac{15gx}{13}\text{ J} \quad \longleftarrow \tan\theta = \tfrac{5}{12} \Rightarrow \sin\theta = \tfrac{5}{13}$$

So, change in total mechanical energy = $-181.5 + \dfrac{15gx}{13}$ J

The only external force doing work on the particle is the frictional force, F.
So you need to find the work done by F. First, resolve perpendicular to the slope:

$$R - 3g\cos\theta = 0 \Rightarrow R = 3g \times \tfrac{12}{13} = \frac{36g}{13}$$

$$F = \mu R = \tfrac{1}{3} \times \frac{36g}{13} = \frac{12g}{13} \qquad \tan\theta = \tfrac{5}{12} \Rightarrow \cos\theta = \tfrac{12}{13}$$

Work done by $F = Fs = \dfrac{12g}{13} \times -x = -\dfrac{12gx}{13}$ J $\qquad$ Displacement is negative because the particle is moving in the opposite direction to F.

Using the work-energy principle: change in total mechanical energy = Work done by F

So: $-181.5 + \dfrac{15gx}{13} = -\dfrac{12gx}{13} \Rightarrow \dfrac{27gx}{13} = 181.5 \Rightarrow x = \dfrac{181.5 \times 13}{27g} = 8.917\ldots = \textbf{8.92 m}$ (3 s.f.)

b) Find the speed of the particle when it returns to A.

The particle moves from A, up to B and back down to A, so overall change in G.P.E. = 0

So, the change in total mechanical energy between the first and second time the particle

is at A is just the change in Kinetic Energy, i.e. Final K.E. − Initial K.E. = $\tfrac{1}{2}mv^2 - \tfrac{1}{2}mu^2$

Work done on the particle = $Fs = F \times -2x$ $\longleftarrow$ The particle has travelled the distance AB twice and is always moving in the opposite direction to the frictional force.

$$= \frac{12g}{13} \times -2(8.917\ldots) = \textbf{−161.3\ldots J}$$

Using the work-energy principle: $u = 11$ ms^{-1}, as this is the speed of the particle when it's first at A.

$$\tfrac{1}{2} \times 3 \times v^2 - \tfrac{1}{2} \times 3 \times 11^2 = -161.3\ldots \Rightarrow \tfrac{3}{2}v^2 = 181.5 - 161.3\ldots \Rightarrow v = \textbf{3.67 ms}^{-1} \text{ (3 s.f.)}$$

The Work-Energy Principle

The work-energy principle sometimes needs to be **applied** to a **whole system**, not just a single particle. An example is **two particles connected** to each other by a string on a **pulley**.

Example: A particle P (mass 2 kg), on a 20° rough slope, is attached to a light, inextensible string. The string is on a frictionless pulley at the top of the slope. At the other end of the taut string, hanging off the slope, is particle Q (mass 3 kg). Particle Q falls 4 m from rest, reaching a speed of 4.7 ms⁻¹. Find the work done on the system by friction.

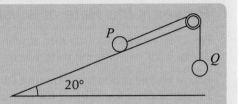

Find the change in K.E. and the change in G.P.E. for Q and P.

Q: change in K.E. $= \frac{1}{2}mv^2 - \frac{1}{2}mu^2 \Rightarrow \frac{1}{2} \times 3 \times 4.7^2 = $ **33.135 J**

change in G.P.E. $= mgh \Rightarrow 3 \times 9.8 \times -4 = $ **−117.6 J**

P: change in K.E. $= \frac{1}{2}mv^2 - \frac{1}{2}mu^2 \Rightarrow \frac{1}{2} \times 2 \times 4.7^2 = $ **22.09 J**

To find vertical distance P has moved: $h = 4 \sin 20°$

change in G.P.E. $= mgh \Rightarrow 2 \times 9.8 \times 4 \sin 20° = $ **26.814... J**

The work done by friction is equal to the change in mechanical energy of the whole system.

Total change in mechanical energy $= 33.135 - 117.6 + 22.09 + 26.814... = $ **−35.560... J**

Work done by friction $= $ **−35.6 J** (3 s.f.)

Practice Questions

Q1 State the principle of conservation of mechanical energy.
Explain why you usually need to model an object as a particle if you are using this principle.

Q2 A jubilant cowboy throws his hat vertically upwards with a velocity of 5 ms⁻¹. Use conservation of mechanical energy to find the maximum height the hat reaches above the point of release. Take $g = 9.8$ ms⁻².

Q3 State the work-energy principle. Explain what is meant by an 'external force'.

Q4 A cyclist of mass 92 kg is cycling up a hill that is inclined at 35°. The cyclist passes point A travelling at 7 ms⁻¹. 50 m after A she passes point B, travelling at 5 ms⁻¹. Find the total change in mechanical energy of the cyclist from point A to point B.

Exam Questions

Q1 A particle of mass 0.3 kg slides from rest down an initially smooth slope, inclined at 40° to the horizontal. When the particle is moving at 20 ms⁻¹, the slope becomes rough.

a) By using conservation of energy, find the distance the particle travelled before reaching the rough part of the slope. [6 marks]

b) When the particle reaches the rough part of the slope, it experiences a constant resistive force of 23 N. Use the work-energy principle to find the distance down the rough part of the slope the particle has travelled when its speed is reduced to 1 ms⁻¹. [5 marks]

Q2 A particle of mass 2 kg is projected up a rough slope inclined at an angle of 40° to the horizontal. The particle travels past point A at 14 ms⁻¹, and travels another 12 m up the slope before coming to rest at point B.

a) Find the coefficient of friction between the particle and the slope. [6 marks]

b) Show that after coming to rest at point B the particle slides back down the slope. [2 marks]

Does this mean we can save energy by doing less work...

There's more than one way to go about answering some of these questions... But don't worry — if the question doesn't tell you what method to use, you'll get marks for using any correct method. Correct being the key word.

Power

The last part of this section — oh boy I'm excited. It's all about power... unlimited power.
Well, not unlimited, but you get the idea. Let's get going...

Power *is the* Rate *at which* Work *is done on an Object*

Power is a measure of the **rate at which a force does work on an object.**
The unit for power is the **watt**, where 1 watt (1 W) = 1 joule per second.

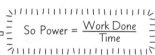

So Power = $\dfrac{\text{Work Done}}{\text{Time}}$

For an **engine** producing a **tractive (driving) force** of F newtons, and moving a vehicle at a speed of v ms^{-1}, the power in watts can be found using the formula:

$$\boxed{\textbf{Power} = \textbf{\textit{F}} \times \textbf{\textit{v}}}$$

Power = $\dfrac{\text{Work Done}}{\text{Time}} = \dfrac{\text{Force} \times \text{Distance}}{\text{Time}} = \text{Force} \times \text{Velocity}$

This is the formula you'll end up using most of the time — those examiners can't resist a question about engines.
But don't forget what power means, just in case they throw you a wild one — it's the **rate of doing work**.

Example:

A train of mass 500 000 kg is travelling along a straight horizontal track with a constant speed of 20 ms^{-1}. The train experiences a constant resistance to motion of magnitude 275 000 N.

a) Find the rate at which the train's engine is working. Give your answer in kW.

b) The train now moves up a hill inclined at 2° to the horizontal. If the engine continues to work at the same rate and the magnitude of the non-gravitational resistance to motion remains the same, find the new constant speed of the train.

a) Call the driving force of the train T N and the speed of the train u ms^{-1}.
Resolve parallel to find T:
$T - 275\,000 = m \times 0$
So $T = 275\,000$ N
Power = $T \times u = 275\,000 \times 20 = \textbf{5500 kW}$

b) Call the new driving force T' and resolve parallel to the slope:
$T' - 275\,000 - 500\,000g \sin 2° = m \times 0$
$\Rightarrow T' = 275\,000 + 500\,000g \sin 2° = 446\,007.5...$ N

Power = $T' \times v$
$5\,500\,000 = 446\,007.5... \times v \quad \Rightarrow \quad v = \dfrac{5\,500\,000}{446\,007.5...} = \textbf{12.3 ms}^{-1}$ (3 s.f.)

Example:

A tractor of mass 3000 kg is moving down a hill inclined at an angle of θ to the horizontal, where $\sin \theta = \frac{1}{24}$. The acceleration of the tractor is 1.5 ms^{-2} and its engine is working at a constant rate of 30 kW. Find the magnitude of the non-gravitational resistance to motion at the instant when the tractor is travelling at a speed of 8 ms^{-1}.

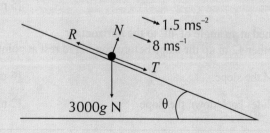

Use Power = $F \times v$ to find T:

Add the component of weight, as the tractor is moving down the slope.

$30\,000 = T \times 8 \Rightarrow T = 3750$ N

Resolve parallel to the slope: $T + mg\sin \theta - R = ma$

$3750 + (3000 \times 9.8 \times \frac{1}{24}) - R = 3000 \times 1.5$

$R = 3750 + 1225 - 4500$

$R = \textbf{475 N}$

There is acceleration here, so this term doesn't disappear for once.

Power

Be prepared for a *Variable Resistive Force*

There's a good chance you'll get a power question where the resistive force isn't constant — it'll be **dependent on the velocity** of whatever's moving. Like the examples on the previous page, these questions require resolving of forces and the careful use of $F = ma$.

Example:

A car of mass 1200 kg travels on a straight horizontal road. It experiences a resistive force of magnitude $30v$ N, where v is the car's speed in ms^{-1}. The maximum speed of the car on this road is 70 ms^{-1}. Find:

a) the car's maximum power,

b) the car's maximum possible acceleration when its speed is 40 ms^{-1}.

a) When the car is travelling at its maximum speed, acceleration is zero, and so the driving force of the car, T, must be equal to the resistive force, i.e. $T = 30v$.

Now use Power = Force × Velocity to give $P = 30v^2 = 30 \times 70^2 = $ **147 kW**

b) Call the new driving force of the car F.

Power = Force × Velocity $\Rightarrow F = \dfrac{147\,000}{40} = 3675$ N

Resolve forces horizontally:

$3675 - 30v = ma$

$3675 - (30 \times 40) = 1200a \Rightarrow a = $ **2.06 ms^{-2}** (3 s.f.)

Maximum acceleration will only be possible when the engine is working at maximum power.

Practice Questions

Q1 A tiger is running at a constant speed of 15 ms^{-1}. The total magnitude of the resistive forces acting on the tiger is 120 N. Find the rate at which the tiger is working.

Q2 A woman and her go-kart together weigh 100 kg. She is travelling on level ground. Find the power of the go-kart whilst it is travelling at 4 ms^{-1}, and accelerating at a rate of 1 ms^{-2}. You can ignore resistive forces.

Q3 A motorbike and rider experience a resistive force of $15v$ N.
What is the maximum speed of the motorbike given that it has a maximum power of 37.5 kW?

Q4 A car travelling at 70 kmh^{-1} is working at a rate of 125 kW.
Find the magnitude of the driving force of the car.

Exam Questions

Q1 A van of mass 2700 kg is travelling at a constant speed of 16 ms^{-1} up a road inclined at an angle of 12° to the horizontal. The non-gravitational resistance to motion is modelled as a single force of magnitude of 800 N. Find the rate of work of the engine. [4 marks]

Q2 A van of mass 1500 kg moves up a road inclined at an angle of 5° to the horizontal. The van's engine works at a constant rate of 25 kW and the van experiences a resistive force of magnitude kv N, where k is a constant and v is the van's speed in ms^{-1}. At the point where the van has speed 8 ms^{-1}, its acceleration is 0.5 ms^{-2}.

a) Show that $k = 137$ to 3 s.f. [4 marks]

b) Using $k = 137$, show that U, the maximum speed of the van up this road, satisfies the equation:
$U^2 + 9.35U - 182 = 0$, where coefficients are given to 3 s.f. [4 marks]

All together now — Watt's the unit for power...

These power questions all revolve around the use of $F = ma$, $P = Fv$ and maybe the occasional Power = Work ÷ Time. Learn these and you're set for life. Well, maybe not life, but at least your exams. And what is life without exams?

Elastic Energy

This page is all about stretching stuff. Exciting or what?

Use **Hooke's Law** to find **Tension** in a **String** or **Spring**

1) **Hooke's law** is a formula for finding the **tension** (T) in a string or spring that has been **stretched** a distance x. You need to **learn** this formula — you won't be given it in the exam.

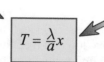

$$T = \frac{\lambda}{a}x$$

You can also use this formula to find the force in a spring which has been compressed a distance x.

2) a is the **natural length** of a spring or elastic string — i.e. its length when it is not being stretched.

You might see the natural length denoted by l in Hooke's law instead.

3) The **modulus of elasticity** (λ) is a measure of **how easily** something can be **stretched elastically** (so that it will return to its original shape when the force is removed). If T has units of N, then the units of λ will also be N.

Example: A wooden block is suspended in equilibrium from an elastic string. The string is extended from its natural length of 5 m to a length of 8 m. Given that the modulus of elasticity of the string is 30 N, find the mass of the block.

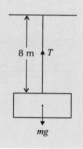

Use **Hooke's law** to find the **tension** in the string: $\quad T = \frac{\lambda}{a}x = \frac{30}{5} \times (8 - 5) = 18$ N.

The block is in **equilibrium**, so resolving forces vertically: $\quad T = mg \Rightarrow 18 = mg$
$$\Rightarrow m = 18 \div 9.8 = \textbf{1.84 kg} \text{ (3 s.f.)}$$

Elastic Potential Energy is energy stored in a Stretched String or Spring

1) When an elastic string (or spring) is stretched, the **work done** in stretching it is converted into **Elastic Potential Energy** (E.P.E.), which is **stored** in the string.

The E.P.E. stored in a compressed spring can be found exactly the same way.

2) You've already seen that W, the work done by a constant force over a distance x m, is given by $W = Fx$. But tension in an elastic string is not constant — it's a **variable force**.

3) To find the **work done** by a variable force, you need to **integrate the force** with respect to **distance**, i.e. $W = \int F \, dx$.

4) This can be used to find a **formula for E.P.E.** It's another formula you need to know I'm afraid. But even worse, you could be asked to **derive** it in the exam. I know — absolutely shocking.

The formula for Elastic Potential Energy

From Hooke's law, the **tension** in an elastic string extended a distance of x m is: $T = \frac{\lambda}{a}x$

So, **work done against tension**:

$$W = \int T \, dx = \int \frac{\lambda}{a}x \, dx = \frac{\lambda}{2a}x^2 + C$$

When the extension is zero, no work has been done, so C has to be zero.

The **potential energy** stored in the string is equal to the work done, so

$$\boxed{\text{E.P.E.} = \frac{\lambda}{2a}x^2}$$

This is the baby you've got to learn.

Holding his favourite rock always reduced Peter's tension.

Elastic Energy

You can find the **Work Done** between **Two Stretched Points**

Example: An elastic string has a natural length of 8 m. If it is extended by x_1 it reaches point A and if it is extended by x_2 it reaches point B. Given that the modulus of elasticity is 80 N, find the work done in stretching the string from point A to point B in terms of x_1 and x_2.

Work done from A to B = work done from equilibrium to B – work done from equilibrium to A

$$W \text{ (from } A \text{ to } B) = \frac{\lambda}{2a}x_2^{\,2} - \frac{\lambda}{2a}x_1^{\,2} \Rightarrow W = \frac{\lambda}{2a}(x_2^{\,2} - x_1^{\,2})$$

$$W = \frac{80}{2 \times 8}(x_2^{\,2} - x_1^{\,2}) \Rightarrow W = 5(x_2^{\,2} - x_1^{\,2}) \text{ J}$$

For **Systems** in **Equilibrium** you need to **Resolve Forces**

Example: A particle is attached to a horizontal ceiling by an elastic string and an inelastic string that pulls it horizontally with a force of 6 N. As a result the angle formed between the ceiling and the elastic string is 75°.

   a)   Find the tension in the elastic string.

a)   Resolve the forces to get $T \cos 75° = 6 \Rightarrow T = 6 \div \cos 75° \Rightarrow T = \textbf{23.2 N}$ (3 s.f.)

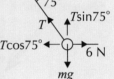

The elastic string is stretched such that it is 1.5 times its natural length.

   b)   Find λ.

b) $T = \frac{\lambda}{a}x = \frac{\lambda}{a} \times \frac{a}{2} = \frac{\lambda}{2} \Rightarrow \lambda = 2T = \textbf{46.4 N}$ (3 s.f.)

      The stretched string is one and a half times its natural length, so the extension is one half of the natural length.

Practice Questions

Q1 A shoe of mass 1.2 kg is suspended in equilibrium from a light elastic string. The string has a natural length of 4 m. Given that the modulus of elasticity of the string is 15 N, find the length of the string.

Q2 The elastic potential energy stored in an elastic string is 1.25 J. The string has a natural length of 2 m and has been stretched to a length of 2.5 m. Find the modulus of elasticity of the string.

Q3 A particle is hanging from a light elastic string attached to a ceiling. The natural length of the string is 3 m and the modulus of elasticity is 12 N. The particle hangs 4.5 m below the ceiling. Find the work done against tension to pull the particle down a further 1.4 m.

Exam Question

Q1 A block of mass 3 kg is attached to one end of a light elastic string of natural length 2 m. The other end of the string is attached to a fixed point A. The weight of the block extends the length of the string to 5 m. The system is in equilibrium, with the block hanging directly below A. Find:

   a)   the modulus of elasticity of the string,   [3 marks]

   b)   the elastic potential energy in the string.   [2 marks]

Now stretch, release that tension...

...and get ready for more examples — woohoo. But before that, make sure you can derive the formula for elastic potential energy from Hooke's law. And remember, work done against tension is equal to the elastic potential energy.

More Elastic Energy Problems

Mechanical Energy *also includes* **Elastic Potential Energy**

We can no longer ignore the E.P.E. term from the equation on p.159. So:

Total Mechanical Energy = Kinetic Energy + Gravitational Potential Energy + Elastic Potential Energy

1) Including the extra term in the equation opens up a whole new **array of exciting questions** which you could be asked about the **Principle of Conservation of Mechanical Energy** and the **Work-Energy Principle** from p.159-p.160.

2) It's nothing scary — just remember that if the only forces acting on a particle are its **weight** and **tension** in an **elastic** string or spring, then the total mechanical energy will be **constant**.

3) And if any other forces **are** acting on a particle, the **work done by them** is equal to the **change in total mechanical energy**. Simples.

Example:

One end of a light elastic string is attached at point O to a smooth plane inclined at an angle of 30° to the horizontal, as shown.
The other end of the string is attached to a particle of mass 8 kg.
The string has a natural length of 1 m and its modulus of elasticity is 40 N.
The particle is released from rest at O and slides down the slope.

'Taut' means that the string is stretched to some length greater than its natural length.

a) Find the length of the string when the particle's acceleration is zero.

b) The string extends to a total length of y m before the particle first comes to rest. Show that $y^2 - 3.96y + 1 = 0$.

c) Hence find the distance from O at which the particle first comes to rest.

The particle is held at point A, 3 m down the slope from O, where it is released from rest and moves up the slope with speed v ms^{-1}.

d) Show that, while the string is taut, the particle's motion satisfies the equation $v^2 = -5z^2 + 19.8z - 14.4$, where z is the particle's distance from O down the slope.

e) Find the speed of the particle at the point where the string becomes slack.

a) Resolve parallel to the slope to find the **tension** in the string, T:

$$T - mg\sin 30° = 8 \times 0 \Rightarrow T = 8 \times 9.8 \times \sin 30° = 39.2 \text{ N}.$$

Now use **Hooke's law** to find the **length of extension** at this point:

$$T = \frac{\lambda}{a}x \Rightarrow x = \frac{Ta}{\lambda} = \frac{39.2 \times 1}{40} = 0.98 \text{ m}.$$

So the length of the string at this point is $a + x = 1 + 0.98 = \textbf{1.98 m}$.

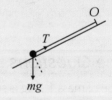

b) The particle starts and ends at rest, so the change in the particle's **kinetic energy** is zero. So, by the **conservation of mechanical energy**: Change in G.P.E. = Change in E.P.E.

G.P.E. lost $= mgh = 8 \times 9.8 \times y \sin 30° = 39.2y$.

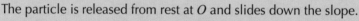

E.P.E. gained $= \frac{\lambda}{2a}x^2 = \frac{40}{2 \times 1} \times (y - 1)^2 = 20(y - 1)^2$

The total length of the extended string is y m, and its natural length is 1 m, so the length of extension is (y − 1) m.

So $20(y - 1)^2 = 39.2y \Rightarrow y^2 - 2y + 1 = 1.96y \Rightarrow y^2 - 3.96y + 1 = 0$.

c) Solving $y^2 - 3.96y + 1 = 0$ using the **quadratic formula** gives $y = \textbf{3.69}$ or $\textbf{0.271}$ (3 s.f.).

0.271 can be ignored as we're told that the string is **extended**, so y must be **greater than 1** (the natural length of the string). So the particle is first stationary when it is **3.69 m** from O (3 s.f.).

d) At point A, the particle has **no K.E.** and **no G.P.E.** (if the level of A is taken as the 'base level').

So, total mechanical energy $= 0 + 0 + \text{E.P.E.} = \frac{\lambda}{2a}x^2 = \frac{40}{2 \times 1} \times (3 - 1)^2 = \textbf{80 J}$

By the conservation of mechanical energy, during the motion of the particle after release from A:

$$\frac{\lambda}{2a}x^2 + mgh + \frac{1}{2}mv^2 = 80 \Rightarrow 20(z - 1)^2 + 78.4(3 - z)\sin 30° + 4v^2 = 80,$$

(3 − z) sin 30° is the vertical distance between A and the particle's current position.

which rearranges to $v^2 = -5z^2 + 19.8z - 14.4$ — as required.

e) The string becomes **slack** when it is no longer stretched, i.e. when it is at its **natural length**. So, substitute $z = 1$ into the equation from part d) and solve for v:

$$v^2 = -5 + 19.8 - 14.4 \Rightarrow v = \textbf{0.632 ms}^{-1} \text{ (3 s.f.)}$$

More Elastic Energy Problems

Example: A particle on a horizontal floor is attached to one end of a light elastic string. The string is also horizontal, with its other end attached to a point 12 m away on a vertical wall. The string has a modulus of elasticity of 40 N and a natural length of 9 m. Given that the particle is in limiting equilibrium and the coefficient of friction between the particle and the floor is $\frac{1}{15}$, what is the mass of the particle?

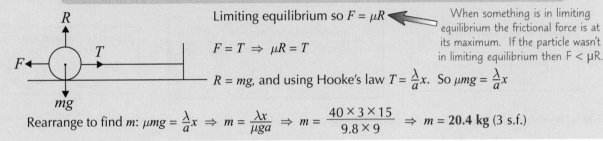

Limiting equilibrium so $F = \mu R$

When something is in limiting equilibrium the frictional force is at its maximum. If the particle wasn't in limiting equilibrium then $F < \mu R$.

$F = T \Rightarrow \mu R = T$

$R = mg$, and using Hooke's law $T = \frac{\lambda}{a}x$. So $\mu mg = \frac{\lambda}{a}x$

Rearrange to find m: $\mu mg = \frac{\lambda}{a}x \Rightarrow m = \frac{\lambda x}{\mu g a} \Rightarrow m = \frac{40 \times 3 \times 15}{9.8 \times 9} \Rightarrow m = \textbf{20.4 kg}$ (3 s.f.)

Example: A particle of mass 1.5 kg is suspended from a point (O) on a horizontal ceiling by a light elastic string which has a natural length of 3 m and a modulus of elasticity of 30 N. The particle hangs in equilibrium at point A, where OA is 4 m. The particle is pulled downwards to point B, where OB is 7 m, and then released from rest. Find the particle's maximum speed as it moves from B to A.

The maximum speed of the particle will be at A, the equilibrium position.

Using conservation of mechanical energy: E.P.E.$_{(B)}$ + K.E.$_{(B)}$ + G.P.E.$_{(B)}$ = E.P.E.$_{(A)}$ + K.E.$_{(A)}$ + G.P.E.$_{(A)}$

$$\frac{\lambda}{2a}x_B^2 + 0 + 0 = \frac{\lambda}{2a}x_A^2 + \frac{1}{2}mv^2 + mgh$$

$$\frac{30}{2\times 3} \times (7-3)^2 + 0 + 0 = \frac{30}{2\times 3} \times (4-3)^2 + \frac{1}{2} \times 1.5v^2 + 1.5 \times 9.8 \times (7-4)$$

$$80 = 5 + 0.75v^2 + 44.1 \Rightarrow v = \sqrt{\frac{80 - 5 - 44.1}{0.75}} \Rightarrow v = \textbf{6.42 ms}^{-1} \text{ (3 s.f.)}$$

Practice Questions

Q1 A particle is attached to a light elastic string on a smooth plane inclined at 40° to the horizontal. The other end of the string is attached to a point further up the plane. The particle is in equilibrium and has a mass of 1.2 kg. Given that the natural length of the string is 4 m and the modulus of elasticity is 60 N, what is the length of the string?

Q2 A particle of mass 5 kg is attached to a light elastic string. The other end of the string is attached to point O on a horizontal ceiling. The particle is dropped from point O and the furthest distance it reaches below O is 5.44 m. Given that the string has a natural length of 2 m, find the modulus of elasticity of the string.

Exam Question

Q1 A block of weight 10 N is attached to one end of a light elastic string, the other end of which is O, a point on a vertical wall. The block is placed on a rough horizontal surface where the coefficient of friction between the block and the surface is $\mu = 0.5$. The string has natural length 5 m and modulus of elasticity 50 N.

a) The block is held a horizontal distance d m from O, where $d > 5$. Find an expression for the elastic potential energy of the system in terms of d. [2 marks]

The block is released from rest d m from O. The subsequent motion results in the block coming to rest just as it returns to O.

b) Find d. [7 marks]

c) State two assumptions that have to be made for the model used in this question to be valid. [2 marks]

I'm just Hooked on elastic potential energy...

All in all quite a nice little topic, if you ask me. You need to know the formulas, and the Principle of Conservation of Mechanical Energy always crops up somewhere along the way. As long as you're down with that, then it's all good.

Collisions

Oh yeah, it's time for some colliding particles — that's right. If you like things loud and dramatic, think demolition balls and high speed crashes. If you're anything like me though you'll be picturing a nice sedate game of snooker.

The **Coefficient of Restitution** is always between **0 and 1**

When two particles collide in a **direct impact** (i.e. they're moving on the **same straight line**), the speeds they bounce away at depend on the **coefficient of restitution**, *e*. This is known as **Newton's Law of Restitution**, and looks like this:

Speed of Approach $= u_A - u_B$

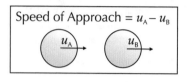

$$e = \frac{\text{speed of separation of particles}}{\text{speed of approach of particles}}$$

$$e = \frac{v_B - v_A}{u_A - u_B}$$

Speed of Separation $= v_B - v_A$

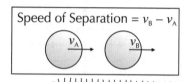

1) The value of *e* depends on the **material** that the particles are made of.

2) *e* always lies between **0 and 1**.

3) When *e* = **0** the particles are called '**inelastic**', and they'll **coalesce**.

4) When *e* = **1** the particles are 'perfectly elastic' and they'll bounce apart with **no loss of relative speed**.

> *Balls of modelling clay would be near the e = O end of the scale, while ping pong balls are nearer to e = 1.*

Example: Two particles collide as shown. Find the coefficient of restitution.

> *Think of 'left to right' as positive, and so particles travelling 'right to left' will have a negative velocity.*

1) Firstly, work out the speeds of approach and separation, taking care with positives and negatives:
Speed of approach $= u_A - u_B = 5 - (-7) = 12$ ms^{-1}.
Speed of separation $= v_B - v_A = 2 - (-4) = 6$ ms^{-1}.

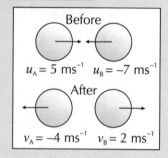

2) Use $e = \dfrac{\text{speed of separation of particles}}{\text{speed of approach of particles}}$:

$e = \dfrac{6}{12} = 0.5$. So the coefficient of restitution is **0.5**.

For **Two Unknown Speeds** — use **Momentum Conservation** too

Often you'll be **given** the value of *e* and asked to find the **velocities** of **both particles** either before or after impact. As there are **two unknowns**, you'll need to use the formula for **conservation of momentum** (on p.150) along with the Law of Restitution to form **simultaneous equations**.

Example: Two particles, *A* and *B*, are moving in opposite directions in the same straight line, as shown. If $e = \frac{1}{3}$, find the velocities of both particles after impact.

$m_A = 4$ kg $m_B = 12$ kg

$u_A = 10$ ms^{-1} $u_B = -2$ ms^{-1}

1) Use $e = \frac{v_B - v_A}{u_A - u_B}$ to get the first equation:

$$\frac{1}{3} = \frac{v_B - v_A}{10 - (-2)} \Rightarrow v_B - v_A = 4. \text{ Call this equation 1.}$$

2) Use $m_A u_A + m_B u_B = m_A v_A + m_B v_B$ to get the second equation:
$(4 \times 10) + (12 \times -2) = 4v_A + 12v_B$
$\Rightarrow 16 = 4v_A + 12v_B \Rightarrow v_A + 3v_B = 4.$ Call this **equation 2**.

3) **Equation 1 + equation 2** gives:
$4v_B = 8$, so $v_B = 2$ ms^{-1} (i.e. 2 ms^{-1} going left to right).

4) Substituting in **equation 1** gives:
$2 - v_A = 4$, so $v_A = -2$ ms^{-1} (i.e. 2 ms^{-1} going right to left).

Collisions

The *Law of Restitution* also works with a *Smooth Plane Surface*

Particles don't just collide with each other. They can collide with a **fixed flat surface** — such as when a ball is kicked against a **vertical wall**, or dropped onto a **horizontal floor**.

As long as the surface can be modelled as **smooth** (i.e. no friction) and **perpendicular** to the **motion of the particle**, the law can be simplified to:

In the mathematical model we're using, momentum is not conserved in collisions with a fixed surface — only in collisions between things that are free to move.

$$e = \frac{\text{speed of rebound of particle}}{\text{speed of approach of particle}} = \frac{v}{u}$$

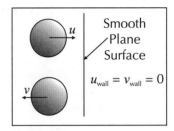

Smooth Plane Surface

$u_{\text{wall}} = v_{\text{wall}} = 0$

Example: A ball rolling along a smooth horizontal floor at 6 ms⁻¹ hits a smooth vertical wall, with a coefficient of restitution $e = 0.65$.

a) Find the speed of the ball as it rebounds.

BEFORE
$u = 6$ ms⁻¹
$e = 0.65$

AFTER
v

Using $e = \frac{v}{u}$:

$0.65 = \frac{v}{6} \Rightarrow v = 0.65 \times 6 = 3.9$ ms⁻¹.

So the ball rebounds at a speed of **3.9 ms⁻¹**.

Piece of cake.

b) How could this model be refined?

Friction between the ball and the floor could be introduced to improve the model.

Use the *Laws of Motion* for things being *Dropped*

Things get a tiny bit trickier when a particle is dropped onto a **horizontal surface** because acceleration under gravity comes into play. You should be pretty nifty with **equations of motion** now though — just remember to use them here.

Example: A basketball is dropped vertically from rest at a height of 1.4 m onto a horizontal floor. It rebounds to a height of 0.9 m. Find e for the impact with the floor.

1) Modelling the ball as a particle, and assuming the floor is smooth, we can use $e = \frac{v}{u}$.
   For the diagram shown, this would be $e = \frac{u_2}{v_1}$, as we need the velocity **just before** the impact (v_1) and the velocity **just after** (u_2).

2) Using $v^2 = u^2 + 2as$ **before** the impact with the floor (where $a = g \approx 9.8$ ms⁻²):
   $v_1^2 = 0 + 2 \times 9.8 \times 1.4 = 27.44$
   $\Rightarrow v_1 = 5.238$ ms⁻¹ to 4 s.f.

3) Using $v^2 = u^2 + 2as$ **after** the impact with the floor (where $a = -g$ since the motion is against gravity):
   $0 = u_2^2 + 2 \times -9.8 \times 0.9$
   $\Rightarrow u_2 = 4.2$ ms⁻¹.

4) Finally, we can find e: $e = \frac{u_2}{v_1} = \frac{4.2}{5.238} = \mathbf{0.802}$ to 3 s.f.

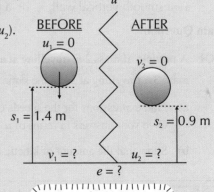

BEFORE
$u_1 = 0$
$s_1 = 1.4$ m
$v_1 = ?$

AFTER
$v_2 = 0$
$s_2 = 0.9$ m
$u_2 = ?$
$e = ?$

There's loads about using the equations of motion in A-level Mechanics as well.

Collisions

Kinetic Energy is only Conserved in Perfectly Elastic Collisions

For any collision where $e < 1$, some **kinetic energy** will be **lost** (it changes into things like **heat** and **sound**). The formula for working out **how much** has been lost is fairly straightforward:

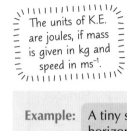

The units of K.E. are joules, if mass is given in kg and speed in ms⁻¹.

$$\text{Loss of K.E. on Impact} = \text{Total K.E. before} - \text{Total K.E. after}$$
$$= (\tfrac{1}{2}m_1u_1^2 + \tfrac{1}{2}m_2u_2^2) - (\tfrac{1}{2}m_1v_1^2 + \tfrac{1}{2}m_2v_2^2)$$

Example: A tiny stationary cannon fires a ball in a straight line across a smooth horizontal table, as shown. The ball collides directly with another, stationary, ball with $e = 0.7$, and moves away from this collision at 7.5 ms⁻¹.

$m_c = 0.05$ kg $m_1 = m_2 = 0.001$ kg

a) Find the loss of K.E. when the balls collide.

1) We first need to find u_1 (the speed of the fired ball before it hits the other) and v_2 (the final speed of the other ball). Use the law of restitution and conservation of momentum (as on p.168) where $e = 0.7$, $v_1 = 7.5$, and $u_2 = 0$.

2) $e = \frac{v_2 - v_1}{u_1 - u_2} \Rightarrow 0.7 = \frac{v_2 - 7.5}{u_1 - 0} \Rightarrow v_2 - 0.7u_1 = 7.5$ (**eqn 1**).

   $m_1u_1 + m_2u_2 = m_1v_1 + m_2v_2$ and since $m_1 = m_2$, they cancel:
   $u_1 + 0 = 7.5 + v_2 \Rightarrow u_1 - v_2 = 7.5$ (**eqn 2**).

   Eqn 1 + eqn 2: $0.3u_1 = 15 \Rightarrow u_1 = 50$ ms⁻¹.

   Sub in **eqn 2:** $50 - v_2 = 7.5 \Rightarrow v_2 = 50 - 7.5 = \mathbf{42.5}$ **ms⁻¹.**

3) Finally, putting all the values in the K.E. formula:

   $\text{Loss of K.E.} = (\tfrac{1}{2}m_1u_1^2 + \tfrac{1}{2}m_2u_2^2) - (\tfrac{1}{2}m_1v_1^2 + \tfrac{1}{2}m_2v_2^2)$
   $= \tfrac{1}{2}m[(u_1^2 + u_2^2) - (v_1^2 + v_2^2)]$
   $= \tfrac{1}{2} \times 0.001 \times [(50^2 + 0^2) - (7.5^2 + 42.5^2)]$
   $= 0.31875 = \mathbf{0.319}$ **J** to 3 s.f.

b) Find the K.E. gained by firing the cannon.

1) Since both the cannon and the ball are stationary before firing, there is no initial K.E. The gain in K.E. is simply $\tfrac{1}{2}m_cv_c^2 + \tfrac{1}{2}m_1v_1^2$, where v_1 is the speed of the ball after firing, i.e. 50 ms⁻¹, as calculated in part a). You need to work out the velocity of the cannon (v_c) though.

2) Momentum is conserved so:
   $m_cu_c + m_1u_1 = m_cv_c + m_1v_1$
   $\Rightarrow 0 + 0 = 0.05v_c + (0.001 \times 50)$
   $\Rightarrow v_c = -(0.001 \times 50) \div 0.05 = -1$ **ms⁻¹.**
   (i.e. the cannon moves backwards at 1 ms⁻¹).

3) Gain in K.E. $= \tfrac{1}{2}m_cv_c^2 + \tfrac{1}{2}m_1v_1^2$
   $= (\tfrac{1}{2} \times 0.05 \times (-1)^2) + (\tfrac{1}{2} \times 0.001 \times 50^2)$
   $= 1.275 = \mathbf{1.28}$ **J** to 3 s.f.

Practice Questions

Q1 Find the <u>loss in kinetic energy</u> when a particle of mass 2 kg travelling at 3 ms⁻¹ collides directly with a stationary particle of mass 3 kg on a smooth horizontal plane surface, where $e = 0.3$.

Q2 Two particles travelling directly towards each other at the <u>same speed</u> collide. The impact causes one particle to <u>stop</u>, and the other to go in the <u>opposite direction</u> at <u>half</u> its original speed. Find the value of e.

Q3 A particle of mass 1 kg travelling at 10 ms⁻¹ on a smooth horizontal plane has a collision where $e = 0.4$. Find the particle's <u>rebound speed</u> if it collides head-on with:
a) a smooth vertical wall,   b) a particle of mass 2 kg travelling at 12 ms⁻¹ towards it.

Exam Question

Q1 A particle of mass $2m$, travelling at a speed of $3u$ on a smooth horizontal plane, collides directly with a particle of mass $3m$ travelling at $2u$ in the same direction. The coefficient of restitution is $\frac{1}{4}$.

a) Find expressions for the speeds of both particles after the collision. Give your answers in terms of u. [4 marks]

b) Show that the amount of kinetic energy lost in the collision is $\frac{9mu^2}{16}$. [4 marks]

Dating Tip #107 — Avoid them if they're on the rebound...

Just when you were thinking this section was a load of balls, along come walls and floors to shake things up a bit. The Law of Restitution is a pretty straightforward formula, but chances are there'll be added complications in the exam questions. Learn how to tackle the types of question on these last three pages and you'll be laughing.

Successive Collisions

You've had an easy ride so far in this section, but now it's time to fasten your seatbelt, don your crash helmet, and prepare for some pretty scary collisions. Don't say I didn't warn you...

Solve **Successive** Collisions **Step by Step**

Think of this as a **multi-particle pile-up**. One particle collides with another, which then shoots off to collide with a third. No extra maths required, but quite a bit of **extra thinking**.

Example: Particles P, Q and R are travelling at different speeds along the same smooth straight line, as shown. Particles P and Q collide first ($e = 0.6$), then Q goes on to collide with R ($e = 0.2$).

a) What are the velocities of P, Q and R after the second collision?

1) Take things step by step. Forget about R for the moment and concentrate on the first collision — the one between P and Q:

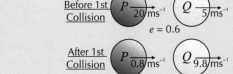

Use $e = \dfrac{v_{Q1} - v_{P1}}{u_{P1} - u_{Q1}}$ first: $0.6 = \dfrac{v_{Q1} - v_{P1}}{20 - 5}$

$\Rightarrow v_{Q1} - v_{P1} = 9$ (**equation 1**).

Then use $m_P u_{P1} + m_Q u_{Q1} = m_P v_{P1} + m_Q v_{Q1}$:

$(0.1 \times 20) + (0.4 \times 5) = 0.1 v_{P1} + 0.4 v_{Q1}$

$\Rightarrow 4 = 0.1 v_{P1} + 0.4 v_{Q1} \Rightarrow v_{P1} + 4 v_{Q1} = 40$ (**equation 2**).

> There are lots of velocities to find here so label them clearly — e.g. v_{Q1} is the final velocity of Q after collision 1, etc.

Equation 1 + equation 2 gives:
$5 v_{Q1} = 49 \Rightarrow v_{Q1} = 9.8$ ms^{-1}.

Substituting in **equation 1** gives:
$9.8 - v_{P1} = 9 \Rightarrow v_{P1} = 9.8 - 9 = 0.8$ ms^{-1}.

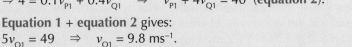

Before 1st Collision

After 1st Collision

$e = 0.6$

2) For the second collision, which is between Q and R: $e = \dfrac{v_{R2} - v_{Q2}}{u_{Q2} - u_{R2}}$.

u_{Q2} is the same as the velocity of Q after the first collision — you found this above (9.8 ms^{-1}), so:

$0.2 = \dfrac{v_{R2} - v_{Q2}}{9.8 - (-1)} \Rightarrow v_{R2} - v_{Q2} = 2.16$ (**equation 3**).

Then $m_Q u_{Q2} + m_R u_{R2} = m_Q v_{Q2} + m_R v_{R2}$:

$(0.4 \times 9.8) + (2 \times -1) = 0.4 v_{Q2} + 2 v_{R2}$

$\Rightarrow 1.92 = 0.4 v_{Q2} + 2 v_{R2} \Rightarrow 0.2 v_{Q2} + v_{R2} = 0.96$ (**equation 4**).

Equation 4 – equation 3 gives:
$1.2 v_{Q2} = -1.2 \Rightarrow v_{Q2} = -1$ ms^{-1}.

Substituting in **equation 3** gives:
$v_{R2} - (-1) = 2.16 \Rightarrow v_{R2} = 2.16 - 1 = 1.16$ ms^{-1}.

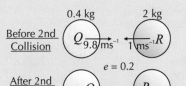

Before 2nd Collision

$e = 0.2$

After 2nd Collision

3) Velocities after both collisions are:
$P = 0.8$ ms^{-1}, $Q = -1$ ms^{-1} and $R = 1.16$ ms^{-1}:

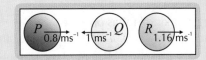

b) After P and Q collide again will there be any further collisions?

Use $e = \dfrac{v_{Q3} - v_{P3}}{u_{P3} - u_{Q3}}$ first: $0.6 = \dfrac{v_{Q3} - v_{P3}}{0.8 - (-1)}$

$\Rightarrow v_{Q3} - v_{P3} = 1.08$

$\Rightarrow 0.1 v_{Q3} - 0.1 v_{P3} = 0.108$ (**equation 1**).

Then use $m_P u_{P3} + m_Q u_{Q3} = m_P v_{P3} + m_Q v_{Q3}$:

$(0.1 \times 0.8) + (0.4 \times -1) = 0.1 v_{P3} + 0.4 v_{Q3}$

$\Rightarrow -0.32 = 0.1 v_{P3} + 0.4 v_{Q3}$ (**equation 2**).

Equation 1 + equation 2 gives:
$0.5 v_{Q3} = -0.212 \Rightarrow v_{Q3} = -0.424$ ms^{-1}, $v_{P3} = -1.504$ ms^{-1}.

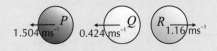

So there will be **no further collisions** as Q is travelling slower than P and will not catch up to it, and Q and R are travelling in opposite directions.

Successive Collisions

Particles may have Successive Rebounds before coming to Rest

Example: A ball falls from a height of 10 m and rebounds several times from the ground, where $e = 0.8$ for each impact. Find the height the ball reaches after each of the first three bounces, stating any assumptions.

1) Some **assumptions** — the ball is a **particle**, **air resistance** can be ignored, it falls **vertically** onto a **horizontal**, **smooth**, **plane** surface, under a **constant acceleration** downwards of $g = 9.8$ ms⁻².

2) For each bounce use $v^2 = u^2 + 2as$ to find the approach speed to the ground and the Law of Restitution, $e = \frac{v}{u}$, to find the rebound speed (p.169). Then use $v^2 = u^2 + 2as$ again to find the height the ball reaches (s) after the bounce.

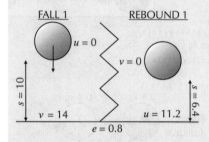

BOUNCE 1

Falling: (Taking 'down' as positive.)
$v^2 = u^2 + 2as$ where $u = 0$, $a = 9.8$ and $s = 10$:
$v^2 = 0 + (2 \times 9.8 \times 10)$ ⇒ $v = \sqrt{2 \times 9.8 \times 10} = 14$ ms⁻¹.

Colliding:
$e = \frac{v}{u}$ ⇒ $v = eu$, where v is the velocity just after the impact, $e = 0.8$ and u is the velocity just before the impact (i.e. 14 ms⁻¹ as found above).
⇒ $v = 0.8 \times 14 = 11.2$ ms⁻¹ (upwards).

Rebounding: (Taking 'up' as positive.)
Set v to zero here because we want → $v^2 = u^2 + 2as$, where $v = 0$, $a = -9.8$, and u is the velocity to know how far it will go upwards (with an acceleration of −g) before it stops and falls back down.
just after the impact (i.e. 11.2 ms⁻¹ as found above).
$0 = 11.2^2 + (2 \times -9.8)s$ ⇒ height of first rebound = $s = \frac{11.2^2}{2 \times 9.8} = 6.4$ m.

BOUNCE 2

If you're not convinced, put the numbers in the equation of motion again to see for yourself.

Falling: (Taking 'down' as positive.)
The motion as the ball rises then falls is **symmetrical** — it covers the same distance under the same acceleration on the 2nd fall as it did on the 1st rebound.
So it hits the floor the second time with the same speed it left it at, 11.2 ms⁻¹.

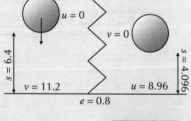

Colliding:
Again, $v = eu$, where v is the velocity after the 2nd impact, $e = 0.8$ and $u = 11.2$ ms⁻¹ (velocity just before impact).
$v = 0.8 \times 11.2 = 8.96$ ms⁻¹ (upwards).

Rebounding: (Taking 'up' as positive.)
$v^2 = u^2 + 2as$, where $v = 0$, $u = 8.96$ (velocity after impact) and $a = -9.8$:
$0 = 8.96^2 + (2 \times -9.8)s$ ⇒ height of second rebound = $s = \frac{8.96^2}{2 \times 9.8} = 4.10$ m (3 s.f.)

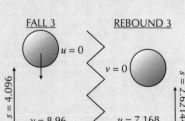

"Did someone say 'bounce'?"

BOUNCE 3

Falling: (Taking 'down' as positive.)
Using the symmetry of the vertical motion, velocity just before 3rd impact = velocity after 2nd impact = 8.96 ms⁻¹.

Colliding:
$v = eu$, where v is the velocity after the 3rd impact, $e = 0.8$ and $u = 8.96$ ms⁻¹ ⇒ $v = 0.8 \times 8.96 = 7.168$ ms⁻¹ (upwards).

Rebounding: (Taking 'up' as positive.)
$v^2 = u^2 + 2as$, where $v = 0$, $u = 7.168$ and $a = -9.8$:
$0 = 7.168^2 + (2 \times -9.8)s$

height of third rebound = $s = \frac{7.168^2}{2 \times 9.8} = 2.62$ m (3 s.f.)

NB: The rebound heights form a geometric progression with common ratio e². You could use the sum to infinity formula (from A-level Pure Maths) to work out the total distance the bouncing particle will travel before stopping.

Successive Collisions

Successive Collisions may involve a Vertical Plane Surface

Example: Particle R is moving on a smooth horizontal surface towards a smooth vertical wall at 1.3 ms⁻¹. Particle Q is in line with R travelling at 1 ms⁻¹ in the opposite direction. R collides with the wall at a right angle. How big would e have to be for this impact to allow R to collide with Q?

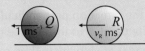

1) Think things through carefully. Q is currently going at 1 ms⁻¹ in the **opposite direction**. To hit Q, R needs to bounce off the wall with a rebound speed **higher** than 1 ms⁻¹, so it can '**catch up**'. So $v_R > 1$.

2) For the impact with the wall, $e = \frac{v_R}{u_R}$ $\Rightarrow$ $v_R = eu_R$, and so $eu_R > 1$.

3) $u_R = 1.3$ ms⁻¹, so: $\qquad 1.3e > 1$

$$\Rightarrow e > \frac{1}{1.3} = 0.7692...$$

4) So, to 3 s.f., e must be **higher than 0.769** for R to collide with Q.

Practice Questions

Q1 Particles A (mass 1 kg), B (4 kg) and C (5 kg) travel in the same direction along a straight line on a smooth horizontal surface at speeds of $3u$, $2u$ and u, respectively.
If A collides with B first ($e = \frac{1}{4}$), then B with C ($e = \frac{1}{3}$), determine whether A and B will collide <u>again</u>.

Q2 A stationary particle drops vertically from a height of 1 m and rebounds from a smooth horizontal plane surface with $e = 0.5$. Find the <u>height</u> that it reaches after its first, second and third bounce.

Q3 Particles A (mass 3 kg), B (1.5 kg) and C (2 kg) are free to move along the same frictionless, horizontal straight line. Initially, particle A is travelling at 3 ms⁻¹ and particles B and C are at rest. If the coefficient of restitution between A and B is 0.5 and the speed of C after B has collided with it is 2.25 ms⁻¹, find the coefficient of restitution between B and C.

Exam Questions

Q1 Particles P (of mass $2m$) and Q (of mass m), travelling in a straight line towards each other at the same speed (u) on a smooth horizontal plane surface, collide with a coefficient of restitution of $\frac{3}{4}$.

a) Show that the collision reverses the direction of both particles, with Q having eight times the rebound speed of P. [6 marks]

Following the collision, Q goes on to collide with a smooth vertical wall, perpendicular to its path. The coefficient of restitution for the impact with the wall is e_{wall}. Q goes on to collide with P again on the rebound from the wall.

b) Show that $e_{wall} > \frac{1}{8}$. [3 marks]

c) Suppose that $e_{wall} = \frac{3}{5}$. If after the second collision with P, Q continues to move away from the wall, but with a speed of 0.22 ms⁻¹, find the value of u, the initial speed of both particles, in ms⁻¹. [7 marks]

Q2 Two particles of mass 0.8 kg and 1.2 kg are travelling in the same direction along a smooth horizontal plane surface with speeds of 4 ms⁻¹ and 2 ms⁻¹ respectively until they collide. After the collision the 0.8 kg mass has a velocity of 2.5 ms⁻¹ in the same direction. The 1.2 kg mass then continues with its new velocity until it collides with a mass of m kg travelling with a speed of 4 ms⁻¹ in the opposite direction to it.

Given that both particles are brought to rest by this collision, find the mass m. [4 marks]

Bouncin's what particles do best...

That's as complex as it gets — just break it down into steps, bounce by bounce. It's a bit like those dance mat games, except less sweaty. And I doubt you'll find Madonna doing mechanics in one of her videos, dressed in a pink leotard...

Oblique Impacts

Don't let the title worry you — there's nothing too difficult on this page. It's pretty similar to what was on the last page, but now the collisions are at funny angles. It's time to get your trig on.

In an *Oblique Impact* with a *Plane*, *Impulse* acts *Perpendicular* to the plane

1) When an object collides with a smooth plane at an **oblique** angle (i.e. not perpendicular to the surface), the **impulse** on the object acts **perpendicular** to the plane. This means that to **calculate the impulse** you only need to consider the component of **velocity** that's **perpendicular** to the plane.

   Check out page 151 if you need a reminder about impulse.

2) The component of the object's velocity in the direction **perpendicular to the plane** is changed by the collision. The component of velocity **parallel** to the surface remains **unchanged**.

3) The **direction** of the perpendicular component of velocity will be **reversed** by the collision (because the object is moving away from the surface after the collision instead of towards it).

4) The **Law of Restitution** still applies in oblique collisions. The **magnitude** of the perpendicular component of velocity after the collision is the original magnitude multiplied by e, the **coefficient of restitution** between the object and the surface.

5) The **angle of deflection** is the angle between the **direction** the particle **would have been going in** if it had continued in its **original direction** and the **new direction** it is travelling in. To **calculate** angle of deflection **add** the angle at which the object **collides** with a surface to the angle with which it **leaves** the surface.

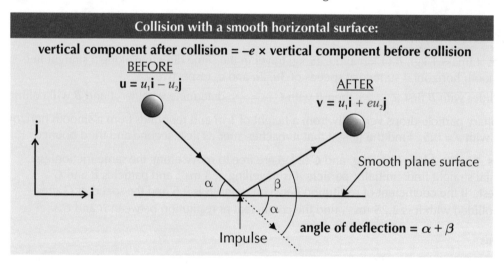

Collision with a smooth horizontal surface:

vertical component after collision = $-e \times$ vertical component before collision

BEFORE
$\mathbf{u} = u_1\mathbf{i} - u_2\mathbf{j}$

AFTER
$\mathbf{v} = u_1\mathbf{i} + eu_2\mathbf{j}$

Smooth plane surface

Impulse

angle of deflection = $\alpha + \beta$

6) Finding the components of velocity and using the above facts gives:

   Parallel: $u \cos \alpha = v \cos \beta$ **(eqn 1)**,   Perpendicular: $eu \sin \alpha = v \sin \beta$ **(eqn 2)**

   (eqn 2) ÷ (eqn 1) $\Rightarrow \dfrac{eu \sin \alpha}{u \cos \alpha} = \dfrac{v \sin \beta}{v \cos \beta} \Rightarrow \boxed{e \tan \alpha = \tan \beta} \longleftarrow$ Since $e \leq 1$, $\beta \leq \alpha$.

   This equation is useful for calculating the angle of deflection.

Example: A ball is rolling on the ground and hits a wall with velocity $12\mathbf{i} - 8\mathbf{j}$ ms⁻¹ (where **i** is parallel to the wall and **j** is perpendicular to the wall), and rebounds at an angle of $\beta°$ to **i**. By modelling the wall as a smooth plane surface with coefficient of restitution $e = 0.5$, find the speed v of the ball after the collision, and the angle of deflection.

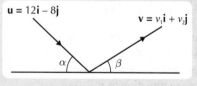

$\mathbf{u} = 12\mathbf{i} - 8\mathbf{j}$
$\mathbf{v} = v_1\mathbf{i} + v_2\mathbf{j}$

1) The wall is parallel to **i**, so the component of velocity in this direction is **unchanged**, i.e. $v_1 = 12$.

2) Perpendicular to the wall, the component of the velocity is **reversed** and **multiplied by** e, so $v_2 = -0.5(-8) = 4$.

3) So the velocity of the ball after the collision is $\mathbf{v} = 12\mathbf{i} + 4\mathbf{j}$ ms⁻¹.

4) Use Pythagoras to find the speed after the collision:
   $v = \sqrt{12^2 + 4^2} = \mathbf{12.6}$ ms⁻¹ (3 s.f.)

5) You can now calculate the angle of deflection
   $\tan \alpha = \dfrac{8}{12} \Rightarrow \alpha = 33.6...°$ $\tan \beta = \dfrac{4}{12} \Rightarrow \beta = 18.4...°$

6) Angle of deflection $= 33.6...° + 18.4...° = \mathbf{52.1°}$ (3 s.f.)

Oblique Impacts

Kinetic Energy is Lost in Collisions that Aren't Perfectly Elastic

Kinetic energy is lost in any collision where $e < 1$ — in the real world that's basically everything.

Example: A smooth uniform sphere of mass 0.15 kg moves on a smooth horizontal plane with velocity $(7\mathbf{i} - 8\mathbf{j})$ ms^{-1}. It collides with a smooth wall that is parallel to $\mathbf{i}$. The coefficient of restitution between the wall and the sphere is 0.4. Find the change in the sphere's kinetic energy due to the collision.

Find the velocity after the collision:

$\mathbf{i}$ component: $v_1 = 7$, $\mathbf{j}$ component: $-e \times (-8) = 0.4 \times 8 = 3.2$

$\mathbf{v} = (7\mathbf{i} + 3.2\mathbf{j})$ ms^{-1}

Use Pythagoras to find u^2 and v^2:

$u^2 = 7^2 + (-8)^2 = 113$, $v^2 = 7^2 + 3.2^2 = 59.24$

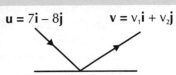
$\mathbf{u} = 7\mathbf{i} - 8\mathbf{j}$ $\mathbf{v} = v_1\mathbf{i} + v_2\mathbf{j}$

Use K.E. $= \frac{1}{2}mv^2$ to find the change in kinetic energy:

K.E. before collision: $\frac{1}{2} \times 0.15 \times 113 = 8.475$ J

K.E. after collision: $\frac{1}{2} \times 0.15 \times 59.24 = 4.443$ J

Change in K.E.: $4.443 - 8.475 = \mathbf{-4.032}$ **J**

The plane and wall were modelled as smooth — a refined model, with rough surfaces, would give a greater change in K.E than the answer here.

Use Trig to find components Parallel and Perpendicular to the Surface

Some questions won't be in vector form. In this case you need to resolve the velocities perpendicular and parallel to the surface. Just make sure you know which is which...

Example: A smooth uniform ball is dropped vertically onto a smooth surface inclined at 30°. When it collides with the surface it is travelling at $14\sqrt{2}$ ms^{-1}. The ball bounces off the surface at an angle of 45° to it, with a speed of 14 ms^{-1}. Find the coefficient of restitution between the ball and the surface.

1) Resolve the velocities before and after the collision, parallel and perpendicular to the surface.

Before collision:

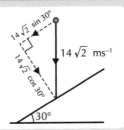
$14\sqrt{2}\sin 30°$ $14\sqrt{2}$ ms^{-1} $14\sqrt{2}\cos 30°$ 30°

After collision:

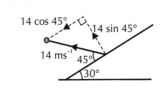
$14\cos 45°$ $14\sin 45°$ 14 ms^{-1} 45°   30°

2) Use the Law of Restitution in the direction perpendicular to the surface:

$$-e \times -14\sqrt{2}\cos 30° = 14\sin 45° \Rightarrow e = \frac{14\sin 45°}{14\sqrt{2}\cos 30°} \Rightarrow e = \frac{1}{\sqrt{3}} \text{ or } \mathbf{0.577} \text{ (3 s.f.)}$$

Practice Questions

Q1 A ball of mass 0.5 kg is travelling on a horizontal surface at $9\mathbf{i} - 4\mathbf{j}$ ms^{-1} when it collides with a wall parallel to $\mathbf{i}$. It rebounds with a velocity of $9\mathbf{i} + 2.5\mathbf{j}$ ms^{-1}. Find the change in kinetic energy and the angle of deflection.

Q2 A uniform sphere is travelling on a smooth horizontal plane. It collides with a wall at an angle of 25° and speed 15 ms^{-1}. Given that $e = \frac{3}{5}$, find the speed after the collision.

Exam Questions

Q1 A particle of mass 1 kg is moving on a horizontal surface when it collides with a wall. It hits the wall at an angle of 45° and with speed $u = 3\sqrt{2}$ ms^{-1}. It rebounds at an angle of 30°. Find:

   a) the coefficient of restitution (e) between the particle and the wall,   [2 marks]

   b) the kinetic energy lost by the particle in the collision.   [6 marks]

Q2 A ball of mass 1.2 kg is dropped vertically onto a surface which is inclined at 27°. When it hits the surface it is travelling at 13 ms^{-1}. Given that $e = 0.7$, find the magnitude of the impulse received by the ball.   [4 marks]

Feel like you're on a collision course with your exams?

Just remember if you're not given an object's velocity in terms of $\mathbf{i}$ and $\mathbf{j}$ vectors you're gonna have to do a bit of trig.

Successive Oblique Impacts

This might be starting to sound familiar by now. More collisions, more calculations, more fun...

Particles may have **More Than One Collision**

You just have to break it down step by step, collision by collision — it's useful to **draw diagrams** for each collision. The velocity must always be resolved **parallel** and **perpendicular** to the **surface** involved in the collision — and these **won't** always be in line with **i** or **j**.

Example:

A smooth uniform sphere is projected along a smooth horizontal floor. It collides with one smooth wall, and then collides with a second smooth wall.
The two walls are at an angle of 110° to one another.
The sphere has an initial speed of 7 ms⁻¹ and hits the first wall at an angle of 40°. The coefficient of restitution between the sphere and each wall is $\frac{3}{4}$. Find the speed of the sphere after it has collided with the second wall.

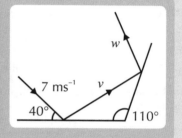

1) Consider the first collision:

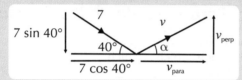

$$v_{para} = 7 \cos 40° \text{ ms}^{-1}$$

$$v_{perp} = 7 \sin 40° \times \frac{3}{4} = \frac{21}{4} \sin 40° \text{ ms}^{-1}$$

2) Find the speed after the first collision, and the angle at which the sphere bounces off.

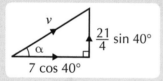

$$v = \sqrt{(7 \cos 40°)^2 + \left(\frac{21}{4} \sin 40°\right)^2} \implies v = 6.3358... \text{ ms}^{-1}$$

$$\tan \alpha = \frac{\frac{21}{4} \sin 40°}{7 \cos 40°} \implies \alpha = \tan^{-1} \frac{\frac{21}{4} \sin 40°}{7 \cos 40°} \implies \alpha = 32.183...°$$

You could also use tan $\alpha = e \tan 40°$

3) Use angles in a triangle to find the angle with which the sphere collides with the second wall.

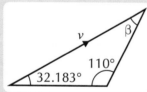

$$\beta = 180° - 110° - 32.183...° \implies \beta = 37.816...°$$

4) Then consider the second collision:

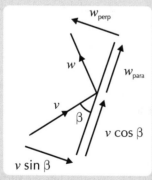

$$w_{para} = v \cos \beta$$
$$= 6.3358... \cos 37.816...° = 5.005... \text{ ms}^{-1}$$

$$w_{perp} = v \sin \beta \times \frac{3}{4}$$
$$= 6.3358... \sin 37.816...° \times \frac{3}{4} = 2.913... \text{ ms}^{-1}$$

5) Find the speed after the second collision:

$$w = \sqrt{(5.005...)^2 + (2.913...)^2} \implies w = 5.79 \text{ ms}^{-1} \text{ (3 s.f.)}$$

Successive Oblique Impacts

Example: A particle of mass 2.5 kg is travelling on a smooth horizontal plane. It collides with one smooth wall, then collides with a second smooth wall which is perpendicular to the first. The particle's initial velocity is $\mathbf{u} = 6\mathbf{i} - 3.5\mathbf{j}$ ms^{-1}. The coefficient of restitution between the particle and the first wall is $\frac{3}{5}$ and the coefficient of restitution between the particle and the second wall is $\frac{2}{5}$.

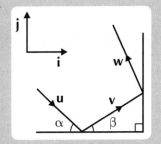

a) Find the angle of deflection of the first collision.

b) Find the difference between the initial kinetic energy of the particle and its final kinetic energy after both collisions.

a) Use the Law of Restitution to find the velocity after the first collision.

$\mathbf{u} = 6\mathbf{i} - 3.5\mathbf{j}$ Let $\mathbf{v} = v_1\mathbf{i} + v_2\mathbf{j}$

$v_1 = 6$ and $v_2 = -3.5 \times -\frac{3}{5} = 2.1 \Rightarrow \mathbf{v} = 6\mathbf{i} + 2.1\mathbf{j}$ ms^{-1}

Then use the i and j components of **u** and **v** to find α and β...

$\tan \alpha = \dfrac{3.5}{6} \Rightarrow \alpha = \tan^{-1}\dfrac{3.5}{6} \Rightarrow \alpha = 30.25...°$

$\tan \beta = \dfrac{2.1}{6} \Rightarrow \beta = \tan^{-1}\dfrac{2.1}{6} \Rightarrow \beta = 19.29...°$

... and add them together to get the angle of deflection.

angle of deflection = $30.25...° + 19.29...° = $ **49.5°** (3 s.f.)

b) For the second collision, the j component is parallel to the wall and the i component is perpendicular.

$\mathbf{v} = 6\mathbf{i} + 2.1\mathbf{j}$ ms^{-1} Let $\mathbf{w} = w_1\mathbf{i} + w_2\mathbf{j}$

$w_1 = 6 \times -\frac{2}{5} = -2.4$ and $w_2 = 2.1 \Rightarrow \mathbf{w} = -2.4\mathbf{i} + 2.1\mathbf{j}$

Use Pythagoras to find the initial and final speeds, then work out the K.E.

$u^2 = 6^2 + (-3.5)^2 = $ **48.25** and $w^2 = (-2.4)^2 + 2.1^2 = $ **10.17**

Difference in K.E. $= \frac{1}{2}mu^2 - \frac{1}{2}mw^2$

$= \frac{1}{2}(2.5)(48.25) - \frac{1}{2}(2.5)(10.17) = $ **47.6 J**

Practice Questions

Q1 A ball is travelling on a smooth horizontal plane with velocity $6.4\mathbf{i} - 4.8\mathbf{j}$ ms^{-1}. It collides with a smooth wall parallel to **i**, then collides with a second smooth wall which is perpendicular to the first. The coefficient of restitution between the ball and each of the walls is $\frac{3}{4}$.

a) Find the velocity of the ball after the second collision.

b) Find the angle of deflection in the second collision.

Q2 A smooth sphere is travelling on a smooth horizontal surface. It collides with one smooth wall at an angle of 35°, then collides with a second smooth wall. The angle between the first wall and the second wall is 115°. The coefficient of restitution between each wall and the sphere is $\frac{1}{3}$.
Find the angle with which the sphere collides with the second wall.

Exam Question

Q1 a) A ball is rolling along a smooth horizontal surface. It collides with one smooth wall, then collides with a second smooth wall which is at an angle of 115° to the first. Just before the first collision, the ball has a velocity of $-3\mathbf{i} + 6\mathbf{j}$ ms^{-1}. The angle at which the ball leaves the surface of the first wall is 38.7°.

The coefficient of restitution between the ball and the first wall is e and the coefficient of restitution between the ball and the second wall is $2e$.

Find the speed of the ball after the second collision. [8 marks]

b) How would your answer to (a) be affected if the floor was not modelled as smooth? [1 mark]

A smooth plane — for more aerodynamic flying...

When dealing with multiple collisions, just break them down into separate collisions and you're golden. Make sure you pay attention to which components are parallel and which are perpendicular once you've switched walls though.

Oblique Collisions of Spheres

You're almost there... the last two pages of mechanics. It's pretty tricky — you'll have to combine a lot of the things you've learnt over the last few pages, but I believe in you. So strap in and get ready for more collisions...

The **Impulse** acts along the **Line Of Centres**

1) An **oblique collision** between two spheres occurs when they're **not** travelling along the same straight line when they collide.

2) All the situations you will have to deal with will involve **smooth spheres** with the **same radius**.

3) When such spheres collide in a **horizontal plane**, the **straight line** that passes through their centres is parallel to the plane. The **impulse** acts in the direction of this **line of centres**.

4) This means that the **velocity** components **parallel** to the line of centres will **change**, but the **velocity** components **perpendicular** to the line of centres will **remain the same**.

5) So **Newton's Law of Restitution** (from p.168) applies **parallel** to the **line of centres**.

That's a different line of centres — they still like collisions though.

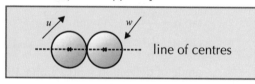

line of centres

6) In collisions between two spheres **momentum is conserved** since they are free to move.

7) As on p.174, the **angle of deflection** is the angle between the direction the sphere **would have been** going in if it had not collided, and the direction it is travelling in **after** the collision.

Use **Simultaneous Equations** to find the **New Velocities**

Problems involving oblique collisions of spheres often involve **two unknowns**. In these situations you'll need to use **conservation of momentum** and the **Law of Restitution** to form **simultaneous equations**.

You can also work out the loss of **kinetic energy** in oblique collisions — you'll need to find the total K.E. **before** and **after**, just as you would for spheres colliding in a straight line (see p.170).

Example: Two smooth uniform spheres (A and B) with the same radius are moving on a smooth horizontal surface. Sphere A has mass 3 kg and velocity $4\mathbf{i} + 3\mathbf{j}$ ms^{-1}. Sphere B has mass 2 kg and velocity $-2\mathbf{i} + 7\mathbf{j}$ ms^{-1}. The two spheres collide and at the instant of the collision the line joining the centres of the spheres is parallel to $\mathbf{i}$. The coefficient of restitution between the two spheres is $\frac{1}{3}$.

Find the velocity of B after the collision, the angle of deflection of B, and the change in B's kinetic energy due to the collision.

1) The collision happens parallel to $\mathbf{i}$, which means the $\mathbf{j}$ component will remain the same after the collision, but the $\mathbf{i}$ component will change.

2) Using conservation of momentum (page 154) for the $\mathbf{i}$ components:
$$m_A v_{Ai} + m_B v_{Bi} = m_A u_{Ai} + m_B u_{Bi} \longleftarrow \text{ } u_{Ai} \text{ denotes the } \mathbf{i} \text{ component}$$
$$3v_{Ai} + 2v_{Bi} = (3 \times 4) + (2 \times -2) = 8 \text{ (eqn 1)} \quad \text{of the initial velocity of A, etc.}$$

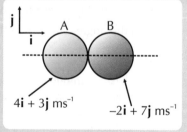

$4\mathbf{i} + 3\mathbf{j}$ ms^{-1} $-2\mathbf{i} + 7\mathbf{j}$ ms^{-1}

3) Using the equation for the coefficient of restitution (page 168) in the $\mathbf{i}$ direction: $\quad e = \dfrac{v_{Bi} - v_{Ai}}{u_{Ai} - u_{Bi}}$

$$\Rightarrow \frac{1}{3} = \frac{v_{Bi} - v_{Ai}}{4 + 2} \Rightarrow v_{Bi} - v_{Ai} = 2 \text{ (eqn 2)}$$

4) (eqn 1) + 3 (eqn 2) $\Rightarrow 5v_{Bi} = 14 \Rightarrow v_{Bi} = 2.8$
velocity of B after collision = **2.8i + 7j ms^{-1}**

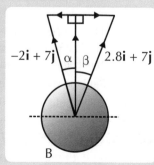

$-2\mathbf{i} + 7\mathbf{j}$ α β $2.8\mathbf{i} + 7\mathbf{j}$

B

5) $\alpha = \tan^{-1}\left(\frac{2}{7}\right) = 15.94...°$ $\beta = \tan^{-1}\left(\frac{2.8}{7}\right) = 21.80...°$
angle of deflection = $\alpha + \beta$ = **37.7°** (3 s.f.)

6) Change in K.E. of B = $\frac{1}{2}m(v_B^2 - u_B^2)$
$$= \frac{1}{2} \times 2 \times [2.8^2 + 7^2 - ((-2)^2 + 7^2)] = \textbf{3.84 J} \text{ (3 s.f.)}$$

Oblique Collisions of Spheres

Example: A and B are smooth spheres, with A of mass 0.5 kg and B of mass 0.6 kg. Both spheres have a radius of 0.065 m. They are moving on a smooth horizontal plane.

The spheres move towards each other along parallel lines, with the centre of the spheres 0.12 m apart. They eventually collide.

Before the collision, A is travelling at 3 ms⁻¹ and B is travelling at 2.5 ms⁻¹. The coefficient of restitution between the spheres is $\frac{1}{4}$. Find the speed of A after the collision.

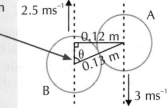

1) You'll need to know the **angle** θ between the line of centres and the direction of motion to resolve the velocities relative to the line of centres.

   The hypotenuse of the triangle is the sum of the radii of the two spheres: 0.065 m + 0.065 m = 0.13 m

   Length of missing side of triangle: $\sqrt{0.13^2 - 0.12^2} = 0.05$ m

   $\sin \theta = \frac{0.12}{0.13} = \frac{12}{13}, \quad \cos \theta = \frac{0.05}{0.13} = \frac{5}{13}$

2) Resolve the initial velocities **parallel** and **perpendicular** to the **line of centres**:

   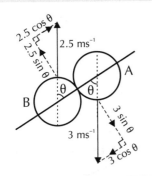

3) After the collision, the component of A's velocity **perpendicular** to the line of centres is still $3 \sin \theta = \frac{36}{13}$.

4) Using conservation of momentum for the **parallel** components:
   $m_A u_A + m_B u_B = m_A v_A + m_B v_B$
   $(0.5)(3 \cos \theta) + (0.6)(-2.5 \cos \theta) = 0.5 v_A + 0.6 v_B$
   $0 = 0.5 v_A + 0.6 v_B \text{ (eqn 1)}$

5) Using the coefficient of restitution equation and the values of $\cos \theta$ found earlier:
   $e = \frac{1}{4} \Rightarrow \frac{1}{4} = \frac{v_B - v_A}{3 \cos \theta + 2.5 \cos \theta} \Rightarrow \frac{55}{104} = v_B - v_A \text{ (eqn 2)}$

6) (eqn 2) × 0.6 $\Rightarrow \frac{33}{104} = 0.6 v_B - 0.6 v_A \text{ (eqn 3)}$
   (eqn 1) − (eqn 3) $\Rightarrow -\frac{33}{104} = 1.1 v_A \Rightarrow v_A = -\frac{15}{52}$

7) Combining the parallel and perpendicular components of A to find the speed: $\sqrt{\left(-\frac{15}{52}\right)^2 + \left(\frac{36}{13}\right)^2} = 2.78 \text{ ms}^{-1} \text{ (3 s.f.)}$

Practice Questions

Q1 Two smooth spheres of the same radius collide on a smooth horizontal surface. Initially, sphere A (0.5 kg) has velocity $5\mathbf{i} + 3\mathbf{j}$ ms⁻¹ and sphere B (0.7 kg) has velocity $-2\mathbf{i} + 6.3\mathbf{j}$ ms⁻¹. When they collide the line of centres of the spheres is parallel to $\mathbf{i}$. The coefficient of restitution is $\frac{1}{3}$. Find the speed of sphere A after the collision.

Q2 Two particles, P (0.5 kg) and Q (1 kg), collide on a smooth horizontal plane. Before the collision, particle P has velocity $5\mathbf{i} + 3\mathbf{j}$ ms⁻¹. After the collision, particle P has velocity $5\mathbf{i} - 4\mathbf{j}$ ms⁻¹ and Particle Q has velocity $\mathbf{i} + \mathbf{j}$ ms⁻¹. Find: a) the velocity of Q before the collision b) the loss in kinetic energy of the whole system.

Q3 Ball B (1 kg) and ball C (0.5 kg) are smooth and have the same radius. Ball B travels at 7 ms⁻¹ on a smooth plane before it collides with ball C. At the moment of collision, C is stationary and B is travelling at an angle of 42° to the line of centres of the balls. The coefficient of restitution is $\frac{3}{5}$. Find the speed of ball C after the collision.

Exam Question

Q1 Two smooth balls with the same radius are travelling towards each other along a smooth horizontal surface. Ball A has mass 0.5 kg and ball B has mass 0.25 kg. When they collide, A is travelling at an angle of 30° to the line of centres and B is travelling at an angle of 60° to the line of centres, as shown on the diagram. Both balls are travelling at 5 ms⁻¹.

The coefficient of restitution between the balls is $\frac{1}{2}$.

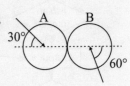

Find the speed of B after the collision and the angle of deflection of B. [10 marks]

Don't look so (o)bleak — you've made it to the end of the section...

These collisions between spheres are all about the line of centres. Make sure you know where it is for any collision you're looking at — you'll need to resolve the velocities relative to it. After that it's just some simultaneous equations...

Algorithms

Welcome to the wonderful world of Decision Maths. And what a good decision it was too. These first pages are on algorithms, which aren't as scary as they sound. You've probably come across them before without knowing it.

Algorithms *are sets of* Instructions

An **algorithm** is just a fancy mathematical name for a **set of instructions** for **solving** a problem. You come across lots of algorithms in everyday life — **recipes**, **directions** and **assembly instructions** are all examples of algorithms.

1) Algorithms start with an **input** (e.g. in a recipe, the input is the raw ingredients).
   You carry out the algorithm on the input, following the instructions **in order**.

2) Algorithms have an **end result** — something that you **achieve** by carrying out the algorithm (e.g. a cake).

3) This means that algorithms will **stop** when you've reached a **solution**, or produced your **finished product**.
   They'll often have a **stopping condition** — an **instruction** that tells you to stop when you've reached a certain point.

4) Algorithms are often written so that **computers** could follow the instructions, but you might see some written in **pseudo-code**.

> Pseudo-code is a bit like computer programming language, but less formal — it's a set of brief instructions written for a person (not a computer).

Algorithms can be used to solve **mathematical problems** too.

- The **input** in a mathematical algorithm is the **number** (or numbers) you start with.
  Your **end result** is the **final number** you end up with — this'll be the **solution** to the original problem.

- It's a good idea to **write down** the numbers each instruction produces in a **table** — sometimes the algorithm will **tell you** when to do this. This table is called a **trace table**.

Algorithms can be written as Flow Charts

Instead of giving instructions in **words**, some algorithms are written as **flow charts**. There are three different types of **boxes** which are used for different things:

(Start / Stop)   [Instruction]   < Decision >

The boxes are connected with **arrows** to guide you through the flow chart. 'Decision' boxes will ask a question, and for each one you have a **choice** of arrows, one arrow for '**yes**' and one for '**no**', which will take you to another box. Sometimes flow charts will include a loop which takes you back to an earlier stage in the chart. Loops are a way of **repeating steps** until the algorithm is **finished**.

Example: a)   Complete a trace table for the flow chart below, for $a = 10$.
              b)   Interpret what the algorithm does.

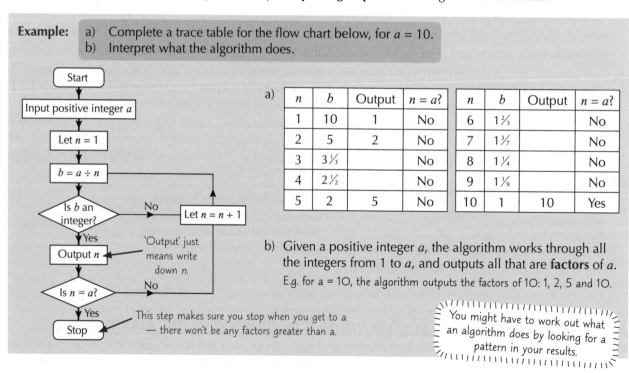

a)

n	b	Output	$n = a$?	n	b	Output	$n = a$?
1	10	1	No	6	$1\frac{2}{3}$		No
2	5	2	No	7	$1\frac{3}{7}$		No
3	$3\frac{1}{3}$		No	8	$1\frac{1}{4}$		No
4	$2\frac{1}{2}$		No	9	$1\frac{1}{9}$		No
5	2	5	No	10	1	10	Yes

b)   Given a positive integer a, the algorithm works through all the integers from 1 to a, and outputs all that are **factors** of a.
     E.g. for $a = 10$, the algorithm outputs the factors of 10: 1, 2, 5 and 10.

> You might have to work out what an algorithm does by looking for a pattern in your results.

Algorithms

The **Order** of an algorithm tells you how **Efficient** it is

You can find how **long** an algorithm takes to run and **compare** it to another to decide which is better:

1) The **size** of an algorithm is the **number of inputs** you have — so for an algorithm like the **bubble sort** (see p.182), the size is **how many numbers** you have in your list. The size of an algorithm is usually written as n.

2) How **long** an algorithm takes to run is measured by its **efficiency** — this will be a **function of n** (e.g. $n^2 - n$). The time it takes depends on **how many operations** the algorithm involves — if there are lots of operations, it'll take **longer**. You can **determine** the efficiency of an algorithm by considering the **worst-case scenario** (i.e. the **maximum** number of times you'll need to **run the algorithm** or carry out a particular **operation** for n inputs).

3) The **order** (or **complexity**) of an algorithm is a way of comparing how **efficient** algorithms are.

4) You work out the order by looking at the **highest power** of n in the function:

- If the highest power is **1**, e.g. $5n + 2$, the algorithm is of **linear** order (you'd write it as O(n) or order 1).
- If the highest power is **2**, e.g. $5n^2 + 6n$, the algorithm is of **quadratic** order (you'd write O(n^2) or order 2).
- If the highest power is **3**, e.g. $n^3 + 2n^2 + 3n$, the algorithm is of **cubic** order (you'd write O(n^3) or order 3).

5) The order tells you how the **time** changes as the size (n) increases. If n is **doubled**, a linear order algorithm will take about **twice as long**, a **quadratic** order algorithm will take about $2^2 = $ **4 times** as long and a cubic order algorithm will take about $2^3 = $ **8 times** as long.

> **Example:** A computer uses a quadratic algorithm. It takes 1.8 seconds to carry out the algorithm on a set of 50 numbers. Estimate how long it will take when there are 250 numbers.
>
> In this example, $n = 50$. $250 = 5 \times 50$, so you have to multiply the time by $5^2 = 25$ as the algorithm is quadratic. So when there are 250 numbers, it will take about $1.8 \times 25 = $ **45 s** to carry out the algorithm.

Practice Questions

Q1 Use the Russian Peasant algorithm (shown below) to multiply 17 and 56.

1) Write down two numbers you are multiplying in a table. Call them x and y.
2) Divide x by 2 and write down the result underneath x, ignoring any halves.
3) Multiply y by 2 and write down the result underneath y.
4) Repeat steps 2) - 3) for the numbers in the new row. Keep going until the number in the x column is 1.
5) Work down your table and cross out every row that has an even value for x.
6) Add up the remaining numbers in the y column to give xy.

Q2 An algorithm has order O(n^2). If it takes 0.4s to apply the algorithm to a set of 20 numbers, approximately how long will it take on a set of 60 numbers?

Exam Question

Q1 Consider the following algorithm:

Step 1: Input A, B with A < B
Step 2: Input N = 1
Step 3: Calculate C = A ÷ N
Step 4: Calculate D = B ÷ N
Step 5: If both C and D are integers, output N
Step 6: If N = A, then stop.
    Otherwise let N = N + 1 and go back to Step 3

a) Carry out the algorithm with A = 8 and B = 12. Record your results. [3 marks]

b) (i) What does this algorithm produce? [1 mark]

(ii) Using your answer to part (i) or otherwise, write down the output that would be produced if you applied the algorithm to A = 19 and B = 25. Explain your answer. [2 marks]

Get into the groove of the algo-rhythm...

Say you had a cubic algorithm faster than a speeding bullet. If you doubled the size of the problem, it would take $2^3 = 8$ times as long, which means it would now be faster than a high-speed train, but not as fast as a bullet — good if you're trying to rescue someone tied to the train tracks, less good if you're trying to rescue someone from a bullet.

Sorting Algorithms

You've probably been able to sort things into alphabetical or numerical order since you were knee-high to a hamster, but in Decision Maths you need to know how to sort things using algorithms. At least it'll be easy to check your answer.

A **Bubble Sort** compares **Pairs** of numbers

The **bubble sort** is an **algorithm** that **sorts numbers** (or **letters**). It's easy to do, but it can be a bit fiddly, so **take care**.

The Bubble Sort

1) Look at the **first two numbers** in your list. If they're in the right order, you don't have to do anything with them. If they're the wrong way round, **swap** them. It might help you to **make note** of which numbers you swap each time.

2) Move on to the **next** pair of numbers (the first will be one of the two you've just compared) and **repeat step 1**. Keep going through the list until you get to the last two numbers. This set of comparisons is called a pass.

3) When you've finished the first pass, go back to the beginning of the list and **start again**. You won't have to compare the **last pair** of numbers, as the last number is now in place. Each pass has **one less comparison** than the one before it. When there are **no swaps** in a pass, the list is in **order**.

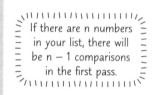
If there are n numbers in your list, there will be n – 1 comparisons in the first pass.

Stop when there are **No More Swaps**

It's called the bubble sort because the highest numbers **rise** to the end of the list like **bubbles** (apparently). It'll all be a lot easier once you've been through an example...

Example: Use a bubble sort to write the numbers 14, 10, 6, 15, 9, 21, 17 in ascending order.

First pass:

<u>14, 10</u>, 6, 15, 9, 21, 17	14 and 10 compared and swapped
10, <u>14, 6</u>, 15, 9, 21, 17	14 and 6 compared and swapped
10, 6, <u>14, 15</u>, 9, 21, 17	14 and 15 compared — no swap
10, 6, 14, <u>15, 9</u>, 21, 17	15 and 9 compared and swapped
10, 6, 14, 9, <u>15, 21</u>, 17	15 and 21 compared — no swap
10, 6, 14, 9, 15, <u>21, 17</u>	21 and 17 compared and swapped
10, 6, 14, 9, 15, 17, 21	**End of first pass.**

At the end of the first pass, the highest number has moved to the end of the list.

At the end of the second pass the list is: 6, 10, 9, 14, 15, 17, 21.

At the end of the third pass the list is: 6, 9, 10, 14, 15, 17, 21.

This list is in order, but the algorithm isn't complete... it needs to carry out a final pass to check there are <u>no swaps</u>...

On the fourth pass there are no swaps, so the numbers are in **ascending order**.

You might have to make **Lots** of **Passes** and **Comparisons**

1) If there are *n* numbers in the list, the **maximum** number of **passes** you might have to make is *n*. On each pass, you'd only get **one** number in the **right place**.

2) On the **first** pass, you have to make $n - 1$ comparisons, with a **maximum** of $n - 1$ swaps. On the **second** pass, you'll have to make $n - 2$ comparisons, as one number is in place from the first pass. On the **third** pass, there'll be $n - 3$ comparisons etc.

- The bubble sort algorithm has a **maximum** of $(n - 1) + (n - 2) + (n - 3) + ... + 1$ comparisons.
- This sum can be found using the formula for the **first *k* whole numbers**, $S_k = \frac{1}{2}k(k + 1)$.
- Use $k = n - 1$ in the formula to get $\frac{1}{2}(n - 1)n$ or $\frac{1}{2}n^2 - \frac{1}{2}n$.
- The highest power is 2, so the bubble sort is of **quadratic order** ($O(n^2)$).

3) If you have to make the **maximum** number of **swaps**, it means that the original list was in **reverse order**.

4) You can also use the algorithm to put numbers in **descending** order — on each comparison, just put the **higher** number **first** instead.

Sorting Algorithms

A *Quick Sort* breaks the list into *Smaller Lists*

The **quick sort algorithm** works by choosing a **pivot** (see below) which **breaks down** the list into two **smaller lists**, which are then broken down in the **same way** until the numbers are in order.

The Quick Sort

1) Choose a **pivot**. Move any numbers that are **less** than the pivot to a new list on the left of it and the numbers that are **greater** to a new list on the **right**. Don't change the **order** of the numbers though.

2) **Repeat step 1)** for each of the smaller lists you've just made. You'll need **new pivots** for the new lists.

3) Continue until each of the smaller lists contain only **one item**.

The pivot should be the '**middle**' item in the list. In a list of n items:

- If n is **odd**, the middle item is the $\frac{1}{2}(n + 1)$th item. For $n = 7$, the pivot is the $\frac{1}{2}(7 + 1) = $ 4th item in the list.

- If n is **even**, the middle item is the $\frac{1}{2}(n + 2)$th item. For $n = 8$, the pivot is the $\frac{1}{2}(8 + 2) = $ 5th item in the list.

Example: Sort the numbers 54, 36, 29, 45, 56, 39 into ascending order using a quick sort.

There are **6 items** in the list, which means the **pivot** is the $\frac{1}{2}(6 + 2) = $ **4th item** in the list. So the pivot is **45**.

Now make new lists by moving numbers < 45 to the **left**, and numbers > 45 to the **right**. Don't reorder the numbers, just write them in the order they appear in the original list. **Circle** 45 to show it's in the correct place.

These are all the numbers < 45 (in the same order as in the original list).   36, 29, 39, (45) 54, 56   These are all the numbers > 45 (in the same order as in the original list).
$\underbrace{\qquad}_{l_1}$ $\underbrace{\qquad}_{l_2}$

The list has been divided into smaller lists, l_1 and l_2. There are 3 items in l_1, so the pivot is the 2nd item (29). There are only 2 items in l_2, so the pivot is the 2nd item (56). Rearranging around the new pivots gives:

(29) 36, 39, (45) 54, (56)   The pivots are in the right place now.
$\underbrace{\qquad}_{l_3}$ $\underbrace{\quad}_{l_4}$

The list l_4 only has one item in it, so 54 is in the correct place.
There are now 2 items in l_3, so the pivot is the 2nd item (39). 36 is already on the correct side of 39:

(29) 36, (39) (45) (54) (56)
$\underbrace{\;}_{l_5}$

The list l_5 only has one item in it, so 36 is in the correct place. The list is now sorted.

Practice Questions

Q1 Use a bubble sort to sort 72, 57, 64, 54, 68, 71 in ascending order. How many passes do you need to make?

Q2 What is the maximum number of comparisons you'd need to make if you use a bubble sort on 10 numbers?

Q3 Sort the numbers 0.8, 1.2, 0.7, 0.5, 0.4, 1.0, 0.1 into ascending order using a quick sort.

Exam Questions

Q1 a) Determine the order of a quick sort. [4 marks]

    b) Use a quick sort to arrange the numbers below into ascending order. Show the pivots you use at each step.
      77 83 96 105 78 89 112 80 98 94 [5 marks]

Q2 A list of six numbers is to be sorted into ascending order using a bubble sort.

    a) Which number(s) will definitely be in the correct position after the first pass? [1 mark]

    b) Write down the maximum number of passes and the maximum number of swaps needed to sort a list of six numbers into ascending order. [2 marks]

My dog's out of sorts — I think algorithm to the vets...

You might be thinking it'd be easier to sort numbers just by looking, but the point of these algorithms is that you could get a computer to do it all for you. Computers could manage millions of numbers, but you'll have to sort just a few.

Bin Packing Algorithms

Packing to go on holiday is a pain. You've got so much to fit in your suitcase, and there's always the risk of the shampoo leaking... luckily, there's some packing algorithms to help (OK, maybe not holiday packing, but you could adapt them?).

Algorithms can be used to Pack Items into Bins

1) In **bin packing problems**, you have a set of items that you need to fit into the **minimum** number of **bins**.
2) One of the most common examples is fitting **boxes** of **different heights** on top of each other into **bins** of a **given height**. You need to arrange the boxes to use the **fewest bins possible**.
3) Other examples include things like cutting specified **lengths of wood** from **planks** of a fixed length (you want to **minimise** the number of planks used), or loading items of different **weights** into **lorries** that have a **maximum weight capacity** (again, you want to use the **smallest** number of lorries possible).
4) An **optimal solution** is one that uses the **least possible number of bins**. There's often more than one possible optimal solution.

Because the optimal solution has the least possible no. of bins, it also has the least wasted space.

The First-Fit algorithm puts the items in the First Bin they'll go in

The first-fit algorithm is **quick** and **easy**, but it probably **won't** give you an **optimal solution**. Here's how it works:

1) Take the **first item** in the list and put it in the **first bin**.
2) Move on to the next item, and put it in the **first bin** it'll **fit** into.
   It might fit in the first bin, or you might have to move on to **another bin**.
3) Repeat step 2) until **all** the items are in a bin. For each item, try the **first bin** before you move on to the next.

> **Example:** Seven gifts need to be packed into paper bags, which can hold no more than 150 g.
> Use the first-fit algorithm to sort the gifts below into bags, saying
> how many bags are needed and how much space is wasted.
>
> A: 90 g   B: 75 g   C: 30 g   D: 65 g   E: 120 g   F: 45 g   G: 60 g
>
> Bag 1:   A: 90 g, C: 30 g   space left: ~~60 g~~ 30 g
> Bag 2:   B: 75 g, D: 65 g   space left: ~~75 g~~ 10 g
> Bag 3:   E: 120 g   space left: 30 g
> Bag 4:   F: 45 g, G: 60 g   space left: ~~105 g~~ 45 g
>
> *B won't fit in bag 1, as there's only 60 g left after A, so it goes in bag 2. However, C < 60 g, so it fits in bag 1.*
>
> So the gifts can fit into **4 bags**, with 30 + 10 + 30 + 45 = **115 g wasted**.

The First-Fit Decreasing algorithm needs the items in Descending Order

1) The **first-fit decreasing** algorithm is **similar** to the **first-fit** algorithm but you need items in **descending order** first.
2) You can do this by using one of the **sorting algorithms** on pages 182-183.
3) Once you've got your ordered list, you just carry out the **first-fit algorithm** from above.
4) The first-fit decreasing algorithm usually gives you a **better solution** than the first-fit algorithm, but it still might **not** be **optimal**.

> **Example:** Ribbon comes in rolls of length 5 m. For the lengths of ribbon given below, use the first-fit decreasing algorithm to work out how the lengths can be cut from the rolls. You should also say how many rolls are needed and how much ribbon is wasted. All lengths are in metres.
>
> 2.5   1.9   2.9   3.1   2.7   2.2   1.8   2.0
>
> First, use a **sorting algorithm** to put the lengths **in order**. The new list is:
>
> 3.1   2.9   2.7   2.5   2.2   2.0   1.9   1.8
>
> Now use the **first-fit algorithm** to sort the lengths into rolls:
>
> Roll 1:   3.1, 1.9   length left: ~~1.9~~ 0
> Roll 2:   2.9, 2.0   length left: ~~2.1~~ 0.1
> Roll 3:   2.7, 2.2   length left: ~~2.3~~ 0.1
> Roll 4:   2.5, 1.8   length left: ~~2.5~~ 0.7
>
> *If you solved this problem using the first-fit algorithm, you'd use 5 rolls and waste 5.9 m of ribbon.*
>
> The ribbon can be cut from **4 rolls**, with 0 + 0.1 + 0.1 + 0.7 = **0.9 m wasted**.

Bin Packing Algorithms

The **Full-Bin** packing algorithm usually wastes the **Least Space**

The **full-bin packing algorithm** needs a bit more **work** than the other two, but it's more likely to produce an **optimal solution**. However, it can be quite **hard** to do if you've got a lot of items.

1) In the full-bin algorithm, first you need to **look** at the items and find items that will **add up** to give a **full bin**. You just have to do this **by eye**, so it can get a bit tricky.

2) Once you've **filled** as many bins as you can, you use the **first-fit algorithm** (see previous page) to put the rest of the items in the **remaining spaces** in the bins.

> **Example:** Boxes of the same length and width need to be packed in bins of height 2.5 m. Use the full-bin packing algorithm to pack the boxes, say how many bins are used and how much space is wasted. The heights of the boxes (in metres) are:
>
> 0.7   1.1   1.2   2.3   0.8   1.4   0.9   1.0   2.5
>
> Just by looking at the heights, you can see that 0.7 + 0.8 + 1.0 = 2.5, 1.1 + 1.4 = 2.5 and 2.5 = 2.5, so you can fill **3 bins** straight away. Then use the **first-fit algorithm** to pack the remaining boxes.
>
> | Bin 1: | 0.7, 0.8, 1.0 | space left: 0 | Bin 4: | 1.2, 0.9 | space left: ~~1.3~~ 0.4 |
> | Bin 2: | 1.1, 1.4 | space left: 0 | Bin 5: | 2.3 | space left: 0.2 |
> | Bin 3: | 2.5 | space left: 0 | | | |
>
> So, the boxes can be packed into **5 bins**, with 0.4 + 0.2 = **0.6 m** wasted space.

The **Lower Bound** gives a **Minimum** for the **Number of Bins** you'll need

1) To work out the **lower bound**, you **add up** the heights / weights etc. of the items, and **divide** the total by the **capacity** of **one bin**.

2) Always **round up** your answer — if you get a lower bound of 2.25, you'd need a **minimum** of **3 bins** (you wouldn't fit the items in 2 bins).

3) A lower bound doesn't mean you can definitely fit the items into this number of bins — you'll need **at least** this, but possibly **more**. In other words, the optimal solution will **not necessarily** match the lower bound...

4) ... but if your solution **does match** the lower bound, you know it's definitely **optimal**. For the example above, the lower bound is 11.9 ÷ 2.5 = 4.76 = 5 bins. The solution is 5 bins, so it is an **optimal solution**.

Practice Question

Q1 Items of weights 5 kg, 11 kg, 8 kg, 9 kg, 12 kg, 7 kg need to be packed into boxes with a max. weight of 15 kg.
  a) Find a lower bound for the number of boxes needed.
  b) Pack the items into the boxes using the following algorithms. For each, say how many boxes are needed, how much space is wasted and if the solution is optimal (if you can):
     (i)   first-fit algorithm   (ii) first-fit decreasing algorithm   (iii) full-bin packing algorithm

Exam Question

Q1 A joiner has planks of wood that are 3 m long.
  He needs to cut pieces of wood in the following lengths: 1.2 m 2.3 m 0.6 m 0.8 m 1.5 m 1.0 m 0.9 m 2.5 m

  a) Use the first-fit bin packing algorithm to fit the lengths of wood onto the planks.
     State how many planks are needed and how much wood is wasted.   [3 marks]

  b) (i) Use the full-bin packing algorithm to fit the lengths of wood onto the planks.
         State how many planks are needed and how much wood is wasted.   [3 marks]

     (ii) Is this solution optimal? Explain your answer.   [3 marks]

Don't forget to pack your pyjamas...

So, 'first-fit' is the quickest algorithm but doesn't give the best solution, 'first-fit decreasing' needs a little more work but usually gives a better solution, and the 'full-bin' algorithm is the hardest but is more likely to give an optimal solution.

Graphs

You probably reckon you're an old pro at graphs. But the graphs coming up are rather different. For a start, there's not a scrap of squared paper in sight. Fret not — soon they'll be as familiar to you as a bar chart.

Graphs have Points Connected by Lines

Here's the definition of a graph:

> A **graph** is made up of **points** (called **vertices** or **nodes**) joined by **lines** (called **edges** or **arcs**).

The 'Edge de Triomphe' didn't sound as gallant.

1) Graphs can be used to **model** or **solve** real-life problems. For example:

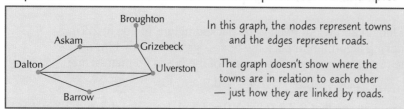

In this graph, the nodes represent towns and the edges represent roads.

The graph doesn't show where the towns are in relation to each other — just how they are linked by roads.

2) **Weighted graphs**, or **networks**, have a number associated with each edge (called the edge's **weight**). Weights often give you **lengths** — like in this network showing points in a nature reserve and the lengths of the footpaths joining them. They sometimes give you **costs**, or **times** too.

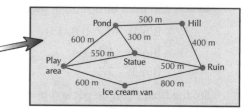

3) Sometimes edges have **directions**, e.g. to show one-way streets. If they do, they're called **directed edges** and the graph is a **digraph** or a **directed graph**.

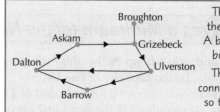

The edges on this digraph show the bus routes between the towns. A bus goes from Dalton to Askam, but not from Askam to Dalton.

There's no direction on the edge connecting Broughton and Grizebeck, so the buses run in both directions.

4) **Subgraphs** are just bits of another graph. If you take a graph, and rub a few bits out, then you're left with a subgraph. The posh definition is: "A **subgraph** of graph *G* is a graph where all the vertices and edges belong to *G*."

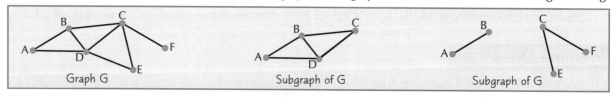

The Degree of a Vertex is the Number of Lines coming off it

1) Here's the formal definition:

> The **order**, **degree** or **valency** of a vertex is the number of edges connected to it.

Example: Calculate the degree of each vertex in the graph below.

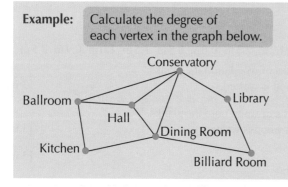

Vertex	Degree
Ballroom	3
Billiard Room	2
Conservatory	4
Dining Room	4
Hall	3
Kitchen	2
Library	2

Rules of Degrees

The sum of the degrees is always double the number of edges.
(It's a count of how many edge ends there are.)

So, the sum of degrees is always even.

Here, there are 10 edges and the sum of the degrees is 20 (2 × 10).

2) A vertex with an **odd degree** is called an **odd vertex**, and one with an **even degree** is — wait for it — **even**.

3) The **number** of **even** and **odd** vertices in a graph is important for **route inspection algorithms** (see p.198-201) — there are **two odd** vertices in this example (the Ballroom and Hall), and the rest are **even**.

Graphs

There's a lot of **Terminology** to learn

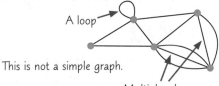

A loop

This is not a simple graph.

Multiple edges between vertices.

Simple Graphs have **No Loops** or **Multiple Edges**

Graphs can have **more than one edge** between a pair of vertices.
There can also be **loops** connecting vertices to themselves.

Graphs **without** any loops or multiple edges between vertices are called **simple graphs**.

Graphs can be **Connected** or not connected

Two vertices are **connected** if there's a path between them — the path can pass through **other vertices**.
A graph is **connected** if **all** its vertices are connected.

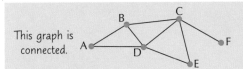

This graph is connected.

This graph is <u>not</u> connected — you can't get from some vertices to others, e.g. there's no path between B and C, or E and A.

A **connected graph** can be described as **Eulerian** or **semi-Eulerian** (or **neither**) — there's more on this on p.198.

In a **Complete** graph all the **Vertices** are **Directly Connected**

Each vertex in a **complete graph** is joined **directly** to every other vertex by exactly one edge.
The notation K_n is used for a complete graph with n nodes. The **number of edges** for the graph $K_n = \frac{1}{2}n(n-1)$.

This is K_4 — it has $\frac{1}{2} \times 4 \times 3 = 6$ edges.

This is K_5 — it has $\frac{1}{2} \times 5 \times 4 = 10$ edges.

Bipartite Graphs have **Two Sets** of Vertices

Bipartite graphs have **two sets** of vertices — an edge can **only** join a vertex in **one set** to a vertex in the **other set**.

The notation $K_{m,n}$ is used for a **complete** bipartite graph — each of the m vertices in the first set must connect to each of the n vertices in the other. The **number of edges** for the graph $K_{m,n} = m \times n$.

This is the complete bipartite graph $K_{3,4}$. Nodes A, B, C are in one set, and nodes 1, 2, 3, 4 are in the other.

Planar Graphs can be drawn so that no **Edges Cross** each other

The edges in a planar graph can only **meet another edge at a vertex** (i.e. none of their edges **cross**).
Be really careful if you're asked to say if a graph is **planar or not**:

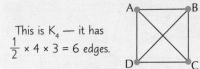

This doesn't look planar...

...but it can be redrawn like this: (There are still 4 vertices each connected to the other 3.)

...or like this.

The planarity algorithm (p.189) is one way of testing if a graph is planar.

Isomorphic Graphs are **Identical** graphs

A graph is **isomorphic** to another graph if the **vertices** and **edges** are all **connected** in exactly the **same way**:

Example: Explain why graphs G and H below are isomorphic.

Graph G   **Graph H**

Relabel the nodes in Graph G (call it Graph G'):

Graphs G' and H **only** have **edges** between vertices **1 and 2**, **2 and 3**, **3 and 4**, and **4 and 1**.

So the graphs are **isomorphic**.

Graph G'

Section 28 — D1: Algorithms and Graph Theory

Graphs

Walks, Paths and Cycles are types of Route in a Graph

① Walk

1) A walk is a **sequence of edges** that flow on, end to end.
2) You can go through vertices and along edges **more than once**.
3) On graph G on the right, **BCDBCE** is a walk, as is **ABDAB**.

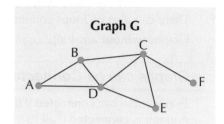

Graph G

② Path

1) A path is also a **sequence of edges** that flow on, end to end.
2) The only thing is, you **can't** go through a vertex more than once.
3) On graph G, possible paths include **ABDECF** or **CBAD**.
   DCECF **isn't** a path as you'd go through vertex C **twice**.

③ Cycle

1) A **cycle** (or **circuit**) is a **closed path**. The **end** vertex is the same as the **start** vertex.
2) On graph G, **ABDA** is a cycle. Other cycles are **ABCDA** and **CEDBC**.

> You still have to follow the rules for paths — you can't go through a vertex twice.

A Hamiltonian Cycle goes through each Vertex Once

1) A **Hamiltonian cycle** is a **cycle** which goes through **each vertex exactly once** — it **does not** have to use every **edge**.
2) Like all cycles, it brings you **back to the start vertex**.
3) Not all graphs contain Hamiltonian cycles — those that do are called **Hamiltonian graphs**.

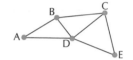

This is a Hamiltonian graph — ABCEDA is one example of a Hamiltonian cycle.

Practice Questions

Q1 Look at the graph on the right.
   a) Draw two subgraphs of the graph.
   b) Explain why this graph is: i) simple   ii) planar
   c) Describe a possible path and a possible cycle in the graph.
   d) List the degree of each vertex.
      Explain the link between the number of edges and the sum of the degrees.

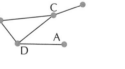

Q2 How many Hamiltonian cycles are there in the following complete graphs:
   a) K_3 b) K_4?
   Note: a Hamiltonian cycle is the same as another if you travel the same edges in the same direction.

So, for K_3, ABCA is the same Hamiltonian cycle as BCAB and CABC.

Exam Question

Q1 Look at Figure 1 below.

Figure 1

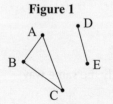

   a) State the number of edges that would need to be added to Figure 1 to make the graph connected.

   [1 mark]

   b) What is the sum of the orders of the vertices in Figure 1?

   [1 mark]

   c) Explain why it is impossible to add edges to Figure 1 so that all vertices have an odd order.

   [2 marks]

And your leg bone's connected to your foot bone...

Graphs are all over the place — the London Underground map is one. Memorising all the Tube stations won't help you for the exam, but all those lovely graph definitions will. You'll need them very, very soon, so learn them and then scribble them down from memory. Then check back to see if you've missed any.

The Planarity Algorithm

If you've ever thought: "Hmm, I wonder if there is an algorithm to test if a graph is planar," then you're in the right place.

The **Planarity Algorithm** tests if a graph is **Planar**

The **planarity algorithm** uses a Hamiltonian cycle to test whether or not a graph is **planar**:

(1) Find a Hamiltonian cycle:
It's important that the graph has a **Hamiltonian cycle** or you **can't use** the algorithm.

(2) Draw the Hamiltonian cycle as a polygon:
Space the vertices out, as you'll need room to draw the other arcs.

(3) Split the other arcs into two lists:
Draw the **remaining arcs** and split them into **two lists**, called 'inside' and 'outside' like so:

- Choose a starting arc to put it in the 'inside' list.
- If an arc crosses just 'inside' arcs, put them in the 'outside' list.
- If an arc crosses just 'outside' arcs, put them in the 'inside' list.

This step will become clear in the example below.

(4) Determine if the graph is planar:
If you **can** separate the arcs this way into two lists, then the **graph is planar**...
...but if an arc has to **cross** both an 'inside' and 'outside' arc, then the **graph is not planar**.

Example: Use the planarity algorithm to determine if graph *G* is planar.

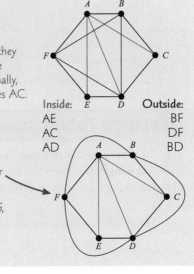

You could use any correct Hamiltonian cycle here.

1) Choose ABCDEFA as the Hamiltonian cycle.

2) Draw ABCDEFA as a polygon.

3) Start with AE as an inside arc. BF and DF are 'outside' arcs as they cross AE. Then, AC and AD are 'inside' arcs as they cross BF. Finally, BD is an 'outside' arc as it crosses AC.

4) The arcs are separated into two lists, so **graph G is planar**.

You can draw the 'outside' arcs outside of the polygon, to get a planar version of the original graph.

If CF was a connected arc in graph G, you'd get a graph that wasn't planar. It would have to cross 'inside' arcs, AD and AE, and 'outside' arc, BD.

Inside: Outside:
AE   BF
AC   DF
AD   BD

Practice Question

Q1 Use the planarity algorithm to determine whether the graphs on the right are planar.

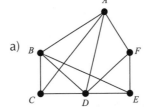

a)

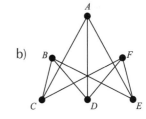

b)

Exam Question

Q1 Take AGFEBCDA as the Hamiltonian cycle to answer the following question.

Use the planarity algorithm to determine whether Figure 1 is planar.
You must show all of your working. [4 marks]

Figure 1

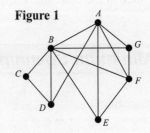

You can't spell planarity without P-A-R-T-Y...

Planar graphs are actually dead useful in the "real world" (*shudder*) — connecting subway stations or components on a circuit board is much easier and safer if you don't have to cross over any tracks or wires.

Spanning Trees and Kruskal's Algorithm

The stuff in the last section might seem like it was dreamed up by bored mathematicians to provide you with useless facts to learn. But this minimum spanning tree stuff is actually rather handy in the real world.

Trees are *Graphs* that have *No Cycles*

They also have to be **connected graphs** (see p.187). Both graphs here are connected — but **only** the first is a **tree**.

This is a tree — there are no cycles.

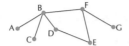

This one <u>isn't</u> a tree — there's a cycle (BDEFB.)

This is also a tree, and coincidentally, it has no cycles in it.

Spanning Trees are *Subgraphs* that include *All Vertices*

1) They also have to be a **tree** (obviously...).

2) Spanning trees include **all** the **vertices** of the graph — so if you're asked to draw a **spanning tree of a graph**, you can only delete **edges** from the original graph.

3) The number of **edges** in a spanning tree is always **one less** than the number of **vertices**.

4) Like most things in this section, a few diagrams speak a thousand words...

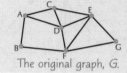

The original graph, G.

A spanning tree of G. There's no cycle, and it contains all the vertices from G.

Another spanning tree of G. There are plenty more that could be drawn too.

Distance Tables show the *Weights* between Vertices

1) To draw a **distance table** from a weighted digraph (p.186), go through each space in the table and write down the **weight** between the two vertices. You only include **direct links** — don't start adding weights together.

2) Be really careful with **directed edges**. A weight on a directed edge only goes in **one** cell of the table, as below.

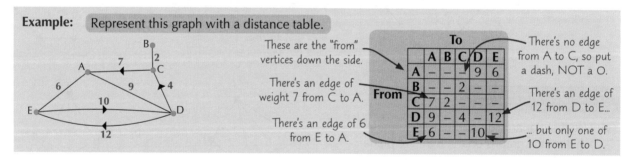

Example: Represent this graph with a distance table.

These are the "from" vertices down the side.

There's an edge of weight 7 from C to A.

There's an edge of 6 from E to A.

From

		To			
	A	B	C	D	E
A	–	–	–	9	6
B	–	–	2	–	–
C	7	2	–	–	–
D	9	–	4	–	12
E	6	–	–	10	–

There's no edge from A to C, so put a dash, NOT a 0.

There's an edge of 12 from D to E...

... but only one of 10 from E to D.

3) If you're asked to draw a **digraph** from a distance table, mark the **vertices**, then go through the table, adding **edges** and **weights** in. If a weight only appears **once** in the table, the edge must be directed, so add an arrow.

Distance tables may be written as a matrix and called distance matrices.

A *Minimum Spanning Tree* is the *Shortest* way to Connect All the Points

Remember — an arc is just another name for an edge.

A **minimum spanning tree** (MST) is a spanning tree where the total weight of the arcs is as **small as possible**.

Minimum spanning trees come in handy for cable or pipe-laying companies. If they need to connect several buildings in a town, say, they'd want to find the **cheapest path** — this may be the **shortest** route, or have the **easiest** ground to dig up.

An MST is also known as a minimum connector.

Spanning Trees and Kruskal's Algorithm

Kruskal's Algorithm Finds Minimum Spanning Trees

Being absolutely certain that you've got the minimum spanning tree is tricky, so using an algorithm helps.

Kruskal's Algorithm

1) List the arcs in **ascending order of weight**.
2) Pick the arc of **least weight** — this starts the tree.
3) Look at the **next arc** in your list.
   - if it forms a cycle, **don't** use it and go on to the next arc.
   - if it **doesn't** form a cycle, add it to the tree.
4) Repeat step 3 until you've joined **all** the vertices.

This is a 'greedy algorithm'. You make the choice that seems best at each stage, without worrying about later choices.

If there are n vertices in a network, there will always be $(n - 1)$ arcs in an MST.

Example: Use Kruskal's algorithm to find a minimum spanning tree for this graph.

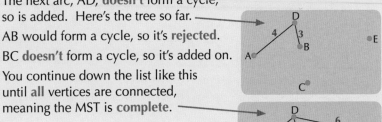

Arc	Weight	Used?
BD	3	✓
AD	4	✓
AB	4	✗
BC	5	✓
AC	5	✗
DE	6	✓
CE	8	✗

You could put AD and AB in either order, because they're the same weight.

1) The **shortest** arc is **BD**, so that starts the tree.
2) The next arc, AD, **doesn't** form a cycle, so is added. Here's the tree so far.
3) AB would form a cycle, so it's **rejected**.
4) BC **doesn't** form a cycle, so it's added on.
5) You continue down the list like this until **all** vertices are connected, meaning the MST is **complete**.

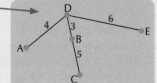

You'll often be asked to find the weight of your MST. This is easy — just add all the weights up. So the weight of this MST is 3 + 4 + 5 + 6 = 18.

There are often **a few different** MSTs that can be found for a network — and you might be asked to find them.

In the list above, <u>AB</u> could have been used instead of AD, or AC instead of BC. All the different combinations of these arcs give **three more MSTs**:

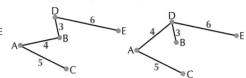

Practice Question

Q1 a) Draw the graph corresponding to this distance table.
   b) Find three spanning trees of this graph.

To

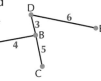

	A	B	C	D	E
A	–	1	2	–	–
B	–	–	–	4	–
C	2	–	–	–	–
D	–	4	–	–	6
E	–	–	7	–	–

From (to the left of the table)

Exam Question

Q1 a) Use Kruskal's algorithm to find and sketch a minimum spanning tree for the graph on the right. List the arcs in the order in which you added them to your tree. [4 marks]
   b) Two arcs are deleted from the graph. AD is now an arc in the minimum spanning tree for the graph. Name the arcs which have been deleted, justifying your answer. [2 marks]

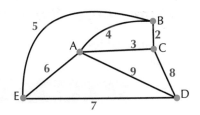

Don't follow Kruskal's example of doing the bare minimum...

Lots of shiny new maths here for you to learn. Spanning trees and distance tables will be making more appearances later on, so make sure you know what they are and how to find them. You've already seen loads of algorithms but you've still got plenty more to come, so make sure you understand Kruskal's before you move on to the others.

Prim's Algorithm

Prim's algorithm does exactly the same job as Kruskal's algorithm. I'd love to say you only need to learn the one you like best, but that'd be a fib. You've got to learn them both, of course.

Prim's Algorithm *Finds Minimum Spanning Trees Too*

Prim's Algorithm

1) Pick a vertex, **any vertex** — this **starts** the tree.
2) Choose the arc of **least weight** that'll join a vertex **in the tree** to one **not yet** in the tree.
3) Repeat step 2 until you've joined **all** the vertices.

> If there's more than one to pick from, just choose whichever you like.

Example: Use Prim's algorithm to find a minimum spanning tree for the network on the right.

> You don't have to check for cycles like you did with Kruskal's algorithm. Connecting to a vertex outside the tree will never make a cycle (one less thing to worry about).

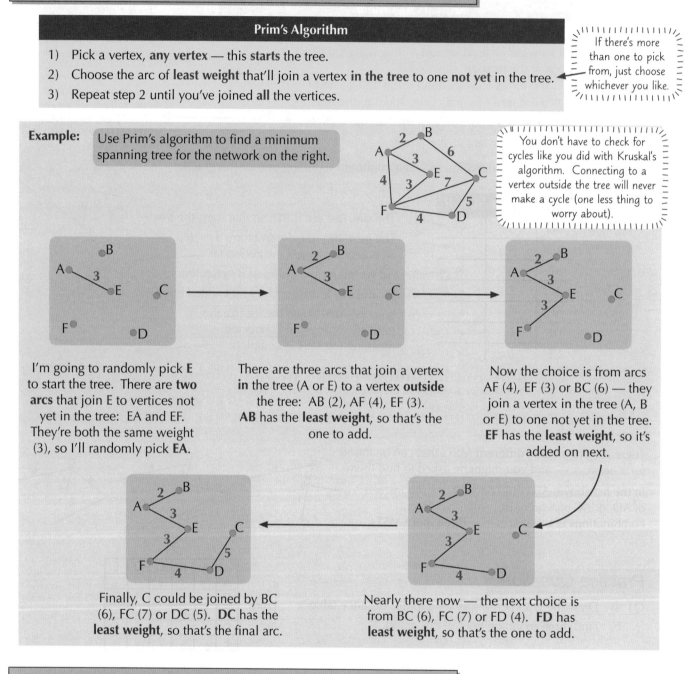

I'm going to randomly pick **E** to start the tree. There are **two arcs** that join E to vertices not yet in the tree: EA and EF. They're both the same weight (3), so I'll randomly pick **EA**.

There are three arcs that join a vertex **in** the tree (A or E) to a vertex **outside** the tree: AB (2), AF (4), EF (3). **AB** has the **least weight**, so that's the one to add.

Now the choice is from arcs AF (4), EF (3) or BC (6) — they join a vertex in the tree (A, B or E) to one not yet in the tree. **EF** has the **least weight**, so it's added on next.

Finally, C could be joined by BC (6), FC (7) or DC (5). **DC** has the **least weight**, so that's the final arc.

Nearly there now — the next choice is from BC (6), FC (7) or FD (4). **FD** has least weight, so that's the one to add.

Prim's Algorithm *Can be Used on* **Distance Tables**

Distance tables can be input onto a computer, which is why Prim's algorithm can be pretty useful. You're probably thinking 'I'm not a computer', but if you fool the examiner into thinking you are then they'll give you full marks...

Prim's Algorithm for Distance Tables

1) Pick **any vertex** to start the tree.
2) Cross out the **row** for the new vertex and circle the **column** for it.
3) Look for the **smallest weight** that's in **ANY circled column** AND **isn't** yet crossed out. Circle it. This is the **next arc** to add to the tree. The row it's in gives you the **new vertex**.
4) **Repeat** steps 2 and 3 until all the rows are crossed out.

Prim's Algorithm

Example: Use Prim's algorithm to find a minimum spanning tree for the graph represented by this distance table.

	A	B	C	D	E
A	–	4	–	3	3
B	4	–	5	–	6
C	–	5	–	8	7
D	3	–	8	–	2
E	3	6	7	2	–

Pick a **starting vertex** — A is as good as any. **Cross out** the A row and **circle** the A **column**.

The **smallest number** in the A column that isn't deleted is **3**. This actually appears twice, so circle **either** of them.
The first arc to add is AD (weight 3).

D is the new vertex, so **cross out** the D row and **circle** the D **column**.

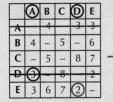

The **smallest number** in the A or D columns that isn't deleted is **2**, so circle it.
The second arc to add is DE (weight 2).

E is the new vertex, so **cross out** the E row and **circle** the E **column**.

The **smallest number** in the A, D or E columns that isn't deleted is **4**, so circle it.
The third arc to add is AB (weight 4).

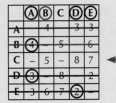

B is the new vertex, so **cross out** the B row and **circle** the B **column**.

The **smallest number** in the A, B, D or E columns that isn't deleted is **5**.
The fourth arc to add is BC (weight 5).

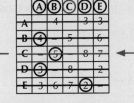

After crossing out the **final row**, you know you've **finished**.

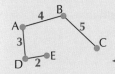

Here's the **MST** for the distance table.
Its total weight = 2 + 3 + 4 + 5 = 14

Practice Questions

Q1 The distance table on the right represents a weighted graph. Starting from vertex A, use Prim's algorithm to find a minimum spanning tree.

Q2 The graph on the right shows how long it takes, in minutes, to cycle between five destinations A, B, C, D and E. Use Prim's algorithm to sketch a minimum spanning tree for the graph.

	A	B	C	D	E
A	–	29	13	20	23
B	29	–	31	25	27
C	13	31	–	22	23
D	20	25	22	–	43
E	23	27	23	43	–

Exam Question

Q1 a) The graph on the right shows flight times in hours between seven worldwide destinations A–G. Use Prim's algorithm to find and sketch a minimum spanning tree for the graph. **[3 marks]**

b) Delete vertex D and all arcs connected to it, and convert the new graph to a distance table. Starting from vertex B, use Prim's algorithm for distance tables to find a minimum spanning tree for the new graph. List the arcs in the order you find them and give the weight of your spanning tree. **[5 marks]**

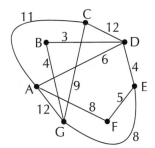

Prim's algorithm probably won't end up using Noah's arc...

Examiners love asking questions comparing Kruskal's and Prim's algorithms, so remember: They both find minimum spanning trees, and they both find the same arcs in the end, but they might find them in a DIFFERENT order.

Dijkstra's Algorithm

This is another of those algorithms that look really, really complicated. But when you've learnt the steps, you can string them together pretty rapidly. This one does a different job from the last two, so don't just skim the first bit.

Dijkstra's Algorithm Finds the Shortest Path between one pair of Vertices

If you're driving between **two cities** with a complicated road network between them, it's good to be able to work out which route is **quickest** (just like satnavs do).

Dijkstra's Algorithm

1) Give the **Start vertex** the **final value '0'.** ◄——— *Once you've given a vertex a final label, you can't change it.*

2) Find all the vertices without final values that are **directly connected** to the vertex you've just given a final value to. Give each of these vertices a **working value**.

> Working value = Final value at previous vertex + weight of arc between previous vertex and this one.

If one of these vertices already has a working value, replace it **ONLY** if the new working value is **lower**.

3) Look at the **working values** of vertices that **don't** have a final value yet. Pick the **smallest** and make this the **final value** of that vertex. ◄——— *If two vertices have the same smallest working value, pick either.*

4) Now repeat steps 2 and 3 until the **End vertex** has a **final value** (this is the shortest path length).

5) Trace the route **backwards** (from the End vertex to the Start vertex). An arc is on the path if:

> Weight of arc = Difference in final values of the arc's vertices

Example: Use Dijkstra's algorithm to find the shortest route between A and G.

In the exam, you'll be given a version of the graph with **boxes** like this to complete. Here's what goes in each box:

Vertex	Order of labelling	Final value
Working values		

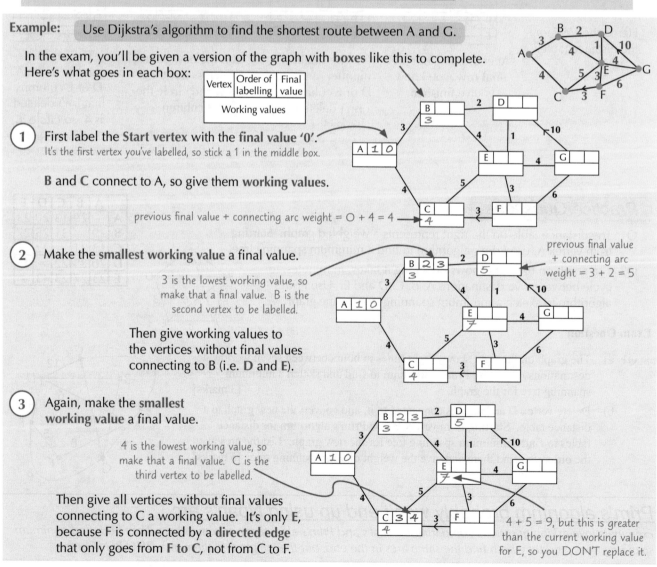

1 First label the **Start vertex** with the **final value '0'.** It's the first vertex you've labelled, so stick a 1 in the middle box.

B and **C** connect to A, so give them **working values**.

previous final value + connecting arc weight = 0 + 4 = 4

2 Make the **smallest working value** a final value.

3 is the lowest working value, so make that a final value. B is the second vertex to be labelled.

previous final value + connecting arc weight = 3 + 2 = 5

Then give working values to the vertices without final values connecting to B (i.e. **D** and **E**).

3 Again, make the **smallest working value** a final value.

4 is the lowest working value, so make that a final value. C is the third vertex to be labelled.

Then give all vertices without final values connecting to C a working value. It's only **E**, because F is connected by a **directed edge** that only goes from **F to C**, not from C to F.

4 + 5 = 9, but this is greater than the current working value for E, so you DON'T replace it.

Section 29 — D1: Algorithms on Graphs

Dijkstra's Algorithm

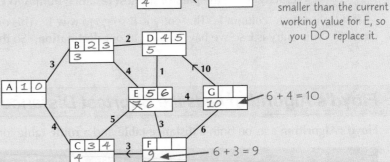

4 You're probably getting the idea now. Make the smallest working value a **final value**. In this case it's **5** (making D the **4th** vertex to be labelled).

Give all vertices without final values connecting to D a working value. It's only **E** in this case. (G is connected by a **directed edge** running in the opposite direction. And of course B **already** has a final value.)

5 + 1 = 6 (you're coming from vertex D this time). This is smaller than the current working value for E, so you DO replace it.

5 E has the **smallest** (in fact, the only) **working value** (6), so make that its **final value**.

Give the vertices connecting to E (F and G) working values.

6 + 4 = 10

6 + 3 = 9

6 F has the **smallest working value** (9), so make that its final value.

9 + 6 = 15. This is greater than the current working value for G, so you leave it as 10.

G (the **End vertex**) is the only vertex left. Make its working value the **final value** — this is the length of the **shortest route**.

7 Now it's time to figure out the **route**. An arc's on the path if:

> Weight of arc = Difference in final values of arc's vertices

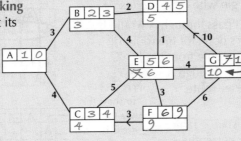

Working backwards from G (the **End vertex**):

- The arc **EG** is on the path, because the **difference** in the final values of E and G is **4**, which is the length of the arc **EG**.
- The arc **DE** is on the path, because the **difference** in the final values of D and E is **1**, which is the length of the arc **DE**.
- And so on, all the way back to **A**.

So the **shortest route** from A to G is **ABDEG**.

Practice Question

Q1 a) Use Dijkstra's algorithm to find the shortest path between E and A on this graph.

b) What is the weight of this path?

c) A new arc is added from G to A, with an integer weight. The shortest route from E to A now goes through G. What is the maximum weight of this arc?

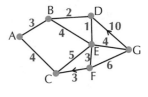

Exam Question

Q1 The following graph represents roads between eight points of interest A-H in a city. The number on each arc is the time it takes, in minutes, to walk along each road.

a) Use Dijkstra's algorithm to find the quickest route between A and H. [5 marks]

b) A bridge is built from E to H. How long must the bridge take to walk if the quickest route that uses the bridge is as long as the route you found in part a)? [2 marks]

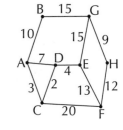

Who needs a Satnav when you've got Dijkstra's algorithm...

Some questions in the exam may have more than one shortest route. If so, make sure you give all of them.

Floyd's Algorithm

If getting from A to B wasn't fun enough, how does getting from everywhere to everywhere else sound...

Route Tables *show the path you've taken*

Route tables are also known as route matrices.

In a **route table**, the 'from' vertices go down the side and the 'to' vertices go along the top, just like a distance table.
They're used in Floyd's algorithm to represent a path from one vertex to another.
Each **cell** tells you the next **vertex** in the **path** and a path **finishes** when you get to the **final** vertex.

Example: The route table shows the shortest routes between 5 vertices. Give the path of shortest distance from A to E.

Start from **row A, column E**. This entry is **B** so go to **row B**. This entry is **D** so go to **row D**. This entry is **E** so we have arrived at our **destination**. So the path is **ABDE**.

To

From

	A	B	C	D	E
A	A	B	B	B	B
B	A	B	C	D	D
C	D	D	C	D	E
D	B	B	C	D	E
E	A	B	C	D	E

Floyd's Algorithm *finds the* Shortest Distance *between* Every *pair of* Vertices

Floyd's Algorithm acts on both a **distance table** and a **route table** for each graph.

Floyd's Algorithm

Steps 2 and 3 together form one iteration.

1) Pick the **vertex** in the **top row** to begin with (here, vertex **A**).
2) Check if any of the **routes** that **don't** pass through A would be **shorter** if they **did**. Here's how that's done for the route **IJ**:
   - Length of current shortest known route from I to J = **X**.
   - Length of route from I to J passing through A = $Y_1 + Y_2$.
   - If $Y_1 + Y_2 < X$, then this is a **shorter route**.
3) For each shorter route found:
   - Replace X with $Y_1 + Y_2$ in the **distance table**.
   - In the **route table**, put the letter currently in **row I, column A** into **row I, column J**.
4) Repeat steps 2-3 for the vertex in the **next row**.

To show the route from I to J needs to head towards A by the shortest known route.

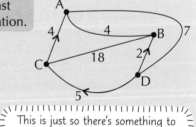

A lot to take in there. I think it's time for a great big example...

Example: For the following graph, use Floyd's algorithm to find a table of least distances. Show both the distance and route tables after each iteration.

In the exam, they'll give you the **initial distance** and **route tables**.
For this example, they look like this:

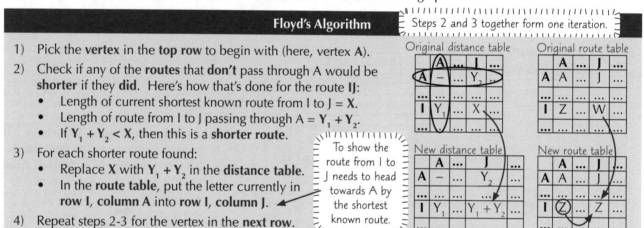

	A	B	C	D
A	–	4	∞	7
B	4	–	18	∞
C	4	18	–	∞
D	7	2	5	–

For Floyd's algorithm, ∞ is used where there is no direct route.

	A	B	C	D
A	A	B	C	D
B	A	B	C	D
C	A	B	C	D
D	A	B	C	D

Even when there's no route between two vertices, the route table is always completely filled in.

This is just so there's something to work with — Floyd's algorithm finds and corrects any incorrect entries.

- For the first **iteration** start with **vertex A**, and see if any routes would be **shorter** if they went through **A**:
  - B-C = 18, B-A-C = BA + AC = 4 + ∞ = ∞ ⇒ B-A-C > B-C ✗ not shorter, so leave both tables how they are.
  - B-D = ∞, B-A-D = BA + AD = 4 + 7 = 11 ⇒ B-A-D < B-D ✓ shorter, so replace ∞ with 11 in the distance table and put an A in the corresponding position in the route table.
  - C-B = 18, C-A-B = 4 + 4 = 8 ⇒ C-A-B < C-B ✓
  - C-D = ∞, C-A-D = 4 + 7 = 11 ⇒ C-A-D < C-D ✓
  - D-B = 2, D-A-B = 7 + 4 = 11 ⇒ D-A-B > D-B ✗
  - D-C = 5, D-A-C = 7 + ∞ = ∞ ⇒ D-A-C > D-C ✗

Make sure the examiner can clearly see where you've made your changes — square brackets should do the trick.

Every **route** that doesn't pass through **A** has been checked, so the **first** iteration is done. These two tables will be the ones that are marked in the exam.

	A	B	C	D
A	–	4	∞	7
B	4	–	18	[11]
C	4	[8]	–	[11]
D	7	2	5	–

	A	B	C	D
A	A	B	C	D
B	[A]	B	C	[A]
C	[A]	[A]	C	[A]
D	A	B	C	D

Floyd's Algorithm

- For the second **iteration**, see if any routes would be **shorter** if they went through **B**:

  - A-C = ∞, A-B-C = 4 + 18 = 22 ⇒ A-B-C < A-C ✓
  - A-D = 7, A-B-D = 4 + 11 = 15 ⇒ A-B-D > A-D ✗
  - C-A = 4, C-B-A = 8 + 4 = 12 ⇒ C-B-A > C-A ✗
  - C-D = 11, C-B-D = 8 + 11 = 19 ⇒ C-B-D > C-D ✗
  - D-A = 7, D-B-A = 2 + 4 = 6 ⇒ D-B-A < D-A ✓
  - D-C = 5, D-B-C = 2 + 18 = 20 ⇒ D-B-C > D-B ✗

  For this iteration, get the shortest known distances between points from the table at the bottom of the previous page (and don't worry that some routes aren't direct).

  So the tables after the **second** iteration will look like this.

	A	B	C	D
A	–	4	[22]	7
B	4	–	18	11
C	4	8	–	11
D	[6]	2	5	–

	A	B	C	D
A	A	Ⓑ	[B]	D
B	A	B	C	A
C	A	A	C	A
D	[B]	Ⓑ	C	D

- For the third **iteration**, see if any routes would be **shorter** if they went through **C**:

  - A-B = 4, A-C-B = 22 + 8 = 30 ⇒ A-C-B > A-B ✗
  - A-D = 7, A-C-D = 22 + 11 = 33 ⇒ A-C-D > A-D ✗
  - B-A = 4, B-C-A = 18 + 4 = 22 ⇒ B-C-A > B-A ✗
  - B-D = 11, B-C-D = 18 + 11 = 29 ⇒ B-C-D > B-D ✗
  - D-A = 6, D-C-A = 5 + 4 = 9 ⇒ D-C-A > D-A ✗
  - D-B = 2, D-C-B = 5 + 8 = 13 ⇒ D-C-B > D-B ✗

  So the tables after the **third** iteration will look like this.

	A	B	C	D
A	–	4	22	7
B	4	–	18	11
C	4	8	–	11
D	6	2	5	–

	A	B	C	D
A	A	B	B	D
B	A	B	C	A
C	A	A	C	A
D	B	B	C	D

- For the fourth **iteration**, see if any routes would be shorter if they went through **D**:

  - A-B = 4, A-D-B = 7 + 2 = 9 ⇒ A-D-B > A-B ✗
  - A-C = 22, A-D-C = 7 + 5 = 12 ⇒ A-D-C < A-C ✓
  - B-A = 4, B-D-A = 11 + 6 = 17 ⇒ B-D-A > B-A ✗
  - B-C = 18, B-D-C = 11 + 5 = 16 ⇒ B-D-C < B-C ✓
  - C-A = 4, C-D-A = 11 + 6 = 17 ⇒ C-D-A > C-A ✗
  - C-B = 8, C-D-B = 11 + 2 = 13 ⇒ C-D-B > C-B ✗

  So the tables after the **fourth** iteration will look like this.

	A	B	C	D
A	–	4	[12]	7
B	4	–	[16]	11
C	4	8	–	11
D	6	2	5	–

	A	B	C	D
A	A	B	[D]	Ⓓ
B	A	B	[A]	Ⓐ
C	A	A	C	A
D	B	B	C	D

Since there's been an **iteration** for **each vertex**, the **algorithm is finished** and you can see the **shortest path** between **every** pair of vertices using the **route table** and how **long** each of them is using the **distance table**.

For example, the **shortest route** from **A** to **D** is direct and has a distance of **7**.
The shortest route from **B** to **C** is **BADC** and has a distance of **16**.

Practice Questions

Q1 The route table on the right shows the shortest routes between 5 vertices. ABDE is an indirect quickest route from A to E. List the other 6 quickest routes that are indirect.

	A	B	C	D	E
A	A	B	B	B	B
B	A	B	C	D	D
C	D	D	C	D	E
D	B	B	C	D	E
E	A	B	C	D	E

Q2 Use Floyd's algorithm to find the table of least distances for the following distance table. Write down the corresponding route table.

	A	B	C
A	–	2	4
B	3	–	8
C	7	3	–

Exam Question

Q1
a) Draw a distance table for the graph on the right. [2 marks]

b) Use Floyd's algorithm for the graph to perform two iterations on the distance table you found in part a).
Show both the distance and route tables after each iteration. [6 marks]

c) State the shortest route from A to D found by the algorithm so far. [2 marks]

d) Determine the order of Floyd's algorithm. [3 marks]

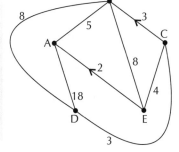

All these algorithms — I feel like a computer...

You need to know the similarities and differences between Floyd's and Dijkstra's algorithms. They both find the shortest distance between two vertices, but Dijkstra's algorithm finds the shortest distances from one vertex to all the others, whereas Floyd's algorithm finds the shortest distance between every pair of vertices.

Route Inspection Problems

The route inspection problem is also called the Chinese postman problem. (It's named after a Chinese guy called Kwan Mei-Ko who worked on it in the 1960s. He wasn't a postman though — he was a mathematician.)

The **Route Inspection Algorithm** finds the **Shortest Path** covering **All Edges**

1) Route inspection problems ask you to find the **shortest route** through a connected network that goes along **each edge**, before returning (usually) to the **starting point**.

2) It's the route that, say, a railway engineer would take if she had to **inspect** all the tracks.

3) In **postman** terms, the postman wants to find the **shortest route** that allows him to deliver letters to **every street** in a city, and brings him back to his **starting point** for a cup of tea.

4) And you'll never guess what. There are **algorithms** for solving these types of problems.

5) The first step is always to consider whether the graph is **Eulerian**, **semi-Eulerian**, or **neither**. Here's what that means...

A pre-1960s postman still manages to raise a smile, despite walking further than he has to each day.

Connected graphs can be **Eulerian**, **Semi-Eulerian** or **Neither**

| If **all** the vertices in a **connected** graph have an **even degree**, the graph is **Eulerian**. |

The degree, order or valency of a vertex is the number of edges connected to it (see page 186).

1) These three graphs are all **Eulerian**. Every vertex is **even**.

The numbers show the degrees.

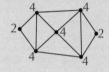

2) Eulerian graphs are **traversable**. This means it's **always possible** for you to start at **any point**, draw along each edge **exactly once** without taking your pen off the paper, and end up back at your **starting position**. Not every route works, but there'll definitely be some that do.

3) Or to look at it another way, if the graph represents **roads**, it's possible to walk down each of them **exactly once** before getting back to your **starting point**.

> **Example:** Find a route that traverses the graph on the right.
>
> The graph is Eulerian. So you can start at any point.
> A possible route is: AGDBCDEGBAFEA.
> Another route is: EDCBDGAFEABGE.

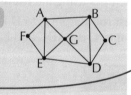

No matter which route you take, it'll always involve meeting the same number of vertices (13 in this case).

| If **exactly two vertices** have an **odd degree**, and the rest are even, the graph is **semi-Eulerian**. |

4) These three graphs are all **semi-Eulerian**. There are exactly **two odd** vertices.

5) Semi-Eulerian graphs are **semi-traversable**. This means it's possible to go along every edge on the graph **exactly once**, but **only** if you start at one odd vertex and end up at the **other** odd vertex.

> **Example:** Find a route that traverses the graph on the right.
>
> This graph is semi-Eulerian, so you have to start and end at the odd vertices (A and D).
> A possible route is: ABDCA around the square, then ABDCA around the circle, then across the diagonal to D.

6) If a graph has **more than two odd vertices** like the ones on the right, it is **non-Eulerian** and you **can't** traverse it.

7) There's **no route** that travels along each edge exactly once. You have to go along some of them **twice**.

8) **Disconnected** graphs are **always** non-Eulerian.

Route Inspection Problems

Eulerian Graphs are the most straightforward

Eulerian graphs can be traversed, so you can go down **each** edge **exactly once**. This means that the length of the inspection route is found by just **adding up** all the **edge weights**.

When finding an inspection route, you can go along some edges more than once if you have to.

Inspection routes sometimes start and finish at different points (see p.200). Exam questions will be clear about what you need to find.

> Length of inspection route in an Eulerian graph = Weight of network

> **Example:**   Find an inspection route for the network on the right.
>   Your route must start and finish at A. State the length of the route.
>
>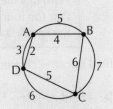
>
> The graph is Eulerian — the vertices all have even degrees (they're all 4).
> So the graph is traversable, and a possible route is: **ABCDABCDA** (once round the quadrilateral, then once round the circle).
> Length of the route = sum of weights = 4 + 6 + 5 + 2 + 5 + 7 + 6 + 3 = **38**

Walking on Both Sides of the street makes it an Eulerian Network

1) Sometimes, the usual route inspection problem is **changed** so that the person has to go down **each path twice**. Perhaps they'll be inspecting each pavement, or delivering leaflets to both sides of the streets.

2) This actually makes it **easier** to solve. It effectively **doubles** the edges at each vertex, making all the vertices effectively **even**. The network is now **Eulerian**, so you can **traverse** it, and the length of the inspection route will just be **double the weight** of the network.

> **Example:**   The graph represents the streets in an estate, and the numbers represent the lengths of each street in hundreds of metres. A feather-duster salesman decides to go down each street twice, once on each side. What is the length of his route?
>
>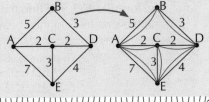
>
> Weight of original network = 26
> Weight of doubled network = 26 × 2 = 52
> Length of new route = **5200 metres**, or **5.2 km**.
>
> A was an odd vertex with 3 edges connected to it. It's now effectively even with 6 edges connected to it.

Semi-Eulerian Graphs are a bit trickier

In semi-Eulerian networks, you have to repeat **the shortest path** between the two **odd vertices** in an inspection route. You can think of it as adding arcs to make the network **Eulerian** so that it can be traversed.

This formula lets you find the length of the inspection route:

> Length of inspection route in a semi-Eulerian graph   =   Weight of network   +   Weight of the shortest path between the two odd vertices

> **Example**   Find an inspection route for the network on the right.
>   Your route must start and finish at B. State the length of the route.
>
>
>
> The graph is semi-Eulerian — the odd vertices are A and D.
> The shortest path between them is **AED**, of length **10** (5 + 5).
> So extra edges **AE** and **ED** are added.
> A possible path is **BCDEFABDEAEB**.
>
> This is worked out just by looking at the different possibilities, i.e. 'by inspection'.
>
> The weight of the network = 3 + 6 + 4 + 5 + 4 + 3 + 5 + 4 + 8 = **42**
> Length of inspection route = Weight of network + Weight of shortest path between odd vertices
>   = 42 + 10 = **52**

You only have to do this if you want to **start and end** at the **same vertex**. If you can pick and choose, just start at one odd vertex and end at the other. Then the length of the route will **equal** the network's weight.

Route Inspection Problems

Learn the **Route Inspection Algorithm** for **Non-Eulerian** networks

1) Non-Eulerian networks have **more than** two odd vertices.

2) But the exam board promises **not** to set a network question involving more than four odd vertices, and networks **never** have odd numbers of odd vertices. So you **only** have to worry about doing this stuff with **four odd vertices**.

> **Finding the shortest inspection route for a non-Eulerian network:**
> With this method you can start at **any vertex**, and you'll end up at the **same one**.
> **Pair** the four odd vertices in all the possible ways, find the pairing that gives you the **smallest total**, then **repeat the paths** between these pairs of vertices.

3) This'll all become clearer with an example.

Example: Find an inspection route for the network below.
Your route must start and finish at E. State the length of the route.

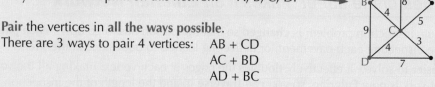

1) Pick out the vertices with **odd degrees**.
   They're marked in pink on this network — A, B, C, D. ⟶

2) **Pair** the vertices in **all the ways possible**.
   There are 3 ways to pair 4 vertices:
   $$AB + CD$$
   $$AC + BD$$
   $$AD + BC$$

3) Work out the **minimum total distance** for each pairing.

   E.g. for AB + CD, you find the smallest distance between AB, and the smallest distance between CD, and add them together:

   $$AB + CD = 5 + 4 = 9$$
   $$AC + BD = 8 + 8 = 16$$
   $$AD + BC = 12 + 4 = 16$$

   > There are loads of paths from A to D. By inspection, ACD is shortest (8 + 4 = 12), so use that one.

4) Pick the pairing with the **smallest total distance**.
   With a length of 9, it's **AB + CD** that has the smallest total.
   AB and CD will be the paths you repeat in the inspection route.

5) Add **extra edges** along each path in your pair.
   Add edges to repeat the path between **A and B** and to repeat the path between **C and D**.

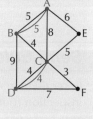

6) The graph is now **Eulerian** — so you can find an **inspection route** through it.
   A possible route starting and finishing at E is **EABDCABCFDCE**.

7) Add the **lengths of the new edges** to the **weight of the network** to get the length of the inspection route.
   The length of the route = weight of network + length of extra edges = 51 + 9 = **60**

   > Alternatively, you could just add up all the edges on your path.

   > Weight of network = 5 + 6 + 8 + 4 + 5 + 9 + 4 + 7 + 3 = 51

Starting and Finishing at **Different Odd Vertices** Always **Shortens** the Route

In a network with **four odd vertices**, the shortest route which goes down each path at least once always involves **starting at one odd vertex** and **ending at a different odd vertex**.

> **Finding the shortest inspection route starting and ending at different points of your choice:**
> You **start at one odd vertex** and **end at another odd vertex**, so you only have to **repeat the path** between **one pair** of vertices. You want this path to be **as short as possible**.

Route Inspection Problems

Example: A postman wants to travel along each street in a housing estate. He can start his journey at any point, and end it at any point. The graph represents the streets in the estate, and the numbers represent the lengths of each street in hundreds of metres.

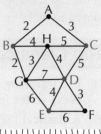

(a) State the vertices that the postman could start at to minimise his journey.

There are four odd vertices, and you're going to **start and end** at **two of them**, so this leaves one pair of odd vertices. You have to **repeat the path** between these two vertices, so make sure it's the **shortest possible**.

The odd vertices are **B, C, D, E**.

The distance between each possible pair is: BC = 5, BD = 8, BE = 8, CD = 5, CE = 9, DE = 4

The distance between **D and E** is shortest, at only 4. So that's the path you need to repeat. So you start at **either** vertex **B or C**, and end at the other.

> ⟋⟋⟋⟋⟋⟋⟋⟋⟋⟋⟋⟋⟋⟋⟋⟋⟋⟋⟋⟋⟋⟋⟋
> Work these out by inspection
> ⟍⟍⟍⟍⟍⟍⟍⟍⟍⟍⟍⟍⟍⟍⟍⟍⟍⟍⟍⟍⟍⟍⟍

(b) Find the length of his journey.

You just have to repeat the path between D and E.

So, total length of journey = weight of network + path between D and E
$$= 54 + 4 = 58$$

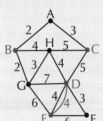

Weight of network = 54

Always **check the units** — the weights represent **hundreds of metres**, so the journey is actually **5800 metres** long, or **5.8 km**.

Practice Questions

Q1 A graph has 4 nodes with the following degrees: $2^x - 1$, 2^{x-1}, $2x - 1$ and $2(x - 1)$, where $x > 1$ is an integer. Is the graph Eulerian, semi-Eulerian or neither? Justify your answer.

Q2 Decide whether the following graphs are Eulerian or semi-Eulerian. Find an inspection route for each, and calculate how long this route is. Your routes must start and end at the vertex A.

a)
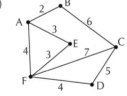

b)
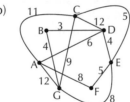

c)
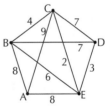

Exam Questions

Q1 The diagram below shows the distances between towns in miles. The combined length of all the roads is 106 miles. Jamie is inspecting the hedgerows along the roads. He needs to go along each road, starting and finishing at A.

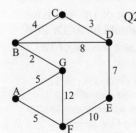

a) Find the length of Jamie's route if he wishes to minimise his distance travelled. **[6 marks]**

b) There are ice-cream shops at points C and E. If Jamie follows his optimal route, how many times will he pass an ice-cream shop? **[2 marks]**

c) Jamie decides it would be better if he went along each road twice. What is the length of his new optimal route? **[2 marks]**

Q2 The diagram shows the paths in a park, and the time taken to walk them in minutes. Alice the park keeper needs to walk down each path to check for storm-damaged trees.

a) If Alice can start and finish wherever she wants, find one route she could follow in order to check every path as quickly as possible. **[5 marks]**

b) Find the time taken for this route, given that the weight of the graph is 56 minutes. **[1 mark]**

c) A path is built from A to B and now Alice wants to walk down every path, starting and finishing at A. The walk now takes 79 minutes. Find how long it takes to walk down the path AB. **[6 marks]**

How's your network? — dunno, the fish just sort of get caught in it...

When faced with a route inspection problem, the first thing you should be asking yourself is how many vertices have odd degrees? Once you know that, you'll know which scenario you're in and then it's just a matter of computation.

Travelling Salesman Problems

In the last section, you met the Chinese postman problem. Well, this section's all about the travelling salesman problem (TSP). I'm not sure where the salesman is from exactly, but he sure does get around...

The **Classical TSP** is all about finding the **Shortest Hamiltonian Cycle**

1) In a **travelling salesman problem**, you need to visit **every vertex** in a network.

2) A **classical** TSP aims to find the **shortest** route that allows you to visit each vertex **exactly once** and end up back at your **starting point** — classical TSPs always involve **complete networks** (see page 187). The route you find will be a **Hamiltonian cycle** (see page 188).

Example:

Two possible Hamiltonian cycles starting from A are: AEDCBA (length 13) and ACBDEA (length 15).

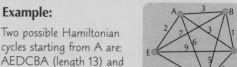

3) There isn't an algorithm guaranteed to find the **shortest** Hamiltonian cycle. And it's not practical to test each one, as the number of possible Hamiltonian cycles for complete graphs **rises dramatically** each time you add a vertex. ◄───

10 vertices means well over 100 000 Hamiltonian cycles — a lot for even a computer to consider.

4) Instead, you find a **lower and upper bound**, then a **reasonably good solution** between them. Luckily, there are **algorithms** for finding the lower and upper bound.

> **Tackling classical travelling salesman problems:**
>
> 1) Find the **lower bound** by using the **Lower Bound algorithm** (unfortunately, it doesn't have a more interesting name).
>
> 2) Find a Hamiltonian cycle using the **Nearest Neighbour algorithm** (see page 204) — this is an **upper bound**.
>
> 3) Then: **Lower bound ≤ minimum weight of Hamiltonian cycle ≤ upper bound**

Practical Travelling Salesman Problems **Aren't** quite so clear-cut

1) **Practical TSPs** involve someone wanting to find the **shortest route** by which they can visit **every vertex** of a network and end up **back at their starting point**. This route is known as a **tour**.

2) This **sounds** like it's exactly the same as the classical problem, but it can have **big differences**.

There **Isn't** Always a **Hamiltonian Cycle**

1) If a graph **isn't complete**, it might **not** have any Hamiltonian cycles. So to visit **all** the vertices, you have to **repeat** some of them.

2) You have to **add edges** to turn the graph into a **complete graph** which you can tackle using the **classical method**.

The shortest distance between A and B.

Example:

There's no Hamiltonian cycle in this graph, so a salesman visiting cities A-D would need to go through one of them twice (e.g. ACBDCA)....

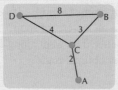

...so add edges to make a complete graph.

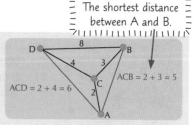

3) By inspection, the Hamiltonian cycle **ADCBA** is as **short** as you can get, with a weight of **18**. You have to **interpret** this in the **context** of the practical problem though — the actual route would be ACDCBCA, which **isn't** a **Hamiltonian cycle**. This only involves the **original edges**, but it still has a weight of 18.

There Might be **Shortcuts**

If the sum of the weights of **two sides** of a triangle in the network is **less** than the weight of the **third side**, then you end up with this type of situation:

In the classical TSP, the "triangle inequality" holds — this says that no side of a triangle can be longer than the combined length of the other two.

A Hamiltonian cycle here is ABCA (length 15). But it's actually quicker to visit all the vertices by repeating A — ABACA (length 14).

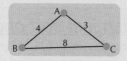

So when solving a practical TSP you have to replace weights with the lengths of any shortcuts.

Travelling Salesman Problems

The **Lower Bound Algorithm** involves finding a **Minimum Spanning Tree**

1) The **Lower Bound algorithm** calculates the **minimum possible weight** for a Hamiltonian cycle in the network.

2) There might **not** be a Hamiltonian cycle of this weight, but there **definitely won't be a shorter one**.

> **The Lower Bound Algorithm**
> 1) Choose a **vertex**, say A (you'll be told which one in an exam question).
>   Find the **two lowest weight edges** joined to vertex A. Call their weights x and y.
> 2) **Delete vertex A** and all the **edges** joined to it. This is your '**reduced network**'.
>   Now find a **minimum spanning tree** (minimum connector) for the rest of
>   the network and work out its **weight**. Call this **W**.
> 3) The **Lower Bound** = $W + x + y$

You do this with either Kruskal's or Prim's algorithm (see p191-192).

Example: By deleting vertex E, find a lower bound for the travelling salesman problem on this network.

1) The **two lowest weights** joined to E are AE (3) and DE (2).
   So $x = 3$ and $y = 2$.

2) **Delete** vertex E and the incident edges.
   Now find a **minimum spanning tree** for
   the reduced network. I'm going to use
   Prim's algorithm, because I like it best.

Edges joined to a vertex are said to be incident to it.

- Pick a vertex, **any vertex** — this **starts** the tree.
  I'll start with A, ta.
- Choose the arc of **least weight** that'll join a vertex **in the tree** to one
  not yet in the tree. Repeat this until you've joined **all** the vertices.
  That'll be AD (2), then AC (4), then BD (4).

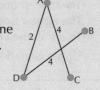

The **weight, W,** of the minimum spanning tree is $2 + 4 + 4 = $ **10**.

3) The **Lower Bound** = $W + x + y = 10 + 3 + 2 = $ **15**

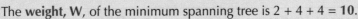

3) If you're asked to find a lower bound from a **distance matrix**, start by crossing out the **row** and **column** of
   the deleted vertex. Then just use **Prim's algorithm** to find the minimum spanning tree (as on page 193).

The **Largest** lower bound is the **Best**

1) Remember: **lower bound ≤ minimum weight of a Hamiltonian cycle ≤ upper bound**

2) A **small range** of possible weights for the optimum
   route is **more useful** than a large range — so you
   want your **lower bound** to be as **large** as possible.

3) To get the best lower bound, you should **repeat the
   algorithm** deleting a **different vertex** each time.
   Then you can pick the **largest** of the lower bounds.

*On the network above, you get these lower bounds
(check them — I'll send you a talking bunny if you find an error):
Deleting A: lower bound = 17, deleting B: lower bound = 18,
deleting C: lower bound = 18, deleting D: lower bound = 17.
So 18 is the best lower bound.*

The **Smallest** upper bound is the **Best**

> The Length of Any Known Route is an Upper Bound

1) If the first route you find has a length of **20**, this is your **initial upper bound**.
   You know it's a possible solution, but you don't know if it's the optimum one.

2) If you find another route that has a length of **22**, then the upper bound **stays** at 20 — it's still the best so far.

3) But if you find a route with a length of **17**, then this is an **improvement** so it becomes the new **upper bound**.

4) If you find a route which has the **same weight** as your **lower bound**, then the lower bound and
   the upper bound will be the **same**, so you know you've stumbled upon an **optimum route**.

5) Looking for routes by inspection is boring though, so you get to learn an algorithm instead...

Travelling Salesman Problems

The **Nearest Neighbour Algorithm** finds a Hamiltonian cycle

1) The **Nearest Neighbour algorithm** finds a reasonable solution to the travelling salesman problem — it **might not be the best** one though. In any case, it gives you an **upper bound** to try to beat.

2) With the Nearest Neighbour algorithm, you basically choose the **unvisited** vertex **closest** to you each time. Once you've been to **all** the vertices, you go along the edge that takes you **straight back** to the starting point.

> **The Nearest Neighbour Algorithm**
> 1) Choose a starting vertex (you'll usually be told which one to use in an exam question).
> 2) Choose the **nearest unused vertex**.
> 3) Repeat Step 2 until you've visited **each vertex**.
> 4) Finish the Hamiltonian cycle by **returning to the starting vertex**.

Example: The graph shows the durations in hours of train journeys between five Russian towns. Ben wants to visit all five towns, spending the minimum amount of time on trains. Apply the Nearest Neighbour algorithm, starting at vertex A, to find an upper bound for Ben's optimum route.

The graph is complete and shows the minimum durations between each town.

Applying the Nearest Neighbour algorithm **from A**:

The closest vertex to A is **D** (2 hours).
The closest unused vertex to D is **E** (2 hours).
The closest unused vertex to E is **C** (7 hours).
The closest unused vertex to C is **B** (7 hours).
That's all the vertices visited, so back to **A** (6 hours).

Upper bound = total duration of ADECBA = **24 hours.**

> The starting vertex for the Nearest Neighbour algorithm is just for applying the algorithm. The route doesn't have to start there. E.g. Ben could start this route at D and go DECBAD.

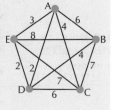

Starting from a **Different Vertex** sometimes gives a **Different Result**

1) Applying the Nearest Neighbour algorithm from **vertex C** on the above graph gives you the route **CADEBC**, which has a duration of **23 hours**.

2) This is **shorter** than the first one, so it becomes the new **upper bound**.

> Ideally, you'd try the algorithm from each vertex, then pick the smallest upper bound. But you won't be expected to do all that in an exam.

You can use the **Nearest Neighbour Algorithm** directly on a **Matrix**

1) Exam questions often give you the weights between vertices in **distance matrix form** (see p190).

2) Here's an example of how to apply the **Nearest Neighbour algorithm** to the matrix:

Example: Poppy is on holiday in New York and wants to see landmarks A, B, D, E and F. The time that it takes in minutes to get between each place on public transport is given in the matrix. Use the Nearest Neighbour algorithm, starting from her hotel at point C, to find an upper bound for Poppy's route.

From\To	A	B	C	D	E	F
A	—	5	35	5	10	15
B	10	—	10	20	20	35
C	45	15	—	10	30	25
D	20	10	5	—	5	10
E	40	25	15	35	—	40
F	35	20	25	30	20	—

(1) Find **vertex C** in the 'From' column, and look across to find the **lowest number** (the time taken to get to the closest vertex). It's **10 mins to D**, so D is the next vertex in the route.

You don't want to go to D again, so cross out this column.
You don't want to go to C again until the end, so cross out that column too so you don't get muddled.

From\To	A	B	C	D	E	F
A	—	5	35	5	10	15
B	10	—	10	20	20	35
C	45	15	—	10	30	25
D	20	10	5	—	5	10
E	40	25	15	35	—	40
F	35	20	25	30	20	—

(2) Now you're at **D**, so find D in the 'From' column, and look across to find the shortest time to an **unvisited vertex** (i.e. not C). This is **5 mins to E**, so E is the next vertex in the route. So far the route is CDE.

Now cross out column E so you don't accidentally revisit it.

From\To	A	B	C	D	E	F
A	—	5	35	5	10	15
B	10	—	10	20	20	35
C	45	15	—	10	30	25
D	20	10	5	—	5	10
E	40	25	15	35	—	40
F	35	20	25	30	20	—

(3) Keep going with this until **all** the vertices are visited, then return to the **start vertex** (C).

F is the last vertex visited — it's then 25 mins back to C.

The whole route is **CDEBAFC**, which takes 90 minutes. So 90 minutes is an upper bound.

Travelling Salesman Problems

Sometimes the Nearest Neighbour Algorithm is a **Bit Rubbish**

You Might End Up with **Really Long Distances** at the End

1) The Nearest Neighbour algorithm is a **greedy algorithm**, so you choose the best option **at any one moment**, rather than thinking about what's best in the long run.

2) This can mean you end up having to go along **really long** edges at the end. You'll often be able to see a better route just by looking.

Example: Use the Nearest Neighbour algorithm, starting from vertex A, to find an upper bound for the classical travelling salesman problem for the network below.

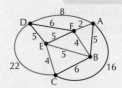

Applying the algorithm from A gives AFBECDA, which has a weight of 45.

But that route zigzags, then goes along the really long route from C to D. Using common sense, you'd go in the circular route ABCEDFA (or AFDECBA). This has a weight of only 28.

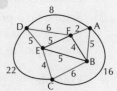

Or you might come to a **Grinding Halt**

Sometimes the algorithm **stalls** and you **don't** get a complete Hamiltonian cycle, even if the graph does contain one.

Often, the algorithm **will work** if you **change** the start vertex though.

For a **practical TSP**, this failure can be avoided altogether by **adding edges** to turn the graph into a **complete graph** (see page 202).

Example: Show that the Nearest Neighbour algorithm, starting from vertex A, fails on this network.

Applying the algorithm from A gives ABEF, but then it **stalls**. You can't get to C or D.

But starting from E, the algorithm works — you get the route EFABCDE.

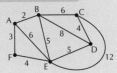

Practice Questions

Q1 Show that the Nearest Neighbour algorithm fails to provide an upper bound in the classical TSP when started at the vertex C for this graph:

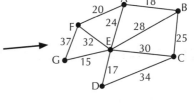

Q2 In terms of visiting landmarks in a city (such as in the example on the previous page), give two potential differences between a solution to the classical TSP and a solution to the practical TSP.

Q3 Convert this graph into a complete graph so that it can be treated as a classical travelling salesman problem.

Exam Questions

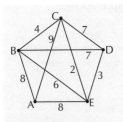

Q1 The graph on the left shows the distance in km between 5 hotels, A-E. Adam wants to find the shortest route that visits every hotel at least once, starting and finishing at the same hotel.

a) Performing the Lower Bound algorithm on vertices B, C, D and E yields the results 23, 23, 24 and 24 respectively. Perform the Lower Bound algorithm on the vertex A, and hence find the best lower bound for the route. [4 marks]

b) Add edges to the graph in order to make it complete, then perform the Nearest Neighbour algorithm starting at the vertex D. Hence find the smallest range in which the length of the optimal route can lie given that performing the Nearest Neighbour algorithm with starting vertices A, B, C and E yields the results 28, 28, 29 and 32 respectively. [4 marks]

	A	B	C	D	E
A	–	29	24	15	23
B	29	–	31	25	27
C	24	31	–	22	23
D	15	25	22	–	43
E	23	27	23	43	–

Q2 This distance matrix tells you how long it takes in minutes to travel between 5 monuments in a city. The optimal tour is the one that visits all 5 monuments at least once in the least time, starting and finishing at the same point.

a) By deleting vertex D and all of its arcs, find a lower bound for the optimal tour. [3 marks]

b) Find a nearest neighbour tour from the vertex D. [2 marks]

Everybody needs good Nearest Neighbour algorithms...

It's a bit disappointing that there's not a magical algorithm to find the optimum solution, like there was with the Chinese postman problem and the finding the shortest route with Dijkstra's algorithm thingamajig. But you can't have everything.

Activity Networks

Critical path analysis is a way of planning a project, making sure that tasks are done in the correct order and reducing the amount of time wasted. The first thing you need to consider is which jobs need doing first.

Precedence Tables *show which activities need doing* Before *others*

1) Complicated projects involve lots of different activities that have to be done in a **specific order**. Often there will be a range of tasks that can't be started until others are finished.

2) For example, if you're building a house, you can't put the roof on until the walls are built, and you can't build the walls until the foundations are in place. If you want to get the house built as **quickly** and **cheaply** as possible, you have to do a lot of **planning** (there's no point in the decorator turning up on the same day as the bricklayer and hanging around for 3 months).

3) Setting up a **precedence table** can help organise a project so that the smallest possible amounts of time and money are wasted. They show what activities must be **finished** before others are **started**. They're not as exciting as an episode of Futurama, but they're pretty easy to draw...

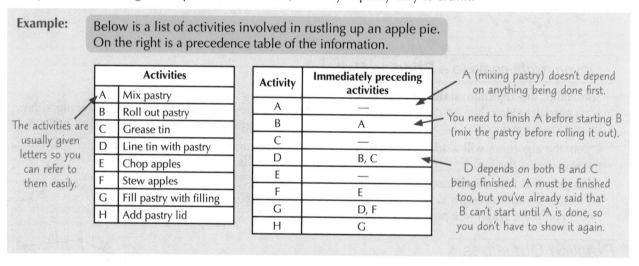

Example: Below is a list of activities involved in rustling up an apple pie. On the right is a precedence table of the information.

	Activities
A	Mix pastry
B	Roll out pastry
C	Grease tin
D	Line tin with pastry
E	Chop apples
F	Stew apples
G	Fill pastry with filling
H	Add pastry lid

The activities are usually given letters so you can refer to them easily.

Activity	Immediately preceding activities
A	—
B	A
C	—
D	B, C
E	—
F	E
G	D, F
H	G

A (mixing pastry) doesn't depend on anything being done first.

You need to finish A before starting B (mix the pastry before rolling it out).

D depends on both B and C being finished. A must be finished too, but you've already said that B can't start until A is done, so you don't have to show it again.

Activity Networks *show the information* More Clearly

1) Precedence tables are OK, but they're not great. Putting the information in an **activity network** makes it easier to understand, and it looks more impressive too.

2) In activity networks, '**arcs**' represent the **activities**, and '**nodes**' represent the **completion of activities** or '**events**'.

3) The nodes are **numbered** as they're added to the network. The first one is numbered **zero** and is called the **source node**. The final node is called the **sink node**.

4) Constructing activity networks can be quite awkward — here's one for the **apple pie example** above:

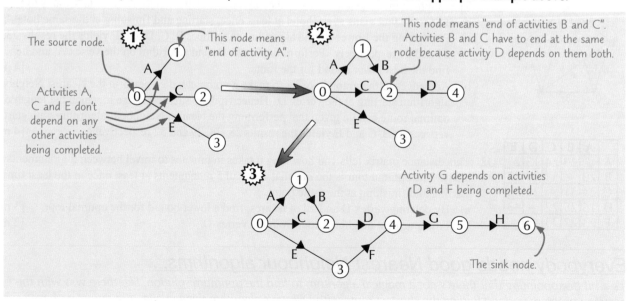

The source node.

This node means "end of activity A".

This node means "end of activities B and C". Activities B and C have to end at the same node because activity D depends on them both.

Activities A, C and E don't depend on any other activities being completed.

Activity G depends on activities D and F being completed.

The sink node.

Activity Networks

Dummies help show the Order that activities must be done in

1) **Dummy activities** are sometimes needed to convert the information in a precedence table to an activity network. They **aren't real** activities — they have **no duration** and don't cost any money. They're shown with **dotted lines**.

2) They're used to show that an activity relies on **two previous activities**, without the need for another activity.

3) The information in the following **precedence table** can't be shown on an activity network without a **dummy**:

Activity	Immediately preceding activities
A	—
B	A
C	—
D	A, C

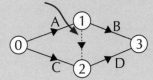

The dummy activity shows that activity **A** must be done **before** activity **D**.

Activity D must come after the completion of activities A <u>AND</u> C. B doesn't depend on C being completed though.

Example: Show the information in the table in an activity network. (It's a tricky one that needs two dummies.)

Activity	Immediately preceding activities
A	—
B	—
C	—
D	A
E	B, C
F	C
G	D
H	D, E, F

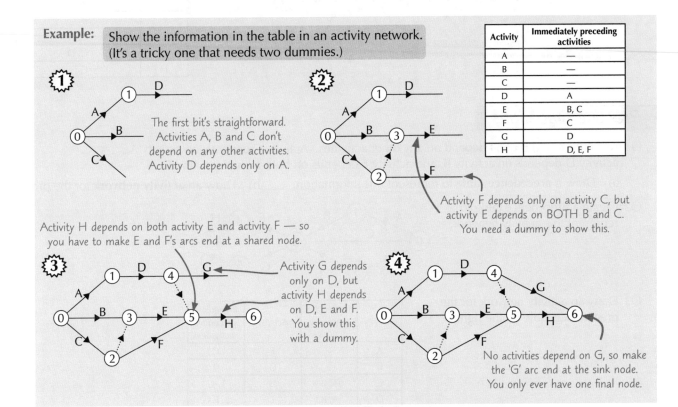

The first bit's straightforward. Activities A, B and C don't depend on any other activities. Activity D depends only on A.

Activity F depends only on activity C, but activity E depends on BOTH B and C. You need a dummy to show this.

Activity H depends on both activity E and activity F — so you have to make E and F's arcs end at a shared node.

Activity G depends only on D, but activity H depends on D, E and F. You show this with a dummy.

No activities depend on G, so make the 'G' arc end at the sink node. You only ever have one final node.

There can only ever be One Activity between the Same Two Events

No two activities can be shown between the <u>same pair of events</u>.

In other words each activity must be shown between a different pair of nodes.

You sometimes need a **dummy** to help you stick to this rule:

Example:

Activity	Immediately preceding activities
A	—
B	A
C	A
D	B, C

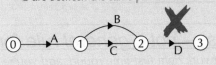

You can't do it like this. Activities B and C are between the same pair of nodes.

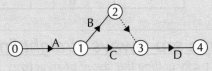

A dummy activity solves the problem.

Activity Networks

An Activity Network can be used to Create a Precedence Table

1) You can also go in the other direction, and use an activity network to create a precedence table.

2) For each activity, its **immediately preceding activities** are the ones that lead into (or point towards) the node it's coming from.

Example: Create a precedence table for the activity network below.

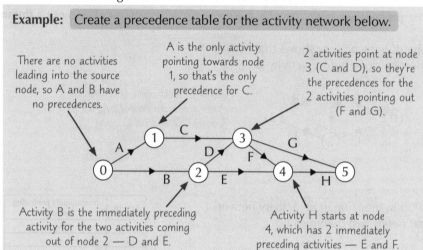

There are no activities leading into the source node, so A and B have no precedences.

A is the only activity pointing towards node 1, so that's the only precedence for C.

2 activities point at node 3 (C and D), so they're the precedences for the 2 activities pointing out (F and G).

Activity B is the immediately preceding activity for the two activities coming out of node 2 — D and E.

Activity H starts at node 4, which has 2 immediately preceding activities — E and F.

Activity	Immediately preceding activities
A	—
B	—
C	A
D	B
E	B
F	C, D
G	C, D
H	E, F

Practice Questions

Q1 Activities A and B don't depend on any other activities. Activity C depends on activity A, activity D depends on activity B, and activity E depends on both activities C and D.

    a) Draw a **precedence table** to represent this information.   b) Draw an **activity network** for the project.

Q2 Create a precedence table to represent this activity network.

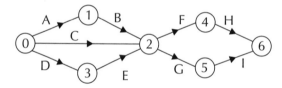

Q3 Draw an activity network for the precedence table on the right.

Activity	Immediate preceding activities	Activity	Immediate preceding activities
A	—	F	C
B	—	G	D
C	A, B	H	E, G
D	A, B	I	E, F, G
E	C		

Exam Question

Q1 This precedence table contains information about a project.

Activity	Immediate preceding activities	Activity	Immediate preceding activities
A	—	F	D
B	—	G	E
C	A	H	F, G
D	B, C	I	F, G
E	B	J	H, I

    a) Draw an activity network to show the information, using exactly two dummies.

                    [5 marks]

    b) Explain why each dummy is needed.

                    [2 marks]

Arcs are always straight lines — not a general rule for life...

It's tricky getting the layout of an activity network right first time round, and you're likely to have to do some rubbing out — so draw your activity network in pencil. Getting the layout right does get easier the more you practise though.

Critical Paths

When planning real projects, you normally have a <u>deadline</u> to work to. So <u>how long</u> each activity takes is important.

Each **Activity** has a **Duration**

1) The **duration** of an activity is **how long** it takes to complete.

The durations are given in brackets.
They can have the units hours, days, weeks, etc.
Remember dummy activities have no duration.

2) Each node or 'event' has an **early event time** and a **late event time**:

An event is the completion of an activity or activities (see page 206).

EARLY EVENT TIME — the **earliest time** you can reach an event. It depends on the durations of the **preceding activities**.	**LATE EVENT TIME** — the **latest time** you can get to an event **without** increasing the duration of the entire project.

3) The convention is to use **boxes** at each node to show the early and late event times.

3 ← The early event time goes in the top box.

6 ← The late event time goes in the bottom box.

Use a **Forward Pass** to find the **Early Event Times**

1) Start at the **source node** — its early event time is **0**. Then move through the network.

2) For each event, add the **duration** of the **preceding activity** to the **early event time** of the **previous event**.

3) If there's a **choice of paths** to an event, use the **biggest number**.

The example below will show you how to do a **forward pass** (times are in hours):

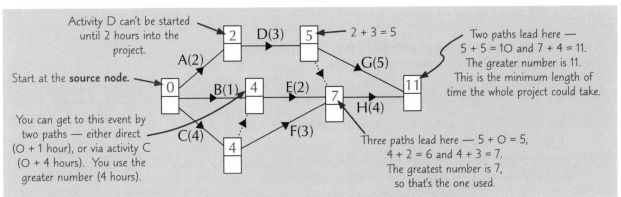

Activity D can't be started until 2 hours into the project.

Start at the **source node**.

You can get to this event by two paths — either direct (0 + 1 hour), or via activity C (0 + 4 hours). You use the greater number (4 hours).

Two paths lead here — 5 + 5 = 10 and 7 + 4 = 11. The greater number is 11. This is the minimum length of time the whole project could take.

Three paths lead here — 5 + 0 = 5, 4 + 2 = 6 and 4 + 3 = 7. The greatest number is 7, so that's the one used.

Then use a **Backward Pass** to find the **Late Event Times**

1) Start at the **sink node** — its late event time is the **same** as its **early event time**. Then move **backwards** through the network, towards the source.

2) This time, you **subtract** the activity's duration from the event that follows it.

3) If there's a **choice of paths**, use the **smallest number**.

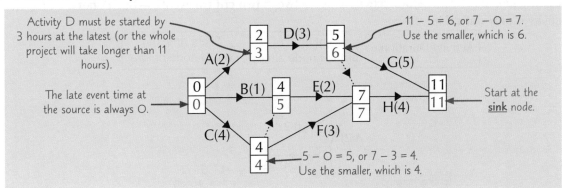

Activity D must be started by 3 hours at the latest (or the whole project will take longer than 11 hours).

The late event time at the source is always 0.

11 − 5 = 6, or 7 − 0 = 7. Use the smaller, which is 6.

Start at the **sink** node.

5 − 0 = 5, or 7 − 3 = 4. Use the smaller, which is 4.

Critical Paths

Critical Activities must be completed *Within* their allotted time

All the activities for a project have to be done, but with some of them you can **take your time** and **still meet** the deadline. With other activities you **can't** — these are the **critical** ones.

> - If the duration of a **critical activity** increases, the duration of the whole project increases by the same amount.
> - A **critical path** runs from the source node to the sink node and is made up of **critical activities**. The **nodes** lying on this path are called **critical events**.

1) All the nodes on a **critical path** have the same **early and late event times**.

2) This means they **MUST** be started at a particular time — there's no 'slack'.

3) **Adding up** the **durations** of the activities on the critical path gives you the duration of the **whole project** or the **'critical time'**.

Example: Find the critical activities and the length of the critical path for this network.

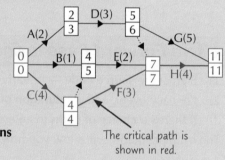

1) Look for the **nodes** where the **early** and **late event times** are the **same** — the **critical activities** lie **between** these nodes: **C, F and H**.

   NB: here all activities between critical nodes are critical — if the duration of any of them increases, the duration of the whole project will increase. But in certain situations that's not the case (see the part of a network shown at the bottom of the page).

2) **Reading** the value from the **sink node**, or **adding** up the **durations** of the critical activities, gives the length of the **critical path**:
   4 + 3 + 4 = **11 hours**

The critical path is shown in red.

4) You can have an activity network with **more than one** critical path. The critical paths will all have the same durations.

Example: Find the critical paths in this activity network.

1) Find the critical nodes and critical activities using the method in the example above.

2) Identify routes from the source node to the sink node that only involve critical activities. There are two here:

   Critical path 1 is activities **A, D, G and I**.

   Critical path 2 is activities **C, F, and J**.

   Critical path 1 has length 2 + 3 + 2 + 4 = 11 and critical path 2 has length 4 + 5 + 2 = 11 — you can see from the **sink node** or by looking at **either path** that the **critical time** is **11**.

Activities *Between* critical events *Aren't* always critical

1) In the really simple network below, **activity B** lies between **two critical events** — but it's **not** a critical activity.

2) An activity is **only critical** if:

$$\text{Activity Duration} = \text{Event time of critical node after} - \text{Event time of critical node before}$$

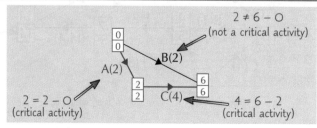

$2 \neq 6 - 0$
(not a critical activity)

$2 = 2 - 0$
(critical activity)

$4 = 6 - 2$
(critical activity)

Critical Paths

The **Total Float** of an activity is **How Long** it can be **Delayed** for

1) The **total float** of an activity is the **maximum amount of time** you can **delay starting it** if the whole project is still going to be **completed on time**.

2) There's a lovely formula for it: | Total float of an activity = latest finish time – duration – earliest start time |

Example: Calculate the total float for the activities below.

a)
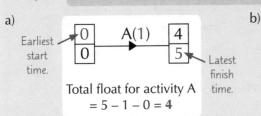
Earliest start time.
Latest finish time.

Total float for activity A
= 5 – 1 – 0 = **4**

You can start A at any time in the first 4 hours without making the project take longer than planned.

b)
| 2 | B(3) | 5 |
| 3 | | 6 |

Total float for activity B
= 6 – 3 – 2 = **1**

You can only delay starting B for an hour after its earliest start time.

c)
| 4 | C(3) | 7 |
| 4 | | 7 |

Total float for activity C
= 7 – 3 – 4 = **0**

C is a critical activity. The total float of a critical activity is always zero — you can't delay starting it without extending the project time.

Practice Questions

Q1 a) What numbers should replace the red letters *a–g* in this activity network?

b) i) Explain what is meant by a critical path.
ii) Identify <u>both</u> critical paths.

c) Explain why activity E **isn't** a critical activity.

d) State the critical time for the project (times are in hours).

e) Work out the total float for activities B, E and I.

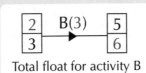

Q2 Identify the critical path(s) in the network on the right.

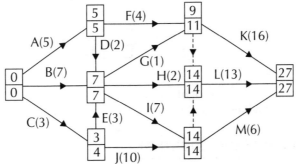

Exam Question

Q1 The network on the right shows the activities involved in a process. The number in brackets on each arc gives the time, in days, taken to complete the activity.

a) Calculate the early time and the late time for each event. Show them on a copy of the diagram. [3 marks]

b) Determine the critical activities and the length of the critical path. [2 marks]

c) Calculate the total float on each of activities F and G. Show your working. [3 marks]

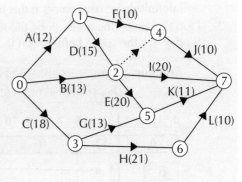

Critical path: You're walking on me all wrong...

Check at the end that your early event times are all less than or equal to your late event times. Remember, use the biggest numbers to work out early event times, and the smallest numbers to work out late event times.

Gantt Charts and Resource Histograms

*The Gantt chart, Henry Gantt's greatest triumph. I bet his mum was proud... If you're doing **AS Level**, once you've learnt this page, skip to the questions on p.214 — you **don't** need to know about resource histograms.*

Gantt Charts show possible Start and Finish Times for activities

1) **Gantt charts** are also called **cascade charts**. They let you show the **possible time periods** that each activity can happen in for the project to be completed on time.

2) Here's how to plot a single activity on a Gantt chart:

P has a duration of 4 hours. If it starts at 1 hour, it'll finish at 5 hours.

$\boxed{\begin{smallmatrix}1\\3\end{smallmatrix}}$ P(4) $\boxed{\begin{smallmatrix}5\\7\end{smallmatrix}}$ Total float for activity P = 7 − 4 − 1 = 2

The earliest P can start is 1 hour into the project.

The latest P can finish is at 7 hours.

The total float is 2 hours.

3) This example shows a whole activity network plotted on a Gantt chart:

Example: Display this information on a Gantt chart. The times are all shown in hours.

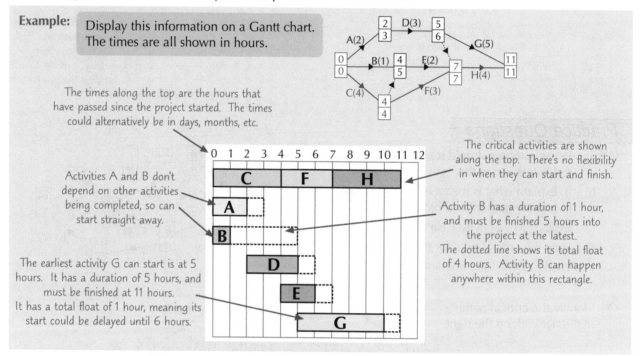

The times along the top are the hours that have passed since the project started. The times could alternatively be in days, months, etc.

Activities A and B don't depend on other activities being completed, so can start straight away.

The earliest activity G can start is at 5 hours. It has a duration of 5 hours, and must be finished at 11 hours. It has a total float of 1 hour, meaning its start could be delayed until 6 hours.

The critical activities are shown along the top. There's no flexibility in when they can start and finish.

Activity B has a duration of 1 hour, and must be finished 5 hours into the project at the latest. The dotted line shows its total float of 4 hours. Activity B can happen anywhere within this rectangle.

4) The solid activity rectangles can slide **right** — as long as they stay within the **dotted rectangles**. But sliding them might affect **other activities**. E.g. if A is delayed by an hour, then D and G must be delayed too.

You have to Interpret Gantt charts too

1) You'll sometimes be asked what activities will be happening at a particular time. Some activities will **definitely** be happening at this time, whereas other activities only **might** be happening.

2) Don't forget — the times along the top indicate the number of days or hours that have **elapsed**. So day 4 is the space **before** 4 on the scale.

Example: Which activities will definitely be happening and which might be happening at noon on day 4 of the 12-day project shown below?

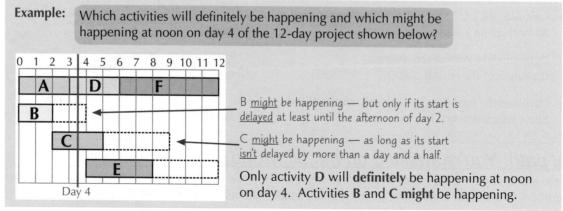

B might be happening — but only if its start is delayed at least until the afternoon of day 2.

C might be happening — as long as its start isn't delayed by more than a day and a half.

Only activity **D** will **definitely** be happening at noon on day 4. Activities **B** and **C** might be happening.

Section 31 — D1: Critical Path Analysis

Gantt Charts and Resource Histograms

Resource Histograms show How Many People are needed at any time

1) Strictly, **resource histograms** show the '**quantity of resources**' needed at any moment.
   It's usually the **number of people**, but it could be, e.g., machines or space.

2) Resource histograms are drawn from **Gantt charts** — and it makes things a lot
   easier if you draw your resource histogram **right under** the Gantt chart.

3) Sometimes activities require **more than one person**. The **number of people** needed
   for each activity will be shown either in a table or on the Gantt chart.
   This example shows the Gantt chart and a resource histogram for the activity network shown:

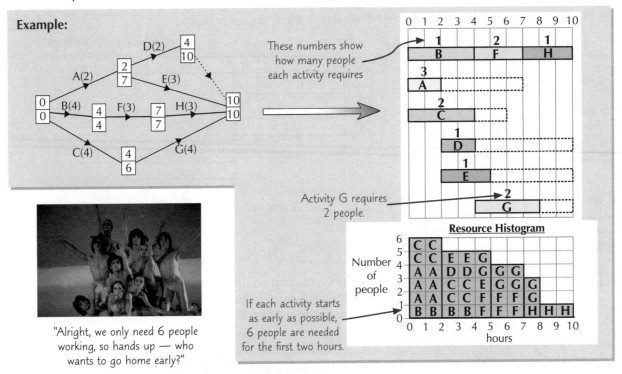

Example:

These numbers show how many people each activity requires

Activity G requires 2 people.

"Alright, we only need 6 people working, so hands up — who wants to go home early?"

If each activity starts as early as possible, 6 people are needed for the first two hours.

Resource Histogram

Sometimes there's only a certain Number of People available

1) The resource histogram above shows that **6 people** are needed at the start of the
   project, but this gradually tails off, and only **1 person** is needed for the last two hours.

2) This is fine **in theory**, but a company might **not** have 6 available workers (and even if
   they have, the workers mightn't bother getting out of bed for just two hours' work).

3) It's sometimes possible to **shift activities** so that there isn't such a peak of people
   needed at one time — this is called **resource smoothing** or **resource levelling**.

Example: Show how the activities for the project above can be reorganised so that no more than 4 people
are needed at any one time and the project can still be completed within the critical time.

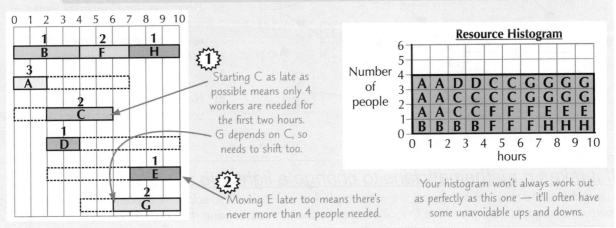

①
Starting C as late as possible means only 4 workers are needed for the first two hours.
G depends on C, so needs to shift too.

②
Moving E later too means there's never more than 4 people needed.

Resource Histogram

Your histogram won't always work out as perfectly as this one — it'll often have some unavoidable ups and downs.

Section 31 — D1: Critical Path Analysis

Gantt Charts and Resource Histograms

Q1 a) State the float, if any, of the activities in this Gantt chart.
   b) Identify the critical activities in the Gantt chart.

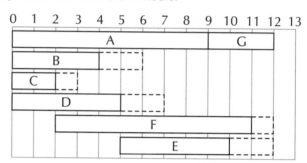

Q2 The Gantt chart for a project is shown below, where the times are in hours.

   a) Which activities will definitely be happening in the first 3 hours?
   b) Which activities could be happening in the 7th hour?
   c) Which activities will definitely be happening after 10 hours?

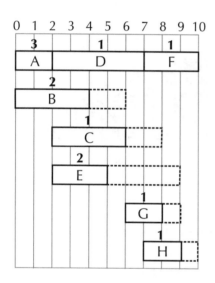

Q3 The Gantt chart on the left is for a different project, with times given in hours, and the number of workers required for each activity shown in bold.

   a) Construct a resource histogram for the project, assuming that each activity starts as soon as possible.
   b) Use resource levelling to show that the project can be completed within the critical time using only four workers.

Exam Question

Q1 A project is represented by this activity network. The durations are given in days.

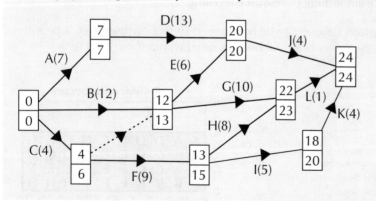

   a) Draw a Gantt chart for the project.
      [3 marks]

   b) Draw a resource histogram for the activity network, given that each activity requires only one worker and starts as soon as possible.
      [3 marks]

   c) How many workers are needed to complete the project in the critical time?
      [1 mark]

If it takes n mathematicians to change a lightbulb...

Gantt charts and resource histograms are useful tools, but you do need to add a bit of common sense when applying them to a situation. You often have to look at what resources you have and then do a bit of juggling to make it all work.

Scheduling

Gantt charts are useful for working out how many people are needed to complete a project on time.
An employer wouldn't want to have people standing about, because they're all going to want to be paid.

Scheduling Diagrams show how many Workers are needed

1) Scheduling diagrams show **which activities** are assigned to each worker,
   and **how many workers** are needed to complete the project by the deadline.

2) There are some **rules** to follow when you're scheduling workers:

   - Assume that **each activity** requires **one worker**.
   - Once a worker starts an activity, they have to **carry on** with it until it's finished.
     They **can't** break off from the activity to get another one started.
   - Assume that once a worker finishes one activity, they're ready to start on
     another **immediately** — workers in Decision Maths don't need a lunch break.
   - If there's a **choice of activities** for a worker, they should always start on the one
     that must be **finished soonest** (which has the earliest late event time).

Example: The Gantt chart on the right is for a project
that must be completed in 12 hours.
Schedule the activities and determine the
minimum number of workers required.

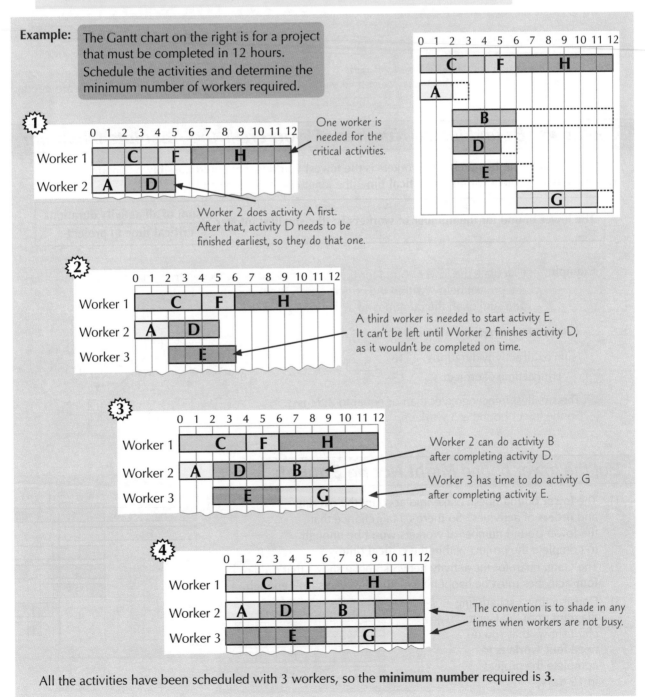

① One worker is
needed for the
critical activities.

Worker 2 does activity A first.
After that, activity D needs to be
finished earliest, so they do that one.

② A third worker is needed to start activity E.
It can't be left until Worker 2 finishes activity D,
as it wouldn't be completed on time.

③ Worker 2 can do activity B
after completing activity D.

Worker 3 has time to do activity G
after completing activity E.

④ The convention is to shade in any
times when workers are not busy.

All the activities have been scheduled with 3 workers, so the **minimum number** required is **3**.

Scheduling

You can make a Scheduling Diagram from an Activity Network

Example: Schedule the activities in the network to find how many workers are needed (times are in weeks).

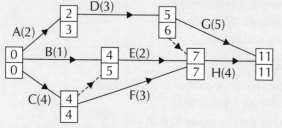

Start by identifying the **critical path** — C F H, and assign one worker to it.

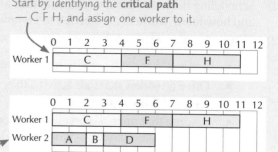

Worker 2 can start with either A or B. Activity A has the **earlier late event time**, so assign them to that. You can then put them on B or D — B is more 'urgent', so that's their next task. After this they can complete activity D too, before its late event time of 6 weeks.

Now you're left with two activities. E has to start before 5 weeks, so that needs a third worker to complete it, but G can wait until 6 weeks to start — you can assign this to either the second or third worker.

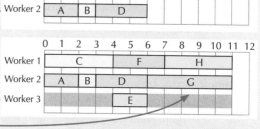

So **3 workers** are needed.

The Lower Bound for the Number of Workers is the Absolute Minimum

The **lower bound** for the number of workers is the **fewest workers** that could **possibly** be enough to complete the project within the **critical time** (the length of the critical path).

> The lower bound for the number of workers is: the smallest integer $\geq \dfrac{\text{sum of all activity durations}}{\text{critical time of project}}$

Example: Calculate the lower bound for the number of workers needed to complete the project below within the critical time. The times are all in days. The sum of all the durations of activities is 38 days.

Critical time of project = 15 days

$$\frac{\text{sum of all activity durations}}{\text{critical time of project}} = \frac{38}{15} = 2.53$$

The smallest integer greater than or equal to 2.53 is 3. So the lower bound is **3 workers**.

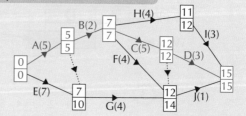

But the lower bound Might Not be Enough

1) The **lower bound** doesn't take into account the **overlap** and **orders** of activities. So there's a fair chance that the lower bound number of workers **won't** be enough to complete the project within the **critical time**.

2) The Gantt chart for the activity network above shows that on day 11, **four** activities **must** be happening — three workers **isn't enough**.

3) Constructing a **scheduling diagram** from the Gantt chart shows that you do need **four workers** to complete the project in **15 days**.

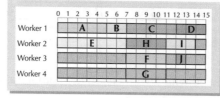

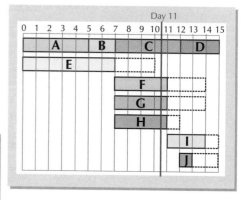

Scheduling

Without **Enough** workers, the project will take **Longer**

1) If you don't have enough workers, the project will take **longer than its critical time**.
2) If you're creating a scheduling diagram for **fewer** than the minimum number of workers, it's best to do it from the **activity network** so you don't miss any precedences.

Example: Only two workers are available to complete the project represented in the previous example. Schedule the activities in the minimum number of days.

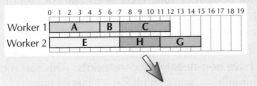

Worker 1 starts activity A, Worker 2 starts activity E.
Worker 1 finishes first and does activity B (it has to be completed sooner than the other activities, and the activities it depends on (just A) are finished).
Worker 2 finishes activity E and goes on to activity H (using the same logic as before).

This system carries on until all the activities are scheduled. The whole project takes 19 days.

Practice Question

Q1 a) The Gantt chart for a project is shown on the right. Find the lower bound for the number of workers needed to complete the project in the critical time.

b) Construct a scheduling diagram from the Gantt chart. The project should be completed in the critical time with the fewest workers possible.

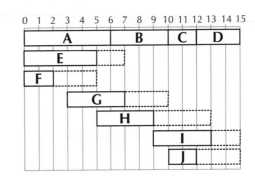

Exam Question

Q1 The diagram shows an activity network for a project.
The duration of each activity is shown in days. The sum of all the activity times is 112 days.

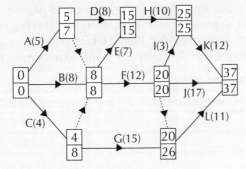

a) There are two critical paths for this network. State them both. [2 marks]

b) Find a lower bound for the number of workers required to complete the project in the critical time. Show your working. [2 marks]

c) Which activities must be happening on day 23 for the project to be completed in the critical time? Explain how you know this. [2 marks]

d) Schedule the activities so that the project is completed in the minimum number of days. You must use as few workers as possible. [3 marks]

e) The supervisor realises at midday on day 14 that activity D has not yet been started. Determine if the project can still be finished on time. Explain your answer. [2 marks]

You're getting through in leaps and lower bounds...

The lower bound assumes that the tasks can all be slotted together neatly. But when some activities depend on others, it doesn't usually work that way. Remember to round up to an integer — because you can't have part of a worker.

Linear Programs

*Linear programming is a way of solving problems that have lots of inequalities. If you're doing **AS Level**, once you've mastered this page, go straight to the practice questions — you **don't** need to learn about slack and surplus variables.*

Linear Programming aims to produce an Optimal Solution to a Problem

You might use **linear programming** to find the solution that gives the **maximum profit** to a manufacturer, for example, based on **conditions** that would affect it, such as **limited time** or **materials**. Before you start having a go at linear programming problems, there are a few **terms** you need to know.

1) In any problem, you'll have things that are being **produced** (or **bought** or **sold**, etc.) — e.g. jars of jam or types of books. The **amount** of each thing is represented by x, y, z, etc. — these are called the **decision variables**.

2) The **constraints** are the **factors** that **limit** the problem, e.g. a limited amount of workers available. The constraints are usually written as **inequalities** in terms of the **decision variables** (although sometimes they can be written as equations). The problems you'll face will have **non-negativity constraints**. This just means that the decision variables **can't** be **negative**. It makes sense really — you can't have –2 jars of jam.

3) The **objective function** is what you're trying to **maximise** or **minimise** (e.g. maximise **profit** or minimise **cost**). It's usually in the form of an **equation** written in terms of the **decision variables**.

4) A **feasible solution** is a solution that **satisfies** all the **constraints**. It'll give you a **value** for each of the **decision variables**. On a **graph**, the **set** of feasible solutions forms the **feasible region** (see p.220).

5) You're aiming to **optimise** the objective function — that's finding a solution within the feasible region that maximises (or minimises) the **objective function**. This is the **optimal solution**, and there can be **more than one** (see p.223).

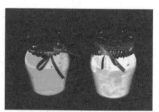

Negative two jars of jam.

Put the Information you're given in a Table

Linear programming questions can look a bit confusing because you're given a lot of **information** in one go. But if you put all the information in a **table**, it's much easier to work out the **inequalities** you need.

> **Example:** A company makes garden furniture, and produces both picnic tables and benches. It takes 5 hours to make a picnic table and 2 hours to paint it. It takes 3 hours to make a bench and 1 hour to paint it. In a week, there are 100 hours allocated to construction and 50 hours allocated to painting. Picnic tables are sold for a profit of £30 and benches are sold for a profit of £10. The company wants to maximise their weekly profit.

Putting this information into a table gives:

Item of furniture	Construction time (hours)	Painting time (hours)	Profit (£)
Picnic table	5	2	30
Bench	3	1	10
Total time available:	100	50	

Now use the table to identify all the different parts of the problem and come up with the inequalities:

- The **decision variables** are the **number of picnic tables** and the **number of benches**, so let x = number of picnic tables and y = number of benches.

- The **constraints** are the **number of hours available** for **each stage** of manufacture. Making a picnic table takes 5 hours, so x tables will take $5x$ hours. Making a bench takes 3 hours, so y benches will take $3y$ hours. There are a total of 100 hours available. From this, you get the inequality $5x + 3y \leq 100$. Using the same method for the painting hours produces the inequality $2x + y \leq 50$. You also need $x, y \geq 0$. ◄ *Don't forget the non-negativity constraints.*

- The **objective function** to be **maximised** is profit. Each picnic table makes a profit of £30, so x tables make a profit of £30x. Each bench makes a profit of £10, so y benches make a profit of £10y. Let P be the profit, then the aim is to maximise $P = 30x + 10y$.

We haven't actually **found** the maximum profit in the example above — you'll see how to do this later on in this section. But **setting up** the constraints is just as important — in fact, some exam questions ask you to **only** write the constraints and **not** to solve. (As always, make sure you read the question **carefully**...)

Linear Programs

Slack and Surplus Variables turn Inequalities into Equations

1) '**Slack**' is the amount of a resource that's left **unused**. For example, if you're buying bricks and have a **budget** of £200, but you end up only spending £170, then you have a **slack** of £30.

2) Slack can be included in a **constraint** by using a **slack variable** — this turns the inequality into an **equation**. Slack variables can only be used when the **decision variables** are constrained by an **upper limit**. For example, the constraint $2x + y \leq 25$ could be **rewritten** to include a slack variable s_1: $2x + y + s_1 = 25$.

3) '**Surplus**' is the amount of **excess** resource that you have. For example, if you had to buy at least 1900 bricks, but you end up buying 2000, then you have a **surplus** of 100 bricks.

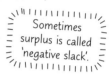
Sometimes surplus is called 'negative slack'.

4) A **surplus variable** also turns an inequality into an equation. They can only be used when the decision variables are constrained by a **lower limit**. E.g. the constraint $4a + 5b \geq 100$ could be **rewritten** to include a surplus variable s_2: $4a + 5b - s_2 = 100$.

5) You will only ever get **either** a slack variable **or** a surplus variable in a constraint — **never** both.

6) Slack and surplus variables are always **non-negative** — i.e., $s_1 \geq 0$, $s_2 \geq 0$.

> **Example:** Turn the following constraints into equations using slack and surplus variables:
>
> a) $-5x + 4y \leq 17$ $\Rightarrow$ $-5x + 4y + s_1 = 17$ where $s_1 \geq 0$ is a slack variable.
>
> b) $y \geq 4$ $\Rightarrow$ $y - s_2 = 4$ where $s_2 \geq 0$ is a surplus variable.
>
> *You should state whether your variable is slack or surplus.*
>
> c) $5 \leq x + 2y$ $\Rightarrow$ $5 = x + 2y - s_3$ where $s_3 \geq 0$ is a surplus variable.
>
> d) $x + z = 4$ — this is already an equation so there's no slack or surplus — it **stays as it is**.

Practice Question

If you're doing AS Level, you only need to do Practice Question 1 and Exam Question 1.

Q1 The constraints of a linear program are: $x, y \geq 0$, $40x + 25y \geq 200$, $x + y \leq 6$.
Suggest a real-life scenario that could be represented by this linear program.

Exam Questions

Q1 Anna is selling red and white roses at a flower stall. She buys the flowers from a wholesaler, where red roses cost 75p each and white roses cost 60p each. Based on previous sales, she has come up with the following constraints:
- She will sell both red roses and white roses.
- Between 45% and 55% of the roses she will sell will be red.
- She will sell a total of at least 100 flowers.

Anna wishes to minimise her costs.
Let x be the number of red roses she buys and y be the number of white roses she buys.
Formulate this information as a linear programming problem. Write out the constraints as inequalities and identify a suitable objective function, stating how it should be optimised.
You do not need to solve this problem. [6 marks]

Q2 A company makes laminated posters, in small and large sizes. It takes 10 minutes to print each large poster, and 5 minutes to print each small poster. There is a total of 250 minutes per day allocated to printing. It takes 6 minutes to laminate a large poster and 4 minutes for a small poster, with a total of 200 minutes per day allocated to laminating. The company wants to sell at least as many large posters as small, and they want to sell at least 10 small posters. Large posters are sold for a profit of £6 and small posters are sold for a profit of £3.50. Write this out as a linear programming problem using equations.
Identify any decision variables, constraints, slack and surplus variables and an objective function.
You do not need to solve this problem. [7 marks]

Forget profit — my objective function is to maximise picnic...

In fancy examiner speak, the example on the previous page could be written like this: "maximise $P = 30x + 10y$ subject to the constraints $5x + 3y \leq 100$, $2x + y \leq 50$ and $x, y \geq 0$". Watch out for constraints such as 'there have to be at least twice as many benches as picnic tables — this would be written as $2x \leq y$. It can all be quite confusing at first...

Feasible Regions

This page is a bit like the graphical inequality problems you came across at GCSE. If you're not that keen on graphs, or if the mere thought of them brings you out in a rash, don't worry — they're only straight-line graphs.

Drawing **Graphs** can help solve **Linear Programming Problems**

Plotting the constraints on a **graph** is probably the easiest way to **solve** a linear programming problem — it helps you see the **feasible solutions** clearly. Get your ruler and graph paper ready.

1) Draw each of the **constraints** as a **line** on the graph. All you have to do is **change** the **inequality sign** to an **equals sign** and plot the line. If you find it easier, **rearrange** the equation into the form $y = mx + c$.

2) Then you have to **decide** whether the feasible solutions will be **above** or **below** the line. This will depend on the **inequality sign** — **rearrange** the inequality into the form $y = mx + c$, then think about which sign you'd use. For $y \leq mx + c$ (or $<$), you want the bit **underneath** the line, and if it's $y \geq mx + c$ (or $>$) then you want the bit **above** the line. If you're not sure, put the **coordinates** of a point on one side of the line (e.g. the origin) into the equation and see if it **satisfies** the inequality.

3) Once you've decided which side you want, **shade** the region you **don't want**. This way, when you've put all the constraints on the graph, the **unshaded region** (the bit you want) will be easy to see.

4) If the inequality sign is $<$ or $>$, use a **dashed or dotted line** — this means the line is **not included** in the region. If the inequality sign is $\leq$ or $\geq$ then use a **normal** line, meaning the line is **included** in the region.

5) Once you've drawn **all** the constraints on the graph, you'll be able to solve the problem. Don't forget the **non-negativity constraints** — they'll limit the graph to the **first quadrant**.

The **Unshaded Area** is the **Feasible Region**

Your finished graph should have an area, **bounded** by the lines of the **constraints**, that **hasn't** been **shaded**. This is the **feasible region** — the **coordinates** of any point inside the **unshaded area** will satisfy **all** the **constraints**.

Example: On a graph, show the constraints $x + y \leq 5$, $3x - y \geq 2$, $y > 1$ and $x, y \geq 0$. Label the feasible region R.

Rearranging the inequalities into '$y = mx + c$' form and choosing the appropriate inequality sign gives: $y \leq 5 - x$, $y \leq 3x - 2$ and $y > 1$. The non-negativity constraints $x, y > 0$ are represented by the x- and y-axes.

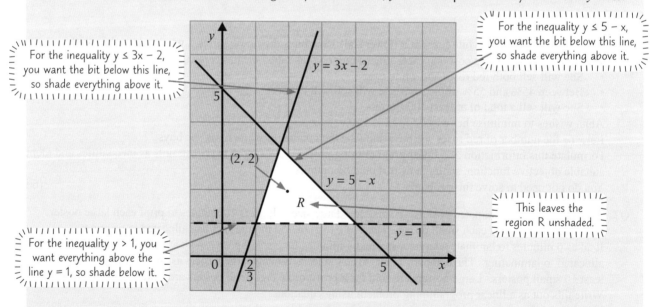

For the inequality $y \leq 5 - x$, you want the bit below this line, so shade everything above it.

For the inequality $y \leq 3x - 2$, you want the bit below this line, so shade everything above it.

This leaves the region R unshaded.

For the inequality $y > 1$, you want everything above the line $y = 1$, so shade below it.

To check that R is the feasible region, take a point inside R, and check that it satisfies all the inequalities. Taking the point $(2, 2)$ gives:

- $x + y = 2 + 2 = 4 \leq 5$
- $3x - y = 3 \times 2 - 2 = 4 \geq 2$
- $y = 2 > 1$ and $x = 2 \geq 0$.

All of the inequalities are satisfied, so R **is the feasible region**.

Feasible Regions

Some problems need Integer Solutions

1) Sometimes it's fine to have **non-integer solutions** to linear programming problems — for example, if you were making different **fruit juices**, you could realistically have 3.5 litres of one type of juice and $4\frac{1}{3}$ litres of another.

2) However, if you were making **garden furniture**, you couldn't make 3.5 tables and $4\frac{1}{3}$ benches — so you need **integer solutions**.

3) You won't always be **told** whether a problem needs integer solutions — you might have to **work it out** for yourself. It's common sense really — just think about whether you can have a **non-integer amount** of the **decision variables**.

> **Example:** Look at the Example on the previous page. Find all the integer solutions in the feasible region R.
>
>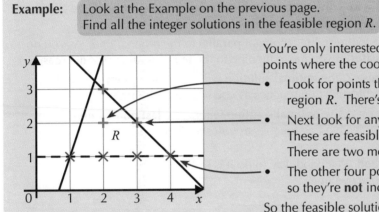
>
> You're only interested in the **integer solutions**, i.e. points where the coordinate **grid lines** shown cross.
>
> - Look for points that lie **entirely within** the region R. There's just one here — (2, 2).
> - Next look for any that lie on the **boundary** of R. These are feasible only if they're on **solid lines**. There are two more here — (2, 3) and (3, 2).
> - The other four points are on a **dashed line**, so they're **not** included in the feasible region R.
>
> So the feasible solutions are: **(2, 2), (2, 3) and (3, 2)**.

Practice Questions

Q1 Give an example of one problem that doesn't require integer solutions, and an example of one that does.

Q2 A furniture company makes armchairs and sofas.
- It takes 5 hours to build an armchair frame, and 8 hours to build a sofa frame. There is a total of 320 hours per month allowed for frame building.
- It takes 10 hours to upholster an armchair and 20 hours to upholster a sofa, with at least 180 hours spent on upholstery each month.
- The manager wants to sell at least half as many armchairs as sofas.
- She also wants to sell at least 10 armchairs.

Let x and y represent the number of armchairs and sofas made respectively. Show the constraints for this problem on a coordinate grid. Label the feasible region R.

Exam Questions

Q1 The graph on the right shows the constraints of a linear programming problem. The feasible region is labelled R. Including the non-negativity constraints, find the inequalities that produce R. **[5 marks]**

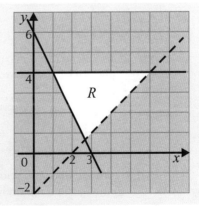

Q2 On graph paper, draw a graph showing the following constraints:
$2x + y \leq 10$, $x + y \leq 8$, $3x + y \leq 12$ and $2y \geq x$, given that x and y are weights of fruit in kg. Label the feasible region R. **[5 marks]**

It's feasible that I might become a film star...

Although it's possible that you might get a linear programming problem with more than two variables, you won't have to draw graphs for those ones. You'll only have to graph two-variable problems. The axes that you'll be asked to draw on in the exam might not have the same scales, so you need to be extra careful when plotting your lines on them.

The Objective Line Method

Don't throw away your graphs just yet — you still need them for the next few pages. You're now getting on to the really useful bit — actually solving the linear programming problem. About time...

Draw a line for the **Objective Function**

All the points in the **feasible region** (see previous page) satisfy all the **constraints** in the problem. You need to be able to work out which point (or points) also **optimises** the **objective function**. The objective function is usually of the form $Z = ax + by$, where Z either needs to be **maximised** (e.g. profit) or **minimised** (e.g. cost) to give the **optimal solution**.

The Objective Line Method
1) Draw the **straight line** $Z = ax + by$, choosing a **fixed value** of Z (a and b will be given in the question). This is called the **objective line**.
2) Imagine moving the line to the **right**, keeping it **parallel** to the original line. As you do this, the value of Z **increases** (if you move the line to the **left**, the value of Z **decreases**).
3) If you're trying to **maximise** Z, the **optimal solution** will be the **last point** within the **feasible region** that the objective line touches as you slide it to the **right**.
4) If you're trying to **minimise** Z, the **optimal solution** will be the **last point** within the **feasible region** that the objective line touches as you slide it to the **left**.

This is sometimes called the **ruler method**, as a good way to do it is to slide a ruler over the graph **parallel** to the objective line.

The objective lines have the **Same Gradient**

When you draw your **first** objective line, you can use **any value** for Z. Pick one that makes the line **easier** to draw — e.g. let Z be a **multiple** of both a and b so that the **intercepts** with the axes are **easy** to find.

Example: Using the Example from page 220, maximise the profit $P = 2x + 3y$.

1) First, **choose** a value for P, say $P = 6 \Rightarrow 6 = 2x + 3y$. So the **objective line** goes through $(3, 0)$ and $(0, 2)$. **Draw** this line on the graph.

2) Imagine **sliding** the objective line to the **right**, keeping the objective line parallel to its starting position. When it reaches the last point within R, then P is **maximised**.

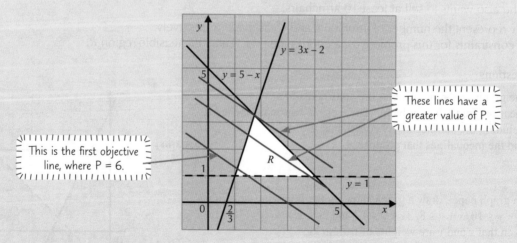

3) From the diagram, you can see that the **last** point the objective line touches in the feasible region is the **intersection** of the lines $y = 5 - x$ and $y = 3x - 2$.

Solve the equations simultaneously — substitute $y = 5 - x$ into $y = 3x - 2$:

$$5 - x = 3x - 2 \Rightarrow 7 = 4x \Rightarrow x = \frac{7}{4} \Rightarrow y = 5 - \frac{7}{4} = \frac{13}{4}.$$

So at the point $\left(\frac{7}{4}, \frac{13}{4}\right)$, the maximum value of $P = 2\left(\frac{7}{4}\right) + 3\left(\frac{13}{4}\right) = \textbf{13.25}$

The Objective Line Method

There might be **More Than One** optimal solution

1) If the objective line is **parallel** to one of the **constraints**, you might end up with a **section of a line** that gives the **optimal solution**.

2) If this happens, **any point** along the line is an optimal solution (as long as it's **inside** the **feasible region**).

3) This shows that there can be **more than one** optimal solution to a problem.

You can find **Integer Solutions** using the **Objective Line Method**

As you saw on page 221, **non-integer** solutions might not be appropriate — e.g. if x and y were cars or sheds (no one wants to buy half a shed). Luckily, you can easily **adapt** the objective line method to find **integer solutions**.

Example: The optimal solution to the problem on the previous page occurred at $\left(\frac{7}{4}, \frac{13}{4}\right)$. Find the optimal <u>integer</u> solution.

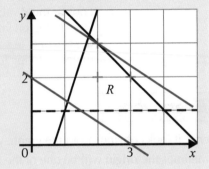

1) Instead of looking at the **feasible region**, we need to look at the **set of feasible points**.

2) Consider the feasible integer solutions that were found in the Example on page 221.

3) As before, draw an initial **objective line** by picking a value for P — e.g. $P = 6$.

4) **Slide** the objective line to the right until it reaches the last point in the set of feasible points. At this point, P is **maximised**.

5) So P has an optimal integer solution at the point (2, 3).

⇒ The maximum value of P with integer solutions is $(2 \times 2) + (3 \times 3) = \mathbf{13}$.

It could be possible for P to be an **integer** while x and y are **non-integers** — for instance, the point $\left(2\frac{1}{2}, 2\frac{1}{3}\right)$ in the above Example gives $P = 12$, but this is **not** an integer solution. Remember that the **decision variables** x and y must **also** be integers, **not** just P.

Practice Questions

Q1 In the Example on page 222, suppose that you wanted to <u>minimise</u> the objective function $Q = x + y$.
   a) Explain why (1, 1) is <u>not</u> a feasible integer solution.
   b) Find the optimal integer solution.

Q2 Look back at Practice Question 2 on page 221. Armchairs are sold for a profit of £150 and sofas are sold for a profit of £75. By using the objective line method, find the optimal solution.

Exam Question

Q1 A company grows Christmas trees to two different heights — 'indoor' and 'outdoor'. They have enough land to grow 300 indoor trees. Outdoor trees require twice as much space as indoor trees.
The cost of water throughout the growing season is £4 per indoor tree and £5 per outdoor tree, and the company has a £1000 water budget. The cost of insecticides is £2 per indoor tree and £8 per outdoor tree, with a budget of £1000.
The company makes £2 profit on each indoor tree and £5 on each outdoor tree, and wishes to maximise its profit (assuming all trees are sold).

   a) If the company grows x indoor trees and y outdoor trees, write down the objective function, stating clearly whether it should be maximised or minimised. [1 mark]

   b) Show that the insecticide constraint is $x + 4y \leq 500$, and list all the other constraints. [4 marks]

   c) Draw a graph of the feasible region. Use the objective line method to solve the problem. [6 marks]

The optimal solution is an integer? I object...

When using the objective line method, don't forget about the pesky dotted lines — if the last point the objective line touches is on a dotted line then this isn't a feasible solution. To find the optimal solution, you'll have to slide the objective line back a tiny little bit. If sliding rulers on a page isn't your thing though, try the method on the next page...

The Vertex Method

If you object to using the objective line, there is another method. This one uses a lot more simultaneous equations, but you don't have to worry about keeping the ruler parallel or stopping global warming or anything like that.

Optimal Solutions are found at Vertices

The **optimal solution** for the example on the previous page was found at a **vertex** of the **feasible region**. This isn't a coincidence — if you have a go at some more linear programming problems, you'll find that the optimal solutions **always** occur at a vertex (or an **edge**) of the feasible region. This gives you another way to solve the problem.

The Vertex Method

1) Find the x- and y-values of the **vertices** of the **feasible region**. You do this by solving the **simultaneous equations** of the **lines** that **intersect** at each vertex.

2) Put these values into the **objective function** $Z = ax + by$ to find the value of Z.

3) Look at the Z values and work out which is the **optimal value**. Depending on your objective function, this might be either the **smallest** (if you're trying to **minimise** Z) or the **largest** (if you're trying to **maximise** Z).

> If two vertices A and B produce the same Z value, this means that all points along the edge AB are also optimal solutions.

Test Every vertex

1) Even if it looks **obvious** from the graph, you still have to **test** each vertex of the feasible region.

2) Sometimes the **origin** will be one of the vertices — it's really easy to test, as the objective function will just be equal to 0 there. Don't forget vertices on the **x-** and **y-axes** too.

Example: Minimise $Z = 8x + 9y$, subject to the constraints $2x + y \geq 6$, $x - 2y \leq 2$, $x \leq 4$, $y \leq 4$ and $x, y \geq 0$.

Drawing these constraints on a graph produces the diagram below, where A, B, C and D are the vertices of the feasible region R:

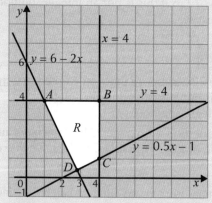

> In these cases, you just read off the coordinates from your graph.

- Point A is the intersection of the lines $y = 6 - 2x$ and $y = 4$, so A has coordinates $(1, 4)$.
- Point B is the intersection of the lines $x = 4$ and $y = 4$, so B has coordinates $(4, 4)$.
- Point C is the intersection of the lines $x = 4$ and $y = 0.5x - 1$, so C has coordinates $(4, 1)$.
- Point D is the intersection of the lines $y = 6 - 2x$ and $y = 0.5x - 1$,

$$\Rightarrow 6 - 2x = 0.5x - 1 \Rightarrow \frac{5}{2}x = 7 \Rightarrow x = \frac{14}{5} \Rightarrow y = 6 - \frac{28}{5} = \frac{2}{5}, \text{ so } D \text{ has coordinates } \left(\frac{14}{5}, \frac{2}{5}\right).$$

Putting these values into the objective function $Z = 8x + 9y$:

At A: $Z = (8 \times 1) + (9 \times 4) = 44$.

At B: $Z = (8 \times 4) + (9 \times 4) = 68$.

At C: $Z = (8 \times 4) + (9 \times 1) = 41$.

At D: $Z = (8 \times \frac{14}{5}) + (9 \times \frac{2}{5}) = 26$.

So the minimum value of Z is 26, which occurs when $x = \frac{14}{5}$ and $y = \frac{2}{5}$.

The Vertex Method

The **Optimal Integer Solution** may **Not** be found at a **Vertex**

1) It's easy to forget that **not all** the integer solutions near the optimal vertex will be **inside** the **feasible region** — you can check if they are either **by eye** on an **accurate graph**, or by putting the **coordinates** into each of the **constraints**.

2) Once you've done that, you can plug the coordinates that **are** in the feasible region into the **objective function** and see which is the **optimal integer solution**.

You might have to check the points near more than one vertex to be sure you've found the optimal integer solution.

Example: A company makes baby clothes. It makes x sets of girls' clothes and y sets of boys' clothes, for a profit per set of £6 and £5 respectively, subject to the constraints $x + y \leq 9$, $3x - y \leq 9$, $y \leq 7$ and $x, y \geq 0$. Maximise the profit, $P = 6x + 5y$.

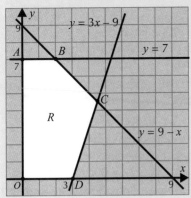

The feasible region is the area $OABCD$, with coordinates $O(0, 0)$, $A(0, 7)$, $B(2, 7)$, $C\left(\frac{9}{2}, \frac{9}{2}\right)$ and $D(3, 0)$.

The value of P at each vertex is O: £0, A: £35, B: £47, C: £49.50 and D: £18.

The maximum value of P is £49.50, which occurs at $C\left(\frac{9}{2}, \frac{9}{2}\right)$. $\frac{9}{2} = (4.5, 4.5)$

However, making 4.5 sets of clothes is not possible, so an integer solution is needed.

The integer coordinates near C are (4, 5), (5, 5), (5, 4) and (4, 4). (5, 5) and (5, 4) don't satisfy the constraint $3x - y \leq 9$, so are outside the feasible region.

At (4, 5), $P = £49$, and at (4, 4), $P = £44$, so £49 is the maximum profit.

So the company needs to make **4 sets of girls' clothes** and **5 sets of boys' clothes** to make the **maximum profit of £49**.

Practice Question

Q1 a) Find the value of $P = 2x + 3y$ at each vertex A, B and C of the feasible region, R, in the graph on the right.

b) State the maximum and minimum values of P within R and the coordinates at which they occur.

c) Find the maximum and minimum values of P within R if x and y represent the number of tables and chairs sold respectively.

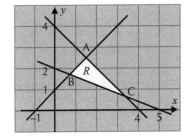

Exam Question

Q1 The graph on the right shows the constraints of a linear programming problem. The feasible region is labelled R.

a) Including the non-negativity constraints, find the inequalities that represent R. [5 marks]

b) Find the coordinates of each vertex of R. [3 marks]

The aim is to minimise $C = 4x + y$.

c) Find the vertex which leads to the smallest value of C and explain why this isn't the optimal solution to the problem. [3 marks]

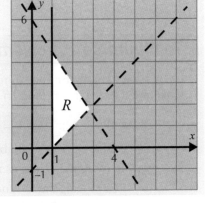

Wow, this is a revision guide and a half...

Some questions might give you two different objective functions and ask you to minimise cost and maximise profit for the same set of constraints. The vertex method is really useful here, as once you've worked out the coordinates of the vertices, you can easily put the values into both objective functions without having to do any more work.

The Simplex Method

Don't be fooled — the Simplex method isn't as simple as its name would have you believe. Also, from now on, there's no such thing as tables — they're called tableaux now. And yes, you do have to pronounce that in a French accent.

The Simplex Method uses Slack Variables

1) The **Simplex method** is another way of solving **linear programming problems**. Instead of drawing a **graph**, you put all the information into a **tableau** (not a table) and solve it from there. The **method's** on the next page.

2) The **constraints** that are entered into the tableau must take the form of **equations**. But most linear programming problems involve constraints that take the form of **inequalities** — this is a complete disaster.

3) Not really — introduce **slack variables** (see page 219) to turn all the inequalities into equations.

> The Simplex method only works with "less than" constraints — i.e. ones that include a "≤" sign.

Put the Variables into Columns in your Tableau

1) To set up the tableau, you need to put each **variable** in a **separate column**. One for x, one for y (and one for w and/or z, if it's a **3 or 4-variable** problem), and one for **each** of the **slack variables**. For the Simplex method to work, **all** of these variables must be **non-negative**.

2) You'll also need a column for the **basic variables (B.V.)**. In each row, there will be one variable that **doesn't** appear in any other row — this is the basic variable for that row.

3) Most **rows** in your tableau will represent one of the **constraints**.

4) The bottom row will be the **objective function**, so a P (or whatever you're trying to maximise) goes in the bottom row of the basic variable column. You need to **rearrange** the objective function to get **all** the variables on the **same side** (so $P = 3x + 2y$ becomes $P - 3x - 2y = 0$).

5) For the other rows, the entries are the coefficients of the variables in the corresponding constraints — that'll be x and y (and maybe w and z), and **one** of the **slack variables** (if the rows represent **inequality** constraints).

6) There should be a column for the **value** of each equation — this will always be **0** for the **objective function** at the beginning of a Simplex problem.

> **Example:** Set up the following linear programming problem as a tableau:
> Maximise $P = 3x + 2y + 5z$ subject to the constraints $x + y - z \le 12$, $3x + 4y + 2z \le 18$, $x, y, z \ge 0$.
>
> First, add in the slack variables: $x + y - z \le 12$ becomes $x + y - z + s_1 = 12$
> and $3x + 4y + 2z \le 18$ becomes $3x + 4y + 2z + s_2 = 18$, where $s_1, s_2 \ge 0$.
> Then rearrange the equation for P: $P = 3x + 2y + 5z$ becomes $P - 3x - 2y - 5z = 0$. Now put this into a tableau:
>
> s_1, s_2 and P only appear in one equation each, so they go in the B.V. column in the row that they appear.
>
> | B.V. | x | y | z | s_1 | s_2 | Value |
> |------|-----|-----|-----|-------|-------|-------|
> | s_1 | 1 | 1 | −1 | 1 | 0 | 12 |
> | s_2 | 3 | 4 | 2 | 0 | 1 | 18 |
> | P | −3 | −2 | −5 | 0 | 0 | 0 |
>
> This is the constraint $x + y - z + s_1 = 12$.
>
> This is the constraint $3x + 4y + 2z + s_2 = 18$.
>
> This row represents the equation for P.

To Minimise a problem, make the objective function Negative

If you have to **minimise** something using the Simplex method, you make the objective function **negative** and **maximise** it (using the method on the next page). The **tableau** for a **minimising problem** will look something like this:

> **Example:** Minimise $C = 2x - 3y$ subject to the constraints $4x + y \le 32$, $6x + 5y \le 45$, $x, y \ge 0$.
>
> Add in the slack variables to get $4x + y + s_1 = 32$ and $6x + 5y + s_2 = 45$, where $s_1, s_2 \ge 0$.
> To minimise C, use its negative — call this C': so $C = 2x - 3y$ gives $C' = -2x + 3y$.
> Rearranging the C' function to get the variables on the same side gives $C' + 2x - 3y = 0$.
> Putting all this into a tableau gives:
>
> | B.V. | x | y | s_1 | s_2 | Value |
> |------|-----|-----|-------|-------|-------|
> | s_1 | 4 | 1 | 1 | 0 | 32 |
> | s_2 | 6 | 5 | 0 | 1 | 45 |
> | C' | 2 | −3 | 0 | 0 | 0 |
>
> You'd now use the Simplex method on the next page to maximise this problem and find a maximum value for C'. As $C = -C'$, min $C = -$max C'.

The Simplex Method

You have to choose **Pivots** from the **Tableau**

Choosing a **pivot** is the next step in **solving** a linear programming problem (once you've set up the **tableau**). It's important that you get this bit right, as it'll affect the rest of the solution if it's wrong.

Choosing a Pivot

1) Look at the **bottom row** of your tableau (the row for the **objective function**). Pick a column that has a **negative value** in the bottom row (let's say you've picked column x for the rest of this method).

2) Now **divide** each number in the **value column** by the corresponding x-value. **Ignore** the **bottom row**, as the value is 0 here. Choose the x-value that gives the **smallest positive solution** when the number in the value column is divided by it. This is your **pivot.** ← *If you get a negative value when you divide, you can't use this as your pivot.*

3) The row that your pivot is in is called the **pivot row.**

Example: Choose a pivot for the following tableau:

Because the Simplex method only works with "≤" constraints, every additional variable is a slack variable.

1) First, look at the bottom row. The y-value is the only negative one, so pick the y-column.

2) Now divide each of the numbers in the value column by the y-value in the same row:
$18 \div 2 = 9$, $15 \div 3 = 5$
and $20 \div -4 = -5$. ← *You can't use the negative solution.*
The smallest positive value is 5, so 3 is your pivot.

B.V.	x	y	s_1	s_2	s_3	Value
s_1	3	2	1	0	0	18
s_2	2	③	0	1	0	15
s_3	5	−4	0	0	1	20
P	4	−1	0	0	0	0

3) Circle the 3 in the y-column. The 's_2' row contains the pivot so it is the pivot row.

Use your **Pivots** to **Solve** the problem

Choosing a pivot is only the **beginning**... Don't panic if you don't understand this method as you read it — it'll make more sense as you go through the **worked example** on the next page.

The Simplex Method

1) a) First, choose a **pivot** (see above).
   b) Then replace the **basic variable** entry in the pivot row with the variable in the **pivot column** (the pivot variable).
   c) **Divide** the whole of the **pivot row** by the pivot — this'll make the **new value** of the pivot **1**.
   d) Finally make all the **other values** in the **pivot column 0** — you do this by **adding** or **subtracting multiples** of the **original pivot row** to all the other rows. This will give you a **new tableau**.

This is one iteration of the Simplex method.

2) **Repeat** step 1 for the other **decision variables** which have a **negative value** in their **bottom row** (i.e. if you used the x-column first, repeat for the y- and maybe z- and w- columns), using the **new tableau**. You need to choose a **new pivot** each time.

If there are no negative values in the bottom row at this stage, you've reached the optimum solution — see below.

3) You should end up with a tableau in which **each** decision variable column has just a **single 1** (the other column entries should be **0s**). The 1s should be in **different rows**.

4) You can now work out the values of the decision variables from your **final tableau**. The **value** in the **bottom row** will be the **maximum value** of P.

Example:

Suppose this was your final tableau...
The bottom row gives $P + 2s_1 + 3s_2 = 14$.
But s_1 and s_2 are both ≥ 0, so to get the maximum value of P, you have to set s_1 and s_2 equal to O. This makes $P = 14$.
The top row gives $x + 2s_2 = 5$ — but $s_2 = O$, so $x = 5$.
Now the second row gives $y + \frac{1}{2}s_1 = 3$. But we've made $s_1 = O$, so $y = 3$.

B.V.	x	y	s_1	s_2	Value
x	①	0	0	2	⑤
y	0	①	½	0	③
ⓟ	0	0	2	3	⑭

Hugo and Jeanne were enjoying their tableau for two and knew they weren't constrained by time.

The Simplex Method

Solve Linear Programming Problems using the Simplex Method

I told you that Simplex wasn't as easy as it sounds, but the best way to understand the Simplex method is to follow through a **worked example**, then have a go for yourself.

Example: Jonny is making cakes to sell at a fair. Baking a small cake takes 1 hour and baking a large cake takes 2 hours. Decorating a small cake takes 2 hours, and decorating a large cake also takes 2 hours. There are 4 hours' baking time available and 6 hours' decorating time. A small cake sells for a profit of £2 and a large cake sells for a profit of £3. Given that he sells them all, use the Simplex method to calculate how many of each type of cake he should make, in order to maximise his profits.

1) First, set this up as a linear programming problem:
Let x = number of small cakes and y = number of large cakes.
So you want to maximise $P = 2x + 3y$, subject to the constraints $x + 2y \leq 4$, $2x + 2y \leq 6$, where $x, y \geq 0$.

If you ever have negative numbers in the Value column (apart from in the P row) then something has gone wrong.

2) Then add in the slack variables:
$x + 2y \leq 4$ becomes $x + 2y + s_1 = 4$, and $2x + 2y \leq 6$ becomes $2x + 2y + s_2 = 6$, where $s_1, s_2 \geq 0$.
Now rearrange the objective function to get all the variables on one side:
$P - 2x - 3y = 0$.

3) Put all the equations into the initial tableau:

4) Choose the pivot:
Both the x- and y- columns have negative values in the last row, so you could use either. Using the x-column:
$4 \div 1 = 4$, $6 \div 2 = 3$.
$3 < 4$, so use $x = 2$ as your pivot (and circle it).

B.V.	x	y	s_1	s_2	Value	
s_1	1	2	1	0	4	(a)
s_2	②	2	0	1	6	(b)
P	−2	−3	0	0	0	(c)

Now divide the pivot row by 2 to make the x-value 1. Then add and subtract multiples of the original pivot row (row (b) above) to the other rows to make the x-values 0:

To make the x-value in the 1st row 0, you need to take away half of row (b) from row (a).

This is the first iteration.

Now x only appears in one equation, so it goes in the basic variable column.

B.V.	x	y	s_1	s_2	Value	
s_1	0	①	1	$-\frac{1}{2}$	1	$(d) = (a) - \frac{1}{2}(b)$
x	1	1	0	$\frac{1}{2}$	3	$(e) = (b) \div 2$
P	0	−1	0	1	6	$(f) = (c) + (b)$

To make the x-value in the bottom row 0, you need to add row (b) to row (c).

5) Choose a pivot from this new tableau for the y-column:
$1 \div 1 = 1$, $3 \div 1 = 3$, so use $y = 1$ in row (d) as the pivot. There's no need to do $6 \div -1$ as it'll give a negative value.

Now you have to make the pivot in the y-column 1, and the y-values in all the other rows 0 by adding or subtracting multiples of row (d). Replace the entry in the B.V. column with your pivot variable, y.

This is the second iteration.

B.V.	x	y	s_1	s_2	Value	
y	0	1	1	$-\frac{1}{2}$	1	$(g) = (d)$
x	1	0	−1	1	2	$(h) = (e) - (d)$
P	0	0	1	$\frac{1}{2}$	7	$(i) = (f) + (d)$

This time, the y-value is already 1, so you don't have to do anything to the pivot row.

6) Now you're ready to read off the solutions:
Row (i) gives $P + s_1 + \frac{1}{2}s_2 = 7$. To maximise P, let $s_1, s_2 = 0$, giving $P = 7$. (g) gives $y + s_1 - \frac{1}{2}s_2 = 1$, so $y = 1$ (as $s_1, s_2 = 0$). (h) gives $x - s_1 + s_2 = 2$, so $x = 2$. So P is maximised when $x = 2$ and $y = 1$, and this gives a P value of 7.

7) So to maximise his profits, Jonny needs to make **2 small cakes** and **1 large cake**, which will make him a **£7 profit**.

You might end up with Spare Capacities too

It's important to recognise that having spare capacities doesn't necessarily mean you haven't found your optimal solution.

1) Most of the time you'll have to set the **slack variables** to **0** to get the maximum value for P, like in the example above.

2) But if your final tableau has a positive value in the bottom row of a **decision variable** column, you'll have to set that variable to 0 instead in order to **maximise** P. This might mean you'll end up with non-zero slack variables.

3) Non-zero slack variables correspond to having **spare capacities**. There's an example with spare capacities at the top of the next page.

The Simplex Method

Example: The following tableau is obtained when Jonny bakes cakes for a different fair. Maximise P using the Simplex method.

B.V.	x	y	s_1	s_2	Value
y	2	1	$\frac{1}{2}$	0	6
s_2	2	0	0	1	2
P	3	0	2	0	10

There aren't any negative values in the bottom row, so you can read off the solution straight away.

1) From row 3 you get $P + 3x + 2s_1 = 10$. To maximise P, let x, $s_1 = 0$, so that $P = 10$.
2) From row 1 you get $2x + y + \frac{1}{2}s_1 = 6$. You know that x, $s_1 = 0$, so $y = 6$.
3) From row 2 you get $2x + s_2 = 2$. As $x = 0$, this means that $s_2 = 2$.

So Jonny should make **6 large cakes** and **no small cakes** for this fair to make a **maximum profit of £10**. He'd have **2 hours'** decorating time left over.

Practice Questions

Q1 Choose the correct pivot in the following Simplex tableau:→

B.V.	x	y	s_1	s_2	Value
y	2	1	½	0	12
s_2	3	0	–1	1	4
P	1	0	–4	0	35

Q2 a) Fill in the missing values in this tableau:

B.V.	x	y	s_1	s_2	Value
	0	2	1	0	6
	1	3	0	1	2
P	0	1	0	5	28

b) Find the maximum value of P, and the corresponding values of x, y, s_1 and s_2.

Q3 a) Put the following linear programming problem into a tableau:
Maximise $P = 6x + 12y$, subject to the constraints $x + 3y \le 7$, $2x + 3y \le 8$, $x, y \ge 0$.
b) Use the Simplex method to solve the problem.
c) The objective function is changed to $P = -3x + 12y$. Explain in words how you would minimise this new objective function, subject to the same constraints, using the Simplex method.

Exam Questions

Q1 A linear programming problem is given by:
Minimise $C = 2x - 4y + 3z$, subject to the constraints
$x + y + z \le 16$, $3x + 2y - z \le 20$, $4x - 5y + z \le 25$ and $x, y, z, \ge 0$.

a) Set up an initial Simplex tableau to show this information. [4 marks]

b) Explain why your pivot has to come from the y-column, and state the value of the pivot. [2 marks]

c) Using your tableau, carry out one iteration of the Simplex method.
State the value of C you have found at this stage. [5 marks]

Q2 A decorating company decorates rooms defined as small or large.
- Each room has to be painted and wallpapered.
- Painting a small room takes 1 day, and painting a large room takes 3 days.
- Wallpapering a small room takes 2 days, and wallpapering a large room takes 4 days.
- There are 15 days' painting time and 22 days' wallpapering time available.
- The company makes a profit of £50 on every small room decorated, and £120 on every large room.

a) Write out the 3 constraints for this linear programming problem. [3 marks]

The company wants to maximise their profits.

b) State the objective function to be maximised. [1 mark]

c) Set up a Simplex tableau to show this information. [3 marks]

d) Use the Simplex method to solve the linear programming problem. Start by choosing a pivot from the x-column.
Interpret your results within the context of the problem. [8 marks]

You're Simplex the best...

The Simplex method is harder than drawing the graph, but at least you can use it to solve problems with more than two variables. Still, it's not perfect — you can't even use it for ≥ inequalities. If only there were two other methods that were even more difficult and only a little bit more useful than this one...

Two-Stage Simplex

More Simplex method for you. Because four pages of Simplex just isn't enough...

The **Two-Stage Simplex Algorithm** uses **Artificial Variables**

1) One limitation of the original Simplex method is that it doesn't work if some **constraints** involve the "$\geq$" sign e.g. $x + 2y \geq 5$. To get around this problem the two-stage Simplex algorithm introduces **artificial variables**.

2) Artificial variables are added to all "$\geq$" and "$=$" constraints in order to **make (0, 0) a feasible solution**. For example, $x = 0$ and $y = 0$ doesn't satisfy $x + 2y \geq 5$, but it can satisfy $x + 2y + t_1 \geq 5$ by setting $t_1 \geq 5$.

3) Artificial variables are usually labelled t_1, t_2, ... etc. and are **always non-negative**.

> **Example:** Turn the following set of constraints into equations suitable for the two-stage Simplex algorithm.
>
> a) $-5x + 4y \geq 17 \quad \Rightarrow \quad -5x + 4y - s_1 = 17$ where $s_1 \geq 0$ is a surplus variable.
> This then becomes $-5x + 4y - s_1 + t_1 = 17$ where $t_1 \geq 0$ is an artificial variable.
>
> b) $y \geq 4 \quad \Rightarrow \quad y - s_2 = 4$ where $s_2 \geq 0$ is a surplus variable.
> This then becomes $y - s_2 + t_2 = 4$ where $t_2 \geq 0$ is an artificial variable.
>
> c) $x + z = 4 \quad \Rightarrow \quad x + z + t_3 = 4$ where $t_3 \geq 0$ is an artificial variable.

Remember, surplus variables are added to make every "$\geq$" inequality into an equation (see page 219).

The **First Stage** seeks to **Minimise** the **Artificial Variables**

Artificial variables can **never** be a part of the **optimal solution** — at the end of the algorithm their value must be 0.

Stage One of the Two-Stage Simplex Algorithm
1) Convert all the **inequalities** to **equations** using **slack, surplus** and **artificial variables**.
2) Introduce a new **objective function** $Q = t_1 + t_2 + ...$ where t_1, t_2, ... are the artificial variables.
3) **Minimise** Q (i.e. maximise $-Q$, see p.226). If the minimum value of Q is 0 then $t_1 = t_2 = ... = 0$. This means a **solution** to the original problem **exists**, and you can move on to the **second stage** by **eliminating the artificial variables**.
4) If $\min(Q) > 0$, **the original problem has no solution**.

> **Example:** Perform stage one of the two-stage Simplex algorithm on the following linear programming problem:
> Maximise $P = 4x + 3y + 2z$, where x, y and z satisfy: $\quad x + y + z \leq 40, \quad 2x + y - z \geq 10,$
> $-y + 2z \geq 10, \quad x, y, z \geq 0$

1) Firstly, rewrite the inequalities as equations using slack, surplus and artificial variables:
$x + y + z \leq 40$ becomes $x + y + z + s_1 = 40$, $\quad 2x + y - z \geq 10$ becomes $2x + y - z - s_2 + t_1 = 10$,
$-y + 2z \geq 10$ becomes $-y + 2z - s_3 + t_2 = 10$ and you need $x, y, z, s_1, s_2, s_3, t_1, t_2 \geq 0$
You want to minimise $Q = t_1 + t_2$, so maximise $-Q = -t_1 - t_2$.

2) Form equations for the artificial variables: $t_1 = 10 - 2x - y + z + s_2$ and $t_2 = 10 + y - 2z + s_3$

3) Use the artificial variables to define your new objective function Q.
Use this to find $-Q$ and then put all the variables on one side of the objective function.
$Q = t_1 + t_2 = 20 - 2x - z + s_2 + s_3 \Rightarrow -Q = -20 + 2x + z - s_2 - s_3 \Rightarrow -Q - 2x - z + s_2 + s_3 = -20$

The right-hand side of the equation for Q won't be 0.

4) Perform the original Simplex algorithm on the objective function $-Q$ and the three constraints:

B.V.	x	y	z	s_1	s_2	s_3	t_1	t_2	Value
s_1	1	1	1	1	0	0	0	0	40
t_1	②	1	−1	0	−1	0	1	0	10
t_2	0	−1	2	0	0	−1	0	1	10
$-Q$	−2	0	−1	0	1	1	0	0	−20

Use column x, row t_1 as your pivot in the first iteration.

B.V.	x	y	z	s_1	s_2	s_3	t_1	t_2	Value
s_1	0	$\frac{1}{2}$	$\frac{3}{2}$	1	$\frac{1}{2}$	0	$-\frac{1}{2}$	0	35
x	1	$\frac{1}{2}$	$-\frac{1}{2}$	0	$-\frac{1}{2}$	0	$\frac{1}{2}$	0	5
t_2	0	−1	②	0	0	−1	−1	1	10
$-Q$	0	1	−2	0	0	1	1	0	−10

Use column z, row t_2 as your pivot in the second iteration.

B.V.	x	y	z	s_1	s_2	s_3	t_1	t_2	Value
s_1	0	$\frac{5}{4}$	0	1	$\frac{1}{2}$	$\frac{3}{4}$	$-\frac{1}{2}$	$-\frac{3}{4}$	$\frac{55}{2}$
x	1	$\frac{1}{4}$	0	0	$-\frac{1}{2}$	$-\frac{1}{4}$	$\frac{1}{2}$	$\frac{1}{4}$	$\frac{15}{2}$
z	0	$-\frac{1}{2}$	1	0	0	$-\frac{1}{2}$	0	$\frac{1}{2}$	5
$-Q$	0	0	0	0	0	0	1	1	0

To maximise $-Q$ (and minimise Q), set $t_1 = t_2 = 0$.
So our **original problem has a feasible solution**.

Two-Stage Simplex

The Second Stage just uses the original Simplex method

1) Now you know the original problem **has** a solution, all that's left to do is find the **optimal solution**.

2) First, rewrite the original **objective function** in terms of the **non-basic variables** found in stage 1.
(Non-basic variables are all of the variables that **don't** appear in the $B.V.$ column of the tableau.)

3) Then obtain a **new** tableau by replacing the $-Q$ objective function with this rewritten objective function and **delete** the two **artificial variable columns**.

   If you're minimising P don't forget to switch from P to $-P$.

4) Finally, perform the **original Simplex method** on your new tableau.

Example: Perform stage 2 of the two-stage Simplex algorithm for the problem stated on the previous page.

1) Start by rewriting the original objective function in terms of the non-basic variables found in stage 1.
From the tableau at the bottom of the last page, the non-basic variables are y, s_2 and s_3.
The objective function, $P = 4x + 3y + 2z$, is currently in terms of x, y and z, so you need to read the tableau to find x and z in terms of y, s_2 and s_3:

   Remember $t_1 = t_2 = 0.$

   From row x: $x + \frac{1}{4}y - \frac{1}{2}s_2 - \frac{1}{4}s_3 = \frac{15}{2}$ $\Rightarrow x = \frac{15}{2} - \frac{1}{4}y + \frac{1}{2}s_2 + \frac{1}{4}s_3$

   From row z: $-\frac{1}{2}y + z - \frac{1}{2}s_3 = 5$ $\Rightarrow z = 5 + \frac{1}{2}y + \frac{1}{2}s_3$

   $\Rightarrow P = 4x + 3y + 2z = 4(\frac{15}{2} - \frac{1}{4}y + \frac{1}{2}s_2 + \frac{1}{4}s_3) + 3y + 2(5 + \frac{1}{2}y + \frac{1}{2}s_3) = 40 + 3y + 2s_2 + 2s_3$

   $\Rightarrow P - 3y - 2s_2 - 2s_3 = 40.$

2) Now make this the new objective function row and delete the artificial variable columns.
Leave the 3 constraint rows as they are to obtain the new tableau.

3) Perform the original Simplex method on this tableau to find the maximum value of P:

B.V.	x	y	z	s_1	s_2	s_3	Value
s_1	0	$\frac{5}{4}$	0	1	$\frac{1}{2}$	$\frac{3}{4}$	$\frac{55}{2}$
x	1	$\frac{1}{4}$	0	0	$-\frac{1}{2}$	$-\frac{1}{4}$	$\frac{15}{2}$
z	0	$-\frac{1}{2}$	1	0	0	$-\frac{1}{2}$	5
P	0	-3	0	0	-2	-2	40

The first 3 rows are copied from the last tableau on the previous page.

Use column s_2, row s_1 as your pivot in this iteration.

B.V.	x	y	z	s_1	s_2	s_3	Value
s_2	0	$\frac{5}{2}$	0	2	1	$\frac{3}{2}$	55
x	1	$\frac{3}{2}$	0	1	0	$\frac{1}{2}$	35
z	0	$-\frac{1}{2}$	1	0	0	$-\frac{1}{2}$	5
P	0	2	0	4	0	1	150

In order to maximise P, as before, you need to set $y = s_1 = s_3 = 0$, which gives $P = 150$.
This is obtained by making $x = 35$, $z = 5$ and $s_2 = 55$.

Practice Question

Q1 Turn the following set of constraints into equations suitable for the two-stage Simplex algorithm using slack, surplus and artificial variables: $3x - 2y \leq 14$, $x \geq 2$, $x + 2y \geq 5$, $x + 2z = 6$ and $x, z \geq 0$.

Exam Question

Q1 The tableau obtained at the end of stage one of the two-stage Simplex algorithm for a linear programming problem is shown on the right.
In this tableau, Q is the sum of the artificial variables in the problem.
a) Show that this problem has a solution. [2 marks]
b) Given that the objective function is $P = x + y + z$, find the optimal solution for this linear programming problem. [7 marks]

B.V.	x	y	z	s_1	s_2	s_3	t_1	t_2	Value
s_1	2	0	0	1	2	2	-2	-2	4
z	1	0	1	0	-1	-1	1	1	12
y	0	1	0	0	0	-1	0	1	4
$-Q$	0	0	0	0	0	0	1	1	0

Stage 1 — pass the D1 exam. Stage 2 — never think about Simplex again...

Remember that all the artificial variables have to be 0 for the linear programming problem to have a solution. Otherwise, you'll come up with values for your decision variables that don't satisfy the constraints in the problem.

The Big-M Method

One more method for you to remember. You might feel like you've done enough already, but this is the last topic in the book so one more method can't hurt. Unless you're reading this back to front, in which case, this is the first of many.

M is an **Arbitrary**, **Large**, **Real** number

The **big-M method** is a lot like the two-stage Simplex algorithm — it has **one stage** to find out whether or not the problem has a solution and another stage to find what the **optimal solution** is. Although, with the big-M method, stage two is just reading off the values you obtained in stage 1.

The Big-M Method

1) Convert all the **inequalities** to **equations** using **slack, surplus and artificial variables**.

2) Write each of the artificial variables, t_i, in terms of the other variables.

3) **Modify the objective function** by adding $-Mt_i$ to it, for each artificial variable t_i — use the **same positive constant M** for **all** artificial variables.

> With minimising problems, make the objective function negative first and then add $-Mt_i$.

4) **Maximise** the modified objective function using the original **Simplex** method.

   • To check if the simplex method is complete, make M **arbitrarily large** (i.e. as big as you can imagine).

   • If making M this big means that all numbers in the **objective function row** (excluding the value column) are **non-negative**, then the Simplex method is **complete**.

   • You can then read off your **optimal solution** to the **modified problem**.

5) If this optimal solution contains any artificial variables then the **original problem** has **no solutions**.

6) If not, then this is an optimal solution to the original problem as well.

Example: Perform the big-M method for the following linear programming problem:

Minimise $P = 2x + 3y$ where x and y satisfy: $\quad -2x - y \geq -16 \qquad x + 3y \geq 20$
$$x + y = 10 \qquad\qquad x, y \geq 0$$

1) Firstly, rewrite the inequalities as equations using slack, surplus and artificial variables:
   $-2x - y \geq -16 \Rightarrow 2x + y \leq 16$ which becomes $2x + y + s_1 = 16$,
   $x + 3y \geq 20$ becomes $x + 3y - s_2 + t_1 = 20$,
   $x + y = 10$ becomes $x + y + t_2 = 10$, and you need $x, y, s_1, s_2, t_1, t_2 \geq 0$.

> If a constraint has a negative right-hand side (like this one), multiply the whole constraint by -1 (and reverse the inequality sign).

2) Write t_1 and t_2 in terms of the other variables: $t_1 = 20 - x - 3y + s_2$ and $t_2 = 10 - x - y$

3) You want to minimise P, so maximise $P' = -P = -2x - 3y$.
   Modify the objective function $P' = -2x - 3y - Mt_1 - Mt_2$.
   $\Rightarrow P' = -2x - 3y - M(20 - x - 3y + s_2) - M(10 - x - y) = -2x - 3y + 2Mx + 4My - Ms_2 - 30M$
   $\Rightarrow P' + x(2 - 2M) + y(3 - 4M) + Ms_2 = -30M$

4) Perform the original Simplex method on the objective function P' and the three constraints:

B.V.	x	y	s_1	s_2	t_1	t_2	Value	
s_1	2	1	1	0	0	0	16	(a)
t_1	1	③	0	−1	1	0	20	(b)
t_2	1	1	0	0	0	1	10	(c)
P'	$2 - 2M$	$3 - 4M$	0	M	0	0	$-30M$	(d)

Remember, M can be very large, so $2 - 2M$ and $3 - 4M$ could still be negative, so another iteration is required. Using column y, row t_1 as the pivot in the first iteration gives:

> In the big-M method, the value column doesn't always start with a O in the objective function row.

B.V.	x	y	s_1	s_2	t_1	t_2	Value	
s_1	$\frac{5}{3}$	0	1	$\frac{1}{3}$	$-\frac{1}{3}$	0	$\frac{28}{3}$	$(e) = (a) - \frac{1}{3}(b)$
y	$\frac{1}{3}$	1	0	$-\frac{1}{3}$	$\frac{1}{3}$	0	$\frac{20}{3}$	$(f) = \frac{1}{3}(b)$
t_2	$\frac{2}{3}$	0	0	$\frac{1}{3}$	$-\frac{1}{3}$	1	$\frac{10}{3}$	$(g) = (c) - \frac{1}{3}(b)$
P'	$1 - \frac{2M}{3}$	0	0	$1 - \frac{M}{3}$	$\frac{4M}{3} - 1$	0	$-\frac{10M}{3} - 20$	$(h) = (d) - (1 - \frac{4M}{3})(b)$

The numbers in the x and s_2 columns of the objective function row are still negative for big enough M.
So using column x, row t_2 as the pivot in the second iteration gives the tableau at the top of the next page.

The Big-M Method

B.V.	x	y	s_1	s_2	t_1	t_2	Value
s_1	0	0	1	$-\frac{1}{2}$	$\frac{1}{2}$	$-\frac{5}{2}$	1
y	0	1	0	$-\frac{1}{2}$	$\frac{1}{2}$	$-\frac{1}{2}$	5
x	1	0	0	$\frac{1}{2}$	$-\frac{1}{2}$	$\frac{3}{2}$	5
P'	0	0	0	$\frac{1}{2}$	$M-\frac{1}{2}$	$M-\frac{3}{2}$	-25

$(i) = (e) - \frac{5}{2}\,(g)$

$(j) = (f) - \frac{1}{2}\,(g)$

$(k) = \frac{3}{2}\,(g)$

$(l) = (h) - (\frac{3}{2} - M)(g)$

1) M can now be set **large enough** $(M > \frac{3}{2})$ so that all the numbers in the objective function row (except in the value column) are **non-negative**. So now you can read off the solution to the **modified problem**.

2) Since the numbers in the s_2, t_1 and t_2 columns are all positive for big enough M in the objective function row, to **maximise** P', set $s_2 = t_1 = t_2 = 0$. As the **modified problem** has a solution with $t_1 = t_2 = 0$, the **optimal solution** to the modified problem is the optimal solution to the **original problem** as well:

3) So $s_2 = t_1 = t_2 = 0 \Rightarrow P' = -25 \Rightarrow P = 25$. This is obtained by making $x = y = 5$ and $s_1 = 1$.

The **Big-M Method** can be used to show that an LP problem has **No Solutions**

Example: The tableau below is obtained using the big-M method for the LP problem:
Maximise $P = x + y$ where x and y satisfy: $x + 3y \le 11$, $x \ge 3$ and $y \ge 3$.
Using the big-M method, show that this LP problem has no solutions.

All the numbers in the **objective function row** (except in the value column) are **non-negative** for big enough M ($M > 2$), so you can read off the solution to the **modified problem** straight away.

- P is maximised when $s_1 = s_2 = s_3 = t_1 = 0$.
- This corresponds to $x = 3$, $y = \frac{8}{3}$ and $t_2 = \frac{1}{3}$.

But since the optimisation of P in the modified problem occurs when $t_2 \ne 0$, the **original problem** has no solutions.

B.V.	x	y	s_1	s_2	s_3	t_1	t_2	Value
x	1	0	0	-1	0	1	0	3
t_2	0	0	$-\frac{1}{3}$	$-\frac{1}{3}$	-1	$\frac{1}{3}$	1	$\frac{1}{3}$
y	0	1	$\frac{1}{3}$	$\frac{1}{3}$	0	$-\frac{1}{3}$	0	$\frac{8}{3}$
P	0	0	$\frac{1}{3}M + \frac{1}{3}$	$\frac{1}{3}M - \frac{2}{3}$	M	$\frac{2}{3}M + \frac{2}{3}$	0	$\frac{17}{3} - \frac{1}{3}M$

Practice Question

Q1 Modify the objective function in the following linear programming problem using the big-M method:
Maximise $P = x + 5y$ subject to the constraints $3x + 4y \le 6$, $x + 3y \ge 2$, $4x + 3y \ge 6$ and $x, y \ge 0$.
You should not attempt to solve this problem.

Exam Question

Q1 A linear programming problem in x and y is described as follows.
Maximise $P = x + 6y$ subject to the constraints $x + 3y \le 12$, $2x + 4y \ge 18$, $x + y = 9$ and $x, y \ge 0$.
a) Set up the initial tableau for a big-M solution to this problem. [5 marks]
After two iterations the tableau below is obtained.

B.V.	x	y	s_1	s_2	t_1	t_2	Value
y	0	1	1	$\frac{1}{2}$	$-\frac{1}{2}$	0	3
x	1	0	-2	$-\frac{3}{2}$	$\frac{3}{2}$	0	3
t_2	0	0	1	1	-1	1	3
P	0	0	$4 - M$	$\frac{3}{2} - M$	$2M - \frac{3}{2}$	0	$21 - 3M$

b) Using column s_2, row t_2 as your pivot, perform another iteration on this tableau. [4 marks]
c) Explain why no further iterations are necessary. [1 mark]
d) Using your final tableau, explain why the original problem must have a solution. [1 mark]
e) Find the maximum value of P and the corresponding values of each of the variables. [1 mark]

Is there any chance that the M stands for Method...

When deciding whether or not you need to perform another iteration during stage one of the big-M method, try making M crazy big — say 1 000 000 000. If all the variables in the objective function row are non-negative for this value of M, then you're ready to evaluate your tableau and decide whether or not the original problem has a solution.

Modelling and Problem Solving

Modelling and problem solving are two of the three overarching themes of the A-level Further Maths course (the third being proof, which is covered in Section 1). This means that they could come up in exam questions on <u>any</u> topic.

A *Mathematical Model* simplifies a *Real-life Situation*

A **mathematical model** is a mathematical description of a real-life situation. Modelling involves **simplifying** the situation so that you can understand its behaviour and predict what is going to happen.

Modelling in maths generally boils down to using an **equation** or a **set of equations** to predict what will happen in real life. You'll meet it in **all** areas of the course including differential equations in **pure maths** (see Section 9), moving objects in **mechanics** (see Sections 23-27) and probability distributions in **statistics** (see Sections 17-22).

Models use *Assumptions*

Models are always **simplifications** of the real-life situation. When you construct a model, you have to make **assumptions**. In other words, you **ignore** or **simplify** some factors that might affect the real-life outcome, in order to keep the maths simpler. For example:

- A population growth model might ignore the fact that the population will eventually run out of **food**, because that won't happen in the **time period** you're modelling.
- A model for the speed of a moving object might ignore **air resistance**, because that would make the maths much **more complicated**, or because you might only want a **general result** for objects of all shapes and sizes.
- Probability distributions based on past data often assume the **conditions** in future trials will be the **same** as when the past data was recorded.

Example: Leon owns a gooseberry farm. This week, he had 5 workers picking fruit, and they picked a total of 1000 punnets of gooseberries. Leon wants to hire more workers for next week. He predicts that next week, if the number of workers on his farm is w, the farm will produce p punnets of gooseberries, where $p = 200w$.
Suggest three assumptions Leon has made in his model.

This is a model because it is a prediction of how many punnets will be produced — the actual number could be higher or lower. The model predicts that the average number of punnets produced per worker each week will be the same. For example:

- There will be enough gooseberries to fill 200 punnets per worker, however many workers he employs.
- The weather is good enough to allow each worker to work the same number of hours each week.
- Any new workers he employs will work at the same speed, on average.

There are lots more possible answers here.

You might have to *Criticise* or *Refine* a model

An important part of the modelling process is **refining** a model. This usually happens after the model has been **tested** by comparing it with real-world outcomes, or if you find out some **extra information** that affects the model. Refining a model usually means changing some of the **assumptions**. For example:

- You might adjust a population growth model if you found that **larger populations** were more susceptible to **disease**, so grew more slowly.
- You might decide to refine a model for the speed of an object to take into account the **friction** from the surface the object is travelling over.
- You might adjust a probability distribution if you collect **more data** which changes the **relative frequency** of the outcomes.

You could be asked to criticise or evaluate a model — e.g. you might need to assess if any assumptions are unrealistic.

Example: (cont.) Leon discovers that the weather forecast for next week is bad, and his workers are only likely to be able to pick gooseberries for half the number of hours they did this week. How should the model be refined?

If the workers can only pick for half the time, they'll probably pick half as many gooseberries.

The refined model would be $p = 200w \div 2 \Rightarrow p = 100w$.

Modelling and Problem Solving

Problem Solving questions are more Challenging

Some maths questions can be straightforward to answer — you're told what maths you need to use, then you use it to get a solution. 'Problem solving' questions are those tricky ones where you have to work out for yourself exactly what maths you need to do.

> Problem solving questions include:
> - questions that don't have 'scaffolding' (i.e. they're not broken down into parts a), b), c) etc.),
> - questions where the information is disguised (e.g. a 'wordy' context, or a diagram),
> - questions that need more than one area of maths,
> - questions that test if you actually understand the maths as well as being able to use it.

The Problem Solving Cycle can be Useful for maths questions

When it's not obvious what you're supposed to do with a question, you can use the **problem solving cycle**. This breaks the problem up into the following steps:

1. **Specify the problem**
   The first thing to do is work out what the question is actually asking. The question might be phrased in an unusual way or it might be written in a 'wordy' context, where you need to turn the words into maths.

2. **Collect information**
   Write down what you know. All the information you need to answer the question will either be given in the question somewhere (possibly on a diagram), or it'll require facts that you should already know.

3. **Process and represent information**
   When you know what you're trying to find out, and what you already know, you can do the calculation to answer the question.

4. **Interpret results**
   Don't forget to give your answer in terms of the original context. The result of your calculation won't necessarily be the final answer.

5. **Repeat (if necessary)**

1. Specify the problem
5. Repeat the cycle if necessary
2. Collect information
4. Interpret results
3. Process and represent information

When you're doing an exam question, it's unlikely that you'll need to repeat the problem solving cycle once you've calculated the answer — just be aware that it's part of the general problem solving process.

You could also be asked to evaluate the accuracy or limitations of your solutions.

Example: Armand cuts out a semicircle from a rectangular sheet of cardboard measuring 20 cm by 40 cm and throws the rest away. The cardboard he throws away has an area of 398.08 cm². How long is the straight side of the semicircle?

1) What are you trying to find? *The length of the straight side of a semicircle is the diameter of the circle, which is twice the radius.*

2) What do you know? *The total area of the sheet of cardboard is 20 cm × 40 cm.*
   398.08 cm² was thrown away, so the rest is the area of the semicircle. The area of a semicircle = $\frac{1}{2}$ × area of a circle = $\frac{1}{2}\pi r^2$.

3) Do the maths. Area of semicircle = $(20 \times 40) - 398.08 = 800 - 398.08 = 401.92$ cm²
   So: $401.92 = \frac{1}{2}\pi r^2$
   $\Rightarrow r^2 = 401.92 \times 2 \div \pi = 803.84 \div \pi \Rightarrow r = \sqrt{803.84 \div \pi}$ cm
   $\Rightarrow d = 2r = 2 \times \sqrt{803.84 \div \pi} = 31.99... = 32.0$ cm (3 s.f.)

4) Give the answer in the context of the question. The length of the straight side of the semicircle is **32.0 cm** (3 s.f.).

99% of modelling jobs require A-level Further Maths...

You can apply the problem solving cycle to all sorts: 1. Need to pass Further Maths exam. 2. Buy CGP revision guide. 3. Knuckle down and get revising. 4. Do some questions and check your answers. 5. Get the kettle on and repeat.

Exam Structure and Technique

Good exam technique can make a big difference to your mark, so make sure you read this stuff carefully.

Get familiar with the **Exam Structure**

For **A-level Further Mathematics**, you'll be sitting **four papers**.
Each paper has the **same** examination time, number of marks and weight.

Paper 1 — Core Pure Mathematics 1 **1.5 hours** 75 marks	**25%** of your A-level	Covers material from **Sections 1-9** of this book.
Paper 2 — Core Pure Mathematics 2 **1.5 hours** 75 marks	**25%** of your A-level	Covers material from **Sections 1-9** of this book.
Paper 3 — Further Mathematics Option 1 **1.5 hours** 75 marks	**25%** of your A-level	Covers material from **Sections 10-32** of this book.
Paper 4 — Further Mathematics Option 2 **1.5 hours** 75 marks	**25%** of your A-level	Covers material from **Sections 17-32** of this book.

The specific **Paper 3** and **Paper 4** that you do will depend on the **two options** you've studied — one paper for each option. You'll have done **two** from the following list: Further Pure Mathematics 1, Further Statistics 1, Further Mechanics 1, Decision Mathematics 1, Further Pure Mathematics 2, Further Statistics 2, Further Mechanics 2 and Decision Mathematics 2. You can only take a '2' option if you've taken the corresponding '1' option — e.g. you can only do Further Statistics 2 if you've done Further Statistics 1. This book covers the Core Pure content, as well as all the '1' options, but doesn't cover the '2' options.

If you're doing **AS-level**, you'll take **two papers**. **Paper 1** is on **Core Pure Mathematics**, and **Paper 2** will cover **both** of your **options** (see above). Each paper is worth **80 marks** (**50%** of the course), and lasts **1 hour 40 minutes**.

Some formulas are given in the **Formula Booklet**

In the exam, you'll be given a **formula booklet** that lists some of the formulas you might need.
The relevant ones for the parts of the course covered in this book are shown on pages 278-282.
You don't need to learn these formulas but you do need to know **how to use** them.

The formula booklet also includes **statistical tables** — the relevant ones are given on pages 283-289.

Be **Careful** with **Calculations**

You should always show your **calculations** for all questions — you may get some marks for your **method** even if you get the answer wrong. But you should bear the following in mind:

1) You should give your final answer to the number of **decimal places** or **significant figures** given on the **front** of each exam paper, unless the **question** specifies otherwise. Writing out the unrounded answer, then your rounded answer shows that you know your stuff.

2) Don't **round** your answer until the **very end**. A lot of calculations in Further Maths are quite **long**, and if you round too early you could introduce errors to your final answer. When using a **calculator** you can **store** full decimals, which you can then use in further calculations.

3) For some questions, you can use your calculator to **check** your answer. Just make sure you've included **all** the working out first, so you don't lose any marks.

4) Your calculator **must**:
   - have an **iterative** function,
   - be able to compute **summary statistics** and **probabilities** from **statistical distributions**,
   - be able to do **matrix calculations** for matrices with order up to at least **3 × 3**.

5) **Calculators** that manipulate algebra, do symbolic differentiation and integration or have retrievable formulas stored in them are **banned** from the exam.

6) If you're not sure whether your calculator is allowed, **check** with your teacher or exam board.

Exam Structure and Technique

Manage Your Time sensibly

1) The **number of marks** tells you roughly **how long** to spend on a question — you've got just over a minute per mark in the exam. If you get stuck on a question for too long, it may be best to **move on** so you don't run out of time for the others.

2) You don't have to work through the paper **in order** — you could leave questions on topics you find harder until last.

Make Sure You Read the Question

1) It sounds obvious, but it's really important you read each question **carefully**, and give an answer that matches what you've been asked.

2) Look at **how many marks** a question is worth before answering. It'll tell you roughly **how much information** you need to include.

3) Look for **key words** in the question — often the first word in the question. These give you an idea of the **kind of answer** you should write. Some of the commonly used key words are given in the table below:

Key words	Meaning in the exam
Find / Calculate / Determine	These are general terms that could be used for pretty much **anything**. You should always **give working** to show how you found the answer.
Estimate	This is found in questions where there is some element of **uncertainty** or **approximation** — often in **modelling** questions. It still requires you to show all your working and handle the maths **accurately**.
Solve	When given an **equation**, solving means finding the **value(s)** of the **variable** (e.g. x or a).
State / Write down / Give	No working is required — often for an **assumption**, **reason** or **example**.
Explain	You must give **reasons**, not just a description — these **can** include **calculations** as part of your explanation.
Show that	You're given a **result** that you have to show is true. Because you're given the answer, you should include **every step** of your working.
Prove	Use a **logical argument** to show the statement or equation you're asked to prove is true.
Plot	**Accurately** mark points on a graph or draw a line of best fit.
Sketch	Draw a diagram showing the **main features** of the graph. This doesn't have to be drawn to **scale**, but will need to include some of the following: correct **shape**, x- and y- **intercepts**, **asymptotes**, and **turning points**.
Verify	You're given a numerical **solution** to a problem, and you have to **show** that it really is a solution — usually by **substituting** it into an equation from earlier in the question.
Comment	Following a **modelling** calculation or statistical **test**, you might be asked to **evaluate** or **criticise** the model somehow. Think about the **real world practicality** of the model.
Hence	Use the **previous statement** or **question** part to answer the next bit of the question. 'Hence or otherwise' means there's another way to answer the question — so if you can't quite see what they want you to do with the 'hence' bit, you can solve it another way and still get all the marks (but be aware that the other way might take longer).
Exact	If a question asks for an **exact value**, don't round. This usually means giving an answer in terms of something like e, ln, or π, a **square** (or other) **root**, or a **fraction** you can't write as a terminating decimal.

The last gag in the book is always a disappointment...

Revising exam technique doesn't sound the most exciting thing in the world (monkey tennis?), but it will actually make a big difference to your mark. In fact, exam technique is a skill that you can master — next time you do an exercise, try to apply the stuff you've seen on these pages to the questions. You'll be glad that you did when you're in the exam.

Answers

Section 1 — CP: Proof

Page 3 — Proof

Practice Questions

1   Let $f(n) = 15^n - 3^n$.
For $n = 1$, $f(1) = 15^1 - 3^1 = 12$, which is divisible by 12.
Assume it's true for $n = k$, so $f(k) = 15^k - 3^k$ is divisible by 12.
For $n = k + 1$, $f(k + 1) = 15^{k+1} - 3^{k+1} = 15 \times 15^k - 3 \times 3^k$
$= (12 + 3) \times 15^k - 3 \times 3^k = 12 \times 15^k + 3(15^k - 3^k) = 12 \times 15^k + 3f(k)$
Both of the terms 12×15^k and $3f(k)$ are divisible by 12 and therefore
$f(k + 1) = 15^{k+1} - 3^{k+1}$ is divisible by 12.
We have shown that if the statement is true for $n = k$, then it is true for $n = k + 1$. Since we have shown it to be true for $n = 1$, it must be true for all positive integers n.

2   Let $f(n) = 4^n + 7^n + 10^n$.
For $n = 0$, $f(0) = 4^0 + 7^0 + 10^0 = 3$, which is divisible by 3.
Assume true for $n = k$, i.e. $f(k) = 4^k + 7^k + 10^k$ is divisible by 3.
For $n = k + 1$, $f(k + 1) = 4^{k+1} + 7^{k+1} + 10^{k+1}$
$= 4 \times 4^k + 7 \times 7^k + 10 \times 10^k = 4 \times 4^k + (4 + 3) \times 7^k + (4 + 6) \times 10^k$
$= 4f(k) + 3 \times 7^k + 6 \times 10^k$
All three terms are divisible by 3, so $f(k + 1)$ is divisible by 3.
We have shown that if the statement is true for $n = k$, then it is true for $n = k + 1$. Since we have shown it to be true for $n = 0$, it must be true for all $n \in \mathbb{Z}_0^+$.

3   Let $f(n) = 2^{6n} + 3^{2n-2}$.
For $n = 1$, $f(1) = 2^6 + 3^0 = 64 + 1 = 65$, which is divisible by 5.
Assume true for $n = k$, so $f(k) = 2^{6k} + 3^{2k-2}$ is divisible by 5.
For $n = k + 1$, $f(k + 1) = 2^{6(k+1)} + 3^{2(k+1)-2} = 2^6 \times 2^{6k} + 3^2 \times 3^{2k-2}$
$= 64 \times 2^{6k} + 9 \times 3^{2k-2} = (55 + 9) \times 2^{6k} + 9 \times 3^{2k-2} = 55 \times 2^{6k} + 9f(k)$
Both terms are divisible by 5 and so $f(k + 1)$ is divisible by 5.
We have shown that if the statement is true for $n = k$, then it is true for $n = k + 1$. Since we have shown it to be true for $n = 1$, it must be true for all $n \in \mathbb{N}$.

4   Let $f(n) = 2^{n+2} + 3^{2n+1}$.
For $n = 0$, $f(0) = 2^2 + 3^1 = 4 + 3 = 7$, which is divisible by 7.
Assume true for $n = k$, so $f(k) = 2^{k+2} + 3^{2k+1}$ is divisible by 7.
For $n = k + 1$, $f(k + 1) = 2^{(k+1)+2} + 3^{2(k+1)+1} = 2 \times 2^{k+2} + 3^2 \times 3^{2k+1}$
$= 2 \times 2^{k+2} + 9 \times 3^{2k+1} = 2 \times 2^{k+2} + (7 + 2) \times 3^{2k+1}$
$= 2f(k) + 7 \times 3^{2k+1}$
Both terms are divisible by 7, so $f(k + 1)$ is divisible by 7.
We have shown that if the statement is true for $n = k$, then it is true for $n = k + 1$. Since we have shown it to be true for $n = 0$, it must be true for all non-negative integers n.

5   Let $f(n) = 3^{2n+2} + 8n - 9$.
If $n = 1$, $f(1) = 3^{2 \times 1 + 2} + 8 \times 1 - 9 = 81 + 8 - 9 = 80$, which is divisible by 8.
Assume true for $n = k$, i.e. $f(k) = 3^{2k+2} + 8k - 9$ is divisible by 8.
For $n = k + 1$, $f(k + 1) = 3^{2(k+1)+2} + 8(k + 1) - 9$
$= 3^2 \times 3^{2k+2} + 8k + 8 - 9 = 9 \times 3^{2k+2} + 8k - 9 + 8$
$= (8 + 1) \times 3^{2k+2} + 8k - 9 + 8 = f(k) + 8 \times 3^{2k+2} + 8$
All three terms are divisible by 8, so $f(k + 1)$ is divisible by 8.
We have shown that if the statement is true for $n = k$, then it is true for $n = k + 1$. Since we have shown it to be true for $n = 1$, it must be true for all $n \in \mathbb{Z}^+$.

Exam Questions

There's usually more than one way to show the divisibility in the inductive step. You'll still pick up the marks if your algebra is correct and thoroughly shows the divisibility required. But you will need the base step, the assumption about n = k and the concluding statement to be pretty similar to what we have here.

1   Let $f(n) = (2^{3n-3})(3^{n-1}) - 1$.
For $n = 2$, $f(2) = (2^{3 \times 2 - 3})(3^{2-1}) - 1 = 8 \times 3 - 1 = 23$, which is divisible by 23 **[1 mark]**.
Assume that $f(k) = (2^{3k-3})(3^{k-1}) - 1$ is divisible by 23 **[1 mark]**.
For $n = k + 1$, $f(k + 1) = (2^{3(k+1)-3})(3^{(k+1)-1}) - 1$
$= 2^3(2^{3k-3}) \times 3(3^{k-1}) - 1 = 24(2^{3k-3})(3^{k-1}) - 1$ **[1 mark]**
$= (23 + 1)(2^{3k-3})(3^{k-1}) - 1 = 23(2^{3k-3})(3^{k-1}) + f(k)$ **[1 mark]**
So $f(k + 1)$ is divisible by 23 since it is the sum of terms which are divisible by 23.
We have shown that if the statement is true for $n = k$, then it is true for $n = k + 1$. Since we have shown it to be true for $n = 2$, it must be true for all integers $n \geq 2$ **[1 mark]**.

2   Let $f(n) = 2^{2n+1} + 4(7^n)$.
When $n = 1$, $f(1) = 2^{2 \times 1 + 1} + 4(7^1) = 8 + 28 = 36$, which is divisible by 6 **[1 mark]**.
Assume the statement is true for $n = k$, so $f(k) = 2^{2k+1} + 4(7^k)$ is divisible by 6 **[1 mark]**.
When $n = k + 1$, $f(k + 1) = 2^{2(k+1)+1} + 4(7^{k+1}) = 2^2 \times 2^{2k+1} + 4(7^{k+1})$
$= 4 \times 2^{2k+1} + 7 \times 4(7^k)$ **[1 mark]**
$= 4 \times 2^{2k+1} + (4 + 3) \times 4(7^k) = 4f(k) + 12(7^k)$ **[1 mark]**
So $f(k + 1)$ is divisible by 6 since it is the sum of terms which are divisible by 6.
We have shown that if the statement is true for $n = k$, then it is true for $n = k + 1$. Since we have shown it to be true for $n = 1$, it must be true for all $n \geq 1$ **[1 mark]**.

Section 2 — CP: Complex Numbers

Page 5 — Complex Numbers

Practice Questions

1 a) $\text{Re}(z) = 3$, $\text{Im}(z) = 2$, $z^* = 3 - 2i$
   b) $\text{Re}(z) = -11$, $\text{Im}(z) = -8$, $z^* = -11 + 8i$
   c) $\text{Re}(z) = 5$, $\text{Im}(z) = 0$, $z^* = 5$
   d) $\text{Re}(z) = 0$, $\text{Im}(z) = 17$, $z^* = -17i$

2 a) $4 + 5i$ b) $10 + 24i$ c) $\dfrac{-1}{5} + \dfrac{3}{5}i$

3 a) $z^* = 6 + 3i$, $zz^* = 45$ b) $z^* = -8 - 2i$, $zz^* = 68$
   c) $z^* = -14i$, $zz^* = 196$ d) $z^* = 12$, $zz^* = 144$

Exam Questions

1 a) $2z_1 = 6 + 8i$ **[1 mark]**
      $2z_1 - z_2 = (6 - 1) + (8 + 2)i = 5 + 10i$ **[1 mark]**
   b) $(3 + 4i)(3 - 4i) = 9 + 16 = 25$ **[1 mark]**,
      $(1 - 2i)(1 + 2i) = 1 + 4 = 5$ **[1 mark]**
      $25 \times 5 = 125$ **[1 mark]**
   c) $\dfrac{3 + 4i}{1 - 2i} = \dfrac{(3 + 4i)(1 + 2i)}{(1 - 2i)(1 + 2i)}$ **[1 mark]**
      $= \dfrac{(3 - 8) + (4 + 6)i}{5} = \dfrac{-5 + 10i}{5}$ **[1 mark]**
      $= -1 + 2i$ **[1 mark]**

2 a) Let $z = a + bi$, then $z^* = a - bi$.
      $3iz^* + 4z = -1 - 6i \Rightarrow 3i(a - bi) + 4(a + bi) = -1 - 6i$.
      $\Rightarrow (3b + 4a) + (3a + 4b)i = -1 - 6i$
      $\Rightarrow$ ①: $3b + 4a = -1$, ②: $3a + 4b = -6$ **[1 mark]**
      $4 \times$ ① $= 12b + 16a = -4$, ③
      $3 \times$ ② $= 9a + 12b = -18$ ④
      Subtract ④ from ③:
      $\Rightarrow 7a = 14 \Rightarrow a = 2 \Rightarrow b = \dfrac{-1 - 4 \times 2}{3} = -3$ **[1 mark]**
      $\Rightarrow z = 2 - 3i$ **[1 mark]**
   b) Let $z = a + bi$, then $z^* = a - bi$.
      $4iz - 2z^* = 28 - 14i \Rightarrow 4i(a + bi) - 2(a - bi) = 28 - 14i$.
      $\Rightarrow (-4b - 2a) + (4a + 2b)i = 28 - 14i$
      $\Rightarrow$ ①: $-4b - 2a = 28$, ②: $4a + 2b = -14$ **[1 mark]**
      $2 \times$ ① $= -8b - 4a = 56$ ③
      Add ③ to ②:
      $\Rightarrow -6b = 42 \Rightarrow b = -7 \Rightarrow a = -(2(-7) + 14) = 0$ **[1 mark]**
      $\Rightarrow z = -7i$ **[1 mark]**
   c) Let $z = a + bi$.
      $z^2 = i \Rightarrow (a + ib)^2 = a^2 - b^2 + (2ab)i = i$
      $\Rightarrow a^2 - b^2 = 0$ and $2ab = 1$ **[1 mark]**
      $(a^2 - b^2) = 0 \Rightarrow a = \pm b \Rightarrow \pm 2b^2 = 1 \Rightarrow b^2 = \pm \dfrac{1}{2}$
      b is real $\Rightarrow b^2 = -\dfrac{1}{2}$ has no solutions $\Rightarrow a = b$ **[1 mark]**
      $b^2 = \dfrac{1}{2} \Rightarrow a = b = \pm \dfrac{1}{\sqrt{2}} = \pm \dfrac{\sqrt{2}}{2}$ **[1 mark]**
      $\Rightarrow z = \pm \left(\dfrac{\sqrt{2}}{2} + \dfrac{\sqrt{2}}{2}i \right)$ **[1 mark]**

Answers

Answers

Page 7 — Complex Roots of Polynomials

Practice Questions

1 a) $1 + 7i$ b) $-2i$ and $-2 - 5i$

2    $f(x) = x^2 - 2x + 2$

3 a) 1 real root and 2 complex roots
   b) 2 real roots and 2 complex roots
   c) No real roots and 2 complex roots
   d) 4 real roots and no complex roots

4   Complex roots always come in pairs, so there could never be an equation that had 3 complex roots but there could be an equation that had two pairs of complex roots.

Exam Questions

1    $(3 - i)$ is a root $\Rightarrow (3 + i)$ is a root **[1 mark]**
$\Rightarrow (x - (3 - i))(x - (3 + i))$ **[1 mark]**
     $= x^2 - 6x + 10$ is a factor of $g(x)$ **[1 mark]**

$$\frac{x^4 - 2x^3 + 15x^2 - 134x + 290}{x^2 - 6x + 10} = x^2 + 4x + 29$$

You can use algebraic long division here.
[2 marks — 1 mark for a correct method, 1 mark for a correct answer]

The 2 other roots are $x = \dfrac{-4 \pm \sqrt{4^2 - (4 \times 1 \times 29)}}{2}$ **[1 mark]**

$= \dfrac{-4 \pm \sqrt{16 - 116}}{2} = -2 \pm 5i$ **[1 mark]**

2 a) $ax^2 - 2x^2 \equiv -4x^2 \Rightarrow a = -2$ **[1 mark]**
     $-2b = -26 \Rightarrow b = 13$ **[1 mark]**

   b) One root is at $x - 2 = 0 \Rightarrow x = 2$ **[1 mark]**
The 2 other roots are $x = \dfrac{2 \pm \sqrt{(-2)^2 - (4 \times 1 \times 13)}}{2}$ **[1 mark]**

$= \dfrac{2 \pm \sqrt{4 - 52}}{2} = 1 \pm 2\sqrt{3}\,i$ **[1 mark]**

3    $f(1 - 3i) = 0 \Rightarrow f(1 + 3i) = 0$ as complex roots occur in conjugate pairs **[1 mark]**.
So $f(x) = (x - 2)(x - (1 + 3i))(x - (1 - 3i))$
     $= (x - 2)(x^2 - 2x + 10)$ **[1 mark]** $= x^3 - 4x^2 + 14x - 20$
$\Rightarrow p = -4$, and $q = 14$ **[1 mark]**

Page 9 — Argand Diagrams

Practice Questions

1

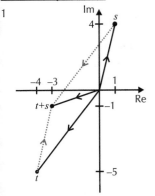

2 a) $\sqrt{61}$ b) $4\sqrt{2}$ c) 7   d) 9
3 a) -1.25 b) 2.82   c) 0   d) -1.57

Exam Questions

1 a)

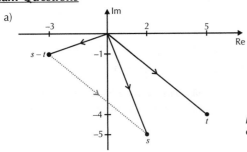

[1 mark for each of s, t and s − t]

b) $st = (2 - 5i)(5 - 4i) = 10 - 25i - 8i + 20i^2 = -10 - 33i$ **[1 mark]**
$\Rightarrow |st| = |-10 - 33i| = \sqrt{10^2 + 33^2}$ **[1 mark]**
     $= \sqrt{1189}$ **[1 mark]**

c) $\arg(s) = -\tan^{-1}\left(\dfrac{5}{2}\right) = -1.19029...$ radians **[1 mark]**
$\arg(t) = -\tan^{-1}\left(\dfrac{4}{5}\right) = -0.67474...$ radians **[1 mark]**
$st = -10 - 33i$, from part b).
$\Rightarrow \arg(st) = -[\pi - \tan^{-1}\left(\dfrac{33}{10}\right)] = -1.86503...$ radians
$= -1.190 + (-0.675) = \arg(s) + \arg(t)$ **[1 mark]**

2 a) $|z|^2 = 8^2 + b^2 = 10^2 \Rightarrow b^2 = 100 - 64 = 36$
$\Rightarrow b = \sqrt{36} = 6$ **[1 mark]**

   b)

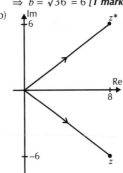

[2 marks available for z and z* both correct — otherwise, 1 mark for two lines that are symmetrical about the Re-axis]

c) $\arg(z) = -\tan^{-1}\left(\dfrac{6}{8}\right) = -0.64$ radians **[1 mark]**
$\arg(z^*) = \tan^{-1}\left(\dfrac{6}{8}\right) = 0.64$ radians **[1 mark]**

3   One root is $-3 + i \Rightarrow$ another is $(-3 + i)^* = -3 - i$
One root is $4 - 2i \Rightarrow$ another is $(4 - 2i)^* = 4 + 2i$
[1 mark for both missing roots]

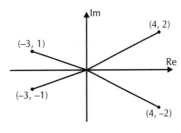

[1 mark for each correct conjugate pair of complex roots drawn]

Page 11 — Modulus-Argument Calculations

Practice Questions

1 a) $5\sqrt{17}\,[(\cos(-0.68) + i\sin(-0.68)]$
   b) $\sqrt{109}\,[(\cos(1.86) + i\sin(1.86)]$
   c) $\sqrt{145}\,[(\cos(-2.30) + i\sin(-2.30)]$
2    $0 + 30i$
3    $\dfrac{8}{3}[\cos(\dfrac{17\pi}{40}) + i\sin(\dfrac{17\pi}{40})]$

Exam Questions

1 a) $r = \sqrt{(-5)^2 + 12^2} = 13$ **[1 mark]**
$\theta = \tan^{-1}\left(\dfrac{12}{5}\right) = 1.1760... \Rightarrow \arg(z) = \pi - 1.1760...$
$= 1.9655... = 1.97$ (2 d.p.) **[1 mark]**
$z = 13(\cos(1.97) + i\sin(1.97))$ **[1 mark]**

b) $z^* = -5 - 12i = 13(\cos(-1.9655...) + i\sin(-1.9655...))$
$\Rightarrow 2z^* = 26(\cos(-1.9655...) + i\sin(-1.9655...))$ **[1 mark]**
$z^2 = z \times z$, so $|z^2| = |z|^2$ and $\arg(z^2) = \arg(z) + \arg(z) = 2\arg(z)$
$z^2 = 13^2(\cos(2 \times 1.9655...) + i\sin(2 \times 1.9655...))$
$2 \times 1.9655...$ is not in the correct range, so subtract 2π.
$= 169(\cos(-2.3520...) + i\sin(-2.3520...))$ **[1 mark]**
$\Rightarrow \dfrac{2z^*}{z^2} = \dfrac{26}{169}(\cos(-1.9655... - (-2.3520...))$
$\quad\quad\quad\quad\quad\quad + i\sin(-1.9655... - (-2.3520...)))$

$= \dfrac{2}{13}(\cos(0.3864...) + i\sin(0.3864...))$

$= \dfrac{2}{13}(\cos(0.39) + i\sin(0.39))$ (2 d.p.)
[1 mark for correct operations on r and θ, 1 mark for correct final answer to 2 d.p.]

Answers

c) $\sqrt{-5+12i} = x + iy \Rightarrow (x+iy)^2 = -5 + 12i$ **[1 mark]**

$\Rightarrow x^2 - y^2 + 2yxi = -5 + 12i$

$\Rightarrow x^2 - y^2 = -5, \ 2yxi = 12i$ **[1 mark]**

$\Rightarrow yx = 6 \Rightarrow y = \dfrac{6}{x}$

$\Rightarrow x^2 - (\dfrac{6}{x})^2 = -5 \Rightarrow (x^2)^2 - 36 = -5x^2 \Rightarrow (x^2)^2 + 5x^2 - 36 = 0$

$\Rightarrow (x^2 - 4)(x^2 + 9) = 0. \ x$ is real $\Rightarrow x = \pm 2 \Rightarrow y = \pm 3$

[1 mark for a correct method to solve simultaneous equations, 1 mark for correct values]

$\sqrt{-5+12i} = \pm (2 + 3i)$

$\Rightarrow 2 + 3i = \sqrt{13}\,(\cos(0.98) + i\sin(0.98)),$

$-2 - 3i = \sqrt{13}\,(\cos(-2.16) + i\sin(-2.16))$

[1 mark for correct r, 1 mark for correct θ in each case]

2 a) $z_1 = \sqrt{13}\,(\cos(0.59) + i\sin(0.59))$

[1 mark for correct r, 1 mark for correct θ]

$z_2 = \sqrt{34}\,(\cos(-2.11) + i\sin(-2.11))$

[1 mark for correct r, 1 mark for correct θ]

b) $r = \sqrt{\dfrac{13}{34}}, \ \theta = 0.59 - (-2.11) = 2.70$

[1 mark for correct r, 1 mark for correct θ]

$\dfrac{z_1}{z_2} = \sqrt{\dfrac{13}{34}}\,\big(\cos(2.70) + i\sin(2.70)\big) = -0.56 + 0.26i$

[1 mark for correct answer]

Page 13 — Complex Loci

Practice Questions

1 a) Circle centred at (0,0) with radius 6

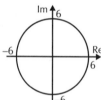

b) Straight line with equation $x = -2$

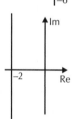

c) Half-line, starting at $(-2, -2)$ with equation $y = -\sqrt{3}x - 2(\sqrt{3} + 1)$ where $x \le -2, \ y \ge -2$

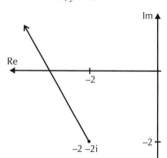

2 a)

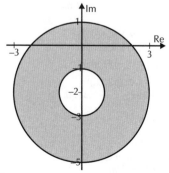

b)

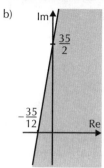

c)

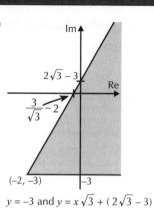

$y = -3$ and $y = x\sqrt{3} + (2\sqrt{3} - 3)$

Exam Questions

1 $|z - 12i| = 2|z - 9| \Rightarrow x^2 + (y - 12)^2 = 2^2((x - 9)^2 + y^2)$ **[1 mark]**

$\Rightarrow x^2 + y^2 - 24y + 144 = 4x^2 - 72x + 324 + 4y^2$

$\Rightarrow 3x^2 + 3y^2 + 24y + 180 = 0 \Rightarrow x^2 - 24x + y^2 + 8y + 60 = 0$

$\Rightarrow (x - 12)^2 - 144 + (y + 4)^2 - 16 + 60 = 0$

$\Rightarrow (x - 12)^2 + (y + 4)^2 = 100 = 10^2$ **[1 mark]**

$\Rightarrow$ The locus of P is a circle **[1 mark]**, centred at $(12, -4)$ with radius 10 **[1 mark]**

2 a)

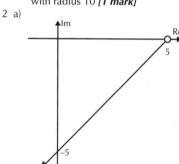

[1 mark for line starting at (5, 0) with nothing drawn beyond y > 0 and x > 5]

[1 mark for straight line y = x – 5]

The locus excludes the endpoint (5, 0).

b) If $z = x + iy$ then $|z + 4 + 3i| = 6 \Rightarrow (x + 4)^2 + (y + 3)^2 = 6^2 = 36$ **[1 mark]**

$\arg(z - 5) = -\dfrac{3\pi}{4} \Rightarrow y = x - 5,$ from part a)

$\Rightarrow (x + 4)^2 + (x - 5 + 3)^2 = 36$ **[1 mark]**

$\Rightarrow x^2 + 8x + 16 + x^2 - 4x + 4 - 36 = 0$

$\Rightarrow 2x^2 + 4x - 16 = 0 \Rightarrow x^2 + 2x - 8 = 0$

$\Rightarrow (x + 4)(x - 2) = 0 \Rightarrow x = 2 \text{ or } x = -4$ **[1 mark]**

$x = 2 \Rightarrow y = 2 - 5 = -3 \Rightarrow z = 2 - 3i$ **[1 mark]**

$x = -4 \Rightarrow y = -4 - 5 = -9 \Rightarrow z = -4 - 9i$ **[1 mark]**

3 $\{z \in \mathbb{C} : |z - 2i| > |z|\}$ represents the set of points (x, y) such that:

$x^2 + (y - 2)^2 > x^2 + y^2 \Rightarrow x^2 + y^2 - 4y + 4 > x^2 + y^2$

$\Rightarrow -4y + 4 > 0 \Rightarrow 4y < 4 \Rightarrow y < 1$

$\{z \in \mathbb{C} : \dfrac{3\pi}{4} \le \arg(z - 2) \le \pi\}$ represents

the set of points (x, y) such that:

$\dfrac{3\pi}{4} \le \arg((x - 2) + yi) \le \pi \Rightarrow \dfrac{3\pi}{4} \le \tan^{-1}\!\left(\dfrac{y}{x - 2}\right) \le \pi$

$\Rightarrow \tan\dfrac{3\pi}{4} \le \dfrac{y}{x - 2} \le \tan\pi \Rightarrow -1 \le \dfrac{y}{x - 2} \le 0.$ Since $\dfrac{3\pi}{4} > \dfrac{\pi}{2}$

and $\pi > \dfrac{\pi}{2}, x$ is restricted to $x \le 2 \Rightarrow x - 2 \le 0.$ So multiplying

$-1 \le \dfrac{y}{x - 2} \le 0$ through by $x - 2$, flips both signs and we obtain:

$2 - x \ge y \ge 0.$ Therefore the correct region is as follows:

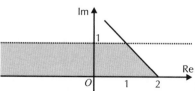

[1 mark for each bounding line y = 1, y = 0 and y = –x +2]

[1 mark correct area shaded, 1 mark for all else left unshaded]

Answers

Page 15 — Exponential Form of Complex Numbers

Practice Questions

1. Any 3 values of θ of the form $2k\pi$ where k is an integer.

2. a) $5\sqrt{17}\,e^{-0.68i}$ b) $\sqrt{109}\,e^{1.86i}$ c) $\sqrt{145}\,e^{-2.30i}$

3. a) $st = 10e^{-i\frac{\pi}{56}}$, $\frac{t}{s} = \frac{5}{2}e^{-i\frac{15\pi}{56}}$ b) $st = 12e^{i\frac{5\pi}{12}}$, $\frac{t}{s} = \frac{4}{3}e^{i\frac{11\pi}{12}}$

4. a) $\cos\theta = \dfrac{e^{i\theta}+e^{-i\theta}}{2}$, $\sin\theta = \dfrac{e^{i\theta}-e^{-i\theta}}{2i}$

$$\Rightarrow \cos^2\theta + \sin^2\theta = \left(\frac{e^{2i\theta}+2+e^{-2i\theta}}{4}\right)+\left(\frac{e^{2i\theta}-2+e^{-2i\theta}}{-4}\right)$$

$$= \frac{2+2}{4}+\frac{e^{2i\theta}-e^{2i\theta}}{4}+\frac{e^{-2i\theta}-e^{-2i\theta}}{4}=1$$

b) $\cos\theta = \dfrac{e^{i\theta}+e^{-i\theta}}{2}$, $\sin\theta = \dfrac{e^{i\theta}-e^{-i\theta}}{2i}$

$$\Rightarrow 2\cos\theta\sin\theta = 2\times\left(\frac{e^{2i\theta}-1+1-e^{-2i\theta}}{4i}\right)=\frac{e^{2i\theta}-e^{-2i\theta}}{2i}$$

$$= \frac{1}{2i}(\cos 2\theta + i\sin 2\theta)-(\cos(-2\theta)+i\sin(-2\theta))=\frac{2i\sin 2\theta}{2i}=\sin 2\theta$$

5. Anything of the form $e^{-\pi(1+2k)}$ for integer values of k e.g. :
$(-1)^i = (e^{i\pi})^i = e^{i^2\pi}=e^{-\pi}=0.0432$ (3 s.f.)

Exam Questions

1. $r = \sqrt{3^2+(3\sqrt{3})^2}=\sqrt{36}=6$ **[1 mark]**

$\theta = \tan^{-1}\left(\frac{-3\sqrt{3}}{3}\right)=-\frac{\pi}{3}$ **[1 mark]**

$\Rightarrow 3-(3\sqrt{3})i = 6e^{-i\frac{\pi}{3}}$ **[1 mark]**

2. $32\left(\cos\left(-\frac{3\pi}{8}\right)+i\sin\left(-\frac{3\pi}{8}\right)\right)=32e^{-i\frac{3\pi}{8}}$

$\Rightarrow [32\left(\cos\left(-\frac{3\pi}{8}\right)+i\sin\left(-\frac{3\pi}{8}\right)\right)]^4 = (32e^{-i\frac{3\pi}{8}})^4$ **[1 mark]**

$= 32^4\,e^{4\times(-i\frac{3\pi}{8})}=(2^5)^4\,e^{-i\frac{3\pi}{2}}=2^{20}\,e^{i\frac{\pi}{2}}$ **[1 mark]**

$= 2^{20}(\cos\frac{\pi}{2}+i\sin\frac{\pi}{2})$ **[1 mark]**

Page 18 — De Moivre's Theorem

Practice Questions

1. $0+i=i$
2. $2^{14}\left(\cos\left(\frac{\pi}{3}\right)+i\sin\left(\frac{\pi}{3}\right)\right)$
3. $(\cos k\pi)^n = (\cos k\pi + i\sin k\pi)^n$ as $\sin k\pi = 0$ for every integer, k.
$\Rightarrow \cos^n(k\pi)=\cos kn\pi + i\sin kn\pi = \cos kn\pi$ by de Moivre's theorem.
4. $(\cos\theta+i\sin\theta)^{-n}=((\cos\theta+i\sin\theta)^n)^{-1}=(\cos n\theta + i\sin n\theta)^{-1}$ by assumption.

$$\frac{1}{\cos n\theta + i\sin n\theta}=\frac{\cos n\theta - i\sin n\theta}{(\cos n\theta + i\sin n\theta)(\cos n\theta - i\sin n\theta)}$$

$$= \frac{\cos n\theta - i\sin n\theta}{(\cos^2 n\theta + \sin^2 n\theta)}=\cos n\theta - i\sin n\theta = \cos(-n\theta)+i\sin(-n\theta)$$

$n\geq 0 \Rightarrow -n\leq 0$. So de Moivre's theorem holds for all negative integers.

Exam Questions

1. $z^n - z^{-n}=2i\sin n\theta \Rightarrow \frac{z-z^{-1}}{2i}=\sin\theta$ by setting $n=1$ **[1 mark]**

$\Rightarrow \sin^3\theta = \left(\frac{z-z^{-1}}{2i}\right)^3 = \frac{z^3-3z+3z^{-1}-z^{-3}}{8i^3}$ using binomial expansion

[1 mark for attempt at expansion, 1 mark for carrying it out correctly]

$$= \frac{(z^3-z^{-3})-3(z-z^{-1})}{-8i}=\frac{2i\sin 3\theta}{-8i}-\frac{6i\sin\theta}{-8i}$$

by setting $n=3$ and $n=1$ respectively **[1 mark]**

$\Rightarrow \sin^3\theta = \frac{1}{4}(3\sin\theta - \sin 3\theta)$ as required **[1 mark]**

2. a) $\cos 6\theta + i\sin 6\theta = (\cos\theta + i\sin\theta)^6$

$= \cos^6\theta + 6i\cos^5\theta\sin\theta + 15i^2\cos^4\theta\sin^2\theta + 20i^3\cos^3\theta\sin^3\theta$
$+ 15i^4\cos^2\theta\sin^4\theta + 6i^5\cos\theta\sin^5\theta + i^6\sin^6\theta$ **[1 mark]**

$= \cos^6\theta + 6i\cos^5\theta\sin\theta - 15\cos^4\theta\sin^2\theta - 20i\cos^3\theta\sin^3\theta$
$+ 15\cos^2\theta\sin^4\theta + 6i\cos\theta\sin^5\theta - \sin^6\theta$

Equate the imaginary parts:
$\sin 6\theta = 6\cos^5\theta\sin\theta - 20\cos^3\theta\sin^3\theta + 6\cos\theta\sin^5\theta$ **[1 mark]**

$= 6\cos^4\theta(\sin\theta\cos\theta)-20\cos^2\theta\sin^2\theta(\sin\theta\cos\theta)+6\sin^4\theta(\sin\theta\cos\theta)$

$= 3(1-\sin^2\theta)^2\sin 2\theta - 10(1-\sin^2\theta)\sin^2\theta\sin 2\theta + 3\sin^4\theta\sin 2\theta$

[1 mark, for using $\cos^2\theta + \sin^2\theta = 1$, 1 mark for using $2\sin\theta\cos\theta = \sin 2\theta$]

$= \sin 2\theta(3 - 6\sin^2\theta + 3\sin^4\theta - 10\sin^2\theta + 10\sin^4\theta + 3\sin^4\theta)$

$= \sin 2\theta(3 - 16\sin^2\theta + 16\sin^4\theta)$

$\Rightarrow \sin 6\theta = \sin 2\theta(3-16\sin^2\theta + 16\sin^4\theta)$ **[1 mark]**

b) $\sin 6\theta = \sin 2\theta \Leftrightarrow \sin 2\theta \neq 0$ and $(3-16\sin^2\theta + 16\sin^4\theta)=1$ **[1 mark]**
or $\sin 6\theta = \sin 2\theta = 0$ **[1 mark]**

$(3-16\sin^2\theta + 16\sin^4\theta)=1 \Rightarrow (\sin^2\theta)^2 - \sin^2\theta + \frac{1}{8}=0$ **[1 mark]**

Using the quadratic formula $\sin^2\theta = \dfrac{1\pm\sqrt{(-1)^2-4\times 1\times\frac{1}{8}}}{2}$

$= \frac{1}{2}\pm\frac{\sqrt{2}}{4}\Rightarrow\sin\theta = \pm\sqrt{\frac{1}{2}\pm\frac{\sqrt{2}}{4}}$ **[1 mark]**

$\Rightarrow \theta = \pm 0.39\,(\pm\frac{\pi}{8}),\,\pm 1.18\,(\pm\frac{3\pi}{8}),\,\pm 1.96\,(\pm\frac{5\pi}{8}),\,\pm 2.75\,(\pm\frac{7\pi}{8})$

[1 mark, can be in exact form given in brackets]
or $\sin 6\theta = \sin 2\theta = 0 \Rightarrow \theta = 0,\,3.14\,(\pi),\,\pm 1.57\,(\pm\frac{\pi}{2})$
[1 mark, can be in exact form given in brackets]

3. Use de Moivre's theorem:

$$\sum_{k=0}^{\infty}\left(\frac{1}{3}\right)^k(\cos k\theta + i\sin k\theta)=\sum_{k=0}^{\infty}(\frac{1}{3}(\cos\theta + i\sin\theta))^k$$ **[1 mark]**

$$= \frac{1}{1-\frac{1}{3}(\cos\theta + i\sin\theta)}$$ using the infinite geometric sum formula

[1 mark]

Multiply top and bottom by $[1-\frac{1}{3}(\cos\theta + i\sin\theta)]^*$

$$\frac{1}{1-\frac{1}{3}(\cos\theta + i\sin\theta)}=\frac{1}{(1-\frac{1}{3}\cos\theta)-\frac{1}{3}i\sin\theta}$$

$$= \frac{(1-\frac{1}{3}\cos\theta)+\frac{1}{3}i\sin\theta}{\left((1-\frac{1}{3}\cos\theta)-\frac{1}{3}i\sin\theta\right)\left((1-\frac{1}{3}\cos\theta)+\frac{1}{3}i\sin\theta\right)}$$ **[1 mark]**

$$= \frac{(1-\frac{1}{3}\cos\theta)+\frac{1}{3}i\sin\theta}{(1-\frac{1}{3}\cos\theta)^2+\frac{1}{9}\sin^2\theta}=\frac{(1-\frac{1}{3}\cos\theta)+\frac{1}{3}i\sin\theta}{1-\frac{2}{3}\cos\theta + (\frac{1}{9}\cos^2\theta + \frac{1}{9}\sin^2\theta)}$$

$$= \frac{(1-\frac{1}{3}\cos\theta)+\frac{1}{3}i\sin\theta}{\frac{10}{9}-\frac{2}{3}\cos\theta}$$ (using $\cos^2\theta + \sin^2\theta = 1$) **[1 mark]**

$$= \frac{9-3\cos\theta}{10-6\cos\theta}+i\frac{3\sin\theta}{10-6\cos\theta}$$ **[1 mark]**

Page 21 — Roots of Unity

Practice Questions

1. $1,\,0.31+0.95i,\,-0.81+0.59i,\,-0.81-0.59i,\,0.31-0.95i$

2. $\sqrt[4]{12},\,i\sqrt[4]{12},\,-\sqrt[4]{12},\,-i\sqrt[4]{12}$
3. $0.96+0.29i,\,-0.29+0.96i,\,-0.96-0.29i,\,0.29-0.96i$
4. a) Because every positive real number x has a real nth root $\sqrt[n]{x}$ for every integer n.
b) As there is a line of symmetry through each vertex, there is a line of symmetry about the real axis which always contains one vertex (as in part a). Therefore if $a+bi$ is a point on the n-gon then $a-bi$ must be a point on the n-gon by this symmetry. Hence $(a+ib)^n = \alpha \Rightarrow (a-ib)^n = \alpha$

Answers

Exam Questions

1 First find $2 - 2\sqrt{3}\,i$ in exponential form:

$r = \sqrt{2^2 + (-2\sqrt{3})^2} = \sqrt{16} = 4$,

and $\tan^{-1}\left(\frac{2\sqrt{3}}{2}\right) = \frac{\pi}{3}$, so $\theta = -\frac{\pi}{3}$ *[1 mark]*

$\Rightarrow 2 - 2\sqrt{3}\,i = 4e^{-i\frac{\pi}{3}} = 4e^{-i\left(\frac{\pi}{3} + 2\pi k\right)} = 4e^{-i\frac{\pi}{3}(6k+1)}$ *[1 mark]*

Let $z = re^{i\theta}$. Then we want to find:

$z^4 = r^4 e^{i4\theta} = 4e^{-i\frac{\pi}{3}(6k+1)}$, where $k = 0, 1, 2, 3$

Equate parts: $r^4 = 4 \Rightarrow r = \sqrt{2}$

and $e^{i4\theta} = e^{-i\frac{\pi}{3}(6k+1)} \Rightarrow 4\theta = -\frac{\pi}{3}(6k+1) \Rightarrow \theta = -\frac{\pi}{12}(6k+1)$

So $z = \sqrt{2}\,e^{-i\frac{\pi}{12}(6k+1)}$. Evaluate for each value of k.

$k = 0$: $z = \sqrt{2}\,e^{-i\frac{\pi}{12}} = 1.37 - 0.37i$

$k = 1$: $z = \sqrt{2}\,e^{-i\frac{7\pi}{12}} = -0.37 - 1.37i$

$k = 2$: $z = \sqrt{2}\,e^{-i\frac{13\pi}{12}} = -1.37 + 0.37i$

$k = 3$: $z = \sqrt{2}\,e^{-i\frac{19\pi}{12}} = 0.37 + 1.37i$

[1 mark for two correct values, 2 marks for all four]

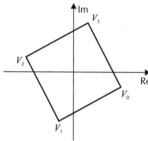

Where V_k is the vertex of the square with a value of k, as found above.
[1 mark for all points plotted correctly]

2 $1 + \omega + \omega^2 + \dots + \omega^{n-1} = \sum_{k=0}^{n-1} \omega^k = \left(\frac{1 - \omega^n}{1 - \omega}\right)$

by the geometric series formula *[1 mark]*

But ω is an nth root of unity so $\omega^n = 1$ *[1 mark]*

and since $n \neq 1$, $\omega \neq 1$ so $1 - \omega \neq 0$

$\Rightarrow 1 + \omega + \omega^2 + \dots + \omega^{n-1} = \left(\frac{1 - \omega^n}{1 - \omega}\right) = \frac{0}{1 - \omega} = 0$ *[1 mark]*

3 Let $z = re^{i\theta} \Rightarrow z^3 = r^3 e^{3i\theta} = 27i$ *[1 mark]*

$27i = 27\left(\cos\left(\frac{\pi}{2}\right) + i\sin\left(\frac{\pi}{2}\right)\right) = 27e^{i\frac{\pi}{2}} = 27e^{i\frac{5\pi}{2}} = 27e^{-i\frac{3\pi}{2}} = \dots$

[1 mark]

$\Rightarrow r^3 = 27, \Rightarrow r = 3$

$\Rightarrow 3i\theta = i\frac{\pi}{2}, i\frac{5\pi}{2}, -i\frac{3\pi}{2} \Rightarrow \theta = \frac{\pi}{6}, \frac{5\pi}{6}, -\frac{\pi}{2}$

$z = 3e^{i\frac{\pi}{6}}, z = 3e^{i\frac{5\pi}{6}}, z = 3e^{-i\frac{\pi}{2}}$. *[1 mark for 1 correct solution, 2 marks for all 3 correct solutions]*

4 The point $(-1, -\sqrt{3})$, corresponds to $-1 - i\sqrt{3}$ on the Argand diagram. Write this in exponential form:

$r = \sqrt{(-1)^2 + (-\sqrt{3})^2} = 2$ and $\tan^{-1}\sqrt{3} = \frac{\pi}{3}$, so $\theta = -\frac{2\pi}{3}$

So $-1 - i\sqrt{3} = 2e^{-i\frac{2\pi}{3}}$ *[1 mark]*

The other 4 points are evenly spaced around the circle with radius 2 at intervals of $\frac{2\pi}{5}$, so they have the exponential

forms $2e^{-i\frac{4\pi}{15}}, 2e^{i\frac{2\pi}{15}}, 2e^{i\frac{8\pi}{15}}, 2e^{i\frac{14\pi}{15}}$ *[1 mark]*

Write these in the form $a + bi$:

$2e^{-i\frac{4\pi}{15}} = 2\left(\cos\left(-\frac{4\pi}{15}\right) + i\sin\left(-\frac{4\pi}{15}\right)\right) = 1.34 - 1.49i$

$2e^{i\frac{2\pi}{15}} = 2\left(\cos\left(\frac{2\pi}{15}\right) + i\sin\left(\frac{2\pi}{15}\right)\right) = 1.83 + 0.81i$

$2e^{i\frac{8\pi}{15}} = 2\left(\cos\left(\frac{8\pi}{15}\right) + i\sin\left(\frac{8\pi}{15}\right)\right) = -0.21 + 1.99i$

$2e^{i\frac{14\pi}{15}} = 2\left(\cos\left(\frac{14\pi}{15}\right) + i\sin\left(\frac{14\pi}{15}\right)\right) = -1.96 + 0.42i$

[1 mark for two correct values, 2 marks for all four correct values]

Convert these back to coordinates:
$(1.34, -1.49), (1.83, 0.81), (-0.21, 1.99), (-1.96, 0.42)$
[1 mark for correctly converting back to coordinates]

Section 3 — CP: Matrices

Page 24 — Matrices

Practice Questions

1 a) $\begin{pmatrix} 3 & 9 \\ 9 & 15 \end{pmatrix}$ **b)** $\begin{pmatrix} -1 & 1 \\ -3 & -1 \end{pmatrix}$ **c)** $\begin{pmatrix} 1 & -1 \\ 3 & 1 \end{pmatrix}$

2 a) $\begin{pmatrix} 6 & -6 \\ -3 & 3 \end{pmatrix}$ **b)** $\begin{pmatrix} 0 & \frac{1}{2} \\ 1 & \frac{1}{4} \end{pmatrix}$ **c)** $\begin{pmatrix} -8 & 2 \\ 4 & -1 \end{pmatrix}$ **d)** $\begin{pmatrix} -2 & 2 \\ 7 & -7 \end{pmatrix}$

3 a) **N** and **S**, **P** and **R** **b)** **N** **c)** None
d) The possible products are: **MQ, NP, NR, NS, PM, PQ, QN, QP, QR, QS, RM, RQ, SN, SP, SR**. (The square matrices **M**, **N** and **S** can also be multiplied by themselves.)

Exam Questions

1 When $n = 1$, the RHS $= \begin{pmatrix} 1 & 1 & 3(1-1) \\ 0 & 0 & 3 \\ 0 & 0 & 1 \end{pmatrix} = \begin{pmatrix} 1 & 1 & 0 \\ 0 & 0 & 3 \\ 0 & 0 & 1 \end{pmatrix} = \mathbf{M} = $ LHS

So the statement is true for $n = 1$ *[1 mark]*.
Assume the statement is true for $n = k$, i.e.

$\begin{pmatrix} 1 & 1 & 0 \\ 0 & 0 & 3 \\ 0 & 0 & 1 \end{pmatrix}^k = \begin{pmatrix} 1 & 1 & 3(k-1) \\ 0 & 0 & 3 \\ 0 & 0 & 1 \end{pmatrix}$ *[1 mark]*

Then $\mathbf{M}^{k+1} = \mathbf{M}\mathbf{M}^k = \begin{pmatrix} 1 & 1 & 0 \\ 0 & 0 & 3 \\ 0 & 0 & 1 \end{pmatrix}\begin{pmatrix} 1 & 1 & 3(k-1) \\ 0 & 0 & 3 \\ 0 & 0 & 1 \end{pmatrix}$ *[1 mark]*

$= \begin{pmatrix} 1 & 1 & 3(k-1)+3 \\ 0 & 0 & 3 \\ 0 & 0 & 1 \end{pmatrix}$ *[1 mark]* $= \begin{pmatrix} 1 & 1 & 3k-3+3 \\ 0 & 0 & 3 \\ 0 & 0 & 1 \end{pmatrix}$

$= \begin{pmatrix} 1 & 1 & 3k \\ 0 & 0 & 3 \\ 0 & 0 & 1 \end{pmatrix} = \begin{pmatrix} 1 & 1 & 3((k+1)-1) \\ 0 & 0 & 3 \\ 0 & 0 & 1 \end{pmatrix}$ *[1 mark]*

If the statement is true for $n = k$ then it has been shown to be true for $n = k + 1$. As we know it to be true for $n = 1$, it is true for all positive integers n *[1 mark]*.

2 a) $\mathbf{AB} = \begin{pmatrix} 3y + 0 \times 1 & 3 \times 2 + 0z \\ xy + 1 \times 1 & 2x + z \end{pmatrix} = \begin{pmatrix} 3y & 6 \\ xy + 1 & 2x + z \end{pmatrix} = \begin{pmatrix} 3 & 6 \\ 1 & 2 \end{pmatrix}$

[1 mark]

Comparing elements:
$3y = 3$
$xy + 1 = 1$
$2x + z = 2$ *[1 mark]*
$\Rightarrow y = 1, x = 0, z = 2$ *[1 mark]*

b) $\mathbf{BA} = \begin{pmatrix} 3y + 2x & 2 \\ 3 + xz & z \end{pmatrix} = \begin{pmatrix} 3 & 2 \\ 3 & 2 \end{pmatrix}$ *[1 mark, using your values of x, y, z]*

Page 27 — Matrix Transformations

Practice Questions

1 a) $\begin{pmatrix} 0 & 1 \\ 1 & 0 \end{pmatrix}$ **b)** $\begin{pmatrix} k & 0 \\ 0 & k \end{pmatrix}$ **c)** $\begin{pmatrix} 1 & 0 \\ 0 & r \end{pmatrix}$ **d)** $\begin{pmatrix} 0 & -1 \\ 1 & 0 \end{pmatrix}$

2 a) $\begin{pmatrix} -1 & 0 & 0 \\ 0 & 1 & 0 \\ 0 & 0 & 1 \end{pmatrix}$ **b)** $\begin{pmatrix} \cos\alpha & 0 & \sin\alpha \\ 0 & 1 & 0 \\ -\sin\alpha & 0 & \cos\alpha \end{pmatrix}$

3 a) Reflection in the line $y = -x$
b) Anticlockwise rotation about the origin through an angle of 0.927 radians (3 s.f.)
c) No change
The identity matrix in any dimension always represents no transformation.
d) Reflection in the plane $z = 0$, i.e. the (x,y)-plane

4 a) $\begin{pmatrix} 2\cos\theta & -\sin\theta \\ 2\sin\theta & \cos\theta \end{pmatrix}$

b) $(2\sqrt{3}, 2), (-1, \sqrt{3}), (-2\sqrt{3}, -2), (1, -\sqrt{3})$

Answers

Exam Questions

1 a) $S = PRRQ$ *[1 mark]*

$$= \begin{pmatrix} \frac{3}{7} & \frac{2}{7} \\ \frac{1}{7} & \frac{3}{7} \end{pmatrix}\begin{pmatrix} 0 & 2 \\ 1 & 1 \end{pmatrix}\begin{pmatrix} 0 & 2 \\ 1 & 1 \end{pmatrix}\begin{pmatrix} 11 & -3 \\ -5 & 2 \end{pmatrix} = \begin{pmatrix} \frac{2}{7} & \frac{8}{7} \\ \frac{3}{7} & \frac{5}{7} \end{pmatrix}\begin{pmatrix} 0 & 2 \\ 1 & 1 \end{pmatrix}\begin{pmatrix} 11 & -3 \\ -5 & 2 \end{pmatrix}$$

$$= \begin{pmatrix} \frac{8}{7} & \frac{12}{7} \\ \frac{5}{7} & \frac{11}{7} \end{pmatrix}\begin{pmatrix} 11 & -3 \\ -5 & 2 \end{pmatrix} = \begin{pmatrix} 4 & 0 \\ 0 & 1 \end{pmatrix}$$

[2 marks for correct answer, otherwise 1 mark for correct method of matrix multiplication]

b) A stretch of scale factor 4 parallel to the x-axis *[1 mark]*

2 $\arccos\left(-\frac{1}{2}\right) = \frac{2\pi}{3}, \frac{4\pi}{3}$

$\arcsin\left(-\frac{\sqrt{3}}{2}\right) = \frac{4\pi}{3}, \frac{5\pi}{3}$ *[1 mark for all four angles seen]*

The student is wrong because

$\sin\left(\frac{2\pi}{3}\right) \neq -\frac{\sqrt{3}}{2}$ **OR**

the transformation takes (1, 0) to bottom-left quadrant but $\frac{2\pi}{3}$ would rotate (1, 0) to the top-left quadrant **OR**

$\frac{2\pi}{3}$ is not a common angle of $\arccos\left(-\frac{1}{2}\right)$ and $\arcsin\left(-\frac{\sqrt{3}}{2}\right)$

[1 mark]

The correct transformation is an anticlockwise rotation, centred about the origin, through an angle $\frac{4\pi}{3}$.

[1 mark — allow any angle of the form $\frac{4\pi}{3} + 2k\pi$]

You could also describe this transformation as a **clockwise** rotation, centred at the origin, through an angle $\frac{2\pi}{3}$.

Page 29 — Invariant Points and Lines

Practice Questions

1 a) $(x, 0)$, i.e. the x-axis   b) $(0, 0)$ c) $(0, y, 0)$, i.e. the y-axis
2 a) $y = mx$ for any m, and $x = 0$, i.e. all lines through the origin
   b) $y = c$ for any c, i.e. all lines parallel to the x-axis, and $x = 0$
   c) i) $y = mx$, all lines through the origin   ii) No invariant lines
3 a) $y = 0, y = -x$ b) $y = x, y = -x$ c) No invariant lines

Exam Question

1 a) An invariant line is a line for which the image under the transformation of all points on the line are themselves on the line *[1 mark]*, whereas a line of invariant points is a line consisting of points which are their own image (invariant) under the transformation *[1 mark]*.

b) Invariant points are the points (x, y) satisfying

$R\begin{pmatrix} x \\ y \end{pmatrix} = \begin{pmatrix} x \\ y \end{pmatrix} \Rightarrow \begin{pmatrix} 2 & -1 \\ 2 & 4 \end{pmatrix}\begin{pmatrix} x \\ y \end{pmatrix} = \begin{pmatrix} x \\ y \end{pmatrix}$ *[1 mark]*

This gives the simultaneous equations
$2x - y = x$ and $2x + 4y = y$ *[1 mark]*
$\Rightarrow x = y \Rightarrow 6x = x \Rightarrow x = y = 0$,
i.e. (0, 0) is the only invariant point *[1 mark]*

c) The position vector of a general point on the line $y = mx$ is $\begin{pmatrix} t \\ mt \end{pmatrix}$
[1 mark]

The image under T of this point is

$R\begin{pmatrix} t \\ mt \end{pmatrix} = \begin{pmatrix} 2 & -1 \\ 2 & 4 \end{pmatrix}\begin{pmatrix} t \\ mt \end{pmatrix} = \begin{pmatrix} 2t - mt \\ 2t + 4mt \end{pmatrix} = \begin{pmatrix} t(2 - m) \\ t(2 + 4m) \end{pmatrix}$ *[1 mark]*

The equation of the image line is $y = \frac{2 + 4m}{2 - m}x$ *[1 mark]*

An invariant line will have the same gradient as the image line so
$m = \frac{2 + 4m}{2 - m}$ *[1 mark]*
$\Rightarrow m^2 + 2m + 2 = 0$, which has no real solutions so there are no invariant lines *[1 mark]*

Page 31 — Determinants

Practice Questions

1 a) -52 b) $4\sqrt{2} - 44$,   c) $\frac{760}{3}$ d) -96
2   279

3 a) 0   b) 0   c) -11 d) 11   e) 77

Exam Question

1   Since **S** is singular, det $\mathbf{S} = \begin{vmatrix} x - 2a & 2b & x^2 \\ 1 & a & a - 2x \\ 0 & b & x^2 - ax \end{vmatrix} = 0$ *[1 mark]*

Combine rows/columns to obtain common factors:

new $C_3 = $ old $C_3 + xC_1$:

$\begin{vmatrix} x - 2a & 2b & x^2 + x(x - 2a) \\ 1 & a & a - 2x + x(1) \\ 0 & b & x^2 - ax + x(0) \end{vmatrix} = \begin{vmatrix} x - 2a & 2b & 2x^2 - 2ax \\ 1 & a & a - x \\ 0 & b & x^2 - ax \end{vmatrix}$ *[1 mark]*

$= \begin{vmatrix} x - 2a & 2b & 2x(x - a) \\ 1 & a & -(x - a) \\ 0 & b & x(x - a) \end{vmatrix}$

$= (x - a)\begin{vmatrix} x - 2a & 2b & 2x \\ 1 & a & -1 \\ 0 & b & x \end{vmatrix}$ *[1 mark]*

new $R_1 = $ old $R_1 - 2R_3$:

$(x - a)\begin{vmatrix} (x - 2a) - 0 & 2b - 2b & 2x - 2x \\ 1 & a & -1 \\ 0 & b & x \end{vmatrix} = (x - a)\begin{vmatrix} x - 2a & 0 & 0 \\ 1 & a & -1 \\ 0 & b & x \end{vmatrix}$

[1 mark]

$= (x - a)(x - 2a)\begin{vmatrix} 1 & 0 & 0 \\ 1 & a & -1 \\ 0 & b & x \end{vmatrix}$ *[1 mark]*

$= (x - a)(x - 2a)(ax + b)$ *[1 mark]*

$\Rightarrow x = a, x = 2a, x = -\frac{b}{a}$ *[1 mark]*

Page 33 — Inverting Matrices

Practice Questions

1 a) $\frac{1}{3}\begin{pmatrix} 0 & 3 \\ 1 & -2 \end{pmatrix}$ b) No inverse   c) $\frac{1}{2}\begin{pmatrix} 1 & 1 \\ -1 & 1 \end{pmatrix}$

d) $\frac{1}{10}\begin{pmatrix} 8 & 2 & -4 \\ 7 & -2 & -1 \\ -12 & 2 & 6 \end{pmatrix}$ e) No inverse

2 a) $X = A^{-1}C = \begin{pmatrix} 1 & 1 \\ -\frac{1}{3} & -1 \end{pmatrix}$ b) $X = CA^{-1} = \frac{1}{3}\begin{pmatrix} -1 & 5 \\ 1 & 1 \end{pmatrix}$

c) $X = D^{-1}E = \frac{1}{10}\begin{pmatrix} 22 & 4 & 2 \\ 18 & 6 & 3 \\ -28 & 4 & 2 \end{pmatrix}$ d) $X = ED^{-1} = \frac{1}{5}\begin{pmatrix} 13 & 2 & -4 \\ 5 & 0 & 0 \\ 6 & -1 & 2 \end{pmatrix}$

3   $\frac{1}{7}\begin{pmatrix} 27 \\ -11 \end{pmatrix} \Rightarrow \left(\frac{27}{7}, -\frac{11}{7}\right)$

Use $\begin{pmatrix} 2 & 3 \\ 1 & -2 \end{pmatrix}\begin{pmatrix} x \\ y \end{pmatrix} = \begin{pmatrix} 3 \\ 7 \end{pmatrix}$ and the inverse of the transformation matrix.

Alternatively, you could also solve the simultaneous equations
$2x + 3y = 3$, $x - 2y = 7$.

4   $(AB)(B^{-1}A^{-1}) = A(BB^{-1})A^{-1} = AIA^{-1} = AA^{-1} = I$
But $(AB)(AB)^{-1} = I$ by the definition of inverse
So $(AB)^{-1} = B^{-1}A^{-1}$

Exam Questions

1 a) i) The determinant of singular **M** is
$a(0 - 1) - x(2 - x) + 2(1 - 0) = -a - 2x + x^2 + 2$
$= x^2 - 2x + (2 - a) = 0$ *[1 mark]*

So $x = \frac{2 \pm \sqrt{4 - 4(2 - a)}}{2}$ *[1 mark]* $= 1 \pm \sqrt{a - 1}$ *[1 mark]*

ii) For **M** to exist, x must exist and this is only true if $a - 1 \geq 0$, i.e. $a \geq 1$ *[1 mark]*

b) $M = \begin{pmatrix} 2 & x & 2 \\ 1 & 0 & 1 \\ x & 1 & 2 \end{pmatrix}$.

det $M = 2(0 - 1) - x(2 - x) + 2(1 - 0) = x^2 - 2x$ *[1 mark]*

Answers

Minor determinants:

$A = \begin{vmatrix} 0 & 1 \\ 1 & 2 \end{vmatrix} = -1,$ $B = \begin{vmatrix} 1 & 1 \\ x & 2 \end{vmatrix} = 2 - x,$ $C = \begin{vmatrix} 1 & 0 \\ x & 1 \end{vmatrix} = 1,$

$D = \begin{vmatrix} x & 2 \\ 1 & 2 \end{vmatrix} = 2x - 2,$ $E = \begin{vmatrix} 2 & 2 \\ x & 2 \end{vmatrix} = 4 - 2x,$ $F = \begin{vmatrix} 2 & x \\ x & 1 \end{vmatrix} = 2 - x^2,$

$G = \begin{vmatrix} x & 2 \\ 0 & 1 \end{vmatrix} = x,$ $H = \begin{vmatrix} 2 & 2 \\ 1 & 1 \end{vmatrix} = 0,$ $I = \begin{vmatrix} 2 & x \\ 1 & 0 \end{vmatrix} = -x$ *[1 mark]*

Matrix of cofactors: $\begin{pmatrix} -1 & x-2 & 1 \\ 2-2x & 4-2x & x^2-2 \\ x & 0 & -x \end{pmatrix}$ *[1 mark]*

Adjoint matrix: $\begin{pmatrix} -1 & 2-2x & x \\ x-2 & 4-2x & 0 \\ 1 & x^2-2 & -x \end{pmatrix}$ *[1 mark]*

$M^{-1} = \frac{1}{x^2-2x} \begin{pmatrix} -1 & 2-2x & x \\ x-2 & 4-2x & 0 \\ 1 & x^2-2 & -x \end{pmatrix}$ *[1 mark]*

2 If matrix **M** is involutory, then $M = M^{-1} \Rightarrow MM = M^2 = I$. *[1 mark]*
So $ABCB^2A^3 = I \Rightarrow ABCB^2A^2A = I \Rightarrow ABCA = I$ *[1 mark]*
Left-multiply by **A** and right-multiply by **A**: $AABCAA = AA$
$\Rightarrow BC = I$ *[1 mark]*
$\Rightarrow B = C^{-1}$. But as B and C are both involutory, then $B = C$. *[1 mark]*

Page 35 — Matrices and Simultaneous Equations
Practice Questions

1 a) $x = \frac{1}{5}, y = -2, z = -\frac{7}{5}$

b) Infinitely many solutions: $x = \frac{1}{4}(t + 3), y = \frac{1}{4}(1 - t), z = t$

c) No solutions

d) Infinitely many solutions: $x = s - t + 3, y = s, z = t$

e) No solutions

2 a) Intersection at a unique point $\left(\frac{1}{5}, -2, -\frac{7}{5}\right)$.

b) Intersection on a line — the first two planes are the same.

c) Three parallel planes.

d) The three planes are all the same.

e) The second and third planes are parallel — both intersect the first plane but not each other.

Exam Question

1 x = volume of gravel, y = volume of clay, z = volume of soil
$x + y + z = 2,$
$x = 2y$
$1.05y + 1.002z = 1.1$
[2 marks for correct set of linear equations, otherwise 1 mark for an attempt to set up 3 equations in 3 unknowns]

In matrix form, this is $\begin{pmatrix} 1 & 1 & 1 \\ 1 & -2 & 0 \\ 0 & 1.05 & 1.002 \end{pmatrix} \begin{pmatrix} x \\ y \\ z \end{pmatrix} = \begin{pmatrix} 2 \\ 0 \\ 1.1 \end{pmatrix}$

[2 marks for correct matrix equation, otherwise 1 mark for setting up some equation of the form Mx = c]

$\begin{pmatrix} x \\ y \\ z \end{pmatrix} = \begin{pmatrix} 1 & 1 & 1 \\ 1 & -2 & 0 \\ 0 & 1.05 & 1.002 \end{pmatrix}^{-1} \begin{pmatrix} 2 \\ 0 \\ 1.1 \end{pmatrix}$ *[1 mark]*

$= \begin{pmatrix} 1.02453... & -0.02453... & -1.02249... \\ 0.51226... & -0.51226... & -0.51124... \\ -0.53680... & 0.53680... & 1.53374... \end{pmatrix} \begin{pmatrix} 2 \\ 0 \\ 1.1 \end{pmatrix}$

$= \begin{pmatrix} 0.92433... \\ 0.46216... \\ 0.61349... \end{pmatrix}$ *[1 mark]*

Spend on gravel: $0.92433... \times 160 = £147.89$
Spend on clay: $0.46216... \times 150 = £69.33$
Spend on soil: $0.61349... \times 135 = £82.82$ *[1 mark]*

Section 4 — CP: Further Algebra and Functions

Page 37 — Roots of Polynomials
Practice Questions

1 a) -10.5 b) -3 c) -4

2   $3x^3 + 5x^2 + 21x - 30 = 0$

3 a) $\alpha + \beta = -8, \alpha\beta = 22$ b) $\frac{10}{11}$

4   $\frac{7}{9}$

Exam Questions

1 $(4 + \alpha)(4 + \beta)(4 + \gamma) = (16 + 4\alpha + 4\beta + \alpha\beta)(4 + \gamma)$ *[1 mark]*
$= 64 + 16\alpha + 16\beta + 4\alpha\beta + 16\gamma + 4\alpha\gamma + 4\beta\gamma + \alpha\beta\gamma$
$= 64 + 16(\alpha + \beta + \gamma) + 4(\alpha\beta + \alpha\gamma + \beta\gamma) + \alpha\beta\gamma$ *[1 mark]*
Using the coefficients of the equation, $\alpha + \beta + \gamma = -\frac{4}{2} = -2,$
$\alpha\beta + \alpha\gamma + \beta\gamma = \frac{14}{2} = 7$ and $\alpha\beta\gamma = \frac{-11}{2} = 5.5.$
So $(4 + \alpha)(4 + \beta)(4 + \gamma) = 64 + 16 \times (-2) + 4 \times 7 + 5.5 = 65.5$ *[1 mark]*

2 First expand $(\alpha + \beta + \gamma)^3$:
$(\alpha + \beta + \gamma)^3 = \alpha^3 + \beta^3 + \gamma^3 + 3\alpha^2\beta + 3\alpha^2\gamma + 3\beta^2\alpha + 3\beta^2\gamma + 3\gamma^2\alpha + 3\gamma^2\beta + 6\alpha\beta\gamma$ *[1 mark]*
Now factorise to get $\alpha^3 + \beta^3 + \gamma^3$ in terms of $\alpha + \beta + \gamma, \alpha\beta + \alpha\gamma + \beta\gamma,$ and $\alpha\beta\gamma$:
$(\alpha + \beta + \gamma)^3 =$
$\alpha^3 + \beta^3 + \gamma^3 + 3(\alpha + \beta + \gamma)(\alpha\beta + \alpha\gamma + \beta\gamma) - 3\alpha\beta\gamma$ *[1 mark]*
The double bracket gives an extra $3\alpha\beta\gamma$, so this is subtracted to give the correct expression.

Rearrange to get:
$\alpha^3 + \beta^3 + \gamma^3 =$
$(\alpha + \beta + \gamma)^3 - 3(\alpha + \beta + \gamma)(\alpha\beta + \alpha\gamma + \beta\gamma) + 3\alpha\beta\gamma$ *[1 mark]*
Using the coefficients of the equation, $\alpha + \beta + \gamma = g,$
$\alpha\beta + \alpha\gamma + \beta\gamma = 0$ and $\alpha\beta\gamma = -h.$
So $\alpha^3 + \beta^3 + \gamma^3 = g^3 - 3 \times g \times 0 + 3 \times (-h) = g^3 - 3h$ *[1 mark]*

3 Looking at the coefficient of x^3, $\alpha + \beta + \gamma + \delta = 12.$
So $\gamma + \delta = 12 - 2 - 6 = 4$ *[1 mark]*.
Looking at the constant in the equation, $\alpha\beta\gamma\delta = 60.$
So $2 \times 6 \times \gamma\delta = 60 \Rightarrow \gamma\delta = 5$ *[1 mark]*
Now find r:
$-r = \alpha\beta\gamma + \alpha\beta\delta + \alpha\gamma\delta + \beta\gamma\delta$ *[1 mark]*
$= \alpha\beta(\gamma + \delta) + (\alpha + \beta)(\gamma\delta)$ *[1 mark]*
$= 2 \times 6 \times 4 + (2 + 6) \times 5$ *[1 mark]* $= 48 + 40 = 88$
So $r = -88$ *[1 mark]*.

Page 39 — Related Roots
Practice Questions

1   $3x^2 + 16x + 144 = 0$
2   $x^3 - 14x + 27 = 0$
3   $y^3 - 3y^2 + 19y - 9 = 0$
4   $y^4 - 12y^3 + 63y^2 - 162y + 175 = 0$

Exam Questions

1 Using the coefficients of the equation:
$\alpha + \beta + \gamma = \frac{2}{3}$
$\alpha\beta + \alpha\gamma + \beta\gamma = \frac{-4}{3}$
$\alpha\beta\gamma = -\frac{-6}{3} = 2$ *[1 mark for all three correct]*
Find the sum of the new roots:
$(3\alpha + 2) + (3\beta + 2) + (3\gamma + 2) = 3(\alpha + \beta + \gamma) + 6 = 8$
Find the sum of pairs of the new roots:
$(3\alpha + 2)(3\beta + 2) + (3\alpha + 2)(3\gamma + 2) + (3\beta + 2)(3\gamma + 2)$
$= 9\alpha\beta + 6\alpha + 6\beta + 4 + 9\alpha\gamma + 6\alpha + 6\gamma + 4 + 9\beta\gamma + 6\beta + 6\gamma + 4$
$= 9(\alpha\beta + \alpha\gamma + \beta\gamma) + 12(\alpha + \beta + \gamma) + 12 = -12 + 8 + 12 = 8$
Find the product of the new roots:
$(3\alpha + 2)(3\beta + 2)(3\gamma + 2) = (9\alpha\beta + 6\alpha + 6\beta + 4)(3\gamma + 2)$
$= 27\alpha\beta\gamma + 18\alpha\beta + 18\alpha\gamma + 12\alpha + 18\beta\gamma + 12\beta + 12\gamma + 8$
$= 27\alpha\beta\gamma + 18(\alpha\beta + \alpha\gamma + \beta\gamma) + 12(\alpha + \beta + \gamma) + 8$
$= 54 - 24 + 8 + 8 = 46$
[1 mark for the correct method of finding the sum, sum of pairs, and product of the new roots.]

Answers

So in the new equation, $-\frac{b}{a} = 8$. So let $a = 1$ and $b = -8$.

Then $\frac{c}{a} = 8$, so $c = 8$ and $-\frac{d}{a} = 46$, so $d = -46$.

[1 mark for using the previous results to find the coefficients of the new equation]

So the new equation is $y^3 - 8y^2 + 8y - 46 = 0$

[2 marks — 1 mark if at least two of the coefficients of y^2, y and the constant are correct, 2 marks if the full equation is correct.]

OR

By substitution:

Let $y = 3\alpha + 2$, so $\alpha = \frac{y-2}{3}$ *[1 mark]*.

So $3\left(\frac{y-2}{3}\right)^3 - 2\left(\frac{y-2}{3}\right)^2 - 4\left(\frac{y-2}{3}\right) - 6 = 0$ *[1 mark]*

Expand the brackets:

$\frac{1}{9}(y^3 - 6y^2 + 12y - 8) - \frac{2}{9}(y^2 - 4y + 4) - \frac{4}{3}(y - 2) - 6 = 0$

Multiply by 9 and simplify:

$y^3 - 6y^2 + 12y - 8 - 2(y^2 - 4y + 4) - 12(y - 2) - 54 = 0$ *[1 mark]*

$y^3 - 8y^2 + 8y - 46 = 0$

[2 marks — 1 mark if at least two of the coefficients of y^2, y and the constant are correct, 2 marks if the full equation is correct.]

2 a) Substitute $x = 1 - 2u$ into $5x^4 + 11x + 8 = 0$:

$5(1 - 2u)^4 + 11(1 - 2u) + 8 = 0$ *[1 mark]*

$5(1 - 8u + 24u^2 - 32u^3 + 16u^4) + 11 - 22u + 8 = 0$

$80u^4 - 160u^3 + 120u^2 - 62u + 24 = 0$ *[1 mark]*

$40u^4 - 80u^3 + 60u^2 - 31u + 12 = 0$

b) If $x = 1 - 2u$ then $u = \frac{1-x}{2}$, so if α, β, γ, and δ are the roots

of the equation in terms of x then $\frac{1-\alpha}{2}$, $\frac{1-\beta}{2}$, $\frac{1-\gamma}{2}$ and $\frac{1-\delta}{2}$

are the roots of the equation in terms of u. *[1 mark]*

$\frac{1-\alpha}{2} + \frac{1-\beta}{2} + \frac{1-\gamma}{2} + \frac{1-\delta}{2} = -\frac{-80}{40} = 2$ *[1 mark]*

$\left(\frac{1-\alpha}{2}\right)\left(\frac{1-\beta}{2}\right)\left(\frac{1-\gamma}{2}\right)\left(\frac{1-\delta}{2}\right) = \frac{12}{40} = \frac{3}{10}$ *[1 mark]*

Page 41 — Summation of Series

Practice Questions

1 The statement to prove is $\sum_{r=1}^{n} r = \frac{1}{2}n(n+1)$.

When $n = 1$, LHS $= \sum_{r=1}^{1} r = 1$ and RHS $= \frac{1}{2}(1)(1+1) = 1$.

So the statement is true for $n = 1$.

Assume the statement is true when $n = k$, so $\sum_{r=1}^{k} r = \frac{1}{2}k(k+1)$.

Then, when $n = k + 1$,

$\sum_{r=1}^{k+1} r = \sum_{r=1}^{k} r + (k+1) = \frac{1}{2}k(k+1) + (k+1) = \frac{1}{2}(k+1)(k+2)$
$= \frac{1}{2}(k+1)((k+1)+1)$

We have shown that if the statement is true for $n = k$, then it is true for $n = k + 1$. Since we have shown it to be true for $n = 1$, it must be true for all $n \geq 1$.

2 The statement to prove is $\sum_{r=1}^{n}(r-1)(r+2) = \frac{1}{3}n(n+4)(n-1)$.

When $n = 1$, LHS $= \sum_{r=1}^{1}(r-1)(r+2) = (1-1) \times (1+2) = 0$

and RHS $= \frac{1}{3}(1)(1+4)(1-1) = 0$.

So the statement is true for $n = 1$.

Assume the statement is true when $n = k$,

so $\sum_{r=1}^{k}(r-1)(r+2) = \frac{1}{3}k(k+4)(k-1)$.

Then, when $n = k + 1$,

$\sum_{r=1}^{k+1}(r-1)(r+2) = \sum_{r=1}^{k}(r-1)(r+2) + (k+1-1)(k+1+2)$

$= \frac{1}{3}k(k+4)(k-1) + k(k+3) = \frac{1}{3}k[(k+4)(k-1) + 3(k+3)]$

$= \frac{1}{3}k[k^2 + 3k - 4 + 3k + 9] = \frac{1}{3}k[k^2 + 6k + 5] = \frac{1}{3}k(k+5)(k+1)$

$= \frac{1}{3}((k+1) - 1)((k+1) + 4)(k+1) = \frac{1}{3}(k+1)((k+1) + 4)((k+1) - 1)$

We have shown that if the statement is true for $n = k$, then it is true for $n = k + 1$. Since we have shown it to be true for $n = 1$, it must be true for all $n \geq 1$.

3 The statement to prove is $\sum_{r=1}^{n} \frac{1}{(r+1)(r+2)} = \frac{n}{2(n+2)}$.

When $n = 1$, LHS $= \sum_{r=1}^{1} \frac{1}{(r+1)(r+2)} = \frac{1}{(1+1)(1+2)} = \frac{1}{6}$

and RHS $= \frac{1}{2(1+2)} = \frac{1}{6}$.

So the statement is true for $n = 1$.

Assume the statement is true when $n = k$,

so $\sum_{r=1}^{k} \frac{1}{(r+1)(r+2)} = \frac{k}{2(k+2)}$.

Then, when $n = k + 1$,

$\sum_{r=1}^{k+1} \frac{1}{(r+1)(r+2)} = \sum_{r=1}^{k} \frac{1}{(r+1)(r+2)} + \frac{1}{(k+1+1)(k+1+2)}$

$= \frac{k}{2(k+2)} + \frac{1}{(k+2)(k+3)} = \frac{k(k+3) + 2}{2(k+2)(k+3)} = \frac{k^2 + 3k + 2}{2(k+2)(k+3)}$

$= \frac{(k+1)(k+2)}{2(k+2)(k+3)} = \frac{k+1}{2(k+3)} = \frac{k+1}{2((k+1)+2)}$

We have shown that if the statement is true for $n = k$, then it is true for $n = k + 1$. Since we have shown it to be true for $n = 1$, it must be true for all $n \geq 1$.

4 The statement to prove is $\sum_{r=1}^{n} 3^r = \frac{3}{2}(3^n - 1)$.

When $n = 1$, LHS $= \sum_{r=1}^{1} 3^r = 3^1 = 3$ and

RHS $= \frac{3}{2}(3^1 - 1) = \frac{3}{2} \times 2 = 3$.

So the statement is true for $n = 1$.

Assume the statement is true when $n = k$, so $\sum_{r=1}^{k} 3^r = \frac{3}{2}(3^k - 1)$.

Then, when $n = k + 1$,

$\sum_{r=1}^{k+1} 3^r = \sum_{r=1}^{k} 3^r + 3^{k+1} = \frac{3}{2}(3^k - 1) + 3^{k+1} = \frac{3}{2}(3^k - 1 + 2 \times 3^k)$

$= \frac{3}{2}(3 \times 3^k - 1) = \frac{3}{2}(3^{k+1} - 1)$

We have shown that if the statement is true for $n = k$, then it is true for $n = k + 1$. Since we have shown it to be true for $n = 1$, it must be true for all $n \geq 1$.

Exam Questions

1 The statement to prove is $\sum_{r=1}^{n} r^2(r+1) = \frac{1}{12}n(n+1)(n+2)(3n+1)$.

When $n = 1$, LHS $= \sum_{r=1}^{1} r^2(r+1) = 1^2(1+1) = 2$ and

RHS $= \frac{1}{12}(1)(1+1)(1+2)(3 \times 1 + 1) = \frac{1}{12} \times 1 \times 2 \times 3 \times 4 = 2$.

So the statement is true for $n = 1$ *[1 mark]*.

Assume the statement is true when $n = k$,

so $\sum_{r=1}^{k} r^2(r+1) = \frac{1}{12}k(k+1)(k+2)(3k+1)$ *[1 mark]*.

Then, when $n = k + 1$,

$\sum_{r=1}^{k+1} r^2(r+1) = \sum_{r=1}^{k} r^2(r+1) + (k+1)^2(k+1+1)$

$= \frac{1}{12}k(k+1)(k+2)(3k+1) + (k+1)^2(k+2)$ *[1 mark]*

$= \frac{1}{12}(k+1)(k+2)[k(3k+1) + 12(k+1)]$

$= \frac{1}{12}(k+1)(k+2)[3k^2 + 13k + 12]$ *[1 mark]*

$= \frac{1}{3}(k+1)(k+2)(k+3)(3k+4)$

$= \frac{1}{3}(k+1)((k+1)+1)((k+1)+2)(3(k+1)+1)$ *[1 mark]*

We have shown that if the statement is true for $n = k$, then it is true for $n = k + 1$. Since we have shown it to be true for $n = 1$, it must be true for all $n \geq 1$ *[1 mark]*.

2 a) The statement to prove is $\sum_{r=1}^{n} r(r-3) = \frac{1}{3}n(n+1)(n-4)$.

When $n = 1$, LHS $= \sum_{r=1}^{1} r(r-3) = 1 \times (-2) = -2$

and RHS $= \frac{1}{3}(1)(1+1)(1-4) = \frac{1}{3} \times 1 \times 2 \times (-3) = -2$.

So the statement is true for $n = 1$ *[1 mark]*.

Assume the statement is true when $n = k$,

so $\sum_{r=1}^{k} r(r-3) = \frac{1}{3}k(k+1)(k-4)$ *[1 mark]*.

Answers

Then, when $n = k + 1$,

$$\sum_{r=1}^{k+1} r(r-3) = \sum_{r=1}^{k} r(r-3) + (k+1)(k+1-3)$$

$$= \frac{1}{3} k(k+1)(k-4) + (k+1)(k-2) \text{ [1 mark]}$$

$$= \frac{1}{3} (k+1)[k(k-4) + 3(k-2)] = \frac{1}{3} (k+1)[k^2 - k - 6] \text{ [1 mark]}$$

$$= \frac{1}{3} (k+1)(k+2)(k-3) = \frac{1}{3} (k+1)((k+1)+1)((k+1)-4) \text{ [1 mark]}$$

We have shown that if the statement is true for $n = k$, then it is true for $n = k + 1$. Since we have shown it to be true for $n = 1$, it must be true for all $n \geq 1$ **[1 mark]**.

b) If $\sum_{r=1}^{k} r(r-3) = 10 \sum_{r=1}^{n} r$ then

$$\frac{1}{3} n(n+1)(n-4) = 10 \times \frac{1}{2} n(n+1) \text{ [1 mark]}$$

$$\Rightarrow \frac{1}{3} (n-4) = 5 \text{ [1 mark]} \Rightarrow n - 4 = 15 \Rightarrow n = 19 \text{ [1 mark]}$$

3 a) The statement to prove is $\sum_{r=1}^{n} r(r!) = (n+1)! - 1$.

When $n = 1$, LHS $= \sum_{r=1}^{1} r(r!) = 1 \times 1! = 1$ and

RHS $= (1+1)! - 1 = 2! - 1 = 2 - 1 = 1$.
So the statement is true for $n = 1$ **[1 mark]**.
Assume the statement is true when $n = k$,

so $\sum_{r=1}^{k} r(r!) = (k+1)! - 1$ **[1 mark]**.

Then, when $n = k + 1$,

$$\sum_{r=1}^{k+1} r(r!) = \sum_{r=1}^{k} r(r!) + (k+1)((k+1)!)$$

$$= (k+1)! - 1 + (k+1)((k+1)!) \text{ [1 mark]}$$

$$= (k+1)!(1 + (k+1)) - 1 = (k+1)!(k+2) - 1 \text{ [1 mark]}$$

$$= (k+2)! - 1 = ((k+1)+1)! - 1 \text{ [1 mark]}$$

We have shown that if the statement is true for $n = k$, then it is true for $n = k + 1$. Since we have shown it to be true for $n = 1$, it must be true for all $n \geq 1$ **[1 mark]**.

b) $\sum_{r=1}^{n} r(r!) = 23 \Rightarrow (n+1)! - 1 = 23 \Rightarrow (n+1)! = 24$ **[1 mark]**

$4! = 24$ **[1 mark]**, so $n + 1 = 4 \Rightarrow n = 3$ **[1 mark]**

Page 43 — Using Summations
Practice Questions

1 $\sum_{r=1}^{n} r^2(r-4) = \sum_{r=1}^{n} r^3 - 4 \sum_{r=1}^{n} r^2 = \frac{1}{4} n^2(n+1)^2 - 4 \times \frac{1}{6} n(n+1)(2n+1)$

$$= \frac{n(n+1)}{12}(3n(n+1) - 8(2n+1)) = \frac{n(n+1)}{12}(3n^2 + 3n - 16n - 8)$$

$$= \frac{n(n+1)}{12}(3n^2 - 13n - 8)$$

2 a) Write as partial fractions:

$$\frac{1}{r(r+1)} = \frac{A}{r} + \frac{B}{r+1} = \frac{A(r+1) + Br}{r(r+1)} = \frac{(A+B)r + A}{r(r+1)}$$

Equating coefficients: $A + B = 0$ and $A = 1 \Rightarrow B = -1$

So $\frac{1}{r(r+1)} = \frac{1}{r} - \frac{1}{r+1}$.

So $\sum_{r=1}^{n} \frac{1}{r(r+1)} = \sum_{r=1}^{n} \left(\frac{1}{r} - \frac{1}{r+1} \right) =$

$1 - \frac{1}{2} + \frac{1}{2} - \frac{1}{3} + \frac{1}{3} - \frac{1}{4} + \dots + \frac{1}{n-2} - \frac{1}{n-1} + \frac{1}{n-1} - \frac{1}{n} + \frac{1}{n} - \frac{1}{n+1}$

$$= 1 - \frac{1}{n+1} = \frac{n+1-1}{n+1} = \frac{n}{n+1}$$

b) $\frac{13}{204}$

3 $\sum_{r=1}^{n} r = \sum_{r=1}^{n} \frac{1}{2}(r(r+1) - r(r-1)) = \frac{1}{2} \sum_{r=1}^{n} (r(r+1) - r(r-1))$

$$= \frac{1}{2} [1 \times 2 - 1 \times 0 + 2 \times 3 - 2 \times 1 + 3 \times 4 - 3 \times 2 + \dots$$
$$\dots + (n-2)(n-1) - (n-2)(n-3) + (n-1)n - (n-1)(n-2)$$
$$+ n(n+1) - n(n-1)]$$

The only non-zero term that doesn't cancel is $n(n+1)$.

So $\sum_{r=1}^{n} r = \frac{1}{2} n(n+1)$.

Exam Questions

1 a) $4 + \sum_{r=1}^{n} (r+1)(r+4) = 4 + \sum_{r=1}^{n} (r^2 + 5r + 4)$

$$= 4 + \sum_{r=1}^{n} r^2 + 5 \sum_{r=1}^{n} r + 4 \sum_{r=1}^{n} 1 \text{ [1 mark]}$$

$$= 4 + \frac{1}{6} n(n+1)(2n+1) + 5 \times \frac{1}{2} n(n+1) + 4n$$

[1 for using both the r and r² summation formulas, 1 mark for the term 4n]

$$= \frac{1}{6} n(n+1)(2n+1) + \frac{5}{2} n(n+1) + 4(n+1) \text{ [1 mark]}$$

$$= \frac{1}{6} (n+1)(n(2n+1) + 15n + 24) \text{ [1 mark]}$$

$$= \frac{2}{6} (n+1)(n^2 + 8n + 12) = \frac{1}{3} (n+1)(n+2)(n+6) \text{ [1 mark]}$$

2 a) Let $\frac{2}{(r+2)(r+3)(r+4)} = \frac{A}{(r+2)(r+3)} + \frac{B}{(r+3)(r+4)}$

$$= \frac{A(r+4) + B(r+2)}{(r+2)(r+3)(r+4)}$$

$$= \frac{(A+B)r + (4A+2B)}{(r+2)(r+3)(r+4)}$$

Equating coefficients gives $A + B = 0$ and $4A + 2B = 2$ **[1 mark]**.
$\Rightarrow A = -B \Rightarrow -2B = 2 \Rightarrow B = -1$ and $A = 1$.

So $\frac{2}{(r+2)(r+3)(r+4)} = \frac{1}{(r+2)(r+3)} - \frac{1}{(r+3)(r+4)}$ **[1 mark]**

b) $\sum_{r=1}^{n} \frac{1}{(r+2)(r+3)(r+4)} = \frac{1}{2} \sum_{r=1}^{n} \left[\frac{1}{(r+2)(r+3)} - \frac{1}{(r+3)(r+4)} \right]$

[1 mark]

$$= \frac{1}{2} \left[\frac{1}{3 \times 4} - \frac{1}{4 \times 5} + \frac{1}{4 \times 5} - \frac{1}{5 \times 6} + \frac{1}{5 \times 6} - \frac{1}{6 \times 7} + \dots \right.$$

$$\dots + \frac{1}{(n)(n+1)} - \frac{1}{(n+1)(n+2)} + \frac{1}{(n+1)(n+2)} - \frac{1}{(n+2)(n+3)}$$

$$\left. + \frac{1}{(n+2)(n+3)} - \frac{1}{(n+3)(n+4)} \right] \text{ [1 mark]}$$

$$= \frac{1}{2} \left[\frac{1}{12} - \frac{1}{(n+3)(n+4)} \right] \text{ [1 mark]}$$

$$= \frac{1}{2} \left[\frac{(n+3)(n+4) - 12}{12(n+3)(n+4)} \right] \text{ [1 mark]}$$

$$= \frac{1}{2} \left[\frac{n^2 + 7n}{12(n+3)(n+4)} \right] = \frac{n(n+7)}{24(n+3)(n+4)} \text{ [1 mark]}$$

Page 45 — Maclaurin Series
Practice Questions

1 Let $f(x) = \cos x$. Then:
$f'(x) = -\sin x$, $f''(x) = -\cos x$, $f'''(x) = \sin x$, $f^{(4)}(x) = \cos x$, etc
So $f(0) = 1$, $f'(0) = 0$, $f''(0) = -1$, $f'''(0) = 0$, $f^{(4)}(0) = 1$, etc
Only even derivatives are non-zero at $x = 0$.

So the Maclaurin series is: $f(x) = 1 - \frac{x^2}{2!} + \frac{x^4}{4!} - \dots$

The coefficient of the general term x^{2r} will be $\frac{(-1)^r}{(2r)!}$.

So $\cos x = 1 - \frac{x^2}{2!} + \frac{x^4}{4!} - \dots + \frac{(-1)^r}{(2r)!} x^{2r} + \dots$

2 Let $f(x) = \ln(1 + x)$. Then:

$f'(x) = \frac{1}{1+x}$, $f''(x) = -\frac{1}{(1+x)^2}$,

$f'''(x) = \frac{2}{(1+x)^3}$, $f^{(4)}(x) = -\frac{6}{(1+x)^4}$, $f^{(5)}(x) = \frac{24}{(1+x)^5}$

So $f(0) = \ln(1) = 0$, $f'(0) = 1$, $f''(0) = -1$, $f'''(0) = 2$,
$f^{(4)}(0) = -6$, $f^{(5)}(x) = 24$.

So the Maclaurin series is: $f(x) = x - \frac{x^2}{2!} + \frac{2x^3}{3!} - \frac{6x^4}{4!} + \frac{24x^5}{5!} \dots$

$$= x - \frac{x^2}{2} + \frac{x^3}{3} - \frac{x^4}{4} + \frac{x^5}{5} - \dots$$

The coefficient of the general term x^r will be $\frac{(-1)^{r+1}}{r}$.

So $f(x) = x - \frac{x^2}{2} + \frac{x^3}{3} - \dots + (-1)^{r+1} \frac{x^r}{r} + \dots$

3 Let $f(x) = (1 + x)^n$. Then:
$f'(x) = n(1+x)^{n-1}$, $f''(x) = n(n-1)(1+x)^{n-2}$,
$f'''(x) = n(n-1)(n-2)(1+x)^{n-3}$,
$f^{(4)}(x) = n(n-1)(n-2)(n-3)(1+x)^{n-4}$

Answers

So $f(0) = 1$, $f'(0) = n$, $f''(0) = n(n-1)$, $f'''(0) = n(n-1)(n-2)$
$f^{(4)}(0) = n(n-1)(n-2)(n-3)$
So the Maclaurin Series is:
$$f(x) = 1 + nx + \frac{n(n-1)}{2!}x^2 + \frac{n(n-1)(n-2)}{3!}x^3$$
$$+ \frac{n(n-1)(n-2)(n-3)}{4!}x^4 + \dots + \frac{n(n-1)(n-2)\dots(n-r)}{r!}x^r + \dots$$
$r! = 1 \times 2 \times \dots \times r$, so this is the required result.

4    $\sin x \cos x = x - \frac{2x^3}{3} + \frac{2x^5}{15} + \dots$

You can find this by multiplying together the Maclaurin series for $\sin x$ and $\cos x$.

Exam Questions

1    $\sin x = x - \frac{x^3}{3!} + \frac{x^5}{5!} - \dots$

$e^x = 1 + x + \frac{x^2}{2!} + \frac{x^3}{3!} + \frac{x^4}{4!} + \dots$ **[1 mark]**

Substituting the Maclaurin series for $\sin x$ into the one for e^x gives:

$e^{\sin x} = 1 + \left(x - \frac{x^3}{3!} + \frac{x^5}{5!} - \dots\right) + \frac{1}{2!}\left(x - \frac{x^3}{3!} + \frac{x^5}{5!} - \dots\right)^2$
$+ \frac{1}{3!}\left(x - \frac{x^3}{3!} + \frac{x^5}{5!} - \dots\right)^3 + \frac{1}{4!}\left(x - \frac{x^3}{3!} + \frac{x^5}{5!} - \dots\right)^4 + \dots$ **[1 mark]**

$= 1 + \left(x - \frac{x^3}{3!} + \frac{x^5}{5!} - \dots\right) + \frac{1}{2!}\left(x^2 - \frac{2x^4}{3!} + \dots\right) +$
$\frac{1}{3!}\left(x^3 - \frac{3x^5}{3!} + \dots\right) + \frac{1}{4!}\left(x^4 - \frac{4x^6}{3!} + \dots\right) + \dots$ **[1 mark]**

We only need the first four non-zero terms, so:

$e^{\sin x} = 1 + x - \frac{x^3}{3!} + \frac{x^2}{2!} - \frac{2x^4}{2!3!} + \frac{x^3}{3!} + \frac{x^4}{4!} + \dots$ **[1 mark]**

$= 1 + x + \frac{x^2}{2} - \frac{x^4}{8} + \dots$ **[1 mark]**

Make sure you write out enough terms in the original series to get everything you need. It's always best to write out more to start with, as you might end up cancelling some terms, like we do here with the x^3 terms. Just cut the expression down at the end to get the number of terms the question asks for.

2   Find the Maclaurin series for both sides of Euler's relation:

LHS: $e^x = 1 + x + \frac{x^2}{2!} + \frac{x^3}{3!} + \frac{x^4}{4!} + \frac{x^5}{5!} + \dots$

So $e^{ix} = 1 + ix + \frac{(ix)^2}{2!} + \frac{(ix)^3}{3!} + \frac{(ix)^4}{4!} + \frac{(ix)^5}{5!} + \dots$ **[1 mark]**

$= 1 + ix - \frac{x^2}{2!} - \frac{ix^3}{3!} + \frac{x^4}{4!} + \frac{ix^5}{5!} + \dots$ **[1 mark]**

RHS:

$\cos x = 1 - \frac{x^2}{2!} + \frac{x^4}{4!} - \dots$ $\sin x = x - \frac{x^3}{3!} + \frac{x^5}{5!} - \dots$

So $\cos x + i \sin x = 1 - \frac{x^2}{2!} + \frac{x^4}{4!} - \dots + i\left(x - \frac{x^3}{3!} + \frac{x^5}{5!} - \dots\right)$ **[1 mark]**

$= 1 + ix - \frac{x^2}{2!} - \frac{ix^3}{3!} + \frac{x^4}{4!} + \frac{ix^5}{5!} + \dots$ **[1 mark]**

So LHS = RHS, which proves Euler's relation is true.

3 a) $\ln((1 + 2x)^3(1 - x)) = 3\ln(1 + 2x) + \ln(1 - x)$ **[1 mark]**

The Maclaurin series for $\ln(1 + x)$ is
$\ln(1 + x) = x - \frac{x^2}{2} + \frac{x^3}{3} - \frac{x^4}{4} + \dots$
So $3\ln(1 + 2x) = 3\left(2x - \frac{(2x)^2}{2} + \frac{(2x)^3}{3} - \frac{(2x)^4}{4} + \dots\right)$ **[1 mark]**
$= 6x - 6x^2 + 8x^3 - 12x^4 + \dots$ **[1 mark]**
and $\ln(1 - x) = -x - \frac{x^2}{2} - \frac{x^3}{3} - \frac{x^4}{4} + \dots$ **[1 mark]**

So $\ln((1 + 2x)^3(1 - x))$
$= 6x - 6x^2 + 8x^3 - 12x^4 - x - \frac{x^2}{2} - \frac{x^3}{3} - \frac{x^4}{4} + \dots$
$= 5x - \frac{13x^2}{2} + \frac{23x^3}{3} - \frac{49x^4}{4} + \dots$ **[1 mark]**

b) The Maclaurin series for $\ln(1 + x)$ is valid for $-1 < x \le 1$ **[1 mark]**.
So the Maclaurin series for $3\ln(1 + 2x)$ is valid for $-1 < 2x \le 1$,
which means $-\frac{1}{2} < x \le \frac{1}{2}$ **[1 mark]**.

The Maclaurin series for $\ln(1 - x)$ is valid for $-1 < -x \le 1$, which means $-1 \le x < 1$ **[1 mark]**.
So $\ln((1 + 2x)^3(1 - x))$ is valid for the intersection of these two inequalities, which is $-\frac{1}{2} < x \le \frac{1}{2}$ **[1 mark]**.

Section 5 — CP: Further Calculus

Page 47 — Volumes of Revolution

Practice Questions

1    $\frac{4\pi}{3}$

2   A sphere with radius a, volume $\frac{4}{3}\pi a^3$

3    $\frac{\pi^2}{2}$
     This one's tricky — but you can use the identity $\cos 2A \equiv 2\cos^2 A - 1$ to simplify the integral.

Exam Questions

1    $y = a \sec t \Rightarrow y^2 = a^2 \sec^2 t$

$x = 2t + 1 \Rightarrow \frac{dx}{dt} = 2$

$\Rightarrow V = \pi \int y^2 \frac{dx}{dt} dt = 2\pi a^2 \int \sec^2 t \, dt$ **[1 mark]**

Convert the limits from x to t:

$x = 2t + 1 = 1 + \frac{\pi}{3} \Rightarrow 2t = \frac{\pi}{3} \Rightarrow t = \frac{\pi}{6}$,

$x = 2t + 1 = 1 + \frac{\pi}{2} \Rightarrow 2t = \frac{\pi}{2} \Rightarrow t = \frac{\pi}{4}$

[1 mark for both limits correct]

$2\pi a^2 \int_{\frac{\pi}{6}}^{\frac{\pi}{4}} \sec^2 t \, dt = 2\pi a^2 [\tan t]_{\frac{\pi}{6}}^{\frac{\pi}{4}}$ **[1 mark]**

$= 2\pi a^2 \left(1 - \frac{\sqrt{3}}{3}\right)$ **[1 mark]**

2 a) $V = \pi \int_1^4 y^2 \, dx = \pi \int_1^4 \frac{2}{2x - 1} \, dx$ **[1 mark]**

$= \pi \left[\ln(2x - 1)\right]_1^4$ **[1 mark]**

$= \pi \ln 7 \text{ km}^3$ **[1 mark]**

b) Diameter is $d = 2y = \frac{2\sqrt{2}}{(2x - 1)^{\frac{1}{2}}}$ **[1 mark]**

i) The widest point is at $x = 1$ so $d = 2\sqrt{2} = 2.83 \text{ km}$ **[1 mark]**

ii) The peak is at $x = 4$ so $d = \frac{2\sqrt{2}}{\sqrt{7}} = 1.07 \text{ km}$ **[1 mark]**

Page 48 — Improper Integrals

Practice Questions

1 a) Undefined at the lower limit 0
  b) Undefined at 0, which is in the interval of integration
2   It's an improper integral because the upper limit is infinity.
     The value of the integral is $\frac{1}{12}$.

Exam Question

1 a) I_1 improper as it has a limit of $-\infty$
     I_2 improper as the integrand is undefined at $x = 0$
     [1 mark for both correct]

b) $I_1 = \lim_{a \to -\infty} \int_a^{-1} \frac{1}{x^2} \, dx = \lim_{a \to -\infty}\left[-\frac{1}{x}\right]_a^{-1} = \lim_{a \to -\infty}\left[1 + \frac{1}{a}\right]$ **[1 mark]**
$= 1 + 0 = 1$ **[1 mark]**

$I_2 = \lim_{a \to 0-} \int_{-1}^a \frac{1}{x^2} \, dx = \lim_{a \to 0-}\left[-\frac{1}{x}\right]_{-1}^a = \lim_{a \to 0-}\left[-\frac{1}{a} - 1\right]$ **[1 mark]**

But $-\frac{1}{a} \to \infty$ as $a \to 0-$ so I_2 is undefined. **[1 mark]**

Page 49 — Mean Value of a Function

Practice Questions

1    $\frac{221}{5}$

2   6

3    $18\,000 + \frac{2}{\pi}$

Answers

Exam Questions

1 a) Evaluating at $x = 2$, $2^3 + 3(2)^2 - 4(2) - 12 = 0$ so 2 is a root and $(x - 2)$ is a factor.
$x^3 + 3x^2 - 4x - 12 = (x - 2)(x^2 + 5x + 6)$ *[1 mark]*
$= (x - 2)(x + 2)(x + 3)$ *[1 mark]*

b) $f_{avg} = \dfrac{1}{b-2} \displaystyle\int_2^b 3x^2 + 6x - 4 \ dx = \dfrac{1}{b-2}\left[x^3 + 3x^2 - 4x\right]_2^b$

$= \dfrac{1}{b-2}\left[(b^3 + 3b^2 - 4b) - (2^3 + 3(2)^2 - 4(2))\right]$

$= \dfrac{1}{b-2}(b^3 + 3b^2 - 4b - 12)$ *[1 mark]*

From part (a), this is equal to $(b + 2)(b + 3)$.
So $f_{avg} = (b + 2)(b + 3) = 56$ *[1 mark]*
$\Rightarrow b^2 + 5b + 6 = 56 \Rightarrow b^2 + 5b - 50 = 0$
$\Rightarrow (b + 10)(b - 5) = 0$
$\Rightarrow b = -10, 5$ *[1 mark]*
But $2 \le b$ so $b = 5$ *[1 mark]*

2 a) $f_{avg} = \dfrac{1}{6} \displaystyle\int_0^6 \sin t + 2\cos 3t + \dfrac{t}{t^2 + 3}\ dt$ *[1 mark]*

$= \dfrac{1}{6}\left[-\cos t + \dfrac{2}{3}\sin 3t + \dfrac{1}{2}\ln(t^2 + 3)\right]_0^6$ *[1 mark]*

$= 0.137$ (3 s.f.) *[1 mark]*

b) The model predicts they will make a profit *[1 mark]* since the average value is positive *[1 mark]*.

Page 51 — Calculus with Inverse Trig Functions

Practice Questions

1 a) If $y = \cos^{-1} x$, then $\cos y = x$.

Differentiate with respect to x: $-\sin y \dfrac{dy}{dx} = 1$

$\Rightarrow \dfrac{dy}{dx} = \dfrac{-1}{\sin y} = \dfrac{-1}{\sqrt{1 - \cos^2 y}}$

But $\cos y = x$, so $\cos^2 y = (\cos y)^2 = x^2$, so $\dfrac{dy}{dx} = \dfrac{-1}{\sqrt{1 - x^2}}$.

b) If $y = \tan^{-1} x$, then $\tan y = x$.

Differentiate with respect to x: $\sec^2 y \dfrac{dy}{dx} = 1$

$\Rightarrow \dfrac{dy}{dx} = \dfrac{1}{\sec^2 y} = \dfrac{1}{1 + \tan^2 y} = \dfrac{1}{1 + x^2}$

2 Derivative $\dfrac{-1}{x^2 + 1}$, gradient $-\dfrac{1}{17}$

Exam Questions

1 a) $\displaystyle\int \dfrac{1}{a^2 + x^2}\ dx = \int \dfrac{1}{a^2\left(1 + \dfrac{x^2}{a^2}\right)}\ dx = \int \dfrac{1}{a^2\left(1 + \left(\dfrac{x}{a}\right)^2\right)}\ dx$ *[1 mark]*

Let $\dfrac{x}{a} = \tan u \Rightarrow x = a \tan u$

Then $\dfrac{dx}{du} = a \sec^2 u \Rightarrow dx = a \sec^2 u\ du$ *[1 mark]*

Substituting this in gives: $\displaystyle\int \dfrac{1}{a^2(1 + \tan^2 u)} a \sec^2 u\ du$

$= \displaystyle\int \dfrac{1}{a^2 \sec^2 u} a \sec^2 u\ du = \int \dfrac{1}{a}\ du = \dfrac{u}{a} + C$ *[1 mark]*

But $\dfrac{x}{a} = \tan u \Rightarrow \arctan \dfrac{x}{a} = u$

So $\displaystyle\int \dfrac{1}{a^2 + x^2}\ dx = \dfrac{1}{a}\arctan \dfrac{x}{a} + C$ *[1 mark]*

b) $\displaystyle\int_{-8}^{8} \dfrac{1}{x^2 + 16}\ dx = \dfrac{1}{4}\left[\arctan \dfrac{x}{4}\right]_{-8}^{8} = \dfrac{1}{4}(\arctan 2 - \arctan(-2))$ *[1 mark]*

You know that $\tan(-x) = -\tan x$. Let $y = -\tan x$.
Then $-y = \tan x \Rightarrow \arctan(-y) = x$.
And $y = \tan(-x) \Rightarrow \arctan y = -x \Rightarrow -\arctan y = x$
$\Rightarrow \arctan(-y) = -\arctan y$ *[1 mark]*

So $\dfrac{1}{4}(\arctan 2 - \arctan(-2)) = \dfrac{1}{4}(\arctan 2 - (-\arctan 2))$

$= \dfrac{1}{4}(2 \arctan 2) = \dfrac{1}{2}\arctan 2$ *[1 mark]*

2 a) 77 m occurs at $x = 0.77$ *[1 mark]*
At this point, $y = 0.988... \Rightarrow$ peak of 99 m (to the nearest metre) *[1 mark]*

b) Differentiate the function to find its gradient.
For the arctan term, let $u = 2x$ and use the chain rule:
$\dfrac{d}{dx}\dfrac{1}{2}\arctan 2x = \dfrac{1}{2} \times \dfrac{d}{du}\arctan u \times \dfrac{d}{dx}2x = \dfrac{1}{2} \times \dfrac{1}{1 + u^2} \times 2$

$= \dfrac{1}{1 + 4x^2}$ *[1 mark]*

For the other term, use the product rule:
$\dfrac{d}{dx}\left(x\sqrt{1 - x^2}\right) = \sqrt{1 - x^2}\dfrac{d}{dx}x + x\dfrac{d}{dx}\sqrt{1 - x^2}$

$= \sqrt{1 - x^2} + x\left(\dfrac{1}{2}(-2x)\dfrac{1}{\sqrt{1 - x^2}}\right) = \sqrt{1 - x^2} - \dfrac{x^2}{\sqrt{1 - x^2}}$ *[1 mark]*

So $\dfrac{dy}{dx} = \dfrac{1}{1 + 4x^2} + \sqrt{1 - x^2} - \dfrac{x^2}{\sqrt{1 - x^2}}$

Find the derivative at $x = 0$ *[1 mark]*, as this is the steepest point.
$x = 0 \Rightarrow \dfrac{dy}{dx} = \dfrac{1}{1 + 0} + \sqrt{1 - 0} - \dfrac{0}{\sqrt{1 - 0}} = 1 + 1 + 0 = 2$ *[1 mark]*

Since $2 < 4$, the drop is allowed *[1 mark]*.

Page 53 — Integration with Partial Fractions

Practice Questions

1 $\dfrac{-2}{(x + 1)} + \dfrac{-\dfrac{7}{2}}{(x + 1)^2} + \dfrac{2x + \dfrac{3}{2}}{(x^2 + 1)} \equiv \dfrac{-2}{(x + 1)} - \dfrac{7}{2(x + 1)^2} + \dfrac{4x + 3}{2(x^2 + 1)}$

The denominator contains a repeated linear factor and a quadratic factor so the partial fractions will be of the form $\dfrac{A}{(x + 1)} + \dfrac{B}{(x + 1)^2} + \dfrac{Cx + D}{(x^2 + 1)}$.

2 2.76 (3 s.f.)

3 $\dfrac{1}{\pi}\ln\left(\dfrac{\pi + 1}{\pi - 1}\right) = \ln\left(\left(\dfrac{\pi + 1}{\pi - 1}\right)^{\frac{1}{\pi}}\right)$

Use the second of the standard integrals on the page, putting $a = \pi$.

Exam Questions

1 $\dfrac{3x^2 + 3x + 2}{(3x^2 + 1)(1 - x)} = \dfrac{Ax + B}{(3x^2 + 1)} + \dfrac{C}{(-x + 1)}$

$3x^2 + 3x + 2 = (Ax + B)(-x + 1) + C(3x^2 + 1)$ *[1 mark]*
Use substitution to find A, B and C.
Substituting $x = 1$ gives: $8 = 4C \Rightarrow C = 2$
Comparing constants gives: $2 = B + C = B + 2 \Rightarrow B = 0$
Comparing x terms gives: $3 = A - B = A - 0 \Rightarrow A = 3$ *[1 mark]*

So $\displaystyle\int_2^3 \dfrac{3x^2 + 3x + 2}{(3x^2 + 1)(1 - x)}\ dx = \int_2^3 \dfrac{3x}{(3x^2 + 1)} + \dfrac{2}{(-x + 1)}\ dx$

$= \left[\dfrac{1}{2}\ln(3x^2 + 1) - 2\ln|-x + 1|\right]_2^3$

[2 marks for correct integration, otherwise 1 mark if at least one term integrated correctly]

$= \dfrac{1}{2}\ln 28 - 2\ln 2 - (\dfrac{1}{2}\ln 13 - 2\ln 1)$

$= \dfrac{1}{2}\ln 28 - \dfrac{1}{2}\ln 16 - \dfrac{1}{2}\ln 13$ *[1 mark]*

$= \dfrac{1}{2}[\ln\left(\dfrac{28}{16}\right) - \ln 13] = \dfrac{1}{2}\ln\left(\dfrac{28}{208}\right) = \dfrac{1}{2}\ln\left(\dfrac{7}{52}\right)$ *[1 mark]*

2 a) $f(x) = \dfrac{Ax + B}{(x^2 - 4)} + \dfrac{Cx + D}{(x^2 + 2)}$

$x + 3 = (Ax + B)(x^2 + 2) + (Cx + D)(x^2 - 4)$ *[1 mark]*
Comparing x^3 terms: $0 = A + C \Rightarrow C = -A$
Comparing x^2 terms: $0 = B + D \Rightarrow D = -B$
Comparing x terms: $1 = 2A - 4C = -6C \Rightarrow C = -\dfrac{1}{6}, A = \dfrac{1}{6}$
Comparing constants: $3 = 2B - 4D = -6D \Rightarrow D = -\dfrac{1}{2}, B = \dfrac{1}{2}$ *[1 mark]*

So $f(x) = \dfrac{\dfrac{1}{6}x + \dfrac{1}{2}}{(x^2 - 4)} + \dfrac{-\dfrac{1}{6}x - \dfrac{1}{2}}{(x^2 + 2)}$

Multiply numerators and denominators by 6 and rearrange to obtain required form $f(x) = \dfrac{x + 3}{6(x^2 - 4)} - \dfrac{x + 3}{6(x^2 + 2)}$ *[1 mark]*

You might have done this question differently if you spotted that the first factor in the denominator of f(x) is the difference of two squares. You'll still get the marks if you deal with it this way and get the right answer — but make sure you give your answer in the form that the question asks for.

b) $\int_0^{\sqrt{2}} f(x)\,dx = \frac{1}{6}\int_0^{\sqrt{2}} \frac{x}{x^2-4} + \frac{3}{x^2-4} - \frac{x}{x^2+2} - \frac{3}{x^2+2}\,dx$

$= \frac{1}{6}\left[\frac{1}{2}\ln|x^2-4| + \frac{3}{4}\ln\left|\frac{x-2}{x+2}\right| - \frac{1}{2}\ln|x^2+2| - \frac{3}{\sqrt{2}}\arctan\left(\frac{x}{\sqrt{2}}\right)\right]_0^{\sqrt{2}}$

[3 marks available — 1 mark for the arctan integration, 1 mark for correctly integrating a term to a ln |g(x)|, 1 mark for fully correct integration]

$= \frac{1}{6}\left(\frac{1}{2}\ln 2 + \frac{3}{4}\ln\left|\frac{\sqrt{2}-2}{\sqrt{2}+2}\right| - \frac{1}{2}\ln 4 - \frac{3}{\sqrt{2}}\arctan(1)\right)$

$\quad - \frac{1}{6}\left(\frac{1}{2}\ln 4 + \frac{3}{4}\ln(1) - \frac{1}{2}\ln 2 - \frac{3}{\sqrt{2}}\arctan(0)\right)$

$= \frac{1}{6}\left(\frac{1}{2}\ln 2 + \frac{3}{4}\ln\left|\frac{\sqrt{2}-2}{\sqrt{2}+2}\right| - \ln 2 - \frac{3}{\sqrt{2}}\frac{\pi}{4}\right)$

$\quad - \frac{1}{6}\left(\ln 2 - \frac{1}{2}\ln 2\right)$ *[1 mark]*

$= \frac{1}{6}\left(\frac{3}{4}\ln\left|\frac{(\sqrt{2}-2)(2-\sqrt{2})}{(\sqrt{2}+2)(2-\sqrt{2})}\right| - \frac{1}{2}\ln 2 - \frac{3}{\sqrt{2}}\frac{\pi}{4}\right) - \frac{1}{6}\left(\frac{1}{2}\ln 2\right)$

$= \frac{1}{6}\left(\frac{3}{4}\ln\left|\frac{4\sqrt{2}-6}{2}\right| - \ln 2 - \frac{3\sqrt{2}\pi}{8}\right)$

$= \frac{1}{6}\left(\frac{3}{4}\ln|2\sqrt{2}-3| - \ln 2 - \frac{3\sqrt{2}\pi}{8}\right)$

$= \frac{1}{6}\left(\frac{3}{4}\ln(3-2\sqrt{2}) - \ln 2 - \frac{3\sqrt{2}\pi}{8}\right)$ *[1 mark]*

$= \frac{1}{8}\ln(3-2\sqrt{2}) - \frac{1}{6}\ln 2 - \frac{\sqrt{2}}{16}\pi$ *[1 mark]*

3 a) $\int_0^1 \frac{1}{9-4x^2}\,dx = \frac{1}{4}\int_0^1 \frac{1}{\frac{9}{4}-x^2}\,dx$ *[1 mark]*

$= \frac{1}{4}\left[\frac{1}{2\times\frac{3}{2}}\ln\left|\frac{\frac{3}{2}+x}{\frac{3}{2}-x}\right|\right]_0^1$ *[1 mark]*

$= \frac{1}{4}\times\frac{1}{3}\left[\ln\left|\frac{\frac{3}{2}+1}{\frac{3}{2}-1}\right| - \ln\left|\frac{\frac{3}{2}+0}{\frac{3}{2}-0}\right|\right]$

$= \frac{1}{12}\left[\ln\left(\frac{5}{2}\div\frac{1}{2}\right) - \ln 1\right] = \frac{1}{12}\ln 5$ *[1 mark]*

b) $V = \pi\int_0^1 y^2\,dx = \pi\int_0^1 \frac{1}{9-4x^2}\,dx$ *[1 mark]*

So using part a), $V = \frac{\pi}{12}\ln 5 = 0.421$ (3 s.f.) *[1 mark]*

Section 6 — CP: Further Vectors

Page 55 — Equations of Lines in 3D

Practice Questions

1 $i + 4j - 7k$

2 $6i - 7j + 4k$

3 a) $r = \begin{pmatrix} 4 \\ 1 \\ 2 \end{pmatrix} + \lambda\begin{pmatrix} 3 \\ 1 \\ -1 \end{pmatrix} = 4i + j + 2k + \lambda(3i + j - k)$

b) E.g. $r = \begin{pmatrix} 2 \\ -1 \\ 1 \end{pmatrix} + \lambda\begin{pmatrix} -2 \\ 3 \\ 2 \end{pmatrix} = 2i - j + k + \lambda(-2i + 3j + 2k)$

You might have got a different answer here, if you used (0, 2, 3) for **a** or used (2, −1, 1) − (0, 2, 3) = (2, −3, −2) for **b**.

Exam Questions

1 $l_1: r = 3i - j + 3k + \lambda(5i + 3j + 7k)$ *[1 mark]*
   $l_2: r = i + 7j + 9k + \mu(-2i + 4j + 3k)$ *[1 mark]*

2 a) $(3-1)i + (2-5)j + (1-9)k$ *[1 mark for identifying $\overrightarrow{OB} - \overrightarrow{OA}$]*
   $= 2i - 3j - 8k$ *[1 mark]*

b) Direction vector: $((-2)-(-9))i + (4-9)j + (3-13)k$ *[1 mark]*
   l_1 is $r = -2i + 4j + 3k + \mu(7i - 5j - 10k)$ *[1 mark]*
   You might have got a different answer here, if you used the position vector of point D for **a**, or if you used $\overrightarrow{CD}$ instead of $\overrightarrow{DC}$ for **b**.

c) Work out the equation for the line that passes through AB:
   $r = i + 5j + 9k + \lambda(2i - 3j - 8k)$ *[1 mark]*
   Set up simultaneous equations involving λ and μ *[1 mark]*
   $-2 + 7\mu = 1 + 2\lambda$ $4 - 5\mu = 5 - 3\lambda$ $3 - 10\mu = 9 - 8\lambda$
   Solve for λ and μ $\lambda = 2, \mu = 1$ *[1 mark for each]*
   Plug into either line equation to obtain $5i - j - 7k$ *[1 mark]*
   As in part b), you might have got a different equation for the line through AB, and therefore you might have got different values of λ and μ — but you should still end up with the same final answer.

Page 57 — Scalar Products

Practice Questions

1 a) −5   b) 1

2 21.6° (to 1 d.p.)

3 E.g. $2j + 4k$
   Any vector of the form $ai + bj + ck$ with $3a + 4b - 2c = 0$ is correct here.

Exam Questions

1 Identify b_1 and b_2: $b_1 = 2i - 3j - 8k$, $b_2 = -7i + 5j + 10k$ *[1 mark]*
   $\cos\theta = \frac{b_1 \cdot b_2}{|b_1||b_2|} = \frac{-109}{\sqrt{77}\sqrt{174}}$ *[1 mark for any equivalent form]*
   $\theta = \cos^{-1}\left(\frac{-109}{\sqrt{77}\sqrt{174}}\right) = 160.336...°$ *[1 mark]*
   $180 - 160.336... = 19.7°$ (to 1 d.p.) *[1 mark]*

2 a) $\overrightarrow{OA} \cdot \overrightarrow{OB} = 9 - 8 - 1 = 0$ *[1 mark for attempting scalar product, 1 mark for carrying it out correctly]*
   So $\overrightarrow{OA}$ and $\overrightarrow{OB}$ are perpendicular, so AOB is a right-angled triangle.
   [1 mark for correct explanation]

b) $\angle$ABO is the angle between $\overrightarrow{BO}$ and $\overrightarrow{BA}$.
   $\overrightarrow{BA} = \overrightarrow{OA} - \overrightarrow{OB} = 6j + 2k$ *[1 mark]*
   $\overrightarrow{BO} = -3i + 4j + k$ *[1 mark]*
   $\cos\theta = \frac{\overrightarrow{BO}.\overrightarrow{BA}}{|\overrightarrow{BO}||\overrightarrow{BA}|} = \frac{(0\times-3)+(6\times4)+(2\times1)}{\sqrt{0^2+6^2+2^2}\sqrt{(-3)^2+4^2+1^2}}$ *[1 mark]*
   $= \frac{26}{\sqrt{40}\sqrt{26}} = \frac{\sqrt{65}}{10}$
   $\theta = \cos^{-1}\left(\frac{\sqrt{65}}{10}\right) = 36.3°$ (to 1 d.p.) *[1 mark]*

c) $|\overrightarrow{OC}| = \sqrt{3^2+(-1)^2} = \sqrt{10}$, $|\overrightarrow{OA}| = \sqrt{3^2+2^2+1^2} = \sqrt{14}$,
   $|\overrightarrow{AC}| = \sqrt{(3-3)^2+(-1-2)^2+(0+1)^2} = \sqrt{10}$
   [1 mark for $|\overrightarrow{AC}|$, 1 mark for the other two]
   $|\overrightarrow{OC}| = |\overrightarrow{AC}| \neq |\overrightarrow{OA}|$, so the triangle is isosceles *[1 mark]*.

Page 60 — Plane Geometry

Practice Questions

1 E.g. $r = (3i - 7j - k) + \lambda(-5i + 7j + 5k) + \mu(6i + 4j + 6k)$
   You could also have used Y or Z for **a** and any scalar multiple of $-5i + 7j + 5k$ and $6i + 4j + 6k$ for **b** and **c**,
   or a scalar multiple of $\overrightarrow{YZ} = 11i +3j + k$.

2 $-2x + 3z - 22 = 0$

3 a) 48.0° (to 1 d.p.)   b) 21.9° (to 1 d.p.)

Exam Questions

1 a) $r.n = \begin{pmatrix} -4 \\ 3 \\ 5 \end{pmatrix}.\begin{pmatrix} 1 \\ -3 \\ 5 \end{pmatrix} = -4 - 9 + 25 = 12$ *[1 mark]*
   $\begin{pmatrix} x \\ y \\ z \end{pmatrix}.\begin{pmatrix} 1 \\ -3 \\ 5 \end{pmatrix} = 12 \Rightarrow x - 3y + 5z - 12 = 0$ *[1 mark]*

b) Identify the normal vectors n_1 and n_2: $n_1 = \begin{pmatrix} -3 \\ -2 \\ 3 \end{pmatrix}$, $n_2 = \begin{pmatrix} 1 \\ -3 \\ 5 \end{pmatrix}$
   Let θ be the angle between the normals and ϕ be the angle between the planes. Then:
   $\cos\theta = \frac{n_1 \cdot n_2}{|n_1||n_2|} = \frac{(-3\times1)+(-2\times-3)+(3\times5)}{\sqrt{(-3)^2+(-2)^2+3^2}\sqrt{1^2+(-3)^2+5^2}} = \frac{18}{\sqrt{22}\sqrt{35}}$
   [1 mark]

Answers

$\theta = \cos^{-1}\left(\dfrac{18}{\sqrt{22}\sqrt{35}}\right) = 49.6°$ (to 1 d.p.) *[1 mark]*

$\Rightarrow \phi = 180° - \theta = 130.441...°$

This is the obtuse angle between the planes, so the acute angle is $180° - 130.441...° = 49.6°$ (to 1 d.p.) *[1 mark, has to be 1 d.p.]*

2   Convert $-19x - 29y + 26z - 12 = 0$ into scalar form:

$\mathbf{r}.(-19\mathbf{i} - 29\mathbf{j} + 26\mathbf{k}) = 12$ *[1 mark]*

Find an equation for l_1: $2\mathbf{i} - 8\mathbf{j} - 7\mathbf{k} + \lambda(-\mathbf{i} + 4\mathbf{j} + 9\mathbf{k})$ *[1 mark]*

Identify $\mathbf{b}$ and $\mathbf{n}$: $\mathbf{b} = -\mathbf{i} + 4\mathbf{j} + 9\mathbf{k}$, $\mathbf{n} = -19\mathbf{i} - 29\mathbf{j} + 26\mathbf{k}$ *[1 mark]*

$\sin\phi = \left|\dfrac{\mathbf{b}\cdot\mathbf{n}}{\|\mathbf{b}\|\|\mathbf{n}\|}\right| = 0.319...$ *[1 mark]*

$\phi = \sin^{-1}(0.319...) = 18.62... = 19°$ to the nearest degree *[1 mark]*

Page 63 — Intersections and Distances
Practice Questions

1   3.27 (to 3 s.f.)

2   E.g. $\dfrac{20x-3}{6} = y = \dfrac{10z-31}{22}$

Other equivalent answers are possible.

3   8.14 (to 3 s.f.)

Exam Questions

1   Let l_1 be the equation of the line that passes through $\overrightarrow{AB}$ and l_2 the equation of the line that passes through $\overrightarrow{DC}$.

Then l_1 has equation $\mathbf{r}_1 = 6\mathbf{i} + 4\mathbf{j} + 3\mathbf{k} + \lambda(\mathbf{i} + 3\mathbf{j} - 2\mathbf{k})$,

and l_2 has equation $\mathbf{r}_2 = -2\mathbf{i} - 5\mathbf{j} + \mu(\mathbf{i} + 3\mathbf{j} - 2\mathbf{k})$ *[1 mark]*.

Let X be any point on l_1 and Y be any point on l_2.

$\Rightarrow \overrightarrow{YX} = (8 + (\lambda - \mu))\mathbf{i} + (9 + 3(\lambda - \mu))\mathbf{j} + (3 - 2((\lambda - \mu))\mathbf{k}$ *[1 mark]*

Set $t = \lambda - \mu$. Then when $\overrightarrow{YX}$ is perpendicular to l_1 and l_2:

$((8 + t)\mathbf{i} + (9 + 3t)\mathbf{j} + (3 - 2t)\mathbf{k}).(\mathbf{i} + 3\mathbf{j} - 2\mathbf{k}) = 0$

$\Rightarrow 29 + 14t = 0 \Rightarrow t = -\dfrac{29}{14}$ *[1 mark]*

The perpendicular distance is $|\overrightarrow{YX}|$

$= \sqrt{(8 + t)^2 + (9 + 3t)^2 + (3 - 2t)^2} = \sqrt{\dfrac{1315}{14}} = 9.69$ (2 d.p.) *[1 mark]*

Alternatively, you could have written the equation for one of the lines and found the distance from this line to one of the known vertices on the other line.

2 a) Line l is perpendicular to Π, so it must have the same direction vector as the normal to Π. So the equation of l is:

$\mathbf{r} = 2\mathbf{i} + 11\mathbf{j} - 4\mathbf{k} + \lambda(-2\mathbf{i} + \mathbf{j} + 3\mathbf{k})$ *[1 mark]*

Substitute the line equation into the plane equation to find the value of λ at the point of intersection:

$\begin{pmatrix} 2-2\lambda \\ 11+\lambda \\ -4+3\lambda \end{pmatrix} \cdot \begin{pmatrix} -2 \\ 1 \\ 3 \end{pmatrix} = 9$ *[1 mark]*

$\Rightarrow 4\lambda - 4 + \lambda + 11 + 9\lambda - 12 = 9 \Rightarrow \lambda = 1$ *[1 mark]*

So the position vector of the point of intersection is:

$2\mathbf{i} + 11\mathbf{j} - 4\mathbf{k} + (1)(-2\mathbf{i} + \mathbf{j} + 3\mathbf{k}) = 12\mathbf{j} - \mathbf{k} = (0, 12, -1)$ as required *[1 mark]*

 b) Equation of PQ is $\mathbf{r} = -\mathbf{i} - 3\mathbf{j} + 4\mathbf{k} + \lambda(3\mathbf{i} + 14\mathbf{j} - 8\mathbf{k})$ *[1 mark]*

Let M be an arbitrary point on PQ.

$\Rightarrow \overrightarrow{NM} = (-1 - 0)\mathbf{i} + (-3 - 12)\mathbf{j} + (4 + 1)\mathbf{k} + \lambda(3\mathbf{i} + 14\mathbf{j} - 8\mathbf{k})$

$\Rightarrow \overrightarrow{NM} = (-1 + 3\lambda)\mathbf{i} + (-15 + 14\lambda)\mathbf{j} + (5 - 8\lambda)\mathbf{k}$ *[1 mark]*

NM is perpendicular to PQ if the scalar product of the direction vectors is zero.

So, $((-1 + 3\lambda)\mathbf{i} + (-15 + 14\lambda)\mathbf{j} + (5 - 8\lambda)\mathbf{k}).(3\mathbf{i} + 14\mathbf{j} - 8\mathbf{k}) = 0$

$\Rightarrow -253 + 269\lambda = 0 \Rightarrow \lambda = \dfrac{253}{269}$ *[1 mark]*

The perpendicular distance is $|\overrightarrow{NM}|$

$= \sqrt{(-1 + 3\lambda)^2 + (-15 + 14\lambda)^2 + (5 - 8\lambda)^2} = 3.61$ (to 3 s.f.) *[1 mark]*

Section 7 – CP: Polar Coordinates
Page 67 — Polar Coordinates and Curves
Practice Questions

1 a) $(-5.54, 2.30)$ b) $(0.39, 0.08)$

   c) $(2.73, -1.25)$ d) $(-1.5, -2.60) = \left(-\dfrac{3}{2}, -\dfrac{3\sqrt{3}}{2}\right)$

2 a) $\left(5\sqrt{2}, -\dfrac{\pi}{4}\right)$ b) $\left(2, \dfrac{5\pi}{6}\right)$ c) $\left(4, -\dfrac{2\pi}{3}\right)$

3 a)

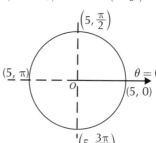

               b)

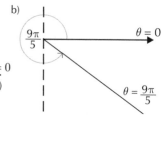

4

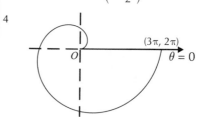

5

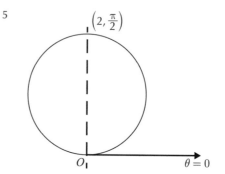

Exam Questions

1   $r \geq 0$ for $0 \leq \theta \leq \dfrac{\pi}{3}$, $\dfrac{2\pi}{3} \leq \theta \leq \pi$ and $\dfrac{4\pi}{3} \leq \theta \leq \dfrac{5\pi}{3}$

The table of values for $0 \leq \theta \leq \dfrac{\pi}{3}$ (one loop) is:

θ	0	$\frac{\pi}{18}$	$\frac{\pi}{12}$	$\frac{\pi}{9}$	$\frac{\pi}{6}$	$\frac{2\pi}{9}$	$\frac{\pi}{4}$	$\frac{5\pi}{18}$	$\frac{\pi}{3}$
r	0	1.5	2.12...	2.59...	3	2.59...	2.12...	1.5	0

The graph can be sketched by plotting these points and using the symmetry of $\sin\theta$.

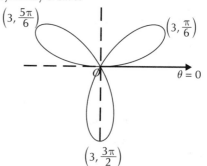

[3 marks available — 1 mark for correct shape, 1 mark for one point labelled correctly, 1 mark for the other two points labelled correctly]

Answers

2 a) $r = 3 \csc\left(\frac{\pi}{6} - \theta\right) \Rightarrow r\sin\left(\frac{\pi}{6} - \theta\right) = 3$

$r\sin\left(\frac{\pi}{6} - \theta\right) = r\left(\sin\frac{\pi}{6}\cos\theta - \cos\frac{\pi}{6}\sin\theta\right)$ *[1 mark]*

$= r\left(\frac{1}{2}\cos\theta - \frac{\sqrt{3}}{2}\sin\theta\right) = \frac{1}{2}(r\cos\theta - \sqrt{3}\,r\sin\theta)$

$x = r\cos\theta$ and $y = r\sin\theta$, so

$\frac{1}{2}(x - y\sqrt{3}) = 3 \Rightarrow y = \frac{\sqrt{3}}{3}x - 2\sqrt{3}$ (or $x - y\sqrt{3} = 6$) *[1 mark]*

b)

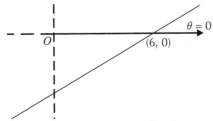

[1 mark for a straight line in the correct position,
1 mark for correctly labelled point]

3 The table of values for $0 \le \theta \le \frac{\pi}{2}$ (one loop) is:

θ	0	$\frac{\pi}{12}$	$\frac{\pi}{8}$	$\frac{\pi}{6}$	$\frac{\pi}{4}$	$\frac{\pi}{3}$	$\frac{3\pi}{8}$	$\frac{5\pi}{12}$	$\frac{\pi}{2}$
r	0	2.12...	2.52...	2.79...	3	2.79...	2.52...	2.12...	0

Since $\sin(2(\theta + \pi)) = \sin(2\theta + 2\pi) = \sin 2\theta$, the values of r in the region $0 \le \theta \le \frac{\pi}{2}$ will be the same as the values of r for $\pi \le \theta \le \frac{3\pi}{2}$.

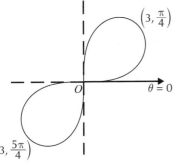

[1 mark for correct shape,
1 mark for each point labelled correctly]

4 The table of values for $0 \le \theta \le \pi$ is:

θ	0	$\frac{\pi}{6}$	$\frac{\pi}{4}$	$\frac{\pi}{3}$	$\frac{\pi}{2}$	$\frac{2\pi}{3}$	$\frac{3\pi}{4}$	$\frac{5\pi}{6}$	π
r	9	8.46...	7.82...	7	5	3	2.17...	1.53...	1

Use symmetry of $\cos\theta$ to reflect the curve in the line $\theta = 0$ and obtain the other half of the graph.

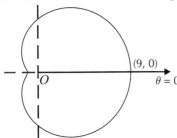

[1 mark for correct shape, 1 mark for correctly labelled point]

Page 69 — Calculus Using Polar Coordinates

Practice Questions

1 Since $\sin\theta \ge 0$ for $0 \le \theta \le \pi$, this is the range of integration. The area enclosed is $\frac{\pi}{4}$.

2 $(3\sqrt{2} + 3, 0)$, $\left(\frac{3\sqrt{2}}{2}, \frac{3\pi}{4}\right)$ and $(3\sqrt{2} - 3, \pi)$

Exam Questions

1 The points that have tangents parallel to the initial line are the points where $\frac{dy}{d\theta} = 0$ *[1 mark]*. So first express y in terms of θ:

$y = r\sin\theta = (\sin\theta + \sqrt{3}\cos\theta)\sin\theta = \sin^2\theta + \sqrt{3}\cos\theta\sin\theta$ *[1 mark]*

$= \left(\frac{1 - \cos 2\theta}{2}\right) + \left(\frac{\sqrt{3}}{2}\sin 2\theta\right)$ *[1 mark]*

$\frac{dy}{d\theta} = \sin 2\theta + \sqrt{3}\cos 2\theta = 0$ *[1 mark]*

$\Rightarrow \sin 2\theta = -\sqrt{3}\cos 2\theta \Rightarrow \tan 2\theta = -\sqrt{3}$

$\Rightarrow 2\theta = -\frac{\pi}{3}, \frac{2\pi}{3} \Rightarrow \theta = -\frac{\pi}{6}, \frac{\pi}{3}$ *[1 mark]*

$\theta = -\frac{\pi}{6} \Rightarrow r = \sin\left(-\frac{\pi}{6}\right) + \sqrt{3}\cos\left(-\frac{\pi}{6}\right) = 1$ *[1 mark]*

$\theta = \frac{\pi}{3} \Rightarrow r = \sin\left(\frac{\pi}{3}\right) + \sqrt{3}\cos\left(\frac{\pi}{3}\right) = \sqrt{3}$ *[1 mark]*

Parallel line $\Rightarrow y = $ constant. So the tangents are at:

$y = r\sin\theta = 1 \times \sin\left(-\frac{\pi}{6}\right) = -\frac{1}{2} \Rightarrow r = -\frac{1}{2}\csc\theta$ *[1 mark]*

and $y = r\sin\theta = \sqrt{3} \times \sin\left(\frac{\pi}{3}\right) = \frac{3}{2} \Rightarrow r = \frac{3}{2}\csc\theta$ *[1 mark]*

2

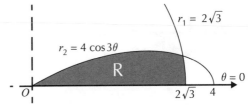

[1 mark for correct shape]

Find the points of intersection between $r_1 = 2\sqrt{3}$ and $r_2 = 4\cos 3\theta$:

$4\cos 3\theta = 2\sqrt{3} \Rightarrow \cos 3\theta = \frac{\sqrt{3}}{2}$ *[1 mark]*

$\Rightarrow 3\theta = \frac{\pi}{6} \Rightarrow \theta = \frac{\pi}{18}$

So the curves intersect at $\left(2\sqrt{3}, \frac{\pi}{18}\right)$ *[1 mark]*

$r_1 \ge 0$ and $r_2 \ge 0$ is satisfied for $0 \le \theta \le \frac{\pi}{6}$, so consider values of θ in this region:

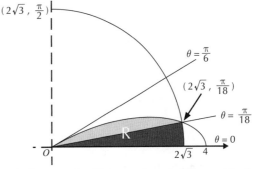

To find the area R, add the area bounded by r_1 and the lines $\theta = 0$ and $\theta = \frac{\pi}{18}$ to the area bounded by r_2 and the lines $\theta = \frac{\pi}{18}$ and $\theta = \frac{\pi}{6}$.

The area bounded by r_1 and the lines $\theta = 0$ and $\theta = \frac{\pi}{18}$

$= \frac{1}{2}\int_0^{\frac{\pi}{18}} (2\sqrt{3})^2 d\theta = \frac{1}{2}\int_0^{\frac{\pi}{18}} 12\, d\theta = [6\theta]_0^{\frac{\pi}{18}} = \frac{\pi}{3}$ *[1 mark]*

The area bounded by r_2 and the lines $\theta = \frac{\pi}{18}$ and $\theta = \frac{\pi}{6}$

$= \frac{1}{2}\int_{\frac{\pi}{18}}^{\frac{\pi}{6}} (4\cos 3\theta)^2 d\theta = \frac{1}{2}\int_{\frac{\pi}{18}}^{\frac{\pi}{6}} 16\cos^2 3\theta\, d\theta = \frac{1}{2}\int_{\frac{\pi}{18}}^{\frac{\pi}{6}} \frac{16(1 + \cos 6\theta)}{2} d\theta$

[1 mark]

$= \int_{\frac{\pi}{18}}^{\frac{\pi}{6}} 4(1 + \cos 6\theta)\, d\theta = \left[4\theta + \frac{2}{3}\sin 6\theta\right]_{\frac{\pi}{18}}^{\frac{\pi}{6}}$ *[1 mark]*

$= \left[\left(\frac{2\pi}{3} + 0\right) - \left(\frac{2\pi}{9} + \left(\frac{2}{3} \times \frac{\sqrt{3}}{2}\right)\right)\right] = \frac{4\pi}{9} - \frac{1}{\sqrt{3}}$ *[1 mark]*

$\Rightarrow$ The area of R $= \frac{\pi}{3} + \frac{4\pi}{9} - \frac{1}{\sqrt{3}} = \frac{7\pi}{9} - \frac{1}{\sqrt{3}} = 1.86611...$

$= 1.87$ to 3 s.f. *[1 mark]*

Answers

3

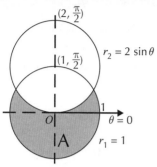

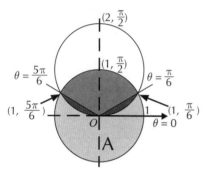

[1 mark for correct shape]

The curves intersect when $2 \sin \theta = 1 \Rightarrow \sin \theta = \frac{1}{2}$ **[1 mark]**

$\Rightarrow \theta = \frac{\pi}{6}, \frac{5\pi}{6} \Rightarrow$ so the curves intersect at $\left(1, \frac{\pi}{6}\right)$ and $\left(1, \frac{5\pi}{6}\right)$.

[1 mark]

$r_1 \geq 0$ and $r_2 \geq 0$ is satisfied for $0 \leq \theta \leq \pi$, so consider values of θ in this region.

To find the area A, find the area of Circle 1 and subtract:

the area bounded by r_1 and the lines $\theta = \frac{\pi}{6}$ and $\theta = \frac{5\pi}{6}$,

the area bounded by r_2 and the lines $\theta = 0$ and $\theta = \frac{\pi}{6}$ and

the area bounded by r_2 and the lines $\theta = \frac{5\pi}{6}$ and $\theta = \pi$.

- The area of Circle 1 $= \pi \times 1^2 = \pi$ **[1 mark]**

- The area bounded by r_1 and the lines $\theta = \frac{\pi}{6}$ and $\theta = \frac{5\pi}{6}$

$= \frac{1}{2} \int_{\frac{\pi}{6}}^{\frac{5\pi}{6}} 1^2 d\theta = \left[\frac{\theta}{2}\right]_{\frac{\pi}{6}}^{\frac{5\pi}{6}} = \frac{\pi}{3}$ **[1 mark]**

- The area bounded by r_2 and the lines $\theta = 0$ and $\theta = \frac{\pi}{6}$

$= \frac{1}{2} \int_{0}^{\frac{\pi}{6}} (2 \sin \theta)^2 d\theta = \int_{0}^{\frac{\pi}{6}} 2 \sin^2 \theta \, d\theta = \int_{0}^{\frac{\pi}{6}} 1 - \cos 2\theta \, d\theta$ **[1 mark]**

$= \left[\theta - \frac{1}{2} \sin 2\theta\right]_{0}^{\frac{\pi}{6}}$ **[1 mark]**

$= \left[\left(\frac{\pi}{6} - \left(\frac{1}{2} \times \frac{\sqrt{3}}{2}\right)\right) - (0)\right] = \frac{\pi}{6} - \frac{\sqrt{3}}{4}$ **[1 mark]**

By symmetry, the area bounded by r_2 and the lines $\theta = \frac{5\pi}{6}$ and $\theta = \pi$ has the same value.

So the area of A $= \pi - \frac{\pi}{3} - 2\left(\frac{\pi}{6} - \frac{\sqrt{3}}{4}\right) = \frac{\pi}{3} + \frac{\sqrt{3}}{2} = 1.91322...$
$= 1.91$ to 3 s.f. **[1 mark]**

Section 8 — CP: Hyperbolic Functions

Page 71 — Hyperbolic Functions

Practice Questions

1 $\sinh 0 = 0$, $\cosh 0 = 1$

2

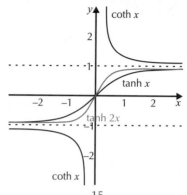

3 a) 548.32   b) $\frac{15}{17}$

4 $2 \sinh x \cosh x = 2 \times \frac{1}{2}(e^x - e^{-x}) \times \frac{1}{2}(e^x + e^{-x}) = \frac{1}{2}(e^x - e^{-x})(e^x + e^{-x})$

$= \frac{1}{2}(e^{2x} + 1 - 1 - e^{-2x}) = \frac{1}{2}(e^{2x} - e^{-2x}) = \sinh 2x$

Exam Questions

1 $1 - \tanh^2 x \equiv 1 - \left(\frac{\sinh x}{\cosh x}\right)^2 \equiv 1 - \frac{\sinh^2 x}{\cosh^2 x}$

$\equiv \frac{\cosh^2 x - \sinh^2 x}{\cosh^2 x}$ **[1 mark]**

$\equiv \frac{1}{\cosh^2 x} \equiv \text{sech}^2 x$ **[1 mark]**

2 RHS $= 2\left(\frac{e^{\frac{x+y}{2}} - e^{\frac{-x-y}{2}}}{2}\right)\left(\frac{e^{\frac{x-y}{2}} + e^{\frac{-x+y}{2}}}{2}\right)$ **[1 mark]**

$= \frac{1}{2}\left(e^{\frac{x+y}{2}} - e^{\frac{-x-y}{2}}\right)\left(e^{\frac{x-y}{2}} + e^{\frac{-x+y}{2}}\right)$

$= \frac{1}{2}(e^x + e^y - e^{-y} - e^{-x})$ **[1 mark]**

$= \frac{1}{2}(e^x - e^{-x}) + \frac{1}{2}(e^y - e^{-y})$ **[1 mark]**

$= \sinh x + \sinh y = $ LHS

3 a)

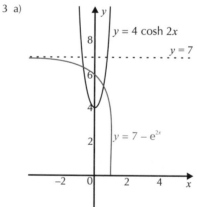

[2 marks available — 1 mark for each correct curve]

Intersection at the axes: $(0,4)$, $(0,6)$ and $(\frac{1}{2}\ln 7, 0)$ **[1 mark]**
Asymptote at $y = 7$ **[1 mark]**

b) $7 - e^{2x} = 4 \cosh 2x = 2(e^{2x} + e^{-2x}) = 2e^{2x} + 2e^{-2x}$ **[1 mark]**
$\Rightarrow 0 = 3e^{2x} + 2e^{-2x} - 7 = 3e^{4x} - 7e^{2x} + 2 = (3e^{2x} - 1)(e^{2x} - 2)$ **[1 mark]**
So $e^{2x} = \frac{1}{3}$ or 2 **[1 mark]**
and therefore $x = \frac{1}{2}\ln\frac{1}{3}$ **[1 mark]** or $\frac{1}{2}\ln 2$ **[1 mark]**

4 $\sinh A \cosh B + \cosh A \sinh B$

$= \frac{(e^A - e^{-A})(e^B + e^{-B})}{2 \quad 2} + \frac{(e^A + e^{-A})(e^B - e^{-B})}{2 \quad 2}$ **[1 mark]**

$= \frac{1}{4}((e^A - e^{-A})(e^B + e^{-B}) + (e^A + e^{-A})(e^B - e^{-B}))$

$= \frac{1}{4}(e^{A+B} + e^{A-B} - e^{-A+B} - e^{-A-B} + e^{A+B} - e^{A-B} + e^{-A+B} - e^{-A-B})$ **[1 mark]**

$= \frac{1}{4}(2e^{A+B} - 2e^{-A-B})$

$= \frac{1}{2}(e^{A+B} - e^{-(A+B)})$ **[1 mark]**

$= \sinh(A + B)$ **[1 mark]**

Answers

5    $\cosh(ix) = \frac{1}{2}(e^{ix} + e^{-ix})$ *[1 mark]*

$$= \frac{1}{2}(\cos x + i \sin x + \cos(-x) + i \sin(-x))\ \textit{[1 mark]}$$

$$= \frac{1}{2}(\cos x + i \sin x + \cos x - i \sin x)\ \textit{[1 mark]}$$

$$= \frac{1}{2}(2 \cos x) = \cos x\ \textit{[1 mark]}$$

Page 73 — Inverse Hyperbolic Functions

Practice Questions

1 a) $\sinh^{-1} x = \ln\left(\frac{1}{2} + \sqrt{\frac{1}{4}+1}\right) = \ln\left(\frac{1+\sqrt{5}}{2}\right)$

     $\cosh^{-1} x$ undefined

     $\tanh^{-1} x = \frac{1}{2}\ln\left|\frac{1+\left(\frac{1}{2}\right)}{1-\left(\frac{1}{2}\right)}\right| = \frac{1}{2}\ln 3$

  b) $\sinh^{-1} x = \ln(\sqrt{2} + \sqrt{3})$

     $\cosh^{-1} x = \ln(\sqrt{2}+1)$

     $\tanh^{-1} x$ undefined

  c) $\sinh^{-1} x = \ln\left(\frac{\pi}{4} + \sqrt{\frac{\pi^2}{16}+1}\right) = \ln\left(\frac{\pi + \sqrt{\pi^2 + 16}}{4}\right)$

     $\cosh^{-1} x$ undefined

     $\tanh^{-1} x = \frac{1}{2}\ln\left(\frac{1+\frac{\pi}{4}}{1-\frac{\pi}{4}}\right) = \frac{1}{2}\ln\left(\frac{4+\pi}{4-\pi}\right)$

2 a)   The domain is $\{x : x \geq 0.5\}$ and the range is $\{y : y \geq 0\}$.

  b)   The domain and range are both $\mathbb{R}$.

  c)   The domain is $\{x : -4 < x < -2\}$ and the range is $\mathbb{R}$.

3 a)   Let $y = \text{arsinh } x$ so then $x = \sinh y = \frac{1}{2}(e^y - e^{-y})$. Rearrange and multiply by e^y: $2xe^y = e^{2y} - 1 \Rightarrow e^{2y} - 2xe^y - 1 = 0$.

     Solve to obtain $e^y = \dfrac{-(-2x) \pm \sqrt{(-2x)^2 - 4(-1)}}{2}$

$$= \frac{2x \pm \sqrt{4(x^2+1)}}{2}$$

$$= x \pm \sqrt{x^2+1}.$$

     Take only the positive root as $e^y > 0$.

     Then $\text{arsinh } x = y = \ln(e^y) = \ln(x + \sqrt{x^2+1})$.

  b)   Let $y = \text{artanh } x$ so then $x = \tanh y = \dfrac{e^y - e^{-y}}{e^y + e^{-y}}$.

$$\Rightarrow x(e^y + e^{-y}) = e^y - e^{-y} \Rightarrow xe^{-y} + e^{-y} = e^y - xe^y$$

$$\Rightarrow e^{-y}(1+x) = e^y(1-x) \Rightarrow \frac{1+x}{1-x} = e^{2y} \Rightarrow e^y = \sqrt{\frac{1+x}{1-x}}$$

$$\Rightarrow \text{artanh } x = y = \ln(e^y) = \ln\left(\sqrt{\frac{1+x}{1-x}}\right) = \frac{1}{2}\ln\left(\frac{1+x}{1-x}\right)$$

4 a)

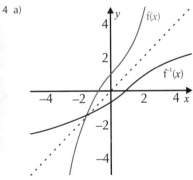

  b)

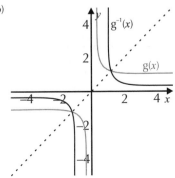

1 a) $\ln\sqrt{5} = \text{artanh } x = \frac{1}{2}\ln\left(\frac{1+x}{1-x}\right)$ *[1 mark]* $= \ln\left(\sqrt{\frac{1+x}{1-x}}\right)$

$$\Rightarrow \sqrt{5} = \sqrt{\frac{1+x}{1-x}} \Rightarrow 5 = \frac{1+x}{1-x}\ \textit{[1 mark]}$$

$$\Rightarrow 5(1-x) = 1+x \Rightarrow 6x = 4 \Rightarrow x = \frac{2}{3}\ \textit{[1 mark]}$$

     arcosh x is not defined as $x < 1$ *[1 mark]*

  b) $\sinh x - 3 \,\text{cosech}\, x = \sinh x - \dfrac{3}{\sinh x} = 2$

$$\sinh^2 x - 2 \sinh x - 3 = 0$$

$$(\sinh x + 1)(\sinh x - 3) = 0$$

$$\Rightarrow \sinh x = -1, 3\ \textit{[1 mark]}$$

     In log form, $x = \ln(-1+\sqrt{2})$ *[1 mark]* and $x = \ln(3 + \sqrt{10})$ *[1 mark]*
     arcosh x is defined only for $x = \ln(3 + \sqrt{10})$ because it is the only value greater than 1 *[1 mark]*

2 a) $h(x) = \tanh^{-1}(\sin^2 x) = \frac{1}{2}\ln\left(\frac{1+\sin^2 x}{1-\sin^2 x}\right)$

                        [1 mark for log form seen anywhere]

     The asymptotes occur at the values of x where $h(x)$ is undefined.

     This happens when $\dfrac{1+\sin^2 x}{1-\sin^2 x}$ is undefined or zero,

     since $\ln 0$ is undefined.

$$\frac{1+\sin^2 x}{1-\sin^2 x} = 0 \Rightarrow 1 + \sin^2 x = 0 \Rightarrow \sin^2 x = -1,$$

     which gives no solutions in the real numbers *[1 mark]*

$$\frac{1+\sin^2 x}{1-\sin^2 x}\ \text{undefined} \Rightarrow 1 - \sin^2 x = 0\ \textit{[1 mark]}$$

$$\sin^2 x = 1$$

$$\sin x = \pm 1$$

     This gives infinite solutions $x = \dots, -\frac{3\pi}{2}, -\frac{\pi}{2}, \frac{\pi}{2}, \frac{3\pi}{2}, \dots$

$$= \frac{\pi}{2} + k\pi \text{ for all integers } k\ \textit{[1 mark]}$$

  b) $h(x) = 0 \Rightarrow \frac{1}{2}\ln\left(\frac{1+\sin^2 x}{1-\sin^2 x}\right) = 0 \Rightarrow \frac{1+\sin^2 x}{1-\sin^2 x} = 1$ *[1 mark]*

$$\Rightarrow 1 + \sin^2 x = 1 - \sin^2 x \Rightarrow 2\sin^2 x = 0 \Rightarrow \sin^2 x = 0$$

     This gives solutions $x = k\pi$ for all $k \in \mathbb{Z}$ *[1 mark]*.

3 a) $f(\theta) = \dfrac{2\cosh\theta + \sinh 2\theta}{1 + 2\sinh\theta + 3\sinh^2\theta - \cosh^2\theta}$ *[1 mark]*

$$= \frac{2\cosh\theta + 2\sinh\theta\cosh\theta}{1 + 2\sinh\theta + 3\sinh^2\theta - \cosh^2\theta}$$

        (using $\sinh 2x \equiv 2\sinh x \cosh x$) *[1 mark]*

$$= \frac{2\cosh\theta + 2\sinh\theta\cosh\theta}{1 + 2\sinh\theta + 2\sinh^2\theta + (\sinh^2\theta - \cosh^2\theta)}$$

$$= \frac{2\cosh\theta + 2\sinh\theta\cosh\theta}{1 + 2\sinh\theta + 2\sinh^2\theta - 1}$$

        (using $\cosh^2 x - \sinh^2 x \equiv 1$) *[1 mark]*

$$= \frac{2\cosh\theta(1+\sinh\theta)}{2\sinh\theta(1+\sinh\theta)}$$

$$= \frac{\cosh\theta}{\sinh\theta} = \coth\theta\ \textit{[1 mark]}$$

  b)   It is invertible because $\dfrac{1}{f(\theta)} = \tanh\theta$ and $\tanh\theta$ is one-to-one.

     Therefore, it is invertible through all its domain, i.e. all the real numbers *[1 mark]*.

  c) $\dfrac{1}{f(\theta)} = \tanh\theta = 1 - 2\tanh^2\theta \Rightarrow 2\tanh^2\theta + \tanh\theta - 1 = 0$

$$(2\tanh\theta - 1)(\tanh\theta + 1) = 0$$

$$\tanh\theta = \frac{1}{2} \text{ or } -1\ \textit{[1 mark]}$$

     But artanh θ is just defined for $-1 < \theta < 1$ so throw away -1 and only take $\tanh\theta = \frac{1}{2}$ *[1 mark]*.

$$\Rightarrow \theta = \text{artanh}\left(\frac{1}{2}\right) = \frac{1}{2}\ln\left(\frac{1+\frac{1}{2}}{1-\frac{1}{2}}\right) = \ln\sqrt{3}\ \textit{[1 mark]}$$

Page 75 — Calculus with Hyperbolics

Practice Questions

1   $\dfrac{d}{dx}\tanh x = \dfrac{d}{dx}\dfrac{\sinh x}{\cosh x} = \dfrac{\cosh^2 x - \sinh^2 x}{\cosh^2 x} = \dfrac{1}{\cosh^2 x} = \text{sech}^2 x$

2   -0.247 (3 s.f.)

3 a) $-\text{sech } x \tanh x$ b) $-\text{cosech } x \coth x$ c) $-\text{cosech}^2 x$

Answers

4 $\dfrac{\sinh \phi}{\sqrt{\cosh^2 \phi + 1}}$

5 $x \sinh x - \cosh x + C$

6 0.064 (3 d.p.)

Exam Questions

1 $\dfrac{dx}{dt} = 6 \cosh 2t, \quad \dfrac{dy}{dt} = 2 \sinh t$

$\Rightarrow \left(\dfrac{dx}{dt}\right)^2 + \left(\dfrac{dy}{dt}\right)^2 = 36 \cosh^2 2t + 4 \sinh^2 t$ *[1 mark]*

Because $\cosh 2t = 1 + 2 \sinh^2 t$ *[1 mark]*,

$\left(\dfrac{dx}{dt}\right)^2 + \left(\dfrac{dy}{dt}\right)^2 = 36(1 + 2\sinh^2 t)(1 + 2\sinh^2 t) + 4\sinh^2 t$ *[1 mark]*

$= 36(1 + 4\sinh^2 t + 4\sinh^4 t) + 4\sinh^2 t$

$= 36 + 148\sinh^2 t + 144\sinh^4 t$ *[1 mark]*

2 $\displaystyle\int_0^1 \dfrac{1}{\sqrt{81x^2 + 4}}\, dx = \int_0^9 \dfrac{1}{\sqrt{u^2 + 4}} \times \dfrac{1}{9}\, du$ *[1 mark]*

$= \dfrac{1}{9}\left[\operatorname{arsinh} \dfrac{u}{2}\right]_0^9$ *[1 mark]* $= \dfrac{1}{9}\left[\ln\left(\dfrac{u}{2} + \sqrt{\left(\dfrac{u}{2}\right)^2 + 1}\right)\right]_0^9$ *[1 mark]*

$= \dfrac{1}{9}\left(\ln\left(\dfrac{9}{2} + \sqrt{\dfrac{81}{4} + 1}\right) - \ln 1\right) = \dfrac{1}{9}\ln\left(\dfrac{9}{2} + \sqrt{\dfrac{85}{4}}\right)$

$= \dfrac{1}{9}\ln\left(\dfrac{9 + \sqrt{85}}{2}\right)$ *[1 mark]*

3 a) $f'(x) = \cosh x + 4 \sinh x$ *[1 mark]*

$= \dfrac{1}{2}(e^x + e^{-x}) + 2(e^x - e^{-x})$

$= \dfrac{5}{2}e^x - \dfrac{3}{2}e^{-x}$

$= \dfrac{1}{2}(5e^x - 3e^{-x})$ *[1 mark]*

b) $\sqrt{10} = \dfrac{1}{2}(5e^x - 3e^{-x}) \Rightarrow 5e^x - 2\sqrt{10} - 3e^{-x} = 0$

$\Rightarrow 5e^{2x} - 2\sqrt{10}\, e^x - 3 = 0$ *[1 mark]*

Using the quadratic formula, $e^x = \dfrac{2\sqrt{10} \pm \sqrt{4 \times 10 - 4 \times 5 \times (-3)}}{2 \times 5}$

$= \dfrac{2\sqrt{10} \pm \sqrt{100}}{10}$

$= \dfrac{1}{5}\sqrt{10} \pm 1$ *[1 mark]*

$\Rightarrow x = \ln\left(\dfrac{1}{5}\sqrt{10} \pm 1\right)$ *[1 mark]*

4 a) Let $x = \cosh u \Rightarrow \dfrac{dx}{du} = \sinh u \Rightarrow dx = \sinh u\, du$ *[1 mark]*

$\Rightarrow \displaystyle\int \dfrac{1}{\sqrt{x^2 - 1}}\, dx = \int \dfrac{\sinh u}{\sqrt{\cosh^2 u - 1}}\, du = \int \dfrac{\sinh u}{\sinh u}\, du$ *[1 mark]*

$= \displaystyle\int 1\, du = u = \operatorname{arcosh} x + C$ *[1 mark]*

$= \ln(x + \sqrt{x^2 - 1}) + C$ *[1 mark]*

b) Area of $R = \displaystyle\int_2^4 \dfrac{1}{\sqrt{x^2 - 1}}\, dx = \ln(4 + \sqrt{15}) - \ln(2 + \sqrt{3})$ *[1 mark]*

$= \ln\left(\dfrac{4 + \sqrt{15}}{2 + \sqrt{3}}\right)$ *[1 mark]*

Section 9 — CP: Differential Equations

Page 77 — First Order Differential Equations

Practice Questions

1 a) $y = \dfrac{k}{x}$

E.g.

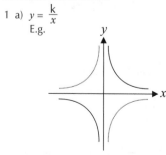

b) $x^2 + y^2 = c^2$

E.g

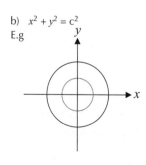

2 a) x^4 b) $\tan x + \sec x$ c) $(\sec x)^{\frac{1}{2}}$

---

3 Let $u = \displaystyle\int P(x)\, dx$. So, $I(x) = e^{\int P(x)\, dx} = e^u$

$\dfrac{dI}{du} = e^u = I$ and $\dfrac{du}{dx} = P(x)$, so by the chain rule

$\dfrac{dI}{dx} = \dfrac{dI}{du} \times \dfrac{du}{dx} = I(x)P(x)$ as required.

Exam Question

1 The equation can be expressed in the form $\dfrac{dC}{dt} + P(t)C = Q(t)$,

so the integrating factor is $e^{\int P(t)\, dt} = e^{\int \frac{1}{\ln 5}\, dt} = e^{\frac{1}{\ln 5}t}$

So $e^{\frac{1}{\ln 5}t} C = \displaystyle\int -10t e^{\frac{1}{\ln 5}t}\, dt$ *[1 mark]*

Let $u = -10t$ and $\dfrac{dv}{dt} = e^{\frac{1}{\ln 5}t}$ and use integration by parts.

$e^{\frac{1}{\ln 5}t} C = \displaystyle\int -10t e^{\frac{1}{\ln 5}t}\, dt$

$= -10(\ln 5)t e^{\frac{1}{\ln 5}t} - \displaystyle\int -10(\ln 5)e^{\frac{1}{\ln 5}t}\, dt$ *[1 mark]*

$= -10(\ln 5)t e^{\frac{1}{\ln 5}t} + 10(\ln 5)^2 e^{\frac{1}{\ln 5}t} + A$ *[1 mark]*

$= 10(\ln 5)(\ln 5 - t)e^{\frac{1}{\ln 5}t} + A$

Divide both sides by $e^{\frac{1}{\ln 5}t}$ to get:

$C(t) = 10(\ln 5)(\ln 5 - t) + A\, e^{-\frac{1}{\ln 5}t}$

$C(0) = 200 \Rightarrow 10(\ln 5)^2 + A = 200 \Rightarrow A = 200 - 10(\ln 5)^2$ *[1 mark]*

So, $C(t) = 10(\ln 5)(\ln 5 - t) + (200 - 10(\ln 5)^2)\, e^{-\frac{1}{\ln 5}t}$ *[1 mark]*

Page 79 — Second Order Differential Equations

Practice Questions

1 a) $y = A \cos 4x + B \sin 4x$ b) $x = Ae^{-7t} + Be^{-8t}$

c) $y = Ae^{-\frac{4}{3}x} + Be^{2x}$

2 $y = (4x - 1)e^{3x}$

Exam Question

1 Rearrange the equation to give $\dfrac{d^2 y}{dx^2} - \delta\dfrac{dy}{dx} + \varepsilon y = 0$.

The auxiliary equation is $\lambda^2 - \delta\lambda + \varepsilon = 0$

$\Rightarrow \lambda = \dfrac{-(-\delta) \pm \sqrt{(-\delta)^2 - 4\varepsilon}}{2} = \dfrac{\delta}{2}$ (since $\delta^2 = 4\varepsilon$) *[1 mark]*

So the general solution is $y = (A + Bx)\, e^{\frac{\delta}{2}x}$ *[1 mark]*

$\dfrac{dy}{dx} = B\, e^{\frac{\delta}{2}x} + \dfrac{\delta}{2}(A + Bx)\, e^{\frac{\delta}{2}x}$

When $x = 0$, $y = A = 0$ *[1 mark]*

When $x = 0$, $\dfrac{dy}{dx} = B + \dfrac{\delta}{2}A = 1 \Rightarrow B = 1$ *[1 mark]*

When $x = 1$, $\ln y = 4$, so $y = (A + B)e^{\frac{\delta}{2}} = e^4 \Rightarrow e^{\frac{\delta}{2}} = e^4 \Rightarrow \delta = 8$ *[1 mark]*

$\varepsilon = \delta^2 \div 4 = 64 \div 4 = 16$ *[1 mark]*

So $y = x\, e^{4x}$ *[1 mark]*

Page 82 — Tougher Second Order Differential Equations

Practice Questions

1 a $\dfrac{d^2 y}{dx^2} + b\dfrac{dy}{dx} + cy$

$= a\dfrac{d^2}{dx^2}(g(x) + h(x)) + b\dfrac{d}{dx}(g(x) + h(x)) + c(g(x) + h(x))$

$= a\dfrac{d^2}{dx^2}g(x) + a\dfrac{d^2}{dx^2}h(x) + b\dfrac{d}{dx}g(x) + b\dfrac{d}{dx}h(x) + cg(x) + ch(x)$

$= a\dfrac{d^2}{dx^2}g(x) + b\dfrac{d}{dx}g(x) + cg(x) + a\dfrac{d^2}{dx^2}h(x) + b\dfrac{d}{dx}h(x) + ch(x)$

$= 0 + f(x) = f(x)$

2 a) $y = A + Be^{2x} + \dfrac{3}{8}\cos 2x - \dfrac{11}{8}\sin 2x$

b) $y = Ae^{2x} + Be^{-2x} - \dfrac{27}{4}e^{\frac{2}{3}x}$

Answers

$y = (4 + 9x)e^{-x} + x^2 - 2x + 3$

Exam Question

a) Write and solve the auxiliary equation:
$\lambda^2 + 2\lambda + 5 = 0$
$b^2 - 4ac = 4 - 4 \times 1 \times 5 = -16 < 0$, so the solution
will be of the form $y = e^{px}(A \cos qx + B \sin qx)$.

$\lambda = \dfrac{-2 \pm \sqrt{2^2 - 4 \times 1 \times 5}}{2} = -1 \pm 2i$ **[1 mark]**

So the complementary function is:
$y = e^{-x}(A \cos 2x + B \sin 2x)$ **[1 mark]**
For the particular integral, try $y = \rho \cos 3x + \sigma \sin 3x$
$\Rightarrow y' = -3\rho \sin 3x + 3\sigma \cos 3x$
$\Rightarrow y'' = -9\rho \cos 3x - 9\sigma \sin 3x$ **[1 mark for y, y' and y'']**
So $-9\rho \cos 3x - 9\sigma \sin 3x + 2(-3\rho \sin 3x + 3\sigma \cos 3x)$
$+ 5(\rho \cos 3x + \sigma \sin 3x) = \sin 3x$ **[1 mark]**
Equating coefficients gives $-4\rho + 6\sigma = 0$ and $-4\sigma - 6\rho = 1$
$\Rightarrow \rho = -\dfrac{3}{26}$ and $\sigma = -\dfrac{1}{13}$ **[1 mark]**
The general solution is CF + PI **[1 mark]**.
So $y = e^{-x}(A \cos 2x + B \sin 2x) - \dfrac{3}{26} \cos 3x - \dfrac{1}{13} \sin 3x$ **[1 mark]**

b) $y(0) = A - \dfrac{3}{26} = 5 \Rightarrow A = \dfrac{133}{26}$ **[1 mark]**

$y' = -2Ae^{-x}\sin 2x - Ae^{-x}\cos 2x + 2Be^{-x}\cos 2x - Be^{-x}\sin 2x$
$\quad + \dfrac{9}{26} \sin 3x - \dfrac{3}{13} \cos 3x$

$y'(0) = -A + 2B - \dfrac{3}{13} = 0 \Rightarrow B = \dfrac{139}{52}$ **[1 mark]**
So, the particular solution is:
$y = e^{-x}(\dfrac{133}{26} \cos 2x + \dfrac{139}{52} \sin 2x)$
$\quad - \dfrac{3}{26} \cos 3x - \dfrac{1}{13} \sin 3x$ **[1 mark]**

Page 85 — Harmonic Motion

Practice Questions

1 $x = 5 \cos 5t + \dfrac{1}{\sqrt{5}} \sin 5t$

2 a) $x = (A + Bt) e^{-\frac{1}{3}t}$ b) The system is critically damped.
3 a) $x = Ae^{(-2+\sqrt{3})t} + Be^{(-2-\sqrt{3})t}$ b) The system is overdamped.
4 $\theta = Re^{-\frac{1}{2}t} \cos(\dfrac{\sqrt{5}}{2} t - \varphi)$

Exam Question

1 a) Take right to be positive.

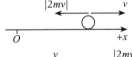

If $v > 0$, the resistive force
is $-|2mv| = -2mv$.

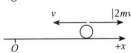

If $v < 0$, the resistive force
is $|2mv| = -2mv$.

In either case, the resistive force is $-2mv$ **[1 mark]**.

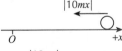

If $x > 0$, the restoring force
is $-|10mx| = -10mx$.

If $x < 0$, the restoring force
is $|10mx| = -10mx$.

In either case, the restoring force is $-10mx$ **[1 mark]**.

In all cases, the particle experiences a net force of
$F_{net} = -2mv - 10mx$ **[1 mark]**
Using $F_{net} = ma$ **[1 mark]** $= m\dfrac{d^2x}{dt^2}$ and $v = \dfrac{dx}{dt}$, gives
$m\dfrac{d^2x}{dt^2} = -2m\dfrac{dx}{dt} - 10mx$ **[1 mark]** as required.

b) Rearrange the DE from part a) to give
$m\dfrac{d^2x}{dt^2} + 2m\dfrac{dx}{dt} + 10mx = 0$
$\Rightarrow \dfrac{d^2x}{dt^2} + 2\dfrac{dx}{dt} + 10x = 0$ **[1 mark]**

Write and solve the auxiliary equation:
$\lambda^2 + 2\lambda + 10 = 0$
$b^2 - 4ac = 4 - 4 \times 1 \times 10 = -36 < 0$, so the solution
will be of the form $x = e^{pt}(A \cos qt + B \sin qt)$.

$\lambda = \dfrac{-2 \pm \sqrt{4 - 4 \times 1 \times 10}}{2} = \dfrac{-2 \pm \sqrt{-36}}{2} = -1 + 3i$ **[1 mark]**
So the general solution for the displacement is
$x = e^{-t}(A \cos 3t + B \sin 3t)$ **[1 mark]**
$x(0) = 6$, so $A = 6$ **[1 mark]**
$v = \dfrac{dx}{dt} = e^{-t}(-3A \sin 3t + 3B \cos 3t) - e^{-t}(A \cos 3t + B \sin 3t)$
$v = 0$ when $t = 0$, so $3B - A = 0 \Rightarrow B = 2$ **[1 mark]**
So $x = e^{-t}(6 \cos 3t + 2 \sin 3t)$ **[1 mark]**

Page 87 — Coupled First Order Differential Equations

Practice Questions

1 $x(t) = Ae^{3t} + Be^t$, $y(t) = Ae^{3t} + 2Be^t$
   You might have got an equally valid pair of solutions,
   $x(t) = Ae^{3t} + \dfrac{B}{2}e^t$, $y(t) = Ae^{3t} + Be^t$ here too.

2 a) $x(t) = \dfrac{5}{2} e^{-3t} + \dfrac{15}{2} e^t$, $y(t) = -\dfrac{5}{2} e^{-3t} + \dfrac{15}{2} e^t$
   b) E.g. both populations will grow without limit, which may be unlikely
      if they are directly competing with each other for food and space.

Exam Question

1 a) The flow of water into and out of each vat is equal, so there
      will be $\dfrac{x}{10}$ and $\dfrac{y}{10}$ g/litre of salt in each vat **[1 mark]**.
      'Rate of salt into A' $= (1 \times 1) + (2 \times \dfrac{y}{10})$g per minute, and
      'rate of salt out of A' $= (3 \times \dfrac{x}{10})$g per minute **[1 mark]**
      So, the net rate of salt in A is $\dot{x} = 1 + \dfrac{2}{10} y - \dfrac{3}{10} x$ ①
      'Rate of salt into B' $= (3 \times \dfrac{x}{10})$g per minute, and
      'rate of salt out of B' $= (2 \times \dfrac{y}{10})$g per minute **[1 mark]**
      So, the net rate of salt in B is $\dot{y} = \dfrac{3}{10} x - \dfrac{2}{10} y$ ②

   b) Multiply and rearrange ② to make x the subject:
      $x = \dfrac{1}{3} (10\dot{y} + 2y) \Rightarrow \dot{x} = \dfrac{1}{3} (10\ddot{y} + 2\dot{y})$ **[1 mark]**
      In ①, $\dfrac{1}{3} (10\ddot{y} + 2\dot{y}) = 1 + \dfrac{2}{10} y - \dfrac{3}{10} (\dfrac{1}{3} (10\dot{y} + 2y))$ **[1 mark]**
      $= 1 + \dfrac{2}{10} y - \dot{y} - \dfrac{2}{10} y$
      $\Rightarrow 10\ddot{y} + 2\dot{y} = 3 - 3\dot{y} \Rightarrow 10\ddot{y} + 5\dot{y} = 3$ **[1 mark]**
      Find the complementary function:
      $10\lambda^2 + 5\lambda = 0 \Rightarrow \lambda(10\lambda + 5) = 0 \Rightarrow \lambda = 0$ or $-\dfrac{1}{2}$ **[1 mark]**
      So $y = A + Be^{-\frac{1}{2}t}$ **[1 mark]**
      A constant is in the CF, so try $y = kt$ for the particular integral.
      $y = kt \Rightarrow \dot{y} = k$ and $\ddot{y} = 0$ **[1 mark]**
      So $5k = 3 \Rightarrow k = \dfrac{3}{5}$
      Therefore the general solution is $y = A + Be^{-\frac{1}{2}t} + \dfrac{3}{5}t$ **[1 mark]**
      $\Rightarrow \dot{y} = -\dfrac{1}{2} Be^{-\frac{1}{2}t} + \dfrac{3}{5}$ **[1 mark]**
      $x = \dfrac{1}{3} (10\dot{y} + 2y)$
      $= \dfrac{1}{3} (-5Be^{-\frac{1}{2}t} + 6 + 2A + 2Be^{-\frac{1}{2}t} + \dfrac{6}{5}t)$ **[1 mark]**
      $= 2 + \dfrac{2}{3}A - Be^{-\frac{1}{2}t} + \dfrac{2}{5}t$ **[1 mark]**
      At $t = 0$, $x = 0$ and $y = 0$ **[1 mark]**
      Because there is no salt in either vat initially.
      $y(0) = A + B = 0 \Rightarrow A = -B$ **[1 mark]**
      $x(0) = 2 + \dfrac{2}{3}A - B = 0 \Rightarrow 3B - 2A = 6$
      $\Rightarrow 5B = 6$ as $A = -B$
      So $B = \dfrac{6}{5}$ and $A = -\dfrac{6}{5}$ **[1 mark]**
      Therefore, the particular solutions are:
      $x = \dfrac{6}{5} - \dfrac{6}{5}e^{-\frac{1}{2}t} + \dfrac{2}{5}t$, $y = -\dfrac{6}{5} + \dfrac{6}{5}e^{-\frac{1}{2}t} + \dfrac{3}{5}t$ **[1 mark]**

Answers

Section 10 — FP1: Further Trigonometry

Page 91 — The t-formulas

Practice Questions

1   $\dfrac{1-\cos\theta}{1+\cos\theta} = t^2$

2 a) $\sin\theta = \dfrac{5}{13}$, $\cos\theta = -\dfrac{12}{13}$, $\tan\theta = -\dfrac{5}{12}$, 2nd quadrant

b) $\sin\theta = \dfrac{21}{29}$, $\cos\theta = \dfrac{20}{29}$, $\tan\theta = \dfrac{21}{20}$, 1st quadrant

c) $\sin\theta = -\dfrac{2\sqrt{2}}{3}$, $\cos\theta = \dfrac{1}{3}$, $\tan\theta = -2\sqrt{2}$, 4th quadrant

3 a) LHS $\equiv \dfrac{1-t^2}{2t} + \dfrac{2t}{1-t^2} \equiv \dfrac{(1-t^2)^2 + 4t^2}{2t(1-t^2)} \equiv \dfrac{1-2t^2+t^4+4t^2}{2t(1-t^2)}$

$\equiv \dfrac{1+2t^2+t^4}{2t(1-t^2)} \equiv \dfrac{(1+t^2)^2}{2t(1-t^2)} \equiv \left(\dfrac{1+t^2}{1-t^2}\right)\left(\dfrac{1+t^2}{2t}\right)$

$\equiv \sec\phi\,\mathrm{cosec}\,\phi \equiv$ RHS

b) RHS $\equiv \dfrac{\left(\dfrac{1+t^2}{2t}\right)}{\left(\dfrac{1+t^2}{2t}\right)-\left(\dfrac{2t}{1+t^2}\right)} \equiv \dfrac{(1+t^2)^2}{(1+t^2)^2 - 4t^2} \equiv \dfrac{(1+t^2)^2}{1+2t^2+t^4-4t^2}$

$\equiv \dfrac{(1+t^2)^2}{1-2t^2+t^4} \equiv \dfrac{(1+t^2)^2}{(1-t^2)^2} \equiv \sec^2\phi \equiv$ LHS

4 a) 1.94 (3 s.f.), 5.43 (3 s.f.)

b) 1.85 (3 s.f.), 2π

The solution 2π comes from checking manually for solutions at the asymptotes of $t = \tan\frac{x}{4}$. These asymptotes are at $x = 2(2n+1)\pi$.

5   $\ln\left|\tan\left(\dfrac{x}{2}\right)\right| + C$ 6 $\dfrac{1}{\sqrt{3}}$

Exam Questions

1   $\sin x = 2\sin\left(\dfrac{x}{2}\right)\cos\left(\dfrac{x}{2}\right)$ *[1 mark]*

$= \dfrac{2\sin\left(\frac{x}{2}\right)\cos\left(\frac{x}{2}\right)}{1} = \dfrac{2\sin\left(\frac{x}{2}\right)\cos\left(\frac{x}{2}\right)}{\sin^2\left(\frac{x}{2}\right)+\cos^2\left(\frac{x}{2}\right)}$ *[1 mark]*

Divide the numerator and denominator by $\cos^2\left(\dfrac{x}{2}\right)$:

$= \dfrac{2\left(\dfrac{\sin\left(\frac{x}{2}\right)\cos\left(\frac{x}{2}\right)}{\cos^2\left(\frac{x}{2}\right)}\right)}{\dfrac{\sin^2\left(\frac{x}{2}\right)}{\cos^2\left(\frac{x}{2}\right)}+\dfrac{\cos^2\left(\frac{x}{2}\right)}{\cos^2\left(\frac{x}{2}\right)}}$ *[1 mark]* $= \dfrac{2\tan\left(\frac{x}{2}\right)}{\tan^2\left(\frac{x}{2}\right)+1} = \dfrac{2t}{t^2+1}$ *[1 mark]*

You'd still get full marks if you worked in the opposite direction.

2 a) Use the substitution $t = \tan\left(\dfrac{x}{4}\right)$ *[1 mark]*

$\Rightarrow x = 4\arctan t \Rightarrow \dfrac{dx}{dt} = \dfrac{4}{1+t^2} \Rightarrow dx = \dfrac{4}{1+t^2}\,dt$

[1 mark for correct dx seen anywhere]

$\displaystyle\int \dfrac{1}{1+\sin\left(\frac{x}{2}\right)+\cos\left(\frac{x}{2}\right)}\,dx = \int \dfrac{1}{1+\left(\frac{2t}{1+t^2}\right)+\left(\frac{1-t^2}{1+t^2}\right)}\left(\dfrac{4}{1+t^2}\right)dt$

[1 mark]

$= \displaystyle\int \dfrac{4}{1+t^2+2t+1-t^2}\,dt = \int \dfrac{4}{2+2t}\,dt = 2\ln|1+t| + C$ *[1 mark]*

$= 2\ln\left|1+\tan\left(\dfrac{x}{4}\right)\right| + C$ *[1 mark]*

b)

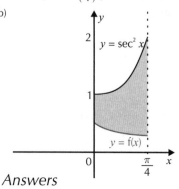

$\displaystyle\int_0^{\frac{\pi}{4}} f(x)\,dx = 2\ln\left|1+\tan\left(\dfrac{\pi}{16}\right)\right| - 2\ln|1+\tan 0|$

$= 0.362829\ldots$ *[1 mark]*

$\displaystyle\int_0^{\frac{\pi}{4}} \sec^2 x\,dx = [\tan x]_0^{\frac{\pi}{4}}$ *[1 mark]* $= 1$ *[1 mark]*

Area $= 1 - 0.362829\ldots$ *[1 mark]* $= 0.637$ (3 s.f.) *[1 mark]*

Section 11 — FP1: Further Calculus II

Page 93 — Taylor Series

Practice Questions

1   $\cos x = -\left(x - \dfrac{\pi}{2}\right) + \dfrac{1}{6}\left(x-\dfrac{\pi}{2}\right)^3 - \dfrac{1}{120}\left(x-\dfrac{\pi}{2}\right)^5 + \ldots$

2   Let $f(x) = e^x$. For any value of n, $f^{(n)}(x) = e^x$ and $f^{(n)}(\ln 3) = e^{\ln 3} = 3$.
So the Taylor series about $x = \ln 3$ is

$e^x = \displaystyle\sum_{n=0}^{\infty} \dfrac{f^{(n)}(\ln 3)}{n!}(x - \ln 3)^n = \sum_{n=0}^{\infty} \dfrac{3}{n!}(x - \ln 3)^n$.

3 a) $\tan x = 1 + 2\left(x - \dfrac{\pi}{4}\right) + 2\left(x - \dfrac{\pi}{4}\right)^2 + \ldots$

b) $\tan\left(\dfrac{\pi}{5}\right) \approx 1 - \dfrac{\pi}{10} + \dfrac{\pi^2}{200}$

c) Error $= |\text{True Value} - \text{Approximation}| = 0.00865$ (3 s.f.)

Exam Question

1 a) Let $f(x) = x^{\frac{1}{3}}$. The first three derivatives of f are:

$f'(x) = \dfrac{1}{3}x^{-\frac{2}{3}}$, $f''(x) = -\dfrac{2}{9}x^{-\frac{5}{3}}$, $f'''(x) = \dfrac{10}{27}x^{-\frac{8}{3}}$ *[1 mark]*

Evaluating these at $x = 8$ gives:

$f(8) = 2$, $f'(8) = \dfrac{1}{12}$, $f''(8) = -\dfrac{1}{144}$, $f'''(8) = \dfrac{5}{3456}$ *[1 mark]*

The Taylor series is therefore:

$x^{\frac{1}{3}} = f(8) + f'(8)(x-8) + \dfrac{f''(8)}{2!}(x-8)^2 + \dfrac{f'''(8)}{3!}(x-8)^3 + \ldots$

[1 mark]

$= 2 + \dfrac{1}{12}(x-8) - \dfrac{1}{288}(x-8)^2 + \dfrac{5}{20736}(x-8)^3 + \ldots$

[1 mark]

b) Setting $x = 7.5$:

$7.5^{\frac{1}{3}} = \sqrt[3]{7.5}$

$\approx 2 + \dfrac{1}{12}(7.5-8) - \dfrac{1}{288}(7.5-8)^2 + \dfrac{5}{20736}(7.5-8)^3$

$= 2 + \dfrac{1}{12}(-0.5) - \dfrac{1}{288}(-0.5)^2 + \dfrac{5}{20736}(-0.5)^3$ *[1 mark]*

$= 2 - \dfrac{1}{24} - \dfrac{1}{1152} - \dfrac{5}{165888}$

$= 1.9574$ (4 d.p.) *[1 mark]*

Page 95 — Limits

Practice Questions

1   2

2   4

3 a) $\dfrac{12}{5}$ b) 14

4 a) $\displaystyle\lim_{x\to 0^+} x\ln x = \lim_{x\to 0^+} \dfrac{\ln x}{\frac{1}{x}} = \lim_{x\to 0^+} \dfrac{\frac{1}{x}}{-\frac{1}{x^2}} = \lim_{x\to 0^+}(-x) = 0$

b) $\displaystyle\lim_{x\to\frac{\pi}{2}^+}(\sec x - \tan x) = \lim_{x\to\frac{\pi}{2}^+} \dfrac{1-\sin x}{\cos x} = \lim_{x\to\frac{\pi}{2}^+} \dfrac{-\cos x}{-\sin x} = 0$

c) $\displaystyle\lim_{x\to 1^+}\left(\dfrac{1}{x-1} - \dfrac{1}{\ln x}\right) = \lim_{x\to 1^+} \dfrac{\ln x - x + 1}{(x-1)\ln x} = \lim_{x\to 1^+} \dfrac{\frac{1}{x}-1}{\frac{-1}{x}+1+\ln x}$

$= \displaystyle\lim_{x\to 1^+} \dfrac{-\frac{1}{x^2}}{\frac{1}{x^2}+\frac{1}{x}} = -\dfrac{1}{2}$

Exam Questions

1   Using the series expansion of $\cos x$:

$\dfrac{p-q\cos x}{x^2} = \dfrac{p-q\left(1-\frac{x^2}{2!}+\frac{x^4}{4!}-\frac{x^6}{6!}+\ldots\right)}{x^2}$ *[1 mark]*

$= \dfrac{p-q+\frac{qx^2}{2!}-\frac{qx^4}{4!}+\frac{qx^6}{6!}-\ldots}{x^2}$

$= \dfrac{p-q}{x^2} + \dfrac{q}{2!} - \dfrac{qx^2}{4!} + \dfrac{qx^4}{6!} - \ldots$ *[1 mark]*

As $x \to 0$, the term $\dfrac{p-q}{x^2} \to \infty$ for all values of p and q other than when $p - q = 0$, i.e. $p = q$. But we are told that the limit is finite so that term cannot tend to ∞ and so it must be the case that $p = q$. In this case, $\dfrac{p-q}{x^2} = 0$ for all x and so $\dfrac{p-q}{x^2} \to 0$. *[1 mark]*

Also, $\displaystyle\lim_{x \to 0} \left(-\dfrac{qx^2}{4!} + \dfrac{qx^4}{6!} - \dots \right) = 0$ *[1 mark]* and therefore:

$$\lim_{x \to 0} \dfrac{p - q\cos x}{x^2} = \lim_{x \to 0} \left(\dfrac{p-q}{x^2} + \dfrac{q}{2!} - \dfrac{qx^2}{4!} + \dfrac{qx^4}{6!} - \dots \right)$$

$$= 0 + \dfrac{q}{2!} - 0 + 0 - \dots$$

$$= \dfrac{q}{2!}$$

$$= 1$$

$\Rightarrow q = 2! = 2, \ p = 2$ *[1 mark]*

Alternatively, you could use L'Hospital's Rule. First notice that as $x \to 0$, the function becomes $\dfrac{p-q}{0}$. This is infinite unless $p = q$, in which case it is an indeterminate of the form $\dfrac{0}{0}$.

2 $x^{\frac{1}{x}} = \exp\left(\ln\left(x^{\frac{1}{x}}\right) \right)$ *[1 mark]*

$$= \exp\left(\dfrac{1}{x} \ln x \right)$$

$$= \exp\left(\dfrac{\ln x}{x} \right)$$ *[1 mark]*

$\displaystyle\lim_{x \to \infty} \ln x = \lim_{x \to \infty} x = \infty$ so we have an indeterminate of the form $\dfrac{\infty}{\infty}$ and we can use L'Hospital's Rule *[1 mark]*:

$$\lim_{x \to \infty} x^{\frac{1}{x}} = \lim_{x \to \infty} \exp\left(\dfrac{\ln x}{x} \right) = \exp\left(\lim_{x \to \infty} \dfrac{\ln x}{x} \right)$$

$$= \exp\left(\lim_{x \to \infty} \dfrac{\left(\frac{1}{x}\right)}{1} \right)$$ *[1 mark]*

$$= e^0$$

$$= 1$$ *[1 mark]*

Page 97 — Leibnitz's Theorem
Practice Questions

1 Putting $n = 1$ into Leibnitz's theorem:

$$\dfrac{d}{dx}(uv) = \sum_{r=0}^{1} \binom{1}{r} u^{(r)}(x) \, v^{(1-r)}(x) = \binom{1}{0} u^{(0)}(x) v^{(1)}(x) + \binom{1}{1} u^{(1)}(x) v^{(0)}(x)$$

$$= u(x) v'(x) + u'(x) v(x), \text{ which is}$$
$$\text{the same as the product rule.}$$

2 a) $(20 - x^2)\sin x + 10x\cos x$

b) $3e^{3x+1}\left(27\ln x + \dfrac{36}{x} - \dfrac{18}{x^2} + \dfrac{8}{x^3} - \dfrac{2}{x^4} \right)$

3 a) Let $u(x) = x^4$ and $v(x) = e^{\sin x}$. The required derivatives are:

$u^{(1)}(x) = 4x^3$ $\quad\quad$ $v^{(1)}(x) = \cos x \, e^{\sin x}$

$u^{(2)}(x) = 12x^2$ $\quad\quad$ $v^{(2)}(x) = \cos^2 x \, e^{\sin x} - \sin x \, e^{\sin x}$

$\Rightarrow \dfrac{d^2}{dx^2}(uv) = x^4(\cos^2 x \, e^{\sin x} - \sin x \, e^{\sin x}) + 2 \times 4x^3 \cos x \, e^{\sin x}$
$$+ 12x^2 e^{\sin x}$$

$$= x^2 e^{\sin x}(x^2 \cos^2 x - x^2 \sin x + 8x \cos x + 12)$$

b) Let $u(x) = \sqrt{x+1} = (x+1)^{\frac{1}{2}}$ and $v(x) = \ln x$. The derivatives are:

$u^{(1)}(x) = \dfrac{1}{2}(x+1)^{-\frac{1}{2}}$ $\quad\quad$ $v^{(1)}(x) = \dfrac{1}{x}$

$u^{(2)}(x) = -\dfrac{1}{4}(x+1)^{-\frac{3}{2}}$ $\quad\quad$ $v^{(2)}(x) = -\dfrac{1}{x^2}$

$\Rightarrow \dfrac{d^2}{dx^2}(uv) = -(x+1)^{\frac{1}{2}} x^{-2} + 2 \times \dfrac{1}{2}(x+1)^{-\frac{1}{2}} x^{-1} - \ln x \, \dfrac{1}{4}(x+1)^{-\frac{3}{2}}$

$$= -\dfrac{(x+1)^{\frac{1}{2}}}{x^2} + \dfrac{1}{x(x+1)^{\frac{1}{2}}} - \dfrac{\ln x}{4(x+1)^{\frac{3}{2}}}$$

$$= \dfrac{-4(x+1)^{\frac{1}{2}}(x+1)^{\frac{3}{2}} + 4x(x+1) - x^2 \ln x}{4x^2(x+1)^{\frac{3}{2}}}$$

$$= \dfrac{-4(x+1)^2 + 4x^2 + 4x - x^2 \ln x}{4x^2(x+1)^{\frac{3}{2}}}$$

$$= \dfrac{-4x^2 - 8x - 4 + 4x^2 + 4x - x^2 \ln x}{4x^2(x+1)^{\frac{3}{2}}}$$

$$= \dfrac{-4x - 4 - x^2 \ln x}{4x^2\sqrt{x+1}^{\,3}}$$

$\Rightarrow \dfrac{d^2}{dx^2}(5uv) = 5 \times \dfrac{d^2}{dx^2}(uv) = -\dfrac{20x + 20 + 5x^2 \ln x}{4x^2\sqrt{x+1}^{\,3}}$

Exam Questions

1 a) Let $u(x) = e^{px}$ and $v(x) = \sin(qx)$.

$\dfrac{dy}{dx} = e^{px} q \cos(qx) + p e^{px} \sin(qx)$ *[1 mark]*

$$= e^{px}(q\cos(qx) + p\sin(qx))$$

$\dfrac{d^2 y}{dx^2} = e^{px}(-q^2 \sin(qx)) + 2 \times p e^{px} q \cos(qx) + p^2 e^{px} \sin(qx)$ *[1 mark]*

$$= e^{px}((p^2 - q^2)\sin(qx) + 2pq\cos(qx))$$

b) $\dfrac{d^2 y}{dx^2} - 2p\dfrac{dy}{dx} + (p^2 + q^2)y$

$= e^{px}((p^2 - q^2)\sin(qx) + 2pq\cos(qx)) - 2pe^{px}(q\cos(qx) + p\sin(qx))$
$$+ (p^2 + q^2)e^{px}\sin(qx)$$ *[1 mark]*

$= e^{px}((p^2 - q^2 - 2p^2 + p^2 + q^2)\sin(qx) + (2pq - 2pq)\cos(qx))$

$= e^{px} \times 0 = 0$ *[1 mark]*

2 a) Let $u(x) = \ln x$ and $v(x) = \dfrac{1}{x}$ *[1 mark for recognition of product]*.

Differentiating u:

$u^{(1)}(x) = \dfrac{1}{x}$, $u^{(2)}(x) = -\dfrac{1}{x^2}$, $u^{(3)}(x) = \dfrac{2}{x^3}$, $\dots$

Generally, $u^{(n)}(x) = (-1)^{n-1}(n-1)! \, x^{-n}$ *[1 mark]* $(n \geq 1)$

Differentiating v:

$v^{(1)}(x) = -\dfrac{1}{x^2}$, $v^{(2)}(x) = \dfrac{2}{x^3}$, $v^{(3)}(x) = -\dfrac{6}{x^4}$, $\dots$

Generally, $v^{(n)}(x) = (-1)^n n! \, x^{-(n+1)}$ *[1 mark]* $(n \geq 0)$.

Applying Leibnitz's theorem:

$$\dfrac{d^n}{dx^n}\dfrac{\ln x}{x} = \sum_{r=0}^{n} \binom{n}{r} u^{(r)}(x)\, v^{(n-r)}(x) = u^{(0)}(x)\, v^{(n)}(x) + \sum_{r=1}^{n} \binom{n}{r} u^{(r)}(x)\, v^{(n-r)}(x)$$

$$= \ln x \, (-1)^n n! \, x^{-(n+1)} + \sum_{r=1}^{n} \binom{n}{r} u^{(r)}(x)\, v^{(n-r)}(x)$$ *[1 mark]*

Evaluating just the sum term:

$$\sum_{r=1}^{n} \binom{n}{r} u^{(r)}(x)\, v^{(n-r)}(x) = \sum_{r=1}^{n} \left\{ \binom{n}{r}(-1)^{r-1}(r-1)! \, x^{-r}(-1)^{n-r}(n-r)! \, x^{-(n-r+1)} \right\}$$

$$= \sum_{r=1}^{n} \left\{ \binom{n}{r}(-1)^{n-1}(r-1)!(n-r)! \, x^{-(n+1)} \right\}$$

$$= \sum_{r=1}^{n} \left\{ \dfrac{n!}{r!(n-r)!}(-1)^{n-1}(r-1)!(n-r)! \, x^{-(n+1)} \right\}$$ *[1 mark]*

$$= \sum_{r=1}^{n} \left\{ (-1)^{n-1}\dfrac{n!}{r} x^{-(n+1)} \right\}$$

The expression we're aiming for has -1 raised only to the power n, not $n - 1$. But $(-1)^{n-1} = (-1)^n(-1)^{-1} = (-1)(-1)^n = -(-1)^n$. So:

$$\sum_{r=1}^{n} \binom{n}{r} u^{(r)}(x)\, v^{(n-r)}(x) = \sum_{r=1}^{n} \left\{ -(-1)^n \dfrac{n!}{r} x^{-(n+1)} \right\}$$

$$= -\sum_{r=1}^{n} \left\{ (-1)^n \dfrac{n!}{r} x^{-(n+1)} \right\}$$ *[1 mark]*

Reintroducing the first term and then factorising:

$$\dfrac{d^n}{dx^n}\dfrac{\ln x}{x} = \ln x \, (-1)^n n! \, x^{-(n+1)} - \sum_{r=1}^{n} \left\{ (-1)^n \dfrac{n!}{r} x^{-(n+1)} \right\}$$

$$= (-1)^n n! \, x^{-(n+1)}\left(\ln x - \sum_{r=1}^{n} \dfrac{1}{r} \right)$$ *[1 mark]*

b) Evaluating the result in part a) at $x = 2$ and $n = 4$:

$$\dfrac{d^4}{dx^4}\dfrac{\ln x}{x} = (-1)^4 \, 4! \, 2^{-(4+1)}\left(\ln 2 - \sum_{r=1}^{4} \dfrac{1}{r} \right)$$ *[1 mark]*

$$= 24 \times \dfrac{1}{32}\left(\ln 2 - \left(1 + \dfrac{1}{2} + \dfrac{1}{3} + \dfrac{1}{4}\right) \right)$$

$$= \dfrac{3}{4}\left(\ln 2 - \dfrac{25}{12} \right) = \dfrac{3}{4}\ln 2 - \dfrac{25}{16}$$ *[1 mark]*

Section 12 —
FP1: Further Differential Equations

Page 99 — Taylor Series and Differential Equations
Practice Questions

1 $y = (x - 1) + \dfrac{1}{2}(x-1)^2 + \dots$

2 $y = 1 + \dfrac{1}{2}(x-1)^2 + \dfrac{1}{3}(x-1)^3 + \dfrac{1}{8}(x-1)^4 + \dots$

Answers

Exam Questions

1. $y'' = (\sin x)y' + 2y$
   $\Rightarrow y''' = (\sin x)y'' + (\cos x)y' + 2y'$ *[1 mark]*
   The initial conditions are $y(\pi) = 1$ and $y'(\pi) = 1$.
   $\Rightarrow y''(\pi) = (\sin \pi)y'(\pi) + 2y(\pi) = 2$ *[1 mark]*
   $\Rightarrow y'''(\pi) = (\sin \pi)y''(\pi) + (\cos \pi)y'(\pi) + 2y'(\pi) = 1$ *[1 mark]*
   $y = y(\pi) + y'(\pi)(x - \pi) + \dfrac{y''(\pi)}{2!}(x - \pi)^2 + \dfrac{y'''(\pi)}{3!}(x - \pi)^3 + \ldots$
   So, $y = 1 + (x - \pi) + (x - \pi)^2 + \dfrac{1}{6}(x - \pi)^3 + \ldots$ as required.
   [1 mark for correct substitution into a series expansion]

2. $y'' = 5xy' - 2y$
   $\Rightarrow y''' = 5xy'' + 5y' - 2y' = 5xy'' + 3y'$ *[2 marks available
   — 1 mark for attempt at using product rule, 1 mark for y'']*
   $\Rightarrow y^{(4)} = 5xy''' + 5y'' + 3y'' = 5xy''' + 8y''$ *[1 mark]*
   $\Rightarrow y^{(5)} = 5xy^{(4)} + 5y''' + 8y''' = 5xy^{(4)} + 13y'''$ *[1 mark]*
   The initial conditions are $y(0) = 0$ and $y'(0) = 2$.
   $\Rightarrow y''(0) = -2y(0) = 0$ *[1 mark]*
   $\Rightarrow y'''(0) = 3y'(0) = 6$
   $\Rightarrow y^{(4)}(0) = 8y''(0) = 0$
   $\Rightarrow y^{(5)}(0) = 13y'''(0) = 78$
   *[1 mark for attempt to find other derivatives at $x = 0$,
   1 mark for all derivatives correct]*
   $y = y(0) + y'(0)x + \dfrac{y''(0)}{2!}x^2$
   $+ \dfrac{y'''(0)}{3!}x^3 + \dfrac{y^{(4)}(0)}{4!}x^4 + \dfrac{y^{(5)}(0)}{5!}x^5 + \ldots$ *[1 mark]*
   A series solution is $y = 2x + x^3 + \dfrac{13}{20}x^5 + \ldots$ *[1 mark]*

Page 101 — Reducible Differential Equations

Practice Questions

1. a) $z = \dfrac{y}{x} \Rightarrow y = xz \Rightarrow \dfrac{dy}{dx} = x\dfrac{dz}{dx} + z$
   $\Rightarrow x\dfrac{dz}{dx} + z = z + z^2 \Rightarrow x\dfrac{dz}{dx} = z^2$

   b) Separate the variables: $x\dfrac{dz}{dx} = z^2 \Rightarrow \dfrac{1}{z^2}dz = \dfrac{1}{x}dx$
   $\Rightarrow \int \dfrac{1}{z^2}dz = \int \dfrac{1}{x}dx \Rightarrow -\dfrac{1}{z} = \ln x + A$
   $\Rightarrow z = -\dfrac{1}{\ln x + A} \Rightarrow y = -\dfrac{x}{\ln x + A}$

2. $y = xz \Rightarrow \dfrac{dy}{dx} = x\dfrac{dz}{dx} + z$
   $\Rightarrow x\dfrac{dz}{dx} + z = \dfrac{x^2 + y^2}{xy - x^2} = \dfrac{x^2 + x^2z^2}{x^2z - x^2} = \dfrac{x^2(1 + z^2)}{x^2(z - 1)}$
   $\Rightarrow x\dfrac{dz}{dx} = \dfrac{(1 + z^2)}{(z - 1)} - z = \dfrac{(1 + z^2) - z(z - 1)}{(z - 1)} = \dfrac{z + 1}{z - 1}$

3. $u = y'' \Rightarrow u' = y'''$
   So $y''' - 25y'' = e^x \Rightarrow u' - 25u = e^x$
   $I(x) = e^{\int -25 dx} = e^{-25x}$
   So $e^{-25x}u = \int e^{-25x}e^x dx = \int e^{-24x}dx = -\dfrac{1}{24}e^{-24x} + C$
   $\Rightarrow u = -\dfrac{1}{24}e^x + Ce^{25x}$
   $y' = \int u\, dx = \int -\dfrac{1}{24}e^x + Ce^{25x}dx = -\dfrac{1}{24}e^x + \dfrac{C}{25}e^{25x} + D$
   $y = \int y'\, dx = \int -\dfrac{1}{24}e^x + \dfrac{C}{25}e^{25x} + D\, dx$
   $= -\dfrac{1}{24}e^x + \dfrac{C}{625}e^{25x} + Dx + E$
   $y = -\dfrac{1}{24}e^x + Ce^{25x} + Dx + E$ where C, D and E are constants.

Exam Questions

1. a) If $x = e^t$, then $\dfrac{dx}{dt} = e^t = x$ *[1 mark]*
   $\dfrac{dy}{dt} = \dfrac{dy}{dx}\dfrac{dx}{dt}$ (by the chain rule) $= x\dfrac{dy}{dx}$ *[1 mark]*
   $\dfrac{d^2y}{dt^2} = \dfrac{d}{dt}\left(\dfrac{dy}{dt}\right) = \dfrac{d}{dx}\left(\dfrac{dy}{dt}\right) \times \dfrac{dx}{dt}$ (by the chain rule) *[1 mark]*
   $= \left(x\dfrac{d^2y}{dx^2} + \dfrac{dy}{dx}\right) \times x$ (by the product rule) *[1 mark]*
   $= x^2\dfrac{d^2y}{dx^2} + \dfrac{dy}{dt}$ (because $x\dfrac{dy}{dx} = \dfrac{dy}{dt}$) *[1 mark]*
   Rearranging gives $x^2\dfrac{d^2y}{dx^2} = \dfrac{d^2y}{dt^2} - \dfrac{dy}{dt}$ *[1 mark]*

Answers

$x = e^t \Rightarrow \ln(x) = t$, so the differential equation can be expressed as
$a\left(\dfrac{d^2y}{dt^2} - \dfrac{dy}{dt}\right) + b\left(\dfrac{dy}{dt}\right) + cy = t$, as required *[1 mark]*.

b) Using part a), $x^2\dfrac{d^2y}{dx^2} - x\dfrac{dy}{dx} - 3y = \ln(x)$ can be expressed as
$\dfrac{d^2y}{dt^2} - \dfrac{dy}{dt} - \dfrac{dy}{dt} - 3y = \dfrac{d^2y}{dt^2} - 2\dfrac{dy}{dt} - 3y = t$ *[1 mark]*
The auxiliary equation is $\lambda^2 - 2\lambda - 3 = 0$ *[1 mark]*
The discriminant $b^2 - 4ac = (-2)^2 - 4 \times 1 \times (-3) = 16 > 0$,
so there are two distinct real roots.
$\lambda^2 - 2\lambda - 3 = 0 \Rightarrow (\lambda - 3)(\lambda + 1) \Rightarrow \lambda = 3$ or $\lambda = -1$ *[1 mark]*
So the complementary function is $y = Ae^{3t} + Be^{-t}$ *[1 mark]*.
For the particular integral, try $y = \beta t + \gamma$ *[1 mark]*.
$\Rightarrow y' = \beta \Rightarrow y'' = 0 \Rightarrow 0 - 2\beta - 3(\beta t + \gamma) = t$ *[1 mark]*
Equate coefficients: $-3\beta = 1 \Rightarrow \beta = -\dfrac{1}{3}$, $-2\beta - 3\gamma = 0 \Rightarrow \gamma = \dfrac{2}{9}$
[1 mark]
So the particular integral is $y = -\dfrac{1}{3}t + \dfrac{2}{9}$ *[1 mark]*
The general solution is $y = CF + PI$:
$y = Ae^{3t} + Be^{-t} - \dfrac{1}{3}t + \dfrac{2}{9}$ *[1 mark]*
But $x = e^t$, so $y = Ax^3 + \dfrac{B}{x} - \dfrac{1}{3}\ln x + \dfrac{2}{9}$ *[1 mark]*

2. $y = xz \Rightarrow y' = xz' + z \Rightarrow y'' = xz'' + z' + z' = xz'' + 2z'$ *[1 mark]*
   Rewrite the DE as $x^2(xz'' + 2z') - 2x(xz' + z) = 2xz(x^2 - 1)$ *[1 mark]*
   $\Rightarrow x^3z'' + 2x^2z' - 2x^2z' - 2xz = 2x^3z - 2xz$
   $\Rightarrow x^3z'' - 2x^3z = 0 \Rightarrow x^3(z'' - 2z) = 0$ *[1 mark]*
   $\Rightarrow x^3 = 0$ or $z'' - 2z = 0$ *[1 mark]*
   The auxiliary equation of $z'' - 2z = 0$ is $\lambda^2 - 2 = 0$ *[1 mark]*
   $\Rightarrow \lambda = \pm\sqrt{2}$ *[1 mark]*
   So, $z = Ae^{\sqrt{2}x} + Be^{-\sqrt{2}x}$ *[1 mark]*
   $y = xz$, so the general solution to L is $y = x(Ae^{\sqrt{2}x} + Be^{-\sqrt{2}x})$ *[1 mark]*

Section 13 — FP1: Coordinate Systems

Page 105 — Parabolas, Ellipses and Hyperbolas

Practice Questions

1. a) $y^2 = 2ax$ b) $\dfrac{x^2}{4a^2} + \dfrac{y^2}{4b^2} = 1$ c) $xy = c^4$
2. Foci: $(0, \sqrt{5})$ and $(0, -\sqrt{5})$
   Directrices: $y = 2\sqrt{5}$ and $y = -2\sqrt{5}$
3. a) $x = \pm2\cosh t$, $y = 2\sqrt{3}\sinh t$ b) $y = \sqrt{3}\,x$ and $y = -\sqrt{3}\,x$

Exam Questions

1. Parabola P has the Cartesian equation $y^2 = 4ax$ *[1 mark]*
   and rectangular hyperbola Q has equation $xy = 2a^2$ *[1 mark]*
   Rearrange: $y = \dfrac{2a^2}{x} \Rightarrow y^2 = \dfrac{4a^4}{x^2}$
   So the curves intersect at the point R when $4ax = \dfrac{4a^4}{x^2}$ *[1 mark]*.
   Simplify to get $a^3 = x^3 \Rightarrow x = a$ *[1 mark]* and $y = 2a$ *[1 mark]*.
   You could also substitute the parametric equations for Q into the Cartesian equation for P and solve for t to find the point of intersection.

2. Putting point Q into the equation: $\dfrac{25}{9a^2} + \dfrac{4}{b^2} = 1$
   Substitute in $b = 3$ and rearrange to find a:
   $\dfrac{25}{9a^2} + \dfrac{4}{9} = 1$ *[1 mark]* $\Rightarrow 25 = 5a^2 \Rightarrow a^2 = 5$ *[1 mark]*
   Use the eccentricity formula: $a^2 = b^2(1 - e^2)$ (as $b > a$) *[1 mark]*
   $\Rightarrow \dfrac{a^2}{b^2} = \dfrac{5}{9} = 1 - e^2 \Rightarrow e^2 = \dfrac{4}{9} \Rightarrow e = \dfrac{2}{3}$ *[1 mark]*

Page 107 — Tangents and Normals to Curves

Practice Questions

1. a) Tangent: $ty - x = at^2$
   Differentiate $y^2 = 4ax$, and use $x = at^2$ to get the gradient as $1/t$.
   Normal: $y + tx = 2at + at^3$
   b) Tangent: $ay\sin t + bx\cos t = ab$
   Normal: $by\cos t - ax\sin t = (b^2 - a^2)\sin t\cos t$
   c) Tangent: $bx\sec t - ay\tan t = ab$
   Normal: $by\sec t + ax\tan t = (b^2 + a^2)\sec t\tan t$

Answers

d) Tangent: $yt^2 + x = 2ct$
Normal: $ty - t^3x = c(1 - t^4)$

2 $\alpha = \text{arsinh}(-6) = \ln(-6 + \sqrt{37})$
The inverse hyperbolic functions are in the formula booklet.

3 The equation for the normal at point P is $y + px = 2ap + ap^3$.
The focus of the parabola is at $(a, 0)$, so $0 + ap = 2ap + ap^3$ at point Z
$\Rightarrow ap + ap^3 = 0 \Rightarrow ap(1 + p^2) = 0$.
As $p^2 \neq -1$ and $a \neq 0$, $p = 0$, so the normal is at $(0, 0)$.

Exam Question

1 a) Find $\dfrac{dy}{dx}$ using implicit differentiation:

$\dfrac{2x}{9} - \dfrac{2y}{16}\dfrac{dy}{dx} = 0 \Rightarrow \dfrac{dy}{dx} = \dfrac{32x}{18y} = \dfrac{16x}{9y}$ **[1 mark]**

So the normal must have gradient of $-\dfrac{9y}{16x}$ **[1 mark]**.
The equation of the normal at point P is:

$y - 4\tan t = -\dfrac{9}{16}\dfrac{4\tan t}{3\sec t}(x - 3\sec t)$
$\qquad = -\dfrac{3\tan t}{4\sec t}(x - 3\sec t)$ **[1 mark]**
$\Rightarrow 4y\sec t - 16\sec t\tan t = -3x\tan t + 9\sec t\tan t$ **[1 mark]**
$\Rightarrow 3x\tan t + 4y\sec t = 25\sec t\tan t$
$\Rightarrow 3x\sin t + 4y = 25\tan t$, as required **[1 mark]**.

b) The eccentricity of a hyperbola satisfies $b^2 = a^2(e^2 - 1)$ **[1 mark]**
(For this question, $a = 3$ and $b = 4$)
Rearrange to find $e^2 = \dfrac{16}{9} + 1 = \dfrac{25}{9} \Rightarrow e = \dfrac{5}{3}$ **[1 mark]**

So, the normal passes through $(9e, 0) = (9 \times \dfrac{5}{3}, 0)$
$\qquad = (15, 0)$ **[1 mark]**
Putting in $x = 15$ and $y = 0$ in the equation for the normal gives:
$45\sin t = 25\tan t$ **[1 mark]**
$\Rightarrow \sec t = \dfrac{45}{25} = \dfrac{9}{5}$ **[1 mark]** (as $\sin t \neq 0$)
$\sec^2 t - 1 = \tan^2 t \Rightarrow \dfrac{81}{25} - 1 = \dfrac{56}{25} = \tan^2 t \Rightarrow \tan t = \dfrac{2\sqrt{14}}{5}$
[1 mark]
You only need to consider the positive square root, since Q is on the positive y-axis.
Let $Q = (0, q)$. The normal also passes through this point, so
$4q = 25\tan t \Rightarrow q = \dfrac{25}{4}\tan t = \dfrac{25}{4} \times \dfrac{2\sqrt{14}}{5} = \dfrac{5\sqrt{14}}{2}$ **[1 mark]**
So the area of ORQ is $\dfrac{1}{2} \times 15 \times \dfrac{5\sqrt{14}}{2} = \dfrac{75\sqrt{14}}{4}$ **[1 mark]**

Page 109 — Loci Problems

Practice Questions

1 E.g.
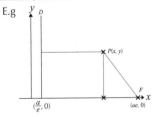

$PF/PD = e \Rightarrow PF = ePD$
$PF = \sqrt{(ae - x^2) + y^2}$ and $PD = x - \dfrac{a}{e}$
Square both sides: $(ae - x)^2 + y^2 = e^2(x - \dfrac{a}{e})^2$
$\Rightarrow a^2e^2 - 2aex + x^2 + y^2 = e^2x^2 - 2aex + a^2$
$\Rightarrow x^2(e^2 - 1) - y^2 = a^2(e^2 - 1)$
Divide by $a^2(e^2 - 1)$: $\dfrac{x^2}{a^2} - \dfrac{y^2}{a^2(e^2 - 1)} = 1$
(Setting $b^2 = a^2(e^2 - 1)$ gives the standard Cartesian equation.)

2 a) The tangent for a rectangular hyperbola (see p.107 Practice Q1d)
is $yt^2 + x = 2ct$.
So the tangent at P is $yp^2 + x = 6p$, and the tangent at Q is $yq^2 + x = 6q$
Subtract both equations to give $y(p^2 - q^2) = 6(p - q)$
$\Rightarrow y = \dfrac{6(p - q)}{(p^2 - q^2)} = \dfrac{6(p - q)}{(p - q)(p + q)} = \dfrac{6}{(p + q)}$
Substitute $\dfrac{6}{(p + q)}$ back into the tangent at P and rearrange to get:
$\Rightarrow x = 6p - \dfrac{6p^2}{(p + q)} = \dfrac{6pq}{p + q}$

b) $y = -x$

3 $\dfrac{4}{x^2} + \dfrac{9}{4y^2} = 1$

4 $16x^2 - 4y^2 = 25$

Exam Question

1 a) The focus of a general parabola $y^2 = 4ax$ is at $(a, 0)$ **[1 mark]**.
So F is at $(1, 0)$ **[1 mark]**
and the gradient of PF and QF will be the same.
Use $\dfrac{y - y_1}{x - x_1} = m: \dfrac{2p}{p^2 - 1} = \dfrac{2q}{q^2 - 1}$ **[1 mark]**
$\Rightarrow p(q^2 - 1) = q(p^2 - 1)$
$\Rightarrow pq^2 - p = qp^2 - q$
$\Rightarrow pq^2 - p - qp^2 + q = 0$
Factorise: $(pq + 1)(q - p) = 0$ **[1 mark]**
P and Q are distinct points, so $p \neq q$.
Therefore $pq + 1 = 0$, which means $pq = -1$ **[1 mark]**.

b) The midpoint R will be at (X, Y) where:
$X = \dfrac{p^2 + q^2}{2}$ **[1 mark]** and $Y = \dfrac{2p + 2q}{2} = p + q$ **[1 mark]**
Eliminate parameters p and q:
$Y^2 = (p + q)^2 = p^2 + 2pq + q^2 = 2X - 2$, since $pq = -1$.
The locus of the point R is $Y^2 = 2(X - 1)$ as required.
**[1 mark for eliminating parameters p and q,
1 mark for getting the required result]**.

Section 14 — FP1: Further Vectors II

Page 111 — Vector Cross Product

Practice Questions

1 a) $12\mathbf{i} - 8\mathbf{j} - 8\mathbf{k}$ b) $-10\mathbf{i} + 10\mathbf{j} - 10\mathbf{k}$

   c) $-(-10\mathbf{i} + 10\mathbf{j} - 10\mathbf{k}) = 10\mathbf{i} - 10\mathbf{j} + 10\mathbf{k}$ as $\mathbf{b} \times \mathbf{a} = -(\mathbf{a} \times \mathbf{b})$

2   $(4\mathbf{i} + \mathbf{j} - \mathbf{k}) \times (-8\mathbf{i} - 2\mathbf{j} + 2\mathbf{k}) = (2 - 2)\mathbf{i} + (8 - 8)\mathbf{j} + (-8 + 8)\mathbf{k} = \mathbf{0}$
   $\Rightarrow$ The vectors are parallel.

3   $(5\mathbf{i} - 2\mathbf{j} + 2\mathbf{k}) \times (-9\mathbf{i} + \mathbf{j} + 3\mathbf{k}) = -8\mathbf{i} - 33\mathbf{j} - 13\mathbf{k}$ is perpendicular to
   both $5\mathbf{i} - 2\mathbf{j} + 2\mathbf{k}$ and $-9\mathbf{i} + \mathbf{j} + 3\mathbf{k}$

Exam Questions

1   $|\overrightarrow{OA}| = |\overrightarrow{OB}| = 4$ so $\sqrt{1^2 + (a_2)^2 + (a_3)^2} = \sqrt{1^2 + (a_2)^2 + (-a_3)^2} = 4$
   $\Rightarrow a_2^2 + a_3^2 = 4^2 - 1^2 = 15$ **[1 mark]**

   The area of OAB = $\dfrac{1}{2}|\mathbf{a} \times \mathbf{b}| = 8$ where $\mathbf{a} = \overrightarrow{OA}$ and $\mathbf{b} = \overrightarrow{OB}$ **[1 mark]**
   $= \dfrac{1}{2}\left\|\begin{matrix} \mathbf{i} & \mathbf{j} & \mathbf{k} \\ 1 & a_2 & a_3 \\ 1 & a_2 & -a_3 \end{matrix}\right\| = \dfrac{1}{2}|-2a_2a_3\mathbf{i} + 2a_3\mathbf{j}| = \dfrac{1}{2}\sqrt{4a_2^2a_3^2 + 4a_3^2}$ **[1 mark]**
   $= \sqrt{a_3^2(a_2^2 + 1)} = 8 \Rightarrow a_3^2(a_2^2 + 1) = 8^2 = 64$
   $a_2^2 + a_3^2 = 15 \Rightarrow a_2^2 + 1 = 16 - a_3^2$
   $\Rightarrow a_3^2(16 - a_3^2) = 64 \Rightarrow (a_3^2)^2 - 16a_3^2 + 64 = 0$ **[1 mark]**
   $\Rightarrow (a_3^2 - 8)^2 = 0 \Rightarrow a_3^2 = 8 \Rightarrow a_3 = \sqrt{8}$ **[1 mark]**
   $\Rightarrow a_2^2 = 15 - 8 = 7 \Rightarrow a_2 = \sqrt{7}$ **[1 mark]**

2   The line AC splits the kite into two congruent triangles,
   ABC and ADC. **[1 mark]**
   So the area of the kite ABCD = 2 × the area of ABC
   (= 2 × the area of ADC)
   $= 2 \times \dfrac{1}{2}|\mathbf{a} \times \mathbf{c}| = |\mathbf{a} \times \mathbf{c}|$ **[1 mark]**
   where $\mathbf{a} = \overrightarrow{BA} = (1 - 5, -3 + 1, 2 - 3) = (-4, -2, -1)$
   and $\mathbf{c} = \overrightarrow{BC} = (17 - 5, -3 + 1, 6 - 3) = (12, -2, 3)$ **[1 mark]**
   (could have used $\mathbf{a} = \overrightarrow{DA}$ and $\mathbf{c} = \overrightarrow{DC}$. The vectors will be different but
   their vector product will be the same)
   $\Rightarrow |\mathbf{a} \times \mathbf{c}| = \left\|\begin{matrix} \mathbf{i} & \mathbf{j} & \mathbf{k} \\ -4 & -2 & -1 \\ 12 & -2 & 3 \end{matrix}\right\| = |(-8, 0, 32)|$ **[1 mark]**
   $= 8|(-1, 0, 4)| = 8\sqrt{(-1)^2 + 4^2}$
   $\Rightarrow$ The area of the kite ABCD = $8\sqrt{17}$ **[1 mark]**

Answers

Page 113 — Scalar Triple Product

Practice Questions

1. $\mathbf{a}.\mathbf{b} \times \mathbf{c} = \begin{vmatrix} 1 & 0 & -6 \\ 8 & 4 & -6 \\ -4 & 1 & -4 \end{vmatrix} = 1\begin{vmatrix} 4 & -6 \\ 1 & -4 \end{vmatrix} - 0\begin{vmatrix} 8 & -6 \\ -4 & -4 \end{vmatrix} + (-6)\begin{vmatrix} 8 & 4 \\ -4 & 1 \end{vmatrix}$

    $= -10 - 0 - 144 = -154$

2. a) $\mathbf{a}.\mathbf{b} \times \mathbf{c} = \begin{vmatrix} a_1 & a_2 & a_3 \\ b_1 & b_2 & b_3 \\ c_1 & c_2 & c_3 \end{vmatrix} = -\begin{vmatrix} a_1 & a_2 & a_3 \\ c_1 & c_2 & c_3 \\ b_1 & b_2 & b_3 \end{vmatrix} = -\mathbf{a}.\mathbf{c} \times \mathbf{b}$

    by the determinant rules (see page 30).
    Similarly:

    $\mathbf{a}.\mathbf{b} \times \mathbf{c} = \begin{vmatrix} a_1 & a_2 & a_3 \\ b_1 & b_2 & b_3 \\ c_1 & c_2 & c_3 \end{vmatrix} = -\begin{vmatrix} b_1 & b_2 & b_3 \\ a_1 & a_2 & a_3 \\ c_1 & c_2 & c_3 \end{vmatrix} = -\mathbf{b}.\mathbf{a} \times \mathbf{c}$

    b) $\mathbf{a}.\mathbf{b} \times \mathbf{c} = \begin{vmatrix} a_1 & a_2 & a_3 \\ b_1 & b_2 & b_3 \\ c_1 & c_2 & c_3 \end{vmatrix} = -\begin{vmatrix} c_1 & c_2 & c_3 \\ b_1 & b_2 & b_3 \\ a_1 & a_2 & a_3 \end{vmatrix} = (-1)^2\begin{vmatrix} c_1 & c_2 & c_3 \\ a_1 & a_2 & a_3 \\ b_1 & b_2 & b_3 \end{vmatrix} = \mathbf{c}.\mathbf{a} \times \mathbf{b}$

    and $\mathbf{a}.\mathbf{b} \times \mathbf{c} = \begin{vmatrix} a_1 & a_2 & a_3 \\ b_1 & b_2 & b_3 \\ c_1 & c_2 & c_3 \end{vmatrix} = -\begin{vmatrix} b_1 & b_2 & b_3 \\ a_1 & a_2 & a_3 \\ c_1 & c_2 & c_3 \end{vmatrix} = (-1)^2\begin{vmatrix} b_1 & b_2 & b_3 \\ c_1 & c_2 & c_3 \\ a_1 & a_2 & a_3 \end{vmatrix} = \mathbf{b}.\mathbf{c} \times \mathbf{a}$

Exam Questions

1. You need vectors $\mathbf{a}$, $\mathbf{b}$ and $\mathbf{c}$ representing edges that meet at one corner. Choosing D as the corner where the edges meet:

    $\mathbf{a} = (5 - 7)\mathbf{i} + (-1 - 5)\mathbf{j} + (3 - 2)\mathbf{k} = -2\mathbf{i} - 6\mathbf{j} + \mathbf{k}$

    $\mathbf{b} = (0 - 7)\mathbf{i} + (4 - 5)\mathbf{j} + (6 - 2)\mathbf{k} = -7\mathbf{i} - \mathbf{j} + 4\mathbf{k}$

    $\mathbf{c} = (2 - 7)\mathbf{i} + (3 - 5)\mathbf{j} + (-3 - 2)\mathbf{k} = -5\mathbf{i} - 2\mathbf{j} - 5\mathbf{k}$ *[1 mark]*

    Volume of Tetrahedron ABC $= \frac{1}{6}|\mathbf{a}.\mathbf{b} \times \mathbf{c}|$

    $= \frac{1}{6}\left|\begin{vmatrix} -2 & -6 & 1 \\ -7 & -1 & 4 \\ -5 & -2 & -5 \end{vmatrix}\right|$ *[1 mark]*

    $= \frac{1}{6}\left|-2\begin{vmatrix} -1 & 4 \\ -2 & -5 \end{vmatrix} - (-6)\begin{vmatrix} -7 & 4 \\ -5 & -5 \end{vmatrix} + \begin{vmatrix} -7 & -1 \\ -5 & -2 \end{vmatrix}\right|$

    $= \frac{1}{6}|-2(5 + 8) + 6(35 + 20) + (14 - 5)|$

    $= \frac{1}{6}|-26 + 330 + 9| = \frac{313}{6}$ *[1 mark]*

2. The parallelepiped has a volume of 53

    $\Rightarrow |\mathbf{a}.\mathbf{b} \times \mathbf{c}| = \left|\begin{vmatrix} 6 & 3 & -1 \\ 3 & -1 & 4 \\ c_1 & 0 & c_3 \end{vmatrix}\right| = 53$ where $\mathbf{a} = \overrightarrow{OA}$, $\mathbf{b} = \overrightarrow{OB}$ and

    $\mathbf{c} = \overrightarrow{OC}$ *[1 mark]*

    $\Rightarrow \left|6\begin{vmatrix} -1 & 4 \\ 0 & c_3 \end{vmatrix} - 3\begin{vmatrix} 3 & 4 \\ c_1 & c_3 \end{vmatrix} + (-1)\begin{vmatrix} 3 & -1 \\ c_1 & 0 \end{vmatrix}\right| = |-6c_3 - 9c_3 + 12c_1 - c_1| =$

    $|11c_1 - 15c_3| = 53$ *[1 mark]*

    The equation for the plane CDEF is $\mathbf{r}.\begin{pmatrix} 4 \\ 0 \\ -2 \end{pmatrix} = 2 \Rightarrow 4c_1 - 2c_3 = 2$

    $\Rightarrow c_3 = 2c_1 - 1$ *[1 mark]*

    $\Rightarrow |11c_1 - 15(2c_1 - 1)| = |-19c_1 + 15| = 53$

    $c_1 < 0 \Rightarrow -19c_1 + 15 > 0 \Rightarrow |-19c_1 + 15| = -19c_1 + 15 = 53$

    $\Rightarrow c_1 = \frac{53 - 15}{-19} = -2$ *[1 mark]*

    $\Rightarrow c_3 = 2 \times (-2) - 1 = -5$ *[1 mark]*

Page 115 — More 3D Geometry

Practice Questions

1. $(\mathbf{r} - (4\mathbf{i} - 2\mathbf{j} + 2\mathbf{k})) \times (3\mathbf{i} + 5\mathbf{j} - 7\mathbf{k}) = \mathbf{0}$

2. $\begin{pmatrix} 1 \\ -4 \\ -4 \end{pmatrix} \times \begin{pmatrix} 2 \\ -5 \\ 3 \end{pmatrix} = \begin{vmatrix} \mathbf{i} & \mathbf{j} & \mathbf{k} \\ 1 & -4 & -4 \\ 2 & -5 & 3 \end{vmatrix} = \begin{pmatrix} -32 \\ -11 \\ 3 \end{pmatrix}$

    $\Rightarrow \mathbf{r}.\begin{pmatrix} -32 \\ -11 \\ 3 \end{pmatrix} = \begin{pmatrix} 3 \\ -3 \\ 1 \end{pmatrix}.\begin{pmatrix} -32 \\ -11 \\ 3 \end{pmatrix} = -96 + 33 + 3 = -60 \Rightarrow \mathbf{r}.\begin{pmatrix} -32 \\ -11 \\ 3 \end{pmatrix} = -60$

Exam Questions

1. Direction cosines are the components of

    $\dfrac{1}{\sqrt{\left(\frac{1}{\sqrt{3}}\right)^2 + (-2)^2}}(\frac{1}{\sqrt{3}}\mathbf{i} - 2\mathbf{j})$ *[1 mark]*

    $= \frac{\sqrt{3}}{\sqrt{13}}(\frac{1}{\sqrt{3}}\mathbf{i} - 2\mathbf{j}) = \frac{1}{\sqrt{13}}\mathbf{i} - \frac{2\sqrt{3}}{\sqrt{13}}\mathbf{j}$ *[1 mark]*

    So the angles between $\mathbf{r}$ and the positive x, y and z-axes are:

    $\theta_x = \cos^{-1}(\frac{1}{\sqrt{13}}) = 1.29$ (2 d.p.)

    $\theta_y = \cos^{-1}(-\frac{2\sqrt{3}}{\sqrt{13}}) = 2.86$ (2 d.p.)

    $\theta_z = \cos^{-1}(0) = 1.57$ (2 d.p.) *[1 mark]*

2. Need to find $\mathbf{a}$, $\mathbf{b}$ and $\mathbf{c}$.

    $\mathbf{a} = \begin{pmatrix} -6 \\ -5 \\ -3 \end{pmatrix}$ (or $\begin{pmatrix} -5 \\ 4 \\ -7 \end{pmatrix}$) and $\mathbf{c} = \begin{pmatrix} -2 \\ 0 \\ 2 \end{pmatrix}$ *[1 mark]*

    $\mathbf{b} = \begin{pmatrix} -5 \\ 4 \\ -7 \end{pmatrix} - \begin{pmatrix} -6 \\ -5 \\ -3 \end{pmatrix} = \begin{pmatrix} 1 \\ 9 \\ -4 \end{pmatrix}$ (or any multiple of $\begin{pmatrix} 1 \\ 9 \\ -4 \end{pmatrix}$) *[1 mark]*

    $\Rightarrow$ The perpendicular distance between l_1 and $l_2 = \dfrac{|(\mathbf{c} - \mathbf{a}) \times \mathbf{b}|}{|\mathbf{b}|}$

    $(\mathbf{c} - \mathbf{a}) = \begin{pmatrix} -2 \\ 0 \\ 2 \end{pmatrix} - \begin{pmatrix} -6 \\ -5 \\ -3 \end{pmatrix} = \begin{pmatrix} 4 \\ 5 \\ 5 \end{pmatrix}$

    $(\mathbf{c} - \mathbf{a}) \times \mathbf{b} = \begin{pmatrix} 4 \\ 5 \\ 5 \end{pmatrix} \times \begin{pmatrix} 1 \\ 9 \\ -4 \end{pmatrix} = \begin{vmatrix} \mathbf{i} & \mathbf{j} & \mathbf{k} \\ 4 & 5 & 5 \\ 1 & 9 & -4 \end{vmatrix} = \begin{pmatrix} -65 \\ 21 \\ 31 \end{pmatrix}$ *[1 mark]*

    $|\mathbf{b}| = \sqrt{1^2 + 9^2 + (-4)^2} = \sqrt{98} = 7\sqrt{2}$

    $|(\mathbf{c} - \mathbf{a}) \times \mathbf{b}| = \sqrt{(-65)^2 + 21^2 + 31^2} = \sqrt{5627}$

    The perpendicular distance between l_1 and $l_2 = \dfrac{\sqrt{5627}}{7\sqrt{2}}$ *[1 mark]*

3. $\mathbf{a} = \begin{pmatrix} 3 \\ -1 \\ 4 \end{pmatrix}$ (or $\begin{pmatrix} 3 \\ 1 \\ 16 \end{pmatrix}$) and $\mathbf{c} = \begin{pmatrix} -2 \\ 5 \\ 2 \end{pmatrix}$ (or $\begin{pmatrix} 2 \\ 6 \\ 1 \end{pmatrix}$) *[1 mark]*

    $\mathbf{b} = \begin{pmatrix} 3 \\ 1 \\ 16 \end{pmatrix} - \begin{pmatrix} 3 \\ -1 \\ 4 \end{pmatrix} = \begin{pmatrix} 0 \\ 2 \\ 12 \end{pmatrix}$ (or any multiple of $\begin{pmatrix} 0 \\ 2 \\ 12 \end{pmatrix}$)

    $\mathbf{d} = \begin{pmatrix} 2 \\ 6 \\ 1 \end{pmatrix} - \begin{pmatrix} -2 \\ 5 \\ 2 \end{pmatrix} = \begin{pmatrix} 4 \\ 1 \\ -1 \end{pmatrix}$ (or any multiple of $\begin{pmatrix} 4 \\ 1 \\ -1 \end{pmatrix}$) *[1 mark]*

    The perpendicular distance between l_1 and $l_2 = \dfrac{|(\mathbf{c} - \mathbf{a}).(\mathbf{b} \times \mathbf{d})|}{|\mathbf{b} \times \mathbf{d}|}$

    $\mathbf{c} - \mathbf{a} = \begin{pmatrix} -2 \\ 5 \\ 2 \end{pmatrix} - \begin{pmatrix} 3 \\ -1 \\ 4 \end{pmatrix} = \begin{pmatrix} -5 \\ 6 \\ -2 \end{pmatrix}$, $\mathbf{b} \times \mathbf{d} = \begin{vmatrix} \mathbf{i} & \mathbf{j} & \mathbf{k} \\ 0 & 2 & 12 \\ 4 & 1 & -1 \end{vmatrix} = \begin{pmatrix} -14 \\ 48 \\ -8 \end{pmatrix}$

    $\Rightarrow |\mathbf{b} \times \mathbf{d}| = \sqrt{(-14)^2 + 48^2 + (-8)^2} = 2\sqrt{641}$ *[1 mark]*

    $(\mathbf{c} - \mathbf{a}).(\mathbf{b} \times \mathbf{d}) = \begin{pmatrix} -5 \\ 6 \\ -2 \end{pmatrix}.\begin{pmatrix} -14 \\ 48 \\ -8 \end{pmatrix} = 374$ *[1 mark]*

    $\Rightarrow$ The perpendicular distance between l_1 and $l_2 = \dfrac{|374|}{|2\sqrt{641}|}$

    $= \dfrac{187}{\sqrt{641}}$ *[1 mark]*

Section 15 — FP1: Further Numerical Methods

Page 117 — Numerical Solution of Differential Equations

Practice Questions

1. a) $y(x_0 + h) = y(x_1) = y_1$

    $\Rightarrow y_1 \approx y(x_0) + hy'(x_0)$, ignoring terms in $y''(x_0)$ and higher.

    Rearrange and divide by h: $y'(x_0) \approx \dfrac{y_1 - y_0}{h}$ as required.

b) Eqn 1: $y_1 = y(x_0 + h) = y(x_0) + hy'(x_0) + \frac{h^2}{2}y''(x_0) + ...$

Eqn 2: $y_{-1} = y(x_0 - h) = y(x_0) - hy'(x_0) + \frac{h^2}{2}y''(x_0) + ...$

Eqn 1 – Eqn 2 $\Rightarrow y_1 - y_{-1} \approx 2hy'(x_0)$,
ignoring terms in $y'''(x_0)$ and higher.

Divide by 2h: $y'(x_0) \approx \frac{y_1 - y_{-1}}{2h}$ as required.

2   E.g. $y(10.1) \approx 2$, using Euler's method with $h = 0.1$.

3    $y(0.2) \approx 2.9325$ (4 d.p.),
You may have a different approximation if you used
Euler's method twice to find y(O.2) here.

4    $y(0.2) \approx 1.4000$ (4 d.p.)

Exam Question

1 a) $\left(\frac{dy}{dx}\right)_0 \approx \frac{y_1 - y_0}{h} \Rightarrow y_1 \approx y_0 + h\left(\frac{dy}{dx}\right)_0$ *[1 mark]*

$\left(\frac{dy}{dx}\right)_0 = 2y_0(x_0{}^2 + x_0 y_0) = 2 \times 1 \times (0.1^2 + 0.1 \times 1) = 0.22$
         [1 mark]

So $y_1 \approx 1 + 0.1 \times 0.22 = 1.022$ *[1 mark]*

b) $\left(\frac{dy}{dx}\right)_1 \approx \frac{y_2 - y_0}{2h} \Rightarrow y_2 \approx y_0 + 2h\left(\frac{dy}{dx}\right)_1$ *[1 mark]*

$\left(\frac{dy}{dx}\right)_1 = 2y_1(x_1{}^2 + x_1 y_1) = 2 \times 1.022(0.2^2 + 0.2 \times 1.022)$ *[1 mark]*
         $= 0.4995...$

So $y_2 \approx 1 + 0.2(0.4995...) = 1.0999$ (4 d.p.) *[1 mark]*

c) $y_2 = y(0.3)$, so $y(0.3) \approx 1.0999$ (4 d.p.) *[1 mark]*

Page 119 — Simpson's Rule

Practice Questions

1 a) 33.0104 (4 d.p.)   b)   256.6590 (4 d.p.)   c)   2.3075 (4 d.p.)

2 a) 126.1528 (4 d.p.)

b) The exact integral is 126, so the error is approximately
126.1528 – 126 = 0.1528 (4 d.p.)

Exam Question

1 a) 5 ordinates $\Rightarrow n = 4$

So, $h = \frac{5 - 4}{4} = \frac{1}{4}$ *[1 mark]*

x	$y = e^{\sqrt{x}}$
$x_0 = 4$	$y_0 = e^{\sqrt{4}}$
$x_1 = \frac{17}{4}$	$y_1 = e^{\sqrt{\frac{17}{4}}}$
$x_2 = \frac{18}{4}$	$y_2 = e^{\sqrt{\frac{18}{4}}}$
$x_3 = \frac{19}{4}$	$y_3 = e^{\sqrt{\frac{19}{4}}}$
$x_4 = 5$	$y_4 = e^{\sqrt{5}}$

[1 mark for list or table of y-values]

$\int_4^5 e^{\sqrt{x}}\, dx \approx \frac{h}{3}[y_0 + 4(y_1 + y_3) + 2y_2 + y_4]$ *[1 mark]*

$\approx \frac{1}{12}[e^{\sqrt{4}} + 4(e^{\sqrt{\frac{17}{4}}} + e^{\sqrt{\frac{19}{4}}}) + 2e^{\sqrt{\frac{18}{4}}} + e^{\sqrt{5}}]$ *[1 mark]*

$= 8.3524$ (4 d.p.) *[1 mark]*

b) $\int_4^5 x + e^{\sqrt{x}}\, dx \approx \int_4^5 x\, dx + 8.3524$ (from part a)

$\int_4^5 x\, dx = \left[\frac{x^2}{2}\right]_4^5 = \frac{25}{2} - \frac{16}{2} = \frac{9}{2}$ or 4.5 *[1 mark]*

So, $\int_4^5 x + e^{\sqrt{x}}\, dx \approx 4.5 + 8.3524 = 12.8524$ (4 d.p.) *[1 mark]*

c) Increase the number of strips used in Simpson's
rule to approximate $\int_4^5 e^{\sqrt{x}}\, dx$ *[1 mark]*.

Section 16 — FP1: Inequalities

Page 121 — Algebraic Inequalities

Practice Questions

1 a) $-3 < x < 0$ or $x > 5$ b) $-3 \le x \le -1$ or $1 \le x \le 3$ c) $-10 \le x < -5$

2    $\{x \in \mathbb{R} : 1 < x < 3\} \cup \{x \in \mathbb{R} : 5 < x < 6\}$

3 a) $x \le -\frac{1}{3}$ or $x \ge 1$ b) $2 < x < 4$ c) $2 < x < 4$

Exam Questions

1   Multiply by $(x + 7)^2(x - 6)^2$: $2x(x + 7)(x - 6)^2 \ge (x + 7)^2(x - 6)$
Write in the form $f(x) \ge 0$: $2x(x + 7)(x - 6)^2 - (x + 7)^2(x - 6) \ge 0$
[1 mark]
Fully factorise the left hand side:
$(x + 7)(x - 6)[2x(x - 6) - (x + 7)] \ge 0$
$\Rightarrow (x + 7)(x - 6)(2x^2 - 12x - x - 7) \ge 0$
$\Rightarrow (x + 7)(x - 6)(2x + 1)(x - 7) \ge 0$ *[1 mark]*

The critical values for $f(x) = 0$ are $x = -7, -\frac{1}{2}$, 6 and 7 *[2 marks*
for all 4 correct values, or 1 mark for at least 2 correct values]
Sketch the graph of $y = f(x)$ to identify the ranges where $f(x) \ge 0$:

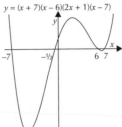

$y = (x + 7)(x - 6)(2x + 1)(x - 7)$

[1 mark for a correct method
to find the range of values]
You could have used the number
line method instead, and tested
values around the critical values.

The graph is greater than or equal to 0 for $x \le -7$, $-\frac{1}{2} \le x \le 6$,
and $x \ge 7$. However, $x \ne -7$ or 6, so the set of values is:
$\{x \in \mathbb{R} : x < -7\} \cup \{x \in \mathbb{R} : -\frac{1}{2} \le x < 6\} \cup \{x \in \mathbb{R} : x \ge 7\}$ *[1 mark]*

2 a) Square both sides to remove the modulus signs:
$\left|\frac{2x}{x - 1}\right| > |x| \Rightarrow \frac{4x^2}{(x - 1)^2} > x^2$ *[1 mark]*
Multiply by $(x - 1)^2$ (which is squared so must be positive):
$\Rightarrow 4x^2 > x^2(x - 1)^2$
Subtract $4x^2$ from both sides: $\Rightarrow 0 > x^2(x - 1)^2 - 4x^2$ *[1 mark]*
Now fully factorise and rearrange as required:
$\Rightarrow 0 > x^2[(x - 1)^2 - 4] \Rightarrow 0 > x^2(x^2 - 2x - 3)$
$\Rightarrow 0 > x^2(x - 3)(x + 1) \Rightarrow x^2(x - 3)(x + 1) < 0$ *[1 mark]*
So $f(x) < 0$, where $f(x) = x^2(x - 3)(x + 1)$ as required.

b) The critical values where $f(x) = 0$ are at $x = -1$, 0, and 3
[2 marks for all 3 correct values, or 1 mark for 2 correct values]
Sketch the graph of $y = f(x)$ to identify the ranges where $f(x) < 0$:

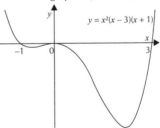

$y = x^2(x - 3)(x + 1)$

[1 mark for a correct method to find the range of values]
The graph is less than 0 for $-1 < x < 3$, but not including $x = 0$
(where $f(x) = 0$), or $x = 1$ (as stated in the question). So the set of
values is: $\{x \in \mathbb{R} : -1 < x < 3, x \ne 0, 1\}$ *[1 mark]*

Section 17 — FS1: Discrete Probability Distributions

Page 123 — Mean and Variance of Discrete Distributions

Practice Questions

1   $k = 0.2$, $E(X) = 2$, $Var(X) = 2$, $E(-2X - 1) = -5$, $Var(-2X - 1) = 8$

2 a) $\frac{1}{8}$ b) $E(Y) = \frac{19}{8}$, $Var(Y) = \frac{63}{64}$

c) $E(2Y - 1) = \frac{15}{4}$, $Var(2Y - 1) = \frac{63}{16}$ d)   63.398 (3 d.p.)

3   $E(aX + b) = E(g(X))$
$= \sum g(x_i)p_i = \sum (ax_i + b)p_i = \sum (ax_i p_i + bp_i) = \sum ax_i p_i + \sum bp_i$
$= a\sum x_i p_i + b\sum p_i = a\sum x_i p_i + b \times 1 = aE(X) + b$

Answers

Exam Question

1 a) You first need to determine the value of k:

$$\frac{k}{0+1} + \frac{k}{1+1} + \frac{k}{2+1} + \frac{k}{3+1} = 1 \Rightarrow \frac{25k}{12} = 1 \Rightarrow k = \frac{12}{25}$$

[1 mark]

Then the probabilities are obtained using $p_i = \frac{\left(\frac{12}{25}\right)}{i+1}$.

This gives $p_0 = \frac{12}{25}$, $p_1 = \frac{6}{25}$, $p_2 = \frac{4}{25}$ and $p_3 = \frac{3}{25}$. *[1 mark]*

The expected number of red lights encountered is

$$E(X) = \left(0 \times \frac{12}{25}\right) + \left(1 \times \frac{6}{25}\right) + \left(2 \times \frac{4}{25}\right) + \left(3 \times \frac{3}{25}\right) = \frac{23}{25}$$

[1 mark]

b) $E(-X+1) = -E(X) + 1 = -\frac{23}{25} + 1 = \frac{2}{25}$ *[1 mark]*

$$E(X^2) = \left(0^2 \times \frac{12}{25}\right) + \left(1^2 \times \frac{6}{25}\right) + \left(2^2 \times \frac{4}{25}\right) + \left(3^2 \times \frac{3}{25}\right)$$

$$= \frac{6}{25} + \frac{16}{25} + \frac{27}{25} = \frac{49}{25}$$ *[1 mark]*

$\text{Var}(X) = E(X^2) - E(X)^2 = \frac{49}{25} - \left(\frac{23}{25}\right)^2 = \frac{49}{25} - \frac{529}{625} = \frac{696}{625}$ *[1 mark]*

So $\text{Var}(-X+1) = (-1)^2\text{Var}(X) = \text{Var}(X) = \frac{696}{625}$ *[1 mark]*

c) $E(\sqrt{X}) = \left(\sqrt{0} \times \frac{12}{25}\right) + \left(\sqrt{1} \times \frac{6}{25}\right) + \left(\sqrt{2} \times \frac{4}{25}\right) + \left(\sqrt{3} \times \frac{3}{25}\right)$

[1 mark]

$= 0 + \frac{6}{25} + 0.226274... + 0.207846... = 0.674$ (3 d.p.) *[1 mark]*

Section 18 — FS1: Poisson and Binomial Distributions

Page 124 — Mean and Variance of Binomial Distribution

Practice Questions

1 a) $\mu = 8$, $\sigma^2 = 4.8$ b) $\mu = 21$, $\sigma^2 = 6.3$ c) $\mu = 0.54$, $\sigma^2 = 0.53352$
2   $n = 50$, $p = 0.02$

Exam Questions

1 a) The number of passers-by is fixed (at 30), the probability of a passer-by taking a leaflet is 0.3 for all passers-by and the event of a passer-by taking a leaflet is independent of any other passer-by.

[1 mark]

b) The number of people the salesman could expect to take a leaflet is $E(X) = np = 30 \times 0.3 = 9$. *[1 mark]*

c) Variance $= np(1-p) = 30 \times 0.3 \times (1-0.3) = 6.3$ *[1 mark]*
Standard deviation $= \sqrt{6.3} = 2.51$ (2 d.p.) *[1 mark]*

2 a) $E(X) = \mu = 25 \times 0.2 = 5$ *[1 mark]*
Using the binomial cdf: $P(X \leq \mu) = P(X \leq 5) = 0.6167$ *[1 mark]*

b) $\text{Var}(X) = \sigma^2 = 25 \times 0.2 \times (1-0.2) = 4 \Rightarrow \sigma = 2$ *[1 mark]*
Using the binomial cdf: $P(X \leq \mu - \sigma) = P(X \leq 3) = 0.2340$ *[1 mark]*

c) Using the binomial cdf:
$P(X < \mu - 2\sigma) = P(X \leq \mu - 2\sigma - 1) = P(X \leq 0) = P(X = 0)$ *[1 mark]*
$= 0.0038$ *[1 mark]*

Page 127 — The Poisson Distribution

Practice Questions

1 a) 0.0063   b) 0.0014   c) 0.0002
  d) 0.0079   e) 0.9921

2 a) i) 8   ii) 8   iii) $\sqrt{8} = 2.83$ (3 s.f.)
  b) i) 12.11   ii) 12.11   iii) 3.48 (3 s.f.)
  c) i) 84.2227   ii) 84.2227   iii) 9.18 (3 s.f.)

3 a) 0.0138   b) 0.4530   c) 0.5925
  d) 0.9970   e) 0.5470   f) 0.1222

4 a) $\text{Po}\left(\frac{100}{3}\right)$ b) $\text{Po}(48\,000)$

Exam Question

1 a) Any two from:
- The birds must arrive at the barn at (on average) a constant rate
- Birds must arrive at the barn singly/one at a time
- Birds must arrive randomly/independently of one another

[2 marks]

b) i) If X represents the number of birds visiting the barn, then X is distributed $X \sim \text{Po}(7)$. *[1 mark]*
Using the Poisson cdf: $P(X < 4) = P(X \leq 3) = 0.0818$ *[1 mark]*

ii) $P(X \geq 7) = 1 - P(X < 7) = 1 - P(X \leq 6)$ *[1 mark]*
$= 1 - 0.4497 = 0.5503$ *[1 mark]*
iii) $P(X = 9) = P(X \leq 9) - P(X \leq 8)$ *[1 mark]*
$= 0.8305 - 0.7291 = 0.1014$ *[1 mark]*
Alternatively, you can use the probability function: $P(X = 9) = \frac{e^{-7} \times 7^9}{9!}$
$= 0.1014$

c) The number of treats eaten by the owl in any one fortnight follows the distribution $\text{Po}(3)$. Let $Y =$ the number eaten in any 28 day period, then $Y \sim \text{Po}(2 \times 3) = \text{Po}(6)$ *[1 mark]*.
Let r be the number of treats in the barn after the birdwatcher adds more. To ensure that the probability of the treats running out is less than 0.05, find r such that $P(Y > r) < 0.05$. *[1 mark]*
$P(Y > r) < 0.05 \Rightarrow 1 - P(Y \leq r) < 0.05 \Rightarrow P(Y \leq r) > 0.95$ *[1 mark]*
Using the Poisson cdf table for $\lambda = 6$:
$P(Y \leq 9) = 0.9161$, $P(Y \leq 10) = 0.9574$
So 10 is the smallest value of r with $P(Y > r) < 0.05$, i.e. the birdwatcher needs to have at least 10 treats in the barn. *[1 mark]*

Page 129 — Poisson Approximation to B(n, p)

Practice Questions

1 a) No — n is not very large and p is not very small
  b) Yes — n is large and p is small, so approximate with $\text{Po}(7)$
  c) No — n is large but p isn't small
  d) No — n is quite small (so you wouldn't need to use an approximation anyway)
  e) Yes — n is enormous and p is tiny, so approximate with $\text{Po}(0.1)$

2   $p = 0.9$ is not small but it is close to 1. Let $W = 80 - Y$.
Then $W \sim \text{B}(80, 0.1)$ and we can approximate W by $\text{Po}(8)$.
This allows us to approximate Y through the relation $Y = 80 - W$.

Exam Question

1 a) The number of call-outs is fixed (= 400), the success of any repair is independent of any other, and the probability of the engineer being unable to fix a fault is constant (= 0.02). *[1 mark]*
This means X (the total number of unsuccessful call-outs) will follow a binomial distribution: $X \sim \text{B}(400, 0.02)$. *[1 mark]*

b) i) The number of call-outs is large *[1 mark]* and the probability that the engineer will be unable to fix the fault is small. *[1 mark]*
ii) $X \sim \text{Po}(8)$ *[1 mark]*
iii) $\mu = \sigma^2 = 8$ *[1 mark]*
iv) P(engineer unable to fix fewer than 10 faults)
$= P(X < 10) = P(X \leq 9) = 0.7166$ *[1 mark]*

c) The approximation is accurate to 2 decimal places. *[1 mark]*

d) If the random variable U represents the number of faults the engineer is able to fix in the advertised timescale when accompanied by his apprentice then $U \sim \text{B}(400, 0.99)$.
Let $V = 400 - U$ represent the number of faults the engineer does not fix in the timescale. Then $V \sim \text{B}(400, 0.01)$. *[1 mark]*
V can be approximated by the distribution $V \sim \text{Po}(4)$. *[1 mark]*
$P(U > 390) = P(400 - V > 390) = P(V < 10)$ *[1 mark]*
$= P(V \leq 9) = 0.9919$ *[1 mark]*

Section 19 — FS1: Geometric & Negative Binomial Distributions

Page 131 — The Geometric Distribution

Practice Questions

1 a) 0.0229 (3 s.f.)   b) 10   c) 90   d) $\sqrt{90} = 9.49$ (3 s.f.)
2   0.000977 (3 s.f.)
3 a) 0.355 (3 s.f.)   b) 0.195 (3 s.f.)   c) 0.0434 (3 s.f.)

Exam Questions

1 a) Let $X =$ number of throws until double six and $p =$ probability of throwing two sixes. Then $X \sim \text{Geo}(p)$. *[1 mark]*
$\mu = \frac{1}{p} = 9 \Rightarrow p = \frac{1}{9}$ *[1 mark]*
Since the dice are identical, the probability of throwing a six on both is $p = p_1 \times p_1$, where p_1 is the probability of throwing a six on one of them. So $p_1 = \frac{1}{3}$. *[1 mark]*

b) i) $P(X = 4) = p(1 - p)^3 = \frac{1}{9} \times \left(\frac{8}{9}\right)^3 = 0.0780$ (3 s.f.) *[1 mark]*

   ii) $P(X \geq 3) = 1 - P(X < 3)$
   $= 1 - (P(X = 1) + P(X = 2))$ *[1 mark]*
   $= 1 - \frac{1}{9} - \frac{8}{81}$
   $= 0.790$ (3 s.f.) *[1 mark]*

2 a) i) Let the random variable X represent the number of householders who support the politician.
   $X \sim B(20, 0.2)$ *[1 mark]*
   $P(X = 2) = {}^{20}C_2 \times 0.2^2 \times 0.8^{18} = 0.136909... = 0.1369$ *[1 mark]*

   ii) Any one from e.g.:
   - Political opinions are unlikely to be independent in a particular area (e.g. wealth/class in an estate or suburb will affect multiple householders' politics).
   - A householder may be undecided on their opinion of the politician (i.e. support/does not support are unlikely to be the only opinions). *[1 mark]*

b) Let the random variable Y represent the number of days the politician canvasses until they have a day where they meet exactly two supporters. Then $Y \sim Geo(0.1369)$. *[1 mark]*
$P(Y = 10) = p(1 - p)^9 = 0.1369(1 - 0.1369)^9 = 0.0364$ *[1 mark]*

Page 133 — The Negative Binomial Distribution

Practice Questions

1 a) 0.001398 (4 s.f.)   b) 0.00004644 (4 s.f.)
  c) 46.7 (1 d.p.)   d) 264.4 (1 d.p.)

2   $r = 3$, $p = \frac{2}{3}$

Exam Question

1 a) The random variable T is the number of rooms visited ("trials") until the sixth towel is taken. We can view a room taking a towel as a "success". So T measures number of trials until the sixth success, so this is a negative binomial distribution *[1 mark]* with parameters $r = 6$, $p = \frac{1}{3}$ *[1 mark]*, i.e. $T \sim NB\left(6, \frac{1}{3}\right)$.

b) $P(T = k) = \binom{k-1}{r-1}p^r(1 - p)^{k-r} = \binom{k-1}{5} \times \frac{1}{3^6} \times \left(\frac{2}{3}\right)^{k-6}$ *[1 mark]*

c) $P(T = 20) = \binom{19}{5} \times \frac{1}{3^6} \times \left(\frac{2}{3}\right)^{14} = 11628 \times \frac{1}{3^6} \times \left(\frac{2}{3}\right)^{14}$
   $= 0.0546$ (3 s.f.) *[1 mark]*

d) If Ken visits at least 9 rooms before visiting the room which takes his final towel, his final towel must be taken at the 10th room or later. This is the event that $T \geq 10$.
$P(T \geq 10) = 1 - P(T \leq 9)$
$= 1 - P(T = 6) - P(T = 7) - P(T = 8) - P(T = 9)$ *[1 mark]*

$= 1 - \binom{5}{5} \times \frac{1}{3^6} \times \left(\frac{2}{3}\right)^0 - \binom{6}{5} \times \frac{1}{3^6} \times \left(\frac{2}{3}\right)^1 - \binom{7}{5} \times \frac{1}{3^6} \times \left(\frac{2}{3}\right)^2$
$\qquad - \binom{8}{5} \times \frac{1}{3^6} \times \left(\frac{2}{3}\right)^3$

$= 1 - 0.0013717... - 0.0054869... - 0.0128029... - 0.0227607...$
$= 0.958$ (3 s.f.) *[1 mark]*

e) P(one or more towels left after 20 rooms)
$= 1 - $ P(all towels used up in the 20 rooms) $= 1 - P(T \leq 20)$
$\approx 1 - 0.70279 = 0.29721$ *[1 mark]*
So P(one or more towels left on three days in a week)
$= $ P(one or more towels left on one day)^3
$= 0.29721^3 = 0.026253... = 0.0263$ (3 s.f.) *[1 mark]*

Section 20 — FS1: Hypothesis Testing

Page 135 — Poisson Hypothesis Tests

Practice Questions

1   Let $\lambda = $ the rate of customers served per 10 minutes.
Then H_0: $\lambda = 8.5$ and H_1: $\lambda \neq 8.5$.
Let $X = $ the number of customers served after the new staff member joins. Then, under H_0, $X \sim Po(8.5)$. $\alpha = 0.1$, so the probability that X lies within each tail should be less than 0.05.
After the new staff member joins, 4 people are served in 10 minutes, which is towards the lower tail, so find:
$P(X \leq 4) = 0.0743...$

Since $0.0743... > 0.05$, there is insufficient evidence at the 10% significance level to reject H_0 and to suggest that the rate of customers served during rush hour has changed.

2 a) $X \sim B(144, 0.0625)$. n is large and p is small, so the binomial distribution can be approximated by $X \sim Po(144 \times 0.0625) = Po(9)$.

b) H_0: $\lambda = 9$ and H_1: $\lambda < 9$. $\alpha = 0.05$
$X \sim Po(9) \Rightarrow P(X \leq 3) = 0.0212...$
$0.0212... < 0.05$, so it's significant at the 5% level.
There is evidence to reject H_0 at the 5% significance level and to suggest that the rate of broken eggs has decreased.

Exam Question

1 a) E.g. The potholes occur at a constant average rate.
/ Each pothole occurs randomly and independently of other potholes *[1 mark for a suitable answer]*.

b) Let $\lambda = $ the rate of potholes per mile of road.
Then H_0: $\lambda = 4$ and H_1: $\lambda \neq 4$. *[1 mark]*
Let $X = $ the number of potholes on a randomly-selected mile of the road. Under H_0, $X \sim Po(4)$.
The probability that X lies within each tail should be as close as possible to 0.025.
Using the Poisson c.d.f. on your calculator:
Lower tail: $P(X = 0) = 0.0183...$ and $P(X \leq 1) = 0.0915...$ *[1 mark]*
Upper tail: $P(X \geq 8) = 1 - P(X \leq 7) = 1 - 0.9488... = 0.0511...$
$\qquad P(X \geq 9) = 1 - P(X \leq 8) = 1 - 0.9786... = 0.0213...$ *[1 mark]*
The critical values are the points at which X would be rejected. Since $P(X = 0)$ and $P(X \geq 9)$ are closer to 0.025 at the lower and upper tails, the critical values are $X = 0$ and $X = 9$. *[1 mark]*
Make sure you give the critical values, not the critical regions.

c) Since $X = 11$ is more extreme than the critical value $X = 9$ (i.e. $11 > 9$), there is evidence at the 5% level that the rate of potholes per mile of road is different in 2017 *[1 mark]*.

d) The actual significance level is the probability of X being in the critical region: $P(X = 0) + P(X \geq 9) = 0.0183... + 0.0213...$
$\qquad = 0.0396$ or 3.96% (3 s.f.) *[1 mark]*.

Page 137 — Geometric Hypothesis Tests

Practice Question

1   Let $p = $ probability that the arcade game awards a prize.
Then H_0: $p = 0.025$ and H_1: $p > 0.025$.
If X is the number of games until the first prize is awarded, then under H_0, $X \sim Geo(0.025)$. $\alpha = 0.1$.
The observed value is 4 and since you'd expect the first prize to be awarded on the $\frac{1}{0.025} = 40^{th}$ game, the p-value is:
$P(X \leq 4) = 1 - (1 - p)^4 = 1 - (1 - 0.025)^4$
$\qquad = 1 - 0.9036... = 0.0963$ (3 s.f.)
Since $0.0963 < 0.1$, the result is (just about) significant.
There is sufficient evidence to reject H_0 at the 10% level, and to suggest that the probability that the arcade game awards a prize is higher than it's supposed to be.
$P(X \leq 4) = 1 - (1 - p)^4$ is a simplification of $P(X = 4) + P(X = 3) + P(X = 2) + P(X = 1)$. You can see similar calculations on page 137.

Exam Questions

1   Let $p = $ probability that a car is black.
Then H_0: $p = 0.2$ and H_1: $p < 0.2$. *[1 mark]*
If X is the number of cars to pass until one is black, then under H_0, $X \sim Geo(0.2)$. *[1 mark]* $\alpha = 0.05$.
The acceptance region is $X < k$, with k such that: $P(X \geq k) < 0.05$
$P(X \geq k) = P(X = k) + P(X = k + 1) + P(X = k + 2) + ...$
$\qquad = p(1 - p)^{k-1} + p(1 - p)^k + p(1 - p)^{k+1} + ...$
$\qquad = p(1 - p)^{k-1}\frac{1}{1 - (1 - p)} = (1 - p)^{k-1} = (0.8)^{k-1}$ *[1 mark]*
Trying different values of k gives:
$P(X \geq 14) = (0.8)^{13} = 0.0549...$ and $P(X \geq 15) = (0.8)^{14} = 0.0439...$
So the acceptance region is $X < 15$. *[1 mark]* Since 10 is inside the acceptance region, the result is not significant. There is insufficient evidence at the 5% level to reject H_0, and to suggest that the probability that a car is black is lower in his area. *[1 mark]*

Answers

2 a) Let p = probability that the ride breaks down on a given day.
Then H_0: $p = 0.1$ and H_1: $p \neq 0.1$. *[1 mark]*
If X is the number of days until the ride breaks down for the first time, then under H_0, $X \sim$ Geo(0.1). *[1 mark]*
$\alpha = 0.01$, so the probability in each tail needs to be less than 0.005. The observed value is 39 and since you'd expect the first breakdown to be on the $\frac{1}{0.1} = 10^{th}$ day, the p-value is:
$P(X \geq 39)$ *[1 mark]* $= (1 - p)^{38} = (1 - 0.1)^{38}$
$\qquad = 0.0182$ (3 s.f.) *[1 mark]*
Since $0.0182 > 0.005$, the result is not significant. There is insufficient evidence to reject H_0 at the 1% level, and to suggest that the probability that the ride breaks down has changed. *[1 mark]*
$P(X \geq 39) = (1 - p)^{38}$ is a simplification of $P(X = 39) + P(X = 40) + ...$
You can see similar calculations on page 137.

b) E.g. The probability that the ride breaks down on any given day is independent of it breaking down on other days.
/ The probability that the ride breaks down on any day is constant.
[1 mark for a suitable answer]

Page 139 — Chi Squared Tests — 1
Practice Questions
1 a) 18.307   b) 7.779   c) 15.086   d) 7.378
2   H_0: uniform distribution is a suitable model for the dice score,
H_1: uniform distribution is not a suitable model for the dice score.

Dice score	1	2	3	4
O_i	113	132	118	137
E_i	125	125	125	125
$\frac{(O_i - E_i)^2}{E_i}$	1.152	0.392	0.392	1.152

$X^2 = \sum \frac{(O_i - E_i)^2}{E_i} = 1.152 + 0.392 + 0.392 + 1.152 = 3.088$
$v = 4 - 1 = 3$.
Using the table with $\alpha = 0.025$, the critical value is $\chi^2_{(3)} = 9.348$.
Since $3.088 < 9.348$, the result is not significant. There is insufficient evidence at the 2.5% level to reject H_0 and to suggest that a uniform distribution is not a suitable model for the dice score.

Exam Question
1   H_0: $X \sim$ Geo(0.78) is a suitable model for the number of party poppers tested until the first one works.
H_1: $X \sim$ Geo(0.78) is not a suitable model for the number of party poppers tested until the first one works. *[1 mark for both]*
Calculate the expected frequencies using the geometric probability function: $E_i = 200 \times P(X = i)$ *[1 mark]*
$E_1 = 200 \times 0.78(1 - 0.78)^0 = 156$
$E_2 = 200 \times 0.78(1 - 0.78)^1 = 34.32$
$E_3 = 200 \times 0.78(1 - 0.82)^2 = 7.5504$ *[1 mark]*
$E_{4\ or\ more} = 200 - 156 - 34.32 - 7.5504 = 2.1296$ *[1 mark]*
$2.1296 < 5$ so combine columns to make '3 or more' column:

X	1	2	3 or more
O_i	154	35	11
E_i	156	34.32	9.68
$\frac{(O_i - E_i)^2}{E_i}$	0.0256...	0.0134...	0.18

[1 mark for correctly combining columns,
1 mark for correctly calculating $(O_i - E_i)^2/E_i$ for each column]
$X^2 = \sum \frac{(O_i - E_i)^2}{E_i} = 0.0256... + 0.0134... + 0.18$
$\qquad = 0.219$ (3 s.f.) *[1 mark]*

The parameter p is estimated from the data, so $v = 3 - 2 = 1$. *[1 mark]*
Using the table with $\alpha = 0.1$, the critical value is $\chi^2_{(1)} = 2.705$.
[1 mark]
Since $0.219 < 2.705$, the result is not significant. There is not sufficient evidence at the 10% level to reject H_0, the hypothesis that $X \sim$ Geo(0.78) is a suitable model for the number of party poppers tested until the first one works. *[1 mark]*

Page 141 — Chi Squared Tests — 2
Practice Question
1   H_0: gender and test result are not associated,
H_1: gender and test result are associated.

E_i	Male	Female	Total
Pass	32.45	26.55	59
Fail	11.55	9.45	21
Total	44	36	80

$X^2 = \sum \frac{(O_i - E_i)^2}{E_i} = \frac{1.45^2}{32.45} + \frac{1.45^2}{26.55} + \frac{1.45^2}{11.55} + \frac{1.45^2}{9.45}$
$= 0.0647... + 0.0791... + 0.1820... + 0.2224... = 0.549$ (3 s.f.)
Using the table with $\alpha = 0.05$, the critical value is $\chi^2_{(1)} = 3.841$.
Since $0.549 < 3.841$, the result is not significant.
There is insufficient evidence at the 5% level to reject H_0 and to suggest that gender and test result are associated.

Exam Question
1 a) $(31 \times 15) \div 100$ *[1 mark]* $= 4.65$ *[1 mark]*
b) The expected frequency for concessions whose review was 'terrible' is less than 5. *[1 mark]*
c) H_0: review and type of visitor are independent,
H_1: review and type of visitor are not independent. *[1 mark]*
$X^2 = 35.7$. After combining 'terrible' and 'poor' there are 4 columns, so $v = (3 - 1)(4 - 1) = 6$. *[1 mark]*
Using the table with $\alpha = 0.01$, the critical value is $\chi^2_{(6)} = 16.812$.
[1 mark] Since $35.7 > 16.812$, the result is significant. There is sufficient evidence at the 1% level to reject H_0 and to suggest that review and type of visitor are not independent. *[1 mark]*

Page 143 — Quality of Tests
Practice Question
1 a) $X \leq 38.2$ and $X \geq 59.8$ (both to 3 s.f.)
b) P(Type I error) = 0.05
The normal distribution is continuous, so the probability of a Type I error is just the significance level.
c) Power = 0.0847 (3 s.f.)

Exam Question
1 a) Nafisa uses $X \sim$ B(100, 0.05). Since $n = 100$ is large and $p = 0.05$ is small, a Poisson approximation is suitable *[1 mark]*.
Paul uses $\lambda = np = 5$, so $Y \sim$ Po(5) *[1 mark]*.
b) The critical region is $Y \leq a$, such that $P(Y \leq a) < 0.05$.
Use the Poisson c.d.f. on your calculator to try different values of a:
$P(Y \leq 1) = 0.0404...$, $P(Y \leq 2) = 0.1246...$ *[1 mark]*
So at the 5% level the critical region is $Y \leq 1$ *[1 mark]*.
c) Size = 0.0404 (3 s.f.) *[1 mark]*
d) The power function is the probability of rejecting H_0: $Y \sim$ Po(λ), for different values of the parameter λ.
Using the Poisson probability function:
Power function = $P(Y \leq 1 \mid Y \sim$ Po(λ)) *[1 mark]*
$= P(Y = 1 \mid Y \sim$ Po(λ)) $+ P(Y = 0 \mid Y \sim$ Po(λ))
$= e^{-\lambda}\frac{\lambda^1}{1!} + e^{-\lambda}\frac{\lambda^0}{0!}$ *[1 mark]* $= e^{-\lambda}(\lambda + 1)$ *[1 mark]*
e) Substitute $p = 0.03$ into Nafisa's power function:
Power = $100(0.03)(0.97)^{99} + (0.97)^{100} = 0.195$ (3 s.f.) *[1 mark]*
Since $p = 0.03$, $\lambda = 100 \times 0.03 = 3$ *[1 mark]*. Substitute $\lambda = 3$ into Paul's power function, which you worked out in part d):
Power = $e^{-3}(3 + 1) = 4e^{-3} = 0.199$ (3 s.f.) *[1 mark]* $0.199 > 0.195$, so you'd recommend Paul's test when $p = 0.03$. *[1 mark]*
If you work out the size of both tests, the size of Nafisa's test is smaller, so on that basis you might recommend her test.

Section 21 — FS1: Central Limit Theorem
Page 145 — The Central Limit Theorem
Practice Questions
1 a) $\overline{X} \approx \sim$ N(4, 0.064)   b) $\overline{X} \approx \sim$ N$\left(\frac{10}{9}, \frac{1}{405}\right)$
c) $\overline{X} \approx \sim$ N(5.5, 0.11)

2 a) 0.1822 (4 d.p.)   b) 0.1284 (4 d.p.)   c) 0.9921 (4 d.p.)

Exam Question

1 a) i) Let T = number of trains the trainspotter sees and
p = probability of a train having the special design = 0.12.
Then $T \sim$ Geo(0.12) *[1 mark]*.
ii) $P(T = 5) = 0.12(1 - 0.12)^{5-1} = 0.0720$ (4 d.p.) *[1 mark]*
iii) $P(T > 2) = 1 - P(T \le 2) = 1 - (P(T = 1) + P(T = 2))$ *[1 mark]*
$= 1 - (0.12 + 0.1056) = 0.7744$ *[1 mark]*
b) i) By the Central Limit Theorem, the sample mean $\overline{T}$ is
approximately normally distributed with mean $\mu = \dfrac{1}{p} = \dfrac{25}{3}$ *[1 mark]*
and variance $\dfrac{\sigma^2}{n} = \dfrac{\left(\dfrac{1-0.12}{0.12^2}\right)}{55} = \dfrac{10}{9}$ *[1 mark]*
$\Rightarrow \overline{T} \approx\sim N\left(\dfrac{25}{3}, \dfrac{10}{9}\right)$
ii) Using the normal cdf: $P(\overline{T} < 7) = 0.1030$ (4 d.p.) *[1 mark]*
iii) Using the normal cdf: $P(\overline{T} > 9) = 0.2635$ (4 d.p.) *[1 mark]*
c) Take a larger sample. *[1 mark]*

Section 22 —
FS1: Probability Generating Functions

Page 147 — Probability Generating Functions

Practice Questions

1 $G_A(t) = 0.2t + 0.15t^2 + 0.5t^3 + 0.15t^4$

2 a) $k = \dfrac{1}{2}$, $P(X = 0) = \dfrac{1}{4}$, $P(X = 1) = \dfrac{1}{8}$, $P(X = 2) = \dfrac{3}{8}$
$P(X = 3) = 0$, $P(X = 4) = \dfrac{1}{4}$, $P(X \ge 5) = 0$
b) i) $\dfrac{1}{8}(2t + t^2 + 3t^3 + 2t^5)$ ii) $\dfrac{1}{8}(2 + t^3 + 3t^6 + 2t^{12})$
iii) $\dfrac{1}{8}(2t^2 + t^4 + 3t^6 + 2t^{10})$

3 The distributions are valid if the probabilities sum to 1.
a) $\sum P(X = x) = \sum P(X = x)1^x = G_X(1) = (1 - p + p \times 1)^n = 1^n = 1$
b) $\sum P(X = x) = \sum P(X = x)1^x = G_X(1) = \dfrac{p \times 1}{1 - (1-p) \times 1} = \dfrac{p}{p} = 1$
c) $\sum P(X = x) = \sum P(X = x)1^x = G_X(1) = \left(\dfrac{p \times 1}{1 - (1-p) \times 1}\right)^r = \left(\dfrac{p}{p}\right)^r = 1$
So each distribution is valid.

Exam Questions

1 a) $G_X(t) = \sum P(X = x) t^x = \sum e^{-\lambda}\dfrac{\lambda^x}{x!} t^x$ *[1 mark]*
$= e^{-\lambda}\sum \dfrac{\lambda^x}{x!} t^x = e^{-\lambda}\sum \dfrac{(\lambda t)^x}{x!}$ *[1 mark]*
The Maclaurin series expansion of e^x is $\sum_r \dfrac{x^r}{r!}$ so $\sum_x \dfrac{(\lambda t)^x}{x!}$ is the
Maclaurin series expansion of $e^{\lambda t}$. *[1 mark]*
$\Rightarrow G_X(t) = e^{-\lambda}e^{\lambda t} = e^{\lambda(t-1)}$ as required *[1 mark]*
b) $G_{3X+5}(t) = t^5 G_X(t^3)$ *[1 mark]* $= t^5 e^{2(t^3-1)}$ *[1 mark]*

2 a) $G_X(1) = \dfrac{1}{26}[(k+3)^2 + 1] = 1$ *[1 mark]*
Solving for k: $(k+3)^2 + 1 = 26 \Rightarrow (k+3)^2 = 25$
$\Rightarrow k + 3 = \pm 5$
$\Rightarrow k = -8$ or $k = 2$ *[1 mark]*
$k > 0$, so k cannot be -8. So $k = 2$ is the only solution. *[1 mark]*
b) $G_X(t) = \dfrac{1}{26}(t^5 + 9t^4 + 6kt^3 + k^2t^2) = \dfrac{1}{26}(t^5 + 9t^4 + 12t^3 + 4t^2)$ *[1 mark]*
So the non-zero probabilities are:
$P(X = 5) = \dfrac{1}{26}$, $P(X = 4) = \dfrac{9}{26}$, $P(X = 3) = \dfrac{6}{13}$, $P(X = 2) = \dfrac{2}{13}$
[2 marks available — 1 mark for attempting to use coefficients of $G_X(t)$, 1 mark for all correct probabilities with no extras]

Page 149 — Using Probability Generating Functions

Practice Questions

1 a) $E(X) = 3.3$, $Var(X) = 8.91$
b) $E(X) = 4$, $Var(X) = 4$

2 $\dfrac{3}{160}$

3 a) $\dfrac{d}{dt}(1 - p + pt)^n = np(1 - p + pt)^{n-1}$
$\Rightarrow E(X) = G_X'(1) = np(1 - p + p)^{n-1} = np(1)^{n-1} = np$
$\dfrac{d}{dt}[np(1 - p + pt)^{n-1}] = n(n-1)p^2(1 - p + pt)^{n-2}$
$\Rightarrow Var(X) = n(n-1)p^2(1)^{n-2} + np - (np)^2$
$= n(n-1)p^2 + np - (np)^2$
$= n^2p^2 - np^2 + np - (np)^2 = np - np^2 = np(1-p)$
b) $\dfrac{d}{dt}\dfrac{pt}{1-(1-p)t} = \dfrac{p[1-(1-p)t] - pt[-(1-p)]}{[1-(1-p)t]^2}$
$= \dfrac{p - (1-p)pt + pt(1-p)}{[1-(1-p)t]^2}$
$= \dfrac{p}{[1-(1-p)t]^2}$
$\Rightarrow E(X) = \dfrac{p}{[1-(1-p)]^2} = \dfrac{p}{p^2} = \dfrac{1}{p}$
$\dfrac{d}{dt}\dfrac{p}{[1-(1-p)t]^2} = -2p[1-(1-p)t]^{-3}[-(1-p)] = \dfrac{2p(1-p)}{[1-(1-p)t]^3}$
$\Rightarrow Var(X) = \dfrac{2p(1-p)}{[1-(1-p)]^3} + \dfrac{1}{p} - \left(\dfrac{1}{p}\right)^2$
$= \dfrac{2p(1-p)}{p^3} + \dfrac{1}{p} - \dfrac{1}{p^2}$
$= \dfrac{2p(1-p) + p^2 - p}{p^3}$
$= \dfrac{2p - 2p^2 + p^2 - p}{p^3} = \dfrac{p - p^2}{p^3} = \dfrac{1-p}{p^2}$

Exam Question

1 a) $G_K(t) = G_X(t) \times G_Y(t)$
$= \dfrac{1}{4}(t + t^2 + t^3 + t^4)e^{6(t-1)}$
[2 marks available — 1 mark for both $G_X(t)$ and $G_Y(t)$ correct, 1 mark for correct product and answer]
b) $G_K'(t) = \dfrac{1}{4}(1 + 2t + 3t^2 + 4t^3)e^{6(t-1)} + \dfrac{1}{4}(t + t^2 + t^3 + t^4) \times 6e^{6(t-1)}$ *[1 mark]*
$= \dfrac{1}{4}e^{6(t-1)}(1 + 2t + 3t^2 + 4t^3 + 6t + 6t^2 + 6t^3 + 6t^4)$
$= \dfrac{1}{4}e^{6(t-1)}(1 + 8t + 9t^2 + 10t^3 + 6t^4)$
$E(X) = G_K'(1) = \dfrac{1}{4}e^0(1 + 8 + 9 + 10 + 6)$ *[1 mark]*
$= \dfrac{1}{4} \times 34 = \dfrac{17}{2}$ *[1 mark]*
$G_K''(t) = \dfrac{1}{4} \times 6e^{6(t-1)}(1 + 8t + 9t^2 + 10t^3 + 6t^4)$
$+ \dfrac{1}{4}e^{6(t-1)}(8 + 18t + 30t^2 + 24t^3)$
[2 marks available — 1 mark for attempting to find second derivative of G, 1 mark for fully correct second derivative]
$= \dfrac{1}{4}e^{6(t-1)}(6 + 48t + 54t^2 + 60t^3 + 36t^4 + 8 + 18t + 30t^2 + 24t^3)$
$= \dfrac{1}{4}e^{6(t-1)}(14 + 66t + 84t^2 + 84t^3 + 36t^4)$
$G_K''(1) = \dfrac{1}{4}(14 + 66 + 84 + 84 + 36) = \dfrac{1}{4} \times 284 = 71$ *[1 mark]*
$Var(X) = G_K''(1) + G_K'(1) - [G_K'(1)]^2$
$= 71 + \dfrac{17}{2} - \dfrac{289}{4}$ *[1 mark]* $= \dfrac{29}{4}$ *[1 mark]*

Section 23 — FM1: Momentum and Impulse

Page 151 — Momentum and Impulse

Practice Questions

1 a) $v = 2\dfrac{1}{4}$ ms^{-1} b) $v = 2\dfrac{1}{9}$ ms^{-1} c) $m = 4$ kg

2 $v = -1\dfrac{2}{3}$ ms^{-1}

Exam Question

1 Before   After

(0.8)→4 (1.2)→2   (0.8)→2.5 (1.2)→v

Total momentum before = $(0.8 \times 4) + (1.2 \times 2)$
Total momentum after = $(0.8 \times 2.5) + 1.2v$
[1 mark for both equations]

Answers

Use conservation of momentum: $3.2 + 2.4 = 2 + 1.2v$ *[1 mark]*
$v = 3$ ms^{-1} *[1 mark]*

Before | After

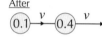

$(1.2 \times 3) + (m \times -4) = (1.2 + m) \times 0$ *[1 mark]*
$3.6 = 4m$
$m = 0.9$ kg *[1 mark]*

Page 153 — Momentum and Impulse Problems
Practice Questions

1   5.12 Ns (3 s.f.)
2   80 ms^{-1}

Exam Question

1 a) Use conservation of momentum *[1 mark]*:

Before | After

$(0.1 \times 0) + (0.4 \times 4) = (0.1 + 0.4)v$ *[1 mark]*
$1.6 = 0.5v$
$v = 3.2$ ms^{-1} *[1 mark]*
b) $(0.4 \times 4) - (0.4 \times 3.2)$ *[1 mark]* $= 0.32$ Ns *[1 mark]*
c) E.g. the balls can be modelled as spherical particles,
the string is light and inextensible, the surface is smooth.
[1 mark for each valid assumption, up to a maximum of 2 marks]

Page 155 — Momentum and Impulse in 2D
Practice Questions

1 a) $\mathbf{v} = 21\mathbf{i} + 51\mathbf{j}$ ms^{-1} b) $\mathbf{v} = -29\mathbf{i} + 11\mathbf{j}$ ms^{-1}
  c) $\mathbf{v} = -9\mathbf{i} - 59\mathbf{j}$ ms^{-1} d) $\mathbf{v} = 41\mathbf{i} + \mathbf{j}$ ms^{-1}
2 a) $\mathbf{Q} = -12\mathbf{i} + 4\mathbf{j}$ Ns   b) 12.6 Ns, to 3 s.f.
  c) 162°, to 3 s.f.
3 a) 2.76 ms^{-1}, to 3 s.f.   b) 1.39 ms^{-1}, to 3 s.f.

Exam Question

1 a) Speed is the magnitude of the velocity.
  So, $(-12a)^2 + (2a)^2 = (\sqrt{37})^2$
  $144a^2 + 4a^2 = 37$ *[1 mark]*
  $\Rightarrow 148a^2 = 37$
  $\Rightarrow a^2 = \frac{37}{148} = \frac{1}{4}$ *[1 mark]*
  $\Rightarrow a = \frac{1}{2}$ as required, since a is positive.
b) $\mathbf{u} = \frac{-12}{2}\mathbf{i} + \frac{2}{2}\mathbf{j} = -6\mathbf{i} + \mathbf{j}$ *[1 mark]*
  $\mathbf{I} = m\mathbf{v} - m\mathbf{u}$,
  $3\mathbf{i} - 8\mathbf{j} = 0.4\mathbf{v} - 0.4(-6\mathbf{i} + \mathbf{j})$ *[1 mark]*
  $3\mathbf{i} - 8\mathbf{j} = 0.4\mathbf{v} + 2.4\mathbf{i} - 0.4\mathbf{j}$
  $0.4\mathbf{v} = 0.6\mathbf{i} - 7.6\mathbf{j}$
  $\Rightarrow \mathbf{v} = 1.5\mathbf{i} - 19\mathbf{j}$ *[1 mark]*.
  So $|\mathbf{v}| = \sqrt{1.5^2 + 19^2}$ *[1 mark]* $= 19.1$ ms^{-1} to 3 s.f. *[1 mark]*.
c) Draw a right-angled triangle of $\mathbf{v}$:

  θ is the angle with the horizontal, so:
  $\theta = \tan^{-1}\left(\frac{19}{1.5}\right)$ *[1 mark]* $= 85.5°$ to 3 s.f. *[1 mark]*.
  As always, a picture helps everything make a lot more sense.

Section 24 — FM1: Work, Energy and Power

Page 158 — Work and Energy
Practice Questions

1   750 J
2   289 kg (3 s.f.)
3   38 000 J (3 s.f.)
4   4.96 ms^{-1} (3 s.f.)
5   12.3 kJ (3 s.f.)

Exam Questions

1 a) Work done = Force × distance moved
  $= 800 \cos 40° \times 320 = 196$ kJ (3 s.f.)
  [3 marks available in total]:
  • *1 mark for using the horizontal component of the force*
  • *1 mark for correct use of formula for work done*
  • *1 mark for correct final answer.*
b) No acceleration vertically, so:
  $R + 800 \sin 40° = mg$
  $R = 1500g - 800 \sin 40° = 14\,185.7...$ N *[1 mark]*
  The resultant force horizontally is $800 \cos 40° - \mu R$ *[1 mark]*
  Work done by resultant force = change in kinetic energy, so:
  $(800 \cos 40° - \mu R) \times 320 = \frac{1}{2} \times 1500 \times (16^2 - 11^2)$ *[1 mark]*
  Rearrange to find μ:
  $\mu = \frac{196\,107.3... - 101\,250}{4\,539\,446.3...} = 0.0209$ (3 s.f.) *[1 mark]*
2 a) Work done = force × distance
  Work done = 66×28
  $= 1848$ J $= 1.85$ kJ (3 s.f.) *[1 mark]*
b) Increase in Kinetic Energy $= \frac{1}{2}m(v^2 - u^2)$
  $= \frac{1}{2} \times 90 \times (6^2 - 4^2)$ *[1 mark]* $= 900$ J *[1 mark]*
  Increase in Gravitational Potential Energy $= mgh$
  $= 90 \times 9.8 \times 28 \sin 30°$ *[1 mark]* $= 12\,348$ J *[1 mark]*

Page 161 — The Work-Energy Principle
Practice Questions

1   "If there are no external forces doing work on an object, the total
    mechanical energy of the object will remain constant."
    You usually need to model the object as a particle because you have
    to assume that the object is not acted on by any external forces such
    as air resistance.
2   1.28 m (3 s.f.)
3   "The work done on an object by external forces is equal to the change
    in the total mechanical energy of that object."
    An external force is any force other than an object's weight.
4   24.8 kJ (3 s.f.)

Exam Questions

1 a) Kinetic energy of the particle when it reaches the rough part:
  K.E. $= \frac{1}{2}mv^2 = \frac{1}{2} \times 0.3 \times 20^2$ *[1 mark]*
  $= 60$ J *[1 mark]*
  The only force acting on the particle is its weight,
  so use the conservation of mechanical energy.
  Let d be the distance travelled down the slope, then:
  G.P.E. $= mgh = mgd \sin 40°$ *[1 mark]*
  Change in K.E. = Change in G.P.E. *[1 mark]*
  $60 - 0 = 0.3 \times 9.8 \times d \sin 40°$ *[1 mark]*
  $\Rightarrow d = 31.7$ m (3 s.f.) *[1 mark]*
b) Particle's change in K.E. while travelling on the rough part:
  $\frac{1}{2} \times 0.3 \times 1^2 - 60 = -59.85$ J *[1 mark]*
  Let x be the distance travelled down the rough part of the slope.
  Then change in G.P.E. while travelling down the rough part $=$
  $-0.3gx \sin 40° = -2.94x \sin 40°$ *[1 mark]*
  Work done on the particle by resistive force $= Fs = -23x$ *[1 mark]*
  By the work-energy principle:
  Work done on the particle = Change in total energy *[1 mark]*
  $-23x = -59.85 - 2.94x \sin 40°$
  Rearrange to find x:
  $x = 2.84$ m (3 s.f.) *[1 mark]*
2 a) Change in Kinetic Energy from A to B:
  Change in K.E. $= \frac{1}{2}mv^2 - \frac{1}{2}mu^2 = 0 - (\frac{1}{2} \times 2 \times 14^2)$
  $= -196$ J *[1 mark]*
  Change in Gravitational Potential Energy from A to B:
  Change in G.P.E. $= mgh = 2 \times 9.8 \times 12 \sin 40°$
  $= 151.1...$ J *[1 mark]*

Answers

Change in Mechanical Energy from A to B:
Change in Mechanical Energy = change in K.E. + change in G.P.E.
$= -196 + 151.184... = -44.8...$ J *[1 mark]*
Find work done by friction.
$R = 2 \times 9.8 \times \cos 40° = 15.0...$ N *[1 mark]*
$F = \mu R$
Work done by friction: $Fs = \mu Rs$
$= \mu \times 15.0... \times -12 = -180.1... \times \mu$
Using the Work-Energy Principle
Change in Mechanical Energy = Work done by F *[1 mark]*
$-44.8... = -180.1... \times \mu$
$\mu = -44.8... \div -180.1... = 0.249$ (3 s.f.) *[1 mark]*

b) Maximum frictional force resisting movement:
$\mu R = 0.248... \times 15.0... = 3.734...$ N *[1 mark]*
The frictional force is resisting the component of the particle's weight acting down the slope: $mg \sin 40° = 12.5...$ N
12.5... N > 3.734... N, so the particle will slide back down the slope *[1 mark]*.

Page 163 — Power

Practice Questions

1   1.8 kW
2   400 W
3   50 ms^{-1}
4   6430 N (3 s.f.)

Exam Questions

1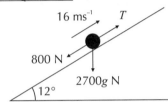

Resolving parallel to the slope using $F = ma$ with $a = 0$:
$T - 800 - 2700g \sin 12° = 0$ *[1 mark]*
So, $T = 6301.3...$ N *[1 mark]*
Power of engine = Driving Force × Velocity
$= 6301.3... \times 16$ *[1 mark]* $= 101$ kW (3 s.f.) *[1 mark]*

2 a) Use Power = $T \times v$
$T = \dfrac{\text{Power}}{v} = \dfrac{25\,000}{8} = 3125$ N *[1 mark]*
Resolve forces parallel to the slope:
$T - kv - mg \sin 5° = ma$
$3125 - 8k - (1500 \times 9.8 \times \sin 5°)$ *[1 mark]* $= 1500 \times 0.5$ *[1 mark]*
$k = \dfrac{1}{8}(3125 - (1500 \times 9.8 \times \sin 5°) - (1500 \times 0.5))$
$= 137$ (3 s.f.) *[1 mark]*

b) From Power = Fv, the driving force of the van's engine at speed U is $\dfrac{25\,000}{U}$ N *[1 mark]*
Again, resolve forces parallel to the slope:
$\dfrac{25\,000}{U} - 137U - 1500g \sin 5° = 0$ *[1 mark]*
Multiply throughout by U:
$25\,000 - 137U^2 - (1500g \sin 5° \times U) = 0$ *[1 mark]*
Rearrange to give: $U^2 + 9.35U - 182 = 0$ (coefficients to 3 s.f.)
[1 mark]

Section 25 — FM1: Strings, Springs and Elastic Energy

Page 165 — Elastic Energy

Practice Questions

1   7.14 m (3 s.f.)
2   20 N
3   12.3 J (3 s.f.)

Exam Question

1 a) The system is in equilibrium, so resolving forces vertically gives
$T = mg$, where T is the tension in the string. Therefore $T = 3g$ *[1 mark]*
So, using Hooke's Law:
$T = \dfrac{\lambda}{a}x = 3g$ *[1 mark]* $\Rightarrow \lambda = \dfrac{3ga}{x} = \dfrac{3 \times 9.8 \times 2}{(5-2)} = 19.6$ N *[1 mark]*

b) E.P.E. $= \dfrac{\lambda}{2a}x^2$
$= \dfrac{19.6}{2 \times 2} \times 3^2$ *[1 mark]* $= 44.1$ J *[1 mark]*

Page 167 — More Elastic Energy Problems

Practice Questions

1   4.50 m (3 s.f.)
2   90.1 N (3 s.f.)

Exam Question

1 a) E.P.E. $= \dfrac{\lambda}{2a}x^2$
$= \dfrac{50}{2 \times 5} \times (d - 5)^2$ *[1 mark]* $= 5(d - 5)^2$ *[1 mark]*

b)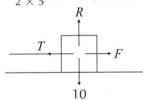

There is no motion vertically, so $R = 10$ N *[1 mark]*
The block is moving, so friction is limiting ⇒
frictional force, $F = \mu R = 0.5 \times 10 = 5$ N *[1 mark]*
Work done by $F = F \times$ distance moved $= -5d$ *[1 mark]*.
There is no change in K.E. or G.P.E. between the start and end of motion, so the only change in mechanical energy is the loss of E.P.E.
By the work-energy principle:
Change in E.P.E. = Work done on block by friction
$\Rightarrow -5(d - 5)^2 = -5d$ *[1 mark]*
The change in E.P.E. is negative because E.P.E. is lost.
Rearranging: $d = d^2 - 10d + 25 \Rightarrow d^2 - 11d + 25 = 0$ *[1 mark]*.
$\Rightarrow d = \dfrac{11 \pm \sqrt{(-11)^2 - 4 \times 1 \times 25}}{2 \times 1}$ *[1 mark]*
$\Rightarrow d = 7.79$ or $d = 3.21$ (each to 3 s.f.)
d must be greater than 5, so $d = 7.79$ m. *[1 mark]*

c) E.g. the block can be modelled as a particle / air resistance can be ignored / the string has no mass.
[2 marks available in total — 1 mark for each valid assumption]

Section 26 — FM1: Elastic Collisions in One Dimension

Page 170 — Collisions

Practice Questions

1   Loss of K.E. = 4.914 J
2   $e = \dfrac{1}{4}$
3   a) $v = 4$ ms^{-1} b) $v = 10.5$ ms^{-1} (3 s.f.)

Exam Question

1 a) Using the Law of Restitution for the collision between particles 1 and 2 gives:
$e = \dfrac{v_2 - v_1}{u_1 - u_2} \Rightarrow \dfrac{1}{4} = \dfrac{v_2 - v_1}{3u - 2u}$ *[1 mark]*
$\Rightarrow v_2 - v_1 = \dfrac{u}{4}$ ...[1]
Using conservation of momentum:
$m_1u_1 + m_2u_2 = m_1v_1 + m_2v_2$
$(2m \times 3u) + (3m \times 2u) = 2mv_1 + 3mv_2$ *[1 mark]*
$\Rightarrow 2v_1 + 3v_2 = 12u$ ...[2]
Equation [1] × 2 gives: $2v_2 - 2v_1 = \dfrac{u}{2}$ ...[3]
Equation [2] + equation [3] gives:
$5v_2 = 12u + \dfrac{u}{2} \Rightarrow v_2 = \dfrac{25u}{2 \times 5} = \dfrac{5u}{2}$ *[1 mark]*.
Substituting in equation [1] gives: $\dfrac{5u}{2} - v_1 = \dfrac{u}{4}$
$\Rightarrow v_1 = \dfrac{5u}{2} - \dfrac{u}{4} = \dfrac{9u}{4}$ *[1 mark]*.

b) Loss of kinetic energy =
$(\frac{1}{2}m_1u_1^2 + \frac{1}{2}m_2u_2^2) - (\frac{1}{2}m_1v_1^2 + \frac{1}{2}m_2v_2^2)$
$= [(\frac{1}{2} \times 2m \times (3u)^2) + (\frac{1}{2} \times 3m \times (2u)^2)] -$
$[(\frac{1}{2} \times 2m \times (\frac{9u}{4})^2) + (\frac{1}{2} \times 3m \times (\frac{5u}{2})^2)]$

Answers

$= (9mu^2 + 6mu^2) - (\frac{81mu^2}{16} + \frac{150mu^2}{16})$

$= (15 - \frac{231}{16})mu^2 = \frac{9mu^2}{16}$.

[4 marks available — 1 mark for correct values in formula for initial kinetic energy, 1 mark for correct values in formula for final kinetic energy, 1 mark for correct calculation of initial and final energy and 1 mark for correct final answer as the difference between the two.]

Page 173 — Successive Collisions

Practice Questions

1 After both collisions:
   A is travelling at $2u = \frac{216u}{108}$, and B is travelling at $\frac{143u}{108}$,
   which means that A is travelling faster than B, so they should collide again.

2 Bounce 1 = 0.25 m
   Bounce 2 = 0.0625 m
   Bounce 3 = 0.0156 m (3 s.f.)

3 $e_{BC} = \frac{3}{4}$

Exam Questions

1 a) Using the Law of Restitution for the collision between P and Q, where P is travelling at u and Q at $-u$ (i.e. in the opposite direction):

$e = \frac{v_Q - v_P}{u_P - u_Q} \Rightarrow \frac{3}{4} = \frac{v_Q - v_P}{u - (-u)}$ *[1 mark]* $\Rightarrow \frac{3}{4} = \frac{v_Q - v_P}{2u}$

$\Rightarrow v_Q - v_P = \frac{3u}{2}$ ...[1]

Using conservation of momentum:

$m_P u_P + m_Q u_Q = m_P v_P + m_Q v_Q$
$2mu - mu = 2mv_P + mv_Q$ *[1 mark]*
$\Rightarrow 2v_P + v_Q = u$ ...[2]

Equation [2] − equation [1] gives:

$3v_P = -\frac{u}{2} \Rightarrow v_P = -\frac{u}{6}$ *[1 mark]*.

Substituting in equation [1] gives:

$v_Q - (-\frac{u}{6}) = \frac{3u}{2} \Rightarrow v_Q = \frac{4u}{3}$ *[1 mark]*.

Since P's velocity was initially positive, and is now negative, and Q's was initially negative but is now positive, the collision has reversed the directions of both particles *[1 mark]*.

$|v_Q| \div |v_P| = \frac{4u}{3} \div \frac{u}{6} = 8$,

so Q is now going 8 times faster than P *[1 mark]*.

b) For the collision with the wall, $e_{wall} = \frac{\text{speed of rebound}}{\text{speed of approach}}$.

Q approaches the wall with a speed of $\frac{4u}{3}$ (from a)),
so if v_{Qwall} is its rebound speed:

$e_{wall} = \frac{v_{Qwall}}{\frac{4u}{3}} \Rightarrow v_{Qwall} = \frac{4ue_{wall}}{3}$ *[1 mark]*.

Since Q collides again with P, v_{Qwall} must be greater than v_P, which is $\frac{u}{6}$ (from a)), so:

$\frac{4ue_{wall}}{3} > \frac{u}{6}$ *[1 mark]* $\Rightarrow e_{wall} > \frac{3u}{6 \times 4u} \Rightarrow e_{wall} > \frac{1}{8}$ *[1 mark]*.

c) If $e_{wall} = \frac{3}{5}$, then (from b)):

$v_{Qwall} = \frac{4ue_{wall}}{3} = \frac{4u \times 3}{3 \times 5} = \frac{4u}{5}$ *[1 mark]*.

Q is now travelling in the same direction as P, which is still travelling at a speed of $\frac{u}{6}$ (from a)), and the particles have a coefficient of restitution of $\frac{3}{4}$, so using the Law of Restitution for the second collision between P and Q:

$e = \frac{v_P - v_Q}{u_Q - u_P} \Rightarrow \frac{3}{4} = \frac{v_P - v_Q}{\left(\frac{4u}{5}\right) - \frac{u}{6}}$ *[1 mark]* $\Rightarrow \frac{3}{4} = \frac{v_P - v_Q}{\frac{19u}{30}}$

$\Rightarrow v_P - v_Q = \frac{19u}{40}$ ...[1]

Using conservation of momentum:

$m_Q u_Q + m_P u_P = m_Q v_Q + m_P v_P$

$\frac{4um}{5} + \frac{2um}{6} = mv_Q + 2mv_P$ *[1 mark]*

$\Rightarrow v_Q + 2v_P = \frac{17u}{15}$ ...[2]

Equation [1] + equation [2] gives:

$3v_P = \frac{193u}{120} \Rightarrow v_P = \frac{193u}{360}$ *[1 mark]*.

Substituting in equation [1] gives:

$\frac{193u}{360} - v_Q = \frac{19u}{40} \Rightarrow v_Q = \frac{193u}{360} - \frac{19u}{40} = \frac{22u}{360}$ *[1 mark]*.

Since $v_Q = 0.22$ ms^{-1}:

$\frac{22u}{360} = 0.22$ *[1 mark]*

$\Rightarrow u = (0.22 \times 360) \div 22 = 3.6$ ms^{-1} *[1 mark]*.

2 Before After

$(0.8 \times 4) + (1.2 \times 2) = (0.8 \times 2.5) + 1.2v$
$3.2 + 2.4 = 2.0 + 1.2v$
$v = 3$ ms^{-1}

Before After

$(1.2 \times 3) + (m \times -4) = (1.2 + m) \times 0$
$3.6 = 4m$
$m = 0.9$ kg

[4 marks available in total:
* *1 mark for using conservation of momentum*
* *1 mark for correct value of v*
* *1 mark for correct workings*
* *1 mark for correct value of m]*

Section 27 — FM1: Elastic Collisions in Two Dimensions

Page 175 — Oblique Impacts

Practice Questions

1 −2.44 J, 39.5° (3 s.f.)

2 14.1 ms^{-1} (3 s.f.)

Exam Questions

1 a) $e = \frac{\tan\beta}{\tan\alpha}$ *[1 mark]*

$= \frac{\tan 30°}{\tan 45°} = \frac{\sqrt{3}}{3} = 0.577$ (3 s.f.) *[1 mark]*.

You could also work out e by finding the final speed (see part (b)) and using the Law of Restitution.

b) The component of the initial speed parallel to the wall is $3\sqrt{2}\cos 45°$ *[1 mark]*. The components of the speed parallel to the wall before and after the collision are equal. Let v be the speed after the collision. Then:

$3\sqrt{2}\cos 45° = v\cos 30°$ *[1 mark]*

$\Rightarrow v = \frac{3\sqrt{2}\cos 45°}{\cos 30°} = \frac{3}{\left(\frac{\sqrt{3}}{2}\right)} = 2\sqrt{3}$ ms^{-1} *[1 mark]*

You could also have found v using the perpendicular components and the Law of Restitution.

Initial kinetic energy $= \frac{1}{2}mu^2$

$= \frac{1}{2}(1)(3\sqrt{2})^2 = 9$ J *[1 mark]*

Final kinetic energy $= \frac{1}{2}mv^2 = \frac{1}{2}(1)(2\sqrt{3})^2 = 6$ J *[1 mark]*

Therefore, the kinetic energy lost is $(9 - 6)$ J $= 3$ J *[1 mark]*.

2 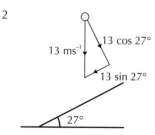

Let u_{perp} and v_{perp} be the components of velocity perpendicular to the slope, before and after the collision. Then:

$u_{perp} = -13\cos 27°$ *[1 mark]*

$v_{perp} = -0.7 \times (-13\cos 27°)$
$= 9.1\cos 27°$ *[1 mark]*

Impulse = $mv_{perp} - mu_{perp}$
= $1.2(9.1 \cos 27° - (-13 \cos 27°))$ *[1 mark]*
= 23.6 Ns (3 s.f.) *[1 mark]*

Page 177 — Successive Oblique Impacts

Practice Questions

1 a) $-4.8\mathbf{i} + 3.6\mathbf{j}$ ms^{-1} b) 114° (3 s.f.)
2   51.9°

Exam Question

1 a) Let α be the angle at which the ball collides with the first wall.

$\tan \alpha = \dfrac{6}{3} = 2$ *[1 mark]*

$e = \dfrac{\tan 38.7°}{\tan \alpha} = \dfrac{\tan 38.7°}{2} = 0.4005...$ *[1 mark]*

Let $\mathbf{v}$ be the velocity after the first collision.

$\mathbf{v} = -3\mathbf{i} + (6 \times -0.4005...)\mathbf{j} = -3\mathbf{i} - 2.403...\mathbf{j}$ *[1 mark]*

$v = \sqrt{3^2 + 2.403...^2} = 3.8440...$ ms^{-1} *[1 mark]*

Now consider the second collision:

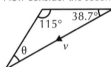

$\theta = 180° - 115° - 38.7° = 26.3°$ *[1 mark]*
Resolve $\mathbf{v}$ relative to the second wall.

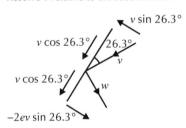

Let $\mathbf{w}$ be the velocity after the second collision.
The component of $\mathbf{w}$ parallel to the surface is
$v \cos 26.3° = 3.446...$ *[1 mark]*
The component of $\mathbf{w}$ perpendicular to the surface is
$-2ev \sin 26.3° = 1.364...$ *[1 mark]*
So $w = \sqrt{3.446...^2 + 1.3645...^2} = 3.71$ ms^{-1} (3 s.f.) *[1 mark]*

b) The answer to (a) will be lower since the friction from the rough floor will lower the speed. *[1 mark]*

Page 179 — Oblique Collisions of Spheres

Practice Questions

1   3.03 ms^{-1} (3 s.f.)

2 a) $\mathbf{i} - 2.5\mathbf{j}$ b) 0.875 J

3   5.55 ms^{-1} (3 s.f.)

Exam Question

1

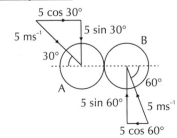

Taking parallel to the line of centres as $\mathbf{i}$ and perpendicular to the line of centres as $\mathbf{j}$.
Before the collision:

$\mathbf{u}_A = 5 \cos 30°\mathbf{i} - 5 \sin 30°\mathbf{j} = \dfrac{5\sqrt{3}}{2}\mathbf{i} - \dfrac{5}{2}\mathbf{j}$ *[1 mark]*

$\mathbf{u}_B = -5 \cos 60°\mathbf{i} + 5 \sin 60°\mathbf{j} = -\dfrac{5}{2}\mathbf{i} + \dfrac{5\sqrt{3}}{2}\mathbf{j}$ *[1 mark]*

Let u_{Ai} and u_{Bi} denote the $\mathbf{i}$ components of the velocities before the collision and v_{Ai} and v_{Bi} denote the $\mathbf{i}$ components of the velocities after the collision. Using the Law of Restitution:

$e = \dfrac{v_{Bi} - v_{Ai}}{u_{Ai} - u_{Bi}} \Rightarrow \dfrac{1}{2} = \dfrac{v_{Bi} - v_{Ai}}{\frac{5\sqrt{3}}{2} - \left(-\frac{5}{2}\right)}$ *[1 mark]*

$\Rightarrow \dfrac{5(1+\sqrt{3})}{4} = v_{Bi} - v_{Ai}$ (eqn 1) *[1 mark]*

Using conservation of momentum:
$m_A u_{Ai} + m_B u_{Bi} = m_A v_{Ai} + m_B v_{Bi}$

$0.5\left(\dfrac{5\sqrt{3}}{2}\right) + 0.25\left(-\dfrac{5}{2}\right) = 0.5v_{Ai} + 0.25v_{Bi}$ *[1 mark]*

$\dfrac{5(2\sqrt{3}-1)}{8} = 0.5v_{Ai} + 0.25v_{Bi}$ *[1 mark]*

$\dfrac{5(2\sqrt{3}-1)}{4} = v_{Ai} + 0.5v_{Bi}$ (eqn 2)

(eqn 1) + (eqn 2) $\Rightarrow \dfrac{15\sqrt{3}}{4} = \dfrac{3}{2}v_{Bi}$

$v_{Bi} = \dfrac{5\sqrt{3}}{2}$

After the collision: $\mathbf{v}_B = \dfrac{5\sqrt{3}}{2}\mathbf{i} + \dfrac{5\sqrt{3}}{2}\mathbf{j}$ *[1 mark]*

Speed of B = $\sqrt{2\left(\dfrac{5\sqrt{3}}{2}\right)^2} = 6.12$ ms^{-1} (3 s.f.) *[1 mark]*

Let θ be the angle between the line of centres and B's direction of travel after the collision.

$\theta = \tan^{-1}\left(\dfrac{\left(\frac{5\sqrt{3}}{2}\right)}{\left(\frac{5\sqrt{3}}{2}\right)}\right) = 45°$ *[1 mark]*

Let the angle of deflection = ϕ
$\phi = 180 - 60 - 45 = 75°$ *[1 mark]*

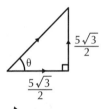

Section 28 — D1: Algorithms and Graph Theory

Page 181 — Algorithms

Practice Questions

1

x	y
17	56
~~8~~	~~112~~
~~4~~	~~224~~
~~2~~	~~448~~
1	896
Total	952

So 17 × 56 = 952

2   3.6 s

Answers

Exam Question

1 a)

N	C	D	Output	N = A?
1	8	12	1	No
2	4	6	2	No
3	$2\frac{2}{3}$	4		No
4	2	3	4	No
5	$1\frac{3}{5}$	$2\frac{2}{5}$		No
6	$1\frac{1}{3}$	2		No
7	$1\frac{1}{7}$	$1\frac{5}{7}$		No
8	1	$1\frac{1}{2}$		Yes

The results are 1, 2 and 4.

[3 marks available in total:
- *1 mark for correct values of C;*
- *1 mark for correct values of D;*
- *1 mark for all three correct outputs]*

b) i) This algorithm produces the common factors of the inputs. *[1 mark]*

ii) The output would be 1 *[1 mark]*, as this is the only common factor of 19 and 25 *[1 mark]*.

Page 183 — Sorting Algorithms

Practice Questions

1 Four passes are needed to sort the numbers.
At the end of the first pass, the list is:
57, 64, 54, 68, 71, 72
At the end of the second pass, the list is:
57, 54, 64, 68, 71, 72.
At the end of the third pass, the list is:
54, 57, 64, 68, 71, 72.
There are no swaps on the fourth pass, so the list is in order.

2 $\frac{1}{2} \times 9 \times 10 = 45$ comparisons.

3 First list: 0.4, 0.1, (0.5), 0.8, 1.2, 0.7, 1.0

Second list: (0.1), 0.4, (0.5), (0.7), 0.8, 1.2, 1.0

Third list: (0.1), (0.4), (0.5), (0.7), 0.8, 1.0, (1.2)

Fourth list: (0.1), (0.4), (0.5), (0.7), 0.8, (1.0), (1.2)

0.1, 0.4, 0.5, 0.7, 0.8, 1.0, 1.2 is the sorted list.

Exam Questions

1 a) For n numbers in a list, a pivot could be chosen so that the other $n-1$ numbers are put in the same list *[1 mark]* (i.e. the pivot is the smallest / largest number in the list). The worst-case scenario is that this happens for each step *[1 mark]*. So, the quick sort would perform $(n-1) + (n-2) + ... + 1$ comparisons *[1 mark]*. The sum of the first $(n-1)$ whole numbers is $\frac{1}{2}(n-1)n$, so the quick sort is $O(n^2)$ *[1 mark]*.

b) There are 10 items in the list, so the pivot is the $\frac{1}{2}(10+2) =$ 6th item = 89 *[1 mark]*. The list becomes:

77, 83, 78, 80, (89), 96, 105, 112, 98, 94 *[1 mark]*
The first small list has 4 items, so the pivot is the $\frac{1}{2}(4+2) =$ 3rd item = 78, and the second list has 5 items, so the pivot is the $\frac{1}{2}(5+1) =$ 3rd item = 112. The list becomes:

77, (78), 83, 80, (89), 96, 105, 98, 94, (112) *[1 mark]*
77 is in a list on its own, so it's in the right place.
The second list now has 2 items, so the pivot is the 2nd item = 80, and the third list has 4 items, so the pivot is the 3rd item = 98. The list becomes:

(77), (78), (80), 83, (89), 96, 94, (98), 105, (112) *[1 mark]*
83 and 105 are in lists on their own, so they are in the correct place. The remaining list has 2 items in it, so the pivot is the 2nd item = 94. The list becomes:

(77), (78), (80), (83), (89), (94), 96, (98), (105), (112) *[1 mark]*
and is now sorted.

2 a) After the first pass, the final (6th) number in the list will be in the correct position. *[1 mark]*

b) There are 6 items, so the maximum number of passes is 6 *[1 mark]*. The maximum swaps is $\frac{1}{2} \times 5 \times 6 = 15$ *[1 mark]*.

Page 185 — Bin Packing Algorithms

Practice Questions

1 a) $5 + 11 + 8 + 9 + 12 + 7 = 52$. $52 \div 15 = 3.467$
So the lower bound is 4 boxes.

b) i)
Box 1: 5, 8	space left: ~~10 kg~~ 2 kg
Box 2: 11	space left: 4 kg
Box 3: 9	space left: 6 kg
Box 4: 12	space left: 3 kg
Box 5: 7	space left: 8 kg

The items are packed in 5 boxes, with 23 kg wasted space. The lower bound is 4 boxes, which means we can't say yet if this solution is optimal or not.

ii) First, reorder the numbers in descending order:
12, 11, 9, 8, 7, 5.
Box 1: 12	space left: 3 kg
Box 2: 11	space left: 4 kg
Box 3: 9, 5	space left: ~~6 kg~~ 1 kg
Box 4: 8, 7	space left: ~~7 kg~~ 0 kg

So the items are packed in 4 boxes, with $3 + 4 + 1 + 0 = 8$ kg wasted space. The lower bound for this problem is 4, so this solution is optimal (and now we can say for definite that part i) is not optimal.

iii) By eye, $8 + 7 = 15$, so this fills one box.
Box 1: 8, 7	space left: 0 kg
Box 2: 5, 9	space left: ~~10 kg~~ 1 kg
Box 3: 11	space left: 4 kg
Box 4: 12	space left: 3 kg

So the items are packed in 4 boxes, with $0 + 1 + 4 + 3 = 8$ kg wasted space. The lower bound for this problem is 4, so this solution is also optimal.
This is actually the same as the answer to part ii) but in a different order — sometimes different methods produce the same solution.

Exam Question

1 a)
Plank 1: 1.2, 0.6, 0.8	space left: ~~1.8~~ ~~1.2~~ 0.4
Plank 2: 2.3	space left: 0.7
Plank 3: 1.5, 1.0	space left: ~~1.5~~ 0.5
Plank 4: 0.9	space left: 2.1
Plank 5: 2.5	space left: 0.5

[1 mark for correct use of the first-fit bin packing algorithm]
So 5 planks are used *[1 mark]* and there is $0.4 + 0.7 + 0.5 + 2.1 + 0.5 = 4.2$ m wasted wood. *[1 mark]*

b) i) By eye, $1.2 + 0.8 + 1.0 = 3$ and $0.6 + 1.5 + 0.9 = 3$ *[1 mark]*, so there are 2 full planks. The rest are placed using the first fit algorithm.
Plank 1: 1.2, 0.8, 1.0	space left: 0
Plank 2: 0.6, 1.5, 0.9	space left: 0
Plank 3: 2.3	space left: 0.7
Plank 4: 2.5	space left: 0.5

[1 mark for correct use of the full-bin packing algorithm]
So 4 planks are used and there is $0.7 + 0.5 = 1.2$ m wasted wood *[1 mark]*.

ii) Calculate the lower bound by adding up all the lengths, dividing by the length of a plank and rounding up.
So $1.2 + 2.3 + 0.6 + 0.8 + 1.5 + 1.0 + 0.9 + 2.5 = 10.8$ *[1 mark]*.
$10.8 \div 3 = 3.6$, so the lower bound is 4. *[1 mark]*
So, the solution is optimal as it matches the lower bound *[1 mark]*.

Page 188 — Graphs

Practice Questions

1 a) E.g.

b) i) There are no loops or multiple arcs.

Answers

ii) The arcs do not cross — they only meet at the vertices.

c) E.g. Path: ADBC, cycle: BCDB

d) A = 1, B = 2, C = 3, D = 3, E = 1
Sum of degrees = double number of edges

2 a) 2   b) 6

Exam Question

1 a) 1 (e.g. AD) *[1 mark]*

b) 8 (2 × number of edges) *[1 mark]*

c) There are 5 vertices, and if they were all odd, the sum of the orders would be odd *[1 mark]*. However, the sum of the orders is double the number of edges, so must be even *[1 mark]*.

Page 189 — The Planarity Algorithm

Practice Question

1 a) E.g. Use ABCDEFA as the Hamiltonian cycle.

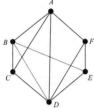

AD, AC and DF are 'inside' arcs.
BE and BD are 'outside' arcs.
So the graph is planar.
You might have had AD, AC and DF as the outside arcs, and BE and BD as the inside arcs instead.

b) E.g. Use ACBDFEA as the Hamiltonian cycle.

AD is an 'inside' arc.
BE is an 'outside' arc.
CF has to cross both AD and BE, so the graph is not planar.

Exam Question

1   E.g.

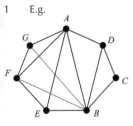

Put AF in the 'inside' list.
Put BG in the 'outside' list as it crosses AF.
Put AE in the 'inside' list as it crosses BG.
Put BF in the 'outside' list as it crosses AE.
AB and BD don't cross any arcs, so put these in the 'inside' list.

The arcs are separated into two lists:

Inside	Outside
AF	BG
AE	BF
AB	
BD	

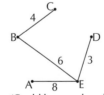

Therefore, the graph is planar.

You could have put BG and BF on the inside list, and AF, AE, AB and BD on the outside list instead.

[4 marks available in total:
* *1 mark for a correct polygon drawn of AGFEBCDA.*
* *1 mark for a correct 'inside' list.*
* *1 mark for a correct 'outside' list.*
* *1 mark for concluding that the graph is planar, or a planar graph is drawn]*

Section 29 — D1: Algorithms on Graphs

Page 191 — Spanning Trees and Kruskal's Algorithm

Practice Question

1 a) E.g.

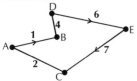

b) Any graph with one arc removed — e.g:

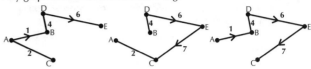

Exam Question

1 a)

Arc	Weight	Used?
BC	2	✓
AC	3	✓
AB	4	✗
BE	5	✓
AE	6	✗
DE	7	✓
CD	8	✗
AD	9	✗

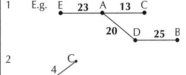

BC, AC, BE, DE *[3 marks if these arcs chosen in this order, otherwise 2 marks for any two correct arcs, or 1 mark for any one correct arc]*

b) AD is the longest arc in the graph, so for it to be in the minimum spanning tree, all other arcs to either A or D must be deleted. *[1 mark]* There are three other arcs to A, so deleting two of them will result in the third being in the minimum spanning tree, not AD.
There are only two other arcs to D, DE and CD, so deleting both of these will result in AD being in the minimum spanning tree.
So the arcs are DE and CD. *[1 mark]*

Page 193 — Prim's Algorithm

Practice Questions

1   E.g.

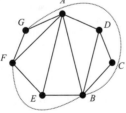

2

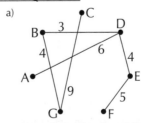

(Could have replaced AE with BA)

Exam Question

1 a)

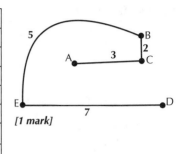

[2 marks for drawing with correct arcs, otherwise 1 mark for any two correct arcs]

Order of arcs found if A was the starting vertex:
AD, BD, DE (or BG), BG (or DE), EF, CG (different starting vertices will give different orders). *[1 mark]*

b)

	A	B	C	E	F	G
A	–	–	11	–	8	12
B	–	–	–	–	–	4
C	11	–	–	–	–	9
E	–	–	–	–	5	8
F	8	–	–	5	–	–
G	12	4	9	8	–	–

[1 mark]

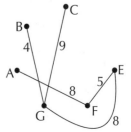

[1 mark]

Answers

Order of arcs BG, EG, EF, AF, CG.
[2 marks for all arcs being added in the correct order, otherwise 1 mark for the first two arcs added in the correct order]

Weight of the minimum spanning tree = 4 + 8 + 5 + 8 + 9 = 34
[1 mark]

Page 195 — Dijkstra's Algorithm

Practice Question

1 a)

EDBA (B and F may be in the opposite order)

b) 6

c) For the shortest route to go through G, EGA < 6 = EDBA.
Since EG = 4, GA < 6 − 4 = 2 ⇒ the maximum weight of GA = 1 (as the weight of GA is an integer).

Exam Question

1 a)

A	1	0		C	2	3		D	3	5		E	4	9
					3				~~7~~ 5				9	

B	5	10		F	6	22		G	7	24		H	8	33
10				~~23~~ 22				24				~~34~~ 33		

[3 marks for correct values in all boxes, otherwise 2 marks for four boxes correct and 1 mark for any two boxes correct]
Since GH = 33 − 24 = 9, GH is an arc on the quickest route.
Since EG = 24 − 9 = 15, EG is an arc on the quickest route.
Since DE = 9 − 5 = 4, DE is an arc on the quickest route.
Since CD = 5 − 3 = 2, CD is an arc on the quickest route.
Since AC = 3 − 0 = 3, AC is an arc on the quickest route. *[1 mark]*
⇒ The quickest route between A and H is ACDEGH. *[1 mark]*

b) The quickest route between A and H takes 33 minutes.
The quickest route between A and E takes 9 minutes. *[1 mark]*
So the bridge between E and H must take 33 − 9 = 24 minutes *[1 mark]*

Page 197 — Floyd's Algorithm

Practice Questions

1 ABC, ABD, BDE, CDB, CDBA and DBA.

2

	A	B	C
A	−	2	4
B	3	−	7
C	6	3	−

	A	B	C
A	A	B	C
B	A	B	[A]
C	[B]	B	C

Exam Question

1 a)

	A	B	C	D	E
A	−	5	∞	18	∞
B	5	−	∞	8	8
C	∞	3	−	3	4
D	18	8	3	−	∞
E	2	8	4	∞	−

[1 mark for correct values, 1 mark for ∞ symbols in the correct cells]

b) For the first iteration start with vertex A, and see if any routes would be shorter if they went through A.
B-C = ∞, B-A-C = BA + AC = 5 + ∞ = ∞ ⇒ B-A-C ≥ B-C ✗
so we leave both tables how they are.
B-D = 8, B-A-D = 5 + 18 = 23 ⇒ B-A-D > B-D ✗
B-E = 8, B-A-E = 5 + ∞ = ∞ ⇒ B-A-E > B-E ✗
C-B = 3, C-A-B = ∞ + 5 = ∞ ⇒ C-A-B > C-B ✗
C-D = 3, C-A-D = ∞ + 18 = ∞ ⇒ C-A-D > C-D ✗
C-E = 4, C-A-E = ∞ + ∞ = ∞ ⇒ C-A-E > C-E ✗
D-B = 8, D-A-B = 18 + 5 = 23 ⇒ D-A-B > D-B ✗
D-C = 3, D-A-C = 18 + ∞ = ∞ ⇒ D-A-C > D-C ✗
D-E = ∞, D-A-E = 18 + ∞ = ∞ ⇒ D-A-E ≥ D-E ✗
E-B = ∞, E-A-B = 2 + 5 = 7 ⇒ E-A-B < E-B ✓
so we replace 8 with 7 in the distance table and put an A in the corresponding position in the route table.

E-C = 4, E-A-C = 2 + ∞ = ∞ ⇒ E-A-C > E-C ✗
ED = ∞, E-A-D = 2 + 18 = 20 ⇒ E-A-D < E-D ✓
So after the first iteration, the distance and route tables are as follows:

	A	B	C	D	E
A	−	5	∞	18	∞
B	5	−	∞	8	8
C	∞	3	−	3	4
D	18	8	3	−	∞
E	2	[7]	4	[20]	−

	A	B	C	D	E
A	A	B	C	D	E
B	A	B	C	D	E
C	A	B	C	D	E
D	A	B	C	D	E
E	Ⓐ	[A]	C	[A]	E

[1 mark for 7 in the EB cell and 20 in the ED cell of the distance table, 1 mark for A in the EB and ED cells of the route table, 1 mark for these changes being the only changes made]
For the second iteration, see if any routes would be shorter if they went through B.
A-C = ∞, A-B-C = 5 + ∞ = ∞ ⇒ A-B-C ≥ A-C ✗
A-D = 18, A-B-D = 5 + 8 = 13 ⇒ A-B-D < A-D ✓
A-E = ∞, A-B-E = 5 + 8 = 13 ⇒ A-B-E < A-E ✓
C-A = ∞, C-B-A = 3 + 5 = 8 ⇒ C-B-A < C-A ✓
C-D = 3, C-B-D = 3 + 8 = 11 ⇒ C-B-D > C-D ✗
C-E = 4, C-B-E = 3 + 8 = 11 ⇒ C-B-E > C-E ✗
D-A = 18, D-B-A = 8 + 5 = 13 ⇒ D-B-A < D-A ✓
D-C = 3, D-B-C = 8 + ∞ = ∞ ⇒ D-B-C > D-C ✗
D-E = ∞, D-B-E = 8 + 8 = 16 ⇒ D-B-E < D-E ✓
E-A = 2, E-B-A = 7 + 5 = 12 ⇒ E-B-A > E-A ✗
E-C = 4, E-B-C = 7 + ∞ = ∞ ⇒ E-B-C > E-C ✗
E-D = 20, E-B-D = 7 + 8 = 15 ⇒ E-B-D < E-D ✓
So after the second iteration, the distance and route tables are as follows:

	A	B	C	D	E
A	−	5	∞	[13]	[13]
B	5	−	∞	8	8
C	[8]	3	−	3	4
D	[13]	8	3	−	[16]
E	2	7	4	[15]	−

	A	B	C	D	E
A	A	Ⓑ	C	[B]	[B]
B	A	B	C	D	E
C	[B]	Ⓑ	C	D	E
D	[B]	Ⓑ	C	D	[B]
E	A	Ⓐ	C	[A]	E

[1 mark for at least two correct changes to the distance table, 1 mark for at least two correct changes to the route table, 1 mark for every entry being correct in both tables]

c) Start at row A and read across to column D — there is a B there. So the route starts AB. *[1 mark]*
Look at row B, column D and you see D. So the route is ABD. *[1 mark]*

d) If a network has *n* vertices, then for each iteration you have to compare *n* − 1 vertices to *n* − 2 vertices.
(You compare every vertex apart from the iteration vertex to every vertex apart from itself and the iteration vertex.) *[1 mark]*
Since there are *n* iterations (there is an iteration for every vertex), there are *n*(*n* − 1)(*n* − 2) comparisons. *[1 mark]*
So Floyd's algorithm is O(n^3). *[1 mark]*

Section 30 — D1: Algorithms on Graphs II

Page 201 — Route Inspection Problems

Practice Questions

1 $2^x − 1$ and $2x − 1$ are odd for every integer $x > 1$.
2^{x-1} and $2(x − 1)$ are even for every integer $x > 1$, so the graph has two odd vertices ⇒ the graph is semi-Eulerian

2 a) Semi-Eulerian. Repeat edges AB and BC.
One possible route is AEFCDFABCBA.
Length of route = Weight of network + 8 = 34 + 8 = 42

b) Eulerian.
One possible route is AFEDCAGCEGBDA.
Length of route = Weight of network = 87

c) Semi-Eulerian. Repeat edges AE and ED.
One possible route is AEDCBACEBDEA.
Length of route = Weight of Network + 11 = 54 + 11 = 65

Exam Questions

1 a) Odd vertices are A, D, E, F. *[1 mark]*
Pairings, and the shortest routes between them, are:
AD + EF = ACD + EF = 12 + 15 = 27

Answers

AE + DF = ACE + DEF = 12 + 21 = 33
AF + DE = ABF + DE = 18 + 6 = 24
[1 mark for pairings, 1 mark for distances]
So the minimum pairing is AF + DE **[1 mark]**
⇒ The length of Jamie's route = 106 + 24 **[1 mark]**
= 130 miles **[1 mark]**

b) C has four edges connected to it, so must be passed through twice.
E has six edges connected to it (including the extra edge along DE),
so must be passed through three times. **[1 mark]**
So Jamie will pass an ice-cream shop 2 + 3 = 5 times **[1 mark]**.
Alternatively, giving an inspection route and drawing the same conclusion is also worth both marks.

c) Since every path is being used twice, the degree of the nodes is doubled, making the graph Eulerian. So the length of the inspection route is twice the weight of the graph. **[1 mark]**
106 × 2 = 212 miles **[1 mark]**.

2 a) Odd vertices are B, D, F, G. **[1 mark]**
BD = 7, BF = 12, BG = 2, DF = 17, DG = 9 and FG = 10 **[1 mark]**
The quickest time is BG **[1 mark]**.
In order to walk for the shortest time, repeat this path and so start at either D or F and end at the other **[1 mark]**.
One possible route is DBCDEFGBGAF **[1 mark]**.

b) Time taken = weight of the network + 2 = 56 + 2 = 58 minutes.
[1 mark]

c) Now the odd vertices are A, D, F, G. **[1 mark]**
The possible pairings are: AD and FG, AF and DG, AG and DF.
For some of these pairings, you can't be sure that a route that includes AB won't be quicker than an existing route, but you can find a lower bound for how long a route including AB could take.
AD and FG: AD > BD = BCD = 7,
              FG > FA + BG = 5 + 2 = 7
              ⇒ AD + FG > 7 + 7 = 14
AF and DG: AF + DG = AF + DCBG = 5 + 9 = 14
AG and DF: AG > BG = 2,
              DF > DB + AF = DCB + AF = 7 + 5 = 12
              ⇒ AG + DF > 2 + 12 = 14
[1 mark for pairings, 1 mark for distances]
So the minimum pairing is AF + DG **[1 mark]**
⇒ Time taken = weight of network + 14 = 79
= (56 + Time for AB) + 14 = 79 **[1 mark]**
⇒ Time for AB = 9 minutes **[1 mark]**

Page 205 — Travelling Salesman Problems
Practice Questions

1   Nearest Neighbour algorithm from C goes to B next, followed by A, F, E then G. The only two vertices connected to G are F and E, which have already been used in the algorithm, so no further progress can be made. But since the vertex D hasn't been visited yet, the algorithm fails.

2   Unlike for the practical TSP, the solution to a classical TSP will only visit each landmark once and no more than once.
The solution to the practical TSP will sometimes be shorter than the solution to the classical TSP.

3
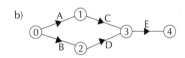

Exam Questions

1 a) Delete the vertex A and each of its arcs, then use Prim's algorithm on the resulting graph. This gives a minimum spanning tree that has edges CE, ED and CB **[1 mark]** and a weight of 2 + 3 + 4 = 9 **[1 mark]**.
The minimum weight of the edges connecting A to the tree (AB and AE) are 8 + 8 = 16. So a lower bound for the optimal route is 16 + 9 = 25 **[1 mark]**.
Since 25 is the highest lower bound, it is the best lower bound **[1 mark]**.

b) Add a vertex from A to D, of length 8 + 3 = 11 **[1 mark]**.
Nearest Neighbour algorithm from D goes to E next, followed by C, B, A then back to D (via E) **[1 mark]**.
This has a length of 3 + 2 + 4 + 8 + 8 + 3 = 28 **[1 mark]**.
Since 28 is the lowest upper bound, it is the best upper bound, so the smallest range in which the length of the optimal route can lie is 25 ≤ length of optimal route ≤ 28 **[1 mark]**.

2 a)

	A	B	C	E
A	–	29	24	23
B	29	–	31	27
C	24	31	–	23
E	23	27	23	–

Starting at vertex A and using Prim's algorithm, a minimum spanning tree is AE, EC and EB **[1 mark]**.
The minimum weight of the edges (DA and DC) connecting D to the tree are 15 + 22 = 37 **[1 mark]**.
So a lower bound is 23 + 23 + 27 + 37 = 110 minutes **[1 mark]**.

b) Nearest Neighbour algorithm from D goes to A next, followed by E, C, B then back to D **[1 mark]**.
This has a length of 15 + 23 + 23 + 31 + 25 = 117 minutes **[1 mark]**

Section 31 — D1: Critical Path Analysis

Page 208 — Activity Networks
Practice Questions

1 a)

Activity	Immediate preceding activities
A	—
B	—
C	A
D	B
E	C, D

b)
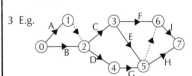

2

Activity	Immediate preceding activities
A	—
B	A
C	—
D	—
E	D
F	B, C, E
G	B, C, E
H	F
I	G

3 E.g.
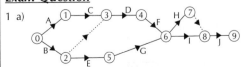

Exam Question

1 a)

[5 marks available — 1 mark for 10 numbered nodes, 1 mark for each correctly placed dummy (2 dummies), 2 marks for other correct precedences. Lose 1 mark for each error.]

Answers

b) The dummy between nodes 2 and 3 is needed to show dependency (that D depends on B and C, but E depends on B only). *[1 mark]*
The dummy between nodes 7 and 8 is needed so that all activities are uniquely represented in terms of their events / no two activities are shown between the same pair of events. *[1 mark]*

Page 211 — Critical Paths
Practice Questions
1 a) $a = 0$, $b = 4$, $c = 9$, $d = 6$, $e = 5$, $f = 13$, $g = 14$
   b) i) A series of activities running from the start to the end of the project (source node to sink node). The activities have zero total float (they are all critical) and if their start is delayed, the entire project time will be extended.
      ii) ACGH and ADJ
   c) E's duration isn't equal to the difference between the time at the node before and the time at the node after.
   d) 14 hours
   e) $B = 6 - 3 - 0 = 3$ hours $E = 10 - 3 - 4 = 3$ hours
      $I = 14 - 1 - 11 = 2$ hours
2   The critical activities are A, B, D, I, L,
    so the critical paths are B I L and A D I L.

Exam Question
1 a)

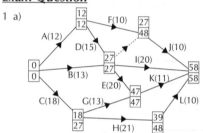

[3 marks available — 1 mark for all top boxes correct, 1 mark for all bottom boxes correct, 1 mark for values increasing in the direction of the arrows.]

   b) Critical activities: ADEK *[1 mark]*
      Length of critical path = 58 days *[1 mark]*
   c) Total float on F = $48 - 10 - 12 = 26$ days
      Total float on G = $47 - 13 - 18 = 16$ days
      [3 marks available — 1 mark for each total float and 1 mark for showing correct working.]

Page 214 — Gantt Charts and Resource Histograms
Practice Questions
1 a) A, E and F have a float of 0.
      B and C have a float of 3.
      D has a float of 4.
   b) A, E and F
2 a) A, B, C and D
   b) D and E might be happening, and A and F will definitely be happening.
   c) F and G
3 a)

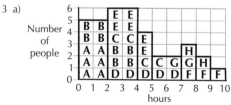

   b) If activities B, E and H are started at the latest possible times, with the other activities starting at the earliest possible times, the resource histogram becomes:

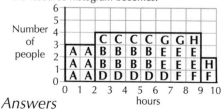

Answers

Exam Question
1 a)

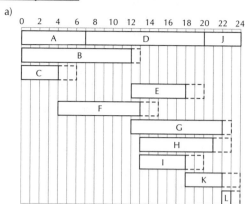

[3 marks available — 1 mark for correct critical activities (ADJ), 2 marks for all other activities and floats correct, otherwise 1 mark for at least six correct.]

   b)

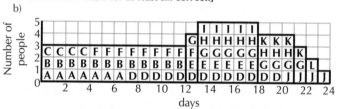

[3 marks available — 1 mark for drawing a suitable histogram, 1 mark for correct bars up to 13 days, 1 mark for the remaining correct bars]

   c) 5 *[1 mark]*

Page 217 — Scheduling
Practice Question
1 a) 3
   b) E.g.

Exam Question
1 a) BEHK *[1 mark]*, BFJ *[1 mark]*.
   b) Lower bound = $112 \div 37 = 3.02...$ *[1 mark]*
      which rounds up to 4 *[1 mark]*
   c) H (critical activity between day 15 and day 25) *[1 mark]*
      J (critical activity between day 20 and day 37) *[1 mark]*
   d) From c) you know you need a minimum of 4 workers.
      E.g.

[3 marks available — 1 mark for every 4 correctly scheduled activities.]

   e) No. *[1 mark]*
      D won't be finished until day 22. Critical activity H must start after 15 days, and depends on D being completed. *[1 mark]*

Section 32 – D1: Linear Programming

Page 219 — Linear Programs
Practice Question
1   E.g. x is the number of bowler hats and y is the number of top hats in a shop. Each bowler hat costs £40 and each top hat costs £25. The shop wants to sell at least £200 worth of the two types of hat, but they only have 6 hat boxes left to pack them in.
    There is no one correct answer for this one — the possibilities are endless. Let your imagination run free.

Answers

Exam Questions

1. The objective is to minimise the cost, $C = 75x + 60y$ *[1 mark]*, in pence, subject to the constraints:
   $x, y > 0$ *[1 mark]* (from the statement that she will sell both red and white roses — x and y can't be 0).
   $0.45(x + y) \leq x$ *[1 mark]* and $0.55(x + y) \geq x$ *[1 mark]*
   This simplifies to $9y \leq 11x$ and $11y \geq 9x$ *[1 mark]* (from the statement that between 45% and 55% of the roses will be red).
   $x + y \geq 100$ *[1 mark]* (from the statement that she will sell a total of at least 100 flowers).

2. Let x be the number of large posters made, and y be the number of small posters made.
   Then x and y are the decision variables *[1 mark]*. The constraints are:
   $10x + 5y + s_1 = 250$, where s_1 is a slack variable *[1 mark]*.
   $6x + 4y + s_2 = 200$, where s_2 is a slack variable *[1 mark]*.
   $x - s_3 = y$, where s_3 is a surplus variable *[1 mark]*.
   $y - s_4 = 10$, where s_4 is a surplus variable *[1 mark]*.
   The objective is to maximise profit, P *[1 mark]*, where $P = 6x + 3.5y$ *[1 mark]*.

Page 221 — Feasible Regions

Practice Questions

1. E.g. maximising the volume of water in three buckets, subject to constraints, would not require integer solutions.
   E.g. minimising the number of cars bought by a company, subject to constraints, would require integer solutions.

2.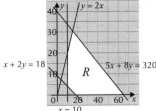

Exam Questions

1. First, the non-negativity constraints are $x, y \geq 0$. The solid line that passes through (0, 6) and (3, 0) has equation $y = 6 - 2x$ (or $2x + y = 6$), and as the area below the line is shaded, the inequality is $2x + y \geq 6$. The dotted line that passes through (2, 0) has equation $y = x - 2$ (or $x - y = 2$), and as the area below the line is shaded, the inequality is $x - y < 2$. The horizontal solid line that passes through (0, 4) has the equation $y = 4$, and as the area above the line is shaded, the inequality is $y \leq 4$.
   [5 marks available — 1 mark for correct non-negativity constraints, 1 mark for each correct line equation and 1 mark for all inequality signs correct]

2.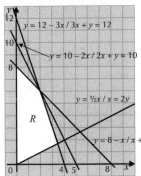
   [5 marks available — 1 mark for each of the four inequality lines (with equations) and 1 mark for the correct feasible region]

Page 223 — The Objective Line Method

Practice Question

1. a) One of the constraints is $y > 1$, so (1, 1) is not a feasible solution.
   b) $Q = 4$, at the point (2, 2)

2. Profit = £9600, at the point (64, 0)

Exam Question

1. a) The objective function is $P = 2x + 5y$, which is to be maximised.
   [1 mark]

b) The insecticide constraint is $2x + 8y \leq 1000$.
   Simplifying, this becomes $x + 4y \leq 500$. *[1 mark]*
   $4x + 5y \leq 1000$ (water constraint) *[1 mark]*
   $x + 2y \leq 300$ (land constraint) *[1 mark]*
   $x, y \geq 0$ (non-negativity constraint) *[1 mark]*

c)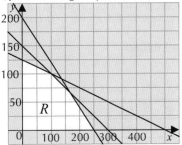
   [4 marks available — 1 mark for each of the three inequality lines and 1 mark for correct feasible region]
   Starting with the objective line $500 = 2x + 5y$
   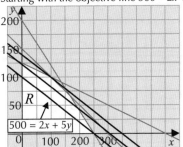
   The last point within the feasible region that the line touches is (100, 100), so the highest value P can take is $(2 \times 100) + (5 \times 100) = £700$. *[1 mark]*
   This can be achieved by planting 100 indoor trees and 100 outdoor trees. *[1 mark]*

Page 225 — The Vertex Method

Practice Question

1. a) At vertex A, $P = 10.5$
   At vertex B, $P = 6.57...$
   At vertex C, $P = 8.66...$
   b) Maximum = 10.5, at the point $\left(\frac{3}{2}, \frac{5}{2}\right)$
   Minimum = 6.57..., at the point $\left(\frac{5}{7}, \frac{12}{7}\right)$
   c) Maximum = 10, at the point (2, 2)
   Minimum = 8, at the point (1, 2)

Exam Question

1. a) First, the non-negativity constraints are $x, y \geq 0$.
   The vertical solid line that passes through (1, 0) has equation $x = 1$ and as the area to the left of the line is shaded, the inequality is $x \geq 1$.
   The dotted line that passes through (0, 6) and (4, 0) has equation $y = 6 - \frac{3}{2}x$, and as the area above the line is shaded, the inequality is $y < 6 - \frac{3}{2}x$ or $\frac{3}{2}x + y < 6$.
   The dotted line that passes through (1, 0) and (0, –1) has equation $y = x - 1$, and as the area below the line is shaded, the inequality is $y > x - 1$ or $x - y < 1$.
   [5 marks available — 1 mark for correct non-negativity constraints, 1 mark for each correct line equation and 1 mark for all inequality signs correct]

b) The intersection of the lines $x = 1$ and $y = 6 - \frac{3}{2}x$ occurs at the point where $x = 1$ and $y = 6 - \frac{3}{2}$, i.e. at $\left(1, \frac{9}{2}\right)$. *[1 mark]*
   The intersection of the lines $x = 1$ and $y = x - 1$ occurs at the point where $x = 1$ and $y = 1 - 1$, i.e. at (1, 0). *[1 mark]*
   The intersection of the lines $y = 6 - \frac{3}{2}x$ and $y = x - 1$ occurs at the point where $x - 1 = 6 - \frac{3}{2}x \Rightarrow \frac{5}{2}x = 7 \Rightarrow x = \frac{14}{5}$.
   So $y = \frac{14}{5} - 1 = \frac{9}{5}$, so the point of intersection is $\left(\frac{14}{5}, \frac{9}{5}\right)$.
   [1 mark]

Answers

c) At $\left(1, \frac{9}{2}\right)$, $C = (4 \times 1) + \frac{9}{2} = \frac{17}{2} = 8.5$.

At $(1, 0)$, $C = (4 \times 1) + 0 = 4$.

At $\left(\frac{14}{5}, \frac{9}{5}\right)$, $C = \left(4 \times \frac{14}{5}\right) + \frac{9}{5} = 13$. *[1 mark]*

The vertex $(1, 0)$ gives the smallest value of C *[1 mark]*, but it isn't in the feasible region, since it doesn't satisfy $x - y < 1$. *[1 mark]*

Page 229 — The Simplex Method

Practice Questions

1   Basic Variable y, column s_1 (with a current value of $\frac{1}{2}$)

2 a)

B.V.	x	y	s_1	s_2	Value
s_1	0	2	1	0	6
x	1	3	0	1	2
P	0	1	0	5	28

b) P is maximised when $y = s_2 = 0$. So $P = 28$.
This corresponds to the values $x = 2$ and $s_1 = 6$.

3 a)

B.V.	x	y	s_1	s_2	Value
s_1	1	3	1	0	7
s_2	②	3	0	1	8
P	−6	−12	0	0	0

b)   Choose column x as the pivot column (y is also an acceptable choice). $8 \div 2 = 4 < 7 \div 1 = 7$, so use row s_2, i.e. the value 2.

B.V.	x	y	s_1	s_2	Value
s_1	0	⓸$\frac{3}{2}$	1	$-\frac{1}{2}$	3
x	1	$\frac{3}{2}$	0	$\frac{1}{2}$	4
P	0	−3	0	3	24

Choose column y as the pivot column. $3 \div \frac{3}{2} = 2 < 4 \div \frac{3}{2} = \frac{8}{3}$.
So use row s_1, i.e. the value $\frac{3}{2}$.

B.V.	x	y	s_1	s_2	Value
y	0	1	$\frac{2}{3}$	$-\frac{1}{3}$	2
x	1	0	−1	1	1
P	0	0	2	2	30

No values in the objective function row are negative so we can read off our solution. P is maximised when $s_1 = s_2 = 0$, so $P = 30$.
This corresponds to $x = 1$ and $y = 2$.

c)   To minimise $P = -3x + 12y$, you'd maximise $P' = 3x - 12y$.
Then min $P = -$max P'.

Exam Questions

1 a)   To minimise C, you need to maximise $C' = -2x + 4y - 3z$. This becomes $C' + 2x - 4y + 3z = 0$. Introducing slack variables to the other equations gives:
$x + y + z + s_1 = 16$, $3x + 2y - z + s_2 = 20$, $4x - 5y + z + s_3 = 25$,
where $s_1, s_2, s_3 \geq 0$. Putting this into the tableau gives:

B.V.	x	y	z	s_1	s_2	s_3	Value	
s_1	1	1	1	1	0	0	16	(a)
s_2	3	2	−1	0	1	0	20	(b)
s_3	4	−5	1	0	0	1	25	(c)
C'	2	−4	3	0	0	0	0	(d)

[1 mark for each correct row of the tableau]
This is a sneaky one — it's a minimising question, so you have to remember to use $C' = -C$ in the tableau.

b)   The y-column is the only column with a negative value in the bottom row, so the pivot must come from there *[1 mark]*.
$16 \div 1 = 16$ and $20 \div 2 = 10$. $10 < 16$, so the pivot is 2 *[1 mark]* (ignore the third row, as this doesn't give a positive value).

c)

B.V.	x	y	z	s_1	s_2	s_3	Value	
s_1	$-\frac{1}{2}$	0	$\frac{3}{2}$	1	$-\frac{1}{2}$	0	6	(e)
y	$\frac{3}{2}$	1	$-\frac{1}{2}$	0	$\frac{1}{2}$	0	10	(f)
s_3	$\frac{23}{2}$	0	$-\frac{3}{2}$	0	$\frac{5}{2}$	1	75	(g)
C'	8	0	1	0	2	0	40	(h)

(e) = (a) $- \frac{1}{2}$ (b), (f) = $\frac{1}{2}$ (b), (g) = (c) $+ \frac{5}{2}$ (b), and (h) = (d) + 2(b)
At this point, the objective function row gives
$C' + 8x + z + 2s_2 = 40$, so the maximum value of C' is obtained by letting $x, z, s_2 = 0$ (as $x, z, s_2 \geq 0$). $C' = 40 \Rightarrow C = -40$.
This corresponds to $s_1 = 6$, $y = 10$ and $s_3 = 75$.
[1 mark for each correct row of the tableau (obtained using correct method), 1 mark for corresponding value of C]

2 a)   Let $x =$ number of small rooms and $y =$ number of large rooms.
The constraint on painting time is $x + 3y \leq 15$ *[1 mark]*.
The constraint on wallpapering time is $2x + 4y \leq 22$ *[1 mark]*.
The non-negativity constraints are $x, y \geq 0$ *[1 mark]*.

b)   The objective function is $P = 50x + 120y$ *[1 mark]*.

c)   The objective function becomes $P - 50x - 120y = 0$.
Adding the slack variables to the constraints gives:
$x + 3y + s_1 = 15$ and $2x + 4y + s_2 = 22$, where $s_1, s_2 \geq 0$.

B.V.	x	y	s_1	s_2	Value	
s_1	1	3	1	0	15	(a)
s_2	②	4	0	1	22	(b)
P	−50	−120	0	0	0	(c)

[1 mark for each correct row of the tableau]

d)   Choose a pivot from the x-column: $15 \div 1 = 15$, $22 \div 2 = 11$. $11 < 15$, so the pivot is 2.

B.V.	x	y	s_1	s_2	Value	
s_1	0	①	1	−0.5	4	(d) = (a) $- \frac{1}{2}$ (b)
x	1	2	0	0.5	11	(e) = (b) ÷ 2
P	0	−20	0	25	550	(f) = (c) + 25(b)

Now choose a pivot from the new y-column: $4 \div 1 = 4$, $11 \div 2 = 5.5$. $4 < 5.5$, so the pivot is 1.

B.V.	x	y	s_1	s_2	Value	
y	0	1	1	−0.5	4	(g) = (d)
x	1	0	−2	1.5	3	(h) = (e) − 2(d)
P	0	0	20	15	630	(i) = (f) + 20(d)

The bottom row gives $P + 20s_1 + 15s_2 = 630$. Let $s_1 = s_2 = 0$, so the maximum value of $P = 630$. The top row gives
$y + s_1 - 0.5s_2 = 4$. As $s_1 = s_2 = 0$, $y = 4$.
The second row gives $x - 2s_1 + 1.5s_2 = 3$, so $x = 3$.
So the maximum profit is £630, which occurs when the company decorates 3 small rooms and 4 large rooms.
[1 mark for choosing the correct x-pivot, 1 mark for correct pivot row in first tableau, 1 mark for obtaining the other rows in first tableau, 1 mark for choosing the correct y-pivot, 1 mark for correct pivot row in second tableau, 1 mark for obtaining the other rows in second tableau, 1 mark for correct P value and 1 mark for correct interpretation of x- and y-values]

Page 231 — Two-Stage Simplex

Practice Question

1    $3x - 2y \leq 14$ becomes $3x - 2y + s_1 = 14$
$x \geq 2$ becomes $x - s_2 + t_1 = 2$
$x + 2y \geq 5$ becomes $x + 2y - s_3 + t_2 = 5$
$x + 2z = 6$ becomes $x + 2z + t_3 = 6$
where $s_1 \geq 0$ is a slack variable, $s_2, s_3 \geq 0$ are surplus variables and $t_1, t_2, t_3 \geq 0$ are artificial variables.

Answers

Exam Question

a) Since every variable in the objective function row is non-negative, there are no more iterations to complete in stage one. *[1 mark]*
From the tableau, $-Q$ can be maximised by setting $t_1 = t_2 = 0$, so a solution to the original problem exists. *[1 mark]*

b) First, identify the non-basic variables. These are the non-zero variables that don't appear in the B.V. column of the final stage one tableau: x, s_2 and s_3.
Then rewrite the objective function, P, in terms of these variables. Since P is in terms of x, y and z, you need to find y and z in terms of x, s_2 and s_3. *[1 mark]*
From row z: $x + z - s_2 - s_3 = 12 \Rightarrow z = 12 - x + s_2 + s_3$
From row y: $y - s_3 = 4 \qquad \Rightarrow y = 4 + s_3$ *[1 mark]*
$\Rightarrow P = x + y + z = x + (4 + s_3) + (12 - x + s_2 + s_3) = 16 + s_2 + 2s_3$
$\Rightarrow P - s_2 - 2s_3 = 16$ *[1 mark]*
So your simplex tableau is:

B.V.	x	y	z	s_1	s_2	s_3	Value
s_1	2	0	0	1	2	②	4
z	1	0	1	0	−1	−1	12
y	0	1	0	0	0	−1	4
P	0	0	0	0	−1	−2	16

Choosing column s_3, row s_1 as your pivot for this iteration gives:

B.V.	x	y	z	s_1	s_2	s_3	Value
s_3	1	0	0	$\frac{1}{2}$	1	1	2
z	2	0	1	$\frac{1}{2}$	0	0	14
y	1	1	0	$\frac{1}{2}$	1	0	6
P	2	0	0	1	1	0	20

[1 mark for correct pivot row, 1 mark for correct numbers in value column, 1 mark for every number in the tableau being correct]
Every variable in the bottom row is now non-negative, so you can read off the solution. Maximising P means setting $x = s_1 = s_2 = 0$.
So the maximum value of $P = 20$.
This corresponds to $y = 6$, $z = 14$ and $s_3 = 2$. *[1 mark]*

Page 233 — The Big-M Method

Practice Question

1 $P = x + 5y$ becomes $P - (1 + 5M)x - (5 + 6M)y + Ms_2 + Ms_3 = -8M$ where s_2, $s_3 \geq 0$ are the surplus variables in the second and third constraints respectively and M is an arbitrary large real number.

Exam Question

1 a) The constraints become $x + 3y + s_1 = 12$, $2x + 4y - s_2 + t_1 = 18$, $x + y + t_2 = 9$ and $x, y, s_1, s_2, t_1, t_2 \geq 0$. *[1 mark]*
$\Rightarrow t_1 = 18 - 2x - 4y + s_2$ and $t_2 = 9 - x - y$ *[1 mark]*
So the modified objective function is $P = x + 6y - Mt_1 - Mt_2$
$= x + 6y - M(18 - 2x - 4y + s_2) - M(9 - x - y)$
$\Rightarrow P = x + 6y - 18M + 2Mx + 4My - Ms_2 - 9M + Mx + My$
$\Rightarrow P = (1 + 3M)x + (6 + 5M)y - Ms_2 - 27M$
$\Rightarrow P - (1 + 3M)x - (6 + 5M)y + Ms_2 = -27M$ *[1 mark]*
So the initial tableau for a big-M solution to this problem is:

B.V.	x	y	s_1	s_2	t_1	t_2	Value
s_1	1	3	1	0	0	0	12
t_1	2	4	0	−1	1	0	18
t_2	1	1	0	0	0	1	9
P	−(1 + 3M)	−(6 + 5M)	0	M	0	0	−27M

[1 mark for correct objective function row, 1 mark for every number in the tableau being correct]

b) The tableau before the iteration is:

B.V.	x	y	s_1	s_2	t_1	t_2	Value	
y	0	1	1	$\frac{1}{2}$	$-\frac{1}{2}$	0	3	(a)
x	1	0	−2	$-\frac{3}{2}$	$\frac{3}{2}$	0	3	(b)
t_2	0	0	1	①	−1	1	3	(c)
P	0	0	$4 - M$	$\frac{3}{2} - M$	$2M - \frac{3}{2}$	0	$21 - 3M$	(d)

After the iteration, the tableau is:

B.V.	x	y	s_1	s_2	t_1	t_2	Value	
y	0	1	$\frac{1}{2}$	0	0	$-\frac{1}{2}$	$\frac{3}{2}$	(e)
x	1	0	$-\frac{1}{2}$	0	0	$\frac{3}{2}$	$\frac{15}{2}$	(f)
s_2	0	0	1	1	−1	1	3	(g)
P	0	0	$\frac{5}{2}$	0	M	$M - \frac{3}{2}$	$\frac{33}{2}$	(h)

(e) = (a) $- \frac{1}{2}$(c), (f) = (b) $+ \frac{3}{2}$(c), (g) = (c) and (h) = (d) $- (\frac{3}{2} - M)$(c)
[1 mark for each correct row of the tableau]

c) Because every variable in the objective function row is non-negative for big enough M (M $> \frac{3}{2}$). *[1 mark]*

d) From the tableau, P is maximised when $s_1 = t_1 = t_2 = 0$, so the original problem has a solution. *[1 mark]*

e) The maximum value of $P = \frac{33}{2}$.
This corresponds to $x = \frac{15}{2}$, $y = \frac{3}{2}$ and $s_2 = 3$. *[1 mark]*

Formulas

The formulas on these pages will be given in your formula booklet in the exam.
You don't need to learn them off by heart, but make sure you can understand and use them all.

Complex numbers

$[r(\cos\theta + i\sin\theta)]^n = r^n(\cos n\theta + i\sin n\theta)$

The roots of $z^n = 1$ are $\omega = e^{\frac{i2k\pi}{n}}$, where $0 \le k \le n - 1$

Mensuration

Surface area of sphere $= 4\pi r^2$

Area of curved surface of cone $= \pi r \times$ slant height

Sequences, Series and Summations

Arithmetic Series:

$$S_n = \frac{1}{2}n(a + l) = \frac{1}{2}n[2a + (n-1)d]$$

Geometric Series:

$$S_n = \frac{a(1 - r^n)}{1 - r}$$

$$S_\infty = \frac{a}{1 - r} \text{ for } |r| < 1$$

Binomial Series:

$$(a + b)^n = a^n + \binom{n}{1}a^{n-1}b + \binom{n}{2}a^{n-2}b^2 + \dots + \binom{n}{r}a^{n-r}b^r + \dots + b^n \quad (n \in \mathbb{N})$$

$$\text{where } \binom{n}{r} = {}^nC_r = \frac{n!}{r!(n-r)!}$$

$$(1 + x)^n = 1 + nx + \frac{n(n-1)}{1 \times 2}x^2 + \dots + \frac{n(n-1)\dots(n-r+1)}{1 \times 2 \times \dots \times r}x^r + \dots \quad (|x| < 1, n \in \mathbb{R})$$

Summations:

$$\sum_{r=1}^{n} r^2 = \frac{1}{6}n(n + 1)(2n + 1) \qquad \sum_{r=1}^{n} r^3 = \frac{1}{4}n^2(n + 1)^2$$

Maclaurin and Taylor Series:

$$f(x) = f(0) + xf'(0) + \frac{x^2}{2!}f''(0) + \dots + \frac{x^r}{r!}f^{(r)}(0) + \dots$$

$$e^x = 1 + x + \frac{x^2}{2!} + \frac{x^3}{3!} + \dots + \frac{x^r}{r!} + \dots \qquad \text{for all values of } x$$

$$\sin x = x - \frac{x^3}{3!} + \frac{x^5}{5!} - \dots + (-1)^r\frac{x^{2r+1}}{(2r+1)!} + \dots \quad \text{for all values of } x$$

$$\cos x = 1 - \frac{x^2}{2!} + \frac{x^4}{4!} - \dots + (-1)^r\frac{x^{2r}}{(2r)!} + \dots \qquad \text{for all values of } x$$

$$\ln(1 + x) = x - \frac{x^2}{2} + \frac{x^3}{3} - \dots + (-1)^{r+1}\frac{x^r}{r} + \dots \qquad \text{for } -1 < x \le 1$$

$$\arctan x = x - \frac{x^3}{3} + \frac{x^5}{5} - \dots + (-1)^r\frac{x^{2r+1}}{(2r+1)} + \dots \quad \text{for } -1 \le x \le 1$$

Trigonometry

$$\sin(A \pm B) \equiv \sin A \cos B \pm \cos A \sin B \qquad\qquad \cos(A \pm B) \equiv \cos A \cos B \mp \sin A \sin B$$

$$\tan(A \pm B) \equiv \frac{\tan A \pm \tan B}{1 \mp \tan A \tan B} \quad \left(A \pm B \ne \left(k + \frac{1}{2}\right)\pi\right)$$

$$\sin A + \sin B = 2\sin\frac{A+B}{2}\cos\frac{A-B}{2} \qquad\qquad \sin A - \sin B = 2\cos\frac{A+B}{2}\sin\frac{A-B}{2}$$

$$\cos A + \cos B = 2\cos\frac{A+B}{2}\cos\frac{A-B}{2} \qquad\qquad \cos A - \cos B = -2\sin\frac{A+B}{2}\sin\frac{A-B}{2}$$

Small Angle Approximations: $\quad \sin\theta \approx \theta \quad\quad \cos\theta \approx 1 - \frac{1}{2}\theta^2 \quad\quad \tan\theta \approx \theta \quad\quad$ where θ is measured in radians.

Formulas and Statistical Tables

Formulas

Hyperbolic Functions

$$\cosh^2 x - \sinh^2 x = 1$$

$$\sinh 2x = 2\sinh x \cosh x$$

$$\cosh 2x = \cosh^2 x + \sinh^2 x$$

$$\text{arsinh } x = \ln(x + \sqrt{x^2 + 1}) \quad \text{for } x \in \mathbb{R}$$

$$\text{arcosh } x = \ln(x + \sqrt{x^2 - 1}) \quad \text{for } x \geq 1$$

$$\text{artanh } x = \tfrac{1}{2}\ln\left(\frac{1+x}{1-x}\right) \quad \text{for } -1 < x < 1$$

Differentiation

First Principles:

$$f'(x) = \lim_{h \to 0} \frac{f(x+h) - f(x)}{h}$$

Quotient rule:

$$\text{for } y = \frac{f(x)}{g(x)}, \quad \frac{dy}{dx} = \frac{f'(x)g(x) - f(x)g'(x)}{(g(x))^2}$$

f(x)	f'(x)
$\tan kx$	$k \sec^2 kx$
$\sec kx$	$k \sec kx \tan kx$
$\cot kx$	$-k \csc^2 kx$
$\csc kx$	$-k \csc kx \cot kx$
$\arcsin x$	$\dfrac{1}{\sqrt{1 - x^2}}$
$\arccos x$	$-\dfrac{1}{\sqrt{1 - x^2}}$
$\arctan x$	$\dfrac{1}{1 + x^2}$

f(x)	f'(x)
$\sinh x$	$\cosh x$
$\cosh x$	$\sinh x$
$\tanh x$	$\text{sech}^2 x$
$\text{arsinh } x$	$\dfrac{1}{\sqrt{1 + x^2}}$
$\text{arcosh } x$	$\dfrac{1}{\sqrt{x^2 - 1}}$
$\text{artanh } x$	$\dfrac{1}{1 - x^2}$

Integration (+ constant)

f(x)	$\int f(x)\,dx$
$\sec^2 kx$	$\dfrac{1}{k}\tan kx$
$\tan kx$	$\dfrac{1}{k}\ln|\sec kx|$
$\cot kx$	$\dfrac{1}{k}\ln|\sin kx|$
$\csc kx$	$-\dfrac{1}{k}\ln|\csc kx + \cot kx|,$ $\dfrac{1}{k}\ln\left|\tan\left(\tfrac{1}{2}kx\right)\right|$
$\sec kx$	$\dfrac{1}{k}\ln|\sec kx + \tan kx|,$ $\dfrac{1}{k}\ln\left|\tan\left(\tfrac{1}{2}kx + \tfrac{\pi}{4}\right)\right|$
$\sinh x$	$\cosh x$
$\cosh x$	$\sinh x$
$\tanh x$	$\ln \cosh x$

a > 0 in the following:

f(x)	$\int f(x)\,dx$
$\dfrac{1}{\sqrt{a^2 - x^2}}$	$\arcsin \dfrac{x}{a} \quad \text{for } |x| < a$
$\dfrac{1}{a^2 + x^2}$	$\dfrac{1}{a}\arctan \dfrac{x}{a}$
$\dfrac{1}{\sqrt{a^2 + x^2}}$	$\text{arsinh } \dfrac{x}{a} = \ln(x + \sqrt{x^2 + a^2})$
$\dfrac{1}{\sqrt{x^2 - a^2}}$	$\text{arcosh } \dfrac{x}{a} = \ln(x + \sqrt{x^2 - a^2}) \text{ for } x > a$
$\dfrac{1}{a^2 - x^2}$	$\dfrac{1}{a}\text{artanh } \dfrac{x}{a} = \dfrac{1}{2a}\ln\left|\dfrac{a+x}{a-x}\right| \text{ for } |x| < a$
$\dfrac{1}{x^2 - a^2}$	$\dfrac{1}{2a}\ln\left|\dfrac{x-a}{x+a}\right|$

Integration by parts: $\displaystyle \int u\frac{dv}{dx}\,dx = uv - \int v\frac{du}{dx}\,dx$

Formulas

Vectors

The Cartesian equation of a straight line passing through point $\mathbf{a} = a_1\mathbf{i} + a_2\mathbf{j} + a_3\mathbf{k}$ with direction vector $\mathbf{b} = b_1\mathbf{i} + b_2\mathbf{j} + b_3\mathbf{k}$ is:

$\dfrac{x - a_1}{b_1} = \dfrac{y - a_2}{b_2} = \dfrac{z - a_3}{b_3} = \lambda$, where λ is variable.

If position vector $\mathbf{a}$ is a fixed point on a plane with normal vector $\mathbf{n} = a\mathbf{i} + b\mathbf{j} + c\mathbf{k}$, the Cartesian equation of the plane is:
$ax + by + cz + d = 0$, where $d = -\mathbf{a.n}$

If position vector $\mathbf{a}$ is a fixed point on a plane and non-parallel direction vectors $\mathbf{b}$ and $\mathbf{c}$ lie in the plane, then the equation of the plane has vector form:

$\mathbf{r} = \mathbf{a} + \lambda\mathbf{b} + \mu\mathbf{c}$, where λ and μ are variable.

If $\mathbf{f}$, $\mathbf{g}$ and $\mathbf{h}$ are position vectors on a plane, and are non-collinear (i.e. all three do not lie on the same line), then the equation of the plane has vector form:

$\mathbf{r} = \mathbf{f} + \alpha(\mathbf{g} - \mathbf{f}) + \beta(\mathbf{h} - \mathbf{f}) = (1 - \alpha - \beta)\mathbf{f} + \alpha\mathbf{g} + \beta\mathbf{h}$,

where α and β are variable.

For a point $\alpha\mathbf{i} + \beta\mathbf{j} + \lambda\mathbf{k}$ and a plane $n_1 x + n_2 y + n_3 z + d = 0$, the perpendicular distance between them is:

$\dfrac{|n_1\alpha + n_2\beta + n_3\lambda + d|}{\sqrt{n_1^2 + n_2^2 + n_3^2}}$

$\mathbf{a} \times \mathbf{b} = |\mathbf{a}||\mathbf{b}|\sin\theta\,\mathbf{n}$ ($\mathbf{n}$ is a unit vector perpendicular to $\mathbf{a}$ and $\mathbf{b}$)

$= \begin{vmatrix} \mathbf{i} & \mathbf{j} & \mathbf{k} \\ a_1 & a_2 & a_3 \\ b_1 & b_2 & b_3 \end{vmatrix} = (a_2 b_3 - b_2 a_3)\mathbf{i} - (a_1 b_3 - b_1 a_3)\mathbf{j} + (a_1 b_2 - b_1 a_2)\mathbf{k}$

$\mathbf{a.b} \times \mathbf{c} = \begin{vmatrix} a_1 & a_2 & a_3 \\ b_1 & b_2 & b_3 \\ c_1 & c_2 & c_3 \end{vmatrix} = \mathbf{b.c} \times \mathbf{a} = \mathbf{c.a} \times \mathbf{b}$

Matrix Transformations

The matrix representing an anticlockwise rotation of θ about the origin:

$\begin{pmatrix} \cos\theta & -\sin\theta \\ \sin\theta & \cos\theta \end{pmatrix}$

Area enclosed by a polar curve

Area $= \dfrac{1}{2}\displaystyle\int_{\alpha}^{\beta} [r(\theta)]^2\, d\theta$

Exponentials and Logarithms

$\log_a x = \dfrac{\log_b x}{\log_b a}$ $e^{x\ln a} = a^x$

Numerical Methods

Trapezium rule: $\displaystyle\int_a^b y\, dx \approx \dfrac{1}{2}h\left[(y_0 + y_n) + 2(y_1 + y_2 + \dots + y_{n-1})\right]$, where $h = \dfrac{b - a}{n}$

The Newton-Raphson iteration for solving $f(x) = 0$: $x_{n+1} = x_n - \dfrac{f(x_n)}{f'(x_n)}$

Kinematics

Constant acceleration equations:

$v = u + at$ $s = ut + \dfrac{1}{2}at^2$ $s = \dfrac{1}{2}(u + v)t$

$v^2 = u^2 + 2as$ $s = vt - \dfrac{1}{2}at^2$

Formulas

Conics

Parabola: *Standard Cartesian equation:* $y^2 = 4ax$ *Parametric equations:* $x = at^2$ and $y = 2at$
Eccentricity: $e = 1$ *Focus:* $(a, 0)$ *Directrix:* $x = -a$

Ellipse: *Standard Cartesian equation:* $\dfrac{x^2}{a^2} + \dfrac{y^2}{b^2} = 1$ *Parametric equations:* $x = a \cos t$ and $y = b \sin t$
Eccentricity: $e < 1$, where $b^2 = a^2(1 - e^2)$ *Foci:* $(\pm ae, 0)$ *Directrices:* $x = \pm \dfrac{a}{e}$

Hyperbola: *Standard Cartesian equation:* $\dfrac{x^2}{a^2} - \dfrac{y^2}{b^2} = 1$ *Parametric equations:* $x = a \sec t$ and $y = b \tan t$
or $x = \pm a \cosh t$ and $y = b \sinh t$

Eccentricity: $e > 1$, where $b^2 = a^2(e^2 - 1)$ *Foci:* $(\pm ae, 0)$ *Directrices:* $x = \pm \dfrac{a}{e}$ *Asymptotes:* $y = \pm \dfrac{b}{a}x$

Rectangular hyperbola: *Standard Cartesian equation:* $xy = c^2$ *Parametric equations:* $x = ct$ and $y = \dfrac{c}{t}$
Eccentricity: $e = \sqrt{2}$ *Foci:* $(\pm\sqrt{2}\,c, \pm\sqrt{2}\,c)$ *Directrices:* $x + y = \pm\sqrt{2}\,c$ *Asymptotes:* $x = 0, y = 0$

Probability

$P(A') = 1 - P(A)$

$P(A \cup B) = P(A) + P(B) - P(A \cap B)$

$P(A \cap B) = P(A)P(B|A)$

$P(A|B) = \dfrac{P(B \mid A)\,P(A)}{P(B \mid A)\,P(A) + P(B \mid A')\,P(A')}$

For independent events A and B:

$P(B|A) = P(B), \quad P(A|B) = P(A), \qquad P(A \cap B) = P(A)P(B)$

Measures of Variation

Interquartile range = IQR = $Q_3 - Q_1$

Standard deviation = $\sqrt{\text{variance}}$

For a set of n values $x_1, x_2, \dots x_i, \dots x_n$:

$S_{xx} = \sum(x_i - \overline{x})^2 = \left(\sum x_i^2\right) - \dfrac{\left(\sum x_i\right)^2}{n}$

Standard deviation = $\sqrt{\dfrac{S_{xx}}{n}}$ or $\sqrt{\dfrac{\sum x^2}{n} - \overline{x}^2}$

Statistical Distributions

The Binomial Distribution: If $X \sim B(n, p)$, then $P(X = x) = \dbinom{n}{x} p^x (1-p)^{n-x}$

Mean of $X = np$ Variance of $X = np(1 - p)$ PGF of $X = (1 - p + pt)^n$

The Poisson Distribution: If $X \sim Po(\lambda)$, then $P(X = x) = \dfrac{e^{-\lambda}\lambda^x}{x!}$

Mean of $X = \lambda$ Variance of $X = \lambda$ PGF of $X = e^{\lambda(t-1)}$

The Geometric Distribution: If $X \sim Geo(p)$ on $1, 2, \dots$ then $P(X = x) = p(1-p)^{x-1}$

Mean of $X = \dfrac{1}{p}$ Variance of $X = \dfrac{1-p}{p^2}$ PGF of $X = \dfrac{pt}{1-(1-p)t}$

The Negative Binomial Distribution: If $X \sim NB(r, p)$ on $r, r+1, \dots$ then $P(X = x) = \dbinom{x-1}{r-1} p^r (1-p)^{x-r}$

Mean of $X = \dfrac{r}{p}$ Variance of $X = \dfrac{r(1-p)}{p^2}$ PGF of $X = \left(\dfrac{pt}{1-(1-p)t}\right)^r$

Sampling Distributions

For a random sample of n observations from $N(\mu, \sigma^2)$: $\dfrac{\overline{X} - \mu}{\sigma / \sqrt{n}} \sim N(0, 1)$

Formulas

Discrete Distributions

For a discrete random variable X with possible values $x_1, x_2, x_3, \ldots$:

Mean = Expected Value $E(X) = \sum x_i P(X = x_i) = \sum x_i p_i$

Variance $= \text{Var}(X) = E(X^2) - [E(X)]^2 = \sum x_i^2 p_i - \left[\sum x_i p_i \right]^2$

For a function $g(X)$: $E(g(X)) = \sum g(x_i) P(X = x_i) = \sum g(x_i) p_i$

The probability generating function of a discrete random variable X is $G_X(t) = E(t^X)$.

$E(X) = G_X'(1)$

$\text{Var}(X) = G_X''(1) + G_X'(1) - [G_X'(1)]^2$

If X and Y are two independent random variables: $G_{X+Y}(t) = G_X(t) \times G_Y(t)$

Chi Squared Tests

For goodness of fit tests and contingency tables, compare $\sum_{i=1}^{n} \frac{(O_i - E_i)^2}{E_i}$ with $\chi^2_{(v)}$.

Statistical Tables

The binomial cumulative distribution function

The values below show $P(X \le x)$, where $X \sim B(n, p)$.

	$p =$	0.05	0.10	0.15	0.20	0.25	0.30	0.35	0.40	0.45	0.50
$n = 5$ $x =$	0	0.7738	0.5905	0.4437	0.3277	0.2373	0.1681	0.1160	0.0778	0.0503	0.0313
	1	0.9774	0.9185	0.8352	0.7373	0.6328	0.5282	0.4284	0.3370	0.2562	0.1875
	2	0.9988	0.9914	0.9734	0.9421	0.8965	0.8369	0.7648	0.6826	0.5931	0.5000
	3	1.0000	0.9995	0.9978	0.9933	0.9844	0.9692	0.9460	0.9130	0.8688	0.8125
	4	1.0000	1.0000	0.9999	0.9997	0.9990	0.9976	0.9947	0.9898	0.9815	0.9688
$n = 6$ $x =$	0	0.7351	0.5314	0.3771	0.2621	0.1780	0.1176	0.0754	0.0467	0.0277	0.0156
	1	0.9672	0.8857	0.7765	0.6554	0.5339	0.4202	0.3191	0.2333	0.1636	0.1094
	2	0.9978	0.9842	0.9527	0.9011	0.8306	0.7443	0.6471	0.5443	0.4415	0.3438
	3	0.9999	0.9987	0.9941	0.9830	0.9624	0.9295	0.8826	0.8208	0.7447	0.6563
	4	1.0000	0.9999	0.9996	0.9984	0.9954	0.9891	0.9777	0.9590	0.9308	0.8906
	5	1.0000	1.0000	1.0000	0.9999	0.9998	0.9993	0.9982	0.9959	0.9917	0.9844
$n = 7$ $x =$	0	0.6983	0.4783	0.3206	0.2097	0.1335	0.0824	0.0490	0.0280	0.0152	0.0078
	1	0.9556	0.8503	0.7166	0.5767	0.4449	0.3294	0.2338	0.1586	0.1024	0.0625
	2	0.9962	0.9743	0.9262	0.8520	0.7564	0.6471	0.5323	0.4199	0.3164	0.2266
	3	0.9998	0.9973	0.9879	0.9667	0.9294	0.8740	0.8002	0.7102	0.6083	0.5000
	4	1.0000	0.9998	0.9988	0.9953	0.9871	0.9712	0.9444	0.9037	0.8471	0.7734
	5	1.0000	1.0000	0.9999	0.9996	0.9987	0.9962	0.9910	0.9812	0.9643	0.9375
	6	1.0000	1.0000	1.0000	1.0000	0.9999	0.9998	0.9994	0.9984	0.9963	0.9922
$n = 8$ $x =$	0	0.6634	0.4305	0.2725	0.1678	0.1001	0.0576	0.0319	0.0168	0.0084	0.0039
	1	0.9428	0.8131	0.6572	0.5033	0.3671	0.2553	0.1691	0.1064	0.0632	0.0352
	2	0.9942	0.9619	0.8948	0.7969	0.6785	0.5518	0.4278	0.3154	0.2201	0.1445
	3	0.9996	0.9950	0.9786	0.9437	0.8862	0.8059	0.7064	0.5941	0.4770	0.3633
	4	1.0000	0.9996	0.9971	0.9896	0.9727	0.9420	0.8939	0.8263	0.7396	0.6367
	5	1.0000	1.0000	0.9998	0.9988	0.9958	0.9887	0.9747	0.9502	0.9115	0.8555
	6	1.0000	1.0000	1.0000	0.9999	0.9996	0.9987	0.9964	0.9915	0.9819	0.9648
	7	1.0000	1.0000	1.0000	1.0000	1.0000	0.9999	0.9998	0.9993	0.9983	0.9961
$n = 9$ $x =$	0	0.6302	0.3874	0.2316	0.1342	0.0751	0.0404	0.0207	0.0101	0.0046	0.0020
	1	0.9288	0.7748	0.5995	0.4362	0.3003	0.1960	0.1211	0.0705	0.0385	0.0195
	2	0.9916	0.9470	0.8591	0.7382	0.6007	0.4628	0.3373	0.2318	0.1495	0.0898
	3	0.9994	0.9917	0.9661	0.9144	0.8343	0.7297	0.6089	0.4826	0.3614	0.2539
	4	1.0000	0.9991	0.9944	0.9804	0.9511	0.9012	0.8283	0.7334	0.6214	0.5000
	5	1.0000	0.9999	0.9994	0.9969	0.9900	0.9747	0.9464	0.9006	0.8342	0.7461
	6	1.0000	1.0000	1.0000	0.9997	0.9987	0.9957	0.9888	0.9750	0.9502	0.9102
	7	1.0000	1.0000	1.0000	1.0000	0.9999	0.9996	0.9986	0.9962	0.9909	0.9805
	8	1.0000	1.0000	1.0000	1.0000	1.0000	1.0000	0.9999	0.9997	0.9992	0.9980
$n = 10$ $x =$	0	0.5987	0.3487	0.1969	0.1074	0.0563	0.0282	0.0135	0.0060	0.0025	0.0010
	1	0.9139	0.7361	0.5443	0.3758	0.2440	0.1493	0.0860	0.0464	0.0233	0.0107
	2	0.9885	0.9298	0.8202	0.6778	0.5256	0.3828	0.2616	0.1673	0.0996	0.0547
	3	0.9990	0.9872	0.9500	0.8791	0.7759	0.6496	0.5138	0.3823	0.2660	0.1719
	4	0.9999	0.9984	0.9901	0.9672	0.9219	0.8497	0.7515	0.6331	0.5044	0.3770
	5	1.0000	0.9999	0.9986	0.9936	0.9803	0.9527	0.9051	0.8338	0.7384	0.6230
	6	1.0000	1.0000	0.9999	0.9991	0.9965	0.9894	0.9740	0.9452	0.8980	0.8281
	7	1.0000	1.0000	1.0000	0.9999	0.9996	0.9984	0.9952	0.9877	0.9726	0.9453
	8	1.0000	1.0000	1.0000	1.0000	1.0000	0.9999	0.9995	0.9983	0.9955	0.9893
	9	1.0000	1.0000	1.0000	1.0000	1.0000	1.0000	1.0000	0.9999	0.9997	0.9990

Statistical Tables

The binomial cumulative distribution function (continued)

	$p =$	0.05	0.10	0.15	0.20	0.25	0.30	0.35	0.40	0.45	0.50
$n = 12$ $x =$	0	0.5404	0.2824	0.1422	0.0687	0.0317	0.0138	0.0057	0.0022	0.0008	0.0002
	1	0.8816	0.6590	0.4435	0.2749	0.1584	0.0850	0.0424	0.0196	0.0083	0.0032
	2	0.9804	0.8891	0.7358	0.5583	0.3907	0.2528	0.1513	0.0834	0.0421	0.0193
	3	0.9978	0.9744	0.9078	0.7946	0.6488	0.4925	0.3467	0.2253	0.1345	0.0730
	4	0.9998	0.9957	0.9761	0.9274	0.8424	0.7237	0.5833	0.4382	0.3044	0.1938
	5	1.0000	0.9995	0.9954	0.9806	0.9456	0.8822	0.7873	0.6652	0.5269	0.3872
	6	1.0000	0.9999	0.9993	0.9961	0.9857	0.9614	0.9154	0.8418	0.7393	0.6128
	7	1.0000	1.0000	0.9999	0.9994	0.9972	0.9905	0.9745	0.9427	0.8883	0.8062
	8	1.0000	1.0000	1.0000	0.9999	0.9996	0.9983	0.9944	0.9847	0.9644	0.9270
	9	1.0000	1.0000	1.0000	1.0000	1.0000	0.9998	0.9992	0.9972	0.9921	0.9807
	10	1.0000	1.0000	1.0000	1.0000	1.0000	1.0000	0.9999	0.9997	0.9989	0.9968
	11	1.0000	1.0000	1.0000	1.0000	1.0000	1.0000	1.0000	1.0000	0.9999	0.9998
$n = 15$ $x =$	0	0.4633	0.2059	0.0874	0.0352	0.0134	0.0047	0.0016	0.0005	0.0001	0.0000
	1	0.8290	0.5490	0.3186	0.1671	0.0802	0.0353	0.0142	0.0052	0.0017	0.0005
	2	0.9638	0.8159	0.6042	0.3980	0.2361	0.1268	0.0617	0.0271	0.0107	0.0037
	3	0.9945	0.9444	0.8227	0.6482	0.4613	0.2969	0.1727	0.0905	0.0424	0.0176
	4	0.9994	0.9873	0.9383	0.8358	0.6865	0.5155	0.3519	0.2173	0.1204	0.0592
	5	0.9999	0.9978	0.9832	0.9389	0.8516	0.7216	0.5643	0.4032	0.2608	0.1509
	6	1.0000	0.9997	0.9964	0.9819	0.9434	0.8689	0.7548	0.6098	0.4522	0.3036
	7	1.0000	1.0000	0.9994	0.9958	0.9827	0.9500	0.8868	0.7869	0.6535	0.5000
	8	1.0000	1.0000	0.9999	0.9992	0.9958	0.9848	0.9578	0.9050	0.8182	0.6964
	9	1.0000	1.0000	1.0000	0.9999	0.9992	0.9963	0.9876	0.9662	0.9231	0.8491
	10	1.0000	1.0000	1.0000	1.0000	0.9999	0.9993	0.9972	0.9907	0.9745	0.9408
	11	1.0000	1.0000	1.0000	1.0000	1.0000	0.9999	0.9995	0.9981	0.9937	0.9824
	12	1.0000	1.0000	1.0000	1.0000	1.0000	1.0000	0.9999	0.9997	0.9989	0.9963
	13	1.0000	1.0000	1.0000	1.0000	1.0000	1.0000	1.0000	1.0000	0.9999	0.9995
	14	1.0000	1.0000	1.0000	1.0000	1.0000	1.0000	1.0000	1.0000	1.0000	1.0000
$n = 20$ $x =$	0	0.3585	0.1216	0.0388	0.0115	0.0032	0.0008	0.0002	0.0000	0.0000	0.0000
	1	0.7358	0.3917	0.1756	0.0692	0.0243	0.0076	0.0021	0.0005	0.0001	0.0000
	2	0.9245	0.6769	0.4049	0.2061	0.0913	0.0355	0.0121	0.0036	0.0009	0.0002
	3	0.9841	0.8670	0.6477	0.4114	0.2252	0.1071	0.0444	0.0160	0.0049	0.0013
	4	0.9974	0.9568	0.8298	0.6296	0.4148	0.2375	0.1182	0.0510	0.0189	0.0059
	5	0.9997	0.9887	0.9327	0.8042	0.6172	0.4164	0.2454	0.1256	0.0553	0.0207
	6	1.0000	0.9976	0.9781	0.9133	0.7858	0.6080	0.4166	0.2500	0.1299	0.0577
	7	1.0000	0.9996	0.9941	0.9679	0.8982	0.7723	0.6010	0.4159	0.2520	0.1316
	8	1.0000	0.9999	0.9987	0.9900	0.9591	0.8867	0.7624	0.5956	0.4143	0.2517
	9	1.0000	1.0000	0.9998	0.9974	0.9861	0.9520	0.8782	0.7553	0.5914	0.4119
	10	1.0000	1.0000	1.0000	0.9994	0.9961	0.9829	0.9468	0.8725	0.7507	0.5881
	11	1.0000	1.0000	1.0000	0.9999	0.9991	0.9949	0.9804	0.9435	0.8692	0.7483
	12	1.0000	1.0000	1.0000	1.0000	0.9998	0.9987	0.9940	0.9790	0.9420	0.8684
	13	1.0000	1.0000	1.0000	1.0000	1.0000	0.9997	0.9985	0.9935	0.9786	0.9423
	14	1.0000	1.0000	1.0000	1.0000	1.0000	1.0000	0.9997	0.9984	0.9936	0.9793
	15	1.0000	1.0000	1.0000	1.0000	1.0000	1.0000	1.0000	0.9997	0.9985	0.9941
	16	1.0000	1.0000	1.0000	1.0000	1.0000	1.0000	1.0000	1.0000	0.9997	0.9987
	17	1.0000	1.0000	1.0000	1.0000	1.0000	1.0000	1.0000	1.0000	1.0000	0.9998
	18	1.0000	1.0000	1.0000	1.0000	1.0000	1.0000	1.0000	1.0000	1.0000	1.0000

Statistical Tables

The binomial cumulative distribution function (continued)

	p =	0.05	0.10	0.15	0.20	0.25	0.30	0.35	0.40	0.45	0.50
n = 25 x =	0	0.2774	0.0718	0.0172	0.0038	0.0008	0.0001	0.0000	0.0000	0.0000	0.0000
	1	0.6424	0.2712	0.0931	0.0274	0.0070	0.0016	0.0003	0.0001	0.0000	0.0000
	2	0.8729	0.5371	0.2537	0.0982	0.0321	0.0090	0.0021	0.0004	0.0001	0.0000
	3	0.9659	0.7636	0.4711	0.2340	0.0962	0.0332	0.0097	0.0024	0.0005	0.0001
	4	0.9928	0.9020	0.6821	0.4207	0.2137	0.0905	0.0320	0.0095	0.0023	0.0005
	5	0.9988	0.9666	0.8385	0.6167	0.3783	0.1935	0.0826	0.0294	0.0086	0.0020
	6	0.9998	0.9905	0.9305	0.7800	0.5611	0.3407	0.1734	0.0736	0.0258	0.0073
	7	1.0000	0.9977	0.9745	0.8909	0.7265	0.5118	0.3061	0.1536	0.0639	0.0216
	8	1.0000	0.9995	0.9920	0.9532	0.8506	0.6769	0.4668	0.2735	0.1340	0.0539
	9	1.0000	0.9999	0.9979	0.9827	0.9287	0.8106	0.6303	0.4246	0.2424	0.1148
	10	1.0000	1.0000	0.9995	0.9944	0.9703	0.9022	0.7712	0.5858	0.3843	0.2122
	11	1.0000	1.0000	0.9999	0.9985	0.9893	0.9558	0.8746	0.7323	0.5426	0.3450
	12	1.0000	1.0000	1.0000	0.9996	0.9966	0.9825	0.9396	0.8462	0.6937	0.5000
	13	1.0000	1.0000	1.0000	0.9999	0.9991	0.9940	0.9745	0.9222	0.8173	0.6550
	14	1.0000	1.0000	1.0000	1.0000	0.9998	0.9982	0.9907	0.9656	0.9040	0.7878
	15	1.0000	1.0000	1.0000	1.0000	1.0000	0.9995	0.9971	0.9868	0.9560	0.8852
	16	1.0000	1.0000	1.0000	1.0000	1.0000	0.9999	0.9992	0.9957	0.9826	0.9461
	17	1.0000	1.0000	1.0000	1.0000	1.0000	1.0000	0.9998	0.9988	0.9942	0.9784
	18	1.0000	1.0000	1.0000	1.0000	1.0000	1.0000	1.0000	0.9997	0.9984	0.9927
	19	1.0000	1.0000	1.0000	1.0000	1.0000	1.0000	1.0000	0.9999	0.9996	0.9980
	20	1.0000	1.0000	1.0000	1.0000	1.0000	1.0000	1.0000	1.0000	0.9999	0.9995
	21	1.0000	1.0000	1.0000	1.0000	1.0000	1.0000	1.0000	1.0000	1.0000	0.9999
	22	1.0000	1.0000	1.0000	1.0000	1.0000	1.0000	1.0000	1.0000	1.0000	1.0000
n = 30 x =	0	0.2146	0.0424	0.0076	0.0012	0.0002	0.0000	0.0000	0.0000	0.0000	0.0000
	1	0.5535	0.1837	0.0480	0.0105	0.0020	0.0003	0.0000	0.0000	0.0000	0.0000
	2	0.8122	0.4114	0.1514	0.0442	0.0106	0.0021	0.0003	0.0000	0.0000	0.0000
	3	0.9392	0.6474	0.3217	0.1227	0.0374	0.0093	0.0019	0.0003	0.0000	0.0000
	4	0.9844	0.8245	0.5245	0.2552	0.0979	0.0302	0.0075	0.0015	0.0002	0.0000
	5	0.9967	0.9268	0.7106	0.4275	0.2026	0.0766	0.0233	0.0057	0.0011	0.0002
	6	0.9994	0.9742	0.8474	0.6070	0.3481	0.1595	0.0586	0.0172	0.0040	0.0007
	7	0.9999	0.9922	0.9302	0.7608	0.5143	0.2814	0.1238	0.0435	0.0121	0.0026
	8	1.0000	0.9980	0.9722	0.8713	0.6736	0.4315	0.2247	0.0940	0.0312	0.0081
	9	1.0000	0.9995	0.9903	0.9389	0.8034	0.5888	0.3575	0.1763	0.0694	0.0214
	10	1.0000	0.9999	0.9971	0.9744	0.8943	0.7304	0.5078	0.2915	0.1350	0.0494
	11	1.0000	1.0000	0.9992	0.9905	0.9493	0.8407	0.6548	0.4311	0.2327	0.1002
	12	1.0000	1.0000	0.9998	0.9969	0.9784	0.9155	0.7802	0.5785	0.3592	0.1808
	13	1.0000	1.0000	1.0000	0.9991	0.9918	0.9599	0.8737	0.7145	0.5025	0.2923
	14	1.0000	1.0000	1.0000	0.9998	0.9973	0.9831	0.9348	0.8246	0.6448	0.4278
	15	1.0000	1.0000	1.0000	0.9999	0.9992	0.9936	0.9699	0.9029	0.7691	0.5722
	16	1.0000	1.0000	1.0000	1.0000	0.9998	0.9979	0.9876	0.9519	0.8644	0.7077
	17	1.0000	1.0000	1.0000	1.0000	0.9999	0.9994	0.9955	0.9788	0.9286	0.8192
	18	1.0000	1.0000	1.0000	1.0000	1.0000	0.9998	0.9986	0.9917	0.9666	0.8998
	19	1.0000	1.0000	1.0000	1.0000	1.0000	1.0000	0.9996	0.9971	0.9862	0.9506
	20	1.0000	1.0000	1.0000	1.0000	1.0000	1.0000	0.9999	0.9991	0.9950	0.9786
	21	1.0000	1.0000	1.0000	1.0000	1.0000	1.0000	1.0000	0.9998	0.9984	0.9919
	22	1.0000	1.0000	1.0000	1.0000	1.0000	1.0000	1.0000	1.0000	0.9996	0.9974
	23	1.0000	1.0000	1.0000	1.0000	1.0000	1.0000	1.0000	1.0000	0.9999	0.9993
	24	1.0000	1.0000	1.0000	1.0000	1.0000	1.0000	1.0000	1.0000	1.0000	0.9998
	25	1.0000	1.0000	1.0000	1.0000	1.0000	1.0000	1.0000	1.0000	1.0000	1.0000

Statistical Tables

The binomial cumulative distribution function (continued)

		$p =$	0.05	0.10	0.15	0.20	0.25	0.30	0.35	0.40	0.45	0.50
$n = 40$	$x =$	0	0.1285	0.0148	0.0015	0.0001	0.0000	0.0000	0.0000	0.0000	0.0000	0.0000
		1	0.3991	0.0805	0.0121	0.0015	0.0001	0.0000	0.0000	0.0000	0.0000	0.0000
		2	0.6767	0.2228	0.0486	0.0079	0.0010	0.0001	0.0000	0.0000	0.0000	0.0000
		3	0.8619	0.4231	0.1302	0.0285	0.0047	0.0006	0.0001	0.0000	0.0000	0.0000
		4	0.9520	0.6290	0.2633	0.0759	0.0160	0.0026	0.0003	0.0000	0.0000	0.0000
		5	0.9861	0.7937	0.4325	0.1613	0.0433	0.0086	0.0013	0.0001	0.0000	0.0000
		6	0.9966	0.9005	0.6067	0.2859	0.0962	0.0238	0.0044	0.0006	0.0001	0.0000
		7	0.9993	0.9581	0.7559	0.4371	0.1820	0.0553	0.0124	0.0021	0.0002	0.0000
		8	0.9999	0.9845	0.8646	0.5931	0.2998	0.1110	0.0303	0.0061	0.0009	0.0001
		9	1.0000	0.9949	0.9328	0.7318	0.4395	0.1959	0.0644	0.0156	0.0027	0.0003
		10	1.0000	0.9985	0.9701	0.8392	0.5839	0.3087	0.1215	0.0352	0.0074	0.0011
		11	1.0000	0.9996	0.9880	0.9125	0.7151	0.4406	0.2053	0.0709	0.0179	0.0032
		12	1.0000	0.9999	0.9957	0.9568	0.8209	0.5772	0.3143	0.1285	0.0386	0.0083
		13	1.0000	1.0000	0.9986	0.9806	0.8968	0.7032	0.4408	0.2112	0.0751	0.0192
		14	1.0000	1.0000	0.9996	0.9921	0.9456	0.8074	0.5721	0.3174	0.1326	0.0403
		15	1.0000	1.0000	0.9999	0.9971	0.9738	0.8849	0.6946	0.4402	0.2142	0.0769
		16	1.0000	1.0000	1.0000	0.9990	0.9884	0.9367	0.7978	0.5681	0.3185	0.1341
		17	1.0000	1.0000	1.0000	0.9997	0.9953	0.9680	0.8761	0.6885	0.4391	0.2148
		18	1.0000	1.0000	1.0000	0.9999	0.9983	0.9852	0.9301	0.7911	0.5651	0.3179
		19	1.0000	1.0000	1.0000	1.0000	0.9994	0.9937	0.9637	0.8702	0.6844	0.4373
		20	1.0000	1.0000	1.0000	1.0000	0.9998	0.9976	0.9827	0.9256	0.7870	0.5627
		21	1.0000	1.0000	1.0000	1.0000	1.0000	0.9991	0.9925	0.9608	0.8669	0.6821
		22	1.0000	1.0000	1.0000	1.0000	1.0000	0.9997	0.9970	0.9811	0.9233	0.7852
		23	1.0000	1.0000	1.0000	1.0000	1.0000	0.9999	0.9989	0.9917	0.9595	0.8659
		24	1.0000	1.0000	1.0000	1.0000	1.0000	1.0000	0.9996	0.9966	0.9804	0.9231
		25	1.0000	1.0000	1.0000	1.0000	1.0000	1.0000	0.9999	0.9988	0.9914	0.9597
		26	1.0000	1.0000	1.0000	1.0000	1.0000	1.0000	1.0000	0.9996	0.9966	0.9808
		27	1.0000	1.0000	1.0000	1.0000	1.0000	1.0000	1.0000	0.9999	0.9988	0.9917
		28	1.0000	1.0000	1.0000	1.0000	1.0000	1.0000	1.0000	1.0000	0.9996	0.9968
		29	1.0000	1.0000	1.0000	1.0000	1.0000	1.0000	1.0000	1.0000	0.9999	0.9989
		30	1.0000	1.0000	1.0000	1.0000	1.0000	1.0000	1.0000	1.0000	1.0000	0.9997
		31	1.0000	1.0000	1.0000	1.0000	1.0000	1.0000	1.0000	1.0000	1.0000	0.9999
		32	1.0000	1.0000	1.0000	1.0000	1.0000	1.0000	1.0000	1.0000	1.0000	1.0000

Statistical Tables

The binomial cumulative distribution function (continued)

	$p =$	0.05	0.10	0.15	0.20	0.25	0.30	0.35	0.40	0.45	0.50
$n = 50$ $x =$	0	0.0769	0.0052	0.0003	0.0000	0.0000	0.0000	0.0000	0.0000	0.0000	0.0000
	1	0.2794	0.0338	0.0029	0.0002	0.0000	0.0000	0.0000	0.0000	0.0000	0.0000
	2	0.5405	0.1117	0.0142	0.0013	0.0001	0.0000	0.0000	0.0000	0.0000	0.0000
	3	0.7604	0.2503	0.0460	0.0057	0.0005	0.0000	0.0000	0.0000	0.0000	0.0000
	4	0.8964	0.4312	0.1121	0.0185	0.0021	0.0002	0.0000	0.0000	0.0000	0.0000
	5	0.9622	0.6161	0.2194	0.0480	0.0070	0.0007	0.0001	0.0000	0.0000	0.0000
	6	0.9882	0.7702	0.3613	0.1034	0.0194	0.0025	0.0002	0.0000	0.0000	0.0000
	7	0.9968	0.8779	0.5188	0.1904	0.0453	0.0073	0.0008	0.0001	0.0000	0.0000
	8	0.9992	0.9421	0.6681	0.3073	0.0916	0.0183	0.0025	0.0002	0.0000	0.0000
	9	0.9998	0.9755	0.7911	0.4437	0.1637	0.0402	0.0067	0.0008	0.0001	0.0000
	10	1.0000	0.9906	0.8801	0.5836	0.2622	0.0789	0.0160	0.0022	0.0002	0.0000
	11	1.0000	0.9968	0.9372	0.7107	0.3816	0.1390	0.0342	0.0057	0.0006	0.0000
	12	1.0000	0.9990	0.9699	0.8139	0.5110	0.2229	0.0661	0.0133	0.0018	0.0002
	13	1.0000	0.9997	0.9868	0.8894	0.6370	0.3279	0.1163	0.0280	0.0045	0.0005
	14	1.0000	0.9999	0.9947	0.9393	0.7481	0.4468	0.1878	0.0540	0.0104	0.0013
	15	1.0000	1.0000	0.9981	0.9692	0.8369	0.5692	0.2801	0.0955	0.0220	0.0033
	16	1.0000	1.0000	0.9993	0.9856	0.9017	0.6839	0.3889	0.1561	0.0427	0.0077
	17	1.0000	1.0000	0.9998	0.9937	0.9449	0.7822	0.5060	0.2369	0.0765	0.0164
	18	1.0000	1.0000	0.9999	0.9975	0.9713	0.8594	0.6216	0.3356	0.1273	0.0325
	19	1.0000	1.0000	1.0000	0.9991	0.9861	0.9152	0.7264	0.4465	0.1974	0.0595
	20	1.0000	1.0000	1.0000	0.9997	0.9937	0.9522	0.8139	0.5610	0.2862	0.1013
	21	1.0000	1.0000	1.0000	0.9999	0.9974	0.9749	0.8813	0.6701	0.3900	0.1611
	22	1.0000	1.0000	1.0000	1.0000	0.9990	0.9877	0.9290	0.7660	0.5019	0.2399
	23	1.0000	1.0000	1.0000	1.0000	0.9996	0.9944	0.9604	0.8438	0.6134	0.3359
	24	1.0000	1.0000	1.0000	1.0000	0.9999	0.9976	0.9793	0.9022	0.7160	0.4439
	25	1.0000	1.0000	1.0000	1.0000	1.0000	0.9991	0.9900	0.9427	0.8034	0.5561
	26	1.0000	1.0000	1.0000	1.0000	1.0000	0.9997	0.9955	0.9686	0.8721	0.6641
	27	1.0000	1.0000	1.0000	1.0000	1.0000	0.9999	0.9981	0.9840	0.9220	0.7601
	28	1.0000	1.0000	1.0000	1.0000	1.0000	1.0000	0.9993	0.9924	0.9556	0.8389
	29	1.0000	1.0000	1.0000	1.0000	1.0000	1.0000	0.9997	0.9966	0.9765	0.8987
	30	1.0000	1.0000	1.0000	1.0000	1.0000	1.0000	0.9999	0.9986	0.9884	0.9405
	31	1.0000	1.0000	1.0000	1.0000	1.0000	1.0000	1.0000	0.9995	0.9947	0.9675
	32	1.0000	1.0000	1.0000	1.0000	1.0000	1.0000	1.0000	0.9998	0.9978	0.9836
	33	1.0000	1.0000	1.0000	1.0000	1.0000	1.0000	1.0000	0.9999	0.9991	0.9923
	34	1.0000	1.0000	1.0000	1.0000	1.0000	1.0000	1.0000	1.0000	0.9997	0.9967
	35	1.0000	1.0000	1.0000	1.0000	1.0000	1.0000	1.0000	1.0000	0.9999	0.9987
	36	1.0000	1.0000	1.0000	1.0000	1.0000	1.0000	1.0000	1.0000	1.0000	0.9995
	37	1.0000	1.0000	1.0000	1.0000	1.0000	1.0000	1.0000	1.0000	1.0000	0.9998
	38	1.0000	1.0000	1.0000	1.0000	1.0000	1.0000	1.0000	1.0000	1.0000	1.0000

Statistical Tables

The Poisson cumulative distribution function

The values below show $P(X \le x)$, where $X \sim Po(\lambda)$.

$\lambda =$	0.5	1.0	1.5	2.0	2.5	3.0	3.5	4.0	4.5	5.0
$x = 0$	0.6065	0.3679	0.2231	0.1353	0.0821	0.0498	0.0302	0.0183	0.0111	0.0067
1	0.9098	0.7358	0.5578	0.4060	0.2873	0.1991	0.1359	0.0916	0.0611	0.0404
2	0.9856	0.9197	0.8088	0.6767	0.5438	0.4232	0.3208	0.2381	0.1736	0.1247
3	0.9982	0.9810	0.9344	0.8571	0.7576	0.6472	0.5366	0.4335	0.3423	0.2650
4	0.9998	0.9963	0.9814	0.9473	0.8912	0.8153	0.7254	0.6288	0.5321	0.4405
5	1.0000	0.9994	0.9955	0.9834	0.9580	0.9161	0.8576	0.7851	0.7029	0.6160
6	1.0000	0.9999	0.9991	0.9955	0.9858	0.9665	0.9347	0.8893	0.8311	0.7622
7	1.0000	1.0000	0.9998	0.9989	0.9958	0.9881	0.9733	0.9489	0.9134	0.8666
8	1.0000	1.0000	1.0000	0.9998	0.9989	0.9962	0.9901	0.9786	0.9597	0.9319
9	1.0000	1.0000	1.0000	1.0000	0.9997	0.9989	0.9967	0.9919	0.9829	0.9682
10	1.0000	1.0000	1.0000	1.0000	0.9999	0.9997	0.9990	0.9972	0.9933	0.9863
11	1.0000	1.0000	1.0000	1.0000	1.0000	0.9999	0.9997	0.9991	0.9976	0.9945
12	1.0000	1.0000	1.0000	1.0000	1.0000	1.0000	0.9999	0.9997	0.9992	0.9980
13	1.0000	1.0000	1.0000	1.0000	1.0000	1.0000	1.0000	0.9999	0.9997	0.9993
14	1.0000	1.0000	1.0000	1.0000	1.0000	1.0000	1.0000	1.0000	0.9999	0.9998
15	1.0000	1.0000	1.0000	1.0000	1.0000	1.0000	1.0000	1.0000	1.0000	0.9999
16	1.0000	1.0000	1.0000	1.0000	1.0000	1.0000	1.0000	1.0000	1.0000	1.0000
17	1.0000	1.0000	1.0000	1.0000	1.0000	1.0000	1.0000	1.0000	1.0000	1.0000
18	1.0000	1.0000	1.0000	1.0000	1.0000	1.0000	1.0000	1.0000	1.0000	1.0000
19	1.0000	1.0000	1.0000	1.0000	1.0000	1.0000	1.0000	1.0000	1.0000	1.0000

$\lambda =$	5.5	6.0	6.5	7.0	7.5	8.0	8.5	9.0	9.5	10.0
$x = 0$	0.0041	0.0025	0.0015	0.0009	0.0006	0.0003	0.0002	0.0001	0.0001	0.0000
1	0.0266	0.0174	0.0113	0.0073	0.0047	0.0030	0.0019	0.0012	0.0008	0.0005
2	0.0884	0.0620	0.0430	0.0296	0.0203	0.0138	0.0093	0.0062	0.0042	0.0028
3	0.2017	0.1512	0.1118	0.0818	0.0591	0.0424	0.0301	0.0212	0.0149	0.0103
4	0.3575	0.2851	0.2237	0.1730	0.1321	0.0996	0.0744	0.0550	0.0403	0.0293
5	0.5289	0.4457	0.3690	0.3007	0.2414	0.1912	0.1496	0.1157	0.0885	0.0671
6	0.6860	0.6063	0.5265	0.4497	0.3782	0.3134	0.2562	0.2068	0.1649	0.1301
7	0.8095	0.7440	0.6728	0.5987	0.5246	0.4530	0.3856	0.3239	0.2687	0.2202
8	0.8944	0.8472	0.7916	0.7291	0.6620	0.5925	0.5231	0.4557	0.3918	0.3328
9	0.9462	0.9161	0.8774	0.8305	0.7764	0.7166	0.6530	0.5874	0.5218	0.4579
10	0.9747	0.9574	0.9332	0.9015	0.8622	0.8159	0.7634	0.7060	0.6453	0.5830
11	0.9890	0.9799	0.9661	0.9467	0.9208	0.8881	0.8487	0.8030	0.7520	0.6968
12	0.9955	0.9912	0.9840	0.9730	0.9573	0.9362	0.9091	0.8758	0.8364	0.7916
13	0.9983	0.9964	0.9929	0.9872	0.9784	0.9658	0.9486	0.9261	0.8981	0.8645
14	0.9994	0.9986	0.9970	0.9943	0.9897	0.9827	0.9726	0.9585	0.9400	0.9165
15	0.9998	0.9995	0.9988	0.9976	0.9954	0.9918	0.9862	0.9780	0.9665	0.9513
16	0.9999	0.9998	0.9996	0.9990	0.9980	0.9963	0.9934	0.9889	0.9823	0.9730
17	1.0000	0.9999	0.9998	0.9996	0.9992	0.9984	0.9970	0.9947	0.9911	0.9857
18	1.0000	1.0000	0.9999	0.9999	0.9997	0.9993	0.9987	0.9976	0.9957	0.9928
19	1.0000	1.0000	1.0000	1.0000	0.9999	0.9997	0.9995	0.9989	0.9980	0.9965
20	1.0000	1.0000	1.0000	1.0000	1.0000	0.9999	0.9998	0.9996	0.9991	0.9984
21	1.0000	1.0000	1.0000	1.0000	1.0000	1.0000	0.9999	0.9998	0.9996	0.9993
22	1.0000	1.0000	1.0000	1.0000	1.0000	1.0000	1.0000	0.9999	0.9999	0.9997

Statistical Tables

Percentage points of the normal distribution

The z-values in the table are those which a random variable
$Z \sim N(0, 1)$ exceeds with probability p, i.e. $P(Z > z) = 1 - \Phi(z) = p$.

p	z	p	z
0.5000	0.0000	0.0500	1.6449
0.4000	0.2533	0.0250	1.9600
0.3000	0.5244	0.0100	2.3263
0.2000	0.8416	0.0050	2.5758
0.1500	1.0364	0.0010	3.0902
0.1000	1.2816	0.0005	3.2905

Percentage points of the chi squared distribution

The values in the table are those which a random variable following the
χ^2 distribution for ν degrees of freedom exceeds with the probability shown.

ν	0.995	0.990	0.975	0.950	0.900	0.100	0.050	0.025	0.010	0.005
1	0.000	0.000	0.001	0.004	0.016	2.705	3.841	5.024	6.635	7.879
2	0.010	0.020	0.051	0.103	0.211	4.605	5.991	7.378	9.210	10.597
3	0.072	0.115	0.216	0.352	0.584	6.251	7.815	9.348	11.345	12.838
4	0.207	0.297	0.484	0.711	1.064	7.779	9.488	11.143	13.277	14.860
5	0.412	0.554	0.831	1.145	1.610	9.236	11.070	12.832	15.086	16.750
6	0.676	0.872	1.237	1.635	2.204	10.645	12.592	14.449	16.812	18.548
7	0.989	1.239	1.690	2.167	2.833	12.017	14.067	16.013	18.475	20.278
8	1.344	1.646	2.180	2.733	3.490	13.362	15.507	17.535	20.090	21.955
9	1.735	2.088	2.700	3.325	4.168	14.684	16.919	19.023	21.666	23.589
10	2.156	2.558	3.247	3.940	4.865	15.987	18.307	20.483	23.209	25.188
11	2.603	3.053	3.816	4.575	5.580	17.275	19.675	21.920	24.725	26.757
12	3.074	3.571	4.404	5.226	6.304	18.549	21.026	23.337	26.217	28.300
13	3.565	4.107	5.009	5.892	7.042	19.812	22.362	24.736	27.688	29.819
14	4.075	4.660	5.629	6.571	7.790	21.064	23.685	26.119	29.141	31.319
15	4.601	5.229	6.262	7.261	8.547	22.307	24.996	27.488	30.578	32.801
16	5.142	5.812	6.908	7.962	9.312	23.542	26.296	28.845	32.000	34.267
17	5.697	6.408	7.564	8.672	10.085	24.769	27.587	30.191	33.409	35.718
18	6.265	7.015	8.231	9.390	10.865	25.989	28.869	31.526	34.805	37.156
19	6.844	7.633	8.907	10.117	11.651	27.204	30.144	32.852	36.191	38.582
20	7.434	8.260	9.591	10.851	12.443	28.412	31.410	34.170	37.566	39.997
21	8.034	8.897	10.283	11.591	13.240	29.615	32.671	35.479	38.932	41.401
22	8.643	9.542	10.982	12.338	14.042	30.813	33.924	36.781	40.289	42.796
23	9.260	10.196	11.689	13.091	14.848	32.007	35.172	38.076	41.638	44.181
24	9.886	10.856	12.401	13.848	15.659	33.196	36.415	39.364	42.980	45.558
25	10.520	11.524	13.120	14.611	16.473	34.382	37.652	40.646	44.314	46.928
26	11.160	12.198	13.844	15.379	17.292	35.563	38.885	41.923	45.642	48.290
27	11.808	12.879	14.573	16.151	18.114	36.741	40.113	43.194	46.963	49.645
28	12.461	13.565	15.308	16.928	18.939	37.916	41.337	44.461	48.278	50.993
29	13.121	14.256	16.047	17.708	19.768	39.088	42.557	45.722	49.588	52.336
30	13.787	14.953	16.791	18.493	20.599	40.256	43.773	46.979	50.892	53.672

Index

Index

Index